PC/Computing 2001 Windows Tips

PC Computing

PC/Computing 2001 Windows Tips

Mike Edelhart
and the Editors of *PC/Computing*

Ziff-Davis Press
Emeryville, California

Editor	Deborah Craig
Technical Reviewer	Richard Ozer
Project Coordinator	Sheila McGill
Proofreaders	Leslie Tilley and Cort Day
Cover Design	Carrie English
Book Design	Peter Tucker
Screen Graphics Editor	Dan Brodnitz
Word Processing	Howard Blechman and Cat Haglund
Page Layout	Sidney Davenport and Bruce Lundquist
Indexer	Julie Kawabata

This book was produced on a Macintosh IIfx, with the following applications: FrameMaker®, Microsoft® Word, MacLink®Plus, Aldus® FreeHand™, Adobe Photoshop™, and Collage Plus™.

Ziff-Davis Press
5903 Christie Avenue
Emeryville, CA 94608

ISBN 1-56276-084-X

Manufactured in the United States of America
10 9 8 7 6 5 4 3

≡ Contents at a Glance

Introduction xxv

PART 1 WINDOWS SECRETS

1. Secrets for Installing and Setting Up Windows 3
2. WIN.INI and SYSTEM.INI: A Complete Reference Guide 35
3. Taming, Troubleshooting, and Turbocharging Windows Hardware 91
4. Expert Management for Dos under Windows 129
5. Maximizing Program Manager and Windows Screen Elements 169
6. Secrets of Windows Accessories 203
7. File Manager 239
8. Managing Fonts and Printing 263
9. Getting Windows Applications to Work Together 289
10. Secrets for Running Windows on Networks 309

PART 2 POWER SECRETS FOR WINDOWS APPLICATIONS

11. Getting the Most from Windows Word Processors 359
12. Spreadsheet Tips 415
13. Drawing and Presentation Package Tips 457
14. Communications Programs 475
15. Windows Enhancements, Utilities, and Programming Tools 487
16. Page Layout Packages 513
17. Personal Productivity Tools 525

Index 545

▬ TABLE OF CONTENTS

Introduction xxv
    What This Book Is xxv
    What This Book Isn't xxv
    Ways to Use This Book xxvi
    Tell Us What You'd Like to Know xxvi

PART 1 WINDOWS SECRETS

    1. Secrets for Installing and Setting Up Windows   **3**
    Tips for Installing Windows 3.1 4
        What You Should Do before Running Setup 4
        Command-Line Switches for Setup 6
        Custom versus Express Setup 6
        Troubleshooting Windows Setup 7
        Moving Windows to a New Location after Installation 9
    Copying Files from Windows Disks without Running Setup 10
    Upgrading Windows 11
        Install Windows 3.1 and Keep Windows 3.0 Intact 12
        Troubleshooting a Windows 3.1 Upgrade Error 12
        Upgrading from Windows 2.0 13
        Reinstalling Windows without Losing Settings 13
    Back Up Your System Files 14
    Removing Windows Components 14
    How to Load Windows on Your PC . . . Best! 14
        Using the WIN Command 14
    Windows' Three Modes and What They Mean to You 17
        Windows Modes and System Requirements 17
        When (If Ever) to Use Real Mode 18
        Making the Most of Standard Mode 18
        Enhancing 386 Enhanced Mode 22

Troubleshooting Problems with Loading Windows
in 386 Enhanced Mode 23
Troubleshooting Problems with Operating Windows
in 386 Enhanced Mode 26
Optional Windows Files 26
111 Windows Files You Can Do Without 27
Remove Drivers and Fonts You Don't Use 28
Remove Support for Standard Mode 29
Remove Support for 386 Enhanced Mode 30
Remove Support for DOS Applications 30
A Few Files to Keep Handy 31
The Many Ways to Skip the Windows Startup Screen 31
Suppress the Startup Screen 31
Another Command-Line Trick to Bypass the Logo 31
Create a Batch File to Bypass the Logo 31
Remove the Logo Permanently by Creating a New WIN.COM 32
Make AUTOEXEC.BAT Skip the Logo for You 32
Replace the Windows Logo with the Image of Your Choice 32
On-line Resources 33
Seek On-line Help 33
Windows Drivers Library 33
Microsoft Knowledge Base 33
Exiting Windows Wisely 33
Fast Windows Shutdown 33
Exiting DOS Programs Quickly in Enhanced Mode 33
How to Quickly Exit DOS Applications in Standard Mode 34

2. WIN.INI and SYSTEM.INI: A Complete
Reference Guide   35
How .INI Files Are Structured 35
Who Does What to Whom? 36
How to Edit an .INI File 37
Tips for Using SYSEDIT 38
A Word about Syntax 39
WIN.INI Line by Line 40
Tips for Editing WIN.INI 41
[Windows] 42
Boolean Values for Editing .INI Files 43
[Desktop] 50

[Extensions] 52

[Intl] 53

[Windows Help] 56

[Ports] 57

[FontSubstitutes] 58

[TrueType] 59

[Sounds] 60

[MCI extensions] 62

[Compatibility] 62

[Fonts] 62

[Network] 62

[Embedding] 63

[Colors] 63

[PrinterPorts] 64

[Devices] 64

[Programs] 65

SYSTEM.INI Line by Line 65

A Word about Syntax 66

Abandon Hope, All Ye Who Edit Here 67

[Boot] 69

[386Enh] 72

[Standard] 86

[NonWindowsApp] 87

3. Taming, Troubleshooting, and Turbocharging
Windows Hardware   91

Optimizing Windows on a 286 PC 91

Beef Up Your RAM 92

Add the Right Kind of RAM 92

Set Up a Disk Cache According to the Applications You Use 92

Get a Fast Hard Disk 93

Pump Up Your Video Card 94

Use TrueType Rather Than Type Managers 94

Use Simple Wallpaper, or None at All 94

Practice Meticulous Disk Housekeeping 94

Printing 95

Give Your System a Break by Turning on Draft Mode 95

Beware the Balky BIOS! 95
    BIOS Problems You Should Know About 96
    EISA Systems BIOS and Extended Memory 97
Hardware Headaches of Particular PCs 97
Memory Secrets 100
    Find Out about Your System's Memory 100
    How Much Memory Should You Have? 100
    Getting the Most from Windows Memory Management 101
    Creative Tricks for Windows Memory 104
    Care and Feeding of TSRs under Windows 105
    Disk Caches and Windows Performance 108
    Working with SMARTDrive 109
Managing Windows COM Ports 111
    Using COM3 or COM4 with Windows 3.1 111
    Using COM3 and COM4 with Windows 3.0 111
    Allow IRQ Sharing 112
    Add Support for More than Four COM Ports 112
Hard-Drive Management for Windows 112
    Golden Rules for Hard-Drive Performance 112
    Maintaining Optimal Hard-Disk Performance 113
    SCSI Hardware and Windows 113
    Windows and Disk-Compression Programs 114
    Setting Up the Windows Swap File 114
Making the Most of Input Devices 116
    Mouse Secrets 116
    Keyboard Tips and Tricks 118
Sharpening Your Windows Display 119
    SVGA Displays 119
    Rooting Out Video Problems 120
    How to Install a New Set of Video Drivers Safely 121
    Get Rid of Old Drivers 122
    Changing Windows Screen Fonts 122
    Make the Cursor Easier to Find by Changing Its Blink Rate 124
Multimedia Tips 124
    Troubleshooting Audio in Windows 124
    Troubleshooting Audio in DOS Sessions 124
    CD-ROM Drives and the Microsoft DOS CD-ROM Extensions 124
    Troubleshooting a CD-ROM Drive 125

Tips for Traveling with Windows 125
   Free Up Valuable Real Estate 125
   LCD Screen Eye Savers 125
   Opt for a Larger Font 126
   Use Keyboard Shortcuts 126
   Customize Style Sheets for Laptop Use 127
   Have Different Printer Drivers Available 127
   Avoid Trouble with Remote-Control Applications 127

4. **Expert Management for DOS under Windows 129**
Installing and Launching DOS Apps under Windows 130
   Ask Windows Setup to Search Out DOS Apps 130
   Installing DOS Programs after Setup 131
   Six Ways to Launch DOS Applications from within Windows 131
   Launch a DOS Application with a Data File Loaded 133
   Windows' Modes and DOS Apps 133
   Mouse Tricks 135
PIFs: DOS Program Control Centers 135
   Check for Predefined PIFs 136
   How to Write the Perfect PIF 136
   Make PIFs for Both Standard and 386 Enhanced Mode 137
   Make Two PIFs for the Same Application 138
   Make PIF Settings Uniform 138
   Protect Shortcut Key Sequences in DOS Apps 138
   Recover Original PIFs 138
   PIF Troubleshooting 138
Establishing Effective DOS Sessions 142
   Optimizing CONFIG.SYS and AUTOEXEC.BAT 142
   Troubleshooting Difficulties with DOS Apps 146
Customizing Sessions Run from Windows' MS-DOS Prompt 148
   Start DOS in a Window 149
   Disable DOS Prompt Instructions 150
   Change the DOS Default Directory 150
   Expand the DOS Environment 150
Copying and Pasting between DOS and Windows 150
   Copy and Paste Text from Full-Screen DOS Applications 151
   Copy and Paste Text in Standard Mode 151
   Copy and Paste in 386 Enhanced Mode 151

Copy DOS Graphics to Windows via the Clipboard 152
Use the Clipboard to Send ASCII Files in DOS Communications
Programs 153
Tips for Working in DOS Programs Running under Windows 153
Change Fonts and Font Sizes for DOS Applications
in Windows 3.1 153
Launch a Batch File from Windows and End in DOS 153
Unzip Files in Windows with Drag and Drop 154
Turn Your Favorite Batch Files into Windows Icons 154
DOS Commands to Avoid 156
Don't Use the MS-DOS Task Swapper 156
Use DOS 5.0's Built-in Help System 156
Three TSR Rules for DOS Applications 157
Run Local TSRs 157
Start DOS Applications with Graphic Logo Full-Screened 157
Tab Through Applications from a Full-Screen DOS Application 157
Three Ways to Speed Up Printing for DOS Applications 158
Assign Hotkeys to Your DOS Applications 158
Easy-to-Remember Hotkeys 158
Run DOS Programs in the Foreground 159
Stop Update Messages to File Manager 159
Switch between DOS and Windows Applications with the Task
List 160
Exit DOS Sessions before Powering Down Your Computer 160
Create a DOS Prompt to Remind You that You're in Windows 160
Create Fun Prompts 161
Bart Simpson 161
Power User 162
Biplane 162
Train 162
Happy Birthday 163
Windows Rules 163
Merry Christmas 163
IBM Logo 164
The Fifth Day of the Week 164
Help 164
Rice Owls 164
ANSI.SYS Metastrings and Graphic Characters 165

ANSI Color Settings 165
Graphics Characters 167

5. Maximizing Program Manager and Windows Screen Elements   **169**

Building and Managing Program Groups 169
   Shortcuts for Program Group Basics 170
   Program Group Strategies 174
   Taming On-Screen Windows 177
   PROGMAN.INI: A Potent Tool 177
Making the Most of the Program Groups That Windows Provides 179
   Tips for Control Panel Control 180
   Redecorate Your Screen with Control Panel's Desktop 182
   Color Secrets 184
   Personalize the Windows 3.1 StartUp Group 188
Icon-ography and Creative Dragging 189
   The Hidden Power of Icons 189
   The Ins and Outs of Dragging and Dropping 193
Savvy Shortcuts for the Screen 194
   Bars and Buttons 194
   Don't Forget the Keyboard 195
Saves and Captures 201
   Screen Savers 201
   Screen Captures 202

6. Secrets of Windows Accessories   **203**

Getting the Time of Day from the Windows Clock 204
   A Timely Icon 205
   Easier Clock-Watching 205
Write Tips 206
   Lines That Don't Disappear 206
   Opt for Optional Hyphens 206
   Change Margins Every Time 206
   Special Searches 207
   Write Keyboard Shortcuts 207
   Write Mouse Shortcuts 207
Hidden Talents of the Windows Calculator 208
   Easy Financial Calculations 208
   A Calculator Limitation You Should Know About 213

Use the Statistics Box to Keep Track of Numbers 213
Calculator Keyboard Shortcuts 214
Calendar 215
Print Blank Calendar Pages 215
Personalize Calendar Output 215
Start Your Day by Previewing Appointments 216
Special Times 217
Calendar Keyboard Shortcuts 218
Cardfile 218
Fit More Cards on a Printed Page 218
Dialing with Cardfile 219
Quick Card Finds 219
Dial Internal Extensions 220
Convert Cards to Text 220
Autodialing Long Numbers in Windows 3.0 220
Cardfile Keyboard Shortcuts 221
Notepad Know-How 221
Turn On Word Wrap 221
Add Time and Date to Printed Documents 222
Format Headers and Footers in Notepad 222
Create a Log of Your Work Day 222
Notepad Keyboard Shortcuts 223
Paintbrush Pointers 223
Quick Duplicates 223
Perfect Lines and Shapes 224
Easy Erasing 224
More Zoom 225
Special Text Effects 226
Paintbrush Keyboard Shortcuts 226
Tapping into Terminal 226
Print Selected Terminal Text 227
Increase the Buffer Size 228
Turn Off Call Waiting 228
Work Around Noisy Phone Lines 228
Run Terminal Maximized 229
Terminal Keyboard Shortcuts 229
Make the Most of the Macro Recorder 229
Avoid the Mouse 230

Use Macros to Resize Windows 230
View Macros 232
Start Recorder Macros from Other Applications 232
Assign Macros to Icons 232
Create Demonstrations with Macro Recorder 232
Assign Macros for Key Combinations 233
Stop Recording Quickly 233
Use Recorder to Assign Shortcut Keys in Windows 3.0 233
Character Map 234
Easy Extended Characters 234
Multimedia Applets 234
Play .WAV Files All the Way Through 235
Sound Recorder Keyboard Shortcuts 235
Solitaire Secrets 235
Surprise Yourself with Random Card Backs 235
Quick Stacks 236
No Missed Opportunities 236
Cheating to Get the Card You Need 236
Keyboard Shortcuts for Windows Accessories 236

7. File Manager   239

File Manager Housekeeping 239
Selecting Files 240
File Tweaks and Traps 241
Take Advantage of Associations 250
Getting the Most from Windows 3.1 File Manager 255
File Manager Drag and Drop Techniques 255
Taming the File Manager Screen 257
File Manager Keyboard Shortcuts 260

8. Managing Fonts and Printing   263

Font Magic 263
Font Housekeeping 263
Advanced Font Secrets 268
TrueType 275
Printer Power 278
Print Manager Secrets 278
Print Manager Keyboard Shortcuts 280
Printer Tips 281

Speed Up PostScript Printing 285
Printer Troubleshooting 285
Responding to Printer Port Error Messages 286

9. Getting Windows Applications to Work
Together   **289**

Basic Windows Integration 289
Load Applications as Icons 289
Make the Windows Clipboard Work for You 290
Use Macros to Integrate Windows Applications 292
Make Sure You Remove Windows Applications Safely 292
Coping with Conflicts 293
The Lingering Spectre of Windows 3.0 UAEs 293
Keep the Dr. Watson Utility on Call 295
Advanced Windows Integration 296
Get the Most from DDE 296
OLE Secrets 298
Application Development Tools for Windows Integration 308

10. Secrets for Running Windows on Networks   **309**

Setup Tips for Network Administrators 309
Optimizing Windows on a Network 310
Using Setup's Command-Line Options 311
Creating a System Settings File to Use with Batch Mode Setup 312
Automating Setup with the SETUP.INF File 319
Automating Setup with the APPS.INF and CONTROL.SRC Files 330
Windows Maintenance on a Network 337
Optimizing Network Performance 343
Fine-tuning Windows Performance on a Network 343
Fine-tuning SYSTEM.INI for Network Use 344
Printing Tips 346
Tips for Specific Networks 349
Novell NetWare Tips 349
3Com Networks 351
Artisoft LANtastic Tips 352
Banyan VINES Tips 353
Microsoft LAN Manager Tips 354
DEC Pathworks 355

PART 2 POWER SECRETS FOR WINDOWS APPLICATIONS

11. Getting the Most from Windows Word Processors   **359**

Ami Professional 359
    Formatting Tips 359
    SmartIcons Tips 360
    Using Handy Ami Pro Macros 361
    Speed Tips 364
    Helpful How-Tos 365
Word for Windows 366
    Text-Manipulation Tips 366
    Formatting Tips 370
    Speed Tips 375
    Table Tips 377
    Toolbar Tips 381
    Macro Tips 382
    Setting Your Own Defaults 385
    Navigation Tips 387
    File Management Tips 388
    Mail Merge Tips 389
    Help Tips 390
    Spell-Checking Tips 391
WordPerfect for Windows 391
    Text Manipulation Tips 392
    Formatting Tips 392
    Button Bar Tips 394
    Keyboard Tips 397
    Navigation Tips 399
    Code Tips 400
    File Management Tips 402
    Table Tips 407
    Speed Tips 408
    Printer Tips 409
    Macro Tips 410
WordStar for Windows 411
    Speed Tips 411
    Formatting Tips 412
    Drawing and Graphics Tips 413

12. Spreadsheet Tips 415

Excel 415
  Start-up and Shutdown Tips 415
  Keyboard Shortcuts 417
  Mouse Tips 418
  Formula and Function Tips 421
  Template Tips 422
  Formatting Tips 423
  Toolbar Tips 425
  Worksheet Tips 427
  Data Entry Tips 428
  Button Tips 429
  Printing Tips 430
  Display Tips 432
Lotus 1-2-3 for Windows 432
  SmartIcon Tips 433
  Worksheet Tips 433
  Tips for Moving, Entering, and Copying Data 435
  Formatting Tips 436
  Formula and Function Tips 439
  SmartPak Tips 441
  Display and Printing Tips 443
  Performance Tips 445
  Tips for Users of Classic 1-2-3 446
  File-Linking Tips 447
Quattro Pro for Windows 447
  Page Tips 447
  Data Entry Tips 449
  Formatting Tips 450
  Tips for Moving Data 452
  Display and Printing Tips 454
  Tips for Quick Access 455

13. Drawing and Presentation Package Tips 457

Aldus Persuasion 457
  Slide and Presentation Tips 457
  System and Operation Tips 459
CorelDRAW! 460

Lotus Freelance for Windows 462
Harvard Graphics for Windows 463
   Drawing and Charting Tips 464
   Presentation and Printing Tips 465
Micrografx Designer, Draw, and Charisma 466
   Tips for Charisma, Draw, and Designer 467
   Tips for Micrografx Designer 468
   Charisma Tips 469
   Windows Draw Tips 470
Microsoft PowerPoint 470
   Drawing Tips 470
   Presentation Tips 471
   Integrating PowerPoint with Other Microsoft Applications 473
Publisher's Paintbrush 474

14. Communications Programs **475**
Procomm Plus for Windows 475
Crosstalk for Windows 476
   Tips for Dialing and On-Line Sessions 476
   Tips for Handling Setup and COM Ports 477
Dynacomm 479
   Scripting Tips 479
   On-Line Session Tips 481
   Troubleshooting Tips 481
Lotus Notes 482
   Address Tips 483
   Mail Tips 483
   Keyboard Shortcuts 485

15. Windows Enhancements, Utilities, and
Programming Tools **487**
Adobe Type Manager 487
   Font Tips 487
   Printing and Problem-Solving Tips 489
Bitstream Facelift 491
   Font Tips 491
   Setup and Operation Tips 492
   Troubleshooting Tips 493

Norton Desktop for Windows 494
  File Tips 495
  Performance Tips 497
  Troubleshooting Tips 499
PC Tools 500
Asymetrix Toolbook 502
  Box and OpenScript Tips 502
  Smart Techniques for Using Toolbook 504
ObjectVision 506
  Data Entry Tips 506
  Timesaving Tips 507
Visual Basic 508
  Function and Routine Tips 509
  Performance Tips 511
Access .INI Files from Visual Basic 512

16. **Page Layout Packages**   **513**
PageMaker 513
  Text Tips 513
  Graphics and Document Tips 515
Ventura Publisher 517
  Formatting Tips 517
  Speed Tips 519
  Troubleshooting Tips 520
Microsoft Publisher 520
  Drawing and Text Tips 521
  Page-Numbering and Exiting Tips 523

17. **Personal Productivity Tools**   **525**
Microsoft Project 525
  Viewing Tips 525
  Task and Task-Sheet Tips 526
  Formatting Tips 528
Microsoft Works 530
  Text Tips 530
  Spreadsheet Tips 531
  Database Tips 532
  Tips for All Works Modules 533

Delrina PerForm Pro 534
  Tool Tips 534
  Form-Design Tips 535
  Data Tips 536
  Performance Tips 536
Polaris Packrat 537
  Searching Tips 537
  Phone Book Tips 537
  Tips for Using Packrat with Other Windows Applications 538
Quicken for Windows 539
  Financial-Tracking Tips 539
  Data Entry Tips 540
Microsoft Money 541
  Customization Tips 541
  Accounting Tips 541
  Navigation Tips 543

Index   **545**

ACKNOWLEDGMENTS

NECESSITY REQUIRES THAT BOOKS CARRY THE PURPORTED AUTHOR'S NAME alone on the cover because acknowledging all the people who actually produced the work wouldn't leave any room for the title. So, here we redress the imbalance.

More so than even a typical book, this is a collaborative effort. To begin with, the project never would have existed without the extraordinarily talented staff of and contributors to *PC/Computing* magazine. Dozens of staff members and literally hundreds of the business computing experts who read *PC/Computing* applied their ingenuity and knowledge toward creating the tips in this book. In a very real sense, this volume is a testament to their talents.

Two of *PC/Computing*'s own deserve special praise. Christine Grech, associate editor, carried the book on her back through a long hot summer and a wild and crazy fall. Christine did the initial research, kept the records, checked the facts, pulled the screen shots, and generally kept the entire unholy process moving forward.

Jean Atelsek, *PC/Computing*'s executive editor, polished the tips into English, read proofs and pages, and generally pushed me around to get my few meager chores done (more or less) on time.

In thanking these two marvelous partners, I must paraphrase Mark Twain: They did all the work…and I did the rest.

Acknowledgment is also due to Harry Blake and Cindy Hudson of ZD Press, who started the whole thing, and to the editorial team of Deborah Craig, Jeff Green, Sheila McGill, and Richard Ozer. Editing me is like brushing a lion's teeth—necessary but not pleasant and kind of dangerous. I commend them all for their steadfastness and courage in the face of mammoth curmudgeonry.

Finally, thanks to all the splendid technologists who created Windows and its cornucopia of software delights. Without them we'd have nothing interesting to say.

 # INTRODUCTION

WHEN WINDOWS 3.0 WAS RELEASED A COUPLE YEARS BACK, THE STAFF AT *PC/Computing* recognized right off that something special had entered our readers' lives. Windows brought a freshness and spirit back to computing that many of us had nearly forgotten since the early, heady days of the PC. But even we who recognized Windows' importance couldn't reckon with just how exhilarating this new graphical environment would be. We soon realized that Windows wasn't just a successful piece of software. It was a phenomenon, one that *PC/Computing* has dedicated itself to tracking ever since.

Simply put, Windows unleashed the greatest sustained creative effort by the largest number of people any of us had ever seen. Windows applications sprouted like mushrooms, each more interesting than the last. And ideas about using the environment better suddenly swirled about our heads like leaves on a blustery autumn afternoon. This book is the result of the distillation of these ideas, tricks, strategies, work arounds, undocumented discoveries, anomalies, fixes, and just plain good sense of *PC/Computing*'s 800,000-plus readers and expert staff.

What This Book Is

Our aim with this book was to create the largest, most extensive treasure trove anywhere of tips for how to get more from using Windows and important Windows applications.

There are many Windows tutorial books today—dozens of guides to the environment's features, scads of advanced programming manuals, and even a few books that contain "secrets" for using Windows better. But this is the first and only book that offers a large number of tips for every facet of Windows and for more than four dozen key Windows programs. This is the biggest collection of hands-on, practical, specific Windows advice ever assembled. All this book contains is tips. No essays. No user stories. No code segments. No long discussions of technical whys and wherefores. We wanted to go for hands-on help here…and nothing but.

What This Book Isn't

An introduction to Windows and its applications.
A technical manual about Windows inner workings or programming.
A tutorial guide.

One man's opinion.

Anything a person of common business acumen couldn't easily follow.

Ways to Use This Book

This book is a logically constructed encyclopedia of Windows tips, thousands of 'em. The tips are broken into two main sections: Windows and Windows applications. In Part 1, Windows Secrets, we move from tips about installing and starting Windows through questions of configuration, maximizing hardware, and all essential areas of Windows operation right up to customizing Windows and working with networks. Each of the chapters in Part 1 contains sections on critical topics, and these in turn are broken down into specific tasks or opportunities. Then we provide tips that apply to that particular subject.

The chapters in Part 2, Power Secrets for Windows Applications, are organized by product type: databases, spreadsheets, utilities, and the like. The main chapter headings direct you to particular applications, and subheadings show you the key areas where that product can be improved. How you use *PC/Computing 2001 Windows Tips* will depend on what you need to accomplish at the moment. Here are some suggestions on ways to get the most out of this book:

To solve a particular problem or improve a specific operation. Use the index or the detailed table of contents to find the area you are interested in. Then study the tips found there. Also, look at the tips in related areas. For example, configuration tips specific to networking are found in the networking section and also appear in sections describing applications that have specific configuration needs. If you don't find what you need, please drop us a note at the address at the end of this Introduction. We'll see what we can dig up to help.

To learn more about how to get more from Windows in ways you might not expect. Turn to the table of contents. Beginning with Chapter 1 through the end of the book, read the chapter titles and headings. Whenever you hit one that catches your fancy, read the tips there. Whenever you find a tip that turns you on, try it. Next time you get frisky, repeat the procedure. Over time, you'll use a lot of the tips in this book, and you'll learn a startling amount about Windows.

To get the most from the Windows applications you use. Concentrate on the early chapters—using a good configuration improves any application—as well as on the hardware chapter, Chapter 3, and the networking chapter, Chapter 10 (if it applies to your situation). Then go to the chapters on the applications you use and read all the tips we offer on them. Reading the tips not only provides you with specific new things to try, it also serves as a closet form of education on how your application works and uses Windows.

Tell Us What You'd Like to Know

If you have a question this book doesn't answer or a tip you'd like to share, get in touch with us c/o Ziff-Davis Publishing Co., 950 Tower Lane, 21st Floor, Foster City, CA 94404.

PART 1

Windows Secrets

3
SECRETS FOR INSTALLING AND SETTING UP WINDOWS

37
WIN.INI AND SYS.INI: A COMPLETE REFERENCE GUIDE

91
**TAMING, TROUBLESHOOTING, AND TURBOCHARGING
WINDOWS HARDWARE**

129
EXPERT MANAGEMENT FOR DOS UNDER WINDOWS

169
**MAXIMIZING PROGRAM MANAGER AND
WINDOWS SCREEN ELEMENTS**

203
SECRETS OF WINDOWS ACCESSORIES

239
FILE MANAGER

263
MANAGING FONTS AND PRINTING

289
GETTING WINDOWS APPLICATIONS TO WORK TOGETHER

309
SECRETS FOR RUNNING WINDOWS ON NETWORKS

1 Secrets for Installing and Setting Up Windows

ONE OF THE GREAT JOYS OF WINDOWS IS THE EFFICIENT WAY IT INSTALLS. THIS is particularly true with Windows 3.1, which neatens and speeds the essentially sound setup procedures of its predecessor. Well, you might ask, if Windows installs so elegantly, who needs tips and secrets for setting up a Windows environment? Aren't installation headaches a blissfully departed characteristic of those dim DOS days of old?

Yes, and no.

Certainly Windows installs far better than DOS ever did. But the automatic nature of Windows' installation demands that the program make assumptions about your computer hardware and personal preferences. In many cases, these presumptions—about everything from the way you want applications arrayed to screen colors and the basic parameters of your memory and I/O setup—will be fine. But for thousands of other users, Windows' default installation will blunt its true power and may even cause operational problems. The tips in this chapter will educate you on every customizable aspect of Windows installation so that *you* can decide whether Windows' automatic choices are the ones you want.

Even more importantly, while Windows installation is marvelous, it's not perfect. No software program can anticipate every option, every nuance in the incredibly varied and complex world of PCs. These potential headaches in getting Windows running aren't bugs; they are more in the nature of disagreements between some systems and Windows' initial demands. If this happens with your PC, you, the user, need to mediate the dispute. This means you have to suffer through trial and error until you figure out precisely what the problem is. Or you can take advantage of the workarounds the experts at *PC/Computing* have already found for you.

Finally, Windows is a magnificent piece of software craftsmanship that has sparked the imaginations of hundreds of thousands. The more adventurous of these Windows experts have poked and prodded around the Windows system and have uncovered any number of ideas that are just neat. You'll find these secrets here too.

The organization of the chapter is straightforward. In the pages that follow, you'll find

■ Tips for installing Windows, including what to do *before* installation, command-line switches for Windows' Setup program, and trouble-shooting solutions

- Advice on upgrading to Windows 3.1 from version 3.0 or from an older version

- Step-by-step instructions on how to reinstall Windows without losing your program groups and other settings

- Information on how to load Windows onto your PC faster

- A discussion of when to use Real mode (Windows 3.0 only), Standard mode, and 386 Enhanced mode, and of how to get the most from each of the three modes

- Hints about which Windows files you can safely delete to reclaim precious hard drive space

- Tips for bypassing the Windows startup screen

- Advice on how best to exit from Windows

Not all of the tips will be valuable for every reader. But something in this chapter will help everyone get more from Windows, right from the start!

Tips for Installing Windows 3.1

If all you want is for Windows 3.1 to run, put Windows Disk 1 in drive A, type **setup**, and choose Express Setup at the first Setup prompt. But if you want Windows to run *your way,* the program offers a host of options and tricks. Unless you are extremely pressed for time, it's a good idea to customize your Windows 3.1 installation. It really doesn't take very long, you'll get better performance, and you'll learn something about Windows and your PC in the process.

What You Should Do before Running Setup

When Windows 3.1 chokes during installation it's seldom the program's fault. Usually, installation problems with Windows have to do with the existing DOS setup. So, to avoid the unexpected, it's a good idea to review the following suggestions for stopping installation problems before they start.

Disable Any TSRs and Programs That You Run from Your AUTOEXEC. BAT or CONFIG.SYS Files   Comment out any memory-resident or other programs you normally run from AUTOEXEC.BAT or CONFIG.SYS, and then reboot your system before installing Windows. Likely candidates include screen savers, virus checkers, and disk caches. If you decide not to remove these programs, Windows may ask you to do so later: Setup automatically searches memory, in addition to your AUTOEXEC.BAT and CONFIG.SYS files, for memory-resident programs that are known to cause problems with Windows.

You can tell in advance whether Setup is going to prompt you to remove a program in one of two ways. If you type **setup /t** at the A: prompt (assuming you're installing Windows from your A drive), SETUP.EXE will scan your system to see if any conflicting programs are currently in memory. If it finds one, it will prompt you to quit Setup and remove all references to the program from your files. Or if you'd like to check the situation for yourself, open the Windows file SETUP.INF (on Windows Disk 1) in a text editor. Look for the sections entitled [incompTSR1] and [incompTSR2]. If your program is there, save yourself the trouble of having to abort Windows Setup by removing the offending program before you begin. After doing this and installing Windows successfully, you can restore the program and see if it works with your system.

The following programs are known to cause problems with Windows 3.1 Setup but should work fine after Windows is installed on your system:

ASP Integrity Toolkit version 3.7

Data Physician Plus version 2.0 (VirAlert); version 3.0 appears to correct this problem

Norton Anti-Virus version 1.0; version 1.5 appears to correct this problem

PC-Kwik version 1.59; version 2.0 appears to address this problem

SoftIce Debugger

Vaccine

VDefend, a PC Tools Deluxe TSR

Virex-PC version 1.11

ViruSafe version 4.0; version 4.5 appears to correct the problem, but its authors recommend that you run ViruSafe with the /C- switch with Windows

Make Sure Your CONFIG.SYS File Is in Order If you're using DOS 5.0, check your CONFIG.SYS file to make sure that your drivers are in the following order: HIMEM.SYS, EMM386.EXE, ANSI.SYS.

Check Your AUTOEXEC.BAT File for DOS Commands That Don't Work Well with Windows If you run DOS's APPEND utility from your AUTOEXEC-.BAT file, remove it, because it interferes with Windows' ability to build the paths it needs to access files. Also comment out any references to the DOS utilities JOIN and SUBST before running Windows Setup. Consider removing these utilities from your AUTOEXEC.BAT file for good, because they can easily confuse Windows as to which files are which and where they actually are. You should also avoid using the SHARE command when installing Windows on your system.

Make Sure That the MOUSE.COM Driver Is Present in Your AUTOEXEC-.BAT File If you'll ever use a mouse with DOS applications running under Windows, add a line to run the MOUSE.COM driver (the driver that lets you use a mouse with DOS applications) to your AUTOEXEC.BAT file before installing Windows. Setup will copy a new version of MOUSE.COM onto your system. If you don't want to automatically load MOUSE.COM from your

AUTOEXEC.BAT because you don't use it often enough, you can remove the statement after Windows is installed.

Command-Line Switches for Setup

When you first install Windows on your PC, you run SETUP.EXE from the DOS prompt. Table 1.1 lists several switches you can use with the SETUP command. Many of these switches pertain to network setup and will be covered in detail in Chapter 10.

TABLE 1.1

Switches for Use with the Windows SETUP Command

Switch	Function
/I	Ignores automatic hardware detection. If you use this switch, you'll have to check the system-setting information and change it manually.
/N	Sets up a shared copy of Windows on a network server.
/A	Starts Administrative Setup, installing Windows files as read-only onto a network.
/B	Sets up Windows with monochrome display attributes.
/T	Searches the drive for incompatible software that should not run at the same time as Setup or Windows 3.1.
/H:*filename*	Runs Batch Mode Setup to install Windows with little or no user interaction. *Filename* is the name of the system-settings file that contains information about the user's configuration.
/O:*filename*	Specifies the SETUP.INF file.
/S:*filename*	Specifies the SETUP.INF file, including a path for the Windows installation disks.

If you can't remember which switch you need to set up Windows 3.1, insert Windows Disk 1 in your floppy drive and type **setup /?** at the DOS prompt. You'll see a list of all of the available switches.

Custom versus Express Setup

You can choose how to install Windows 3.1 on your system. Express Setup requires the least amount of work on your part, while Custom Setup allows for greater customization.

Use Custom Setup for More Control over Your System   Use Custom Setup if any of the following apply:

- You want control over how your CONFIG.SYS and AUTOEXEC-.BAT files are modified.

- You want to specify the directory in which Windows is installed (the default is C:\WINDOWS).

■ You want to specify the language you will work in (the default is American English).

■ You want to make detailed choices about your system configuration. Express Setup detects most kinds of hardware, but Custom Setup provides more options.

■ You want to keep the amount of space Windows uses to a minimum by opting for only the Windows components you'll need. Laptop users who need to use the minimum amount of disk space will especially benefit from Custom Setup. You can nix wallpaper, accessories you'll never use, games, and screen savers.

■ You want to create a permanent swap file on your hard disk, and you don't already have a permanent swap file from Windows 3.0. (By default, Express Setup creates a temporary swap file.)

Before running Custom Setup, be prepared to respond to prompts about what type of printer you have and which port it's connected to; what kind of monitor, mouse (if any), keyboard, and network (if any) you have; the directory where you want to store Windows; which components of Windows you want installed on your system; which applications you have on your hard disk that you'll want to appear in Windows; and changes you want made to your CONFIG.SYS and AUTOEXEC.BAT files.

Speed Installation with Express Setup   To get through Windows Setup in a hurry, choose Express Setup. It takes you through the entire setup process, asking you only to fill in your name and insert floppy disks as needed. You can even use Express Setup if you are upgrading to Windows 3.1 from version 3.0. Express Setup will preserve your Program Groups and update your drivers.

Before running Express Setup, all you need to know is what type of printer you have and which PC port it's connected to (LPT1, for example).

Troubleshooting Windows Setup

Let's be honest. Sometimes, even though you've done all the right stuff—you've done all your homework and prepared your system properly for installation—it *still* won't work under Windows. This is frustrating, but don't let it drag down your self-image. You're okay and your PC is okay, too. The following prescriptives should root out the problem.

Test for Defective Disks   If you're installing Windows and Setup keeps prompting you for the next disk even though you've already put it in the floppy drive, here's how you can check if you have a bad disk: Try inserting the other Windows Setup disks in the floppy drive to see if a disk was mislabeled and the files Setup needs are actually on a different disk. If you're installing Windows from a backup copy, try your original disks to see if the floppies you backed up onto are defective.

To see if you have bad Windows disks, use the DOS DIR command to list the contents of each disk. If you can't get a directory listing, or if you see garbled filenames, the disk may be defective. If the DIR listing looks normal, use the DOS COPY command to copy the files from each Windows disk to a temporary directory on your hard drive. If you receive an error message during this process, you probably have a defective disk. Contact your software dealer for information on how to get replacement disks.

Check for TSR Conflicts   If you didn't remove memory-resident programs before installing Windows, you may be encountering Setup problems because of them. To see if that is the case (or, similarly, if a device driver is causing a problem), boot from a floppy disk and then try running Windows Setup. If you don't already have a boot disk (you should always keep one handy), make one before resuming the Windows installation: Place a floppy disk in drive A and type the command **format a: /s**. Next create basic CONFIG.SYS and AUTOEXEC.BAT files directly on the floppy. Your CONFIG.SYS should look like this:

```
FILES=40
BUFFERS=20
SHELL=C:\DOS\COMMAND.COM /P/E:256
```

You'll also want to include any device drivers that are needed for your computer to boot properly—for example, those for Stacker.

Your AUTOEXEC.BAT should look like this:

```
PATH=C:\;C:\DOS;C:\WINDOWS
PROMPT $P$G
SET COMSPEC=C:\DOS
```

NOTE   This example assumes that COMMAND.COM is located in your DOS directory.

Once you have Windows installed and running, it's a good idea to make backups of your Windows initialization files as well.

What to Do If Your System Hangs   If you're installing Windows and your system hangs, it may be because Setup has a problem identifying your hardware. To turn off automatic hardware detection during the setup routine, type **setup /i** at the A: prompt (assuming your Windows Setup disk is in drive A). With auto-detection disabled, Setup will present you with a standard system configuration for your hardware. You'll have to choose settings manually for the type of computer, video, and keyboard your system has. When you do so, specify that no network or mouse is installed—with these options turned off you'll have a better chance of finishing the setup routine. If you'll be using a network or mouse with your system, you can rerun Setup from within Windows and add these options later.

You can manually select the following PCs during setup:

AST Premium 386/25 and 386/33 (CUPID)

AT&T NSX 20 (Safari Notebook)

AT&T PC

Everex Step 386/25

Hewlett-Packard (all machines)

IBM PS/2 model L40SX

IBM PS/2 model P70

Intel 386 SL-based system with APM

MS-DOS System

MS-DOS System with APM

NCR (all 80386- and 80486-based machines)

NEC PowerMate SX Plus

NEC ProSpeed 386

Toshiba 1200XE

Toshiba 1600

Toshiba 5200

Zenith (all 80386-based machines)

Be Sure You Have Enough Conventional Memory   When installing Windows you may get the error message "Setup Error #S020 Setup is unable to make changes to the Windows configuration file, SYSTEM.INI. These changes are needed to set up Windows. Setup cannot continue." This means your system doesn't have enough conventional memory to complete the setup procedure. To regain enough memory, reboot your computer from a floppy, and then go through Setup again.

Moving Windows to a New Location after Installation

If you want to move Windows to a new drive or system, you probably don't relish the idea of having to rerun Setup and recreate your customized environment. To successfully transfer Windows to a new location, follow these steps:

1. Copy the files in your WINDOWS directory (and \WINDOWS \SYSTEM subdirectory) to the new location.   An easy way to copy your Windows directory structure to a new location (either to a hard disk or to floppies if you have to transfer Windows to a new system) is to use DOS's XCOPY command. For example, to copy your Windows directory to floppies in drive A, you would type

```
xcopy c:\windows a:windows /s /e /m
```

at the DOS prompt. The /S switch tells DOS to copy the subdirectories found below the WINDOWS directory, while the /E switch ensures that even empty subdirectories are copied. Use the /M switch if you're copying your Windows files to floppies—it tells DOS to turn off each file's archive bit as it's being copied. This way, when the first floppy disk fills up and you insert a new one, DOS will know to continue copying where it left off.

Copying Files from Windows Disks without Running Setup

If you're installing Windows and try to copy files from the setup disks, you'll notice that you can't use the files as they are. On the Windows 3.1 disks, certain files—including HIMEM.SYS, RAMDRIVE.SYS, and lots of device drivers—are stored in compressed form with an underscore as the last letter in their filename extension. In Windows 3.0, the files are stored with a dollar sign as the last character in the extension. To copy these files, you need to expand them first.

To decompress HIMEM.SYS in Windows 3.1, for example, copy EXPAND.EXE from Windows Disk 3 and type

```
expand himem.sy_ himem.sys
```

To decompress HIMEM.SYS in Windows 3.0, copy EXPAND.EXE from Windows Disk 2 and type

```
expand himem.sy$ himem.sys
```

EXPAND will create an expanded version of HIMEM.SYS that is the correct one to use.

---

2. Change all directory references to Windows in your .INI files. Open the WIN.INI, SYSTEM.INI, PROGMAN.INI, and the .INI files for other Windows applications in a text editor. Look for any references to the Windows path, and change them to fit the new location. If your text editor has a search feature, you can use that to make the process even easier. Just use the old Windows path as the search string—for example, C:\WINDOWS—and you won't miss any references. Be sure to save the files you change in ASCII format.

3. Change all Windows path references in your Program Manager group (.GRP) files. While you're in your text editor, also change path references in your Program Manager group (.GRP) files. Open each .GRP file and insert the correct Windows path reference. Most of the contents of the .GRP files will look like gobbledygook in a text-editing program, but the references to your Windows path will be in text; just search for C:\WINDOWS, say, if you're moving files from that location. Again, make sure you save your .GRP files in ASCII format.

4. Change references to Windows' path in your AUTOEXEC.BAT file. Another place to change references to the Windows path is in your AUTOEXEC.BAT file. If you move Windows to a new system, you may not have to make any changes since your Windows path will probably still be C:\WINDOWS. However, if you're moving Windows to a different directory or drive (for example, from C to D) you'll need to make this change.

5. Make sure Windows works in the new location. If you've moved Windows to a new location on an existing system, don't delete your old WINDOWS directory and files until you make sure that everything works exactly right. Just check that the references to Windows in your AUTOEXEC.BAT file point to the new location.

6. Make any necessary changes to your setup configuration. If you've moved Windows to a new location on your old hard disk, it's time to reboot your system and run Windows from its new location. However, if you've moved Windows to a different kind of system—for example, from a 386SX to a 486—you should run Windows Setup from the DOS prompt to change the hardware settings for your system before actually starting Windows.

If you are moving Windows to a *new* system it is also important to first disable any permanent swap file by selecting 386 Enhanced from the Control Panel and clicking Virtual Memory. Change the swap file type from Permanent to Temporary or None. Otherwise, Windows will look for the *old* swap file on the *new* system, which may cause it to hang.

7. Check your .PIF files. If you've moved Windows to a new system, your .PIF files might also contain path references that will be incorrect for Windows' new location. You should open these files in the PIF Editor and check that the references are correct.

Upgrading Windows

In some ways, shifting from one version of Windows to another is easier than an installation from scratch; in other ways, it's harder. Keep in mind that with an upgrade you have a golden opportunity either to leave your carefully constructed Windows environment precisely as it is, or to change it for the better.

Install Windows 3.1 and Keep Windows 3.0 Intact

If you're upgrading to Windows 3.1 from Windows 3.0, it's easiest to install 3.1 right on top of the earlier version. But you may have a good reason for keeping Windows 3.0 intact on your system: Maybe you still have some old apps that you need to run in Real mode, or maybe you're just cautious. You could install Windows 3.1 in a separate directory and start over, painstakingly recreating your Program Manager setup. But that's a lot of unnecessary work. Instead, you can copy your program groups from 3.0 over to 3.1.

After you've installed Windows 3.1 on your hard disk (to a directory other than the one containing Windows 3.0), switch back to the WINDOWS 3.0 directory and take stock of your program groups. If any of your Windows 3.0 program groups still have the default Windows names (for example, Main or Accessories) you may want to rename these to differentiate them from their Windows 3.1 counterparts. The default groups in Windows 3.1 contain different programs than in 3.0. (For the exact contents of the new program groups, see Chapter 5's discussion of the PROGMAN.INI file.) If you copy these groups over to Windows 3.1 without changing their names, you'll overwrite icons for the new programs that have been added. Once you've renamed any program groups, back up the Windows 3.0 .GRP files and PROGMAN.INI.

Now open the PROGMAN.INI file in the subdirectory where Windows 3.0 is located, and find the [Groups] section. Print this file so that you can refer to it when you have to edit the PROGMAN.INI file in Windows 3.1.

Return to the directory where you've installed Windows 3.1 and back up the .GRP files and PROGMAN.INI. Then copy the .GRP files from your Windows 3.0 directory to your Windows 3.1 directory. Now you'll need to add references to the Windows 3.1 PROGMAN.INI for these new groups. Refer to the printout of your Windows 3.0 groups, noting that each line specifies a group number. In addition, the line that reads "Order…" refers to the order of the program groups the last time you saved your Program Manager settings. The sequence of the numbers in the Order line doesn't matter; what's important is that for the total amount of groups listed, a corresponding number is noted in the Order line, as shown in Figure 1.1.

Troubleshooting a Windows 3.1 Upgrade Error

You may try to install Windows 3.1 over Windows 3.0 and find yourself unable to complete the installation. If that happens, try this trick before calling technical support or deciding to install Windows 3.1 in its own directory (thereby losing all of your program group settings): Before running Setup again, go into your Windows 3.0 \SYSTEM subdirectory (most likely it's C:\WINDOWS\SYSTEM) and delete the old SETUP.EXE file. Your installation problems may be caused by Windows reading the SETUP.EXE file from the hard disk rather than from the Windows 3.1 floppy disk.

FIGURE 1.1

Editing the PROGMAN.INI file in Windows 3.1 allows you to maintain the custom groups you created in Windows 3.0. For each group listed, a corresponding entry on the Order line is required.

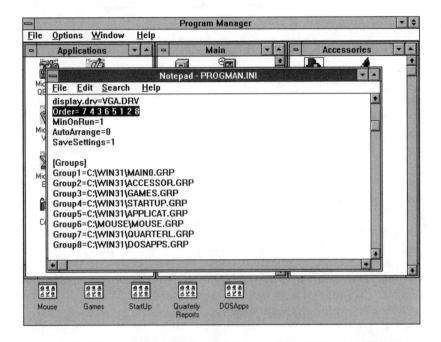

Upgrading from Windows 2.0

If you have Windows 2.0 on your system, not version 3.0, you should delete the old version before installing 3.1. If you try to install 3.1 over 2.0, you may receive an error message telling you it is not possible. But if you insist on going with this process to maintain your Windows environment, delete the files WIN200.BIN and WIN200.OVL from your WINDOWS directory before trying the Windows 3.1 upgrade again.

Reinstalling Windows without Losing Settings

If you have to reinstall Windows onto your system, here's a plan for maintaining your current settings: Install Windows into a new directory, keeping the old one in its original location. Then rename all of the .GRP files in the new directory to .GRN (for new) and all of the .INI files in the new directory to .INN. Next, copy all of the files from the new WINDOWS directory to the old WINDOWS directory, overwriting the original files. If Windows does not run from this setup, try renaming the .INI files to .INO (for original) and the .GRP files to .GRO; then rename the .INN and .GRN files back to .INI and .GRP. Windows should now run on your system.

Back Up Your System Files

Of course, you should always back up your files, but in the case of the system files that Windows depends on, backing up is especially important. You should regularly back up your WIN.INI, SYSTEM.INI, PROGMAN.INI, and any other .INI files (some Windows applications supply their own .INI file). Other candidates for regular backups include your .GRP files.

It's also a good idea to make backups of the WIN.INI and SYSTEM.INI files before you install new Windows applications. If the new application wreaks havoc with your Windows setup, these files will let you easily restore things to the way they were. Copies of your WIN.INI and SYSTEM.INI files are also handy if you want to study the changes a new Windows application makes to them.

Removing Windows Components

Situations change, people change, and PC components change. For a host of reasons, you may want to slim down Windows after the initial installation. No problem. At any time, you can remove Windows components that you don't need and that are taking up valuable disk space. To do so, select the Window Setup icon in the Main group of Program Manager. Choose Options, Add/Remove Windows Components. The dialog box shown in Figure 1.2 enables you to get rid of README files, accessories, games, screen savers, and other miscellaneous files. If you want to trim your Windows files even more, refer to the section "Optional Windows Files," later in this chapter.

How to Load Windows on Your PC . . . Best!

Once you've navigated through Setup and installed Windows properly, you have a variety of modes and options for how to run it. We've included a host of different possibilities here. No one will ever use all of these, but this unique flexibility represents one of Windows' crowning glories.

Using the WIN Command

One of the pleasures of working with Windows programs is that there's nearly always more than one way to get something done. Here are some alternative methods for starting Windows.

Start Windows with Your Favorite Program Open and Running One way to start Windows is with your favorite program in place. To to this you include the program's name as a DOS command-line parameter. For example, to start Windows and then load and open Polaris PackRat, go to the DOS prompt and type:

```
win packrat
```

FIGURE 1.2

Remove Windows components that you don't use by running Windows Setup. You can remove accessories, games, screen savers, README files, and more.

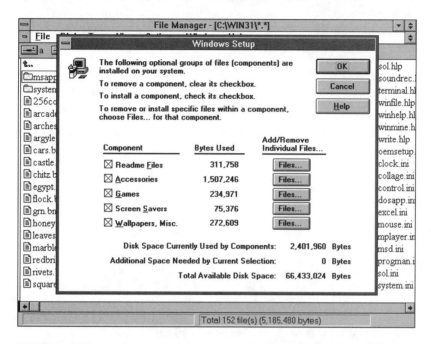

You don't have to include your program's extension, but you do need to make sure Windows can find the program. In this example, if PACKRAT.EXE was not stored in your Windows directory—or in another directory included in your DOS path—you'd need to include a path name before PACKRAT.

 When you start Windows with a command-line parameter, the system itself comes up faster because it skips the opening logo screen.

Launch a File Automatically Every Time You Load Windows You can start either a Windows or a non-Windows program with a command-line parameter. You can also launch Windows with a file in place, in one of two ways. The first way is simply to add the filename after the command-line parameter, as just described. So, if you wanted to open a copy of Excel and load a file called BUDGET.XLS, you could start Windows by typing the following command:

```
win excel budget.xls
```

The second method requires the file's extension to be associated with an application in the [Extensions] section of WIN.INI. Suppose you have a file named TODOLIST.TXT. If you type

```
win todolist.txt
```

at the DOS prompt, Windows loads, runs Notepad, and opens your to-do list, because files with the extension .TXT are associated with Notepad.

Windows Setup creates several other associations, and every time you install a Windows application, more associations are added to the WIN.INI file. You can also make associations manually—just go into Windows' File Manager and select Associate from the File menu. (Associating files is covered in more detail in Chapter 7.)

Check Out Four Other Parameters for the WIN Command   Here are four other handy parameters that you can employ with the WIN command:

- The /3 parameter loads Windows in 386 Enhanced mode, assuming your system meets the basic hardware requirements for Enhanced mode.

- The /S parameter loads Windows in Standard mode, assuming your system meets the basic hardware requirements for Standard mode.

- The /R parameter (for Windows 3.0 only) loads Windows in Real mode.

- The /B parameter (for Windows 3.1 only) generates a file, BOOT-LOG.TXT, that records system messages during startup. This log can be helpful in diagnosing problems you experience loading Windows in either 386 Enhanced or Standard mode.

Use the /D Parameter to Troubleshoot 386 Enhanced Mode   The /D parameter (for Windows 3.1 only) helps you identify conflicts when Windows doesn't start up properly in 386 Enhanced mode. Use the /D parameter with the following variables—try starting Windows using each variable. For more information on using these switches, see the section "Troubleshooting 386 Enhanced Mode," later in this chapter.

- The /D:F parameter turns off 32-bit disk access. If Windows loads properly in 386 Enhanced mode when you use this parameter, chances are you've mistakenly specified (either in the 386 Enhanced section of Control Panel or in your SYSTEM.INI file) that 32-bit disk access should be on, even though your hard disk cannot support 32-bit disk access. This parameter is equivalent to the SYSTEM.INI file setting 32BitDiskAccess=FALSE.

- The D:S parameter specifies that Windows should not use ROM address space between F000:0000 and 1Mb for a breakpoint. If Windows loads properly when you use this parameter, it's likely that a third-party 386 memory manager (such as QEMM-386 or 386Max) has been using the address space at the same time that Windows has been trying to use it. This parameter is equivalent to the SYSTEM.INI file setting SystemROMBreakPoint=FALSE.

- The D:V parameter causes Windows to use the computer's ROM routine to handle interrupts from the hard-disk controller. If Windows loads properly when you use this switch, Windows' own 386 Enhanced routines have been trying unsuccessfully to handle interrupts from your PC's hard-disk controller. This parameter is equivalent to the SYSTEM.INI setting VirtualHDIRQ=FALSE.

■ The D:X parameter makes Windows exclude all upper memory blocks from being used while loading in 386 Enhanced mode. If Windows starts successfully when you use this parameter, there's an upper memory conflict between Windows and another device on your system. This parameter is equivalent to the SYSTEM.INI setting EMMExclude=A000-FFFF.

Windows' Three Modes and What They Mean to You

The best way to run Windows on your system depends both on your hardware setup and on how you plan to use Windows. Windows offers three distinct modes of operation. Here, we examine the strengths and weaknesses of each, and offer tips for troubleshooting Standard and 386 Enhanced modes.

Windows Modes and System Requirements

Which mode you run Windows in depends first on what your hardware is capable of—in particular, the type of processor your PC has, how much RAM is available, and how much hard-disk space is free.

Real Mode (Windows 3.0 only)   Windows' Real mode is the default for Windows 3.0 running on a PC with at least 640K, but less than 1Mb, of RAM. Real mode requires a PC with an 8088 processor or better. Don't expect much if you're running Windows in Real mode. In this mode, Windows 3.0 is hobbled by many of the same performance and memory limitations that plagued pre-3.0 versions of Windows. Task-switching in Real mode requires Windows to swap data out to disk, slowing down operations considerably. Microsoft put Real mode out of business with Windows 3.1, which runs only in Standard or 386 Enhanced mode.

Standard Mode   Standard mode is the default mode for Windows 3.0 or 3.1 running on an 80286 PC with at least 1Mb of RAM. Other requirements for running in Standard mode are 6.5Mb free hard-disk space, EGA or better graphics, and an extended memory driver such as Windows' own HIMEM.SYS. For running Windows 3.1 in Standard mode, Microsoft *recommends* (but doesn't require) at least 2Mb of RAM, 9Mb free hard-disk space, and VGA or better graphics. Among the advantages of Standard mode is that it allows Windows and Windows applications to access all the memory installed on the PC, although DOS applications are still limited to the conventional 640K. Switching between loaded applications is fairly speedy in Standard mode, as long as your PC's memory doesn't become overloaded.

386 Enhanced Mode   386 Enhanced mode is the default mode for Windows 3.0 or 3.1 running on an 80386 or better PC with at least 1.6Mb RAM (640K conventional and 1,024K extended). It also requires 8Mb free hard-disk space, EGA or better graphics, and an extended memory driver such as Windows' HIMEM.SYS. For running Windows 3.1 in 386 Enhanced mode, Microsoft recommends (but does not require) at least 4Mb RAM, 10.5Mb free disk space, and VGA or better graphics.

386 Enhanced mode is the best that Windows has to offer. One advantage it has over Standard mode is that it allows true multitasking (the ability to run more than one program simultaneously) as opposed to task-switching (the ability to have more than one application loaded at once and to switch quickly between them). Another is that 386 Enhanced mode lets you run DOS programs in resizable windows, whereas Standard mode lets you run DOS programs only in full-screen mode.

When (If Ever) to Use Real Mode

If you're running Windows 3.0 in Real mode, you're missing out on the real benefits of Windows. In fact, probably the only reason to use Real mode is if you have old Windows applications (*2.x*) that *require* you to run Windows 3.0 in Real mode. If your system is capable of running in 386 Enhanced mode, you can use the following technique to get the benefits of Windows while running your old applications.

Start Windows 3.0 as you normally would in 386 Enhanced mode. Next, go into the PIF Editor in the Main program group, and create a .PIF file for a DOS session that runs Windows in Real mode. (PIF is short for Program Information File, which is the file Windows uses to configure DOS programs running under Windows.) In the PIF Editor dialog box, enter **C:\WINDOWS\WIN.COM** for the Program Filename. For Optional Parameters, enter **/r** to start Windows in Real mode. Save the .PIF file, naming it WINREAL.PIF, for example. Now, when you want to run old Windows applications, just choose Run from the Program Manager File menu and specify the name of the .PIF file.

Making the Most of Standard Mode

Even though Standard mode doesn't give you access to multitasking and resizable DOS windows, as 386 Enhanced mode does, there are plenty of compelling reasons to use it, no matter how powerful your system is. Use the following guidelines to get the most out of Windows when you're running in Standard mode.

Speed Performance with Standard Mode   If you only run Windows applications, or if you run DOS applications only occasionally, you'll get better performance from Windows by running in Standard mode (type **win /s** at the command line). Although Windows can't provide expanded memory in Standard mode, you can allocate expanded memory *before* loading Windows that will then be available to DOS applications running under Windows, but *only* if you have a physical EMS card, such as AST's RAMPage or Intel's AboveBoard.

You can use either EMM386 or a third-party memory-management utility such as QEMM-386 to allocate expanded memory in this manner.

When you run Windows in Standard mode, you'll also lose the ability to run DOS applications in a window, but you'll get snappier performance because Windows won't chew up processor cycles managing virtual memory.

Use Standard Mode with DOS-Extended Programs   You should also load Windows in Standard mode if you want to run DOS-extended applications—such as AutoCAD, Paradox 3.5, and Lotus 1-2-3 3.1—while in Windows. You cannot run DOS-extended programs like AutoCAD and Paradox 3.5 in 386 Enhanced mode, but if you use Quarterdeck's QEMM memory manager you can still run them effectively in Standard mode. With QEMM's support for the DOS protected-mode interface (DPMI), these applications will have access to the memory they need.

Use a Larger Number of File Handles for Running Standard Mode   If you're running in Standard mode, you should increase the number of file handles that are specified in your CONFIG.SYS file. These file handles are shared among applications in Standard mode. A low number may cause applications that use a large number of file handles, such as databases, to perform poorly or not run at all. Try setting the number to 50 or more for such applications. To do this, change the FILES= line in your CONFIG.SYS to read FILES=50.

Add a RAM Disk If You've Got Memory to Spare   If you have 4Mb of RAM or more on your system, consider setting up a RAM disk. For details on how to do so, see Chapter 3.

To speed up switching to and from DOS applications, add a line to your SYSTEM.INI file that tells Windows exactly where your RAM disk is. In the [NonWindowsApps] section, add the line SwapDisk=*drive,* where *drive* points to your RAM disk. For more on the Windows .INI files, consult Chapter 2.

Troubleshooting Windows in Standard Mode   If you're having trouble running Windows in Standard mode, the following troubleshooting tips will help get you up and running:

1. Check your hardware.   Does your hardware meet the minimum system requirements for running Windows in Standard mode? You'll need at least a 286 system with 1Mb of RAM.

2. Try running in Real mode.   If you're running Windows 3.0, check whether you can at least run in Real mode (type **win /r** at the DOS prompt). If you can run in Real mode but not in Standard mode, you may have a problem with a device driver that was designed for an earlier version of Windows. Drivers for older versions of Windows—including those for keyboard, printer, and video—often prevent Windows 3.0 from running in Standard mode. Try disabling the old drivers and using the ones that came with Windows 3.0. To add the latest drivers, you'll have to run Windows Setup from the DOS prompt. If a more up-to-date driver isn't available on your Windows disks, contact the device's manufacturer or Microsoft for a driver update.

3. Search out conflicts with memory-resident programs. Check your AUTOEXEC.BAT file for conflicts with memory-resident programs, also known as TSRs. If you load any TSRs before starting Windows, remark them out of your AUTOEXEC.BAT file (type **rem** before the command that loads them) and try starting Windows again. Also check that your CONFIG.SYS contains lines specifying an adequate number of file handles and buffers. File handles should be at 30 or more (FILES=30), and buffers should be at 20 or less (BUFFERS=20).

4. Check your version of HIMEM.SYS. Make sure that you're using the version of HIMEM.SYS that comes on your Windows disks. You'll have to expand the file off of the disks for Windows to recognize it. For Windows 3.1, you'll need version 3.01 of HIMEM.SYS or higher. (For instructions on how to expand the file, see the earlier section "Copying Files from Windows Disks without Running Setup.")

5. Update your version of DOS. Are you using the correct version of DOS? If you aren't using DOS 5.0, you may need a new version from your system's manufacturer for your PC to run Windows smoothly. Contact your PC's manufacturer for an updated version, or, even better, install MS-DOS 5.0 over the older version you've been using. Also check that you're using a current version of your system's BIOS—contact your system manufacturer to find out whether you need a new one and, if so, how to get it.

6. Make sure HIMEM.SYS is identifying your PC correctly. HIMEM.SYS may be incorrectly identifying your machine and therefore unable to access extended memory correctly. The A20 handler is the name of the device that tells HIMEM.SYS what kind of machine you're running and which routine to use to access extended memory. At bootup you'll see the line "Installed A20 handler number x." The x is a number from 1 to 8 that specifies the type of machine you're using; for example, a value of 1 identifies an IBM AT or compatible, and a value of 2 identifies a PS/2. The A20 handlers that Windows uses are listed in Table 1.2. Check with your system manufacturer for the A20 handler used by your system. Once you know the setting, force HIMEM.SYS to use it by adding the /M switch after the line that loads HIMEM.SYS in your CONFIG.SYS file. For example, the line

```
DEVICE=C:\DOS\HIMEM.SYS /M:1
```

indicates that you're running Windows on an IBM AT or compatible PC.

TABLE 1.2

A20 Handlers Used in Windows

Number	Name	Computer Type
1	at	IBM AT or compatible
2	ps/2	IBM PS/2
3	ptlcascade	Phoenix Cascade BIOS
4	hpvectra	HP Vectra (A and A+)
5	att6300plus	AT&T 6300 Plus
6	acer1100	Acer 1100
7	toshiba	Toshiba 1600 and 1200 XE
8	wyse	Wyse 12.5 Mhz 286

7. Find out if you're squeezing memory. Your system may require more extended memory. Check the device settings in your CONFIG.SYS file for programs, such as EMM386, that use extended memory. Disable these programs by commenting out the CONFIG.SYS line that loads them (add REM to the beginning of the line), or deduct the amount of memory allocated to them. Then try reloading Windows.

8. Disable RAM shadowing. Disable RAM shadowing if your system supports it. Check your PC's setup program or manual if you're not sure.

9a. Pad your code segments. If you're using a 286 system, you may be unable to run Windows in Standard mode unless you add the following statement to the [Standard] section of your SYSTEM.INI file:

```
PadCodeSegments=1
```

This setting tells Windows to pad code segments with 16 bytes, ensuring that the last instruction in the segment is not too close to the segment limit for your 286 PC. For more details on the Windows .INI files, refer to Chapter 2.

9b. Boot from a clean floppy. Have you made any changes to your system? Deleted any files? Installed any new programs or utilities? Try booting your system from a floppy disk and then running Windows in Standard mode. If you can load Windows after booting from a floppy, the offending element is probably a program or driver that's loaded by your AUTOEXEC.BAT or CONFIG.SYS file. Try commenting out the programs and drivers loaded by these files (add REM at the beginning of the line that loads them), and then add them back one by one to track down the conflicting program. If you've added any peripherals such as printers to your system, try disabling these devices and their drivers and then running Windows.

10. Reinstall Windows. If all else fails, try reinstalling Windows on your system. If you still can't run Windows in Standard mode, contact your system manufacturer.

Enhancing 386 Enhanced Mode

If you have the hardware, 386 Enhanced mode gives you the best Windows has to offer, especially in terms of support for DOS applications. Here's how to use it right.

Use SMARTDrive or Another Disk Cache Set up SMARTDrive or another disk cache on your system to speed up performance. A *disk cache* is a section of memory that keeps recently accessed information available so that your system can get to it faster than if it had to search the hard disk. For guidelines on setting up SMARTDrive, see Chapter 3.

Defragment Your Hard Disk Remember to defragment your hard disk often— for instance, on a weekly basis. A fragmented hard disk greatly affects Windows' performance, especially if you have SMARTDrive or a swap file installed.

Create a Permanent Swap File In 386 Enhanced mode, a swap file lets you use hard-disk space to create virtual memory in addition to the physical memory in your system. For guidelines on setting up a permanent swap file, see Chapter 3.

Change Your SYSTEM.INI To speed up file access by DOS applications running under 386 Enhanced mode, disable the option that allows Windows to monitor disk access by DOS applications and then send update messages to File Manager so that it knows what changes were made. You can turn off this feature by checking your SYSTEM.INI file and making sure the [386Enh] section includes the following line:

```
FileSysChange=off
```

While you've got your SYSTEM.INI open for editing, look for the line ReservePageFrame= in the same section. Turn off this option if you don't need expanded memory for your DOS applications; you'll increase the amount of conventional memory available to them and therefore increase system performance. Chapter 2 includes detailed information on working with Windows .INI files.

Use Standard VGA Opt for VGA display with Windows unless you really need the higher resolution or additional color choices available from an SVGA monitor. If you can do without these extra features, you'll get better performance from your system.

Troubleshooting Problems with Loading Windows in 386 Enhanced Mode

386 Enhanced mode is the most powerful way to operate Windows, but it can also be problematic to load and run properly. Use the following guidelines to solve problems in 386 Enhanced mode. Often these tips involve altering your Windows .INI files, a topic that is covered in depth in the next chapter.

1. Be sure your system meets 386 Enhanced mode requirements.   Does your hardware meet the minimum system requirements for running Windows in 386 Enhanced mode? You'll need at least a 386 system with 2Mb RAM. If you have enough memory, try forcing Windows into 386 Enhanced mode by using the command-line switch /3 with the WIN command. If Windows successfully starts in 386 Enhanced mode only when you use this switch, it's not detecting enough memory in your system. If you're short on RAM, you won't be able to run EMM386 or other memory managers that allow you to load memory-resident programs and device drivers into upper memory blocks, because 386 Enhanced mode remaps extended memory to the upper memory blocks. You can still force Windows into 386 Enhanced mode if you have less than 2Mb of extended memory available, by using the /3 command-line switch, but you should avoid doing so unless absolutely necessary, because performance will suffer.

2. Try starting in Standard mode.   Can you run in Standard mode (or does Windows default to Standard mode)? To see if Windows runs in Standard mode, type **win /s** at the DOS prompt. If you can't run in either Standard mode or Enhanced mode, you may have a program conflict. Have you made any changes to your system since running Windows Setup? Deleted any files? Installed any new programs, utilities, or drivers? Try booting your system from a floppy disk and then running Windows. If you can boot from a floppy, comment out the programs and drivers by adding REM at the front of the lines that load them in your AUTOEXEC.BAT and CONFIG.SYS files. Then try adding the original programs and drivers back to your AUTOEXEC.BAT and CONFIG.SYS files one by one to find the conflicting program.

   Likewise, disable any programs that are automatically loaded when you start Windows. Open your WIN.INI file in Notepad or by running SYSEDIT (from Program Manager choose File, Run, SYSEDIT.EXE), and comment out the load= and run= lines by placing a semicolon in front of them.

   If you're running Windows 3.1, you must also disable the Startup group. To do so, simply select the Startup group icon in Program Manager; choose File, Properties; and change the name of the Startup program group to anything but STARTUP.GRP. Exit Windows and try restarting Windows in 386 Enhanced mode.

   If Windows does start in Standard mode automatically, also try booting the system from a floppy and disabling any programs that start automatically when

Windows is loaded, as just described. Exit Windows and try restarting Windows in 386 Enhanced mode.

3. Check for outdated drivers.   If you've added to your system any peripherals with their own drivers, such as printers, try disabling these and instead use the appropriate device driver that came with Windows. To install this driver, you'll have to run Setup from the DOS prompt. If you can't find a more recent version of the driver on your Windows disks, contact the device's manufacturer or Microsoft for an updated driver.

4. Update your version of DOS.   Are you using the correct version of DOS? If you aren't using DOS 5.0 and your computer is an IBM-compatible, you may require an updated version of DOS from your PC's manufacturer. Contact the manufacturer for the correct version, or better yet install MS-DOS 5.0.

   Also, make sure that you're using the latest BIOS version available for your system; check with your PC's manufacturer to find out whether you have an updated BIOS and how to get a new one if necessary. In addition, be sure you're using the correct version of HIMEM.SYS: Windows 3.1 requires version 3.01 or higher. If you need to retrieve HIMEM.SYS from your Windows disks, you'll have to expand it before you can use it. (See the earlier section "Copying Files from Windows without Running Setup" for instructions.)

5. Make sure HIMEM.SYS is identifying your machine properly.   HIMEM.SYS may be incorrectly identifying your machine and therefore be unable to access extended memory correctly. The A20 handler is the device that tells HIMEM.SYS what kind of machine you're running and which routine to use to access extended memory. At bootup you'll see the line "Installed A20 handler number x," where x is a number from 1 to 8 that specifies the type of machine you're using; for example, a value of 1 identifies an IBM AT or compatible, and a value of 2 identifies a PS/2. The A20 handlers that Windows uses are shown in Table 1.2.

   Check with your system manufacturer for the correct A20 handler for your system. Once you know the setting, force HIMEM.SYS to use it by adding the /M switch to the DEVICE= line in your CONFIG.SYS file that loads HIMEM.SYS. For example, if your system is an IBM AT or compatible, use this line in your CONFIG.SYS file:

```
DEVICE=C:\DOS\HIMEM.SYS /M:1
```

6. Rule out memory conflicts.   You may have a memory conflict between a device and Windows in the upper memory blocks. This occurs if Windows fails to recognize a card or device in upper memory and tries using the same memory range. Try excluding a range of upper memory from use by Windows by editing the EMMExclude= line in the [386Enh] section of your SYSTEM.INI file. To test for such a conflict, try starting Windows from the DOS prompt by typing **win /d:x**. This parameter excludes all of the upper memory blocks from use. (See the earlier section "Use the /D Parameter to Troubleshoot 386 Enhanced Mode," which explains how to diagnose system problems with the /D parameter.)

If Windows is now able to start in 386 Enhanced mode, the problem is a device conflict. Try to find the memory address of the conflicting adapter and narrow the range that you are excluding from use by Windows by including the statement

```
EMMExclude=address range
```

in the [386Enh] section of the SYSTEM.INI file. For example, many high-resolution video boards use the address range above C000 to C7FF, so the SYSTEM.INI would contain the line EMMExclude=C000-C7FF. Likewise, nonstandard video boards often use the range C600-C800; try excluding this range if you have such a board. Do not exclude the entire range (A000-EFFF), because when running in 386 Enhanced mode, Windows tries to reserve space for system maintenance in upper memory. If the space isn't available, the buffers will be placed in conventional memory, resulting in a considerable drop in performance.

If you're loading the EMM386 driver in your CONFIG.SYS, you can exclude memory blocks there by following the DEVICE=EMM386.EXE line with the switch

```
x=address range
```

instead of using EMMExclude in the SYSTEM.INI file.

7. Fine-tune your SYSTEM.INI file.   Try further fine-tuning your SYSTEM-.INI to solve the problem. To the [386Enh] section, add the line VirtualHD-IRQ=Off to the [386Enh] section of the SYSTEM.INI. This statement tells Windows not to terminate interrupts from the hard-disk controller, but instead to use your system's ROM routines to handle these interrupts. Some hard drives can process interrupts correctly only if this setting is off.

8. Check for hardware interrupt conflicts.   If Windows won't run in 386 Enhanced mode, you may have an interrupt conflict between two hardware devices. Remove all hardware devices—such as mouse, modem, and network card—from your system. If you can run Windows in 386 Enhanced mode after removing all the devices, try adding them back one at a time to find the conflict. Once you've found the offending device, trying changing the interrupt it uses.

9. Check for the WINA20.386 file.   Are you using Windows 3.0 and DOS 5.0? Check that the read-only file WINA20.386 is in your root directory. If it's in another directory, you'll have to tell Windows where it is by adding a SWITCHES=/W statement to your CONFIG.SYS file and adding a device statement to the [386Enh] section of your SYSTEM.INI file. For example, if you have moved WINA20.386 to your SYSTEM subdirectory, you should put this statement in the [386Enh] section of SYSTEM.INI:

```
DEVICE=C:\SYSTEM\WINA20.386
```

Reboot your system and Windows should run in 386 Enhanced mode.

If WINA20.386 is missing from your system, you will need to install it from your DOS 5.0 disks.

10. Disable RAM shadowing. Disable RAM shadowing if it's supported by your system; check your PC's setup screen or manual to find out if this is so.

11. Reinstall Windows. Try reinstalling Windows. If you still can't run Windows in 386 Enhanced mode, contact your system manufacturer.

Troubleshooting Problems with Operating Windows in 386 Enhanced Mode

Even if Windows loads smoothly in 386 Enhanced mode, you may notice some problems with the operation of your system when Windows is running. Use these tips to pinpoint the solution.

Hard-Disk Difficulties If you're having hard-disk problems under 386 Enhanced mode and are using a SCSI hard disk (or another nonstandard controller), make sure you're using SMARTDrive. Without SMARTDrive, Windows supports only standard ST506 and ESDI controllers. With SMARTDrive installed, Windows will direct all disk access requests through it and resolve any conflicts.

If you try this and you still have hard-disk problems, try adding the line VirtualHDIRQ=Off to the [386Enh] section of the SYSTEM.INI. This statement tells Windows not to terminate interrupts from the hard-disk controller and to bypass the ROM routines that handle these interrupts. Some hard drives can't process interrupts correctly unless this setting is off.

Internal Stack Overflow If you get an internal stack overflow while in Enhanced mode, check your CONFIG.SYS file for the STACKS= statement. If you're using Windows 3.0 and DOS 3.3 or later, it should read STACKS=0,0. For Windows 3.1 and DOS 3.3 or later, the line should read STACKS=9,256.

Slow Typing If you notice that typing slows down when you are running more than one application in Enhanced mode, increase the priority of a foreground application whenever it receives a keystroke. To do so, add the statement

```
KeyBoostTime=.005
```

(or a larger number) to the [386Enh] section of your SYSTEM.INI file.

Optional Windows Files

The way you want to use Windows on one PC may be different from your intentions on another. You may want to go full bore on that 486 monster at work, but have to sweat every megabyte on your 386SX home machine or that disk-starved notebook. You can tailor which parts of Windows you install to fit your needs and your hardware.

111 Windows Files You Can Do Without

If you travel with Windows on a notebook PC, or if disk space on your desktop system is at a premium, take note of 111 files that you can eliminate and still run Windows 3.1. Table 1.3 lists these files. Many of these same files are found in Windows 3.0, so you can free up disk space with the earlier version too.

TABLE 1.3

111 Nonessential Windows Files

File Extension	Subdirectory	Number of Files	Disk Space Saved	Description
*.BMP	WINDOWS	22	187K	Wallpaper and desktop patterns
*.WAV	WINDOWS	4	80K	Sound effects
*.SCR	WINDOWS	4	58K	Screen Savers
*.WRI	WINDOWS	5	364K	On-line documentation
SOL.*, WINMINE.*	WINDOWS	4	239K	Games
*.MID	WINDOWS	2	74K	Sample MIDI files
CALENDAR.*, CARDFILE.*, CLOCK.*, MPLAYER.*, PACKAGER.*, PBRUSH.*, PRINTMAN.*, RECORDER.*, SOUNDREC.*, WINTUTOR.*	WINDOWS	21	1,020K	Nonessential applications
CALC.*, CHARMAP.*, MSD.*, TERMINAL.*, WRITE.*	WINDOWS	10	714K	Interesting but disposable applications
WINHELP.EXE, *.HLP	WINDOWS	12	724K	Windows Help
*.TXT	WINDOWS	2	27K	Miscellaneous text files
CLIPBRD.*	WINDOWS	2	31K	Clipboard
DRWATSON.EXE	WINDOWS	1	26K	Fault-detection utility
TASKMAN.EXE	WINDOWS	1	4K	Task Manager
SMARTDRV.EXE	WINDOWS	1	43K	SMARTDrive disk cache (delete if you use a third-party cache)
MORICONS.DLL	WINDOWS	1	116K	Dynamic link library with program icons
EMM386.EXE	WINDOWS	1	108K	Expanded memory manager (delete if you aren't loading EMM386.EXE in CONFIG.SYS and you don't need expanded memory for DOS applications).

TABLE 1.3

111 Nonessential Windows Files (Continued)

File Extension	Subdirectory	Number of Files	Disk Space Saved	Description
RAMDRIVE.SYS	WINDOWS	1	6K	Support for RAM drive in extended memory
MODERN.FON, ROMAN.FON, SCRIPT.FON	SYSTEM	3	34K	Little-used vector fonts
COURx.FON, SMALLx.FON, SYMbOLx.FON	SYSTEM	3	105K	Bit-mapped fonts
MCI*.*, MIDI*.*, TIMER.DRV	SYSTEM	5	134K	Multimedia drivers
SYSEDIT.EXE	SYSTEM	1	18K	System editor
xxxLOGO.*	SYSTEM	2	27K	Logo files
MMSYSTEM.DLL	SYSTEM	1	60K	Dynamic link library for playing audio files
DDEML.DLL	SYSTEM	1	36K	Dynamic data exchange library
TOOLHELP.DLL	SYSTEM	1	14K	Dynamic link library for information on Windows internal data, used with the Dr. Watson utility
Totals		111	4,249K	

Remove Drivers and Fonts You Don't Use

In addition to removing any of the preceding 111 files, you can get rid of any fonts and drivers that are installed on your system and that you don't use. For example, maybe you hate the WingDing font, or perhaps you've installed a new printer on your system (which means that the drivers for your old printer are still on disk even though you're not using them).

To remove unwanted fonts, open Control Panel and select the Fonts icon. Select the names of the fonts that you want to get rid of, and make sure that the Delete Font File from Disk option is checked, as shown in Figure 1.3. Choose Remove, and then answer Yes when prompted.

To remove extra printer drivers from your system, open Control Panel and select the Printers icon. Select the printers you don't use, and choose Remove. Likewise, choose the Drivers icon in Control Panel and select and remove any other drivers that you don't need. Unfortunately, this won't delete the actual driver files from your disk; it just deletes the references to them. To delete the files themselves, you'll have to find out their filenames and delete them from File Manager or from the DOS command line.

FIGURE 1.3 ▬▬▬▬▬▬▬▬▬▬▬▬▬▬▬▬▬▬▬▬▬▬▬▬▬▬▬▬▬▬▬▬

Conserve hard-disk space by deleting fonts that you don't need from the Control Panel.
When the Delete Font File From Disk option is selected, the font will be removed from
Windows and deleted from your hard disk.

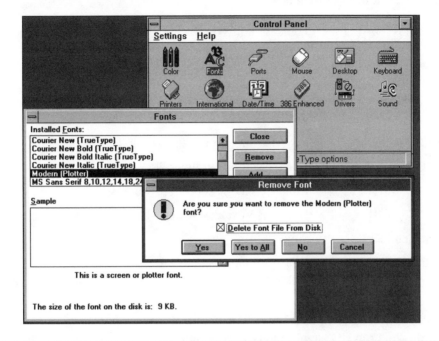

Remove Support for Standard Mode

If you run Windows exclusively in 386 Enhanced mode, you can delete several
more files—the ones that support Standard mode. When deleted, the following
files will yield approximately 183K in disk space. Note that if you do delete any
of these files, you won't be able to run Windows in Standard mode.

DOSX.EXE	Microsoft DOS Extender
DSWAP.EXE	Standard mode support for swapping non-Windows applications
KRNL286.EXE	The Standard mode kernel
WINOLDAP.MOD	Standard mode support for executing non-Windows applications
WSWAP.EXE	Standard mode support for swapping DOS applications
*.2GR	Standard mode grabber file

Remove Support for 386 Enhanced Mode

If you run Windows exclusively in Standard mode, you can delete the following files to disable 386 Enhanced mode support. These files will free up approximately 781K on your hard disk.

CGA40WOA.FON, CGA80WOA.FON, EGA40WOA.FON, EGA80WOA.FON	Fonts for non-Windows applications
CPWIN386.CPL	Support file for the Enhanced mode icon in Control Panel
DOSAPP.FON	Font that supports sizable text in Enhanced mode
*.3GR	Enhanced mode grabber file
*.386	Enhanced mode support drivers
WIN386.EXE	Windows Virtual Machine Manager
WIN386.PS2	Support for PS/2s
WINOA386.MOD	Enhanced mode support for non-Windows applications

Remove Support for DOS Applications

If you don't run DOS applications from Windows—and never plan to—you can also get rid of the following files and free up nearly 300K of disk space:

PIFEDIT.EXE	PIF Editor
*.PIF	.PIF files
APPS.INF	PIF information file
CGA40WOA.FON, CGA80WOA.FON, EGA40WOA.FON, EGA80WOA.FON	Fonts for non-Windows applications
*.2GR, *.3GR	Standard mode and 386 Enhanced mode grabber files
DOSAPP.FON	Font that supports sizable text in 386 Enhanced mode
WINOLDAP.MOD	Standard mode support for executing non-Windows applications
WINOA386.MOD	Enhanced mode support for non-Windows applications
DSWAP.EXE	Standard mode support for swapping non-Windows applications

A Few Files to Keep Handy

In your enthusiasm for freeing up hard-disk space, you may start deleting some Windows files without a moment's hesitation. Here are a few files you might want to keep around. If you don't leave them on your hard drive, you may want to copy them to a floppy in case you want them later.

- MSD.EXE and MSD.INI are two files you need to run the Microsoft Diagnostics Utility. This utility reports on your system memory and drivers.

- DRWATSON.EXE and TOOLHELP.DLL allow you to run the Dr. Watson utility, a tool for detecting General Protection Faults.

- README.WRI, SYSINI.WRI, and WININI.WRI are README files providing information on Windows that became available after the manual was printed. Before deleting these files, you should skim them or consider printing them as a handy reference. (Windows 3.0 also contains the valuable README files README.TXT, SYSINI.TXT, SYSINI2.TXT, SYSINI3.TXT, WININI.TXT, and WININI2.TXT.)

- SYSEDIT.EXE is a text editor that allows easy access to your AUTOEXEC.BAT, CONFIG.SYS, WIN.INI, and SYSTEM.INI files.

The Many Ways to Skip the Windows Startup Screen

One of the most irritating aspects of Windows is waiting to get past the Microsoft advertisement that appears while the program is loading. The next section describes a number of ways to make it disappear.

Suppress the Startup Screen

You can reduce the time Windows takes to load by suppressing the startup screen and cutting straight to the chase. Simply complete the command at the DOS prompt with a space and colon. For example, to load Windows in Standard mode without the startup screen, type **win /s :**.

Another Command-Line Trick to Bypass the Logo

When you start Windows with a command-line parameter to load an application, Windows starts faster because it skips its opening logo screen. You can take advantage of this even if you don't want to start with an open application. Typing **win progman** will launch you directly into Windows' Program Manager.

Create a Batch File to Bypass the Logo

If you use a batch file to start Windows (for example, W.BAT) instead of having to type WIN each time, make it also bypass the Microsoft logo for you. As before, follow the WIN command in the batch file with a space and a colon. This way you can launch Windows, and bypass the logo, just by typing **w** at the DOS prompt.

Remove the Logo Permanently by Creating a New WIN.COM

If you want to remove the Windows logo from your system for good, just copy the WIN.CNF file (which contains the Windows startup code) from your SYSTEM directory to your main WINDOWS directory, renaming it WIN.COM. By doing this you are deleting the original WIN.COM created at setup, which is composed of WIN.CNF, a file that detects the video mode of your system, and another file that actually displays the logo.

Make AUTOEXEC.BAT Skip the Logo for You

If you start programs with either the run= or load= line in the WIN.INI file, you still have to see the Windows logo emblazoned on your screen. Fortunately, you can combine the command-line and WIN.INI methods. If you already start Windows with a command in your AUTOEXEC.BAT file, you might as well make that command read WIN PROGMAN, even if you also use the run= or load= line.

Replace the Windows Logo with the Image of Your Choice

If you prefer not to see the Windows logo every time you boot up, you can go a step further than simply eliminating it. Using some graphical craft, you can actually replace that Microsoft image with the image of your choice. At last, an advertisement for yourself!

The WIN.COM file that starts Windows is actually created from several files: WIN.CNF, VGALOGO.LGO (in a VGA system), and VGA-LOGO.RLE (for a VGA system). The last file is a bitmap file in a compressed format that displays the Windows logo. By substituting any image you like for the logo file, you can have Windows display that image at startup. The only requirement is that the image be in the Run-length encoded format (RLE). You can convert an image such as a .PCX or .BMP file with a graphics-file conversion program. Once the image is renamed to VGALOGO.RLE (or EGALOGO.RLE on your EGA display), you just need to copy it into the WINDOWS\SYSTEM subdirectory. It will be copied over the original Microsoft logo.

To get Windows to rebuild the WIN.COM file, change the display setting for your system in the DOS part of Windows Setup. Run Setup from the DOS prompt, and choose a different setting for the display option. Exit Setup, and then while you're still in DOS run Setup again and select your original display option. The next time you start Windows you should see your custom image on the startup screen.

On-line Resources

Windows is not just a product, it's a community. Never have so many smart people worked so hard and long on behalf of a computer product. As a result, you can find Windows advice in many places besides books like this. (For more information about on-line forums and bulletin boards dedicated to Windows, see Appendix A.)

Seek On-line Help

Check out all of the on-line forums dedicated to Windows users. CompuServe has a several Windows forums, including the Windows New Users forum (GO WINNEW) and the Windows Advanced Users forum (GO WINADV). If you need help with a Windows problem, on-line experts and fellow Windows users will probably have the answer or will help you find it. You'll also find the latest Windows shareware, icon files, and wallpaper files.

Windows Drivers Library

(206) 637-9009
This on-line resource, accessed through the Technical Support Library, provides compatible device drivers for Windows as they become available.

Microsoft Knowledge Base

Available on-line through Compuserve (GO MSKB), Knowledge Base is a collection of thousands of technical articles on Microsoft products written by Microsoft support. You can learn about compatibility, configuration, bugs, workarounds, customization, and more.

Exiting Windows Wisely

We've spent most of this chapter talking about getting *into* Windows. Getting *out* of Windows is even more automatic than starting it. But here again, wise users are aware of the options and dangers that confront them.

Fast Windows Shutdown

Since you probably don't change your Windows layout every day, don't use the Save Settings option upon exiting Windows. When you do want to record a new layout, just hold down the Shift key and choose Exit Windows from the Program Manager File menu. This action forces a rewrite of your group layout without your having to exit Windows.

Exiting DOS Programs Quickly in Enhanced Mode

Windows deliberately makes it difficult for you to exit Windows in Real (for 3.0) or Standard mode with a DOS application active. When your C: prompt is just sitting there, you're in fact running a program called COMMAND.COM, DOS's command-line interpreter. Although it may be frustrating, this feature protects you from ending the Windows session with an unsaved data file open in your DOS application. It's designed this way because of Windows' inability to communicate effectively with DOS applications.

When you tell Windows to shut down, it sends a message to all the Windows applications that are still running. If you have unsaved data in a Windows application—an Excel worksheet or a Word for Windows document, for example—you're given the opportunity to save the data before Windows shuts down.

Because DOS applications cannot respond to these Windows messages, it's conceivable that your DOS window might contain a 1-2-3 spreadsheet, for example, that has not yet been saved. If you exited from Windows without saving the data in the DOS session, you would lose the file—and very likely your composure as well.

If you run Windows in Real or Standard mode, there is no way short of rebooting to exit from Windows with a DOS session still active. On the other hand, if you're running in 386 Enhanced mode, you can order Windows to let you shut down with a DOS program open; the DOS application must be running under the control of a .PIF file.

Here's how to set up a .PIF file for a DOS version of 1-2-3 that will surrender without protest: Double-click on the PIF Editor icon (in the Program Manager's Accessories group), choose File Open, and then load 123.PIF from the WINDOWS directory. (If you don't have a .PIF file for the DOS application, click on the Windows Setup icon in the Main group and choose Options, Set Up Applications.) Next, click on the Advanced button at the bottom of the dialog box. Under Other Options in the Advanced Options dialog box that appears, you'll see a check box labeled Allow Close When Active. Click on this box and then click on OK. Windows will display an error message warning that you might lose data if you set this option. (Of course, caution is warranted when using this powerful option.) Click on OK to clear the dialog box. Then choose File, Save As and save the .PIF file.

Now, the next time you attempt to exit Windows with a 1-2-3 window active, you'll see a different error message: "Application still active. Choose OK to end it." Click on OK, and your Windows session will end without fuss.

How to Quickly Exit DOS Applications in Standard Mode

There is a workaround that lets you exit Windows in Standard mode without having to go into each DOS session you have running. To do so, call up the Windows Task Manager (either by double-clicking on your wallpaper or pressing Ctrl+Esc). In the Task List box, select one of the sessions. Then choose the End Task button. A dialog box informs you that the application is still active, and tells you to select OK if you want to end it. Repeat this process for all of the DOS sessions you have running, and then exit Windows.

2. Win.ini and System.ini: A Complete Reference Guide

THE MULTIFACETED NATURE OF WINDOWS IS CONCENTRATED WITHIN TWO files: WIN.INI and SYSTEM.INI. These files function as intricate control panels through which the sophisticated user can fine-tune Windows in innumerable ways. On the one hand this is a brilliant stroke of program design and one of Windows' big wins. It makes the operating system easily accessible to user, manager, and programs. On the other hand, the density of options in Windows results in two huge, complex files that can prove daunting to the uninitiated. So, as a natural first step on our journey toward total Windows power, we are devoting this early chapter to deciphering the intricacies of Windows' two most important files.

NOTE Both Windows 3.0 and Windows 3.1 have WIN.INI and SYSTEM.INI files, but not every notation is the same in both. We have aimed this chapter at Windows 3.1, the latest version, but we note where a particular aspect is new or changed from Windows 3.0.

WIN.INI and SYSTEM.INI have distinctly different purposes. In broad terms, WIN.INI's purpose is to record your preferences about how you want your system to look and behave. Entries in WIN.INI, for example, tell Windows whether you want to be beeped when you err, what wallpaper you want to use, whether you want your wallpaper tiled or centered, and myriad other details. SYSTEM.INI, in contrast, mostly records information about the nature of your system—the kind of display you're using, the type of network you're connected to, the names of device drivers that Windows will use, and so on.

This distinction, preferences versus system components, is not absolute. Printer and communication ports, for example, are listed in WIN.INI, and SYSTEM.INI handles one crucial matter of preference—the name of the program that will act as your Windows shell. But generally you can think of WIN.INI as the place where customization choices are recorded. If you change the equipment you're using to run Windows, or if you get involved in troubleshooting your system, you'll probably be working with SYSTEM.INI.

How .INI Files Are Structured

WIN.INI and SYSTEM.INI are both plain ASCII text files. Each consists of several sections, and each section is headed by a word or phrase enclosed in brackets, like this:

```
[Desktop]
```

Beneath the bracketed heading come one or more lines consisting of a keyword, an equal sign, and zero or more parameters. A typical entry might look like this:

```
KeyboardSpeed=31
```

If a line has no parameter to the right of the equal sign, Windows uses that line's default value. So, for example, the line

```
KeyboardSpeed=
```

would be equivalent to the line

```
KeyboardSpeed=31
```

because 31 is KeyboardSpeed's default value.

In most cases, Windows also uses a line's default value if that line is omitted. (There are exceptions. If certain lines are removed from SYSTEM.INI, Windows doesn't use defaults; it crashes.) If you want to specify a nondefault value for a line that isn't now in your WIN.INI file, you can simply add the line. For example, the [Desktop] section of your WIN.INI file may not include the lines

```
WallpaperOriginX=
```

and

```
WallpaperOriginY=
```

By adding these lines and specifying values other than 0 (the lines' default value), you can make a wallpaper image appear at some position other than the center of your screen.

Many .INI-file entries require Boolean values. For instance, you can enter True, Yes, On, or 1 to enable an entry's function, and False, No, Off, or 0 to disable the entry's function. (Case doesn't matter.) Any line that begins with a semicolon is treated as a "comment" and disregarded by Windows. You can add as many comment lines as you like. Within any section, the order in which lines appear is immaterial. And within the initialization file as a whole, the order in which sections appear is also immaterial.

Who Does What to Whom?

The majority of the lines in both WIN.INI and SYSTEM.INI are created and maintained by various elements of your Windows software. You do not need to change these items directly; Windows will do it for you.

For example, entries in the [Desktop] section of WIN.INI specify details about the way you want your system to look. Most of these entries are made automatically when you change settings in the Desktop section of Control Panel.

As soon as you click OK after making selections in this part of Control Panel, Control Panel updates your WIN.INI file. The Windows applications you install, like Word for Windows or Ami Pro, may also add lines to WIN.INI to define preferences and other items.

Some customizing choices can only be made by editing your .INI files, however. If you want to change the font used by Windows to display the text beneath your icons, for example, you'll need to modify WIN.INI yourself.

As a rule, changes that are made to an initialization file by some component of Windows, such as Control Panel, take effect immediately. Changes you make yourself are usually not effective until the next time you start Windows. (The Setup program can make changes to SYSTEM.INI that don't take effect until the next startup. But in these cases, Setup presents a button that you can click to automatically restart Windows.)

How to Edit an .INI File

You should remember two rules when editing any of Windows' initialization files: Make a backup first, and don't use a formatting editor. Making a backup gives you a chance to recover if you make a serious mistake—or simply change your mind. Formatting editors (such as most word processing programs) introduce nontext characters into documents and are a good way to damage an .INI file.

The safest way to edit WIN.INI or SYSTEM.INI is to use the System Editor that Microsoft ships with Windows. The formal name for this Windows application is SYSEDIT.EXE. If you don't find an icon for it in your Program Manager group, add one. As an editor, SYSEDIT is a bit primitive; for example, it has a Search command but no Replace. The program has two virtues, however: It creates backups automatically (with the extension .SYD), and it puts no formatting characters in your file.

So, to edit WIN.INI or SYSTEM.INI, follow these steps:

1. Make a backup of the file you're editing. (Although SYSEDIT automatically backs up any file you use it to change, it keeps only the version last saved, which may not be a working version. As a precaution, *always* back up the .INI file you're editing before making any changes.)

2. Run SYSEDIT from either the File Manager (File, Run) or by double-clicking on its icon.

3. Four files appear ready for your perusal, each in its own window: WIN.INI, SYSTEM.INI, AUTOEXEC.BAT, and CONFIG.SYS. Click the window that contains the file you want to edit, and modify the text as you like.

4. Save the file. You can either use SYSEDIT's File, Save command or exit SYSEDIT (Alt+F4) and click on Yes when it asks if you want to save the current changes.

5. Restart Windows so that your changes will take effect.

Tips for Using SYSEDIT

You might think that a text editor built into an operating system that only works with four files isn't of much value. In the case of Windows and SYS-EDIT.EXE, you couldn't be more wrong. Certainly, you could call up WIN.INI, SYSTEM.INI, AUTOEXEC.BAT, or CONFIG.SYS in any text editor when you need to change them. But, in Windows, these files are so important, and you'll be checking them so often, that having all four ready in editable form is a great boon. SYSEDIT also assures that the files are saved in pristine text format, something you might have to double-check when using a word processor. In short, SYSEDIT represents the kind of small, beneficial detail that has set Windows apart as a user-responsive environment.

We explain the basics of using SYSEDIT in the tip "How to Edit an .INI File." Here are some more advanced tricks to use with this unique editor. Try it, you'll like it.

Install SYSEDIT as an Icon   If you like to optimize your system setup by messing around with your AUTOEXEC.BAT CONFIG.SYS, WIN-.INI, and SYSTEM.INI files, you can save steps by adding an icon for SYSEDIT to your desktop, as shown in Figure 2.1. Create the icon by choosing New from the File menu in Program Manager and specifying SYSEDIT.EXE as the command line. Be sure to *always* back up these system files before doing any edits.

Quicker .INI Editing   When making changes to your WIN.INI, PROG-MAN.INI, and SYSTEM.INI files, you probably find yourself scrolling through the document trying to locate the appropriate section. Save time by using the Search function in Notepad, SYSEDIT, or whatever text editor you are using. Search for the opening bracket character ([) that starts each of the files' sections. By using the keyboard equivalent to search for the Next occurrence (F3 in SYSEDIT and Notepad) you'll move through the file much more quickly. Likewise, if you're looking for multiple references to the same application, use the Search function to find them quickly.

Back Up Your INI Files before Installing a New Windows Application   Because many Windows applications make changes to the INI files, it's a good idea to back them up before you install a new application. If you run into a problem and need to remove the application, it's handy to have a reference to see what changes were made to the INI files. With the backups as your guide, you can compare the two files and remove all references to the application.

Use SYSEDIT without a Mouse   If you open up SYSEDIT and attempt to start working on your files without using your mouse, you'll notice that you can't activate the cursor. To do so, switch out of SYSEDIT momentarily using the Alt+Tab key combination. Then press Alt+Tab again to return to SYSEDIT. The cursor will now be active and you can edit without the aid of a mouse.

FIGURE 2.1

Add an icon for the Windows System Editor to your desktop to gain immediate access to your AUTOEXEC.BAT, CONFIG.SYS, SYSTEM.INI, and WIN.INI.

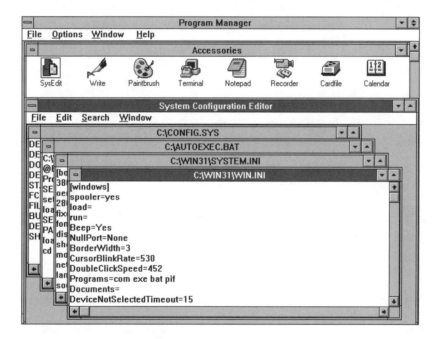

A Word about Syntax

The WIN.INI file is divided into distinct sections, which are always referred to in brackets: [Windows], [Desktop], and so on. Each entry has an equal sign—for example, Device=. Following the equal sign are the parameters that can be used with the entry. If the parameters for the entry consist of a choice between a limited number of discrete values, the choices are demarcated with a pipe character (|), like so: Yes | No.

NOTE   If you must supply a specific value for a parameter, the type of value is noted in italic—for example, *seconds* or *kilobytes*. For each entry, we include the default value in parentheses immediately following the entry—for example, (default: 3).

Table 2.1 includes a brief description of each section of the WIN.INI file.

TABLE 2.1

Sections of the WIN.IN File and What They Do

Section	Description
[Windows]	Affects elements of the Windows environment, including which applications start when you load Windows, the warning beep, printing, the window border width, keyboard speed, mouse settings, and the definition of files as documents or programs
[Desktop]	Controls the appearance of the desktop and the position of windows and icons
[Extensions]	Associates specified types of files with corresponding applications
[Intl]	Describes how to display items for countries other than the United States
[Windows Help]	Lists settings used to specify the default size, placement, and text colors of the Help window and dialog boxes
[Ports]	Lists all available output ports
[FontSubstitutes]	Lists pairs of fonts that are recognized by Windows as interchangeable
[TrueType]	Describes options for using and displaying TrueType fonts
[Sounds]	Lists the sound files assigned to each system event
[MCI extensions]	Associates specified types of files with Media Control Interface devices
[Compatibility]	Includes lines that resolve compatibility issues arising from minor differences between Windows 3.1 and Windows 3.0
[Fonts]	Describes the screen font files that are loaded by Windows
[Network]	Describes network settings and previous network connections
[Embedding]	Lists the server objects used in Object Linking and Embedding (OLE)
[Colors]	Defines colors for the Windows display
[PrinterPorts]	Lists active and inactive output devices to be accessed by Windows
[Devices]	Lists active output devices that provide compatibility with earlier versions of Windows applications
[Programs]	Lists additional paths that Windows will search to find a program file when you try to open an associated data file

We discuss the sections of WIN.INI in the order in which they appear in the table, which is how they should appear in a default Windows setup. Within each of these sections, we include line-by-line options in alphabetical order for easy reference.

WIN.INI Line by Line

This is a section you should *not* skim over. This is real meat. Read it. Savor it. Chew it. If you want to understand how Windows works and what you can do with it, you must understand .INI files *in detail.* Here we examine all the many different sections of WIN.INI and each line within those sections that you may ever want to change. At first glance this may seem like an awful lot of detail to plow through, but persevere. Where Windows is concerned, .INI knowledge is power.

Tips for Editing WIN.INI

Windows sets up its .INI files at setup. However, if you are a sophisticated user—or even just a curious one—you'll want to tinker with the arrangement Windows starts out with. Here are some ideas for editing WIN.INI.

Automate .INI Backups with SYSEDIT   The SYSEDIT program that comes with Windows is a handy way to access your WIN.INI, as well as your SYSTEM.INI, CONFIG.SYS, and AUTOEXEC.BAT files. But there's an added bonus to using SYSEDIT: automatic backups. Every time you make a change to a file with SYSEDIT, it keeps the previous version of your file and marks it with the .SYD extension. So if you're editing your WIN.INI and realize that you've made some mistakes that have overwritten your original file, don't panic. Just rename WIN.SYD to WIN.INI and you're back in business.

Familiarize Yourself with WIN.INI's README Files   The WIN-INI.TXT file that comes with Windows 3.0 and the WININI.WRI file that comes with Windows 3.1 are important documents for those who will be editing their WIN.INI. Skim them on-line, or print a copy of their contents for future reference.

Why It Pays to Keep WIN.INI Slim   Every time you select an option in the Windows Control Panel, the entire WIN.INI file is written to disk. If your file contains unnecessary entries, or if it contains a lot of blank lines between sections, this will slow the process down. Keep WIN.INI as slim as possible, and you won't always be waiting for your hard-disk light to turn off.

How to Make WIN.INI Changes Take Effect without Restarting Windows   If you make changes to your WIN.INI file, you'll have to exit Windows before these changes take effect. And of course this isn't very convenient. To fool Windows into updating the WIN.INI file without exiting Windows, go into the Control Panel. Select an option such as the Keyboard icon, and click on it. Don't change anything; just select OK. You'll hear some hard-disk activity, which means that just by opening the option you've rewritten the WIN.INI file. Your previous changes should now be in effect.

[Windows]

Lines in the [Windows] section affect a variety of factors concerning the appearance and behavior of your system. Almost all of these lines are managed for you by Control Panel.

Beep=Yes | No (default: Yes)   Makes Windows beep to signal various kinds of user errors. If the beeping annoys you, you can turn it off by changing the Beep= line from Yes to No. To do this, open the Sound section of Control Panel and clear the Enable System Sounds check box shown in Figure 2.2.

FIGURE 2.2

Turn off Windows' warning beep by clearing the Enable System Sounds check box in the Sound section of Control Panel.

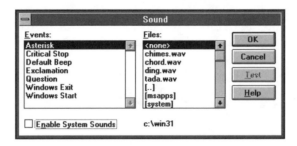

BorderWidth=*number* (default: 3)   Tells Windows how wide to draw the borders around sizable windows. This value can range from 1 to 49. The default is 3, which is also the value that Windows *always* uses for nonsizable windows (dialog boxes, for example). To change the BorderWidth value, open the Desktop section of Control Panel. Enter a new number in the Border Width field at the lower-left corner of the dialog box.

If you're using Windows on a low-contrast LCD screen and have difficulty clicking on window borders, you might want to increase the border width. A setting of 5 or 6 will make the borders much more visible. If you prefer the Twiggy look, reduce the value to 1.

CoolSwitch=0 | 1 (default: 1)   Affects the behavior of the Alt+Tab and Alt+Shift+Tab keyboard combinations. mWith CoolSwitch on (set to 1), when you switch programs by pressing Alt+Tab, Windows displays a box in the center of your screen showing the name and icon of the program you're about to switch to. Alt+Shift+Tab steps you through your apps in reverse order. With CoolSwitch off, Windows displays the program's title bar and window borders (or the icon and icon label, if the program is minimized). As its more formal name (Fast "Alt+Tab" Switching) suggests, CoolSwitch can speed up the switching process because it requires the system to do less graphical work. But its main value is that it lets you see exactly where you're going. If you want to turn CoolSwitch off, open the Desktop section of Control Panel and clear the check box labeled Fast "Alt+Tab" Switching.

Boolean Values for Editing .INI Files

Most of entries in Windows' .INI files are set using Boolean values. You should note that there is more than one acceptable value for enabling or disabling the setting.

To *activate* a setting you can use

- True
- Yes
- On
- 1

To *disable* a setting you can use

- False
- No
- Off
- 0

The values are not case-sensitive.

CursorBlinkRate=*milliseconds* (default: 530)   Governs the speed at which Windows blinks the cursor in text documents, spreadsheet cells, and other editable fields. The default is 530 milliseconds per blink. You might want to slow it down, if you find the cursor blink distracting, or speed it up if you're working at a screen where the cursor is sometimes hard to find. To change this value, open the Desktop section of Control Panel and adjust the scroll bar in the lower-right corner of the dialog box (shown in Figure 2.3).

The range of values available when you use Control Panel's scroll bar is 200 through 1200 (although those values are not visible in Control Panel). A value of 200 gives you a very fast blink, and 1200 gives you almost none at all. You may use blink rates outside that range by modifying WIN.INI directly. For example, you could make the cursor seem to stop blinking altogether by setting CursorBlinkRate to some large number, such as 50000, but this is not advisable. The cursor has two phases of equal duration—on and off. If you make the on phase long, you will have equally long periods when the cursor is invisible. For best results, stick to the range that Control Panel offers.

DefaultQueueSize=*number* (default: 8)   Specifies the maximum number of messages that can be held in an application's message queue. Your WIN.INI file probably does not include this line (which means your system is using the default value). This line is included primarily for the benefit of developers who want to test their applications under varying conditions. As an end user, you should have no need to modify this line.

FIGURE 2.3

The Cursor Blink Rate section in the lower-right corner of Control Panel's Desktop dialog box allows you to change the blinking rate of your cursor.

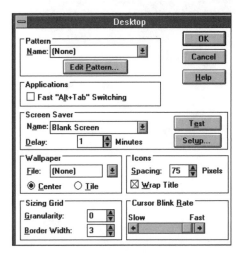

Device=*output-device-name, device-driver, port-connection* Records your current default printer setting, as specified in the Printer section of Control Panel. The line consists of three arguments separated by commas, like this:

```
Device=HP LaserJet Series II,HPPCL,LPT1:
```

The first argument is the name of the printer; this is how you'll see your printer identified in your applications' printer-selection dialog boxes. The name must match an entry in the [Devices] section of WIN.INI (described later in this chapter). The second argument is the filename of your printer's driver file, minus its .DRV extension. The third argument is the name of the printer port to which the default printer is assigned. This entry must match an entry in the [Ports] section of WIN.INI (also covered later in the chapter).

DeviceNotSelectedTimeout=*seconds* (default: 15) Specifies the default amount of time that Windows will wait for an off-line printer to be connected before issuing a timeout error. To increase or decrease this setting for all your printers, edit this line in WIN.INI. To override the default for one particular printer, use the Connect option under the Printers icon in Control Panel.

Documents=*extensions* (default: none) Specifies the extensions of files to be regarded by Windows as documents. Specify each extension without a period, and use spaces to separate extensions, like this:

```
Documents=abc xyz 123
```

If the Documents= line in your WIN.INI file includes extensions that also appear in the [Extensions] section (covered later), you may safely remove them from this line. All [Extensions] extensions are automatically treated as documents.

You might want to put an extension on the Documents= line if that extension is associated with more than one application. If you have two programs that create .DOC files, for example, you might find it inconvenient to associate .DOC with either program. By adding that extension to the Documents= line, however, you can still include your .DOC files in File Manager views that are filtered to display documents only.

DosPrint=Yes | No (default: No)   Makes Windows send printer output directly to hardware ports, rather than printing via the DOS Interrupt 21 file-access services. This results in faster performance, but requires complete hardware compatibility. If you are able to print from DOS but not from Windows (and you have a properly installed Windows printer driver), try changing this setting from No to Yes. You can do that by opening the Printers section of Control Panel, selecting any installed printer driver, clicking the Connect button, and clearing the Fast Printing Direct to Port check box shown in Figure 2.4. (Note: This setting was introduced with Windows 3.1.)

FIGURE 2.4

Clearing the Fast Printing Direct to Port check box in Control Panel's Printer dialog box prohibits Windows from sending output directly to the printer port.

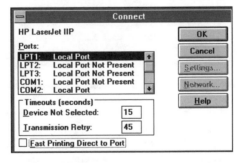

DoubleClickHeight=*pixels* (default: 4)

DoubleClickWidth=*pixels* (default: 4)   Specify the amount you can move the mouse between the two clicks of a double-click. If you move the mouse more than 4 pixels (by default) in either direction, Windows regards your action as two single clicks. To make Windows more tolerant, add these lines to WIN.INI and specify values greater than 4.

DoubleClickSpeed=*milliseconds* (default: 452)   Determines the maximum time that can elapse between the two clicks of a double-click. If the amount of time between double-clicks exceeds this value, Windows regards your action as two single clicks. To increase the double-click tolerance, open the Mouse section of Control Panel and adjust the Double Click Speed scroll bar.

KeyboardDelay=*milliseconds* (default: 2)   Specifies the length of time you have to press a key before it begins to repeat. (Note: This line was introduced with Windows 3.1.) To make your keyboard begin repeating sooner, reduce this value or open the Keyboard section of Control Panel and move the top scroll bar to the right.

KeyboardSpeed=*number* (default: 31)   Determines the speed at which a key repeats when you hold it down. The higher the number, the faster your keyboard repeats. The default setting, 31, is also the highest accepted value. To change the repetition speed, open the Keyboard section of Control Panel and adjust the lower scroll bar, shown in Figure 2.5.

FIGURE 2.5

Change the speed at which a key repeats by adjusting the Repeat Rate scroll bar in Control Panel's Keyboard dialog box; test the new rate in the text box below.

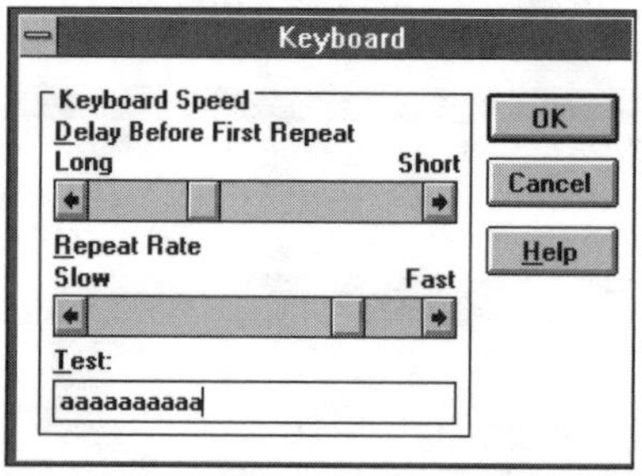

Keyboard
Keyboard Speed
Delay Before First Repeat
Long   Short
Repeat Rate
Slow   Fast
Test:
aaaaaaaaaa

OK   Cancel   Help

Load=*filename(s)* (default: none)   Can be used to name any programs that you want to run minimized at the beginning of each Windows session. If the program is not stored in your WINDOWS directory, your SYSTEM directory, or another directory in your DOS path, include the full path. Use the space character to separate programs if you specify more than one.

If you're using Program Manager as your Windows shell, you don't need to add startup programs on this line. To load an application or document automatically at startup, put its icon in a program group called Startup. The Load= line is included for compatibility with earlier versions of Windows. The installation routines of certain applications may add entries to this line (or to Run=, discussed later in the chapter).

If your default shell is not Program Manager, you may be able to use the Load= line to specify startup programs. File Manager, MS-DOS Executive, Norton Desktop for Windows, and some other shell programs look for information on the Load= line at startup to load the specified programs. Not all shell programs do this, however.

MenuDropAlignment=0 | 1 (default: 0)   Tells Windows whether to align drop-down menus flush left or flush right with their titles. The default setting produces left alignment. If you want to be different, you can edit WIN.INI and change the setting to 1. (You will probably need to add the line to your [Windows] section.) See Figure 2.6 to see what the result looks like.

FIGURE 2.6

Editing the MenuDropAlignment entry in the WIN.INI file lets you change the side on which drop-down menus align; a setting of 1 makes them align to the right.

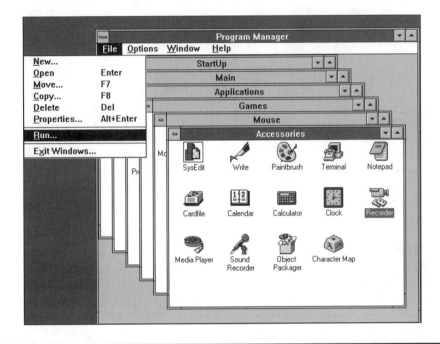

MenuShowDelay=*milliseconds* (default: 0 on 386 and 486 computers, 400 on 286 computers)   Determines the length of time Windows waits after you click any menu bar item before it drops the menu. On 286 computers, Windows uses a 400-millisecond delay to avoid jerky menu behavior as you pass the mouse across the menu bar with a menu already open. (If you move the mouse beyond a menu before it drops, the drop is canceled.) If you find the delay irksome, reduce the value in this line in WIN.INI. (You will probably need to add the line, and then specify a nondefault parameter value.)

MouseSpeed = 0 | 1 | 2 (default: 1)

MouseThreshold1=*pixels* (default: 5)

MouseThreshold2=*pixels* (default: 10)   Govern the acceleration characteristics of your mouse. If MouseSpeed is 0, the relationship between mouse movement and pointer movement is constant. If MouseSpeed is 1, you get one level of acceleration, meaning anytime you move the mouse more than Threshold1 pixels between mouse interrupts, the pointer begins traveling twice as fast. If MouseSpeed is 2, the ratio of pointer travel to mouse travel quadruples whenever the mouse is moved more than Threshold2 pixels between interrupts.

The easiest way to adjust these settings is by choosing options in the Mouse section of Control Panel. Because not all variations of the three settings are available via Control Panel, however, you may want to fine-tune your mouse's behavior by editing WIN.INI.

MouseTrails=*number* (default: 0)   Causes Windows to display trailing images of the mouse pointer as it moves across the screen when a MouseTrails setting of between 1 and 7 is used. The *number* parameter specifies the number of images that appear. Using MouseTrails may help you follow the pointer on an LCD display. The only Windows-supplied display drivers for which this option is available are EGA, VGA, and SuperVGA. Depending on your mouse driver, you may be able to change the setting via the Mouse section of Control Panel. If you do not see a Mouse Trails option there, or if the Mouse Trails option is dimmed, edit the MouseTrails line in WIN.INI.

NetWarn=0 | 1 (default: 1)   Displays a warning message any time the network is unavailable at the start of a session if you have configured Windows to run on a network and NetWarn is set to 1. If you don't want the warning, disable the Network Warnings option in the Network section of Control Panel.

NullPort=*string* (default: "None")   Earlier versions of Windows did not permit you to assign more than one printer to the same printer port. If you had two printers and only one port, you had to assign one of them to the null port. The NullPort line in WIN.INI specified the name of the null port. Its default was "None," but you could change it to *zip*, *nada*, or anything else. In Windows 3.1, this line is strictly an anachronism. If it appears in your Win 3.1 WIN.INI file, you may safely remove it.

Programs=*extensions* (default: com exe pif bat scr)   Specifies the extensions of files for Windows to regard as programs. Specify each extension without a period, and use spaces to separate extensions, like this:

```
Programs=abc xyz 123
```

Only file types identified as programs can be executed from within Windows. Thus, a simple way to make your system inoperable is to remove the exe extension from the Programs= line. (Be sure you have a backup of WIN.INI handy before you try this.)

As long as pif is included in the list of program extensions, from File Manager you can run a .PIF file to launch the DOS application with which it is associated. Just double-click on the .PIF filename.

Run=*filename(s)* (default: none)   Names any programs that you want to run in open windows at the beginning of each Windows session. If the program is not stored in your WINDOWS directory, your SYSTEM directory, or another directory in your DOS path, include the full path. Use the space character to separate programs if you specify more than one.

If your default shell is not Program Manager, you may be able to use the Run= line to specify startup programs. File Manager, MS-DOS Executive, Norton Desktop for Windows, and some other shell programs look for information on the Run= line at startup and load the specified programs. Not all shell programs do this, however.

ScreenSaveActive=0 | 1 (default: 0)   Determines whether Windows should activate one of its screen savers when your system is idle. The default turns off use of a screen saver. To turn screen-saving on, use the Desktop section of Control Panel. If you're using a third-party screen saver, leave this switch off.

ScreenSaveTimeOut=*seconds* (default: 120)   Specifies the length of time Windows waits when your system is idle before activating the current screen saver. (Note: This setting was introduced with Windows 3.1.) The default is two minutes. To change this value, use the Desktop section of Control Panel.

Spooler=Yes | No (default: Yes)   Determines whether printing is managed by Print Manager. If you change the value to No, Windows may complete a print job more quickly, but you will be able to print only one job at a time. To turn spooling off, open the Printers section of Control Panel and clear the Use Print Manager check box, as shown in Figure 2.7.

FIGURE 2.7

Clear the Use Print Manager check box in Control Panel's Printers dialog box to turn off Windows print job management.

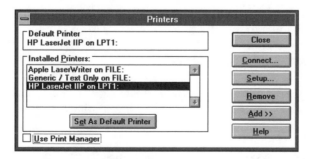

SwapMouseButtons=0 | 1 (default: 0)   Specifies your primary mouse button. If SwapMouseButtons is 0 (the default), the left button is primary. To make the right button primary, check the box labeled Swap Left/Right Buttons in the Mouse section of Control Panel.

TransmissionRetryTimeout=*seconds* (default: 45)   Specifies the default amount of time that Windows will wait for acknowledgment while transmitting data to a printer. (If the printer in use is a PostScript device, Windows waits twice the length of time specified by TransmissionRetryTimeout.) If this time elapses, Windows issues a timeout error. To increase or decrease this setting for all your printers, edit this line in WIN.INI. To override the default for one particular printer, modify the printer's RetryTimeout entry in the [PrinterPorts] section of WIN.INI (see below), or change the Transmission Retry value in the Connect dialog box of the Printers option in Control Panel.

[Desktop]

The [Desktop] section records preferences about the appearance of your Windows desktop. Most of the items in this section are managed automatically by the Desktop section of Control Panel.

GridGranularity=*number* (default: 0)   Lets you position application windows anywhere you please. If you set GridGranularity to a nonzero value, your windows are forced to align along an imaginary grid. Values from 1 to 49 are permitted; each increment increases the coarseness of the grid by 8 pixels both horizontally and vertically. This feature can help if you need precise positioning, but it has no effect on the placement of icons or document windows. To change the setting in Control Panel's Desktop dialog box, change the Granularity number near the lower-left corner (in the Sizing Grid box).

IconSpacing=*pixels* (default: 77)   Determines the horizontal spacing used by Windows in response to an Arrange Icons command. If you want more space between your icons, increase the IconSpacing value. To do so, use the Spacing setting in Control Panel's Desktop dialog box.

If you've used a version of Windows earlier than 3.1, you probably sometimes needed to increase the default value to avoid having icon labels overlap. In version 3.1, a simpler solution is to let Windows wrap icon titles. (IconTitle-Wrap is covered in a moment.) Even with IconTitleWrap on (set to 1), however, you may sometimes experience overlapping icon titles, particularly if you minimize applications containing maximized document windows. In that case, the icon title text includes the name of the current document as well as the name of the application. The solution? Increase the horizontal distance between icons, as explained here, and the vertical distance, too, as explained shortly.

IconTitleFaceName=*fontname* (default: MS Sans Serif)   Specifies the font that Windows uses to display icon titles. For a different look, edit this line in WIN.INI and specify another font (from the list that appears in the [Fonts] section of WIN.INI).

IconTitleSize=*number*(default: 8)   Specifies the point size of the font used to display icon title text. If you have trouble reading icon titles on a high-resolution screen, try editing this line of WIN.INI to increase their value.

IconTitleWrap=0 | 1 (default: 1)   Wraps long icon titles onto two or three lines, if necessary, to fit within the space defined by IconSpacing. If you object, clear the Wrap Title check box in the Desktop section of Control Panel.

IconVerticalSpacing=*pixels* (default: depends on other settings)   Determines the vertical spacing Windows uses in response to an Arrange Icons command. The default depends on your IconTitleSize setting and display driver. To increase or decrease the default spacing, edit this line of WIN.INI.

Pattern=b1 b2 b3 b4 b5 b6 b7 b8 (default: "(None)")   Records any desktop background pattern you specify via the Desktop section of Control Panel. The numeric values represent a bitmap 8 pixels high and 8 pixels wide. To change the pattern, use Control Panel's Desktop dialog box. You can either select a built-in pattern from the drop-down list or click the Edit Pattern button and design your own.

TileWallpaper=0 | 1 (default: 0)   Determines whether the current wallpaper is centered (the default) or tiled. To change the setting, use the Desktop section of Control Panel.

Wallpaper=*filename* (default: "(None)")   Specifies the filename and path of your current wallpaper bitmap. To change the setting, use the Desktop section of Control Panel.

Although the Desktop dialog box does not include a Browse button, you are not limited to bitmaps stored in your Windows directory. Just add the drive and directory when you specify the filename.

WallpaperOriginX=*number* (default: 0)

WallpaperOriginY=*number* (default: 0)   Tile wallpaper images beginning at the upper-left corner of your screen and continuing rightward and downward until the screen is filled. By specifying values other than zero for WallpaperOriginX= and WallpaperOriginY=, you can begin the tiling at some other location. The *number* parameter for WallpaperOriginX specifies a horizontal offset, in pixels, from the upper-left corner. The *number* parameter for WallpaperOriginY specifies a vertical offset from the upper-left corner.

These lines also affect the position of centered wallpaper. If the coordinates are 0,0 (or the lines are omitted from WIN.INI), your wallpaper is centered around the midpoint of your screen. Nonzero coordinates produce alternative centering points measured from the upper-left corner. Low values for both coordinates, for example, would position the image near the upper-left corner, as shown in Figure 2.8.

FIGURE 2.8

Changing the WIN.INI settings WallpaperOriginX= and WallpaperOriginY= allows you to specify coordinates for your wallpaper; this Windows logo wallpaper is tiled at coordinates of 12 and 12.

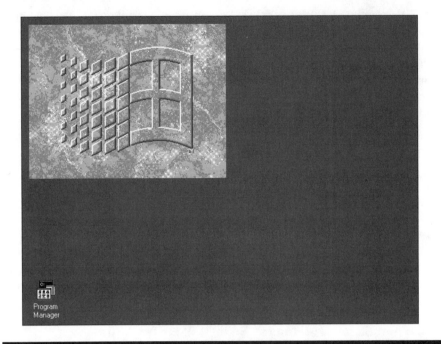

[Extensions]

The [Extensions] section can contain any number of lines of the form

```
extension=command-line
```

Each line associates a class of document files with an application. A line associating .INI files with Notepad, for example, would look like this:

```
ini=notepad.exe ^.ini
```

When you run a document file whose extension is listed here, Windows launches the associated application, and the application loads your document. You can run a file by double-clicking on it in a File Manager window or by means of a shell program's File, Run command. You can associate as many extensions as you want with a specific application here, but you can't associate a given extension with more than one application.

The Windows Setup program automatically creates associations for many of the Windows "applets." Your [Extensions] section therefore may already include entries for .WRI, .TXT, .CAL, and others. Other applications' installation programs also commonly modify this section.

Many associations are also recorded in the Windows registration database. (The *registration database* is a binary file, REG.DAT, that records both simple file associations and information used by Windows for object linking and embedding.) If an extension is associated in both the [Extensions] section of WIN.INI and the registration database, Windows disregards the entry in [Extensions].

The safest way to create or modify an association, therefore, is to use File Manager's File, Associate command. That command updates both the registration database and the [Extensions] section of WIN.INI.

[Intl]

Settings in the [Intl] section record your preferences regarding the display of numbers, dates, and times. Entries that begin with an "i" must be integers. Entries that begin with an "s" must be strings (text). All entries can be set from the International section of Control Panel. Defaults listed here are for systems installed in the United States.

Certain Windows programs that existed originally in DOS versions have their own extensive international formatting commands and may use these in preference to your WIN.INI settings. Lotus 1-2-3 for Windows is an example.

iCountry=*country-code* (default: 1)   Specifies the country whose standard settings you want to use. The *country-code* should be the country's international telephone code in all cases except Canada. To specify Canada, use the number 2. The default setting, 1, specifies the United States.

iCurrDigits=*number* (default: 2)   Specifies the number of digits that should appear after the decimal separator in currency-formatted values. (The decimal separator is either a period or a comma, depending on the iCountry setting.)

iCurrency=*number* (default: 0)   Specifies the position of the currency symbol. (The symbol itself is determined by the sCurrency line.) Use 0 to put the symbol before the number, 1 to put it after the number, 2 to put it before the number (with a space between the symbol and the number), or 3 to suppress the display of the currency symbol.

iDate=*number* (default: depends on iCountry setting)   Specifies the date format Windows should use. Values may be 0 (mm/dd/yy), 1 (dd/mm/yy), or 2 (yy/mm/dd). This line is provided for compatibility with Windows 2.*x*. If you have it in your WIN.INI file, you may safely delete it.

iDigits=*number* (default: 2)   Specifies the number of digits to be displayed to the right of the decimal separator.

iLZero=0 | 1 (default: 0)   Specifies whether a single leading 0 should appear to the left of the decimal separator in values between -1 and +1.

iMeasure=0 | 1 (default: 1)   Specifies your choice of metric (0) or English (1) measurement.

iNegCurr=*number* (default: 0)   Governs the display of negative currency values. The currency symbol and decimal separator are determined by the sCurrency and iCountry settings. Table 2.2 lists each value and how it displays negative currency values.

TABLE 2.2

Negative Currency Value Settings Used with the iNegCurr= Setting in WIN.INI's [Intl] Section

Value	Display
0	($123.45)
1	–$123.45
2	$–123.45
3	$123.45–
4	(123.45$)
5	–123.45$
6	123.45–$
7	123.45$–
8	–123.45 $
9	–$ 123.45
10	123.45 $–

iTime=*number* (default: 0)   Specifies your choice of a 12-hour (0) or 24-hour (1) clock.

iTLZero=*number* (default: 0)   Specifies whether a leading 0 should appear before single-digit time values. Change this value to 1 if you want the zero.

s1159=*string* (default: AM)   Specifies the characters that should appear after ante-meridian times when a 12-hour clock is in use. Some programs (Excel, for example) will use only the first four characters of *string*.

s2359=*string* (default: PM)   Specifies the characters that should appear after post-meridian times when a 12-hour clock is in use.

sCountry=*string* (default: United States)   Specifies the name of the country whose standard values you want to use.

sCurrency=*string* (default: $)   Specifies your choice of currency symbol.

sDecimal=*string* (default: .)   Specifies your choice of decimal separator.

sLanguage=*string* (default: enu)   Specifies your choice of standard language. Some Windows applications use this information to determine which sorting sequence or spelling checker to use. Acceptable values include those in Table 2.3.

TABLE 2.3

Acceptable Values for the Windows Standard Language Setting in the [Intl] Section of WIN.INI

Value	Language
dan	Danish
deu	German
eng	International English
enu	American English
esn	Modern Spanish
esp	Castilian Spanish
fin	Finnish
fra	French
frc	Canadian French
isl	Icelandic
ita	Italian
nld	Dutch
nor	Norwegian
ptg	Portuguese
sve	Swedish

sLis=*string* (default: ,)   Specifies your choice of punctuation to separate items in a list.

sLongDate=*format* (default: dddd, MMMM dd, yyyy)   Specifies your choice of long-date format. Acceptable symbols and their meanings are listed in Table 2.4.

sShortDate=*format* (default: M/d/yy)   Specifies your choice of short-date format. The symbols are the same as for sLongDate (see Table 2.4).

TABLE 2.4

Symbols Used for the Date Settings in WIN.INI's [Intl] Section

Symbol	Meaning
d	Day number, without leading 0
dd	Day number, with leading zero
ddd	Weekday, abbreviated
dddd	Weekday, spelled out
M	Month number, without leading 0
MM	Month number, with leading 0
MMM	Month name, abbreviated
MMMM	Month name, spelled out
yy	Year, in two-digit form
yyyy	Year, in four-digit form

sThousand=*string* (default: ,)   Specifies your choice of punctuation to appear between three-digit groups in numbers greater than 999.

sTime=*string* (default: :)   Specifies your choice of punctuation to use in time values, such as 12:34.

[Windows Help]

The [Windows Help] section of WIN.INI records settings that determine the size and placement of the Help window and its dialog boxes, including the color of text that displays a Help macro, pop-up window (used for glossary definitions), or new screen of information.

M_WindowPosition=[*upper_left_x, upper_left_y, width, height,* 0 | 1]
Specifies the default position and size of the main Help window. The first two parameters specify the x and y coordinates of the window's upper-left corner. The third and fourth parameters specify the width and height of the window, in pixels. The fifth parameter is 1 if the window is maximized and 0 if it isn't (if 0, Winhelp uses the default width and height). The five parameters are enclosed within a pair of brackets. You do not need to edit WIN.INI to set these values. Simply position the Help window the way you want it to appear in the future. When you close the Window, Winhelp updates your WIN.INI file.

H_WindowPosition=[*upper_left_x, upper_left_y, width, height,* 0 | 1]
Specifies the default position and size of the Help system's History dialog box. The parameters work as they do for M_WindowPosition, except that the fifth parameter has no effect because the History dialog box cannot be maximized.

A_WindowPosition=[*upper_left_x, upper_left_y, width, height,* 0 | 1]
Specifies the default position and size of the Help system's Annotate dialog box. The parameters work as they do for M_WindowPosition, except that the fifth parameter has no effect because the Annotate dialog box cannot be maximized.

C_WindowPosition=[*upper_left_x, upper_left_y, width, height,* 0 | 1]
Specifies the default position and size of the Help system's Copy dialog box. The parameters work as they do for M_WindowPosition, except that the fifth parameter has no effect because the Copy dialog box cannot be maximized.

IFJumpColor=*r g b* Specifies the color of Winhelp's "inter-file" jump text. This is the text that, when clicked, leads to a new panel of information taken from a different help file. The three parameters specify red, green, and blue color values and must be in the range 0 to 255. If you choose a combination of settings that would produce a dithered color on your display adapter, Windows uses the nearest available solid color.

To change this setting, you must edit WIN.INI. The first time you change it, you'll probably need to add the line to your WIN.INI file. If you want to restore the original color settings, you can either delete the line from your file or just delete the three color values, leaving the keyword and equal sign with no parameters.

IFPopupColor=*r g b* Specifies the color of Winhelp's "inter-file" pop-up hot text—the text that, when clicked, generates a pop-up window taken from another file. The parameters work as they do for IFJumpColor.

JumpColor=*r g b* Specifies the color of Winhelp's "intra-file" jump text. This is the text that, when clicked, leads to a new panel of information taken from the same help file. The parameters work as they do for IFJumpColor.

MacroColor=*r g b* Specifies the color of text that, when clicked, runs a Help-file macro. The parameters work as they do for IFJumpColor.

PopupColor=*r g b* Specifies the color of Winhelp's "intra-file" pop-up hot text—the text that, when clicked, generates a pop-up window that usually defines terms. The parameters work as they do for IFJumpColor.

[Ports]

The [Ports] section of WIN.INI lists your system's serial and printer ports, as well as the communication parameters in effect for your serial ports. You may list as many as ten ports.

Use the Ports section of Control Panel to specify communications parameters. WIN.INI will record your settings, using the following syntax:

```
portname:=baud-rate, parity, word-length, stop-bits [[,p]
```

Acceptable entries include the following:

```
LPTn:=
COMn=
EPT:=
FILE:=
filename.ext=
LPTn.ext=
LPTn.ext=path
```

Use LPT*n*:= to specify a parallel printer port. Be sure to include the colon and the equal sign. This line takes no parameters.

Use EPT:= to specify an IBM Personal Pageprinter. This line takes no parameters.

Use FILE:= if you want to be able to print to disk. This line takes no parameters. If the current printer is attached to a port named FILE:, Windows prompts you for a filename and then directs output to that file. You can use File Manager or the DOS COPY command to transfer the file's contents to a physical printer.

Use *filename.ext=* if you want to print to a particular filename. Windows will not prompt in this case.

Use LPT*n.ext=* to bypass Windows' normal method of printing direct to port. (See the DOSPrint= line, under the [Windows] heading, discussed earlier.) For example, if you sometimes want to use the MS-DOS Interrupt 21 services when printing to your first parallel port, you could include the line

```
LPT1.DOS=
```

(Do *not* include a colon after the port number. This line doesn't take any parameters, either.) It makes no difference which three characters you use for the extension. (If you have upgraded from earlier versions of Windows, you may find a line such as LPT1.OS2 in your WIN.INI file. This is exactly equivalent to LPT1.DOS, which was introduced with Windows 3.1.)

Because the name LPT1.DOS does not include a colon, Windows regards it as a filename. Output directed to such a name is handed off to DOS as though it were redirected to an ordinary disk file. However, DOS sees the first four characters as a printer device and handles the data accordingly. The result is output directed to the printer via the DOS interrupts.

[FontSubstitutes]

The [FontSubstitutes] section, introduced with Windows 3.1, provides a list of font aliases. Each entry has the following form:

```
font-name=font-name
```

Windows includes four entries by default:

Helv=MS Sans Serif

Tms Rmn=MS Serif

Times=Times New Roman

Helvetica=Arial

Helv and Tms Rmn were bitmapped fonts included with Windows versions prior to 3.1. Their Windows 3.1 equivalents are MS Sans Serif and MS Serif. So, for example, if you open a document formatted in Helv under Windows 3.0, Windows will use MS Sans Serif instead (provided you haven't removed these default [FontSubstitutes] entries).

If you regularly receive documents showing bitmapped fonts that remain on your system, substitute them for TrueType equivalents. Name all the fonts you receive in documents from other people, and pair each with a TrueType alternative. Note, however, that if you type the name of a non-TrueType font resident on your system into an application's font box, it will still format correctly. In other words, you'll see the non-TrueType font, not the TrueType equivalent you specified in WIN.INI.

[TrueType]

The [TrueType] section of the WIN.INI file was added with version 3.1 because this version marked the first appearance of the TrueType fonts it describes. TrueType fonts are Microsoft's answer to PostScript. Both produce lettering that is scalable: Characters can be sized, altered, and manipulated in ways that standard, static characters cannot.

OutlineThreshold=*pixels-per-em* (default: 256)   Specifies a "crossover" point at which TrueType characters are rendered from outlines into bitmaps via GDI (Graphics Device Interface) calls, rather than via the TrueType rasterizer. The TrueType rasterizer is faster.

If this threshold is set too high, characters with a large point size (say, 61-point type—particularly in highly decorative fonts—on a 300 dpi printer) may not be rendered. Microsoft recommends that you not set the threshold higher than 300. If you get blank spaces on a printout where you expect to see characters, try editing WIN.INI and reducing the OutlineThreshold value.

TTEnable=0 | 1 (default: 1)   Determines whether TrueType fonts are available. The default setting enables TrueType fonts for your applications. To disable TrueType, use the Fonts section of Control Panel, click the TrueType button, and clear the Enable TrueType Fonts check box, as shown in Figure 2.9.

FIGURE 2.9

Clear the Enable TrueType check box in Control Panel's Fonts section to disable the use of TrueType fonts.

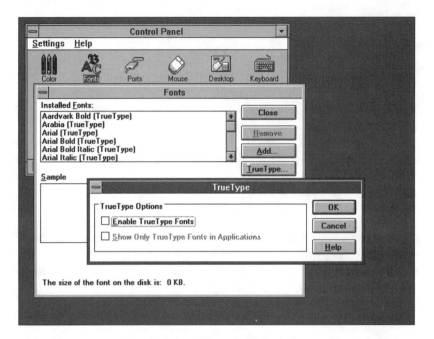

TTIfCollisions=0 I 1 (default: 0) Determines which font Windows uses in the rare circumstance when a TrueType font and a non-TrueType font have identical names and identical character sets. The default setting causes Windows to use the non-TrueType font.

TTOnly=0 I 1 (default: 0) Determines whether *only* TrueType fonts appear in your applications' font dialog boxes. The default setting makes all fonts on your system available to your applications. Windows 3.1's built-in TrueType fonts look great—they're scalable to any point size between 4 and 127 points, and they can be downloaded to your printer for true WYSIWYG output. If you like what you see, banish the jaggies forever by specifying that your Windows applications list only TrueType fonts: Open the Fonts section of Control Panel, click the TrueType button, and select the check box labeled Show Only True-Type Fonts in Applications.

[Sounds]

The [Sounds] section records the mapping of system events to sound files established via the Sound section of Control Panel. The section may contain one or more lines of the format:

```
system-event=filename,description
```

A typical line might look like this:

```
SystemStart=C:\WINDOWS\MMDATA\GONG.WAV,SystemStart
```

In this line, the event known internally to windows as SystemStart has been mapped to a waveform file named GONG, stored in the directory C:\WINDOWS\MMDATA. When the SystemStart event occurs, Windows plays the specified waveform file. The last parameter on the line, also SystemStart in this example, is the description of the event as it appears in the Events list in Control Panel's Sound dialog box. Normally, this last parameter is identical to the keyword at the beginning of the WIN.INI line, but you could change it to something else if you wanted to. You could change SystemStart to Startup, for example.

Ordinarily, however, there's no particular reason to edit this section of WIN.INI. Simply assign events to sound files in Control Panel, and WIN.INI will be updated for you.

You must have a properly installed Windows-supported sound board or the Microsoft speaker driver to be able to play .WAV files. If your computer does not have either of these, the Events and Files list boxes in the Sound section of Control Panel will be dimmed, as shown in Figure 2.10, and you will probably not have a [Sound] section in your WIN.INI file.

FIGURE 2.10

If you do not have a sound board or the Microsoft speaker driver installed on your system, the list boxes in Control Panel's Sound section will be unavailable to you.

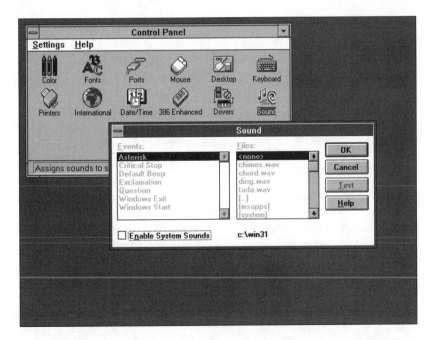

[MCI extensions]

The [MCI extensions] section, introduced in Windows 3.1, may include one or more lines of the following format:

```
extension=mcidevice-type
```

Typical examples look like this:

```
wav=waveaudio
mid=sequencer
rmi=sequencer
mmm=animation
```

These lines, which are entered automatically by the Windows Setup program, tell Windows how to render multimedia files. You should never need to edit this section.

[Compatibility]

The [Compatibility] section includes lines that resolve compatibility issues arising from minor differences between Windows 3.1 and Windows 3.0. The keyword on each line is the name of an application, and the parameter is a hexadecimal value, like this:

```
CHARISMA=0X2000
```

The Setup program automatically creates more than two dozen [Compatibility] entries when you install Windows 3.1 (whether or not you have the affected applications on your system). Other applications' installation routines may add lines of their own. You should not edit or delete the entries in this section.

[Fonts]

The [Fonts] section records the names of the screen fonts loaded by Windows at the start of each session. Each entry has the following format:

```
font-name=font.filename
```

The *font-name* is the name of the font as it appears in Windows dialog boxes. The *font.filename* is the name of the file that contains the font's specifications.

Be aware that simply adding a new entry to the [Fonts] section of WIN.INI does not make the font available. To make a screen font available, you must install it via the Fonts section of Control Panel.

[Network]

Unlike DOS, which never really got its arms around networking, Windows accepts the presence of LANs as part of its natural milieu. This section of WIN.INI allows pinpoint description of key aspects of a network connection for a Windows session.

drive=*network-server-and-share*   Tells Windows which network connections to restore at the start of each session. To change this line, use the Network Connections command on File Manager's Disk menu.

InRestoreNetConnect=0 I 1 (default: 1)   Tells Windows whether to restore network connections at startup. To change, use the Networks section of Control Panel. If the Network dialog box for your network doesn't include a reconnect option, change this line to 1 to reconnect to the network at startup.

port=*network-printer-path*   Defines the path and port for a network printer. To change, open the Printers section of Control Panel, select the appropriate printer driver, click the Connect button, and then click the Network button.

[Embedding]

The [Embedding] section, added to WIN.INI in Windows 3.1, may include one or more lines of the following format:

```
object=description, description, program file, format
```

These lines define classes of objects that may be embedded in OLE client applications. A typical example might look like this:

```
ExcelWorksheet=Microsoft Excel Worksheet,Microsoft Excel Worksheet,C:\EXCEL
```

The information in this section duplicates information kept in the registration database (REG.DAT) and is provided for compatibility with applications that don't assume you're using Windows 3.1. You should never have to edit this section of WIN.INI.

Although this section may eventually become an anachronism, don't delete it from your WIN.INI file. Many OLE client programs (to allow for the possibility that you're using Windows 3.0) read object information from WIN.INI, not from the registration database.

[Colors]

The [Colors] section records the color preferences that you have specified in the Color section of Control Panel. The section contains 21 lines of the following format:

```
component=r g b
```

The *component* keyword names an element of your Windows user interface, and the *r*, *g*, and *b* parameters specify red, green, and blue color values. These parameters must be in the range 0 to 255.

Because Control Panel takes care of this section of WIN.INI for you, there is ordinarily no reason to edit this section yourself. You might conceivably want to go into this part of WIN.INI if you needed to match a custom color scheme on someone else's machine. In that case, you could copy the [Colors] values from your colleague's WIN.INI file into your own.

Named color schemes—the ones that Windows supplies and any you create yourself—are not recorded in WIN.INI. Instead, they're stored in the [Color schemes] section of the CONTROL.INI file.

[PrinterPorts]

The [PrinterPorts] section specifies which port(s) each of your printer drivers is attached to, and what timeout settings are in effect.

Control Panel fills out this section for you automatically when you connect printer drivers to printer ports and adjust their timeout settings. Certain applications, such as Winfax and Publisher's Powerpak, add virtual ports for themselves in this section as well. You should never need to edit this section directly.

The [PrinterPorts] section may include one or more lines of the following format:

```
device=driver,port,DeviceTimeout,RetryTimeout[, other ports …]
```

A typical entry might look like this:

```
HP LaserJet Series II=HPPCL,LPT1:,15,45
```

Device is the name of your printer, as it appears on a device= line in the [Windows] section of WIN.INI.

Driver is the name of your printer's driver file, without the .DRV extension. If this file is not in your WINDOWS\SYSTEM subdirectory, the full path must be included.

Port is the name of a port listed in the [Ports] section of your WIN.INI file.

DeviceTimeout specifies the amount of time that Windows will wait for this printer to be put on line before issuing a timeout error.

RetryTimeout specifies the default amount of time that Windows will wait for acknowledgment while transmitting data to a printer.

If you have a printer connected to more than one port, each connection will appear on that printer's *device=* line. For example, if your LaserJet Series II is attached to both FILE: and LPT1:, the line might look like this:

```
HP LaserJet Series II=HPPCL,FILE:,15,45,LPT1:,15,45
```

[Devices]

The [Devices] section is included for compatibility with Windows 2.*x* applications. In Windows 2.*x*, it served a purpose comparable to that now served by [PrinterPorts]. You should never need to edit this section directly. Do not delete or comment out this section, however. Applications that do not require Windows 3.1 may look for information here rather than in the [PrinterPorts] section.

The [Devices] section may contain one or more lines of the following format:

```
device=driver,port,[,other ports … ]
```

The *device* parameter is the name of a printer as identified on a *device=* line in the [Windows] section of WIN.INI and as it appears in your applications' printer-selection dialog boxes. The *driver* parameter is the name of your printer's driver file, without its .DRV extension.

If you have a printer connected to more than one port, each connection will appear on that printer's *device=* line. For example, if your LaserJet Series II is attached to both FILE: and LPT1:, the line might look like this:

```
HP LaserJet Series II=HPPCL,FILE:,LPT1:
```

[Programs]

The [Programs] section, not to be confused with the Programs= line of the [Windows] section, provides a mechanism for expanding your DOS PATH environment variable. If you try to run a document file (by double-clicking in a File Manager window, for example) and Windows cannot locate the document's associated .EXE file, you will be prompted to provide the path of that .EXE file. After launching your file, Windows will then create an entry like the following in the [Programs] section of WIN.INI:

```
program file=drive:directory\program file
```

For example, suppose you move NOTEPAD.EXE to C:\WINDOWS\-TINYAPPS, a directory not included in your AUTOEXEC.BAT file's path= statement. The next time you try to run JOTTINGS.TXT, Windows will ask you where NOTEPAD.EXE is located. After you tell it, Windows will create a [Programs] section in WIN.INI, if one is not there already, and will add the following line:

```
notepad.exe=c:\windows\tinyapps\notepad.exe
```

You should never need to edit this section directly.

SYSTEM.INI Line by Line

Windows' SYSTEM.INI file primarily records information about the makeup of your PC—its display, drivers, network, and so on. As a result, anyone who wants to understand the deep, inner workings of Windows needs a full knowledge of SYSTEM.INI. The following pages list the lines in SYSTEM.INI that you are most likely to want to change at some point in your use of Windows 3.1. Study them well; they are vital for a full understanding of this environment.

Because SYSTEM.INI describes the deep workings of Windows, it's potentially dangerous. You should change settings in SYSTEM.INI only when you completely understand what you are doing and why. Some parts of SYSTEM-.INI should never be changed by the user. We list those sections in this chapter. Some of these entries are modified for you automatically by the Windows Setup program, Control Panel, or the installation routines included with third-party applications.

If you look through your own SYSTEM.INI file, you will probably find a number of lines that are not listed here. Some of these install drivers essential to your system. Others (those whose parameters begin with an asterisk) identify virtual device drivers for 386 Enhanced mode that are actually incorporated into WIN386.EXE. All of the lines we chose to omit are lines that you should not tinker with or delete, unless you're willing to reinstall Windows altogether if something goes awry.

A Word about Syntax

Like WIN.INI, the SYSTEM.INI file is divided into distinct sections, the names of which are always enclosed within brackets ([Boot], [386Enh], and so on). Each entry has an equal sign—for example, Shell=. Following the equal sign are the parameters you can use with the entry. If the parameters for the entry consist of a choice between a limited number of discrete values, the choices are demarcated with a pipe character (|), like so: Off | On. If you must supply a specific value for a parameter, the type of value is noted in italic—for example, *filename* or *seconds*. For each entry, we include the default value in parentheses immediately following the entry—for example, (Default: 16).

Table 2.5 provides a brief description of the sections that appear in SYSTEM.INI.

TABLE 2.5

The Sections That Make Up SYSTEM.INI

Section	Description
[Boot]	Lists drivers and Windows modules
[Keyboard]	Contains information about the keyboard
[Boot.description]	Lists the names of devices you can change using Windows Setup
[386Enh]	Contains information used by Windows in 386 Enhanced mode
[Standard]	Contains information used by Windows in Standard mode
[NonWindowsApp]	Contains information used by non-Windows applications
[MCI]	Lists Media Control Interface (MCI) drivers (this section was introduced with Windows 3.1)
[Drivers]	Contains a list of aliases (or names) assigned to installable driver files (this section was introduced with Windows 3.1)

We discuss the sections of SYSTEM.INI in the order in which they appear in Table 2.5, which is how they should appear in a default Windows setup. The line-by-line discussion includes only four sections, however—[Boot], [386Enh], [Standard], and [NonWindowsApp]—because it is inadvisable to edit the other sections, as we will discuss next. We have described those sections of SYSTEM.INI that well-informed users can tamper with to their benefit. Within each of these sections, we include line-by-line options in alphabetical order for easy reference.

Abandon Hope, All Ye Who Edit Here

As we mentioned at the beginning of the chapter, it's important to realize that the majority of the settings in the SYSTEM.INI file should not be casually edited. Such tinkering could literally kill your Windows session. In Table 2.6, to make sure there is no question about it, we list those sections and lines of SYSTEM.INI that you should touch only at your peril.

TABLE 2.6

Sections and Specific Entries of SYSTEM.INI That You *Should Not* Edit

Section	Entry
[Boot]	286grabber=*filename*
	386grabber=*filename*
	CachedFileHandles=*number*
	Display.drv=*filename*
	Drivers=*filename I aliasname*
	keyboard.drv=*filename*
	language.dll=*libraryname*
	mouse.drv=*filename*
	network.drv=*filename*
	system.drv=*filename*
[Keyboard]	keyboard.dll=*filename*
	oemansi.bin=*filename*
	subtype=*number*
	-type=*number*
[Boot.description]	The whole section
[386Enh]	A20EnableCount=*number*
	BkGndNotifyAtPFault=0 I 1
	Device=*filename I *devicename*
	Display=*filename I *devicename*
	EBIOS=*filename I *devicename*

TABLE 2.6

Sections and Specific Entries of SYSTEM.INI That You *Should Not* Edit (Continued)

Section	Entry
	EISADMA=0 I 1 I *channel.size*
	HardDiskDMABuffer=*kilobytes*
	IdleVMWakeUpTime=*seconds*
	IgnoreInstalledEMM=0 I 1
	InDOSPolling=0 I 1
	Keyboard=*filename I *devicename*
	KybdPasswd=0 I 1
	Local=*devicename*
	LPTnAutoAssign=*seconds*
	LRULowRateMult=*number*
	LRURateChngTime=*milliseconds*
	LRUSweepFreq=*milliseconds*
	LRUSweepLen=*length-in-pages*
	LRUSweepLowWater=*number*
	LRUSweepReset=*milliseconds*
	MapPhysAddress=*range*
	MaxBPs=*number*
	MaxDMAPGAddress=*address*
	MinUnlockMem=*kilobytes*
	Mouse=*filename I *devicename*
	Network=*filename I *devicename*
	NMIReboot=0 I 1
	NoWaitNetIO=0 I 1
	OverlappedIO=0 I 1
	PageOverCommit=*megabytes*
	PerformBackfill=0 I 1
	PSPIncrement=*number*
	ReserveVideoROM=0 I 1
	ROMScanThreshold=*number*
	ScrollFrequency=*number*
	SGrabLPT=*port-number*
	SyncTime=0 I 1

TABLE 2.6

Sections and Specific Entries of SYSTEM.INI That You *Should Not* Edit (Continued)

Section	Entry
	SystemROMBreakPoint=0	1
	SysVMEMSLimit=*number	kilobytes*
	SysVMEMSLocked=0	1
	SysVMEMSRequired=*kilobytes*
	SysVMV86Locked=0	1
	SysVMXMSLimit=*number	kilobytes*
	SysVMXMSRequired=*kilobytes*
	TimerCriticalSection=*milliseconds*
	TranslateScans=0	1
	TrapTimerPorts=0	1
	UniqueDOSPSP=0	1
	UseInstFile=0	1
	VideoBackgroundMsg=0	1
	VideoSuspendDisable=0	1
	WindowUpdateTime=*milliseconds*
	WOAFont=*font-filename*
	XlatBufferSize=*kilobytes*
	XMSUMBInitCalls=0	1
[Standard]	PadCodeSegments=0	1
	StackSize=*kilobytes*
[NonWindowsApp]	GlobalHeapSize=*kilobytes*
[MCI]	The whole section
[Drivers]	The whole section

[Boot]

The [Boot] section contains information about some basic settings that are established when Windows starts. Most importantly, this is where the shell—the program that controls the Windows screen—is loaded. Usually this is the Windows Program Manager, although alternatives are available, as discussed in Chapter 5.

Comm.drv=*filename* (default: comm.drv)   Specifies the filename of the serial communications driver in use. The Windows 3.1 default driver is named

COMM.DRV. A number of third-party communications programs install their own replacement drivers for COMM.DRV.

If you upgrade a Windows 3.0 system that uses a third-party communications driver, the Windows 3.1 Setup program does not replace that driver with Microsoft's COMM.DRV, because your software may depend on the third-party driver. However, if you are running Windows 3.1 in Enhanced mode with a communications driver designed for Windows 3.0, you may need to add the line COMMDrv30=On to the [386Enh] section of SYSTEM.INI (discussed later in the chapter).

To replace a third-party communications driver with Microsoft's COMM-.DRV, you may need to make other changes to the [386Enh] section of SYSTEM.INI (because some third-party products also install their own virtual communications drivers). You should contact your communications vendor for details.

Fixedfon.fon=*filename* (default: depends on display driver)   Specifies the system font used by Windows 2.*x* running under Windows 3.1. If you have older applications that use monospaced fonts for all their text, you may be able to modernize them by changing this line.

To make Notepad use a proportionally spaced font on a VGA system, try setting Fixedfon.fon to VGASYS.FON. Valid entries are raster font files with a .FON extension. The specified file should be in your SYSTEM directory.

Fonts.fon=*filename* (default: depends on display driver)   Specifies the system font Windows uses for menus and dialog boxes. Windows is shipped with versions of this font for various resolutions of display. You may switch to any other available system font by specifying its name on the Fonts.fon= line. The specified font must be classified by Windows as a system font and must be in your SYSTEM directory. (The Windows-supplied system fonts are named EGASYS.FON, VGASYS.FON, and 8514SYS.FON.)

If you specify an invalid font, Windows will not start, and you will have to reboot your computer.

For another way to change the Windows menu font (one that is not limited to fonts of the system class), see the entry describing the [Fonts] section of WIN-.INI, earlier in the chapter.

Oemfonts.fon=*filename* (default: depends on display driver)   Specifies the name of the font the Clipboard Viewer program uses to display text in OEM Text format. This is a monospaced font that uses the character set native to DOS, rather than the ANSI character set used by all other Windows-supplied fonts (except Symbol). When you copy a block of text to the Clipboard, Windows ordinarily stores it in OEM Text format as well as in Text format. If you then paste into a non-Windows program, the Clipboard supplies the data in OEM Text format instead of Text format. Wherever possible, the appropriate character-value conversions are made so that, for example, accented characters appear the same in the non-Windows program as they did in your Windows application.

The font specified by Oemfonts.fon= is simply the font that the Clipboard Viewer uses when you choose its Display command and select OEM Text. Windows supplies three OEM-class fonts, named EGAOEM.FON, VGAOEM-.FON, and 8514OEM.FON.

The Setup program installs the font appropriate for your display resolution and initializes the Oemfonts.fon= line accordingly. You can change this setting by editing SYSTEM.INI, although there's probably no good reason to do so. If you do edit this line, the specified font must be categorized by Windows as an OEM font, or else Windows will not start and you will need to reboot.

Shell=*filename* (default: PROGMAN.EXE)   Specifies the name of your default shell, which is the program that starts and ends your Windows sessions. This is a required line, so don't delete it or its parameter value. The Windows Setup program automatically makes Program Manager your default shell, but you can switch it to File Manager or another program if you like. (To make File Manager the default, specify WINFILE.EXE.) If the program you specify is not in your WINDOWS directory, your SYSTEM directory, or a directory included in your DOS PATH statement, be sure to supply the full path name.

Nearly any program can act as your default shell. But if the program you specify is not designed to launch other programs, you will turn your Windows system into a single-application environment. That may be convenient at times. If you work only in Excel, for example, you can save yourself some startup time and steps by making Excel your default shell.

Vendors of third-party shells (such as the Norton Desktop for Windows) usually modify the Shell= line for you automatically if you choose to make their programs the default. To restore Program Manager as your default shell, edit the Shell= line and specify PROGMAN.EXE. (Note that you must include *something* on the Shell= line. If you leave it blank or delete the line, Windows won't start.)

Sound.drv=*filename* (default: depends on your system's sound hardware)   Specifies the filename of the sound driver in use.

TaskMan.Exe=*filename* (default: TASKMAN.EXE)   Specifies the program that appears when you press Ctrl+Esc, double-click on the desktop, or choose an application's Switch To command. If this line is omitted or has no parameter value, Windows uses TASKMAN.EXE. Some third-party shells come with their own task-switching programs and modify this line. You may choose to modify it yourself if you want a different program to pop up in response to Ctrl+Esc.

If you make a change to this line and later decide to restore TASK-MAN.EXE as your task switcher, either delete the line altogether or enter TASKMAN.EXE as the *filename* parameter. If you do not enter anything to the right of the equal sign, you get no task switcher.

A trick: You can modify this line for easier access to Solitaire. Just add the line

```
TaskMan.Exe=SOL.EXE
```

to the [Boot] section of your SYSTEM.INI file. Now you can press Ctrl+Esc to get right into your favorite card game, as shown in Figure 2.11.

FIGURE 2.11

Editing the SYSTEM.INI to load Solitaire in place of the Task Manager enables you to instantly call up Solitaire from anywhere in Windows by pressing Ctrl+Esc.

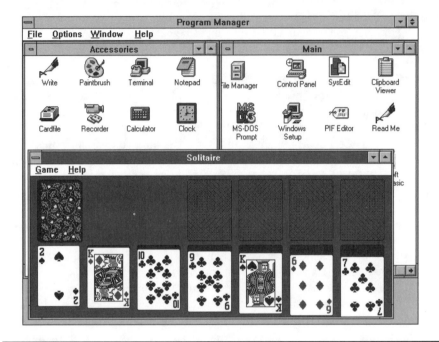

[386Enh]

Windows runs somewhat differently in 386 Enhanced mode than in Standard mode. These changes are primarily aimed at taking the fullest possible advantage of the powers of the 386 processor. The [386Enh] section defines the parameters Windows uses when running in 386 Enhanced mode.

32BitDiskAccess=Off | On (default: Off)   On systems with hard-disk controllers that are 100-percent compatible with the Western Digital 1003 standard, this line determines whether Windows uses its "Fastdisk" technology to bypass the ROM-BIOS disk access services. As the name suggests, Fastdisk may result in quicker disk access. It may also let you run more non-Windows applications at once in 386 Enhanced mode.

When you install it, Windows checks to see if the hardware you're using could benefit from 32-bit disk access. If it can, a check box entitled Use 32-Bit Disk Access is included in the Control Panel's Virtual Memory dialog box. If you use Windows to run DOS applications in 386 Enhanced mode, 32-bit virtual memory is a godsend. It speeds up virtual memory access and doubles your PC's capacity to run DOS apps with background processing. There are some caveats, however: 32-bit disk access works only with Western Digital 1003-compatible hard-disk controllers (which account for 90 percent of them), and it's not safe on battery-operated PCs with power-saving facilities. But unless you're using a laptop or ESDI or SCSI hard disk, use 32-bit access.

To turn Fastdisk on, open the 386 Enhanced section of Control Panel, choose Virtual Memory, choose Change, and then select the check box labeled Use 32-Bit Disk Access. Control Panel records your action on the 32BitDiskAccess line of SYSTEM.INI.

AllEMSLocked=Off | On (default: Off)   If On, this entry prevents Windows from swapping expanded memory to disk and overrides any PIF settings that leave expanded memory unlocked. In most cases, swapping expanded memory to disk does not create problems.

Change this line to On if you use a disk-caching program or DOS device driver that uses expanded memory.

AllVMsExclusive=Off | On (default: Off)   If On, this line forces all non-Windows programs in Enhanced mode to run full screen, regardless of their PIFs. Microsoft recommends using this setting if you're running network or TSR software that isn't fully compatible with Windows 3.1.

Setting this line to On also renders Alt+Enter ineffective at toggling between full and windowed-screen DOS apps.

AltKeyDelay=*seconds* (default: .005)   Specifies the length of time Windows waits to process a keyboard interrupt after it has processed an Alt interrupt. Try increasing this value if you have applications that don't handle the Alt key correctly.

AltPasteDelay=*seconds* (default: .025)   Specifies the length of time Windows waits to paste characters after the Alt key has been pressed. Some applications may require a higher setting than the default.

AutoRestoreScreen=Off | On (default: On)   Specifies whether, when you switch back to a non-Windows program running in 386 Enhanced mode, the program's screen is restored by Windows or by the program. Affects only programs running in VGA display modes that identify themselves to Windows as being able to restore their own screens.

Changing this setting to Off reduces memory use but may also degrade performance, since Windows can usually restore the screen more quickly.

CGANoSnow=Off | On (default: Off)   If On, this entry causes Windows to do some processing to avoid "snow" on a CGA display.

CGA40WOA.FON=*filename* (default in U.S.: CGA40WOA.FON)   Specifies the fixed-pitch font that Windows uses to display non-Windows applications that use a 40-column display with 25 or fewer lines.

CGA80WOA.FON=*filename* (default in U.S.: CGA80WOA.FON)   Specifies the fixed-pitch font Windows uses to display non-Windows applications that use an 80-column display with 25 or fewer lines.

Com1AutoAssign=*number* (default: 2, if port is present)

Com2AutoAssign=*number* (default: 2, if port is present)

Com3AutoAssign=*number* (default: 2, if port is present)

Com4AutoAssign=*number* (default: 2, if port is present)   Determine how Windows behaves when two non-Windows applications or a non-Windows application and a Windows application both want to use a particular COM port at the same time. If *number* is –1, Windows always displays a warning and asks you to decide which application gets the port. If *number* is 0, Windows doesn't arbitrate—any application can use the port at any time. If *number* is greater than 0, Windows gives the port to the application that claims it first. After that application has finished, Windows waits *number* seconds before allowing another application to use the port. *Number* may not be greater than 1000.

NOTE   Windows always arbitrates device contention between Windows applications. The AutoAssign value affects only contention between virtual machines—that is, contention in which at least one of the applications is a non-Windows program.

To change the AutoAssign value for any COM port, open the 386 Enhanced section of Control Panel, shown in Figure 2.12. In the Device Contention section of the dialog box, select the port you want to change. Then choose Always Warn, Never Warn, or Idle.

FIGURE 2.12

Change the Device Contention settings for a COM port by changing the values in Control Panel's 386 Enhanced dialog box.

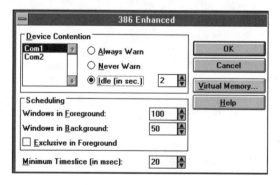

Normally, it's not a good idea to set *number* to 0. However, certain non-Windows print spoolers may require a 0 setting for printers attached to serial ports. Your spooler vendor should advise you if this setting is necessary.

COM1Base=*address* (default: port value in BIOS data area)

COM2Base=*address* (default: port value in BIOS data area)

COM3Base=*address* (default: 3E8h)

COM4Base=*address* (default: port value in BIOS data area) Let you set the base (starting) address for each serial port, in both Standard mode and Enhanced mode. To change them, use the Ports section of Control Panel. Double-click the icon for the port you want to adjust, then click the Settings button and then the Advanced button to specify a base address.

COM1Buffer=*number* (default: 128)

COM2Buffer=*number* (default: 128)

COM3Buffer=*number* (default: 128)

COM4Buffer=*number* (default: 128) Specify the number of characters that Windows buffers on each port. You may need to increase the buffer size if you are losing characters. Before trying this, however, Microsoft recommends that you try setting the Com*x*Protocol line (described in a moment) to XOFF.

If you are using a 16550 Universal Asynchronous Receiver Transmitter (UART) and a non-Windows communications program running in Enhanced mode, you may need to set the communications buffer to 0 to take advantage of the UART's buffer.

COM1FIFO=Off | On (default: On)

COM2FIFO=Off | On (default: On)

COM3FIFO=Off | On (default: On)

COM4FIFO=Off | On (default: On) Determine whether the FIFO buffer of a 16550 UART will be enabled. If you are using an older 16550 UART that does not properly support the FIFO buffer, and you experience problems, try disabling the FIFO buffer for the appropriate port by changing this setting to Off.

COM1IRQ=*number* (default: 4)

COM2IRQ=*number* (default: 3)

COM3IRQ=*number* (default: ISA and EISA, 4; MCA, 3)

COM4IRQ=*number* (default: 3) Specify the interrupt request line (IRQ) that each serial port uses in both Standard and Enhanced mode. To change them, use the Ports section of Control Panel. Double-click the icon for the port you want to adjust, then click the Settings button and then the Advanced button to specify the IRQ you want to use. To disable input for a serial port, specify an IRQ of –1.

COM1Protocol=XOFF | (blank) (default: blank)

COM2Protocol=XOFF | (blank) (default: blank)

COM3Protocol=XOFF | (blank) (default: blank)

COM4Protocol=XOFF | (blank) (default: blank) Determine whether Windows, when running in 386 Enhanced mode, stops simulating characters in a virtual machine on receipt of an XOFF character. If these lines are set to any value other than XOFF, or if the lines are omitted, Windows ignores XOFF characters. If a line is set to XOFF, Windows stops sending characters when it gets an XOFF and resumes when it receives the next character, whatever that may be. You should turn off the protocol setting for any serial port used for binary file transfers. If you are losing text characters at high baud rates, try setting the protocol to XOFF. If you still lose characters, try increasing the associated COM*x*Buffer line (described previously) to a higher value.

COMBoostTime=*milliseconds* (default: 2)   Specifies the length of time a virtual machine is allowed to process a COM interrupt. Try increasing this value if you're losing characters on the screen in a communications program.

COMIrqSharing=Off I On (default: MCA and EISA, On; ISA, Off)   Specifies whether serial ports can share interrupt request lines. If COM1 and COM3 or COM2 and COM4 use the same IRQ on your system, this line should be set to On.

COMdrv30=Off I On (default: Off)   If this line is Off (the default), Windows' virtual communications driver maintains its own copy of the serial communications driver's interrupt handler.

If you're using a communications driver designed for Windows 3.0 (specified by the [Boot] section's COMM.DRV= line discussed earlier), you probably need to change this setting from Off to On. Add the line to SYSTEM.INI if it isn't already there.

DMABufferIn1MB=Off I On (default: Off)   Specifies whether the direct memory access (DMA) buffer should be located in the first megabyte of memory, for compatibility with 8-bit bus-mastering cards.

DMABufferSize=*kilobytes* (default: 16)   Specifies the amount of memory to be reserved for the DMA buffer. Some backup systems may require a higher value than 16. Central Point Software, for example, recommends a setting of 64.

If a NetBIOS network has been installed before Windows starts, Windows uses the larger of this size and the size specified by the NetDMASize line (described in a moment).

If you are using EMM386.EXE with a D= parameter, be aware that Windows ignores this parameter, using the DMABufferSize parameter instead.

DOSPromptExitInstruc=Off I On (default: On)   With this line set to On (or omitted), displays five lines of instructions near the top of the screen when you run a copy of COMMAND.COM (or choose the DOS Prompt icon in Program Manager) in 386 Enhanced mode. These instructions (shown in Figure 2.13) tell you to type **Exit** to quit the DOS session, to press Alt+Tab to switch back to Windows or another application temporarily, or to press Alt+Enter to switch the DOS session between a window and a full screen.

If you find this message vexing, change the DOSPromptExitInstruc line to Off. (You may need to add the line to the [386Enh] section of SYSTEM.INI.)

FIGURE 2.13

Changing the DOSPromptExitInstruc setting in the SYSTEM.INI file gets rid of this message, which reminds you how to return to Windows from a DOS session.

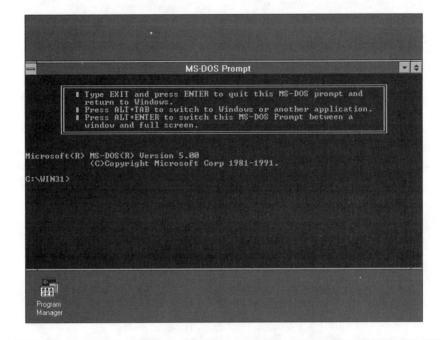

Note that with the prompt turned off, you will still get a copyright message from Microsoft near the top of your DOS session screen. And you will still get a polite message if you try to return from a DOS session by typing **Win**.

DualDisplay=Off I On (default: depends on display adapter) Set this line to On if you want EMM386 to make the B000-B7FF address range available as an upper memory block (UMB).

If you set DualDisplay to On, you must also include the parameter i=B000-B755 in the DEVICE=EMM386.EXE statement of your CONFIG.SYS file.

EGA40WOA.FON=*filename* (default in U.S.: EGA40WOA.FON) Specifies the fixed-pitch font Windows uses to display non-Windows applications that use a 40-column display with more than 25 lines.

EGA80WOA.FON=*filename* (default in U.S.: EGA80WOA.FON) Specifies the fixed-pitch font Windows uses to display non-Windows applications that use an 80-column display with more than 25 lines.

EMMExclude=*paragraph-range* (default: none) Prevents Windows from scanning a designated range of upper memory. This line is most often used for troubleshooting purposes. If you suspect that Windows is trying to locate its expanded-memory page frame or translation buffers in an area already occupied by a hardware adapter or device, you may want to exclude all of high memory by adding the statement EMMExclude=A000-EFFF. If that enables your system to work, you can then try excluding a smaller area of upper memory, continuing in this fashion until you locate the address where the conflict is occurring.

To use EMMExclude, specify the lower and upper boundaries of the region you want to exclude, in hexadecimal notation, with a hyphen separating the two addresses. Windows will round your lower boundary down and your upper boundary up, if necessary, so that the region is an even multiple of 16K. To exclude a smaller region of upper memory, use the ReservedHighMemory= setting, discussed later in this chapter.

EMMInclude=*paragraph-range* (default: none)   Explicitly instructs Windows to scan the designated upper-memory range for free UMBs, overriding any overlapping area specified in an EMMExclude line. You can use this line in conjunction with EMMExclude to locate the source of a UMB conflict.

As it does with EMMExclude, Windows rounds the specified area, if necessary, to cover an even multiple of 16K. To specify a smaller region, use the UsableHighArea setting (described later in this chapter).

Windows will ignore an EMMInclude range if it overlaps with a range excluded by means of EMM386's X= parameter.

EMMPageFrame=*paragraph* (default: none)   Explicitly specifies the starting address for Windows' expanded-memory page frame.

EMMSize=*kilobytes* (default: 64)   Allocates all available memory as expanded memory for the benefit of non-Windows applications that can use expanded memory. The EMMSize line lets you specify a maximum amount to be used as EMS. You would want to do this if an application you're using claims all the available expanded memory, leaving you unable to start any other applications.

If you set this line to 0, Windows allocates no expanded memory but still loads its expanded memory manager. If you really want no expanded memory, use NoEMMDriver=On instead (described in a moment).

FileSysChange=Off | On (default: On for 386 Enhanced mode, Off for Standard mode)   Determines whether File Manager is notified when a non-Windows application creates, deletes, copies, moves, renames, or modifies a file. Performance is faster with this service off. If you run Windows in 386 Enhanced mode and can live without immediate updating of File Manager's records, change this line from On to Off. (You may need to add this line to your [386Enh] section.)

Global=*devicename* (default: none)   Specifies that an MS-DOS device is to be global, which means that one copy of its state is maintained in memory for all virtual machines. By default, all DOS devices other than CON are global. But some device drivers may try to make themselves local. The Global= switch is provided to override any drivers that may cause the system to fail if they are local.

The *device-name* must match the case of the device name exactly as it's listed in CONFIG.SYS, or this entry will not work.

Int28Critical=Off | On (default: On)   If On, indicates that a critical section is needed for handling Int 28h interrupts used by memory-resident software. The default is On because some networks use virtual devices that perform internal task switching in response to Int 28h. If you're not using such software, you may get quicker task switching by setting this switch Off.

IRQ9Global=Off | On (default: Off)   If On, converts IRQ 9 masks to global. Try setting this switch On if you are unable to read from floppy disks in 386 Enhanced mode.

KeyBoostTime=*seconds* (default: .001)   Specifies the length of time an application gets increased priority when it receives a keystroke. Increase this value if your foreground programs respond sluggishly to keystrokes while other programs are running in the background.

KeyBufferDelay=*seconds* (default: .2)   Specifies the length of time Windows waits before pasting keyboard input after the keyboard buffer is full. Try increasing this value if some of your non-Windows programs don't paste Clipboard text correctly.

KeyIdleDelay=*seconds* (default: .5)   Specifies the length of time Windows ignores idle calls after simulating a keystroke to a virtual machine. Reducing this value may speed up keyboard input but may also cause some applications to slow down.

KeyPasteCRSkipCount=*number* (default: 10)

KeyPasteSkipCount=*number* (default: 2)   Govern the delay loop Windows uses to slow down pasting into a virtual machine. Specifically, they determine how many Int 16h calls should return "empty" after a carriage return has been pasted (KeyPasteCRSkipCount) or any other character has been pasted (KeyPasteSkipCount) before Windows pastes another character. Try increasing both values if you are losing characters while pasting into a non-Windows program.

KeyPasteDelay=*seconds* (default: .003)   Specifies the minimum time Windows waits after pasting a character before pasting another character. Try increasing this setting if you are losing characters while pasting.

KeyPasteTimeout=*seconds* (default: .003)   Specifies the length of time Windows gives an application to make the BIOS keyboard-reading calls before Windows switches from its fast-paste (Int 16h) to its slow-paste (Int 9h) mechanism.

KybdReboot=Off I On (default: On) Specifies whether Windows uses a keyboard controller command to reboot the computer in response to Ctrl+Alt+Del. If your computer hangs when you attempt to reboot, change this setting to Off.

LocalLoadHigh=Off I On (default: Off) Determines whether Windows leaves some UMBs free for local use of virtual machines under DOS 5. Don't set this On unless you need local use of UMBs for particular virtual machines.

LocalReboot=Off I On (default: On) If On, enables the Ctrl+Alt+Del keyboard combination to terminate a hung application without rebooting your computer. Leave this switch On unless you relish the prospect of losing data when a program fails.

MaxCOMPort=*number* (default: 4) Specifies the maximum number of communications ports that Windows will support. Increase this value if you use more than four communications ports.

MaxPagingFileSize=*kilobytes* (default: 50% of available disk space) This is one of two SYSTEM.INI lines that govern the maximum size of a temporary swap file, relative to the amount of space available on the designated drive. (The other is MinUserDiskSpace, discussed in a moment.) Windows normally does not permit you to create a temporary swap file larger than half the available disk space. If you're low on disk space, you might want to override this requirement. You can do that by adding the line MaxPagingFileSize to the [386Enh] section of SYSTEM.INI and specifying the number of kilobytes you want to be permitted to use. Then, after restarting Windows, go to the 386 Enhanced section of Control Panel, choose Virtual Memory, choose Change, and specify the size and location of your temporary swap file.

MaxPhysPage=*hexadecimal page number* (default: depends on amount of physical memory Windows detects at startup) Specifies the highest physical page number in memory that Windows will use. Windows initializes this value at startup depending on the amount of physical memory it finds in your system. If you use hardware devices that cannot recognize all of your system's physical memory, you might want to set an explicit ceiling with MaxPhysPage=. (An example of such a device might be an ISA DMA network card that cannot use memory beyond 16Mb.)

MCADMA=Off I On (default: On for MCA computers, Off for all others) Determines whether Windows uses the Micro Channel extensions to DMA. Turn this switch off if you use a Micro Channel computer on which the DMA extensions have not been implemented.

MessageBackColor=*vga color attribute* (default: 1)
MessageTextColor=*vga color attribute* (default: F) Specify the background and foreground colors, respectively, that Windows uses for certain full-screen text

messages—like the message that appears when you press Ctrl+Alt+Del. The defaults give you white characters on a blue background. To change these values, specify a color attribute between 0 and 7 for the background and between 0 and F (in hexadecimal notation) for the foreground.

MinTimeSlice=*milliseconds* (default: 20)   Governs the minimum amount of time a virtual machine is allowed to run before other virtual machines are given the opportunity to claim the processor. Setting this value lower can make multitasking appear smoother, but it will degrade overall performance because Windows will spend more time switching. Note that because all Windows applications run within a single virtual machine, this setting has no effect on the division of processor time between Windows applications.

To change the MinTimeSlice setting, open the 386 Enhanced section of Control Panel and adjust the Minimum Timeslice value. Control Panel will update SYSTEM.INI for you.

MinUserDiskSpace=*kilobytes* (default: 2000)   Specifies the minimum amount of disk space that Windows will leave free when creating a temporary swap file. (This entry has no effect if you have a permanent swap file.) The default, 2K, leaves room for temporary files created by Windows applications as well as for new and enlarged data files. Decrease this value cautiously if you need more room for a temporary swap file.

MouseSoftInit=Off | On (default: On)   Change this setting from On to Off (by editing SYSTEM.INI) if your cursor and screen information sometimes appear distorted when you use a mouse with a non-Windows program running in a window.

NetAsynchFallback=Off | On (default: Off)
NetAsynchTimeout=*seconds* (default: 5.0)   Determine whether Windows attempts to rescue a failing asynchronous NetBIOS request. Normally, if Windows doesn't have enough space in its global network buffer to handle the request, the request fails. If NetAsynchFallback is On, however, Windows allocates a buffer in local memory and prevents any other virtual machine from running until the time specified by NetAsynchTimeout elapses.

NetDMASize=*kilobytes* (default: 32 on MCA computers, 0 on all others)   Specifies the size of the DMA buffer used for NetBIOS transport software, if a NetBIOS network is installed. Windows uses the larger of this setting and the DMABufferSize setting described earlier.

NetHeapSize=*kilobytes* (default: 12)   Determines the size of the conventional-memory buffer that Windows uses in Enhanced mode for transferring data over a network. Increasing this value decreases available conventional memory but may be necessary for some networks. The NetHeapSize value is always rounded up to the next 4K boundary.

NoEMMDriver=Off | On (default: Off)   If On, prevents Windows from loading the driver that makes expanded memory available to non-Windows programs running in 386 Enhanced mode.

If you never require expanded memory for your non-Windows programs, you should change this line to On. Doing so reduces the likelihood that Windows will be unable to place its translation buffers in upper-memory blocks, and may therefore free up more conventional memory for your non-Windows programs. Note that if Windows has to put translation buffers in conventional memory, the buffers reduce available conventional memory in all virtual machines.

PageBuffers=*number* (default: 4)   Specifies the number of 4K page buffers that Windows uses to store asynchronous read and write pages when 32-Bit Disk Access is in use. You may get better Windows performance by increasing this setting.

Paging=Off | On (default: On)   If Off, disables Windows' use of virtual memory. You should change this to Off only if you need the disk space that would be used by a temporary or permanent swap file. To change this line, open the 386 Enhanced section of Control Panel, choose Virtual Memory, and choose Change. Then, in the Type list, choose None.

PagingFile=path-and-filename   (default: C:\WINDOWS\WIN386.SWP)
Specifies the location and name of your temporary swap file. Because this line includes the full path of the file, it overrides any contradictory setting in PagingDrive= (described next). There's probably no reason to change the PagingFile value.

PagingDrive=*drive-letter* (default: the drive on which your SYSTEM.INI file is stored)   Specifies the drive that Windows uses for a temporary swap file. The setting is ignored if you use a permanent swap file. To change this setting, click the Virtual Memory and Change buttons in the 386 Enhanced section of Control Panel and choose a new drive.

PermSwapDOSDrive=*drive-letter* (default: none)   Specifies the drive that Windows uses for a permanent swap file. The setting is ignored if you use a temporary swap file. To change, click the Virtual Memory and Change buttons in the 386 Enhanced section of Control Panel and choose a new drive.

PermSwapSizeK=*kilobytes* (default: none)   Specifies the size of your permanent swap file. To change this setting, click the Virtual Memory and Change buttons in the 386 Enhanced section of Control Panel and specify the desired size in the New Size box.

PerVMFiles=*number* (default: 10)   Sets the number of local file handles allowed for each virtual machine. Note, however, that this setting is ignored if the DOS SHARE utility is installed. Also be aware that the total file handles opened by all virtual machines, plus the file handles specified in your CONFIG-.SYS's FILES statement, may not exceed 255.

If a non-Windows application gives you an error message instructing you to increase the FILES= statement in your CONFIG.SYS, ignore this advice and increase PerVMFiles.

ReflectDOSInt2A=Off | On (default: Off)   Specifies whether Windows should reflect or consume Int 2Ah interrupts. Windows consumes the interrupts and runs more efficiently with this switch off. Turn it on only if you are running memory-resident software that depends on Int 2Ah calls.

ReservedHighArea=*paragraph range* (default: none)   Prevents Windows from scanning a designated range of upper memory. Specify the lower and upper boundaries of the region you want to exclude, in hexadecimal notation, with a hyphen separating the two addresses. Windows rounds your lower boundary down and your upper boundary up, if necessary, so that the region is an even multiple of 4K. This line is similar to EMMExclude (described previously), except that it allows you to exclude smaller areas of memory.

ReservePageFrame=Off | On (default: On)   Tells Windows whether to give preference to the expanded-memory page frame or to translation buffers, if insufficient UMB space for both is available. If this switch is On and Windows can't find enough room in upper memory for both the EMS page frame and the translation buffers, Windows locates the page frame in upper memory (if a contiguous 64K space is available) and puts the translation buffers in conventional memory, thereby reducing the amount of conventional memory available to all virtual machines.

If you never use expanded memory in your DOS applications, it's a good idea to change this setting to Off.

TokenRingSearch=Off | On (default: On)   Determines whether Windows searches for a Token-Ring network adapter on AT-architecture machines. Turn this switch off if you're not using a Token-Ring network and the search interferes with another device.

UsableHighArea=*paragraph range* (default: none)   Explicitly instructs Windows to scan the designated upper-memory range for free UMBs, overriding any overlapping area specified in an EMMExclude line. You can use this line in conjunction with EMMExclude to locate the source of a UMB conflict.

Windows rounds the specified area, if necessary, to cover an even multiple of 4K. To specify a larger region, use EMMInclude.

Windows will ignore a UsableHighArea range if it overlaps with a range excluded by means of EMM386's X= parameter.

UseROMFont=Off | On (default: On)   Determines whether Windows uses the soft font in video ROM to display text in full-screen non-Windows programs, as well as text used in messages that appear when you switch away from non-Windows programs. You should set this switch to Off if you see random dots and shapes on your screen.

According to Microsoft, you should also turn this switch off if you use the VGASwap option with Qualitas's 386Max or BlueMax.

VGAMonoText=Off | On (default: On)   If your applications don't use the monochrome display mode of the VGA adapter, you should set this switch Off. Doing so allows Windows access to an additional upper-memory block, B000 to B7FF. This switch has no effect with systems that don't use a VGA display.

VirtualHDIrq=Off | On (default: On for AT-compatible systems, Off for all others)   If On, allows Windows to virtualize the hard-disk interrupt line, bypassing the ROM BIOS. Virtualization provides better performance but is incompatible with certain hard-disk controllers, as well as certain software products.

Among the products requiring VirtualHDIrq to be set to Off, according to Microsoft, are the Super PC-Kwik cache utility, Borland's Reflex, the Toshiba HARDRAM, various games from Broderbund, Plus Development's HardCard Plus 80 II, and some ESDI hard-disk controllers.

WindowKBRequired=*kilobytes* (default: 256)   Specifies the amount of conventional memory that must be free for Windows to start. If you have trouble starting Windows, try reducing this value.

WindowMemSize=–1 | *kilobytes* (default: –1)   Specifies the amount of conventional memory Windows may use for itself. The default, –1, allows Windows as much conventional memory as it needs.

If you get insufficient-memory messages when you try to run virtual machines on a 2Mb system, try setting WindowMemSize to a value less than 640. (Alternatively, use PIFs and set smaller values for Kb Required.)

WinExclusive=0 | 1 (default: 0)   Allows you to prevent non-Windows applications running in 386 Enhanced mode from operating in the background. With this line set to 1, Windows suspends all non-Windows programs whenever a Windows program is running in the foreground. To change this line, open the 386 Enhanced section of Control Panel and set or clear the Exclusive in Foreground check box.

WinTimeSlice=*foreground, background* (default: 100,50)   Determines the priority given to the Windows virtual machine relative to the non-Windows virtual machine(s) when the Windows virtual machine is running in the foreground and background, respectively. (When both Windows and non-Windows applications are open in 386 Enhanced mode, all the Windows applications together run in one virtual machine, while each non-Windows program runs in its own separate virtual machine.)

Unlike the MinTimeSlice line, whose parameter is measured in milliseconds, WinTimeSlice specifies relative values only. For example, suppose the WinTimeSlice values are 100 and 50 (their defaults) and no DOS programs are running. In this case, the Windows virtual machine gets 100 percent of the processor time, since there are no non-Windows virtual machines.

Now suppose you start two non-Windows programs whose own priority values are also set to 100 and 50. (These values are determined by the application's PIF. If you don't run the program from a PIF, Windows uses the values set in _DEFAULT.PIF, which are 100 and 50 unless you modify them.) While the Windows virtual machine is in the foreground, it will get approximately half of the processing time, as shown by the following expression:

$$\frac{WindowsVM\ Foreground\ Priority}{DOSVM1\ Background\ Priority + DOSVM2\ Background\ Priority}$$

or, in this case,

$$\frac{100}{50 + 50}$$

While the first non-Windows program is running in the foreground, all your Windows applications together will get about one-third of the processing time, as shown by this expression:

$$\frac{WindowsVM\ Background\ Priority}{DOSVM1\ Foreground\ Priority + DOSVM2\ Background\ Priority}$$

or

$$\frac{50}{100 + 50}$$

If you leave your DOS applications' priorities set at 100 and 50 (that is, if you don't specify other values in _DEFAULT.PIF or in any of your applications' PIFs), you can reduce the drag that non-Windows programs running in the background exert on your foreground Windows programs by increasing the *foreground* parameter on the WinTimeSlice line. To do that, open the 386 Enhanced section of Control Panel and adjust the Windows in Foreground value upward. Values from 1 to 10000 are accepted. Similarly, if you find the foreground performance of your non-Windows programs unsatisfactory, you can reduce the WinTimeSlice line's *background* priority by adjusting the Windows in Background value in Control Panel. (To boost the performance of a particular non-Windows program, however, you may find it simpler to increase its foreground priority—or just to run it in Exclusive mode. You can do either of those things by modifying the application's PIF.)

[Standard]

The [Standard] area of SYSTEM.INI defines the parameters Windows uses when running in Standard mode.

FasterModeSwitch=0 | 1 (default: 0)   Allows most 286 computers to switch more quickly between Protected mode and Real mode, thereby improving throughput for Windows running in Standard mode. (This line has no effect on 386 or 486 computers.) The default is 0 because a value of 1 may cause certain early-model IBM PC-ATs and compatibles to hang when Windows starts. You can improve performance on most 286 systems by changing FasterModeSwitch to 1. (Add this line to the [Standard] section if it is not already there.)

You should definitely try setting FasterModeSwitch to 1 if you are losing characters while typing on a Zenith Z-248, losing control of the mouse on an Olivetti M-250-E, or losing characters or experiencing slow performance with Winfax Pro 2.0 on a 286 computer.

Int28Filter=*number* (default: 10)   In Standard mode, this line determines the percentage of Int 28h interrupts that are made visible to applications that were loaded before Windows. With the default setting, Windows makes every tenth interrupt visible. Setting this value higher may improve performance but may also cause problems with certain memory-resident programs.

MouseSyncTime=*milliseconds* (default: 500)   Determines the number of seconds that can elapse between mouse data bytes before Windows assumes a data packet is complete. (This line only affects systems with an IBM PS/2 mouse interface running in Standard mode.)

NetAsynchSwitch=0 | 1 (default: 0, unless an application is running that supports the use of the Task Switcher API by NetBIOS)   Determines, in Standard mode, whether you are allowed to switch away from an application after that application has made an asynchronous NetBIOS call. Because switching away from some applications under these circumstances can cause your system to fail, Windows prevents switching by default.

NetHeapSize=*kilobytes* (default: 8)   Determines the size of the conventional-memory buffer that Windows in Standard mode uses for transferring data over a network. If an application is not running correctly, your network may need a larger buffer than Windows' default. Increasing this value decreases available conventional memory but may be necessary for some networks.

Stacks=*number* (default: 12)   Determines the number of reflector stacks DOSX.EXE uses to map DOS or BIOS interrupts from Real mode to Protected mode.

If you get a "Standard Mode: Stack Overflow" error message, try increasing this value. Acceptable values range from 8 to 64.

[NonWindowsApp]

Windows requires some basic operating information that it can use to run DOS applications. This information focuses primarily on fundamentals for running DOS itself, operating mice in DOS, and other such housekeeping items.

CommandEnvSize=*bytes* (default: 0, with DOS 3.0 or 3.1; with DOS 3.2 or later, the default matches the /e: parameter of the SHELL statement in your CONFIG.SYS, if any) Specifies the size of your DOS environment space. This line can help you out if you get a "not enough environment space" message while trying to run a non-Windows program under Windows. When you launch a DOS application in Windows' 386 Enhanced mode, Windows creates a virtual machine and gives it a copy of DOS with the same amount of environment space as you allocated in your CONFIG.SYS file. The default is 160 bytes or whatever you may have specified with a statement such as this:

```
SHELL=C:\DOS\COMMAND.COM /E:1024
```

You can increase the environment space for all non-Windows applications by adding a CommandEnvSize= line to the [NonWindowsApp] section of SYSTEM.INI. To allocate 2K, for example, enter the line

```
CommandEnvSize=2048
```

You may also use PIFs to increase the environment space for particular non-Windows applications. For example, to run the program WHIZBANG-.EXE in a virtual machine with 2,048 bytes of environment space, you could create a PIF with the following entries:

```
Program Name: COMMAND.COM
Program Title: Whizbang
Program Parameters: /E:2048 /C C:\WHIZ\WHIZBANG.EXE
Startup Directory: C:\WHIZ
```

If the environment space specified via a PIF is larger than that given on the CommandEnvSize= line, Windows allocates the larger amount—but only for the virtual machine launched by that PIF.

DisablePositionSave=0 | 1 (default: 0) Records the window's position, whether it's maximized, and the font it uses, when you quit a non-Windows application running in a window in 386 Enhanced mode. This information is stored in an initialization file called DOSAPP.INI. You can ask Windows not to record this information by choosing the Fonts command on the application's Control menu (while the app is in a windowed display) and clearing the check box labeled Save Settings on Exit.

If you change the DisablePositionSave line in SYSTEM.INI from 0 (its default) to 1, Windows never saves this position and font information. You may need to add the line to SYSTEM.INI to do this. If this line is omitted, Windows assumes its parameter is 0.

FontChangeEnable=0 I 1 (default: 1 on systems that use Windows 3.1 grabbers; 0 on systems that use Windows 3.0 grabbers)   Lets you change the display font used for a non-Windows application running in a window in 386 Enhanced mode. If you are unable to do this, it may be because you are using a display driver and grabber file designed for Windows 3.0. (The grabber is a file that supports the exchange of data in video memory between non-Windows applications and Windows 3.1.) You may be able to rectify the problem by entering FontChangeEnable=1 in the [NonWindowsApp] section of your SYSTEM.INI file. This fix does not work on all display systems, however, and it may cause your mouse pointer to be displayed incorrectly. If it doesn't work, reset FontChangeEnable to 0.

LocalTSRs=*TSRname1,TSRname2*... (default: dosedit,   ced,   pced)   Specifies a list of TSR (terminate-and-stay-resident) programs that may be copied into each running virtual machine. Certain TSRs do not function correctly in virtual machines if they have been loaded before Windows starts. DOSEDIT, for example, assumes that there is only one keyboard buffer, not a separate buffer in each virtual machine. If a TSR that is in memory when you start Windows is included on the LocalTSRs= line, Windows puts a copy of it in each virtual machine you create. Note, however, that some TSR programs do not work if copied into virtual machines in this manner.

MouseInDosBox=0 I 1 (default: 1 if supported mouse driver is loaded; otherwise, 0)   In Windows 3.1, when you run a non-Windows application in a window in 386 Enhanced mode, mouse events are normally passed through to the application. (This is true for most mouse drivers that have the extension .COM or .SYS, provided that your display system uses a Windows 3.1 grabber file.) If you want to select text and copy it to the Clipboard, you must first use the Edit and Mark commands on your application's Control menu. If you prefer to be able to select text directly (without going to the Control menu) and don't mind forgoing your application's own mouse interface, edit the SYSTEM.INI file to change the MouseInDosBox line from 1 to 0.

Screenlines=*number* (default: 25)   Specifies the number of lines displayed on a non-Windows application running full-screen. The default is 25. Provided your display system permits, you may select a 43- or 50-line display by editing the Screenlines line in SYSTEM.INI. This setting may be overridden by the application itself, however.

Swapdisk=*drive:\directory* (default: the directory pointed to by your DOS TEMP environment variable; if no TEMP variable, the root directory of your first hard disk)   When you switch away from a non-Windows application in Standard mode, Windows swaps that program's data to disk, storing it in the directory indicated by the Swapdisk= line. To maximize the efficiency of this process, you can set a DOS environment variable named TEMP to point to your fastest and least-fragmented hard disk. Or you may edit SYSTEM.INI to enter a particular drive and directory on the Swapdisk= line.

If you run Windows in Standard mode and use a RAM disk, you might want to point your TEMP variable to the RAM disk and set Swapdisk= to some other drive and directory. That way, applications that put temporary files in the TEMP directory will be able to use the RAM disk, but you won't be trying to swap entire applications in and out of a RAM drive. (If you point Swapdisk= to a RAM disk that isn't large enough, Windows may force you to reboot.)

The Swapdisk= line has no effect in 386 Enhanced mode.

3 Taming, Troubleshooting, and Turbocharging Windows Hardware

WHEN WINDOWS GETS ACCUSED OF BEING SLOW, HARDWARE INADEQUACIES or conflicts are usually the true cause. Even when Windows is running "well," sophisticated manipulation of hardware can turbocharge performance to achieve the maximum benefit for the user.

Nowhere is this more true than when you have to work with Windows on a 286 PC. Conventional wisdom says it simply isn't worth doing. *Au contraire.* Properly tuned, a 286 PC can handle Windows chores just fine, as we'll demonstrate in this chapter.

The chapter also delves into the mysteries of BIOS, buffers, ports, and drives. But most of all, this chapter focuses on memory. If the key to retail success is location, location, location, the key to Windows success is memory, memory, memory. And we look into the particular problems of multimedia hardware and notebooks, environments that challenge Windows in very different ways.

Windows is high-octane software. This chapter is a tune-up.

Optimizing Windows on a 286 PC

Nowhere does savvy manipulation of hardware have greater impact than with 286 PCs. The myth has evolved that Windows simply will not operate on 286 PCs. The reality is that you *can* run Windows on a 286 PC. The key to accomplishing this goal is to recognize that there is more to your PC than just its processor. Without doubt, the 286 is a weak processor for handling Windows chores. But clever tinkering with memory, drives, and screens can mask many of these limitations. These are the secrets we'll divulge in this section.

However, where Windows and 286 PCs are concerned, it's wise to remain realistic. It's true, for instance, that if you're in the market for a new system you shouldn't consider anything less than a 386SX for solid Windows performance. The price difference between 286 and 386SX systems today is so small as to be of little note, and you get a lot for that extra money. No matter what you do, some Windows programs just won't run well on a 286 because they need more processor horsepower. In addition, a 286 can't run Windows in 386 Enhanced mode, which supports background processing and lets DOS applications run in graphical windows.

But a 286 will let you display more than one Windows program at a time, so that you can switch between them with one click of your mouse. And, although DOS applications occupy the entire screen on a 286 when they're active, you can load several DOS and Windows programs at once and switch among them with a few keystrokes.

Beef Up Your RAM

The first step to making your 286 machine Windows-worthy is to add more RAM. Windows has an insatiable appetite for memory. The Program Manager may report that there are lots of kilobytes free, but that's because Windows swaps program code it doesn't immediately need to disk when it loads or switches applications. If you find yourself looking at the clock waiting for a pull-down menu to appear, Windows is looking for that part of the program on your hard disk.

You may not think you need more memory, but you do. Nothing makes Windows run better than adding 1, 2, or 3 additional megabytes of RAM. If you've got a 1Mb 286, add another megabyte. If your system has 2Mb, go for 4Mb or more. Memory costs so little there's really no excuse for having too little in your system.

Adding more memory doesn't just make your programs run faster, it helps you do more. Although Windows doesn't really multitask on a 286, it can keep two or more programs in memory at the same time. But with less than 2Mb of memory, you probably won't be able to keep entire programs in RAM. Once your machine's RAM is used up, Windows will swap the program code you're not using to disk. As a result, switching from one program to another may take nearly as long as exiting the first and starting the second. With more memory, you'll spend less time waiting and more time working.

Add the Right Kind of RAM

For you to get the most out of Windows, your system must contain a good-sized chunk of extended memory. If you don't have any extra memory yet, add or replace the memory on your motherboard. Not only is this usually the cheapest option, but it generally provides slightly better performance than using add-in memory cards. Adding motherboard memory has become rather simple these days. The RAM comes in plug-in chips called SIMMs that you can buy in any computer or electronics store. These memory modules come in two different formats and several different speeds. Check your PC's documentation for the specs you need to meet. Once you buy the RAM, you simply plug it into open RAM slots, following the order specified in your documentation.

If your motherboard doesn't have any memory-expansion capability, you can still get more memory for your 286 by installing a memory add-in board, such as the Intel AboveBoard. These boards contain their own RAM, plug into slots on your PC's motherboard, and are generally used to provide expanded memory, but they can be set up to provide extended memory instead.

Set Up a Disk Cache According to the Applications You Use

Adding more RAM helps you get better performance, but only if you use it properly. That means setting up a disk cache that is the right size for your applications. Windows automatically installs a cache (SMARTDrive) when you run the Setup program, but Setup usually picks a size that's a compromise for all users. Different kinds of work require different cache sizes. Someone using a word processor needs a larger cache than a spreadsheet maven, for example, because word processing documents and dictionaries are often spooled to disk, whereas entire spreadsheets are kept in memory.

The size of your cache should be as big as you can make it without eating into the memory requirements of Windows and your largest application. That's a tough call to make, because it's almost impossible to know how much memory a Windows program really needs. Unlike DOS programs, Windows programs rarely tell you when they are out of memory. Instead, they just start swapping code to disk, running slower and slower as a result.

The trick is to strike the right balance between free memory and cache memory. A good rule of thumb is to allot no more than one-third of your memory as cache, but maintain a minimum of 1.5Mb for Windows and Windows programs. On a 2Mb 286, make sure your CONFIG.SYS reads

```
DEVICE=SMARTDRV.SYS 512 128
```

The first number represents the size of the cache; the second is SMARTDrive's minimum size. For a 3Mb 286, try 1024 512; for a 4Mb machine, try 1536 512.

These numbers will work well for word processing and simple desktop publishing. If, however, your main application is a memory-intensive program such as a spreadsheet or a drawing package, you should decrease the first number slightly to 384, 768, and 1024, for 2, 3, and 4Mb machines, respectively.

Note that the second number sets SMARTDrive's minimum size. If you work with both memory-intensive and disk-intensive applications, make the second number smaller so that SMARTDRIVE can respond to the changing needs of your work.

Although SMARTDRIVE doesn't offer the level of control of some caching programs, it's more than enough for a 286. It caches all applications, not just Windows programs.

Get a Fast Hard Disk

Along with lots of memory, Windows likes fast hard disks. Windows and Windows programs use a frightening amount of disk space, so now might be a good time to consider dumping that old hard disk and buying a bigger, faster unit. Here's why: When you move from a typical 28- to 40-millisecond AT-class drive to an 18- to 23-millisecond high-speed drive, you'll be able to pull information from the drive 15 to 25 percent faster; this translates into far less time spent starting applications and loading files.

When shopping for a hard disk, look for drives with low average seek times (20 milliseconds or less). Although a fast transfer rate is important, too, Windows usually doesn't read a huge amount of data when it accesses the hard disk, so put your money into fast seek rates.

Pump Up Your Video Card

A chain is only as strong as its weakest link, and a sluggish 8-bit EGA board can slow your whole system to a crawl. No matter how fast your hard disk is, and no matter how much memory you install, Windows absolutely requires a fast VGA card to run well. Unfortunately, most EGA and VGA cards sold before 1990 run about as fast as molasses in Minnesota. Before Windows 3.0, manufacturers optimized their adapters for fast operation in text modes and ignored graphics.

If you have an EGA system, you absolutely must replace your card (and your monitor, unless it's multiscanning) with a VGA adapter. Windows runs optimally on a 286 PC at VGA resolution (640×480), and VGA adapters are inherently faster than EGA. If you already have VGA, you should still consider a newer, faster model, especially if your current adapter is an 8-bit unit.

If you're going to replace your system's video card, check out cards that are referred to as Windows accelerators. These cards contain a graphics coprocessor that takes the load of screen redraw off of the CPU.

But remember, no matter how fast your video card is, it will get bogged down if you put it in a 286 and try to run Windows in 256-color or Super VGA mode. Anything more complex than 640×480 by 16 colors is just too much for any system that runs slower than 33MHz.

Use TrueType Rather Than Type Managers

Windows 3.1 provides TrueType scalable fonts, which are all you should need for 286-level tasks. If you insist on using another type manager with Windows, be prepared to wait. Adobe Type Manager and Bitstream FaceLift simply use too many resources for a 286 PC. Another way to achieve scalable fonts on a LaserJet or other non-PostScript printer is to try a product, such as Zenographics SuperPrint, that offers the same control of printer output, but doesn't scale screen fonts on the fly or let you turn off screen font scaling, which saves your CPU for better things.

You might consider buying a PostScript or PostScript-compatible cartridge for your printer and using the Windows Control Panel to change printers, to an Apple LaserWriter, which is how Windows views all PostScript-equipped printers. You'll get scalable output with no drain on your system and no additional fonts cluttering your hard disk. (This technique is covered fully in Chapter 8.)

Use Simple Wallpaper, or None at All

A single-color background may be boring, but the Windows Program Manager will display faster if it doesn't have to refresh a scene from Fantasia every time you resize a window. Removing wallpaper will also decrease the time it takes to load large Windows programs.

Practice Meticulous Disk Housekeeping

Defragmenting your hard disk helps most applications run faster, and Windows is no exception. When it's running, Windows creates dozens of temporary files to swap code to and from. These files don't necessarily get placed side by side on your disk; in fact, each file may be broken into chunks (called clusters) all over the drive's surface. That's how the DOS file system that underlies Windows crams as much information as possible onto a drive. But when you request a file, all those spread-out clusters have to be reassembled. That takes time, so when a disk is fragmented Windows won't run as fast as it could.

You should run a disk reorganizer every month, even if the rest of your existing files aren't fragmented, to keep large, contiguous areas of your hard disk free. Here's an important caveat, however: Never run the disk defragmenter from within Windows; always return to the native DOS prompt first. If you don't, the attempt by a single program (the defragmenter) to manipulate critical disk files will cause Windows to lock up. DOS lets programs play with drives; Windows, because it tries to share resources among many programs, does not.

Printing

The Print Manager is one of Windows' weakest utilities: It's simply a print spooler that captures application output, stores it in a disk file, and prints it when CPU time is free. As a replacement, look for programs that intercept the output from your application and compress it into a proprietary format that uses less disk space and can be transmitted to the printer more efficiently. Since the files are so much smaller, you spend less time waiting.

Give Your System a Break by Turning on Draft Mode

Finally, you can give your working-at-the-edge 286 machine a break by lightening its graphical load. The less complex the PC's display requirements, the faster everything will run. If, for instance, the Windows application you're using has a Draft mode, use it whenever you can. You'll get better performance if complicated screen elements don't have to be redrawn every time you make a change. Likewise, turn off font scaling until you actually need WYSIWYG output.

Beware the Balky BIOS!

Deep in the heart of every DOS and Windows PC lies a cloistered segment of programming code known as the Basic Input/Output System (BIOS). The BIOS contains basic operating instructions for the PC: what resources it has available, how to configure memory, how to bootstrap itself when the power comes on. Because it handles such elemental aspects of the PC's operation, the BIOS is tremendously sensitive to change. The BIOS must be revised as hardware components such as processors and drives change and as operating systems grow more complex. Thus, an outdated BIOS can render an otherwise splendid Windows PC completely useless.

If your PC refuses to handle Windows, the BIOS is the first place to look. As a rule of thumb, BIOSes dated pre-1988 should be upgraded. Usually, your PC's BIOS displays version information on screen at start-up. If not, you'll find information about the BIOS in your PC's documentation. If you have an old BIOS, avoid frustration by getting an update before the problems start. Contact your system manufacturer for a more recent version and instructions on how to install it in your machine.

BIOS Problems You Should Know About

Since forewarned is forearmed, here is a list you can scan to see if your computer's BIOS has been known to cause problems with Windows. If it has, you should contact your system manufacturer (not the BIOS manufacturer) for a more recent BIOS version that fixes these problems.

- **ALR BIOS and Seagate Drives**   ALR Microchannel computers use a BIOS that is incompatible with Seagate IDE drives. If you are planning on upgrading your ALR hard drive to a popular Seagate IDE hard drive for better Windows performance, you'll need to reconsider.

- **Ami BIOS**   The Ami BIOS dated from 1987 may cause the system to reboot when you attempt to access the floppy drive in Windows File Manager. With an Ami BIOS dated 1989, you may experience unrecoverable application errors, general protection faults, or the system might hang. The Ami BIOS dated 1991 may cause mouse and modem problems.

- **AST BIOS**   On AST Premium 286 machines, the BIOS may cause system lockups, general protection faults, unrecoverable application errors, and, if the PC is hooked up to a network, network errors.

- **Award BIOS**   Award BIOSes prior to version 3.05 may cause floppy-drive read errors.

- **DTK BIOS**   DTK BIOSes prior to version do 35 not allow Windows to run in Enhanced mode.

- **Oak Technology Inc. Video BIOS**   Oak Technology BIOS versions earlier than 2.14 may make your system hang in Enhanced mode.

- **Peak/DM BIOS from Chips and Technologies**   Peak/DM BIOSes prior to version 1.30 may cause general protection faults and unrecoverable application errors.

- **Phoenix BIOS**   Phoenix recommends that any of their BIOSes dated earlier than 1988 should be upgraded to a more recent version. For AT&T 386 machines that use a Phoenix BIOS of 1.10.14 or earlier, you may be unable to run a DOS application in a window. To remedy the situation, reboot the system with the AT&T Customer Test that came with the computer, run the Setup utility, turn off the settings that say Redirect to COM1 and Redirect to COM2, and then save these changes.

- **Toshiba BIOS**   Toshiba T3100/20 systems need a BIOS version of 4.2 or later. Toshiba T3100e systems need a BIOS version 1.70 or later. Toshiba T2200SX systems with a BIOS earlier than version 1.20 may have incompatibility problems with the Trackball mouse plugged into the system's PS/2 port.

- **Tandon BIOS**   Older versions of the Tandon BIOS may cause keyboard failures on PCs running Windows.

- **Wyse BIOS**   The Wyse BIOS has been know to cause the wrong keyboard to be selected during Windows setup. The 84-key keyboard may be mistakenly detected, instead of the correct 101-key keyboard. You'll need to run Windows Setup from DOS (not within Windows) to change this option.

- **Zenith BIOS**   Zenith 386/16 systems need BIOS version 2.6E or later, and the Zenith Turbosport 386 needs BIOS version 2.4D or later.

EISA Systems BIOS and Extended Memory

On some extended industry standard architecture (EISA) systems, not all of the extended memory available is detected by the system's BIOS, meaning that the memory goes unused by Windows. If your system seems unable to address all its memory, this may be the cause. You can eliminate the problem by placing a statement in your CONFIG.SYS file that orders HIMEM.SYS, Windows' memory manager, to use all of this available memory. The line might look like this:

```
DEVICE=C:\DOS\HIMEM/EISA
```

Certain problems between EISA memory and the BIOS involve device drivers or applications that use the same BIOS call as the PC's own system (known, in technical terms, as Interrupt 15h). Some older applications use Interrupt 15h to allocate extended memory to themselves. This was a trick they could get away with in early DOS days. Windows requires that programs use the extended memory specification of HIMEM.SYS to find their place in memory. An Interrupt 15h conflict will freeze your PC at boot time. To determine if you have a driver or application that uses this outmoded memory method, you'll have to check its documentation or talk to the vendor.

If you do have such a driver or application, you can still load it in extended memory by telling HIMEM.SYS to set aside a specific amount of memory for its use. For example, to set aside 256K of extended memory for an application that uses the Interrupt 15h call, add a line to CONFIG.SYS that looks like this:

```
DEVICE=C:\DOS\HIMEM/EISA/INT15=256
```

Hardware Headaches of Particular PCs

Not only BIOS problems, but other small variations in a PC's design can cause problems for Windows. In many cases, testing and cooperation between hardware manufacturers and Microsoft have unearthed problems and resulted in workarounds. Scan the following list to see if your computer has been known to cause problems with Windows and to find out what you can do about them.

- **Acer 1100 Computers and HIMEM.SYS**   If you're using an Acer 1100 computer and the Windows extended memory manager, HIMEM.SYS, you may actually need to tell HIMEM.SYS the model of computer you are using for extended memory management to work properly. The modified line in your CONFIG.SYS file might look like this:

```
DEVICE=C:\DOS\HIMEM.SYS /M:ACER1100
```

■ **Apricot Computers**   If you have an Apricot 386 system running Apricot's DOS 3.3 and you want to run in Enhanced mode, you need to install a console device driver such as ANSI.SYS. Without the driver, Ctrl+Break keystrokes might cause the wrong application to terminate. To install the ANSI.SYS driver from your DOS subdirectory, add the following line to CONFIG.SYS:

```
DEVICE=C:\DOS\ANSI.SYS
```

For Apricot computers in general, you'll need to get special drivers from Apricot to run Windows in Enhanced mode.

■ **AST Rampage Boards and Microchannel PCs**   If your AST Rampage memory expansion board is configured to use both expanded and extended memory and you have a microchannel architecture system (such as a PS/2), you may need to get a driver update. RAMTYPE.SYS drivers prior to version 1.20 will not coexist with other applications that use extended memory. If Windows Setup detects RAMTYPE.SYS, it will remove it from your CONFIG.SYS file.

■ **Compaq Deskpros and SMARTDrive 4.0**   On some Compaq Deskpro 386/16 and 386/20 computers, you may have problems accessing your floppy drives when SMARTDrive 4.0 (the version included in Windows 3.1) is running in upper memory. You can get around this problem by restricting the SMARTDrive buffer to conventional memory. Simply add the /L parameter when SMARTDrive loads in your AUTOEXEC.BAT. The command would look like this:

```
SMARTDRV /L
```

If the problem persists when SMARTDrive is in conventional memory, or if you prefer to keep SMARTDrive in upper memory, you must disable caching on the floppy drives. To do this, you should include the line

```
SMARTDRV A- B-
```

in your AUTOEXEC.BAT file (assuming you have floppy drives A and B).

■ **Epson Computers**   For Epson systems that come with screen-saver utilities, the utility may detect that the system is idle under Windows when it is not. If that's the case, the screen will appear blank, even though Windows and the system still function properly. You'll have to exit Windows and start it again to reactivate the display. If this is a problem with your system, you should disable the Epson screen-saver feature. Check the documentation that came with your system for details on how to do this, or contact Epson.

■ **Everex Computers and Expanded Memory**   If you're using an Everex 386/25 and the Windows expanded memory manager, EMM386, you'll need to exclude a range of memory from being used to map expanded memory. To do so, edit your CONFIG.SYS file. If you're using Windows 3.0 (without DOS 5.0), the file for EMM386 is EMM386.SYS, and the line in your CONFIG.SYS would read

```
DEVICE=EMM386.SYS C600-C7FF
```

For Windows 3.1 and DOS 5.0 users: EMM386 now loads with the file EMM386.EXE and has different parameters than the Windows 3.0 version. The line in your CONFIG.SYS would look like this:

```
DEVICE=EMM386.EXE X=C600-C7FF
```

■ **IBM 7552 Computer and HIMEM.SYS**   If you're using an IBM 7552 Industrial Computer and the Windows extended memory manager, HIMEM.SYS, you may need to indicate to HIMEM.SYS which computer model you are using for extended memory management to work properly. The modified line in your CONFIG.SYS file should read

```
DEVICE=C:\DOS\HIMEM.SYS /M:IBM7552
```

■ **NCR 925 System and EMM386**   If you're using an NCR 925 and the Windows expanded memory manager, EMM386, you'll need to exclude a range of memory from being used to map expanded memory. To do so, edit your CONFIG.SYS file. For Windows 3.0 (without DOS 5.0), the file for EMM386 is EMM386.SYS and the line in your CONFIG-.SYS should be

```
DEVICE=EMM386.SYS E000-EFFF
```

For Windows 3.1 (or DOS 5.0) users, EMM386 now loads with the file EMM386.EXE, which has different parameters from the Windows 3.0 version. The line in CONFIG.SYS should look like this:

```
DEVICE=EMM386.EXE X=E000-EFFF
```

■ **Wyse Computers and HIMEM.SYS**   To get a Wyse computer to work with the Windows extended memory manager, HIMEM.SYS, you need to tell HIMEM.SYS the computer model by placing this line in your CONFIG.SYS file:

```
DEVICE=C:\DOS\HIMEM.SYS /M:WYSE
```

Memory Secrets

A big part of optimizing Windows is knowing how to work with the memory you have. Of course, the only memory in your PC that applications can address is RAM. But your system can configure RAM in several different ways. To get the most from Windows, you'll need a basic understanding of the different forms your PC's memory can take.

Conventional memory is the first 640K (0K through 640K) of memory available on your system. This is the memory where you run regular DOS applications, device drivers, and utilities. Windows itself also runs in conventional memory.

Expanded memory is memory that is mapped by software onto the system's upper memory area (from 640K to 1,024K). This expanded memory is either found on an expanded memory card or, in a 386 system, it is emulated by an expanded memory manager (the Windows expanded memory manager is called EMM386). The expanded memory manager maps the memory in sections of a few thousand bytes, called *pages,* onto the upper memory area. Only DOS applications that are designed to use expanded memory can do so.

Extended memory is the memory beyond the first megabyte. It starts at 1,024K and goes up to the amount of memory the system has installed—for example 4Mb or 8Mb. The first 64K of extended memory is called the *high memory area* (HMA). Windows extended memory manager, HIMEM.SYS, provides access to extended memory and the high memory area.

Find Out about Your System's Memory

Windows 3.1 comes with a handy utility called the Microsoft Diagnostics Utility (MSD). This utility gives you a rundown of system memory and the drivers that are installed on your system. To run MSD, simply type **msd** at the DOS prompt. See Figure 3.1.

How Much Memory Should You Have?

With Windows, the first rule of memory is the more the better. To extract top performance from Windows, the most important step you can take is to install more RAM. At a bare minimum, you'll need 2Mb of RAM. If you plan to run more than one Windows application at a time, you'll need at least 4Mb. For top performance, upgrade your system to 8Mb or more.

FIGURE 3.1

Run the Microsoft Diagnostics Utility included with Windows 3.1 to find out about the available memory on your system.

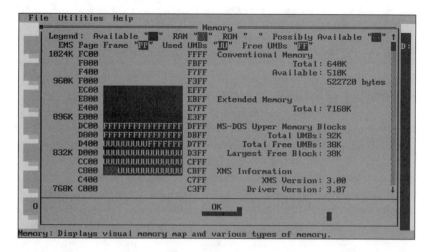

Getting the Most from Windows Memory Management

Working with PC memory is akin to putting together one of those intricate M. C. Escher jigsaw puzzles. Lots of options, lots of confusion, and it's hard to tell when you've put everything together properly. Because Windows sits on top of DOS, it can help memory management look better or perform more automatically, but it can't fundamentally change the confusing (that's the kind word for it) memory scheme DOS perpetuates. The tips that follow are among the most critical for getting maximum performance from a Windows machine. Memory is the foundation for any Windows setup; if it's unstable, so is everything else.

Determine the Best Way to Use EMM386   Don't use EMM386 at all if your regular suite of applications consists of Windows programs and small DOS programs. In that case, Windows will manage the region between 640K and 1,024K—the area containing the upper memory block—just fine by itself. If you use a bulky DOS application that will benefit from a bigger conventional memory space, go ahead and stuff device drivers and TSRs into upper memory with the help of EMM386. But leave some free space: Windows needs a contiguous block of at least 4K for Windows housekeeping chores. If you don't leave enough room in upper memory for these buffers, you'll pay a performance penalty.

Decide Whether You Really Need Expanded Memory   Windows itself does not use expanded memory. If possible, you should reconfigure any expanded memory in your system as extended memory before installing Windows. But some DOS applications, like Lotus 1-2-3 2.*x*, can benefit tremendously from expanded memory (EMS). When Windows runs in Enhanced mode, it automatically creates expanded memory from extended memory as long as there's a contiguous 64K block of memory free in upper memory; you don't need to modify CONFIG.SYS at all. Windows (in Enhanced mode) and DOS need an EMS manager such as EMM386.EXE in order for DOS applications to access EMS memory. To create a 1Mb pool of EMS memory, add this line to your CONFIG.SYS:

```
DEVICE=EMM386.EXE 1024 RAM
```

Convert Expanded Memory to Extended Memory   Some systems' memory expansion boards allow their memory to be configured as either expanded or extended. (For an explanation of the difference between the two, refer to "Memory Secrets" earlier in this chapter.) If you don't require expanded memory (for instance, if you don't run any DOS applications that use it), you'll be wasting the memory configured this way on the board because Windows can't make use of expanded memory. And even if you do have DOS applications that use expanded memory, you should convert the memory to extended memory because Windows can change it back as needed. The expanded memory manager that comes with Windows, EMM386.EXE, can emulate expanded memory when an application requires it.

The line in your CONFIG.SYS that loads the device driver for the memory board must load before the device driver that allows you access to extended memory (for example, HIMEM.SYS) and before the device driver that loads your expanded memory manager (for example, EMM386.EXE). The lines in your CONFIG.SYS file might look like this:

```
DEVICE=C:\EMMBORD.SYS
DEVICE=C:\DOS\HIMEM.SYS
DEVICE=C:\DOS\EMM386.EXE
```

The first line represents the driver for your board.

Find Out What Switches Control EMM386.EXE   To see a list of the switches for controlling EMM386.EXE after it has been loaded, type **EMM386/?** at the DOS prompt.

Troubleshooting EMM386: Invalid Path   If starting Windows in Enhanced mode yields an error message indicating that you have an invalid path for EMM386, Windows may not know where to find EMM386. To fix this problem, add the /Y switch to the line in your CONFIG.SYS that loads EMM386. For example, if it is located in your DOS directory, the line might look like this:

```
DEVICE=EMM386.EXE/Y:C:\DOS\EMM386.EXE
```

Also check that you have specified the correct path for HIMEM.SYS in your CONFIG.SYS.

Troubleshooting EMM386: Testing Whether EMM386 Works If you still get an error message stating that you have an invalid path, you need to see if HIMEM and EMM386 are working on your system. To do this, boot your system from a disk with a CONFIG.SYS file that contains only the commands for loading HIMEM and EMM386. The command that loads EMM386 should exclude the use of expanded memory, as the following does:

```
DEVICE=C:\DOS\EMM386.EXE NOEMS X=A000-EFFF
```

The AUTOEXEC.BAT file on the boot disk should only include a path statement, and a prompt statement if you want one:

```
PATH=C:\DOS
PROMPT $P$G
```

If your computer could not boot from the disk, you might have a problem with HIMEM or your hardware.

Troubleshooting EMM386: Conflicting Programs If you are having problems with EMM386, you may have a memory conflict with another program, device driver, or hardware card. If you think that certain TSRs or drivers may be causing the conflict, load them into conventional memory, not the high memory area, to see if that was the problem. If you think you have a conflict with a hardware device, try to find out the memory address that the card uses and exclude EMM386 from using it with the NOEMS parameter. For example, if your network card uses the D800h-DFFFh memory addresses, the line that loads EMM386 in your CONFIG.SYS would look like this:

```
DEVICE=C:\DOS\EMM386.EXE NOEMS X=D800-DFFF
```

Troubleshooting EMM386: Doesn't Provide Expanded Memory If you receive Out of Memory errors or have problems when running DOS applications from Windows, but you can run Windows applications just fine, Windows may not be providing expanded memory to the applications. To force Windows to do so, edit the line that loads EMM386 in your CONFIG.SYS file to include the RAM parameter. The line would look like this:

```
DEVICE=C:\DOS\EMM386.EXE RAM
```

Using Third-Party Memory Managers with Windows In place of HIMEM-.SYS and EMM386, you can use a third-party memory manager. These memory managers usually offer a wider range of options for accessing the upper memory blocks, and they usually take less conventional memory to run than HIMEM.SYS and EMM386.EXE. But if you are satisfied with your system's performance using the Windows memory managers and don't relish the idea of learning how a new program works, stick with HIMEM.SYS and EMM386.

If you do opt for a third-party memory manager, make sure *not* to use HIMEM.SYS and EMM386. You'll also have to avoid using their commands in your CONFIG.SYS and AUTOEXEC.BAT files. Statements to watch out for include DOS= UMB, DEVICEHIGH, and LOADHIGH.

Creative Tricks for Windows Memory

With enough memory loaded into your Windows PC (more than 4Mb for most Windows users) you can become clever in your uses of RAM. Memory can emulate a disk drive and can provide extra horsepower to your DOS applications.

Set Up a RAM Disk   If you've got memory to spare, add a RAM disk to your system. It will use part of your system memory as a hard disk. RAM disks are faster than regular hard disks because they allow your computer to read information from memory, which it can do much more quickly than reading from a physical drive. However, because a RAM disk exists in memory, it will be lost once your system is turned off. This combination of speed and evanescence makes RAM disks the ideal place for storing TEMP files.

Here are the recommended RAM disk settings for a system that runs Standard mode:

RAM	Disk Size
4Mb	1,024K
5–6Mb	2,048K
7Mb	2,560K
8Mb	3,072K
9Mb	4,099K
10–12Mb	4,096K

DOS Applications, Standard Mode, and Extended Memory   If you run DOS applications that use extended memory in Standard mode, you should make sure to set up a .PIF file for each, specifying the amount of extended memory that the application needs. Keep this setting to the amount of memory that the application actually needs so that Windows can avoid swapping to disk. If you run this DOS application when all of the extended memory is already in use by Windows applications, data that already exists in extended memory will have to be swapped to disk to make way for your program's requirements. The extended memory setting in the PIF Editor is marked XMS Memory.

Troubleshooting Out of Memory Errors   If you keep getting Out of Memory errors even though you're sure that you've got enough available memory, your problem may be with Free System Resources (FSRs). FSRs are composed of two 64K areas of memory, called USER (for input and output information) and GDI (for graphics and printing information), that Windows uses to keep track of system information for the current Windows session. These areas, and not your system memory, may be filling up. You'll have to close some applications or even restart Windows to recover from the shortage.

Remove Fonts to Save Memory   Getting rid of some of Windows' fonts can mean more memory for your applications. But because Windows fonts really don't take up all that much memory, you'll only want to get rid of these if there's nothing else you can do to regain memory. To remove fonts from your system, open the Windows Control Panel and select Fonts. In the resulting dialog box, highlight the names of the fonts you want to remove, and then select Remove. If you change your mind and want to add the fonts back to your system, it's easy to do with the same Fonts dialog box, since you didn't delete them from your hard disk, but just removed them from memory.

Care and Feeding of TSRs under Windows

Because TSRs (memory-resident programs) take up precious memory and can also cause problems when running with Windows, you should approach them with care and caution. To be frank, one of the benefits of Windows is that it allows applications to interact, rendering much of the value of TSRs moot. However, if a TSR offers unmatchable benefit, you can continue to use it with Windows.

The first rule to follow is to load those TSRs you absolutely need from your AUTOEXEC.BAT file. If a TSR is used with only one specific DOS application, don't load it until you are in a DOS session running the application. Better yet, create a batch file that loads the TSR and your DOS application simultaneously.

If a TSR needs to be available to Windows applications and not DOS applications, it must be listed in the WINSTART.BAT file (a batch file that Windows runs whenever it starts in Enhanced mode) so that it will always be loaded when you're in Windows. To create WINSTART.BAT, use Notepad or another text editor. As with any DOS batch file, WINSTART.BAT contains the executable filename of each TSR along with any parameters required to load it. When saved in ASCII format under the name WINSTART.BAT, this file will automatically control the loading of the TSRs. The next time you start Windows in Enhanced mode, the TSRs should be available.

Even if you follow this advice, however, TSRs may not run smoothly under Windows. Here are some tips for avoiding the land mines.

Troubleshooting TSR Compatibility Problems   Windows Setup scans your system for TSRs that cause problems during the setup process, but it doesn't detect TSRs that might cause problems when actually running with Windows. If you add a problematic TSR to your system after Windows is installed, you'll have no way of knowing that you may experience compatibility problems—until they occur.

If you experience system problems that you think may be TSR-related, such as the system crashing or incorrect displays, first check the DOS-based TSRs that load into high memory. To do this, change your AUTOEXEC.BAT file to load these TSRs into conventional memory. If the problem goes away, try loading them back into high memory one by one to isolate the incompatible TSR. If the problem persists, comment out the loading of all TSRs in your AUTOEXEC.BAT file and try restoring them to conventional memory, one by one, until you isolate the incompatible TSR.

If your DOS TSRs pass muster, the problem may be an incompatibility between the program and Windows. Other users have discovered many of these problems through painful experience. Save yourself their trouble by looking at this list of TSRs that have been known to cause problems running with Windows 3.1:

ANARKEY version 4.00

APPEND, the DOS utility

DOSCUE, a command-line editor

GRAPHICS, the DOS utility

JOIN, the DOS utility

LanSight version 2.0, a utility for controlling and monitoring workstations on a Novell network

Lockit version 3.3

MIRROR, the DOS utility

Newspace version 1.07

Norton Utilities version 5.0: Diskreet and Ncache

Norton Utilities version 6.01: DiskMon

Printer Assistant

XGAAIDOS.SYS

The problems these products cause are unpredictable, varying with the situation and the machine. Just note that if any of these TSRs are present on your system they may well be at the root of your problems.

TSRs That Need Special Consideration   Many TSRs in Windows are like prescription drugs: they're fine as long as your follow all instructions. Here are some guidelines for getting the most from TSRs that run with Windows.

- **BOOT.SYS**   BOOT.SYS, a tool for booting under multiple configurations from a menu, creates several sections in CONFIG.SYS and AUTOEXEC.BAT. Windows Setup only modifies the first section in

CONFIG.SYS and AUTOEXEC.BAT. You'll need to modify the other sections manually to use Windows 3.1 with the alternate configurations.

- **Control Panel 2.2**   LaserTools Control Panel version 2.2 might cause your system to hang if you load it from within Windows. Load Control Panel before starting Windows 3.1.

- **Doubledisk 2.5**   Doubledisk version 2.5 creates "phantom" disk drives that Windows 3.1 might try to access. Vertisoft has a utility to make these phantom drives invisible to Windows 3.1. Contact Vertisoft to get this utility.

- **FASTOPEN**   The FASTOPEN DOS utility might need to be removed in low-memory situations for Windows to function properly. FASTOPEN also causes File Allocation Table (FAT) problems when used with disk defragmenting utilities, so be sure to remove FASTOPEN from memory before you defragment your hard disk.

- **KBFLOW**   The LANtastic KBFLOW TSR should not be loaded before you start Windows 3.1. To use KBFLOW, start Windows and then run it.

- **Le Menu 1.0**   Le Menu version 1.0 may cause environment information such as PATH and PROMPT to be lost when you run a DOS application from Windows. If you are going to start Windows from a Le Menu menu option, set it up as a batch file menu option.

- **Logitech Mouse Software 5.0 and 6.0**   The Click and Logimenu programs included in the Logitech Mouse Software, versions 5.0 and 6.0, must be loaded from within a DOS application running under Windows to be available to the DOS application, even if they were previously resident in DOS before Windows was loaded.

- **Norton Utilities 6.01**   If it is on a disk drive, the Ncache program in Norton Utilities 6.01 prevents you from creating a permanent swap file.

- **PC-Tools Deluxe 6.0 and 7.0**   PC-Tools Deluxe version 6.0's Desktop might cause your machine to hang if you launch it from a DOS application running under Standard mode Windows, and might cause your machine to reboot if it's running under Enhanced mode Windows. With PC-Tools Deluxe version 7.0, Desktop should not be run in a DOS session if it was resident before Windows was loaded.

- **Pyro! 1.0**   Pyro! version 1.0 will blank the screen after the delay period has expired if it is loaded before you run Windows.

- **SideKick**   SideKick versions 1.0 and 2.0 and SideKick Plus cause many problems with Windows. For the best results, load SideKick from a PIF under Windows instead of as a TSR.

- **SPEEDFXR**   SPEEDFXR is not compatible with Windows as a TSR, so avoid loading it as one.

- **SUBST**   The DOS SUBST utility works with Windows if you do not add or remove substituted drives while in Windows.

- **Trantor T100**   Trantor T100's Host Adapter Driver (TSCSI.SYS) mistakenly identifies the SCSI hard disk drive as a removable drive. If you try to access this drive in File Manager, your system may crash. Avoid using File Manager with this driver.

Disk Caches and Windows Performance

One of the best uses for any extra memory your PC has is to set up a *disk cache*, an area in memory where data recently drawn from the hard drive is temporarily stored. Caches can vastly improve Windows performance because pulling commonly accessed data from memory is so much faster than drawing it from a drive. Windows comes with its own disk cache program, called SMARTDrive, which is discussed a bit later in this chapter. Numerous commercial disk caches also run with Windows.

Run Your Disk Caches in Extended Memory   Whatever disk cache you have on your system (and you *really* should have one) make sure that it is using extended (not expanded) memory. Windows is more stable if there are no DOS programs that use expanded memory running when it is loaded. SMARTDrive users don't have to worry about this (unless they've edited SMARTDrive's configuration) because SMARTDrive uses extended memory by default.

Tell Windows Where to Store Temporary Files   A disk cache works by creating temporary files of recently accessed data in memory. To make it easy to keep track of these temporary files and to prevent them from littering your root directory and application directories, tell Windows where you'd like them stored. Try putting a line like this in your AUTOEXEC.BAT:

```
SET TEMP=C:\WINDOWS\TEMP
```

Now, whenever you run Windows, it will automatically use the WINDOWS-\TEMP directory for its temporary files. Having all the files in one location also makes it easy for you delete them.

Keep Your TEMP Directory Clean   Deleting unnecessary files keeps Windows and its applications running as efficiently as possible. This holds for temporary files as well. When Windows is not running, delete any files that remain in your TEMP subdirectory, any files that start with the characters ~WOA (application swap files), and any file named WIN386.SWP. Windows usually deletes all of these files in the course of its normal housekeeping, but some may remain if an application or Windows terminates unexpectedly.

Store Your Temporary Files on a RAM Drive   If you have a RAM drive set up on your system, it's a good idea to store your temporary files there so that when your system shuts down, it will take with it all of the temporary files stored on the RAM drive. You'll no longer have to worry about clearing your system of these pesky files.

In your AUTOEXEC.BAT file, point Windows to the location of your RAM drive with a line like the following:

```
SET TEMP= D:
```

Working with SMARTDrive

SMARTDrive is a perfectly adequate disk-caching program that comes with Windows and handles the basics of caching. More sophisticated caches—such as Super PC-Kwik, Norton Cache (included in the Norton Utilities), and the shareware standby HyperDisk—add an extra measure of performance improvement. To add SMARTDrive to your system, add a line to your AUTOEXEC.BAT file invoking it and specifying the correct size for your system. For example, for a system with 4Mb of RAM, the line would read

```
C\WINDOWS\SMARTDRV 2048 1024
```

The first number is the size of the cache when Windows is not loaded, and the second number is the amount that Windows can reduce the cache size to when it is loaded. Here are some recommended settings for SMARTDrive based upon available system memory:

RAM	Setting 1	Setting 2
2Mb	1,024K	512K
3Mb	2,048K	1,024K
4Mb	2,048K	1,024K
5-12Mb	2,048K	2,048K

How to Tell If You Need Double Buffering   Windows' Setup program tries to determine if your system will require double buffering—that is, an increased amount of memory set aside for trading data with your disk drive. If Windows thinks that your system might need double buffering, it installs the double-buffering driver in your CONFIG.SYS file. The line might look like this:

```
DEVICE=C:\WINDOWS\SMARTDRV.EXE /DOUBLE_BUFFER
```

This driver does not actually load SMARTDrive; it merely makes the double-buffering driver available to SMARTDrive when it is loaded. SMARTDrive itself will be loaded from your CONFIG.SYS file.

It's easy to determine if your system does, in fact, need double buffering. From the Windows DOS prompt (not a DOS session), and after SMARTDrive has loaded from your CONFIG.SYS file, type the command **smartdrv**. You will see a screen of information about running SMARTDrive on your system. (See

Figure 3.2.) The buffering column displays the status for each of your drives. If all the entries in this column say "no," you do not need double buffering. In that case, you can save yourself some memory by deleting the line in your CONFIG-.SYS file that loaded the double-buffering driver.

FIGURE 3.2

To determine if your system requires double buffering, type smartdrv at the DOS prompt; the fourth column will specity whether double buffering is needed.

```
C:\WIN31>smartdrv
Microsoft SMARTDrive Disk Cache version 4.0
Copyright 1991,1992 Microsoft Corp.

Cache size: 2,097,152 bytes
Cache size while running Windows: 2,097,152 bytes

               Disk Caching Status
drive    read cache    write cache    buffering
---------------------------------------------------
  A:         yes            no            no
  B:         yes            no            no
  C:         yes            yes           no

For help, type "Smartdrv /?".

C:\WIN31>
```

If double buffering is required on your system, you can achieve the best performance by loading the driver into conventional memory rather than the upper memory blocks. When your system uses double buffering, performance decreases because of the additional memory required for all disk reads and writes. If you loaded the double-buffering driver into the upper memory blocks, you would introduce yet another step into the process, where buffering from the upper memory block to conventional memory would have to take place.

Fine-tuning SMARTDrive 4.0 You can fine-tune SMARTDrive performance on your system by using command-line parameters that set the size of the read-ahead buffer and the size of the chunks of data that SMARTDrive moves at one time. You should type the parameters discussed here on the command line following SMARTDRV.EXE.

The /B switch sets the read-ahead buffer, which tells SMARTDrive how much extra information it should read while doing a read from the disk. For example, if the /B setting is 1024 and an application reads 512K of information from a file, it would read an additional 1,024K of data into buffer memory at the same time (for a total of 1,536K). For the next disk read, SMARTDrive will look in the cache to see if the requested information is already there. The buffer size has to be a multiple of the element size because SMARTDrive can only deal in whole chunks of information.

The /E switch sets the maximum size for each chunk of information (in bytes) that SMARTDrive reads and writes. The default setting for /E is 8,192 bytes, and the other valid settings are 1,024, 2,048, and 4,096. The /E parameter should match the allocation unit size reported by CHKDSK. For example, the command for loading SMARTDrive with a read-ahead buffer of 512K and an element size of 1,024 bytes is

```
C:\WINDOWS\SMARTDRV.EXE /E:1024 /B:512
```

Force SMARTDrive to Write All Data to Disk   Avoid turning off your computer while write-caching is going on, because this may result in a loss of data. If you are not sure whether data was written to disk, or if you need to turn off your system immediately, you can force SMARTDrive to write all of the data to disk by issuing the SMARTDRV /C command at the DOS prompt.

Managing Windows COM Ports

Under DOS, managing communication ports was a true nightmare. Under Windows, it's merely a headache. The Ports icon in the Windows Control Panel generates a relatively easy-to-follow dialog box for setting up basic communications ports. Keep the following tips in mind, however, for high-end communication needs or when unexpected problems crop up.

Using COM3 or COM4 with Windows 3.1

Because there is no common hardware configuration for using COM ports 3 and 4, it is best to avoid using these ports unless both COM1 and COM2 are unavailable. If, however, you need to configure COM3 and COM4 for use with your system, do the following:

Open the Control Panel and select the Ports icon. Choose the port you want to configure—for example, COM3. Choose Settings, and check whether the communications settings meet the hardware requirements for the device that you are configuring on that port. Choose Advanced, and specify the Base I/O Port Address and Interrupt Request Line (IRQ) for the device. If you don't know the correct settings, try using the Default settings.

Using COM3 and COM4 with Windows 3.0

If you happen to be confronting a PC with Windows 3.0, you cannot specify the Base I/O Port Address or Interrupt Request Line (IRQ) for ports. But these settings may be crucial to avoiding conflicts among your PC's peripherals. To specify these settings, you have to edit your SYSTEM.INI file, as explained in Chapter 2. In the [386Enh] section, find the following lines:

```
COM1Base=3F8h
COM2Base=2F8h
COM3Base=2E8h
COM4Base=2E0h
```

For the correct port, specify the address of the hardware you are setting up. This information should be contained in the product's documentation.

Allow IRQ Sharing

If two of your serial ports share the same IRQ lines, you'll also need to specify this in your SYSTEM.INI file. In the [386Enh] section, find the line:

```
COMIrqSharing=Off
```

Change this setting to On to allow for IRQ line sharing.

Add Support for More than Four COM Ports

If you have more than four COM ports on your system, you can edit your SYSTEM.INI file to allow for support of all your COM ports. In the [386Enh] section, find the setting that reads

```
MaxCOMPort=4
```

and change the number 4 to the number of COM ports that you have.

Hard-Drive Management for Windows

Under DOS a hard drive was valuable; under Windows it's essential. Windows will recognize and adjust itself to your hard drive far more easily than DOS did. In Windows your problems won't so much be based on getting your hard drive working as on keeping it operating at peak performance. That is the thrust of these tips.

Golden Rules for Hard-Drive Performance

Here are the six golden rules for keeping your hard disk in trim. Practice them religiously.

- Delete any files that remain in the TEMP directory. This is the directory that applications use to store temporary files.

- Delete any files that start with the characters ~WOA. These files are application swap files that are used by some applications. Normally, Windows deletes these files when you exit the actual applications, but if Windows terminates unexpectedly, these files may still remain.

- Delete any files that start with the characters ~GRB. These files are created by Windows to save screen information before you switch out of a DOS application.

- Delete any file named WIN386.SWP. This file is the temporary Windows swap file. Windows normally deletes it when you exit, but if Windows terminates unexpectedly it may still be there.

- Regularly delete backup files that you no longer need, especially if your applications generate these backup files for you automatically.

- Delete any accessories, help files, games, and wallpaper files that you don't use. For more details about Windows files that you can do without, see Chapter 1.

Maintaining Optimal Hard-Disk Performance

Cleaning out unnecessary files from your hard disk is only part of the hard-disk maintenance you should do regularly. While in DOS (not a Windows DOS session), run the DOS utility CHKDSK to see if you have any lost chains or clusters on your disk. Remember that files aren't stored on your disk in one piece; they are broken into chunks and then reassembled when you call for them. Chains and clusters are chunks of data that have become separated from their host file. If CHKDSK reports that you do have lost clusters, type **chkdsk/f** to run CHKDSK again and have DOS do its best to restore these lost clusters into files.

After you run this command, you will notice files with the extension .CHK on your disk. These files correspond to the number of lost clusters and chains that CHKDSK found. You can even open these files to see what they contain if you think you might want to save some of this information. When you're done, delete these .CHK files.

You should also use a utility program to defragment your hard disk regularly. A fragmented hard disk reduces Windows performance, especially if SMARTDrive is installed or you are using a temporary swap file.

SCSI Hardware and Windows

If you plan to use SCSI hardware with Windows, such as a new hard disk or CD-ROM player, you'll require special device drivers for them. Drivers are usually available from the manufacturer, so be sure to ask at the time of purchase.

If you're using Windows with an SCSI hard disk, make sure that you use SMARTDrive and its double-buffering option. With SMARTDrive installed, Windows will direct all disk access requests through it, eliminating potential hardware conflicts. The double-buffering option means that SMARTDrive adds a memory buffer where physical and virtual addresses are the same.

If your SCSI hard disk uses direct memory access (DMA), you'll need to add the following line to the [386Enh] section of your SYSTEM.INI file:

```
VirtualHDIRQ=false
```

This statement prohibits Windows (running in Enhanced mode) from terminating interrupts from the hard-disk controller and bypassing the ROM routine that handles these interrupts. Turning this setting off ensures that interrupts will be processed correctly.

Windows and Disk-Compression Programs

Disk-compression utilities such as Stacker and SuperStor can be a boon with Windows. These applications shrink data and program code so that you have less to read or write from the hard drive. Performance soars and the size of your hard drive appears to nearly double. However, there are a few things you must keep in mind. You can't create a permanent swap file on a compressed volume, and you can't use SMARTDrive to cache this compressed volume. (Swap files are the subject of the next section, "Setting Up the Windows Swap File.") You can, however, create a permanent swap file on the physical disk that contains the compressed volume, and you can also use SMARTDrive on this physical drive. Also, you should never use a regular disk-defragmentation utility on a compressed volume; use the utility provided with the compression package instead.

If you are using SMARTDrive with the disk-compression program, make sure that SMARTDRV.EXE loads after the program in your CONFIG.SYS file. This ensures that the SMARTDrive is only caching the physical drives on your system. You can also load SMARTDrive from your AUTOEXEC.BAT file with a parameter telling it not to cache the compressed volumes. For example, if E and F are your compressed volumes, the command would read

```
SMARTDRV E- F-
```

If you install the Stacker disk-compression program after Windows is already on your system, you'll have to recreate any TEMP directory that you were using, because Stacker deletes empty subdirectories when it is installed.

Setting Up the Windows Swap File

Just as excess memory can be used to emulate a hard drive (with a RAM disk), excess disk storage can be configured to look like RAM. This "fake" RAM is known as virtual memory. One of the best ways to use virtual memory is to establish a swap file.

Add a Swap File to Your System   In Enhanced mode, a swap file lets you use hard-disk space to create virtual memory in addition to the physical memory in your system. The total swap-file size can be up to three times as large as the amount of physical RAM in your system.

In Windows, Express Setup creates a temporary swap file, which is somewhat slower than the permanent variety, and Custom Setup lets you specify whether you want a temporary or permanent swap file.

If you have disk space to spare, you should install a permanent swap file, but if you're rapidly running out of disk space, a temporary swap file is the way to go. A permanent swap file improves Windows performance because it is contiguous (one large chunk), so access to it requires less overhead than that required for a temporary swap file, which can be all over your hard disk.

Tips for Setting Up a Permanent Swap File   Before you create a permanent swap file, defragment your hard disk with a disk-compacting utility. To create the swap file, choose the 386 Enhanced icon from the Windows Control Panel and click on the Virtual Memory command button. You'll see a series of command buttons on the right; press the Change button. In the resulting dialog box, you'll see the actual size of any existing swap file, a recommended size, and a space to enter the size you want. Type in the swap file size and click on OK. A dialog box will appear, asking you to confirm the new setup. Click on Yes. (See Figure 3.3.)

FIGURE 3.3

Create a permanent swap file to improve system performance by selecting the 386 Enhanced icon in the Control Panel and choosing the Virtual Memory command button.

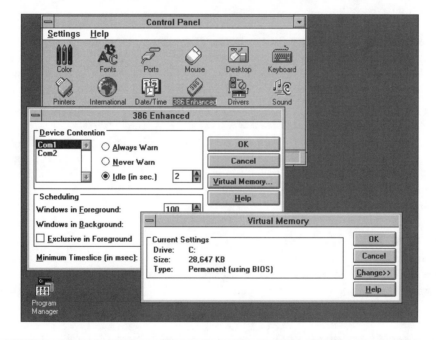

To give your swap file what it needs to run quickly, make sure to use the fastest hard disk on your system, and never swap to a network drive or a RAM disk. A swap file created on a RAM disk is self-defeating because you sacrifice physical memory to create virtual memory.

And *never* delete, move, or rename the hidden files SPART.PAR and 386SPART.PAR. 386SPART.PAR is the actual swap file, while SPART.PAR is a read-only file that tells Windows how large the permanent swap file is and where it is located. The only exception to this rule is that, if you ever receive an error message that says your swap file is corrupted, you should delete the current swap file and create a new one from the Control Panel.

Temporary Swap File Tips   If you're rapidly running out of disk space and would prefer a temporary swap file, Windows lets you edit your SYSTEM.INI file to specify the minimum amount of hard-disk space that will always be available.

For example, to restrict the size of the temporary swap file to the amount of available hard-disk space minus 1Mb, open SYSTEM.INI and add the following line under the [386Enh] section:

```
MinUserDiskSpace=1024
```

Also in the [386Enh] section of the SYSTEM.INI, you can specify where you want to locate the temporary swap file. If you want to set the swap file to an actual filename, you can enter the path and filename after the PagingFile= entry. Or if you prefer to assign the swap file to a specific drive, you can do so in the PagingDrive= entry.

The Best Swap File May Be No Swap File   If you have ample memory on your system (8Mb or more), you may achieve better Windows performance without a swap file. Your system memory may be all that you need to run applications, and Windows won't be slowed down by having to swap to disk.

Making the Most of Input Devices

The keyboard was probably the only peripheral that DOS handled effortlessly. Mice gave DOS some problems. Windows improves operation of both peripherals (its ability to shift to alternate keyboards goes far beyond DOS's, for instance). However, potential problems remain, especially along the DOS-Windows border.

Mouse Secrets

Because DOS handles mice in a clumsy fashion, and because contention can sometimes arise between mice and other peripherals, mouse installations under Windows are sometimes frustrating. The following sections include some suggestions for mouse use under Windows.

Loading the Microsoft Mouse   You can load the Microsoft mouse driver for use with DOS applications one of two ways: from your CONFIG.SYS file with a device command, or from your AUTOEXEC.BAT file as an executable file. It is better to use the MOUSE.COM driver loading from AUTOEXEC.BAT than MOUSE.SYS from CONFIG.SYS. This prevents problems that Windows may have saving the DOS settings for the Control Panel utility that comes with the Microsoft mouse. If you do use MOUSE.SYS and have problems with these settings, make sure that the mouse is being loaded from the mouse directory, not the Windows directory.

Tips for Microsoft Mouse Troubleshooting   If you cannot make your Microsoft mouse work with Windows, Windows may not recognize the mouse on your system. If there is an unused mouse port on your system, Windows may be detecting that instead. Refer to your system documentation or contact your system manufacturer for details on how to disable the unused port. Windows may also fail to recognize your mouse because it thinks that some other hardware hooked up to your computer, such as a scanner or modem, is the mouse. If your mouse is hooked up to COM1 or COM2, try swapping ports to see if this resolves the problem.

If you are using a Microsoft mouse version 8.0 or later, you can edit your mouse initialization file (MOUSE.INI) to tell Windows exactly where the mouse is located. Open the MOUSE.INI file in a text editor, and look for the line that says MouseType=. Table 3.1 lists the settings that you can place after the equal sign to tell Windows where your mouse is.

TABLE 3.1

Indicating the Type of Mouse You Are Using

Setting	Mouse Type
Serial	For a mouse on either COM1 or COM2
Serial1	For a mouse on COM1
Serial2	For a mouse on COM2
PS2	For a mouse on a PS/2-style mouse port
Bus	For an older bus card
InPort	For an InPort card
InPort1	For an InPort card, with Jumper 3 set to primary
InPort2	For an InPort card, with Jumper 3 set to secondary

Using a Logitech Mouse with Windows   Logitech mouse users will probably need to a do a little bit of adjustment to use their mouse with Windows. Even though the Logitech mouse driver in Windows 3.1 works fine, the Logitech drivers also provide other features such as speed and shape of mouse cursor. And some Logitech mice are identified by Windows Setup as Microsoft or IBM PS/2 mice and will use the Microsoft-compatible mouse driver. So to make sure you get the best performance, use the drivers that came with your mouse instead of those provided with Windows.

To use the mouse with DOS applications you need to load the DOS mouse driver, MOUSE.COM, before you load Windows. if you'll be using a mouse with DOS applications on a regular basis, put the command to load MOUSE-.COM in your AUTOEXEC.BAT file. You also need a line to your SYSTEM-.INI file that loads the driver in each DOS session. The line in the [386 Enh] section should read

```
local=PC$MOUSE
```

Cover More Ground with Your Mouse   If you seem to be forever dragging your mouse across the screen to get where you want, speed up the Mouse Tracking Speed in the Mouse Control Panel settings. (Double-click on the mouse icon within the Control Panel.) Moving the speed indicator all the way to the right makes a dramatic difference in the distance you can cover with each hand motion. It also means you won't have to continually pick up your mouse and reposition it to keep it on your mouse pad.

Keyboard Tips and Tricks

Loading the standard QWERTY keyboard under Windows is essentially automatic. But shifting smoothly to alternative keyboards and supercharging keyboard performance take a bit more work.

Change Keyboard Layout to Non-U.S.   If you are using Windows and have to change your keyboard layout often—perhaps you are bilingual and work in two languages regularly—you can change the keyboard layout by selecting the International icon in the Control Panel. Windows will need the Setup disk to copy the new file to your system. You are prompted for the new .DLL file only once. Each successive time that you change the keyboard layout, Windows tells you that a driver is already installed and asks if you want to use the current one or install a new one. See Figure 3.4.

FIGURE 3.4

When you make subsequent keyboard layout changes, you are informed that a driver for that specific country's layout already exists on your system and are asked if you want to use it.

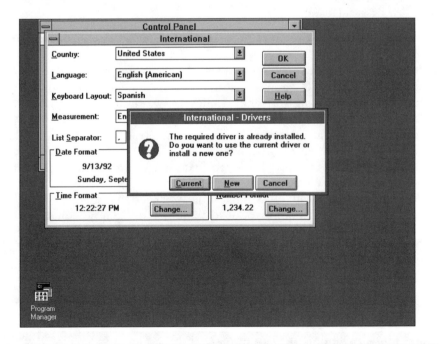

Increase Keyboard Responsiveness If you're running more than one application at a time, your keyboard may not be as responsive as it normally is. You can edit the [386Enh] section of your SYSTEM.INI file to adjust the amount of time allocated to an application when it receives a keystroke. You can set the KeyBoostTime= setting to increase this priority. This line will probably not be in your SYSTEM.INI, so you will have to add it. The default is .001. Try setting it to .005, like this:

```
KeyBoostTime=.005
```

Sharpening Your Windows Display

Yes, Windows is a graphical environment. However, curiously enough, Windows isn't designed for the most advanced display options on PCs today. Big screens, screens with a large number of colors, and displays that go beyond the common VGA standard all can cause Windows headaches. The reason behind this lowest-common-denominator approach to graphical display in Windows seems to be a desire to ensure that the system runs on as many machines as possible, rather than running superbly on fewer leading-edge PCs. That probably makes sense. And you can get your high-end graphics screen humming under Windows if you know what you are doing.

SVGA Displays

Super VGA displays (known as SVGA) have become extremely popular on powerful Windows PCs. These monitors can show more text on screen than VGA displays, and offer far better color resolution and better refresh rates (which translates into screen crispness). The problem is that SVGA isn't a single standard. Rather, it's a loose family of approaches that have in common only the fact that they are more powerful than VGA. Needless to say, this can create problems for users. Here, we offer some advice that applies to SVGA generally. Other possibilities may exist for your particular monitor; use bulletin board services from your manufacturer or vendor literature to get the most from the particular SVGA setup you have. Also, check out the section "Specific Video Board Problems" that follows.

Give Up 256 Colors for Improved Performance If you're using a Super VGA display, you can improve Windows performance by giving up your 256 colors and sharper images and going back to regular VGA. For applications, such as graphic packages, that require the higher resolution and enhanced color support, you'll want to stick with SVGA, but if you're not really using these features it's an unnecessary burden on your system.

However, if your system has a video accelerator board with its own graphics coprocessor, switching from SVGA to VGA will not make much of a difference to system performance.

Switch between SVGA and VGA Resolutions with Batch Files   If you have a display that supports SVGA resolution, you may find yourself switching back and forth between VGA and SVGA depending on the task you are doing. For example, you may use SVGA when you are using a graphics program, but find that VGA's larger text is better for word processing. Instead of having to change the display resolution by running Windows Setup each time, you can create batch files that run Windows in the different modes. When you make these change in Windows Setup, Windows rewrites your SYSTEM.INI file with the new settings. As a result, all you have to do is create and maintain separate SYSTEM.INI files for each display mode you want to run Windows in.

For example, if you are currently running Windows in regular VGA, copy the SYSTEM.INI file and name it something like SYSTEM.VGA. Now run Windows Setup and change the display mode to SVGA. Copy the SYSTEM.INI again, naming it something like SYSTEM.SVG. Next, write batch files that copy these special SYSTEM.INI files to be the current SYSTEM.INI file, and then load Windows. The batch file to run Windows in VGA, which might be called VGA.BAT, would look like this:

```
COPY SYSTEM.VGA SYSTEM.INI
WIN
```

To run Windows from a display mode other than the current one, exit Windows and start the corresponding batch file.

Rooting Out Video Problems

In a situation as confused as video is today, problems are inevitable. Drivers, the programs that describe peripherals to the operating system, are extremely model-specific. The assumptions applications make about how they are being displayed may not be consistent. Of all the areas of Windows, this is the one where troubleshooting is most likely to be necessary.

Tips for Troubleshooting Display Problems   To troubleshoot display problems, you need to know that Windows display drivers actually have three parts: the driver file (*.DRV), which allows your hardware to talk to your software; the grabber files (*.2GR, *.3GR or *.GR2, *.GR3), which support data exchange between Windows and DOS applications; and the virtual display driver (VDD*x*.386), which provides virtual display support for DOS applications running in Enhanced mode.

If you install a third-party display driver, you must make sure that all of these files are updated and added to your WINDOWS\SYSTEM subdirectory. You also need to make sure that the grabber entries in the [boot] section of SYSTEM.INI file are accurate. They are 286grabber= or 386grabber=. The filename of the grabber file should come after the equal sign. For more information on installing video drivers, see the section "How to Install a New Set of Video Drivers Safely" a little later in this chapter.

You may also have problems running a VGA display adapter in Enhanced mode if your video card uses additional memory to enhance its performance. In most cases, Windows detects this memory and excludes it from being used, but you may need to add an emmexclude= entry in the [386Enh] section of SYS-TEM.INI if you are having display problems. This entry specifies the memory address that the card uses.

Specific Video Board Problems There are literally hundreds of video boards available for Windows-capable PCs. Here are some of the known problems for boards from leading manufacturers:

- **Cornerstone Full-Page Display with Type-A Video Card** If you have a Cornerstone Full-Page Display and are using the Type-A video card, you may have problems running DOS applications in Enhanced mode. According to Cornerstone Technical Support, this problem occurs because of a hardware limitation of the Type-A video card. You may need to upgrade to the Type-B video card.

- **STB Powergraph Ergo Video Card and Excel** If you are using the STB Powergraph Ergo video card with Excel 3.0 and Windows, you may experience Uses or General Protection Faults. The Powergraph Ergo video card may also cause your system to freeze if you are using Excel 3.0's Print Preview. To fix these problems, you should get the most recent video driver for the card or upgrade the BIOS on the video card.

- **Quadram VGA Cards and Video Display** If you are using a Quadram VGA video card, you may experience display problems such as being unable to have the DOS prompt in a window, or a corrupted display as a result of the Alt+Tab key combination. To help performance, you should run the DOS command MODE CO80 before or after running Windows. This command tells DOS that you are using a color adapter with an 80-column display.

- **Tseng Labs Video Card in Austin Computers** If your Austin computer has a Tseng Labs video card installed, you'll need to have a BIOS dated 4/90 or later to run Windows.

How to Install a New Set of Video Drivers Safely

When you install a new set of video drivers for Windows, you should avoid directly running the SETUP.INF file that comes with the third-party driver disk. The SETUP.INF is used by Windows Setup to copy the correct files to your system, based on the kind of hardware you have and the choices you make during setup. If you run the SETUP.INF file that came on the driver disk, you risk corrupting your original SETUP.INF file.

Try renaming the SETUP.INF file on your driver disk to OEMSETUP.INF. When you run Setup from DOS and you are prompted for the disk, Windows should find the OEMSETUP.INF file. If this doesn't work, you can accomplish the same thing by hand: Copy all the drivers (they'll have the .DRV extension) from the disk into your WINDOWS\SYSTEM subdirectory. Also copy any files with the .386 or .286 extension to this directory. Open the SETUP.INF file that came on the third-party driver disk in a text editor.

Look for the [display] section, which contains a list of driver filenames and parameters for using them. Find the drivers that you will need, and select this section of text. Copy these lines to the Clipboard, and then open your real SETUP.INF file. In its [display] section, paste the lines at the end of the driver list. You can now run Windows Setup, and these new driver choices should appear.

Get Rid of Old Drivers

If you're trying to sort out video drivers, figuring out which ones were from your old Windows 3.0 installation and which ones belong to Windows 3.1, you can take a look at the dates of the files. Go to the WINDOWS\SYSTEM subdirectory in File Manager and choose View, Sort By Date. You can safely get rid of those driver files that are dated before Windows 3.1 came out (that is, before April 6, 1992).

Changing Windows Screen Fonts

Under DOS we were stuck with a single block-like on-screen font for 10 years. We didn't have WYSIWYG ("what you see is what you get"). We suffered through WYGIWYS ("what you get is what you see"). Windows, too, comes with standard screen fonts for such elements as title bars, but happily you can change them at will.

Changing Windows Screen Fonts by Editing the WIN.INI   You can change the font that Windows uses to display menu text, title bars, and dialog boxes by adding a line to your WIN.INI file. (See Figure 3.5). The system font that Windows uses to display this text is normally defined in the [boot] section of the SYSTEM.INI file. Look for the line that reads something like this:

```
fonts.fon= vgasys.fon
```

However, you can supersede this setting by specifying a different font in the [windows] section of the WIN.INI. Add a line that specifies one of the raster fonts that are installed on your system (located in your WINDOWS\SYSTEM subdirectory). For example, to set the system font to Courier for a VGA display, you would enter a line like the one highlighted in Figure 3.5:

```
SystemFont=coure.fon
```

If you try using one of the vector fonts instead (such as Script), you'll get screen text that's too large.

FIGURE 3.5

Change the font Windows uses to display menu text, title bars, and dialog boxes by editing your WIN.INI file.

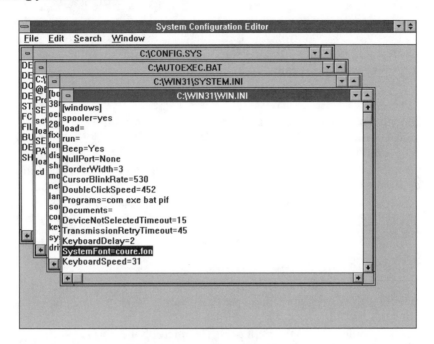

Use Small Fonts on Big Monitors If you're using a Super VGA display and want to get more information on screen at once, change your system fonts to those for a VGA display. Once again, you need to edit the SYSTEM.INI file to do so. Run Windows Setup to select the display mode that you want—for example, SVGA. Next, open your SYSTEM.INI file and in the [boot] section you'll see the entry:

```
fixedfon.fon=8514fix.fon fonts.fon=8514sys.fon
oemfonts.fon=8514oem.fon
```

Change this setting to request those fonts regularly used for a VGA display:

```
[boot]
fixedfon.fon=vgafix.fon fonts.fon=vgasys.fon
oemfonts.fon=vgaoem.fon
```

The next time you use Windows you'll be using these smaller fonts and will get more information on your display at one time.

If you have a VGA display, or if you want even smaller text on your SVGA display, you can use the EGA fonts instead.

Make the Cursor Easier to Find by Changing Its Blink Rate

If you like strong coffee, and you edit text with intensity to match, then increase Windows' cursor blink rate to its maximum. You'll be amazed how much faster you can locate the quickly flashing insertion point on a full page of solid text. From the Windows Control Panel, double-click the Desktop icon. From the Desktop dialog box, move the Cursor Blink Rate slider bar all the way to the right for the fastest blink rate.

Multimedia Tips

Multimedia is an emerging area for Windows. It is a natural extension of the graphical nature of the Windows environment. By combining traditional computer operations with motion and sound, multimedia holds the promise for newly interactive business programs, as well as a union between computing and entertainment. Because it is so new, the course multimedia will take, and what it will mean for business users, remains unclear. Although this book does not focus on this area too heavily, here are a couple of secrets to give you a flavor of what lies ahead.

Troubleshooting Audio in Windows

If you have a sound card and speakers installed on your system, but you don't seem to be getting any sound, there are a few simple things to check before delving into the box for a possible hardware conflict. First, make sure that your speakers are plugged into the right port. The microphone port is often confused with the speaker port. Also, check the volume setting for your sound card. If you have accidentally turned it all the way down, you won't get any sound. Another thing to check is that the speakers have power to operate. Some speakers need batteries, while others need to be plugged into an electrical outlet. You'll also want to check the drivers in the Control Panel to verify that you have the right sound driver installed for your sound card. Lastly, check for IRQ and address conflicts between the sound card and other system hardware.

Troubleshooting Audio in DOS Sessions

If you attempt to run a DOS application that supports sound under Windows, but you get a message that the application won't be able to use audio, you may still be able to get sound. If you are running in Enhanced mode, exit Windows and restart in Standard mode (type **win/s**). You should now have support for sound. In Enhanced mode, Windows takes over your sound hardware and won't give up control to a DOS application.

CD-ROM Drives and the Microsoft DOS CD-ROM Extensions

If you are using a CD-ROM drive with Windows, make sure that you are using a recent version of the Microsoft CD-ROM Extensions (MSCDEX). If your drive is not working properly with Windows, you may need to get a more recent version of MSCDEX. If you are upgrading to version 2.20 or later, be sure to remove the following line from the [386Enh] section of your SYSTEM.INI (it was required for previous versions):

```
device=LANMAN10.386
```

If you use this setting with a recent version of MSCDEX, you may experience time-out and failure problems with the drive. But for versions prior to 2.20 the setting should remain in your SYSTEM.INI.

Troubleshooting a CD-ROM Drive

If your PC doesn't recognize your CD-ROM drive, first check that all of your connections are correct. And if your SCSI drive requires an external terminator, make sure that this is also installed correctly. Verify that you have the Microsoft CD-ROM Extensions (MSCDEX) installed on your system. Also make sure that the directory where MSCDEX is stored is included in your path statement.

Tips for Traveling with Windows

It's tough to work with Windows in the office and go back to DOS on the road. The good news is that notebook computing has increased in power to the point where mobile Windows actually makes sense. Notebook screens achieve VGA quality in readable black and white, and color screens are now emerging. Hard drives as large as 80Mb are not uncommon on notebook computers today. Still, saying that Windows makes sense on notebooks isn't saying that the mobile environment is the same as the desktop. It's not. Windows on the road is a less-equals-more proposition; you want to squeeze the most Windows performance out of the smaller, less powerful, less naturally graphical package of a notebook PC.

Free Up Valuable Real Estate

You're careful not to overpack your suitcase for a weekend, so why stuff the small hard disk on your notebook PC with superfluous Windows files? On a typical 40Mb hard drive, that real estate is just too valuable to waste. If you're not sure you need an accessory or file, keep it on your system. Or remove it but take along your Windows disks just in case. For a list of files that you can trim from your notebook's hard disk, see Chapter 1.

LCD Screen Eye Savers

Running Windows on a tiny monochrome screen adds new meaning to the word eyestrain. Give your pupils a break by fine-tuning the display. For starters, run Setup and choose the VGA with Monochrome Display option. Next, you can optimize your desktop colors for the best results on an LCD screen. If you're a Windows 3.1 user this is merely a matter of selecting one of the four preconfigured LCD color schemes. (See Figure 3.6.) Choose the Color icon from the Control Panel and select the one you want.

FIGURE 3.6

Laptop users will want to select one of the Windows color schemes designed specifically for LCD screens.

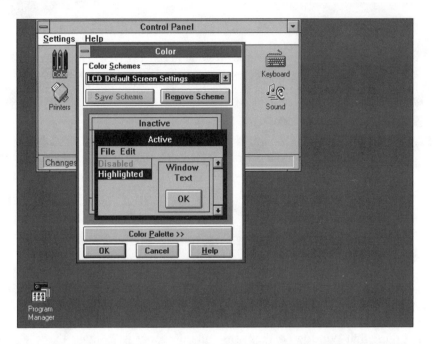

You should also select the Mouse icon while you're in the Control Panel. In the resulting dialog box, you'll find a check box labeled Mouse Trails. Click there, and your mouse pointer will streak across the screen with a satisfyingly visible blur, making it much easier to track on a dim screen. Using a third-party program that enlarges your cursor or changes its shape is another way to make the cursor easier to find.

Opt for a Larger Font

Another simple way to make screens more readable is to use larger fonts. If you're knocking out memos or expense reports while you're on the plane, for example, why not bump up your program's default font size a couple of points? You can always switch back to your usual size when you hook up to a printer. The methods for changing fonts vary from program to program, but you'll find tips on several dozen applications in Part 2 of this book.

Use Keyboard Shortcuts

Before you hit the road, review your favorite programs' keyboard shortcuts. Develop some key-combination macros that replace menu selections three or four mouse clicks deep. And never click on, or cancel in, dialog boxes—Enter and Esc do the job much better. Chances are you won't be able to get by with the keyboard alone, but you can at least minimize your dependence on the clumsy pointer. For maximum convenience on a business trip, you might want to pack two devices—a standard mouse for hotel and client-site use and a trackball for the plane.

Customize Style Sheets for Laptop Use

If the software you use on the road employs style sheets, set up a large default font on the laptop and a smaller one on your desktop machine. In Word for Windows, for example, define the Normal style in the Normal template as, say, 14-point Arial on your laptop and 10-point Arial on your desktop system. When you transfer your work from one machine to the other, the text will change point size automatically.

Have Different Printer Drivers Available

Also make sure that you've got several basic printer drivers installed on your portable system, so that you're prepared to print no matter where you are. You should include the generic driver and an HP LaserJet driver, as well as one for Epson dot-matrix printers. Between these three basic drivers, your bases should be covered.

Avoid Trouble with Remote-Control Applications

If you use remote-control software to run Windows—perhaps you use a program such as pcAnywhere to control your office PC from your home computer or laptop—you've probably run into problems trying to load Windows. So-called remote-control programs work best with character-based applications because there's not much screen data to be transferred from host to remote in order to show the application running on the host PC. With faster modems in particular, screen updates can be so fast that it's easy to forget you're working remotely.

A graphical application such as Windows, however, contains several hundred thousand pixels on each screen. Transferring that much information from one computer to another simply isn't practical for remote operation—you'd have to wait five minutes for the screen to update! None of the vendors of remote-control programs has *yet* mastered the process for Windows.

In the meantime, there is one simple trick that might help you avoid accidentally trying to run Windows across a phone line. Before you leave the office, change the prompt on the host machine to something that will constantly remind you that you're working remotely. For example, you can type

```
PROMPT ** HOST ** $P $G
```

on the host machine before you leave it unattended. Then, when you log on with the remote machine, you'll see the following prompt:

```
** HOST ** D:\123>
```

With luck, this distinctive prompt will cause you to think twice before you try to launch Windows.

Another useful trick is to write a WIN.BAT file for the host computer that will display a message if you try to run Windows on the remote machine. Your batch file might look something like this:

```
CLS
ECHO IF YOU ARE OPERATING REMOTELY, WINDOWS WILL LOCK UP THIS SYSTEM.
ECHO PRESS CTRL-BREAK TO ABORT!
PAUSE
C:\WINDOWS\WIN
```

*E*XPERT MANAGEMENT FOR DOS UNDER WINDOWS

A KEY TO THE STUNNING SUCCESS OF WINDOWS SINCE THE RELEASE OF VERSION 3.0 has been the choices offered to users: You can use Windows (either 3.0 or 3.1) as an entirely new graphical computing environment, complete with sophisticated new Windows applications, or you can use it as a splendid graphical memory manager and program launcher for familiar DOS applications.

This duality has made it much easier for people to begin experimenting with Windows, and has given users a flexibility they not only crave, but require. You can use Windows without making any changes in the applications that handle your critical computing chores. As time goes on, you can migrate smoothly from DOS applications to Windows applications when new programs offer enough significant new benefits to make the change seem worth *your* while.

Windows' dual nature has been a boon, no question. But it means that DOS remains a significant element in the lives of many, if not most, Windows users.

While Windows does a splendid job of handling DOS applications and providing DOS services to users, it's not perfect. How could it be? This is, after all, gnarly, nasty, difficult old DOS we're talking about. DOS is a tough environment on users, and on system software such as Windows as well.

Friction along the boundaries between Windows and DOS creates more confusion and consternation than any other aspect of the new environment, so this chapter offers dozens of effective secrets for taming DOS on your Windows PC, including these:

- Tips for installing and launching DOS applications under Windows, with information on how Windows' modes affect DOS program performance

- The ins and outs of Program Information Files (PIFs), which control every aspect of DOS program operation; includes a guide to troubleshooting common problems

- Advice on establishing effective DOS sessions, with details on how to optimize your AUTOEXEC.BAT and CONFIG.SYS files and how to interpret some common error messages

- Step-by-step instructions on copying and pasting between DOS and Windows applications

- Lots of shortcuts and ingenious workarounds for managing DOS sessions under Windows

We even show how to set up your system so that you *know* whether you're in native DOS or you're running DOS under Windows, a confusion that's a potential cause of fatal errors such as crashing the system by running DOS commands forbidden under Windows.

Installing and Launching
DOS Apps under Windows

The proper handling of DOS applications under Windows is somewhat akin to the correct method for handling rare poisonous snakes—take care and beware. Although adding DOS applications to Windows is simple, the day-to-day practice of actually getting DOS programs to work well with Windows without crashing the system can be vexing. We recommend a step-by-step approach to DOS application management. To begin, let Windows do the work. If things don't go smoothly, get more involved yourself.

Ask Windows Setup to Search Out DOS Apps

Your first opportunity to bring DOS programs into Windows occurs when you install Windows with the Setup program. The Setup program asks if you want it to search your hard disk for programs that have already been installed on your computer. If you answer Yes, Setup looks for the more than 80 DOS applications—including all the chart-leading favorites—that it recognizes, plus any Windows applications. It then lists the programs it finds and asks you to select which ones to install in Program Manager (see Figure 4.1). To add DOS applications, click on the application name in the list on the left and then click on the Add button.

Don't be alarmed if Setup "finds" applications that aren't on your disk. All that means is that one of your programs has the same executable filename as the one Setup thought it found. For instance, the name MP.COM is used by both MousePerfect, a mouse driver for WordPerfect, and Multiplan, Microsoft's spreadsheet. When Setup finds MP.COM, it assumes that it has located Multiplan. Also, the setup routine may identify arcane DOS utilities that are of little value to most users, such as LINK or BASICA. If you don't use them regularly, don't install them in Program Manager—they'll just create clutter. You can easily add them later if necessary.

Once you've indicated your choices, Setup creates two program groups, one called Windows Applications and one called Non-Windows Applications. Then it generates a program item for each application you've selected. In addition, Setup creates a PIF for each DOS application that it installs. The PIF tells Program Manager where to find the application (that is, in which DOS subdirectory on your hard disk it is stored), what the application's executable file is called, and other data relating to the application, including the minimum amount of RAM that must be available before the program can be launched. (For more on PIFs, see the section "PIFs: DOS Program Control Centers" later in this chapter.)

FIGURE 4.1

Setup searches out DOS programs on your hard disk and lets you set them up to run from a Windows PIF file.

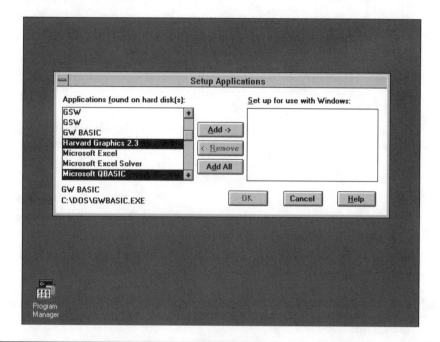

Installing DOS Programs after Setup

You can install more DOS programs at any time after the initial setup. Just select the New command on the Program Manager's File menu and fill in the two-line dialog box with the title you want for the program item and the location and filename of the executable file (or the PIF, if you've created one) needed to run it. Your program will appear with the default DOS icon supplied by Windows, or you can choose a nicer-looking icon, as described in Chapter 5.

To change the icon, highlight it and choose Properties from the File menu. Select Change Icon, and a dialog box will appear. The filename for the icon source file is PROGMAN.EXE by default, meaning that the icons available in Program Manager are the default selection. If you're using Windows 3.1, try MORICONS.DLL, located in the WINDOWS subdirectory.

Six Ways to Launch DOS Applications from within Windows

You can hang on to your beloved DOS applications even if you're using Windows, but stop wasting time exiting Windows to run them. There are at least six ways to run DOS apps from within Windows. Choose the one that works best for you:

- Add an icon to launch your DOS application from the Program Manager. Select New from the Program Manager File menu, specify that you're creating a program item, supply the name you want to appear with the icon, and indicate the path and command you would normally use to execute the program.

- Use File Manager to launch a DOS program by locating the subdirectory containing its executable file and double-clicking on the filename entry (see Figure 4.2).

- If the program has a PIF file—either one you've created or one that Windows put together during Setup—locate it and double-click on the PIF's name in the File Manager.

- Use the Run command on the File menu in Program Manager. When prompted you for the name of the program you want to use, type the name of your application's executable file (including its path) or the name of the PIF that launches it, and then press Enter.

- Select the DOS prompt icon in Program Manager to get to the DOS command line, and then launch your application with the same commands you'd use outside of Windows.

- Or, finally, use third-party alternatives to Program Manager, such as hDC's Power Launcher or Norton Desktop for Windows.

FIGURE 4.2

One way to launch a DOS application from Windows is to double-click on the executable file from within File Manager.

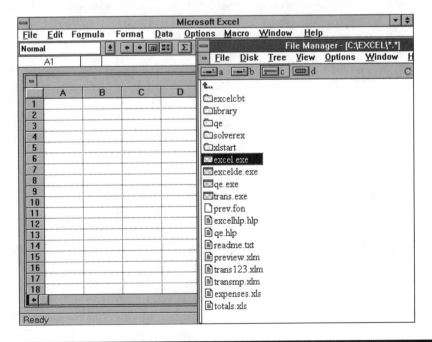

Launch a DOS Application with a Data File Loaded

Windows can launch many DOS programs with a certain file already loaded into them. This capability is automatically enabled for most Windows programs when you install them, but for DOS applications you'll have to modify the WIN.INI file. The [Extensions] section of the WIN.INI file tells Windows what to do when someone tries to run data files with certain filename extensions. Part of that section looks like this:

```
[Extensions]
txt=notepad.exe ^.txt
```

All this little piece of WIN.INI says is that when you double-click on a .TXT file, Windows should launch Notepad and load that file. If you decide that you'd rather edit .TXT files in your favorite DOS editor—say, Norton's NED.EXE—replace the above line in WIN.INI with the following:

```
txt=ned.exe ^.txt
```

Keep in mind that this works only if the executable file is in your current DOS path. If it isn't, change the entry to read

```
txt=ned.pif ^.txt
```

Then create a PIF file for NED.EXE that tells Windows where to find the program.

You can also add new filename extensions to the list to launch other types of programs. For example, to add .WKS files that launch a DOS-based version of 1-2-3, put the following line in WIN.INI's [Extensions] list:

```
wks=123.exe ^.wks
```

WIN.INI is an ordinary text file, so you can use any text editor, including Windows' own Notepad, to modify it.

Windows' Modes and DOS Apps

DOS applications interact with Windows differently in each of Windows' modes. Real mode, which exists only in Windows 3.0, has become outdated. Since the introduction of Windows 3.1, Standard mode represents the common way Windows is used on 286 and low-powered 386 machines. 386 Enhanced mode brings DOS applications much closer to the graphical, shared-screen, multitasking world of Windows by taking advantage of the power of the 80386 microprocessor.

Windows 3.0 Real Mode Isn't Great for DOS Applications Here's a great reason to upgrade to Windows 3.1, if you haven't already: Don't expect much when running your DOS favorites in Windows 3.0's Real mode. DOS applications in Real mode have access to the same 640K of RAM that's available to them under DOS. Unfortunately, Windows itself consumes 60 to 75K of conventional DOS memory when running in Real mode. Only one program can run at a time, whether it's a DOS or a Windows application, and switching from one program to another requires moving data from RAM to disk and back. In fact, in Real mode, Windows 3.0 (and any DOS applications running under it) are hobbled by many of the same performance and memory limitations that plagued earlier versions of Windows.

Standard mode in either Windows 3.0 or 3.1 is a more realistic environment for task-switching among DOS applications. (Task switching means switching from one application to another without having to exit one program and start up the next.)

Run DOS Applications in Standard Mode for Faster Performance   On some occasions, you might actually want to run a lesser Windows mode than your machine can handle. Owners of 386 PCs who are willing to give up 386 Enhanced mode's special multitasking capabilities (see the following tip) will find that Windows applications run 10 to 15 percent faster in Standard mode than in 386 Enhanced mode.

Task-switching in Standard mode is simple enough. Launch one program, and then use it in the foreground for a while. When you're done, minimize its window, and then launch another application. To reactivate the first program, double-click on its icon to bring it into the foreground. You can also use Windows keyboard commands to switch between programs. Pressing Alt+Esc or Alt+Tab switches you from one loaded application to another, and pressing Ctrl+Esc brings up the Windows Task List, a list of loaded applications from which you can choose.

Unfortunately, although Standard mode allows Windows and Windows applications to access all the memory installed on the PC (up to 16Mb), DOS applications are still restricted to the same 640K limitation found in Real mode. Switching among loaded applications is a fairly rapid process, but when memory becomes overloaded, inactive programs go to disk, slowing your work considerably.

Run DOS Applications in 386 Enhanced Mode for True Multitasking   386 Enhanced mode is far and away the most versatile alternative for running DOS applications under Windows. It adds both a complete, disk-based virtual memory manager and background processing to Standard mode's task-switching capabilities. Its superior memory management means that DOS applications use about 10K less memory than they would running on the same machine using standard DOS.

In 386 Enhanced mode, one or more DOS or Windows programs can run in the background while another DOS or Windows application runs in the foreground. Therefore, your PC can execute a large database sort and conduct a file transfer in the background while you continue to work at word processing or some other task in the foreground. (There will be some compromise in performance, of course.)

When you're in Windows and have a DOS application loaded, the application is represented by a DOS icon at the bottom of the screen. You can reactivate the DOS program that the icon represents by double-clicking on it, or you can use the Alt+Tab or Alt+Esc keyboard commands to switch between the DOS program and other programs you have running.

Toggle Enhanced Mode Applications between Windowed and Full-Screen Size   In 386 Enhanced mode, you can run DOS applications either full-screen size or in a resizable window. Press Alt+Enter to toggle between these two modes. If you want your DOS app to start up in a window by default, go to the program's PIF (or create a PIF if there isn't one already, as is described in the next section of this chapter), and select Windowed as the Display Usage option.

Mouse Tricks

Many DOS applications were developed BTM (before the mouse). Back then men were men, women were women, and long keyboard commands were considered sexy. No longer. Today, women are strong, men are sensitive, and application services are expected to be just a mouse click away. Windows offers methods savvy users can employ to bring mouse power to old DOS programs. With them you can install or launch a DOS application with a quick click.

Use the Mouse in DOS Applications in Windows 3.1   In Windows 3.1, you can use a mouse in DOS applications whether they're running full-screen or in a window. But you need to load a DOS mouse driver into memory to do so.

Make sure you're using the most recent version of MOUSE.COM, the Microsoft mouse driver for DOS. Version 8.2 of MOUSE.COM is included with Windows 3.1, but is not automatically installed during setup.

If you retrieve the driver from the Windows disks (it's on Disk 4), remember that you need to expand it before you can use it. To do this, copy EXPAND-.EXE from Windows 3.1 Disk 3 to your \WINDOWS directory. Then, assuming Windows Disk 4 is in drive A, type

```
EXPAND A: MOUSE.CO_ MOUSE.COM
```

EXPAND will create a usable version of the driver in your \WINDOWS directory.

Load the DOS Mouse Driver from a Batch File   If you won't always need the mouse in DOS applications, or if only one specific DOS application calls for it, load the driver from a batch file. You can create a PIF for a batch file that loads just the mouse driver, or, in the case of a single mouse-supported DOS application, loads the driver and application in one batch file.

PIFs: DOS Program Control Centers

Before Windows, DOS programs never had to describe themselves to their PC's system or to any other running applications. When operating, a DOS program *was* its PC's system and there were no other applications running. To integrate these recalcitrant DOS applications into Windows sessions, you must place them in an envelope of descriptive information. This envelope is called a Program Information File, or PIF. Windows provides the framework for building PIFs in a utility called the PIF Editor, which resides in the Program Manager's Main program group. Using it wisely can make DOS applications as "windowable" and as cooperative with other programs as their natures allow.

Check for Predefined PIFs

The Windows APPS.INF file (in Windows 3.1) and the SETUP.INF file (in Windows 3.0) each contain PIF settings for many popular DOS applications; Windows uses these files during setup if you tell it to look for your existing applications. If one of your DOS applications is not listed in these files, check with the DOS application's manufacturer. They may have a PIF available for your application (many manufacturers' bulletin boards will provide these). If not, it may have information on the PIF settings that you should use. Finding this information will save you time trying to fine-tune the performance of your favorite DOS application.

If you didn't let Windows set up PIFs for your DOS applications during the initial setup, it's not too late to do so now. In Program Manager, choose the Setup icon (located in the Main program group) and choose Set Up Applications from the Options menu. Setup will search your disk for all the Windows and DOS applications it recognizes and then give you the option of installing any or all of them. If you want to check whether APPS.INF or SETUP.INF contains a PIF for your DOS application before you rerun Setup, you can open the .INI file in a text editor such as Notepad. These .INF files are located in Windows' SYSTEM subdirectory. If your DOS application isn't listed in the [pif] section, don't waste time running Setup.

How to Write the Perfect PIF

Program Information Files are small settings files that tell Windows where to find and how to load non-Windows applications. When you select Install Applications during Windows setup, Windows creates PIFs for all the non-Windows applications it recognizes on your disk. Here's how to write perfect PIFs for the DOS applications Setup misses:

1. Open the Windows PIF Editor. (It's found in the Main program group in Windows 3.1 and in the Accessories group in Windows 3.0.)

2. Enter the path and filename for your application's executable file on line 1.

3. Enter a title to appear with your application's icon on line 2.

4. On line 3, enter any command-line parameters you'd like to pass to the application.

5. On line 4, enter the directory where the application's executable file is stored.

6. Save the PIF. Change nothing else.

That's it. You're done. You've just created the perfect PIF, or something close enough to perfect that you'll never know the difference. This holds true for about 90 percent of DOS-based applications.

Make PIFs for Both Standard and 386 Enhanced Mode

When you're setting up a PIF file for a DOS application, the available configuration options depend on which Windows mode you're currently running. To have access to all the PIF options available in Standard and 386 Enhanced mode, first go into the Windows PIF Editor (in the Main group in Windows 3.1 and in the Accessories group in Windows 3.0) and fill in all the currently available options. When you're done, select the name of the mode that isn't already checked from the Mode menu at the top of the PIF Editor dialog box. For example, if you're currently running Windows in 386 Enhanced mode, a check mark will appear next to the item 386 Enhanced; click on Standard. A message will tell you that you are not currently running in this mode and that PIF options may not be appropriate; you'll be asked if you want to continue. Choose Yes to display a new PIF dialog box with other options for you to configure. The options that are identical in both modes will already be filled in, based on the options you selected in the first PIF box. See Figure 4.3.

FIGURE 4.3

Access all of the possible PIF settings for Enhanced and Standard modes by changing the setting in the Mode menu; Windows indicates that you are not currently running in this mode, but allows you to establish settings for when you are.

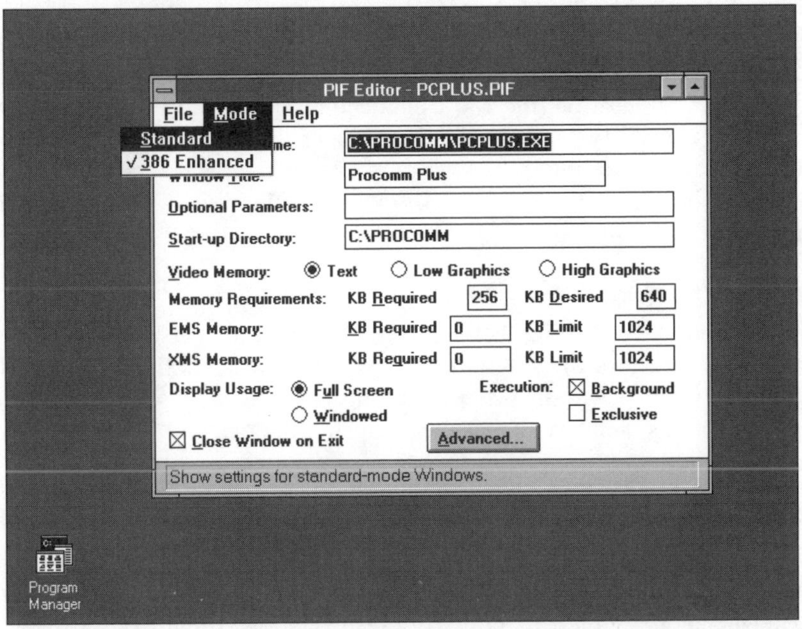

Make Two PIFs for the Same Application

For DOS applications you use frequently, consider making two separate PIFs (and program icons) that allow you to specify different starting directories and memory options. For example, this would come in handy with a DOS spreadsheet program that you use for both work and personal purposes. Start the PIF Editor and enter the program information for the first set of options. Choose Save from the File menu, giving the PIF a descriptive name that will distinguish it from the second one. Now select New from the PIF Editor's File menu and fill in the information for the second set of options, treating it as if it were a separate application (the Program Filename box will contain the same executable file as the first PIF). In Program Manager, add the icons for each PIF to the desired program groups, naming each appropriately so that you'll be able to easily distinguish between the two.

Make PIF Settings Uniform

If everyone at your workplace runs the same DOS applications under Windows, you might want to fine-tune the PIFs for each application and distribute them for everyone's use, especially if the applications have been known to cause problems. This way everyone will be running DOS applications optimized for Windows performance. Likewise, if your company develops its own DOS applications, it's a good idea to add PIFs with the correct settings for running them under Windows.

Protect Shortcut Key Sequences in DOS Apps

If one of your DOS applications uses some of the same shortcut key sequences as Windows itself (like Alt+Tab, Alt+Esc, and Ctrl+Esc), you can reserve these keys for use only by the application by changing the PIF settings. The Standard mode PIF dialog box includes five keyboard combinations that you can reserve for your DOS application; the 386 Enhanced mode Advanced Options dialog box contains seven key combinations that you can reserve for your DOS application. Note that reserving these keys only affects that particular DOS application. Once you return to Windows, the key combinations will revert to their Windows actions.

Recover Original PIFs

If you've modified a PIF file that Windows installed for you at setup, and you then decide to restore the original settings, all is not lost. Simply rerun Windows Setup from the Main program group and select Set Up Applications from the Options menu. You can then reinstall the original PIF over the one you've modified.

PIF Troubleshooting

Any DOS application that doesn't work with the standard PIF settings (see the earlier tip "How to Write the Perfect PIF") will do one of three things: Refuse to load when you use the PIF, crash, or crash Windows. In any of these events, turn to these troubleshooting tips.

And remember, if you're having trouble determining the correct PIF settings for a DOS application, use context-sensitive help. Pressing F1 brings up help for setting each section of the PIF, as shown in Figure 4.4.

FIGURE 4.4

You can access context-sensitive help for the PIF Editor by pressing F1.

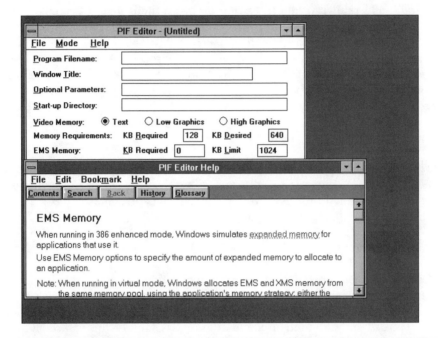

Not Enough Memory Does your program start to load, and then flash a "Not enough memory" message on the screen? You can increase the amount of memory available to your application by shedding a few TSRs or device drivers. Standard mode users can reserve a little more memory for their applications by checking the No Screen Exchange and Prevent Program Switch options in the PIF Editor dialog box. However, this prevents you from switching from your program while it's operating and from copying the contents of its screen to the Windows Clipboard.

Not Enough Memory for High-Resolution DOS Graphics in 386 Enhanced Mode Do you receive an out-of-memory error when running a high-resolution DOS graphics application? Check the program's PIF file: Under Video Memory, select High Graphics, and in the Advanced Options dialog box select Retain Video Memory from Display Options. Also select the Full Screen option.

Maintaining Access to Serial Ports Does your program use one of your PC's serial ports? If you're running in Standard mode, check the appropriate Directly Modifies box in the PIF Editor dialog box for the COM port that it uses.

Note, however, that doing so will prevent you from minimizing the program while it's running. Once you've checked any of the Directly Modifies boxes, you'll have to quit your program before you can return to Windows.

Mouse and Keyboard Problems   Does your mouse no longer work with your program? Write a batch file that loads your mouse driver and then the program, and change your PIF to run the batch file instead of running your program directly.

Do the shortcut key combinations (such as Alt+Tab and Ctrl+Enter) used by your program no longer work? Check the appropriate combinations in the Reserve Shortcut Keys section of the PIF Editor dialog box. If you're running in Standard mode and the special key sequences in your program still don't work, try selecting the Directly Modifies Keyboard check box in the PIF Editor dialog box. (Be aware, however, that this last step will prevent you from switching from your application while it's loaded.)

Putting Data Files Where You Want Them   Do you want to save files created by your DOS program to a directory other than the one in which your application's executable file is stored? Although the first line of the PIF will include the full path of your application's executable file (as in C:\TEXT\TEXT-EDIT.EXE), change the Startup directory in line 4 to be the path in which your data files can be found (C:\TEXT \DATAFILS\).

Clearing Up a Garbled Display   Is your application's screen garbled or incorrectly restored when you switch back to it after it has been iconized? Select the Graphics/Multiple Text option on the Video Mode check box in the PIF Editor dialog box if you're running in Standard mode. (Careful—this will reduce the amount of RAM available to your application.) If you're running in 386 Enhanced mode, click on Advanced Options in the PIF Editor dialog box, and then change the Monitor Ports and Video Memory options one by one until the problem is solved. Also make sure the Monitor Ports options is checked and that Emulate Text Mode is not checked.

Lost or Garbled DOS Data   Does your DOS data become garbled or lost when you're running a DOS application under Windows? Check the Directly Modifies options in the PIF Editor. If the options for the keyboard and COM ports are checked, the DOS application has exclusive control over these resources. Another application cannot simultaneously use the same serial port, and Windows cannot switch from the application. You can also select No Screen Exchange to prevent Windows from updating the screen when you switch back to the DOS application.

Expanded Memory   Does your DOS application require EMS memory that Windows isn't providing? Standard mode users should first try changing the XMS KB Required setting in the program's PIF to –1 (which will allot any EMS memory you've installed to your application, as needed), and then to a specific number (such as 500 for 500K) if that doesn't work. If you want to reserve XMS memory for other applications, enter an upper limit for the EMS RAM your application should be allowed to access in the KB Limit box. In 386 Enhanced mode, Windows automatically provides EMS and XMS memory to applications. However, you can adjust both the Required and Limit settings in the PIF Editor if your application is not operating correctly.

Background Execution and Windowed Display Some applications may crash if suspended while another program becomes active. If your application must continue execution while other applications are running in the foreground, check the Background Execution check box in the PIF Editor dialog box.

Do you want your application to load in a window, not full-screen? Select Windowed for the Display Usage option.

Pasting Data to and from the Clipboard Does your application hang or beep loudly when you paste data into it from the Windows Clipboard? Or are some of the characters not showing up? Deselect the Allow Fast Paste check box in the PIF Editor's Advanced Options dialog box.

Pasting Graphics to and from the Clipboard Are you unable to paste graphic screens from DOS applications to the Clipboard? If you're running in Standard mode, make sure that the No Screen Exchange option in the program's PIF file is not checked. This option prevents Windows from using PrtSc and Alt+PrtSc in DOS applications to paste to the Clipboard. Also check the Reserve Shortcut Keys settings. Make sure that PrtSc and Alt+PrtSc are not checked as reserved keys by the DOS application.

Task Switching Are you unable to switch from a DOS application into Windows? Check the application's PIF file to make sure that Prevent Program Switch isn't checked. If this item is checked, you won't be able to go back to Windows until the DOS session has ended. Also, if you've checked any of the Directly Modifies boxes, task-switching from your DOS application will be disabled; that is, you'll have to quit your DOS program before you can return to Windows.

Running Multiple DOS Applications Can you run DOS applications under Windows individually, but not run two or more DOS programs at the same time? You may have a problem with a conflicting device driver or TSR. One of the DOS applications may have a driver or TSR that requires expanded or extended memory, but the other DOS application may have the EMS Memory Locked or XMS Memory Locked option selected in its PIF file. If so, and if you want to run these DOS applications at the same time, turn off these memory options in the PIF.

DOS Communications Programs If you have problems keeping a modem connection while running a DOS communications program and trying to switch back to Windows, first consider if you're running in Standard mode. Standard mode doesn't allow DOS applications to run in the background; any DOS program is put on hold when you switch to Windows and the connection is terminated.

If you're operating in 386 Enhanced mode, try making these changes to the communications' program PIF: Under Execution, select the Background check box, and in the Advanced Options dialog box, make sure that the Detect Idle Time check box is not checked in the Multitasking Options section.

Last Resorts   If you try these adjustments and your application still doesn't work well under Windows, you may have a serious problem on your hands. Try calling Microsoft's Windows technical support line: (206) 637-7098. Or try calling the application program's developers, because they've no doubt already heard from other frustrated Windows users and may either have suggestions on how to make it work or may be working on an updated version that solves the problem. Finally, if you have access to CompuServe, check the Windows forums—the Windows New Users Forum (Go WINNEW) and the Windows Advanced Users forum (Go WINADV)—or any forum specific to your application to find out whether other users have encountered (and solved) the problem.

Establishing Effective DOS Sessions

DOS doesn't go away when Windows is running; it goes underground. The entire DOS structure becomes a substructure beneath Windows, just a click on the DOS prompt button away from reasserting itself. This means that you must take care to set up DOS properly if you want to get the most from Windows. This is particularly true if you are running DOS applications, which may look like they are part of your Windows screen groups, but actually operate in their traditional DOS sessions. Setting up the proper parameters in the DOS control files, such as CONFIG.SYS and AUTOEXEC.BAT, is essential to getting the most out of Windows.

Optimizing CONFIG.SYS and AUTOEXEC.BAT

Here are some straightforward rules of thumb to consider when setting up your DOS sessions under Windows. In total, they represent something of a refresher course in DOS basics. That may seem out of place in a Windows book, but it's not. When a contractor builds a house, even if it's his 10,000th house, he very carefully measures every angle, moving slowly, and sets the cornerstone with care. The same is true for DOS sessions in Windows. You may know all this material, but review it anyway to make sure you are setting your Windows cornerstone properly.

Upgrade to DOS 5.0   Upgrade to DOS 5.0, and then load it into the high memory area on 386 PCs by making sure HIMEM.SYS and EMM386.SYS are loaded and adding the line DOS=HIGH or DOS=HIGH,UMB to your CONFIG.SYS file just after the lines that load these files. (HIMEM and EMM386 are discussed fully later in this chapter.) If you specify DOS=HIGH,UMB you are also telling DOS to utilize any available sections of reserved memory (called upper memory blocks). Loading DOS high or in upper memory will give you more conventional memory for your DOS applications running under Windows. This procedure leaves only about 19K of DOS code in conventional memory.

Check Your Memory with DOS 5.0's MEM Command   Before you start experimenting with loading drivers, programs, and TSRs into high memory by tinkering with CONFIG.SYS, run the MEM command with the /C switch to see just which programs would benefit most. The /C switch is new to DOS 5.0 and gives you a detailed rundown of how much conventional memory drivers and TSRs are using. If certain programs are taking up too much memory, you can place them in the upper memory blocks by following the steps outlined later in this chapter or using the LOADHIGH and DEVICEHIGH commands.

Load HIMEM.SYS First   Make sure that the line of your CONFIG.SYS file that loads HIMEM.SYS comes before any other commands that load applications or drivers into extended memory.

Set FILES=30 in CONFIG.SYS   Set FILES=30 in your CONFIG.SYS unless you have an application that requires a higher number. Applications that can take advantage of a higher number include databases, which use a large number of file handles.

Set BUFFERS=10 in CONFIG.SYS   If you use Windows' SMARTDrive disk cache, set BUFFERS=10 in your CONFIG.SYS. If you don't use SMARTDrive, set it to 20. Using a higher number of buffers may improve disk access time, but it also uses up more conventional memory. (For more information on Windows's SMARTDrive disk cache, see Chapter 3.)

Free Up Conventional Memory by Loading Device Drivers High   If you're using DOS 5.0, for each device you want to load into the upper memory blocks, your CONFIG.SYS must contain a DEVICEHIGH= command, as in

```
DEVICEHIGH=C:\DOS\RAMDRIVE.SYS
```

Likewise, for each TSR that you want to load into upper memory, your AUTOEXEC.BAT must contain a LOADHIGH command, as in

```
LOADHIGH C:\DOS\DOSKEY.COM
```

If You Can't Load Programs in High Memory under DOS 5.0   To run programs in high memory, the following conditions must be met:

- The PC must be a 386 or greater.

- At least 350K of extended memory must be available.

- CONFIG.SYS must contain the line DEVICE=HIMEM.SYS before any other DEVICE= or DEVICEHIGH= commands.

- CONFIG.SYS must contain either a DOS=UMB or DOS=HIGH, UMB command.

Troubleshooting a Specific Device Driver If you cannot load a specific driver with the DEVICEHIGH command in DOS 5.0, check that the device driver itself works by loading it into conventional memory first. Next try changing the loading order of drivers and TSRs, keeping in mind that some programs require extra memory to load, often up to twice the amount of space they will actually use when resident.

Load EMM386 to Access Expanded Memory If you run DOS applications that require expanded memory, or if you want to access the upper memory blocks, load Windows' EMM386 memory manager in your CONFIG.SYS file. (The expanded memory manager is EMM386.EXE in Windows 3.1, EMM386.SYS in Windows 3.0. The following examples assume you're using Windows 3.1.)

Using the RAM switch with the line that loads EMM386.EXE, as in

```
DEVICE=EMM386.EXE RAM
```

tells the memory manager to simulate expanded memory and manage the upper memory blocks. On the other hand, using the NOEMS switch, as in

```
DEVICE=EMM386.EXE NOEMS
```

prevents access to expanded memory. If none of your DOS applications require expanded memory, use the NOEMS switch to gain an extra 64K in the upper memory blocks that would otherwise be reserved for the expanded memory page frame.

Troubleshooting EMM386 Error If you try to run Windows in 386 Enhanced mode and get the error message "Unable to start Enhanced Mode Windows due to invalid path specification for EMM386," here's what's going on: When you start Windows in 386 Enhanced mode with DOS 5.0's EMM386.EXE driver loaded, Windows attempts to locate the driver. The error message you see is an indication that EMM386.EXE is not in the same location as when the system was started. (This usually happens when you boot from a floppy disk that contains EMM386.EXE and then remove the floppy before starting Windows.)

There are two ways to fix the problem:

■ If possible, modify your CONFIG.SYS so that EMM386.EXE is loaded from the hard disk. For example, if you currently boot from a floppy that contains the statement DEVICE=EMM386.EXE NOEMS, and there is a copy of EMM386.EXE in the DOS directory of drive C, you should change the statement to read

```
DEVICE=C:\DOS\EMM386.EXE NOEMS
```

Then, when Windows looks for EMM386.EXE, it will find it.

■ Use the EMM386.EXE driver's sparsely documented /Y switch to explicitly spell out the path you want to use for EMM386. For example, if it's imperative that you load EMM386.EXE from the floppy, you can still direct Windows to the copy of the driver in C:\DOS by modifying the CONFIG.SYS file to read

```
DEVICE=EMM386.EXE NOEMS /Y=C:\DOS\EMM386.EXE
```

This, too, will eliminate the error message.

Load Only What You Need   In the AUTOEXEC.BAT and CONFIG.SYS files, load only the TSRs, drivers, and programs that you will use regularly. And conserve conventional memory by loading as much as possible into high memory and the upper memory blocks. You can also eliminate the DOS mouse driver altogether; if you have DOS applications that use a mouse, write batch files that load the mouse driver with the application.

Use DOSKEY with Windows   To have access to all of the macros that you've created with DOSKEY, load DOSKEY and the macros you want to use *before* you start Windows. You can do this automatically by adding lines invoking your DOSKEY macros to your AUTOEXEC.BAT file *before* the line that loads Windows. This way, no matter how many DOS sessions you have running, you'll always be able to use your favorite DOSKEY macros.

Optimize Memory Usage via PIFs   An addendum to the memory control possible through CONFIG.SYS is to optimize memory usage by allocating the expanded and extended memory required by DOS applications in a custom PIF. Put specific values in the EMS and XMS memory boxes in the PIF Editor to fine-tune the application's memory needs. By adjusting these settings you may be able to squeeze more applications into high memory by fitting them tightly into the available space.

Streamline Your PATH Statement   Your PATH statement, located in your AUTOEXEC.BAT file, tells DOS where to look for command files. When you install a new DOS or Windows program on your PC, the setup routine often adds the program's directory to your PATH statement. If you have many applications installed, a good chunk of the environment space allocated to the PATH statement is being used up (DOS allocates 127 bytes to the PATH statement). To make the most of this precious real estate, here are a few things you can do:

■ **Keep directory names short.** Your application will usually suggest a standard name for the default directory, but you can specify one that's much shorter. For example, instead of PROCOMM, you could opt for just PRO. If applications that you've already installed have long directory names, rename them in the Windows File Manager and change the name of the directory in the AUTOEXEC.BAT's PATH statement and the program's PIF. For Windows applications, you can rename any references in the WIN.INI file or the application's own INI file.

■ **Eliminate the drive letter.** If all of your applications are in a single drive (in most cases C), you can eliminate the drive letter that precedes every directory listing. For example, instead of

```
PATH=C:\DOS\;C:\WINDOWS;C:\PROCOMM;C:\EXCEL,
```

your PATH could simply read

```
PATH=\DOS;\WINDOWS;\PROCOMM;\EXCEL
```

■ **Keep applications in branches off the root directory rather than in sub-directories that are more deeply nested.** When you install applications, make sure that you do so in a directory that branches directly from the root directory. That way, if the application's directory needs to be in the PATH statement, it will be shorter than if it were nested. For example, instead of installing PROCOMM as a subdirectory of the directory DOSAPPS, so that the PATH statement would have to include C:\DOSAPPS\PROCOMM, install it in just the PROCOMM directory so that the PATH would simply include C:\PROCOMM. If you already have applications installed in subdirectories, move them to new directories and change your PATH statement, PIFs, and INI files to reflect their new locations.

Troubleshooting Difficulties with DOS Apps

As with many areas of Windows, you may feel you've done everything right in setting up your DOS applications, and the system will still give you fits. Here are some of the more common hidden problems to look for as you begin troubleshooting DOS session woes.

Where to Put WINA20.EXE When you install DOS 5.0 on your system, DOS Setup places a file called WINA20.386 in your root directory. If you move it out of the root directory and into a subdirectory, you may no longer be able to run Windows in 386 Enhanced mode. Windows aborts with the error message "You must have the file WINA20.386 in the root of your boot drive to run Windows in Enhanced Mode."

You can put the WINA20.386 file anywhere you wish, but you must let DOS and Windows know where it is by performing these two steps:

1. Add a SWITCHES=/ statement to CONFIG.SYS.

2. Add a DEVICE statement to the [386Enh] section of SYSTEM.INI naming the drive and directory where WINA20.386 is stored.

Suppose you want to move WINA20.386 to C:\SYSTEM. First, copy the WINA20.386 file to the SYSTEM subdirectory. Then use an ASCII text editor to add the statement SWITCHES=/W to your CONFIG.SYS so that DOS will know the file has been moved. Next, go to the directory where Windows is

■ Use the EMM386.EXE driver's sparsely documented /Y switch to explicitly spell out the path you want to use for EMM386. For example, if it's imperative that you load EMM386.EXE from the floppy, you can still direct Windows to the copy of the driver in C:\DOS by modifying the CONFIG.SYS file to read

```
DEVICE=EMM386.EXE NOEMS /Y=C:\DOS\EMM386.EXE
```

This, too, will eliminate the error message.

Load Only What You Need   In the AUTOEXEC.BAT and CONFIG.SYS files, load only the TSRs, drivers, and programs that you will use regularly. And conserve conventional memory by loading as much as possible into high memory and the upper memory blocks. You can also eliminate the DOS mouse driver altogether; if you have DOS applications that use a mouse, write batch files that load the mouse driver with the application.

Use DOSKEY with Windows   To have access to all of the macros that you've created with DOSKEY, load DOSKEY and the macros you want to use *before* you start Windows. You can do this automatically by adding lines invoking your DOSKEY macros to your AUTOEXEC.BAT file *before* the line that loads Windows. This way, no matter how many DOS sessions you have running, you'll always be able to use your favorite DOSKEY macros.

Optimize Memory Usage via PIFs   An addendum to the memory control possible through CONFIG.SYS is to optimize memory usage by allocating the expanded and extended memory required by DOS applications in a custom PIF. Put specific values in the EMS and XMS memory boxes in the PIF Editor to fine-tune the application's memory needs. By adjusting these settings you may be able to squeeze more applications into high memory by fitting them tightly into the available space.

Streamline Your PATH Statement   Your PATH statement, located in your AUTOEXEC.BAT file, tells DOS where to look for command files. When you install a new DOS or Windows program on your PC, the setup routine often adds the program's directory to your PATH statement. If you have many applications installed, a good chunk of the environment space allocated to the PATH statement is being used up (DOS allocates 127 bytes to the PATH statement). To make the most of this precious real estate, here are a few things you can do:

■ **Keep directory names short.** Your application will usually suggest a standard name for the default directory, but you can specify one that's much shorter. For example, instead of PROCOMM, you could opt for just PRO. If applications that you've already installed have long directory names, rename them in the Windows File Manager and change the name of the directory in the AUTOEXEC.BAT's PATH statement and the program's PIF. For Windows applications, you can rename any references in the WIN.INI file or the application's own INI file.

■ **Eliminate the drive letter.** If all of your applications are in a single drive (in most cases C), you can eliminate the drive letter that precedes every directory listing. For example, instead of

```
PATH=C:\DOS\;C:\WINDOWS;C:\PROCOMM;C:\EXCEL,
```

your PATH could simply read

```
PATH=\DOS;\WINDOWS;\PROCOMM;\EXCEL
```

■ **Keep applications in branches off the root directory rather than in sub-directories that are more deeply nested.** When you install applications, make sure that you do so in a directory that branches directly from the root directory. That way, if the application's directory needs to be in the PATH statement, it will be shorter than if it were nested. For example, instead of installing PROCOMM as a subdirectory of the directory DOSAPPS, so that the PATH statement would have to include C:\DOSAPPS\PROCOMM, install it in just the PROCOMM directory so that the PATH would simply include C:\PROCOMM. If you already have applications installed in subdirectories, move them to new directories and change your PATH statement, PIFs, and INI files to reflect their new locations.

Troubleshooting Difficulties with DOS Apps

As with many areas of Windows, you may feel you've done everything right in setting up your DOS applications, and the system will still give you fits. Here are some of the more common hidden problems to look for as you begin trouble-shooting DOS session woes.

Where to Put WINA20.EXE   When you install DOS 5.0 on your system, DOS Setup places a file called WINA20.386 in your root directory. If you move it out of the root directory and into a subdirectory, you may no longer be able to run Windows in 386 Enhanced mode. Windows aborts with the error message "You must have the file WINA20.386 in the root of your boot drive to run Windows in Enhanced Mode."

You can put the WINA20.386 file anywhere you wish, but you must let DOS and Windows know where it is by performing these two steps:

1. Add a SWITCHES=/ statement to CONFIG.SYS.

2. Add a DEVICE statement to the [386Enh] section of SYSTEM.INI naming the drive and directory where WINA20.386 is stored.

Suppose you want to move WINA20.386 to C:\SYSTEM. First, copy the WINA20.386 file to the SYSTEM subdirectory. Then use an ASCII text editor to add the statement SWITCHES=/W to your CONFIG.SYS so that DOS will know the file has been moved. Next, go to the directory where Windows is stored, call up the SYSTEM.INI file with your text editor, locate the [386Enh] section, and add the statement

```
DEVICE=C:\SYSTEM\WINA20.386
```

Save the SYSTEM.INI file and then reboot your system. Windows should run just fine.

Troubleshooting the "Unexpected MS-DOS Error #11" Message   If you receive the "Unexpected MS-DOS Error #11" error message when you try to run a DOS application under Windows 3.1, Windows has tried to execute a file that has an invalid format and the Windows files that support non-Windows applications are corrupted. To fix the problem, copy the grabber file and either WINOLDAP.MOD (if this happens in Standard mode) or WINOA386.MOD (in Enhanced mode) from your original Windows disks. The grabber filename will differ depending on which Windows and video mode you are running in. For example, it's CGA.2GR or VGACOLOR.2GR in Standard mode, and EGA.3GR or VGA.3GR in Enhanced mode. All the grabber files are on Windows 3.1 Disk 1; WINOLDAP.MOD is on Disk 5, and WINOA386.MOD is on Disk 4.

You need to expand these files before you can use them. The files are in compressed form on the disks, with the last character of the uncompressed filename's extension replaced with an underscore. To expand the VGA.3G_ file, for example, copy EXPAND.EXE from Windows 3.1 Disk 3 and type

```
EXPAND VGA.3G_ VGA.3GR
```

EXPAND will create usable versions of the files.

How to Delete a DOS Application   If you want to delete a DOS application, one point to remember about program items is that they merely direct Windows to the location of your application. Nothing you do to a program item—including moving it, deleting it, or renaming it—affects the underlying program file. Conversely, Windows has no way of knowing if you change or move the program files, so it's up to you to keep program items up-to-date. Deleting a DOS application file doesn't change its Windows icon; double-clicking on the icon will simply return a "Program Not Found" error. Also you can still access the application through the File Manager. If you want to actually delete the application, you can do so through the File Manager.

If DOS Application Doesn't Start in the Correct Directory in Windows 3.1   If you're running a DOS application from a PIF and it doesn't start in the directory you've specified, the Working Directory setting in the file's Properties settings may be different from the one you've specified. To check, highlight the program icon in Program Manager and choose Properties from the File menu. The Working Directory setting (shown in Figure 4.5) overrides the Start-up Directory setting in the application's PIF.

FIGURE 4.5

The Working Directory specified in a program item's Properties dialog box overrides the start-up directory specified in its PIF.

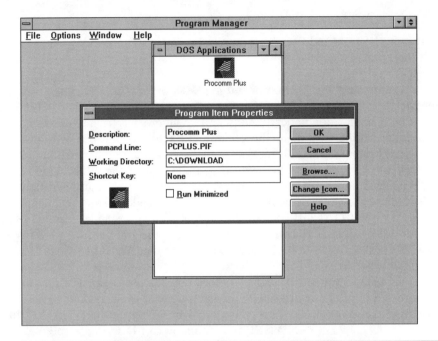

Troubleshooting Font Changes for a Windowed DOS Application If you're unable to change the font size for a DOS application running in a window, the application may be running in graphics mode. You can only change the font for a DOS application running in text mode. If the application is running in text mode and you still can't change the font, there may be a problem with the display driver. For an SVGA monitor, make sure that you are using the SVGA driver that came with Windows, because it supports font changes in windowed DOS applications. If the Windows driver doesn't work with your display and your driver doesn't seem to support font changes, try adding this line to your SYSTEM.INI file:

```
FontChangeEnable=1
```

Note that this setting may cause problems with displaying the mouse pointer.

Customizing Sessions
Run from Windows' MS-DOS Prompt

Even though you should be cautious in establishing DOS sessions running under Windows, you can still play around a little. Gourmet users of DOS under Windows can use these tips to spice up their DOS sessions.

Start DOS in a Window

To start DOS in a window rather than full-screen in 386 Enhanced mode, you have to change the DOSPRMPT.PIF file (in Windows 3.1) or create a new PIF (in Windows 3.0).

In Windows 3.1, the DOSPRMPT.PIF file (the file that runs DOS when you click on the MS-DOS icon in the Main group) is located in the WINDOWS sub-directory. Simply open the PIF in the PIF Editor (located in the Main group in Windows 3.1 and in the Accessories group in Windows 3.0) and change the Display Usage selection from Full Screen to Windowed.

In Windows 3.1, highlight the gray DOS icon in the Main group and select Properties from the File menu. Change the Command Line entry in the dialog box from COMMAND.COM to COMMAND.PIF. Then use the PIF Editor to create COMMAND.PIF. Specify COMMAND.COM as the Program Filename, and set the Display Usage option to Windowed. The next time you click on the DOS icon, DOS will run in a window.

Here's another tip: Certain programs can't be run from a windowed command line. If you need to switch to a full screen temporarily, you can select Settings from the DOS window's Control menu (in the upper-left corner) and choose Window under Display Options.

You can also press Alt+Enter to switch between a small window and a larger full-screen view. See Figure 4.6.

FIGURE 4.6

To temporarily change a DOS session to full-screen size, select Settings from the Control menu and change the Display Options setting to Full Screen or press Alt+Enter.

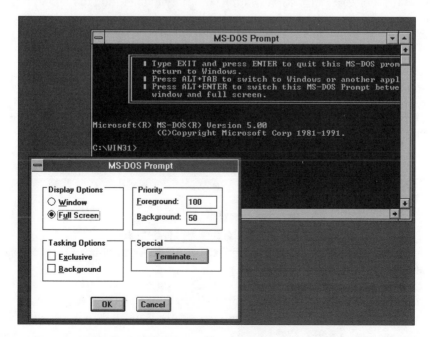

Disable DOS Prompt Instructions

Every time you select the DOS prompt icon to start a DOS session in Windows 3.1, you'll be given instructions on how to exit the DOS session and how to switch to other applications. To disable this message, edit your SYSTEM.INI. The line should read

```
DOSPromptExitInstruc=Off
```

Change the DOS Default Directory

Here's a case where Windows 3.1 is a big improvement over 3.0. When you start a DOS session from Windows 3.0, you end up in the WINDOWS directory by default. To specify a different working directory, highlight the DOS icon in Program Manager and choose Properties from the File menu. The Command Line text box will contain the DOS executable filename COMMAND.COM. The path, including the name of your DOS directory, may also be there. Change the path to include the directory you want DOS to start up in. For example, if the Command Line box reads C:\DOS\COMMAND.COM or simply COMMAND.COM, change it to read

```
C:\DATA\COMMAND.COM
```

if you want DOS to start in the DATA subdirectory. For this trick to work, the working directory you specify must be included in your DOS PATH statement.

In Windows 3.1 this is even easier to do. You can specify a working directory for your DOS session (or for any application) by highlighting the DOS prompt icon, choosing Properties from the File menu, and specifying the Working Directory in the Program Item Properties dialog box that appears.

Expand the DOS Environment

For a DOS application running in 386 Enhanced mode, the environment space available in a DOS session is much less than that set in your CONFIG.SYS file. To have access to the full environment, edit the application's PIF file to launch DOS, specifying the application's executable file and your standard DOS environment as optional parameters. For example, to run Procomm Plus with a DOS environment of 1,024 bytes, the first four lines of the PIF would read like those in Figure 4.7.

Copying and Pasting between DOS and Windows

You can copy and paste data between DOS and Windows applications in Real or Standard mode, but doing so can be a tedious process because you're restricted to copying a full screen at a time from the DOS applications. Windows' 386 Enhanced mode, on the other hand, allows DOS applications to run in resizable, movable windows, so you can copy and paste only as much data as you need.

FIGURE 4.7

This PIF increases the DOS environment from the default set in the CONFIG.SYS file to 1,024 bytes.

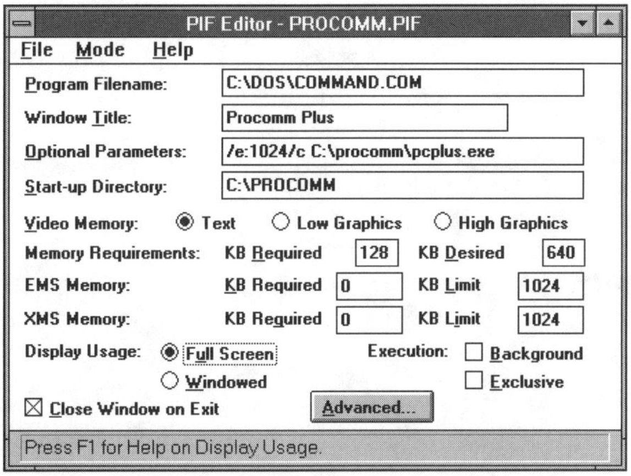

```
─                    PIF Editor - PROCOMM.PIF                  ▼ ▲
 File  Mode  Help

 Program Filename:      C:\DOS\COMMAND.COM
 Window Title:          Procomm Plus
 Optional Parameters:   /e:1024/c C:\procomm\pcplus.exe
 Start-up Directory:    C:\PROCOMM

 Video Memory:      ● Text    ○ Low Graphics    ○ High Graphics
 Memory Requirements:   KB Required   128    KB Desired    640
 EMS Memory:            KB Required   0      KB Limit      1024
 XMS Memory:            KB Required   0      KB Limit      1024
 Display Usage: ● Full Screen        Execution:  ☐ Background
                ○ Windowed                       ☐ Exclusive
 ☒ Close Window on Exit       Advanced...

 Press F1 for Help on Display Usage.
```

Use the following tips for easy cut-and-paste operations, no matter what Windows mode you're working in.

Copy and Paste Text from Full-Screen DOS Applications

The full-screen presentation of DOS programs in Real or Standard mode means that the only amount of data that the Windows Copy command and Clipboard will understand is "all of it." To copy data from a full DOS screen and paste it into a Windows application, press the PrtSc key; this copies the entire DOS screen to the Windows Clipboard. Then switch to the desired Windows program and select Paste from its Edit menu to insert the data from the Clipboard. You might need to clean up the pasted screen by cutting material you didn't really want, such as the menu bar, status line, and Ready indicator from a Lotus 1-2-3 screen.

Copy and Paste Text in Standard Mode

Pasting text from a Windows application to a full-screen DOS application (in Real or Standard mode) is more complicated, and you can't transfer graphics this way. First, place the cursor at the point in the DOS document where you want to paste text. Then use Alt+Tab or Alt+Esc to switch to your Windows application and select and copy the data. Your DOS document will be iconized on the Windows desktop at this point—click on its icon once to activate its Control menu. Choose Paste, and Windows will paste the text at the cursor location in your DOS file.

Copy and Paste in 386 Enhanced Mode

When your DOS application is running in a window (that is, when you're working in 386 Enhanced mode), the copy and paste capabilities work much as they do in a Windows application. Select Edit, Mark from the DOS program's Control menu. See Figure 4.8. (To get to the Control menu, click once on the box in the upper-left corner.) Then, use your mouse to select the range of data you want to copy. Next, select Edit, Copy from the DOS program's Control menu. To paste the selected data into a DOS file, place the cursor at the desired location in that file and use Edit, Paste from the DOS application's Control menu or Paste from any Windows program's Edit menu.

FIGURE 4.8

Select text to be copied from a windowed DOS application to the Windows Clipboard by selecting Edit, Mark from the application's Control menu.

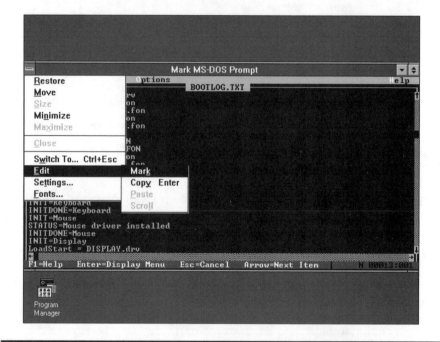

Copy DOS Graphics to Windows via the Clipboard

While running a DOS application in Windows 386 Enhanced mode, you can copy DOS graphics to the Windows Clipboard by pressing the PrtSc key. This copies a bitmap of the DOS screen to the Clipboard. From there you can paste it into Paintbrush or another Windows application and save it. For a windowed DOS application you can copy the entire active window by pressing Alt+PrtSc.

To copy only part of a DOS screen, also run the application in a window. From the Control menu (click once on the box in the upper-left corner of the window), select Edit and choose Mark. With the mouse, select the part of the screen you want to copy. Then choose Edit, Copy from the Control menu.

Use the Clipboard to Send ASCII Files in DOS Communications Programs

You probably still use your DOS communications program even though you've switched to Windows: Why rewrite your custom log-on scripts? But the Windows Clipboard can eliminate your having to save Windows word processing files as "Text Only" before sending them via ASCII-based E-mail. Launch the Windows PIF Editor and load the PIF for your DOS communications program. Select Windowed as the Display Usage option, and then click the Advanced command button and turn on the Allow Fast Paste check box near the bottom of the dialog box. Save your changes to the PIF.

Your DOS communications program will now appear in a resizable window when you launch it. To send a message or document composed on your word processor, copy the message to the Clipboard. Then switch to your communications program, click on its Control menu (in the upper-left corner), and select Edit, Paste. Your message will be entered, with no intermediate text file required.

Tips for Working in DOS Programs Running under Windows

DOS has driven a decade of users mad by being weak and unpredictable, but it has given a generation of users great joy by being flexible. So it is with DOS under Windows. We could offer as many tips for handling DOS in the Windows world as we could for handling DOS on its own. DOS longs to be experimented with. Since we can't run on forever about this subject, however, here is a handful of tips that we thought particularly useful or interesting.

Change Fonts and Font Sizes for DOS Applications in Windows 3.1

Make font sizes larger in windowed DOS applications to make text easier to read, or make the font size smaller to get more text into view at one time. While you're in a DOS application window, click once on the Control menu box in the upper-left corner and select Fonts from the drop-down Control menu. You'll see a menu of screen fonts and sizes that will work in a character-mode DOS screen. (See Figure 4.9.) Unlike the graphical Windows environment, DOS supports few font options. If you have the Save Settings box checked when you exit Windows, the font you choose will be your new default for DOS applications.

Launch a Batch File from Windows and End in DOS

When you run a batch file from Windows (either from a PIF, from the File menu's Run command, or from a program item for a .BAT file), you'll end up back in Windows once the batch file has executed. To remain in DOS instead, make COMMAND.COM the last line of your batch file for starting a new DOS session. From the DOS prompt, type **exit** to return to Windows.

FIGURE 4.9

Use a smaller or larger font for windowed DOS applications by changing the setting accessed through the Control menu box in the DOS application's window.

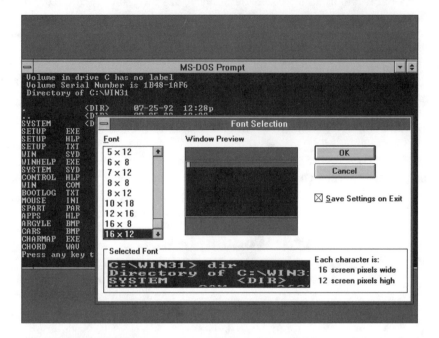

Unzip Files in Windows with Drag and Drop

Follow these steps to unzip files that you've downloaded with your Windows communication program without going into DOS:

1. Create a separate directory for this purpose and make sure that PKUN-ZIP.EXE is in it.

2. Download your zipped files into this directory or move them into it after you're off-line.

3. Go into File Manager and drag the zipped file onto the filename PKUNZIP.EXE.

4. A dialog box will ask "Are you sure you want to start PKUNZIP.EXE using *filename*.ZIP as the initial file?" Choose Yes.

5. Windows starts a DOS session to expand the files and returns to the File Manager when it's all done.

Turn Your Favorite Batch Files into Windows Icons

Experienced Windows users have probably passed this stage already, but those who've recently switched to Windows from plain old DOS may still be exiting

Windows, opening a DOS window, or slogging through directories with the File Manager to use the batch files they once started with a few simple keystrokes. Don't.

You can run your old batch file simply by clicking on an icon. If you have a 386 machine or better and run Windows in 386 Enhanced mode, you'll get a bonus when you run batch files because Windows can multitask DOS programs. This means that the batch file can accomplish work in the background, performing hard-disk backups and the like as you continue your other tasks.

To create an icon that runs a batch file, use the PIF Editor to make a PIF that tells Windows how to run DOS applications. Enter the full path and name of the batch file, as well as a Window Title. If your batch file needs parameters, enter them in the Optional Parameters box. Also enter a Start-up Directory name if a program invoked by your batch file must be started in a particular directory. See Figure 4.10.

FIGURE 4.10

Create an icon that launches a batch file by constructing a PIF for it that contains the proper settings for running the file.

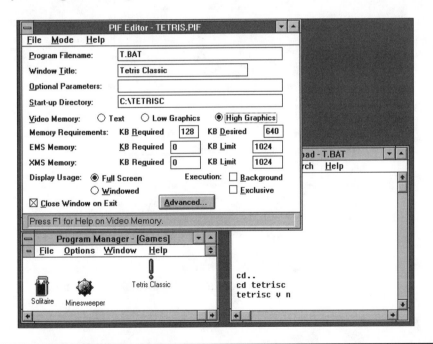

In many cases, you won't need to touch the other options because they're already set for a generic DOS program, but it's a good idea to look through them just in case. For instance, in Standard mode, if the batch file runs any graphics programs, select the radio button that says Graphics/Multiple Text. Likewise, in either mode, if you run any program that needs more than the default amount of

RAM (128K), tell Windows to allocate more RAM by changing the number in the Memory Requirements text box. If you're running Windows in 386 Enhanced mode, you can choose whether the batch file runs full-screen or in a window.

Now that you have a PIF for your batch file, add it to your desktop as an icon: Select New from the File menu, specify Program Item, and enter the description you wish to appear under the batch file's icon (if you enter nothing, the name of the batch file, sans extension, is used to label the icon). Then, in the Command Line text box, enter the name of the PIF (for example, BATCH.PIF). Finally, click on the Change Icon button and browse through the available icons using the View Next button. When you find one you like, click on OK.

That's all there is to it. Now you can run your batch file simply by double-clicking on its icon.

DOS Commands to Avoid

APPEND, ASSIGN, SUBST, and JOIN are DOS commands that you should avoid when running DOS under Windows. They're likely to cause problems because Windows gets confused as to which drives and files are which and where they are. APPEND tells DOS where to look for data files. ASSIGN refers requests for one disk drive to another. JOIN allows one entire drive to be treated as a subdirectory of a separate drive. SUBST (substitute) lets you assign a drive letter to a subdirectory. Windows 3.1 Setup scans your CONFIG.SYS and AUTOEXEC.BAT files for any of these commands and warns you about using them, but if you install them after your initial setup, Windows does not warn you of any danger in using them.

When you're in a DOS session, avoid running CHKDSK/F, FDISK, RECOVER, SELECT, FORMAT C: (or any other drive letter), UNDELETE, or other commands that reorganize a hard disk.

Don't Use the MS-DOS Task Swapper

If you're running Windows, avoid the DOS Task Swapper. The Windows Task List will do the same thing without costing you more conventional memory. Better yet, use Alt+Tab to navigate from task to task.

Use DOS 5.0's Built-in Help System

If you're in a DOS session and you forget the syntax of a DOS command, type

```
HELP command name
```

or

```
command name /?
```

and DOS will provide a description of the command, the proper syntax, and the optional switches available.

Three TSR Rules for DOS Applications

To avoid unnecessary hassles with memory-resident DOS programs, follow these rules:

- If you have a TSR (memory-resident program) that doesn't need to interact with other applications, run it as you would any other DOS application under Windows.

- If you have a TSR that's required by all DOS programs, load it before you start Windows.

- If you have a TSR that's required by all Windows applications and you're running in 386 Enhanced mode, load the TSR using a batch file called WINSTART.BAT (stored in your Windows subdirectory). This way, the TSR will be loaded and available when Windows starts or your AUTOEXEC.BAT file loads it, but it won't take memory away from your DOS programs.

Run Local TSRs

To have access to TSR programs in each DOS session that you run under Windows 3.1, you have to edit the SYSTEM.INI file. In the [NonWindowsApp] section, look for the line LocalTSRs=. You may not already have this line in the file. If you don't, add it to the [NonWindowsApp] section, and after the equal sign add the names of the TSRs you want available during every DOS session, separating each name with a space. Before adding a TSR to the list, you should make sure that it has no problems running under Windows.

If you don't want to edit your SYSTEM.INI file, or if you're running Windows 3.0, you can create a batch file that launches all of your TSRs in a single DOS session. Create the batch file with Notepad and then create a PIF for it. Make sure to include the setting Allow Close When Active in the PIF. This will let you exit from the DOS session but leave the TSRs loaded into memory.

Start DOS Applications with Graphic Logo Full-Screened

Many DOS applications have graphical startup or logo screens, although the application itself may be text-based. These programs, including Lotus 1-2-3, cannot be started in a window in 386 Enhanced mode. The best solution is to start the application at full-screen size (check Full Screen in the application's PIF) and then press Alt+Enter to switch to a window.

Another possibility is to check the DOS program's documentation for parameters that will start the application without displaying the graphics screen.

Tab Through Applications from a Full-Screen DOS Application

When switching out of a DOS program running in full-screen mode, hold down the Alt key and press Tab successively—a title bar at the top of a blank screen will cycle through the names of all applications to which you can switch. This method is quicker than using Alt+Esc, which switches entire windows, loading complete programs as you cycle through applications. It's also faster than pressing Ctrl+Esc, which will switch you to the Windows desktop and call up the Task List.

Three Ways to Speed Up Printing for DOS Applications

There are three things you can do to speed printing from DOS applications running under Windows:

- Don't use Print Manager (a good general rule for DOS apps).

- If you're running in 386 Enhanced mode, make sure that the PIF setting has your DOS application running in Exclusive mode. This will force Windows to allocate the maximum available resources to the DOS print job. If you choose to do this, however, don't print if something is actively running in the background (such as a communications download), because background processing will come to almost a complete stop.

- Load Windows with the /S parameter at the DOS command line to start Windows in Standard mode. You won't be able to multitask your DOS applications, but printing from them should go faster.

Assign Hotkeys to Your DOS Applications

Windows 3.1 allows you to assign hotkeys to your DOS applications, allowing for quick task switching.

In each program's PIF, go to the Advanced Options dialog box and find the last option, Application Shortcut Key. Click on this box and a cursor will appear. Press the key combination that you want to assign to the application. The keystrokes are recorded and appear in the box. Your combinations can include the Ctrl, Alt, and Shift keys. Make the hotkeys easy to remember—use the first letter of the application's name if possible.

When you want to assign a new hotkey to the application, clear away the previous one by placing the cursor in the Application Shortcut Key box and pressing Ctrl+Shift+Backspace.

Easy-to-Remember Hotkeys

If you think you'll forget the hotkeys that you've assigned to DOS applications, you can jog your memory every time you launch the application by annotating the application's icon title with the hotkey combination. To do so, highlight the program's icon in Program Manager, select Properties from the File menu, and in the Description text box, type the name of the hotkey after the program name—for example, type **Excel_Alt+Ctrl+E**. See Figure 4.11. In Windows 3.1, icon titles automatically wrap to the next line, so add blank spaces until the hot-key combo appears in the line beneath the actual description.

Windows 3.1's ability to wrap icon titles provides a convenient way for noting an application's shortcut key below its title.

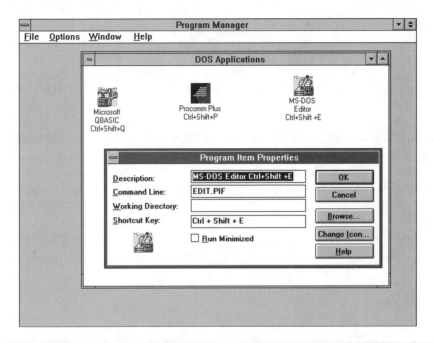

Run DOS Programs in the Foreground

For better overall performance when running DOS applications in 386 En-hanced mode, try running them in the foreground only. To do this, go to the Ex-ecution section of the program's PIF and make sure that the Background box is not checked. If you leave this option unchecked, the application will stop what it's doing when you switch to another task. However, if you want the DOS ap-plication to calculate data or print documents while you're doing something else, the Background box should be checked.

If you'll be running DOS applications in the background and want to exper-iment with the PIF's background and foreground settings, click on the Ad-vanced command button in the PIF Editor and refer to the Multitasking Options at the top of the dialog box. Try increasing or decreasing the values for Back-ground Priority and Foreground Priority by small increments (say 10) at a time.

Stop Update Messages to File Manager

Set FileSysChange=no in the [386Enh] section of SYSTEM.INI to avoid send-ing update messages to File Manager from non-Windows applications. Turning this setting off prevents File Manager from receiving updates every time a DOS application creates, renames, or deletes a file. When this setting is on, system performance often suffers.

Switch between DOS and Windows Applications with the Task List

Windows 3.0 lets you switch easily between standard DOS and Windows applications during a multitasking session. When you are working in a DOS program loaded from Windows, pressing Ctrl+Esc temporarily exits that program and displays the Windows Task List, from which you can select the Windows application you want. When it's time to switch back to your DOS application, simply click on the DOS icon that Windows created for that program when you pressed Ctrl+Esc.

Exit DOS Sessions before Powering Down Your Computer

Never shut off your system while still in a DOS session—you may cause file damage. Always exit the DOS session and return to Windows (by typing **exit** at the DOS prompt), and then exit the Windows session.

Create a DOS Prompt to Remind You that You're in Windows

Some programs, such as Windows 3.0 and XyWrite III Plus, let you temporarily exit, or shell, to DOS without reminding you that you've done so. In such cases, it's easy to forget that the program is still loaded and that there's little room to run another application. You may also forget how to return to the original application once you've shelled out to DOS.

To remedy this situation, modify the batch file that starts the DOS application. First, add a line that changes your prompt to a warning message. Position this line just above the command that invokes the application. After the line that runs the application, include a line that returns the prompt to its normal setting.

The following batch file, which starts Windows 3.1, illustrates this technique:

```
CD \WINDOWS
PROMPT=Type EXIT To Return To
Windows $_$P$G
WIN
PROMPT=$P$G
```

The second line changes the prompt and remains in effect while Windows is running. if you shell to DOS, you'll see the message "Type EXIT To Return To Windows" on one line and the current drive and directory on a second line. The last line resets the prompt when you exit Windows.

Create Fun Prompts

Personalize your DOS environment by setting a special DOS prompt when you're in Windows. Sure, you can add a message reminding you that you're in Windows (as you just learned), but how about something a little more fun? You can create the following prompts using the DOS device driver ANSI.SYS, which controls the display of colors and special graphics characters under DOS. To take advantage of these, the ANSI.SYS driver must be loaded before Windows is run. You can do this by adding the following line to your CONFIG.SYS:

```
DEVICE=C:\DOS\ANSI.SYS
```

Or, if you're using DOS 5.0, load it high:

```
DEVICEHIGH=C:\DOS\ANSI.SYS
```

With ANSI.SYS loaded, you can in turn load Windows from a batch file that sets up a customized DOS prompt at the same time.

All the prompts that follow use *metastrings,* special ANSI.SYS codes that direct various aspects of graphic display. By placing these metastrings in the proper order, you can create an amazing array of small graphic effects.

Combining the ANSI.SYS metastrings with the DOS PROMPT command and any desired text enables you to customize the way the DOS prompt appears in any DOS session. The form is

```
PROMPT text or metastrings
```

or

```
SET PROMPT = text or metastrings
```

By loading Windows from a batch file with the PROMPT command and a unique metastring, you can identify instantly when you are in a Windows DOS session in a graphical way that fits neatly with Windows' character.

In each of these sample ANSI-based prompts, the character # substitutes for a space, so that you can count precisely how many spaces to leave, a critical factor in metastrings. Type the characters on one command line, without a carriage return. See the following sections for details on how to generate graphics characters and colors in these prompts or when you're creating your own.

Bart Simpson

```
PROMPT=$e[1;33m|\/\/\/|$_|$e[6C|$_|###$e[;5;36m0#0$e[;1;33m)$_
C$e[6C_)$_#|#$e[;31m,_
_$e[1;33m|#Command#me,#dude!$_#|###/#$e[m#
```

Power User

```
PROMPT=$e[37;44mP##╔ = = = ╗
  ###$_O##║$e[31;46m█ $e[33;46m█ $e[36;46m█ $e[37;44m║###$_W##╚ ■
  ■ ■ ╝ $_E╔ = = = = = = = = ╗ #$_R╚ = #USER#╚ = $e[36m$g$p$g#
```

See Figure 4.12.

FIGURE 4.12

This Power User prompt is a fun reminder that you're in a DOS session under Windows, not in DOS itself; use one of the many prompts provided in this chapter or create your own with ANSI.SYS to personalize your own DOS sessions.

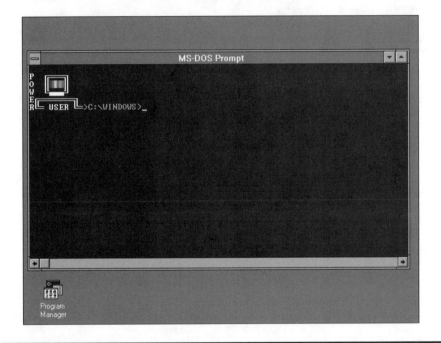

Biplane

```
PROMPT=$e[8C_│_$_= = ╤ = = ╤ = =
  $e[5;31m*$e[0;33m/$e[31;5m*$e[0m= = ╤ = = ╤ = = $_= = # = =
  # = = \#/= = # = = # = = $_$e[7C║ ─ $e[0;33m╗ $e[0m─ ╢ $e[0m#
```

Train

```
PROMPT=$e[44;37;5m$e[16C*$e[0;44;1;31m$_█ █ █ = $e[36m█ █ █ =
  $e[33m█ █ █ = $e[35m█ █ █ ■ █
  $_$e[32;5m° #° #° #° #° #° #° ###° $e[0;1;44;37m$e[1A$p$g#
```

See Figure 4.13.

FIGURE 4.13

Use this colorful train prompt to remind you that you're in a DOS session.

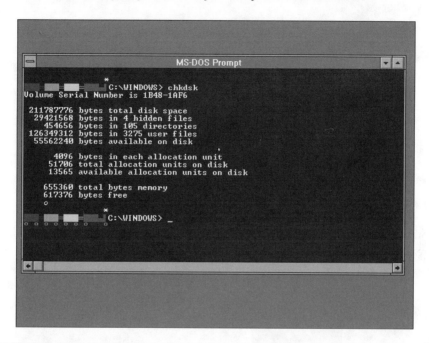

Happy Birthday

```
PROMPT=$e[5;33;40m####******$_$e[0m$e[1;37m####    IIIIII$_$e[33m#
##  IIIIIIIII  $_###  IIIIIIIIII
$_$_$d$_$e[35mHAPPY#BIRTHDAY!###$e[36m$p$g#
```

Windows Rules

```
PROMPT=$e[44;37m#Windows#$e[1B$e[9D■ ■ ■ ■ ■ ■ ■ ■ ■
$e[1B$e[9D■ ■ ■ ■ ■ ■  $e[41m##Rules##  $e[1B$e[9D■ ■ ■ ■ ■
■ ■ ■  $e[1B$e[9D■ ■ ■ ■ ■ ■ ■ ■ ■ ■  $e[40m#$p$g#
```

See Figure 4.14.

Merry Christmas

```
PROMPT=$e[1;5;37m##*$_$e[0;32;40m##■$_#$e[1;31;42m#♪#$_$e[33;
42m#°#o#$e[30;40m$e[K$_##■$_$e[31m#MERRY$_CHRISTMAS!$_$_$e[37
m$p$g#
```

With this special prompt there's no mistaking how you feel about being a Windows power user.

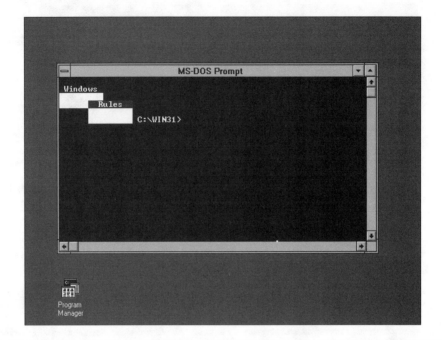

IBM Logo

```
PROMPT=$e[1;34m■ ■ #■■■■■ ■ #■■■ ###■■ ■
#(TM)$_#■###■■■ ■ ###■■■#■#$_#■###■■ ■ ■ ##■##■##$_■
■■ #■■■■■■ ##■■■ #####■■ ■ $e[0m$_$D$_$_$p$g#
```

The Fifth Day of the Week

```
PROMPT=$e[30;47m#### ε###$e[0m$_$e[30;47m########$e[0m$_$e[5;37
;44m#α###α##$e[0m$_$e[5;37;44m###α####$e[0m#$p$g#
```

Help

```
PROMPT=$e[2C┌ = = = = ┐ $_$e[2C‖$e[5;31;42mHELP$e[0m‖$_$e[2C└
= = = = ┘ $_###■■ ■ ■ ■ $_$e[5;31;47m#■#$e[0m$e[32;47m■ ■
#$e[30m├ = ┤ #$e[0m#$p$g#
```

Rice Owls

```
PROMPT=$e[34;1m  $e[9C $_#■ ■ ■ ■ ■ ■ ■ ■ ■ $_#┌■ ¬ ■ ■ ■ ┌ ■
¬ $_# └ # ┘ ■■■ └ # ┘
$_$e[5C■$_$e[37;5m##R#I#C#E$_##O#W#L#S####$e[0m$p$g#
```

ANSI.SYS Metastrings and Graphic Characters

The following tables (Tables 4.1, 4.2, 4.3, and 4.4) list ANSI.SYS metastrings and graphics characters that you can use if you want to try to grow your own Windows DOS prompt. Note that ANSI settings are case-sensitive. Table 4.1 lists ANSI metastrings that you can use when you are devising customized prompts.

TABLE 4.1

ANSI Metastrings to Incorporate into Your Customized Prompts

What Appears in the Prompt	What You Enter
Current time	$t
Current date	$d
Current drive	$n
Current drive and path	$p
Moves cursor to next line (underline character)	$_
I	$b
>	$g
<	$l
Backspaces one character	$h
=	$q

ANSI Color Settings

Use ANSI color metastrings to change your display attributes, such as foreground or background color. The proper syntax is

```
$e[xx;xx;...m
```

where xx is the number for the color attribute (from Table 4.2), and semicolons separate each number. Note that the letter "m" must end the metastring. Table 4.3 lists the display attributes you can use in ANSI metastrings; Table 4.4 lists the ANSI metastrings for cursor positioning.

TABLE 4.2

Color Attributes for Use in ANSI Metastrings

Color	Foreground	Background
Black	30	40
Red	31	41
Green	32	42

TABLE 4.2

Color Attributes for Use in ANSI Metastrings (Continued)

Color	Foreground	Background
Yellow	33	43
Blue	34	44
Magenta	35	45
Cyan	36	46
White	37	47

TABLE 4.3

Display Attributes for Use in ANSI Metastrings

Attribute	Meaning
0	Normal
1	Highlight
4	Underline
5	Blink
7	Inverse

TABLE 4.4

ANSI Metastrings for Cursor Positioning[*]

Action	What You Enter
Moves cursor up	$e[rA
Moves cursor down	$e[rB
Moves cursor right	$e[cC
Moves cursor left	$e[cD
Moves cursor to precise position	$e[r;cf or $e[r;cH
Moves cursor to upper-left corner	$e[H
Clears screen and leaves cursor in upper-left corner	$e[2J
Erases current line from cursor to end of line	$e[K
Records cursor's position	$e[s
Moves cursor to recorded position	$e[u

[*] r = number of rows and c = number of columns.

Graphics Characters

ANSI.SYS can also access the graphics characters at the high end of the ASCII character set (see Table 4.5). These include lines, simple geometric shapes, scientific symbols, and the like. They are listed by number, and can be found in the technical reference manuals for most PCs or in any listing of the ASCII character set, which is the standard alphabet PCs use. To enter any ASCII graphics character into your prompt, hold down the Alt key and then type the character's number using the numeric keypad only (not the numbers across the top of the keyboard). Then release the Alt key. The character should appear.

TABLE 4.5

Use the Numeric Keypad on Your Keyboard to Generate Graphic Characters in Your Fun Prompts

Character Generated	ASCII Code	Character Generated	ASCII Code	Character Generated	ASCII Code
─	196	▓	177	╫	215
┐	191	═	205	╨	208
┌	218	╗	187	╕	184
└	192	╔	201	╒	213
┘	217	╚	200	╘	212
├	195	╝	188	╛	189
┤	180	╠	204	╞	198
┼	197	╣	185	╡	181
│	179	╬	206	╪	216z
┬	194	║	186	╤	209
┴	193	╦	203	╧	207
┌	169	╩	202	∈	238
┐	170	╥	183	∝	224
■	223	╤	214	°	248
▄	220	╙	211	⌡	245
▌	221	╜	189	⌠	244
▐	222	╟	199		
█	219	╢	182		

5 Maximizing Program Manager and Windows Screen Elements

CONVENTIONAL WISDOM HOLDS THAT THE GREAT BENEFIT OF WINDOWS IS graphics. Certainly, Windows is a superb graphics computing environment—a much friendlier, more flexible way to handle computing chores than DOS. But there have been other graphics environments over the years, and none has taken off like Windows.

What really sets Windows apart is its customizability. Great lip service has been paid over the last decade to how valuable PCs are as competitive weapons. But how much advantage could genuinely be attained when all PCs ran the same processor, the same DOS, and the same applications running in precisely the same manner? Nada.

Windows brings the personal back to PC. Because virtually every aspect of Windows can be altered to suit the user's taste—from colors and screen display to intricate arrangements of applications—this is the first environment that actually makes it possible for one PC to run smarter than another. A sophisticated user does not have to become a professional programmer to make Windows utterly unique.

In this chapter, we'll explore the myriad ways you can tinker with the already excellent standard approaches Windows offers—so that you can set off on the exciting journey of making your PC absolutely your own personal property.

Most Windows users will be content with the Windows shell, Program Manager, which is the focus of most of this chapter. However, we should note that third-party applications can serve you just as well or better. If you aren't satisfied with Program Manager, consider alternatives such as the Norton Desktop, hDC's Power Launcher, the uniquely object-oriented WinTools (it's virtually menu-free), or New Wave, from Hewlett-Packard. We examine several of these alternatives in Part 2.

Building and Managing Program Groups

The key to understanding the Program Manager, and the place where Windows most stands apart from all other graphic environments (including the Macintosh) is in its program groups. A program group is an array of icons within a single on-screen window. These icons represent applications. Windows provides several program groups upon startup, including the Main and Startup groups. You can create your own program groups as well.

The icons in a Windows program group are defined as program items: These are Windows-defined objects that contain enough information to tell Windows how to find and launch an application and, optionally, load a particular file. One program item might be labeled Excel and another, with an identical icon, might be labeled First-Quarter Sales. Rather than booting Excel and then calling the file, you can click on the First-Quarter Sales icon to launch the application and load the file in one step.

What's most unique about Windows program groups and the items they contain is that they are not directly tied to directories and other aspects of the traditional file system. DOS applications and Windows applications can reside side by side in a program group. A single application can appear in as many program groups as you wish, even if it resides just once on the hard drive.

Because of this flexibility, you can organize Windows, through the program groups, to reflect any work style you choose. You can group applications by time of day, operating system, function, or letter of the alphabet. And then, you can arrange your display screen to emphasize what you wish and to hide what you use less often.

Program groups provide a new ultimate in user control of the display of application programs.

Shortcuts for Program Group Basics

We won't spend much time in this section on instruction in the absolute basics of creating program groups and manipulating program group windows here. Windows documentation and on-line help handles that task admirably. Our principal focus is on clever ways experienced users have found of speeding tasks. These first tips deal with improving program groups beyond the basics.

Start a Program Group   The only way to start a new program group is from the Program Manager's File menu. Click on New, and a dialog box with two option buttons will appear: Program Group and Program Item. Click on Program Group, and then click on OK. A dialog box will appear, asking for two pieces of information. The Description is the name you'll use to refer to the new group from within Windows—the name that the Program Manager will display whenever the group or its icon is on the screen. The Group File, which is the file where information about the group is stored, can be any DOS filename you want; Windows defaults to a .GRP filename extension and automatically assigns it a DOS filename based on your description if you fail to select an alternative. Click on OK and you'll see a blank window titled with your program group's name.

Add a Program Item to a Group   Once you've created a group, you can fill it with program items in any one of three ways: You can use the Program Manager's File menu, or you can copy or move the program's icon from another program group by dragging it with the mouse.

To use the File menu, select New, make sure Program Item is checked, and click on OK. The Program Item Properties dialog box that comes up at this point differs slightly from the one presented when you create a new program group. The Description becomes Windows' name for the program, while the Command Line is the name of the executable file, including extension and subdirectory, of the application you're putting into the group. If you're not sure of your program's exact name or location, click on the Browse button. Up pops a window containing two list boxes, one for files and one for directories. Use them to find the file-name you seek; then double-click on it. Program Manager will insert the path and filename in the Command Line box. The program you install need not be a Windows program. Program Manager can launch standard DOS applications as well, which should help to ease your transition to the Windows environment.

When you want to move or copy a program item from one group to another, start by opening both group windows. If the windows overlap on the screen, use the Tile command in Program Manager's Window menu to place them side by side. To move the program item, drag its icon from one window to the other by placing the icon on it, then holding down the left mouse button while moving the mouse. If you want to copy it instead, drag the icon while holding down the Ctrl key. You can also copy a program item to the same group if you want to have more than one copy in that group. You might do this, for instance, if you want to load spreadsheets with different documents upon start-up for different kinds of budgeting.

Delete a Program Item from a Group   To delete a program item from a group, click on the program item's icon and then either choose Delete from the Program Manager's File menu or press the Delete key on your keyboard. The same technique works for a program group, but you must "iconize" the group first, by clicking on the Minimize button in the window's upper-right corner. (This isn't necessary if the program group is empty.)

Create Program Groups for Specific Tasks   Don't confine yourself to Windows' default program groups and icons. Set up new groups that fit the way you work. For example, if you start a new project that will be taking up most of your time, you can create a program group just for that task. In the group, place icons representing the applications that you'll be using. If you are working on a presentation for a new client, your group might be named "Acme Proposal." The custom icons you might have in the group would be your presentation program, Persuasion, with the data file of the current presentation you are working on; your word processor, Word for Windows, with the draft proposal loaded; your spreadsheet, Lotus 1-2-3 for Windows, with the most recent sales figures; and the Notepad text editor, with a to-do list (see Figure 5.1). Once you've copied the original program icons into the new group, edit them to use custom icons and load the actual files you'll be using for the project.

To do this, select the icon and choose File, Properties. You can change the name of the application to reflect what it will actually be used for. For example, you could rename the Word for Windows icon Draft—Winword and the Lotus 1-2-3 icon The Numbers—Lotus 123/W. To change the icons, click on Properties in the File menu. Then choose Change Icon, Browse, select an icon source file, such as MORICONS.DLL, and click on OK. You'll be presented with a collection of icons to choose from. (See "Modify Program Item Properties" and "Iconography and Creative Dragging" later in this chapter for more on icon changing.) You'll also want to edit the application's command line to load the specific files you'll be using. To do so, specify the name of the file and its path on the command line. For example, to load the Acme Proposal in Word for Windows, you would use a command line like this:

```
C:\PROPOSAL\ACME.DOC
```

The file ACME.DOC will automatically load when you click on the icon to start Word for Windows.

FIGURE 5.1

Create custom program groups based upon your current projects with custom icons that load your corresponding data files, not just the application.

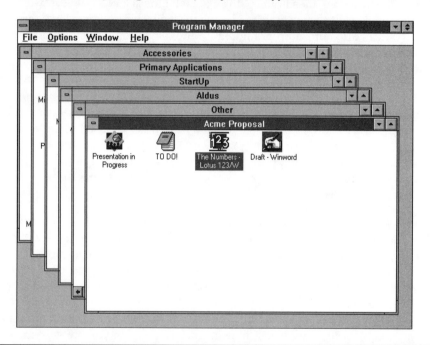

You can start any application's data file from Program Manager, as long as the file is associated with that particular application. The association is based on the data file's extension. For example, if the Acme proposal had an extension not recognized by Windows, such as .PRO, Program Manager would not recognize the file as belonging to Word for Windows. You'll know when this is the case because a DOS icon instead of the regular application icon will appear once you have finished editing the icon's properties.

To remedy the situation, open File Manager and locate the file, ACME-.PRO. From the File menu, choose Associate, and in the dialog box that appears enter the name of the executable file for the application that you want to run with the file loaded. In this case, you would specify WINWORD.EXE. Now when you go back to the ACME.PRO icon in Windows, you can bring up the Properties dialog box again, and then close it. The Word for Windows icon will reappear.

When you are done working on the Acme proposal, you can delete the Acme Proposal group that you created, or simply edit it to reflect the next task.

Streamline Program Groups   Don't clutter program groups with more icons than you can view in a window. It doesn't do you any good to have to navigate through a Program Group window to find your important applications. To keep things tidy, remove those accessories and applications that you seldom use and put them in group that remains minimized. On the rare occasions that you need these items, you can simply open the minimized group to get at them. Putting them out of sight makes for a neater desktop, and allows you to find what you need more quickly.

Start the Day with a Clean Slate   To make sure that your desktop is always in the same condition—with your frequently used applications right where you need them and your seldom used ones out of sight—make sure that the Save Settings option is not selected. In Windows 3.0, the Save Settings option appears when you exit Windows; in Windows 3.1, it is located on the Options menu, where it is called Save Settings on Exit. Use Save Settings when you want to change your program group setup, but deactivate it after the change takes effect. If the Save Settings option is always selected, your desktop will start out the way it looked when you ended your last Windows session.

Toward a Tidier Desktop   Windows' great ability to open lots of files at once is also its greatest trap. How are you going to find anything with 17 layers of windows to sort through?

Two of the choices on Program Manager's Options menu look complicated at first glance, but they are really handy housekeeping tools for tidying your desktop with a keystroke. Both Auto Arrange and Minimize on Use operate only when you click on them to put a check mark beside them.

Auto Arrange prevents your icons from obscuring other icons on the screen. It keeps the Program Item icons in neat rows and columns. Even if you move icons around in a window, if Auto Arrange is selected they will come up in neat rows the next time you open the Program Group.

Minimize on Use reduces the Program Manager to an icon whenever you run an application. This keeps the Program Manager screen and program group windows from distracting you while you work. You'll have to restore the Program Manager to its normal size when you quit the application, but if you tend to keep lots of different documents open, you're better off keeping your desktop uncluttered and making the extra effort to reopen Program Manager when you need it.

If you wish, you can also neaten your Windows screen by arranging your on-screen Windows. From the Program Manager's Windows menu, you can choose to cascade your program groups so that they overlap step-wise, or tile them so that they line up side by side without overlapping.

Modify Program Item Properties   There are three program item properties: Description, Command Line, and icon. You've already encountered the first two when adding a program item, and you can modify them anytime you want by using the Properties option on the Program Manager File menu. Just highlight the program icon and follow the same procedure you used when you first added the item.

If you've copied a program item into the same program group, chances are you want to modify it to load a different file. (See the section "Load a Data File from an Icon," later in this chapter.)

The other property you can modify is the program item's icon. Many Windows applications are shipped with more than one icon. And, if you'd prefer, you can appropriate an icon from another program and assign it to your program.

Especially handy sources for icons are PROGMAN.EXE, the Windows Program Manager, and CONTROL.EXE, the Windows Control Program. Nine nicely drawn icons are available from PROGMAN; 14 are available from CONTROL. Windows 3.1 also comes with the dynamic link library, MORICONS-.DLL, which provides many more icons to choose from. To find icons, use the Program Manager File menu. Click on Properties and then select the Change Icon command button from the Program Item Properties dialog box. You'll see the icons currently associated with the selected file. If you want to see more icons, type:

```
C:\WINDOWS\PROGRAM.EXE
```

in the File Name text box and press Enter. You'll see the icons from that file. You could also type MORICONS.DLL to see the icons in that file.

Spare icons are particularly useful if you're installing standard DOS applications, which have no icons of their own.

Point Browse in the Right Direction   When you use the Browse button in the Program Item Properties dialog box to locate the file you want to place in the Command Line text box, save time by pointing it in the right direction. If you specify a directory in the Working Directory text box before you press the Browse button you'll be taken directly to that directory. See Figure 5.2.

Program Group Strategies

There's more to making the most of Program Manager than just creating program groups. You must also make sure that Program Manager doesn't unduly drain Free System Resources (FSRs). A system resource is a morsel of information stored in a memory compartment allocated to USER.EXE, one of the three principal program modules that make up Windows. That memory region, USER.EXE's local heap, can be no larger than 64K, no matter how many memory chips and disk sectors your system possesses. Each time you open a window, a descriptor file for that window eats up precious resource space.

FIGURE 5.2

Point the Program Manager's Browse option in the right direction by entering the directory to be searched in the Working Directory box.

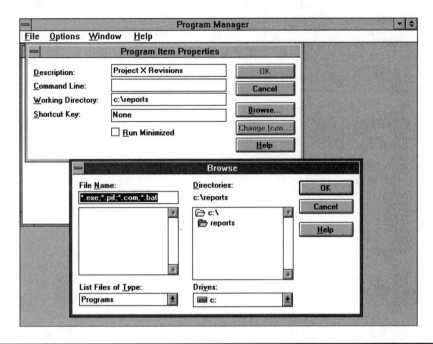

64K would seem to be an ample amount of space for your needs; after all, how many windows will you have open at one time? Unfortunately, however, the definition of a window includes all sorts of graphical objects as well. Dialog boxes and their associated lists, boxes, and buttons are windows. So are icons of all kinds. Other bits of data—information about menus, for example—also end up in the system resource space. Applications usually clean up after themselves when you close them. But on most systems, Program Manager is the one application that never closes, so it never releases its resource space. And you need Program Manager running, since its main business is to display windows in the form of program groups and icons—without it Windows isn't worth running. You must make sure Program Manager leaves enough Free System Resources for your other tasks.

Check the Status of Free System Resources   To check the status of your Free System Resources, open the Help menu in Program Manager and choose About Program Manager. You'll see the amount of memory you have available, and the amount of Free System Resources (expressed as a percentage). To see how much of your FSRs Program Manager alone is using, check About Program Manager when you start Windows, before you launch any programs or do other operations. Your system may run into trouble if FSRs get below 20 or 25 percent.

A Program Manager Diet   To keep the amount of Free System Resources that Program Manager uses to a minimum, do the following:

- Use the About Program Manager command (located on the Program Manager and File Manager Help menus) periodically. The dialog box that appears tells you how much memory and resource space is available. When that number drops below 25 percent, close some programs or documents immediately.

- Keep your Program Manager setup simple. Create one group with the program icons that you use every day; keep other group windows minimized. Icons don't consume resources until the group windows are opened, but once used, the space cannot be reclaimed.

- Launch programs without the use of icons by adding them to the Load= or Run= line of your WIN.INI file or by clicking on their filenames in File Manager. When you launch applications this way, you won't waste the system resources required for their icons and for the other icons located in the same program group.

- Watch out for "resource leakers." Certain programs (including early versions of PowerPoint and PackRat 3.0) do not return all of their resource space when you close the application. Repeatedly opening and closing such applications drains resource space. To check for resource leaks, use the About Program Manager option on Program Manager's Help menu. If your program "leaks," use it sparingly (and complain to the vendor).

- Consider replacing Program Manager with a shell that is less resource intensive.

Save Program Manager Settings without Actually Exiting   If you want to save changes to Program Manager without having to exit and restart Windows, here's a trick to make Windows save your changes. Start a DOS session, switch back to the Program Manager, and attempt to exit by pressing Alt+F4. Windows brings up the dialog box saying that you are exiting Windows (and asking whether changes will be saved). Select Save Changes and then click on OK. Windows attempts to exit and in doing so writes your Program Manager changes to the PROGMAN.INI file. However, when it realizes that you have a DOS session running, it displays a dialog box telling you that you can't exit while there's a DOS application running. You are still in Windows and can keep working along, while your changes have already been written to disk. When you really do exit, make sure the Save Settings option is turned off again. This approach works in both Windows 3.0 and 3.1.

Use the Shift Key to Save Changes   You can save your Program Manager configuration without exiting Windows 3.1 by simply holding down the Shift key while choosing Exit from the File menu. This obviates the need to use the Save Settings on Exit switch on the Options menu and makes saving much simpler and quicker. You may think nothing has happened, since no messages appear, but if you exit and reload Windows, you'll find that the settings have been saved.

Taming On-Screen Windows

Through Program Manager, Windows allows you to be logical in the organization of your applications and efficient in the use of your system; happily, it also allows you to fine-tune the way your PC environment looks. This sounds like a small thing, but it's not. We spend hours in front of our PCs, and yet we've been forced to stare at completely generic screens with no individuality, no style, no personality. No more. Now, you can make your PC wake up each day looking precisely as you wish. More comfortable computing could be the biggest productivity boon of them all!

Broader Borders   If you have a tough time sizing windows because you can't get ahold of their borders with your mouse, increase the border width. To do so, select Desktop from the Control Panel and locate the Sizing Grid box—it's in the lower-left corner of the Desktop dialog box. Increase the number of the Border Width setting (you can choose from 1 to 50) until the borders are large enough for you, and then click on OK.

Window Adjustments   If the Windows layout on your screen looks haphazard, it's easy to fix. Take advantage of Windows' Granularity setting to create an invisible grid to which your windows and icons will align. To adjust the granularity, double-click on the Control Panel's Desktop icon and locate the Granularity setting in the Sizing Grid box (in the lower-left corner of the Desktop dialog box). Click on the up or down arrow to increase or decrease the value in the Granularity text box (from 0 to 49). To see the effect, close the dialog box and move a window. If the granularity is a low value, the window will move in tiny increments. The higher the granularity, the larger the invisible grid that the window snaps to.

PROGMAN.INI: A Potent Tool

Windows uses a file called PROGMAN.INI to set up and manage program groups. As with WIN.INI and SYSTEM.INI (described in Chapter 2), intelligent use of PROGMAN.INI gives the sophisticated user precision control of the screen.

Use Multiple PROGMAN.INI Files   Suppose you sometimes run Windows with a specific set of applications in one mode, and distinct applications in another mode. For example, suppose you are running Windows 3.1 and prefer to run in Standard mode when you're using just Windows applications, but you like to use Enhanced mode for DOS sessions. In this situation, you can create separate PROGMAN.INI files that make the most of your system's resources. Doing this allows you to keep Program Manager uncluttered, while also cutting down on the amount of system resources required for maintaining groups you'll never use.

For example, to create a PROGMAN.INI file for use with DOS applications in 386 Enhanced mode, do the following:

1. In Program Manager, select New from the File menu, check the Program Group radio button, and click on OK. Call the group Enhanced Mode Applications. Click on OK and the group appears.

2. Next, create icons for each application you want included in the group by filling out the Program Item Properties dialog box for each. Alternatively, if icons for the programs already exist in different Program Manager groups, drag the icon from its old location to the newly created group. (See the section "Adding a Program to a Group" earlier in this chapter.)

3. Open the PROGMAN.INI file in Notepad or another text editor, and before you edit it, save it as PROGMAN.ENH (for Enhanced mode). Now find the [Groups] section and delete references to any program groups of applications that you'd never run in Enhanced mode. For example, if your DOS applications were in a group called Enhanced, the entries might look like this:

```
Group1=C:\WINDOWS\OTHER.GRP
Group2=C:\WINDOWS\MICROSOF.GRP
Group3=C:\ENHANCED.GRP
Group4=C:\WINDOWS\MAIN.GRP
```

Deleting the second line, which refers to the group titled Microsoft Applications (which contains only Windows Applications), will remove it from the Program Manager the next time you start up in 386 Enhanced mode, saving resources.

4. After making any changes, save PROGMAN.ENH and now reopen your original PROGMAN.INI file. This time, delete the line that refers to the Enhanced Mode Applications group. Save this edited version of the PROGMAN.INI file as PROGMAN.STD (for Standard mode).

5. Next, create a batch file that lets you run the correct version of PROGMAN.INI when you start Windows. Open a new file in any text editor and type the following lines for the file that will start Windows in Standard mode:

```
COPY C:\WINDOWS\PROGMAN.STD C:\WINDOWS\PROGMAN.INI
WIN /S
```

6. Save this file as WINS.BAT (for Windows, Standard mode).

7. Create another batch file named WINE.BAT (for Windows, Enhanced mode). The lines in that file look like this:

```
COPY C:\WINDOWS\PROGMAN.ENH C:\WINDOWS\PROGMAN.INI
WIN /3
```

8. Now you can type **Wins** to start Windows in Standard mode with your Windows applications available. To start Windows in Enhanced mode without your Microsoft Applications group, type **Wine**.

Restrict Your PROGMAN.INI   In Windows 3.1, the PROGMAN.INI file contains a new section that is intended for network administration, but it can help protect your system from unwanted (or accidental) changes. The [Restrictions] settings allow you to prohibit the Program Manager setup from being changed.

The two applicable entries are NoSaveSettings= and EditLevel=. A No-SaveSettings setting of 1 disables the Save Settings option on the Program Manager's Options menu. With this option, any changes made to the Program Manager's arrangement will not be preserved.

The EditLevel settings specify different levels of access to Program Manager commands. A setting of 1 prevents the creation, deletion, and renaming of program groups by removing the New, Move, Copy, and Delete commands from the Program Manager's File menu only when the Program group option is selected. A setting of 2 prevents the creation or deletion of both program groups and program items by removing the New, Move, Copy, and Delete commands from the Program Manager's File Menu altogether. A setting of 3, in addition to altering menus, prevents you from typing changes to the command lines for program items. A setting of 4 also prevents changes to the program item information. If you select this level, all of the Program Item Properties dialog box options will be dimmed.

To prevent any changes whatsoever to your Program Manager setup, add the [Restrictions] section to PROGMAN.INI (if it does not already exist). Open the file in a text editor, scroll to the end of the file, and add the following entries:

```
[Restrictions]
EditLevel=4
NoSaveSettings=1
```

Making the Most
of the Program Groups That Windows Provides

Windows establishes four program groups automatically at setup: Main, Accessories, Startup, and Games. Main contains the Control Panel, PIF Editor, and other operational programs; Accessories holds small applications that Windows provides (they are discussed in Chapter 6); Startup is empty, but it can be used as a location for applications you would like to run at Windows start-up.

Although the creation of these groups is automatic, they can be used wisely by the savvy user.

Tips for Control Panel Control

Aspects of the Main Program Group are covered in many places in this book. The PIF Editor is discussed in Chapter 4, the File Manager in Chapter 6. Many of the icons in the Control Panel are direct expressions of statements in the *.INI files covered in Chapter 2. Here, we will touch on aspects for controlling the Control Panel itself, then we'll move on to making the most of the Control Panel Desktop, which oversees the look and feel of the Windows screen environment.

Select Settings with Quick Keystrokes   You're probably used to starting Windows applications and accessories by double-clicking on their icons. While you will probably select Control Panel choices with the mouse too, this may not always be the quickest way. If you prefer using the keyboard to the mouse, or if you sometimes have difficulty locating just the right icon from the bunch, you'll want to use the Control Panel's Settings menu to launch the item that you want to use. To access the menu, press Alt+S, and then press one of the following letters that represents the desired Control Panel module:

C	Color
F	Fonts
O	Ports
M	Mouse
D	Desktop
K	Keyboard
P	Printers
I	International
T	Date/Time
N	Network
3	386 Enhanced Mode
R	Drivers
S	Sound

Start the Control Panel from Anywhere in Windows 3.1   When you decide that you suddenly need to change something in Windows, such as the desktop colors, the speed of your mouse, or the fonts that are installed, it isn't always easy getting to the Control Panel and its many icons. If you have several applications open, you may have to hunt around for the program group that contains the Control Panel icon, and then you have to locate the icon you need. But there is an easier way. You can directly access a Control Panel item by using the Run option on the Program Manager's File menu. For example, to open the Control Panel's Desktop icon, you would select Run from the Program Manager's File menu and then type **control desktop** in the Command Line text box, as shown in Figure 5.3. You can use this method for any of the Control Panel icons. Just specify its title after the CONTROL command.

FIGURE 5.3

Directly access Control Panel settings from Program Manager's Run dialog box by following the CONTROL command with the name of the icon to be launched.

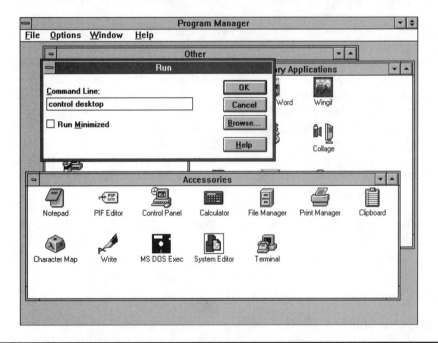

Keep Control Panel Icons Out of Sight in Windows 3.1   If you share your system with other users and don't want them to be able to tamper with your Windows setup, there is a way to keep Control Panel icons out of sight. You can selectively hide Control Panel icons by editing the CONTROL.INI file. To do so, open CONTROL.INI in a text editor such as Notepad and go to end of the file. Now create a new section called [Don't Load] where you list each icon that you want turned off. The setting will look like this:

```
[Don't Load]
Color=1
386 Enhanced=0
Drivers=1
```

Placing either the number 1 or 0 after the equals sign prevents the icon from showing up when the Control Panel loads.

Any options made unavailable this way also won't be able to be accessed via the Program Manager's Run command, as explained in the previous tip. They won't be available until you remove the line from the [Don't Load] section and restart Windows.

Sound Off   Even a jazzy sound assigned to the Windows warning beep can grow tiresome. To turn off this special sound or the regular old Windows warning beep, select the Control Panel's Sound icon, and uncheck the check box that says Warning Beep (Windows 3.0) or Enable System Sounds (Windows 3.1).

Device Contention and Problem Prevention   If you run Windows in Enhanced mode, you'll notice a 386 Enhanced icon in the Control Panel. The first setting in the 386 Enhanced dialog box is for Device Contention. This setting tells Windows whether it should monitor the use of your system's ports. In Windows 3.0 it handled both serial and parallel ports, while in Windows 3.1 it only monitors the serial ports. If a DOS application and a Windows application attempt to use a port at the same time, Windows can warn you of this potential problem. For example, if a Lotus 1-2-3 file and a Microsoft Word for Windows file attempted to print to COM1 at the same time, Windows would tell you to choose to print one document or the other first. To have Windows warn you of a potential conflict, select the Always Warn option button.

Redecorate Your Screen with Control Panel's Desktop

The decoration of the Windows screen is managed by a program within the Control Panel, the Windows Desktop. Here, you can select wallpaper, borders, and textures for your Windows screen. In this section we offer a serving of tasty decorating hints for the Windows desktop.

Wallpaper Choices   By this time, everyone knows about Windows wallpaper, the decoration that lies behind all Windows screen objects. Windows wallpaper can be anything you want it to be: any pattern, any line drawing, any painting, any scanned image.

Windows offers several wallpaper patterns, but as with every colorful and graphic aspect of Windows, you can easily add your own. To access the Windows wallpaper patterns, click on the Desktop icon from the Control Panel and locate the Wallpaper item in the Desktop dialog box. There's a drop-down list of wallpaper filenames carrying the .BMP filename extension, which means they are Windows Paintbrush bitmap files.

Wallpaper patterns can occupy a whole screen or, if they're smaller than a whole screen, can be tiled. The advantage of smaller patterns is that they occupy less disk space and, more importantly, less PC memory when they're in use. All Microsoft-supplied patterns must be tiled, although some are relatively large and require as few as four copies to fill the screen.

Windows wallpaper is easy to create. Because it comes in .BMP format, anything that you can create with Windows Paintbrush is fair game to become wallpaper.

Simply get into the Paintbrush program (it's in the Accessories group window) and draw away. When you're done, save the file in the directory where Windows is stored. Then open the Desktop in the Control Panel and select the Paintbrush file you created from the list in the Wallpaper section of the dialog box to load your new wallpaper onto your desktop. If you don't like what you've got, go back to Paintbrush and give it another shot. We discuss Paintbrush more fully in Chapter 6.

If you don't fancy yourself an artist and don't want to create wallpaper from scratch, there are other ways of obtaining Windows wallpaper. If an image in another Windows application, or even a DOS application (not running in text mode) is to your liking, you can capture the image using the Clipboard and save it as a .BMP file from the Clipboard. For example, say you're running Tetris in a DOS session and think that a shot of falling tiles would make great wallpaper. Press the PrtSc key to capture the image to the Clipboard. Then open Paintbrush and select Paste. The screen image will appear, ready for you to edit or save as a .BMP file. Remember to store the file in the directory where Windows is located so that it will appear as a wallpaper choice in the Control Panel's Desktop dialog box.

You can also scan an image into your PC and convert it to the .BMP format. If your scanner software produces .PCX files, Paintbrush can convert them to .BMP files. Plenty of conversion programs are available, including some that are shipped with scanners that convert files to the .PCX format, so you shouldn't have trouble finding a route to wallpaper compatibility.

Other sources of wallpaper include almost any graphics program that produces, or can be converted to, a compatible file. For example, you might want a business graphic (such as your company's logo) on your screen when you shut down the rest of your applications or convert them to icons. Bulletin boards and on-line services are other great sources for .BMP files to use as wallpaper

Wallpaper versus Patterns   If you're short on memory but still crave that Windows decorator touch, opt for a desktop pattern instead of wallpaper. Patterns use less memory than wallpaper because they contain smaller bitmap images. You can find patterns along with wallpaper in the Control Panel Desktop.

Custom Desktop Patterns   The patterns that come with Windows do liven up your desktop a bit, but you can go one better by editing them to create your own patterns. While you do have to work from one of the original patterns, you'll find that you can essentially get a blank slate in one of two ways. First, go to the Control Panel's Desktop dialog box and select Edit Pattern. You'll see a box containing the selected pattern. Hold down the left mouse button and "wipe" away the pattern as you wish, leaving areas clear. Alternately, you can draw by clicking on clear areas to darken them. Try creating a pattern with your initials as the motif, as we did in Figure 5.4.

FIGURE 5.4

Edit the desktop patterns included with Windows to make your own motif, such as your initials.

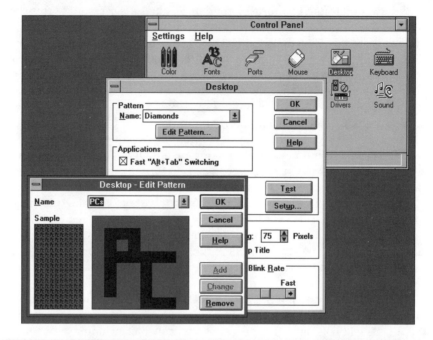

When you create a new pattern, make sure to change the name in the Name Text Box so that you don't overwrite the original pattern. Once you've named your new desktop pattern, you can add it to your list of choices by selecting Add. This is important, because if you forget to press Add and return to the main Desktop dialog box, your work of art will be lost.

Color Secrets

The natural partner for the Windows Desktop dialog box is the Color dialog box, whose icon is also found in the Control Panel. Here, you can select colors for every part of Windows, either from a large palette of predefined colors or by mixing your own hues.

The entire set of Windows colors you use is called a color scheme. There's no limit to the number of Windows color schemes that you can save, swap, and reuse. That means you can use one set of colors in the morning, another for lunch, and a third during the late afternoon.

You'll probably want the most visible elements to be easy on your eyes. To help you choose aesthetically pleasing combinations, Windows provides several predefined color schemes as well as a set of tools for modifying them or creating schemes of your own.

Use Built-In Color Schemes   The default color scheme that comes with Windows is an unexciting combination of blue and gray, but you can use the Control Panel to choose one of the other predefined schemes that suits your taste. Select the Color icon in the Control Panel to bring up the Color dialog box. You'll see the Color Schemes box with Windows Default selected. Scroll through the choices to select another color combination for your desktop. The color scheme names describe their tonal qualities. For example, Bordeaux consists of a series of winelike purples, while the Arizona scheme conjures sandy desert tones, and Ocean paints the screen with sea blues and greens. Simply scroll to one of the set color schemes, and then click OK to put it in action.

Do-It-Yourself Schemes   If you like some but not all of the colors in the scheme you've chosen, you can go back to the Color dialog box to make a modified version. Click on the Color Palette command button, and the half-screen Color dialog box will double in width to present a color table and another drop-down list box containing all the Windows screen elements. Ten graphic elements plus ten text elements make up the Windows desktop, and you can make each element any color you want.

The color table accommodates a wide range of colors in two parts: the larger section, at the top, contains basic colors, while the smaller section, at the bottom, contains boxes in which you can define custom colors. To pick a color for any Windows desktop element, click on the element in the model window on the left side of the screen or select it from the Screen Element drop-down list box on the right side. Then choose a color for the element by clicking on the appropriate color box in the color table. The miniature window on the left changes immediately, revealing the effects of your new color choice.

Windows colors, whether basic or custom, are either solid or nonsolid (nonsolid colors actually consist of a solid color interspersed with pixels of an alternate color). The number of available solid colors depends on the type of video adapter you have.

Change as many colors as you like, and then click the OK button. Your desktop will change colors to reflect the colors you chose. If you like what you see, name and save your custom scheme by clicking the Save Scheme button, entering a name for the scheme, and clicking on OK. Thereafter, it will appear on the list of available set color schemes.

Create Your Own Colors   If you're unhappy with the colors in the basic color table, make your own. When you click on the Define Custom Colors command button in the Color dialog box, a rectangular implementation of a color wheel appears on the left side of the screen, as shown in Figure 5.5. Grab the color cursor and move it until the color sample is the color you want. As you change colors you'll notice the values in the boxes at the bottom of the dialog box change. You can control aspects of colors by entering values here. Finally, you can darken or lighten a hue by moving the arrow along the color bar on the right of the custom color selector dialog box.

FIGURE 5.5

Fine-tune custom colors by entering values in the boxes labeled Hue, Sat, Lum, Red, Green, and Blue and by moving the color bar arrow on the right side of the dialog box.

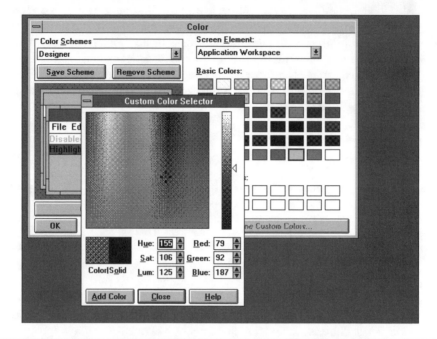

When you've found the color you're looking for, click an unused box in the Custom Colors table to select it, and then click on the Add Color command button. After that, you can use your new color wherever you want.

Add a Pattern to Your Desktop Color   The simplest way to add interest to your desktop is to overlay the color with a textured pattern. Microsoft supplies several patterns with Windows, ranging from a 50-percent gray pattern, which simply alternates colored pixels with white ones, to patterns depicting dogs, flowers, and propellers.

To add a textured pattern, select the Desktop icon from the Control Panel. The Pattern box displays the current desktop pattern in a drop-down list box. Click on the down arrow to list the original Microsoft-supplied choices, select one, and then click on OK. If your desktop is visible and it's painted a color other than white, you'll immediately see the results of the change.

More Color Control for Windows 3.0   Windows 3.1 lets you apply color to more desktop items than version 3.0 does, including those items that define on-screen buttons. (See Figure 5.6.) To change the colors of these elements in Windows 3.0, you'll have to add entries to the [Colors] section of the WIN.INI.

FIGURE 5.6

Windows 3.1 offers more Control Panel options for setting the colors of the desktop than Windows 3.0 does, such as letting you choose the colors of buttons; in Windows 3.0, you can make these changes by editing the WIN.INI file.

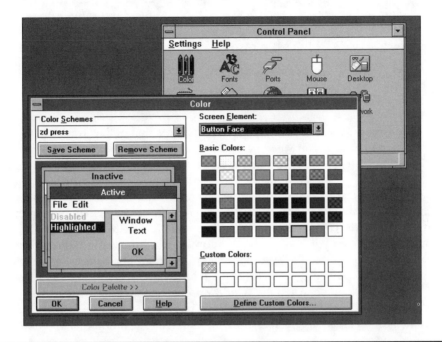

You can use the following settings in the [Colors] section of the WIN.INI to change the color of Windows 3.0 help text:

ButtonFace   Color of the button face

ButtonShadow   Color of the button shadow

ButtonText   Color of the button text

GrayText   Color of text that is unavailable in a menu or dialog box

Hilight   Color of the background of highlighted text

HilightText   Color of the highlighted text itself

The format for each of these settings is to specify the red-green-blue (RGB) value of the color for the desktop element. To find out this setting for the color that you want, open the Color dialog box via the Control Panel. Select Color Palette, and then select Define Custom Colors to open the Custom Color Selector. You'll notice boxes for the Red, Green, and Blue color values, as well as a square palette that lets you drag a cross-like cursor to the desired color. A vertical bar shows the current color listed. Experiment with the three values to come up with the colors you desire. Or if you know the colors you want, drag the cursor to that location. Then jot down the corresponding red-green-blue values for your desired colors so that you can easily edit the WIN.INI file. For example, to set the ButtonFace color to blue and the ButtonText color to black, you would add the following lines to WIN.INI's [Colors] section:

```
ButtonFace=0,0,128
ButtonText= 0,0,0
```

One color choice that you may want to change is that of the GrayText. GrayText is often hard to read when an option isn't available. If you change it to a darker color, at least you'll be able to read what options you're missing out on.

Change the Cursor Color While there is no default option for changing the color of the blinking cursor in Windows, there is a way to change it indirectly. That's because the color of the cursor is always the inverse of the Window Background Color. After you change the Window Background color in the Color dialog box of the Control Panel, you'll have to open an application to see what color the blinking cursor becomes. (The blinking cursor isn't visible in Program Manager.) For example, when the Window background is blue, the cursor is yellow; when the background is yellow, the cursor is blue. Experiment with different background and cursor colors until you find a combination that you like.

Personalize the Windows 3.1 StartUp Group

By placing a program item in Windows 3.1's StartUp group, you can automatically load a program you use every day when you start Windows. But you can go one better by customizing PROGMAN.INI so that any one of your program groups loads automatically. With this method, your regular StartUp group stays intact but is disabled, and you won't have to shuffle the contents of another whole program group into it.

To change the StartUp group, open PROGMAN.INI in Notepad or another text editor. In the [Settings] section, enter the name of the group whose applications you want to load automatically every time you start Windows. For example, if you want to change the StartUp group to the program group entitled Quarterly Report, your PROGMAN.INI might look like this:

```
[Settings]
Window=60 28 565 388 1
SaveSettings=1
MinOnRun=0
AutoArrange=1
Startup="Quarterly Report"
```

This technique is especially handy if you're working on a new project and want to load a suite of files automatically when you start Windows. When you're done with the project, go back to your default StartUp group by deleting the group name you added after Startup=.

Set the Loading Order of the StartUp Group   To change the loading order of the applications in the Program Manager's StartUp group, simply rearrange the order of the icons. The programs are launched in order from left to right.

Bypass the StartUp Group   The StartUp group is a great time-saver because it automatically loads the applications you generally use when you start Windows. But there'll be times when you want to get to Windows without waiting for these applications to load. For example, say you forgot to reply to an e-mail message before you exited Windows, and now you just want to go directly to your e-mail application and dash off a reply. To override the StartUp group applications, press the Shift key while Windows is loading (during the Windows logo screen or on the blank screen if you've disabled the Windows logo). You'll end up in Program Manager and will be able to quickly get to the task at hand.

Recreate the StartUp Group   To restore a StartUp group you deleted accidentally, simply create a new group and name it STARTUP; Windows 3.1 will recognize that it should automatically load the contents of this group at Windows startup.

Icon-ography and Creative Dragging

Windows offers two metaphors for control and identification of your intent: One is an icon, the tiny on-screen picture that represents an application, and the other is motion, the movement of an icon or other screen element from one place to another. By cleverly using both these methods, you can play the Windows screen like an instrument.

The Hidden Power of Icons

Windows applications generally come with their own nifty icons that load automatically. All you have to decide is which program group to place the icon in. However, you can create your own icons, assign new applications to existing icons, and otherwise manipulate these symbols to your own ends.

Create Your Own Icons for DOS Applications   To create your own icons for your favorite DOS applications, you need an icon editor; there are several shareware programs that will do the job nicely, such as Icondraw, Icon Magic, and IconMaster. Once you've created and saved an icon, assigning it to a DOS application is a five-step process:

1. In the non-Windows Applications window (or wherever you've stashed your DOS applications), highlight the program whose icon you want to change by clicking on it once.

2. Select Properties from Program Manager's File menu.

3. Press the Change Icon command button in the Program Item Properties dialog box.

4. In the File Name text box, enter the full path and filename of the .ICO file that contains the icon you created.

5. Click OK twice to confirm your selections.

Bulletin boards and on-line services also include a wide variety of icons that others have created for popular DOS applications. If you look around a bit, you'll undoubtedly find some icons that are just right for your DOS applications.

Adding an Original Icon   You don't have to settle for Program Manager's default DOS icon for character-mode applications. Instead use any image: a picture of Elvis, a golf club, a favorite cartoon character.

All you need is a collection of icons or an icon editor. Both are available on various bulletin board systems. Investigate the file libraries. You'll find dozens of icons (most have the extension .ICO or .ICN) ready for downloading—everything from sober, businesslike icons for leading applications such as 1-2-3, WordPerfect, and dBASE to cartoon characters like Calvin, Hobbes, and Bugs Bunny. Download the likely suspects, decompress them, if necessary, and you're all ready to go.

To attach one of your new icons to an installed application, highlight the application's current icon and select Properties from Program Manager's File menu. Then choose the Change Icon command button in the Program Item Properties dialog box. Your application's filename and its current icon will appear. Replace that filename with the name of the icon file you wish to substitute (HOBBES.ICO, for example). Then press View Next and your new icon will be displayed. If you like what you see, click on OK. The new icon will appear.

Easy-to-Find Icons   If your program groups are cluttered with icons whose names are running into each other, you can use these tips to tidy up. Adjust the icon spacing to allow more room for each icon and its title by selecting Desktop from the Control Panel and changing the icon spacing to a larger number (the minimum is 32). The default is 75 pixels and the maximum is 512, but anything over 100 pixels takes up too much real estate on most monitors. Once you make the adjustment, you'll have to select Arrange Icons to see the new layout. In version 3.1, Desktop also has a Text Wrap option, which permits icon titles that are many lines in length; check this option for more flexibility.

A Timely Icon   Here's a way that you can always see what time it is when you're working in a Windows application—without fooling with the cumbersome default clock display.

Double-click on the Accessories icon and then double-click on Clock. Click on Settings, then on Digital, and then use the Minimize command to reduce the clock display to an icon. This places a relatively small, easy-to-read, working digital clock icon at the bottom of your Windows display. And, of course, you can use your mouse to drag the clock icon anywhere you like.

Start Program Manager as an Icon   You may want to start Program Manager as an on-screen icon instead of as a window. Maybe you've got some great-looking wallpaper that you'd rather look at. You have two options for doing this: You can minimize Program Manager and exit Windows, checking the Save Settings option for this time only. When you do this, the next time you start Windows, Program Manager will be still be minimized. Alternatively, you can edit your WIN.INI file and add the Program Manager's executable file, PROGMAN.EXE, to the Run= line.

Load Applications as Icons   To load a Windows application automatically as an icon, hold down the Shift key while double-clicking on the name of its on-screen icon in the program group. When an application is run this way, its identifying icon is placed at the bottom of the screen for future use rather than being loaded into an active window.

Load a Data File from an Icon   Everyone has a certain method for organizing data files—be it by document type, month, or project. But most people don't store files in the directory of the application that creates them. (This isn't a good idea anyway, because if you upgrade or remove an application the files may get lost in the shuffle.) With many programs, this means you have to switch to the appropriate data file directory every time the program loads. Windows 3.1 eliminates this headache by letting you specify a distinct working directory for the application. From this start, you can move on to creating icons that pull files directly from this directory and automatically load the application that runs them!

In Program Manager, select the icon of an application and choose Properties from the File menu. In the text box labeled Working Directory, enter the path of the directory where you keep most of your current data files. Update the directory as your needs change—for example, when you start a new project.

If you frequently need access to files that don't belong in this working directory, consider making unique icons for those data files that automatically access the proper directory. To do so, choose New from the File menu in the Program Manager, make sure Program Item is selected, and click on OK. Enter a description for the file, and, in the Command Line text box, enter the path and filename of the data file. If you can't remember the exact filename, or if it's buried several subdirectories deep, select the Browse command button to find it. Then select the working directory and choose whether you want a shortcut key to load it quickly.

For this data file to launch its parent application, it must be associated with the application. For example, a Word for Windows document with the default .DOC extension will load automatically, but one with your initials as the extension won't. To associate the file, start File Manager, highlight the data file, and choose Associate from the File menu. In the Associate With list box, select the correct file type, in this case Word Document. For more on File Manager, see Chapter 7.

You can also launch an unassociated file by putting the entire path and filename in the Command Line text box of the Program Item Properties dialog box, following the program filename. For example, you could enter

```
C:\WINWORD\WINWORD.EXE C:\PROPOSAL\COVER.LET
```

Run Multiple Data Files from a Single Icon   Once you've set up an icon to launch a data file and its parent application, make it do double duty. You can launch multiple data files from the same application by adding their names to the Command Line text box in the icon's Program Item Properties dialog box. For example, to launch another letter in addition to the one shown earlier, you would use a command line like this:

```
C:\WINWORD\WINWORD.EXE C:\PROPOSAL\COVER.LET C:\PROPOSAL\NOTES.DOC
```

The filenames must be separated by a single space, and the file directory must be located in your DOS PATH statement. See Figure 5.7.

FIGURE 5.7

Have a single icon launch many data files for an application. In the Program Item Properties dialog box, list the desired filenames, separating them with spaces.

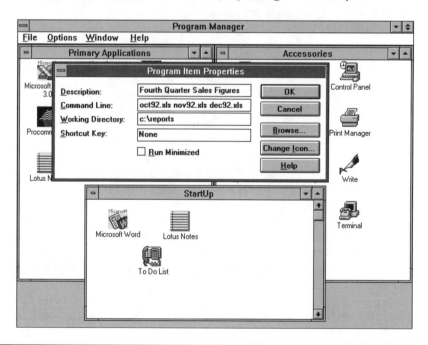

The Ins and Outs of Dragging and Dropping

Clicking isn't the only way to get power from a mouse in Windows. You can also use the mouse to move objects around the screen using Windows' drag and drop capabilities. You drag a file by selecting it with the mouse and then holding down the left mouse button while moving the mouse. You drop the file by releasing the button when the mouse arrives at its destination. Done correctly, this allows you to accomplish with one quick motion what it might take far longer to type or manage with menus. Drag and drop is one of Windows' least understood and used features.

Create an Icon with Drag and Drop   Using the File menu isn't the only way to create an icon. If you have File Manager and Program Manager open, grab the File Manager icon for the file (either an executable file or an associated data file) and drag it to the program group where you want it to be. Drop the file icon, and the Program Manager icon for the application appears in the desired group, as shown in Figure 5.8.

FIGURE 5.8 ▬▬▬▬▬▬▬▬▬▬▬▬▬▬▬▬▬▬▬▬▬▬▬▬▬▬▬▬▬

Create instant program items in a Program Manager group by dragging the appropriate file from the File Manager to the desired location.

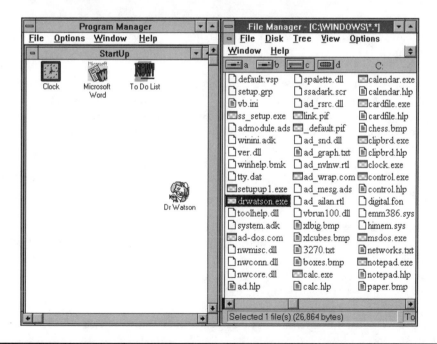

Open a File with Drag and Drop   To open an application file without having to wade through menus, use drag and drop. Here's a trick that works with many, but not all Windows applications. Using Windows File Manager (which is discussed more fully in Chapter 7) select the data file that you want to load and then drag it onto the title bar of an open application. The application will load the file. If the application is not already running, you can drop the file onto the application's icon, and the application will start up, with the data file loaded.

Savvy Shortcuts for the Screen

Menus form the backbone of Windows' interface. You can accomplish some of the tasks faster through alternative routes, however. In this section, we'll look at shortcuts for the mouse and the keyboard.

Bars and Buttons

Power can be found in the bars, buttons, and borders of Windows applications and screen groups. By moving the mouse to these sensitive spots, you can manipulate your programs. Exactly what happens varies by program; experiment with and read the application tips in Part 2.

Double-Click the Title Bar to Maximize a Window   To quickly maximize a Program group window or an application window, double-click on the title bar. If the Window is already maxed, clicking the title bar is equivalent to clicking Restore.

You can also maximize the window by clicking on the Maximize button (the up arrow located in the window's upper-right corner) or in some applications by pressing Ctrl+F10.

Incredible Shrinking Windows   Clicking on an open window's Maximize/Restore button (the arrow in the top right corner) to fit the window to the screen is easier than resizing it with a mouse or using the Control menu's Maximize or Restore command. But because this button is located next to the Minimize button (a down arrow), it's easy to click the wrong one.

Fortunately, there's another way: You can toggle between full-screen display and shared-screen windows by double-clicking anywhere on the program's title bar—a much larger target.

Close a Window Quickly   You can quickly close any window (or even Windows itself) by double-clicking on the Control menu icon—the small rectangular icon on the far left end of the application's title bar. This is a speedy alternative to opening the Windows Control menu and then selecting the Close option or using the Alt+F4 keyboard command.

Do the Windows Shuffle   If you're running only one or two Windows programs at once, calling up the Task List (Ctrl+Esc) and selecting the relevant window isn't the most convenient way to switch between windows or slip out to the Program Manager. It's quicker to shuffle between your open windows by pressing Alt+Tab or Alt+Esc until you find the title bar or icon label you want.

Scroll Bar Secrets   To easily scroll through the information in a window, keep in mind the following mouse shortcuts:

- To move one line up or down, click once on the up or down arrow located at the top and bottom of the vertical scroll bar.

- To move one screen up or down at a time, click in the vertical scroll bar above or below the scroll box.

- To move one screen left or right in the horizontal scroll bar, click left or right of the scroll box.

- To move continuously through the document or list, point to one of the scroll arrows (up, down, left, or right) and hold down the mouse button until you get where you want to be.

- You can also drag the scroll box anywhere you want as you navigate through the window.

Find the Perfect Window Size   When you've got a handful of Windows applications active at once, the perfect window size lets you use just enough of the space below the window to see your other program icons at a glance. Manipulating windows to just the right size can be a real drag (pun intended).

Fortunately, there's a no-fuss way to resize your windows with one touch. First, shrink to icons all applications except for the one that you plan to size. Press Ctrl+Esc to bring up the Task List, and click on Tile (or press Alt+T). Your window will instantly resize to be as large as possible while still leaving room for a row of icons along the bottom of the screen.

Don't Forget the Keyboard

For getting things done in Windows, mice may be nice, but the keyboard is often nicer still. Because they have less distance to travel, fingers are usually more nimble than forearms—provided, of course, that the fingers know where they're going.

Windows comes with a healthy number of built-in keyboard shortcuts. You can increase your Windows agility by getting to know them. Still other keystroke combinations may be well established in your own muscle memory (because of your experience with certain non-Windows programs) but not employed by your favorite applications; you may want to establish these key combinations yourself with the help of Recorder, a keyboard macro recording application bundled with Windows. (Recorder is discussed in Chapter 6.)

The universal shortcuts include those that give you access to menus and those that let you control the size and position of application windows. Both Alt and F10, for example, activate the menu bar in any Windows program. If you're coming to Windows from a DOS program (such as Symphony) that uses F10 for menu access, you don't need to abandon that keyboard habit. On the other hand, you may need to unlearn the use of F10 for executing commands. If you press Fl0 while in the menu system, for example, Windows does not carry out the highlighted command as a MultiMate user might expect; instead, it removes you from the menu bar.

Nearly every Windows program includes an Application Control menu, which contains commands for maximizing, minimizing, restoring, and closing the application window. You activate this menu by clicking the mouse on a bar in a square at the window's upper-left corner. This bar looks like the keyboard's spacebar—a reminder to you that pressing Alt+spacebar also displays this menu.

Document windows, the smaller windows in which you work with files in certain applications, have Document Control menus denoted by a shorter bar in a box. If you think of a short bar as a hyphen, you won't forget that the access combination for Document Control menus is Alt+hyphen.

A substitute for the Application Control menu's Close command, Alt+F4, shuts down the active application. In most programs you can use this key combination (or Esc) to close the current dialog box without saving any changes. If you find a dialog box you can't dismiss with the Escape key, try Alt+F4.

To close the current document window, use Ctrl+F4. To move between open document windows, try Ctrl+F6 or Shift+Ctrl+F6. These procedures should work in all Windows programs that allow multiple documents, even those that don't bother to put a Next Window command on their Document Control menus. Document Control menus typically include shortcuts for maximizing, restoring, moving, and sizing document windows—Ctrl+Fl0, Ctrl+F5, Ctrl+F7, and Ctrl+F8, respectively. If you take Windows on the road without a mouse, you'll do well to learn the control-key shortcuts.

Two very useful shortcuts appear on many programs' Edit menus: Ctrl+Ins for Copy, and Shift+Ins for Paste. If you think of a copy-and-paste operation as an insertion at the target location, you'll be able to remember the second half of these combinations. You might associate the "C" in Ctrl with the "C" in copy. Many Edit menus also offer Del for Clear, and Shift+Del for Cut. Cut puts a copy of the deleted matter on the Clipboard, replacing whatever was there before; Clear, on the other hand, deletes without affecting the Clipboard's contents. Again, a first-letter mnemonic may help you remember the key combination: Think of Shift+Del as a command to Store and Delete.

The keyboard is often superior to the mouse for navigating in list boxes. Pressing an alphabetic or numeric key in a list always takes you to the next item that begins with that letter or number. This seems to be true in all Windows dialog boxes and in some contexts outside of dialog boxes. Anytime your favorite Windows application presents you with an alphabetical list, try the first-letter express; you'll find this method both faster and more accurate than dragging the scroll box.

In most Windows lists, Home, End, Up Arrow, and Down Arrow behave as you would expect. Be wary of PgUp and PgDn, however. While these keys generally scroll by the windowful, some applications treat them as browse rather than navigation keys. In IBM's Current List View, for example, PgDn moves the display without changing the selection. No matter how many PgDns you press, the same item remains selected.

First-Letter Shortcuts   When you press a letter key in a program group, Windows selects the next program item that begins with that letter. For example, in your Accessories group you can skip from Calculator to Calendar to Cardfile to Clock by pressing the letter C successively.

Use Shortcut Keys for Quick Task Switching   In Windows 3.1, a new program item property allows you to specify a shortcut key for each icon. To set these shortcut keys, go to the Program Manager File menu and select Properties. In the Program Item Properties dialog box, you'll see a text box marked Shortcut Key. Click on this text box and type any key or combination. Windows will automatically add Ctrl+Alt to complete the shortcut. These shortcuts allow you to switch between applications quickly. If you've got seven different tasks running simultaneously and you need to get back to your word processor in a hurry, it's simpler to press Ctrl+Alt+W than to use the Alt+Tab key combination five or six times. When you're selecting these shortcuts, try to come up with a key combination that's easy to remember and that reminds of you the application it represents.

Keyboard Shortcuts: Text   You can use the following keyboard shortcuts for text selection and editing:

Keyboard Shortcut	Function
Backspace	Deletes the character to the left of the insertion point, or deletes selected text
Del	Deletes the character to the right of the insertion point, or deletes selected text
Shift+Home	Selects text to the beginning of the line
Shift+End	Selects text to the end of the line
Ctrl+Shift+Right Arrow	Selects next word
Ctrl+Shift+Left Arrow	Selects previous word
Ctrl+Shift+Home	Selects text to the beginning of the document
Ctrl+Shift+End	Selects text to the end of the document
Shift+Left Arrow or Shift+Right Arrow	Cancels the selection of a character
Shift+Up Arrow or Shift+Down Arrow	Selects one line of text up or down; if a line is selected, cancels the selection
Shift+PgUp or Shift+PgDn	Selects text up or down one window; if a window is selected, cancels the selection
Shift+Del	(Cut) Deletes selected text and places it on the Clipboard
Shift+Ins	(Paste) Inserts text from the Clipboard at the insertion point in the active window

Keyboard Shortcut	Function
Ctrl+Ins	(Copy) Makes a copy of selected text and places it on the Clipboard
Alt+Backspace	Undoes the previous editing operation

Keyboard Shortcuts: Characters   You can use the following keyboard shortcuts for character formatting:

Keyboard Shortcut	Function
Ctrl+B	Boldfaces selected characters
Ctrl+I	Italicizes selected characters
Ctrl+U	Underlines selected characters
F5	Normal, turns off bold, italic, and underlining

Keyboard Shortcuts: Cursor   You can use the following cursor movement keys for most Windows applications:

Keyboard Shortcut	Function
Ctrl+Right Arrow	Moves right one word
Ctrl+Left Arrow	Moves left one word
Home	Goes to the beginning of the line
PgUp	Scrolls up one screen
PgDn	Scrolls down one screen
Home	Scrolls to the beginning of the line
End	Scrolls to the end of the line
Ctrl+Home	Scrolls to the beginning of the document
Ctrl+End	Scrolls to the end of the document
Shift+Tab	Moves cursor in opposite direction of Tab

Keyboard Shortcuts: Dialog Boxes   You can use the following keyboard shortcuts for dialog boxes:

Keyboard Shortcut	Function
Tab	Moves from option to option
Shift+Tab	Moves from option to option in reverse order

Keyboard Shortcut	Function
Alt+*letter*	Moves to the option whose underlined letter matches the one you type
arrow key	Moves from option to option, or within a list or text box
Home	Moves to the first item or character in a list or text box
End	Moves to the last item or character in a list or text box
PgUp or PgDn	Scrolls up or down in a list box, one window at a time
Alt+Down Arrow	Opens a drop-down list box
Alt+Up Arrow or Alt+Down Arrow	Selects an item in a drop-down list box
spacebar	Selects or cancels a selection in a list box, or selects or clears a check box
Ctrl+/	Selects all items in a list box
Ctrl+\	Cancels all selections except the current one
Enter	Executes a command button, or chooses an item in a list box and executes the command
Esc or Alt+F4	Closes a dialog box without completing the command
letter	Moves to item in the list box that starts with that letter

Keyboard Shortcuts: Menus   For menu keys (in any application), use Alt or F10 to select the first-level menu on the menu bar. Then use the following keyboard shortcuts for menu selection:

Keyboard Shortcut	Function
letter	Chooses the menu or menu item whose underlined letter you type
Left Arrow or Right Arrow	Moves to the left or right between menus
Up Arrow or Down Arrow	Moves up or down between menu items

Keyboard Shortcut	Function
Enter	Chooses the selected menu item
Esc	Cancels the selected menu
Alt+hyphen	Opens submenu menu

Keyboard Shortcuts: On-Screen Windows   You can use the following keyboard shortcuts to manipulate and move between windows:

Keyboard Shortcut	Function
Alt+spacebar	Opens the Control menu for an application window
Alt+hyphen	Opens the Control menu for a document window
Alt+F4	Closes a window
Alt+Esc	Switches to the next application window or minimized icon, including full-screen programs
Alt+Tab	Switches to the next application window, restoring applications that are running as icons
arrow key	Moves a window if you've chosen Move from the Control menu, or changes the size of a window when you've chosen Size
Ctrl+F6 or Ctrl+Tab	Repeatedly cycles through open group windows and group icons
Ctrl+F4	Closes a group window

Keyboard Shortcuts: Program Manager   The following keyboard shortcuts will work in Program Manager or from within an application that you are running in Windows:

Keyboard Shortcut	Function
Ctrl+Esc	Switches to the Task List
Alt+Esc	Switches to the next application window or the next minimized icon, including full-screen program icons
Alt+Tab	By repeatedly pressing the Tab key as you hold down the Alt key, you can scroll through all current tasks
PrtSc	Copies an image of the screen contents onto the Clipboard

Keyboard Shortcut	Function
Alt+PrtSc	Copies an image of the active window onto the Clipboard. If this doesn't work, try Shift+PrtSc
Alt+F4	Closes the active application window; pressing Alt+F4 from the Program Manager exits you from Windows itself
Alt	Activates the first pad on the Menu bar; pressing Alt again closes it
spacebar	Places an X in any dialog box check box
F1	Activates context-sensitive help and displays the Help Index for the application; if the Help window is open, displays the Help Index; if you need help filling out Windows dialog boxes, F1 usually brings up a Help screen that explains options

The following shortcuts work within Program Manager only:

Keyboard Shortcut	Function
Alt+WC and Shift+F5	Cascades windows
Alt+WT and Shift+F4	Tiles windows
Alt+WA	Arranges icons

Saves and Captures

A smart user wants to save his or her screen in two ways: first, avoiding burned-on impressions from images that stand on the screen unchanged for long periods. This saves the screen from fuzziness and eventual uselessness. In a much different context, a sophisticated Windows user will want, from time to time, to save the visual contents of the screen. Screen savers and screen capture programs accomplish these two tasks, respectively.

Screen Savers

Every good Windows setup should have a screen saver installed and operating. Screen savers are programs that blank the working screen and replace it with some kind of animated graphic. It's good for your screen, avoiding unnecessary wear, and it's secure, keeping your work away from prying eyes. You can use the screen saver that comes in Windows 3.1 (it's found in the Control Panel Desktop) or any of the many commercial products, such as AfterDark or Intermission.

Extra Protection from Windows' Screen Saver   If your workspace is chaotic, Windows 3.1's screen saver password feature offers more than confidentiality: It can prevent unintended text entries when, for example, a hefty report plops onto your keyboard, pressing some of the keys. From the Control Panel Desktop dialog box, click the Setup command button in the Screen Saver section. Turn on the Password Protected option and use the Set Password command button to set a simple, unforgettable password, like the first letter of your name.

Then exit and restart Windows. When a keystroke or mouse movement interrupts the screen saver, the password alert box prevents random keystrokes from affecting your program until the correct password has been entered.

A Screen Saver with a Personal Touch   One of the several screen-saving patterns that comes with Windows 3.1 is called Marquee. By default, it displays the words "Windows 3.1," but you can customize the message, the background color, and the font of Marquee, so there's no excuse not to really personalize Windows. You might want to tell people where you've gone, when you'll be back, or maybe you just need a little push to get yourself back to work. How can you possibly sit there wasting time when your screen saver scrolls the message "Why Aren't You Working on the Anderson Proposal?!" in 50-point black type across your bright red screen every few seconds?

Screen Captures

Once you've got your desktop truly customized, why not capture it so that others can see just how great Windows can look. Use the Clipboard to take a screen capture of your Windows desktop that you can save as a graphic file or printout. Arrange everything the way you want it to look, and then, depending on your keyboard, press a keyboard combination that involves the Print Screen key. For some keyboards, you need to press the Print Screen key once; others require that you press it twice; still others require that you to hold down the Shift key while pressing the Print Screen key. You should be able to tell when the screen has been captured by watching the arrow of your mouse pointer. The arrow will momentarily disappear and then reappear, almost as if a photograph were being taken.

You can verify that your screen has been captured by opening the Clipboard. A copy of your desktop should be inside it. You can then save the capture as a Clipboard file, or open Paintbrush and select Paste from the Edit menu. A picture of your desktop will appear, ready for you save as a .BMP, .PCX or .TK file. Or you can personalize it even further by using some of Paintbrush's drawing and paint tools.

If you notice that only part of the desktop appears when you choose Paste, try pressing Ctrl+O (Zoom) before selecting the Paste command. You'll see a grid-like representation of a full screen. Press Esc and a regular picture of your desktop (zoomed out) will be visible.

6 SECRETS OF WINDOWS ACCESSORIES

TIME WAS WHEN AN OPERATING SYSTEM CAME IN ONE PACKAGE AND APPLICA-tion software came in another. The line between the two was absolute. DOS handled drives, ports, screens, and basic housekeeping; applications took care of everything else. That line is now breaking down. Today, it is common for oper-ating systems, including DR DOS and the most recent release of MS-DOS, to come with small but useful applications built right into them. Windows is a leader in this trend.

Upon setup, Windows presents you with a clock, a calculator, a perfectly competent word processor, a simple but solid communications program, a draw-ing package, and more. None of these programs is as dazzling as the big commer-cial programs developed for Windows, but they're free!

Many Windows users are curiously reluctant to dig into these so-called ap-plets. Part of this is habit: DOS didn't do it, and applications are not operating sys-tems. And part of this is a natural desire to push toward the ultimate in features and performance, which is, after all, one of the major attractions of Windows.

Still, overlooking these small applications is a mistake. If you're like most Windows users, for example, you'll find Terminal, Windows' built-in commu-nications package, to be quite adequate for your communications needs. It does the job—dialing the phone, handling uploads and downloads—and oth-erwise stays out of the way. And it doesn't take precious disk space away from more important applications, as more fully featured Windows communica-tions packages do.

Make the best use of Windows' applets by following the advice in this chap-ter, which includes

- Tips for using the Windows Clock

- Information on how to get the most out of Write, Windows' built-in word processor

- Secrets about the Windows Calculator, including a variety of financial calculations that rival spreadsheet capabilities

- Strategies for using Calendar

- Details on how to take advantage of Cardfile, Windows' utility for man-aging name, address, and phone number information

- Tips for using Notepad, including step-by-step instructions on building an activities log

- Pointers for Paintbrush, Windows' drawing and painting package

- Advice on how to navigate Terminal, Windows' telecommunications program

- Secrets for making the most of the Macro Recorder

- Strategies for using the Character Map

- A few nuggets of information on how to win at Windows Solitaire

All of these useful features are found in the Accessories group window, shown in Figure 6.1. Don't jump past this chapter to get on to the "real" applications. Take a look. There's gold in them thar' applets!

FIGURE 6.1

The Accessories group contains icons for these Windows applets: Write, Paintbrush, Terminal, Notepad, Cardfile, Recorder, Calculator, Clock, Calendar, Media Player, Sound Recorder, Object Packager, and Character Map.

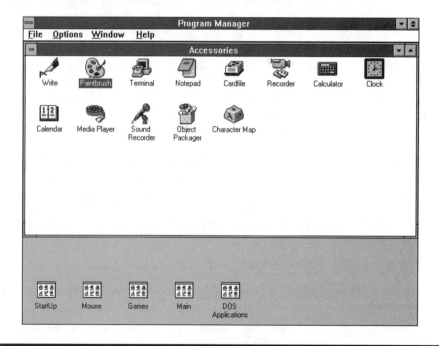

Getting the Time of Day from the Windows Clock

The presence of a clock in Windows may seem mundane, until you think about all the different valuable uses for knowledge of the time. Through this mini-application, Windows can become your timepiece in several different forms.

A Timely Icon

Here's a way that you can always see what time it is when you're working in a Windows application. From the Program Manager, open the Accessories group window and then double-click on the Clock icon. Click on Settings, then on Digital, and then select Minimize from the Control menu to reduce the clock display. (To get to the Clock's Control menu, click once on the box in the upper-left corner of the Clock window.) Or click on the Minimize icon in the Clock's upper-right corner to achieve the same result. This places a relatively small, easy-to-read digital clock icon at the bottom of your screen, as shown in Figure 6.2.

FIGURE 6.2

Keep the Windows Clock minimized (see bottom of screen) so that you can see the time from any application.

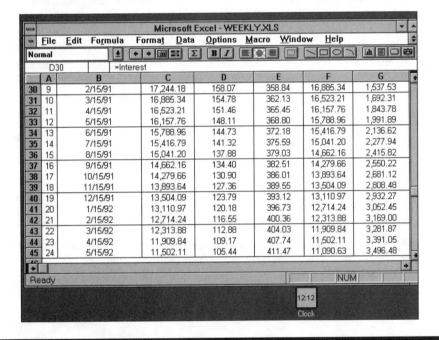

Easier Clock-Watching

You can use your mouse to drag the clock icon anywhere you like, but it will only be visible from another application if the application is not maximized to fill the entire screen or you have chosen the Always On Top option (Windows 3.1 only). To access this option, open the Clock, access the Clock's Control menu by clicking on the box in the upper-left corner of the Clock window or pressing Alt+spacebar, and then click on Always on Top. (If the option has a check mark to its left, it has already been toggled on.) You can then keep the clock minimized or resize it so that it's easier to see but is still unobtrusive.

Write Tips

Windows Write is a fairly full-featured word processor. It falls neatly between the scratch-pad nature of Notepad and the rich document-management capabilities of Microsoft Word. Generally, you would use Notepad for straightforward text work *related to Windows itself*, such as edits of Windows information files. Also, use Notepad for quick text you want to print—that is, for notes. In contrast, you would use Write for straightforward text work you want to share with others, such as memos or simple letters. If your document needs are few, use Write as your day-to-day word processor; it is powerful enough to handle that level of activity.

Lines That Don't Disappear

If you try to create lines in your Write document by choosing Underline from the Character menu (or pressing Ctrl+U) and then pressing the spacebar repeatedly, the lines disappear when you press Enter. To make the underlined spaces stay on the screen, you need to add some kind of text to the end of the blank line. For flawless lines, add a "hard space" at the end of the line to keep the underline intact. After you've entered the number of spaces to create the desired line length, hold down the Alt key and type **0160** on the numeric keypad; then release the Alt key.

Opt for Optional Hyphens

Like most word processors, Write doesn't break words that are too long to fit on one line. Instead, it places the entire word on the next line. If you are using long words, this may create big gaps at the end of your lines. Of course, you can add hyphens manually and split the word yourself by inserting a carriage return. But this will create problems when you edit the document and line lengths change; the word will stay hyphenated even if there is room to accommodate it on a single line. To prevent this from happening, use optional hyphens. Optional hyphens will only be displayed if they are needed (at the end of a line); they won't appear when line lengths change. To insert an optional hyphen in a Write document, press Ctrl+Shift+hyphen.

Change Margins Every Time

Write sets default margins at 1 1/4 inches for the left and right margins and 1 inch for the top and bottom margins. If you are accustomed to using different margins, you'll have to change them every time you create a document because Write doesn't let you set new defaults. You can get around this limitation by creating a template for your documents. Change the margins (select Page Layout from the Document menu) and make any other formatting changes you'd like in the untitled document that is automatically loaded when you start Write.

When you have everything set the way you want, save the file with an easy-to-remember name such as LETRTEMP.WRI. Then, in Program Manager, edit the Program Item Properties for the Write icon. Choose Properties from the Program Manager File menu to bring up the Program Item Properties dialog box. In the Command Line text box, replace WRITE.EXE with the name of your template .WRI file. Now each time you run Write this template will be loaded automatically. Of course, you have to remember to save the new documents you create under different filenames (using the Save As command on the File menu) so that the original template stays unchanged.

Special Searches

Like many full-featured word processors, Write can search for special formatting characters in your documents. When you select Find or Replace from the Find menu, you can specify the following codes to search for and replace formatting in your Write documents (use the shifted 6 key to get the ^ character):

^w   White space (one or more spaces in the document)

^t   Tab

^p   Paragraph mark

^d   A manual page break

You can also use a question mark (?) as a wildcard character in your searches. So, if you're looking for the words "dot" or "doc," you could enter **do?** in the Find What box. Likewise, you could find all references to .SYS files by entering **?.SYS**.

Being able to find and replace these formatting characters is especially handy if you need to strip hard returns from a document that includes line spaces between paragraphs. To do this, first replace all cases where there are consecutive paragraph marks, ^p^p (the end of a real paragraph), with a series of uncommon characters that wouldn't appear elsewhere in the document, such as &88&. Then do a second find-and-replace operation where you replace single paragraph marks (^p) with a space. Once all of these extraneous paragraph marks are removed, do a final find-and-replace operation to replace the temporary characters, in this case &88&, with regular paragraph marks (^p).

Write Keyboard Shortcuts

You can use the keyboard shortcuts in Table 6.1 in Write.

Write Mouse Shortcuts

You can select entire sections of text in Write by using mouse shortcuts. To select an entire line of text, move the mouse pointer to the left of that line and click once. (The mouse pointer should be an arrow rather than an I-beam.) If you want to extend the selection to successive lines, hold down the Shift key while clicking. To select a paragraph, double-click in the left margin next to the desired paragraph. If you want to extend the selection to successive paragraphs, hold down the Shift key while you keep double-clicking. To select the entire document, press the Ctrl key while you click in the left margin.

TABLE 6.1

Write Keyboard Shortcuts

Key	Action
F1	Provides help about Write
Alt+Backspace	Undoes previous operation
F3	Repeats the last find
F4	Goes to a page
F5	Turns off font attributes such as bold and italic
Ctrl+Enter	Inserts page break
Ctrl+B	Selects bold
Ctrl+C	Copies selected text to Clipboard
Ctrl+I	Selects italic
Ctrl+U	Selects underline
Ctrl+V	Pastes material from Clipboard
Ctrl+X	Cuts selected text to Clipboard
Ctrl+Z	Undoes previous operation (including undo operations)
GoTo (5 on the numeric keypad with the Num Lock key turned off)+Up Arrow	Moves to previous paragraph
GoTo+Down Arrow	Moves to next paragraph
GoTo+Left Arrow	Moves to previous sentence
GoTo+Right Arrow	Moves to next sentence
GoTo+PgUp	Moves to previous page
GoTo+PgDn	Moves to next page

Hidden Talents of the Windows Calculator

The Windows Calculator is surprisingly powerful. With a quick mouse click, you can gain access to functionality you might expect only from a spreadsheet. In a sense, the Calculator is a simple, on-screen financial computer.

Easy Financial Calculations

Following are seven financial calculations you can perform using the scientific view of the Windows Calculator. The scientific view provides four calculator buttons: the two parenthesis keys; the x^y (exponent) key; and the ln (natural logarithm) key. Don't worry if you don't remember what an exponent or a logarithm is. This isn't calculus. You just need to know where the buttons are so you can punch them.

To get started, open the Accessories program group window and double-click on the Calculator icon. Then, to display the scientific view of the Calculator, choose the Scientific command from the View menu. Your Calculator should now look like the one shown in Figure 6.3. The formulas outlined in the following sections can be entered with a mouse or from the keyboard.

FIGURE 6.3

The scientific view of the Windows Calculator

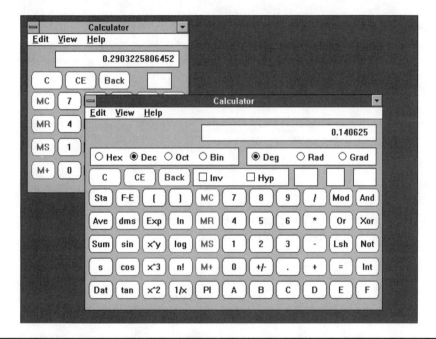

Calculate a Loan Payment   To calculate a loan payment, you need to know the loan amount, interest rate, and number of payments. Suppose, for example, that you were thinking about purchasing or refinancing a home. You already know how much money you want to borrow. And you can flip through the Sunday paper to check out lender rates and terms. That's all you need to calculate a loan payment. The formula is

$$payment = pv*i/(1-(1-i)^\wedge(-n))$$

where *pv* equals the loan balance (present value), *i* equals the interest rate, and *n* equals the number of payments. The calculator keystrokes that you type to solve the formula are

```
pv * i / ( 1 - ( 1 + i ) x^y ( n  +/- ) ) =
```

(Note that +/- is a single key located between zero and the decimal point on the calculator.)

For example, suppose you want to determine the payments on a $100,000, 30-year (or 360-month) mortgage with a 12-percent annual (or 1 percent monthly) interest rate. You would type the following keystrokes.

```
100000 * .01 / ( 1 - ( 1 + .01 ) x^y ( 360 +/- )) =
```

The Calculator display will show 1028.612596926, which means that the loan payment is $1,028.61 when you round to the nearest cent.

Calculate a Loan Balance   You can calculate an outstanding loan balance if you know the loan payment, the interest rate, and the number of remaining payments. You might do this if you were thinking about paying off a car loan and wanted to figure out the current balance. The formula is

$$loan\ balance = (1-(1+i)^{(-n)})/i*pmt$$

where i equals the interest rate, n equals the number of remaining payments, and *pmt* equals the loan payment. The calculator keystrokes are

```
(1 - ( 1 + i ) x^y  ( n +/- ) ) / i * pmt =
```

So, given a car loan in which the monthly payments are $250 and the loan has two years (24 months) of payments left at a 12-percent annual interest rate (1 percent monthly), type these keystrokes:

```
( 1 - ( 1 + .01 ) x^y ( 24 +/- ) )  / .01 * 250 =
```

The Calculator display will show 5310.846814407, so the loan balance equals $5,310.85, rounded to the nearest cent.

Calculate the Future Value of a Lump-Sum Investment   You can calculate the future value of a lump-sum investment if you know the initial investment, the interest rate the investment earns, and the number of years that interest is earned. The formula is

$$future\ investment\ value = pv*(1+i)^n$$

where *pv* equals the initial investment, i equals the annual interest rate, and n equals the number of years that interest is earned.

The Calculator keystrokes that solve this formula are

```
pv * ( 1 + i ) x^y n =
```

For example, if you currently have $10,000 in a mutual fund and expect to earn 10 percent interest annually, you would use this formula to estimate the account balance in ten years:

```
10000 * (1 + .10 ) x^y 10 =
```

The Calculator display will show 25937.424601, so the future investment balance, rounded to the nearest cent, equals $25,937.42. You can also specify the interest rate as a monthly interest rate instead of an annual interest rate and use months instead of years to describe how long the investment will earn interest.

Calculate the Future Value of a Series of Regular Investments You can calculate the future value of a series of equal investments given the annual (or monthly) investment amount, the number of annual (or monthly) investments made, and the annual (or monthly) interest rate. The formula is

future investment value = $((1+i)^\wedge n-1)/ i*pmt$

where *i* equals the annual (or monthly) interest rate, *n* equals the number of years (or months) interest is earned and payments are made, and *pmt* equals the regular payment, or investment, amount.

The Calculator keystrokes are

```
( ( 1 + i ) x^y n - 1 ) / i * pmt
```

For example, if you currently plan to contribute $1,800 a year to your Individual Retirement Account, and you expect to earn 12 percent annually, you could use this formula to calculate the account balance in 20 years:

```
( ( 1 + .12 ) x^y 20 - 1 ) / .12 * 1800 =
```

After you click on the equal sign, the display shows 129694.3963991, which means that the future investment balance, rounded to the nearest dollar, equals $129,694.

Some investments are better when made on a monthly basis rather than annually. An IRA illustrates why. Assume that you still plan to contribute $1,800 a year, but will make your contributions every month. The formula remains the same, but you need to replace the annual figures with figures for $150 a month at 1 percent a month for 240 months, as shown here:

```
( ( 1 + .01 ) x^y 240 - 1 ) / .01 * 150 =
```

The result, 148388.3048081, illustrates that a monthly investment of $150 yields $148,388 over 20 years. In other words, you would earn over $18,000 more by investing monthly rather than annually.

Calculate the Term of a Lump-Sum Investment You can calculate the term of an investment, or the years it will take for an investment to reach a specified future value, if you know the present investment value, the future investment value, and the interest rate the investment will earn. The formula is

term = $\ln(fv/pv)/\ln(1+i)$

where *fv* equals the future investment value, *pv* equals the present investment value, and *i* is the interest rate.

The Calculator keystrokes that solve this formula are

```
( fv / pv ) ln / ( 1 + i ) ln =
```

To calculate how long it would take a $50,000 inheritance earning 14-percent annual interest to grow to $1 million, type the following:

```
( 1000000 / 50000 ) ln / (1 + .14 ) ln  =
```

The Calculator display will show 22.86325269477, which means that it will take roughly 23 years for a $50,000 inheritance to grow to $1 million if it earns 14 percent annually. (If you want greater precision, you can also use a monthly interest rate. In that case, the term calculated would be in months, not years.)

Calculate the Term of an Annuity   You can calculate the term of an annuity—that is, the number of years it will take for a series of regular annual investments to reach a specified future value—if you know the regular investment amount, the future investment value, and the annual interest rate the investments will earn. The formula is

$$term = \ln(1+(i*fv)/pmt)/\ln(1+i)$$

where *fv* equals the future investment value, *pmt* equals the annuity (regular investment amount), and *i* equals the interest rate.

The Calculator keystrokes you type to solve this formula are

```
( 1 + (i * fv) / pmt ) ln / ( 1 + i ) ln =
```

For example, to calculate how many years of annual $5,000 contributions to your 401(k) it would take for you to become a millionaire if your 401(k) earned a 10-percent annual return, you would use this formula:

```
(1 +   (.10  * 1000000) / 5000 ) ln / ( 1+ .10 )   ln =
```

The calculator display will show 31.94330809127, which means that it will take roughly 32 years for a $5,000 annual 401(k) contribution to grow to $1,000,000 if the 401(k) earns 10 percent annually. (If you want greater precision, you can use a monthly interest rate and then specify the regular investment amounts as monthly figures. In that case, the term calculated would be in months rather than years.)

Calculate an Interest Rate   You can calculate the interest rate an investment earns if you know the present investment value, the future investment value, and the number of years (or months) over which interest will be earned. The formula for this calculation is

$$interest\ rate = (fv/pv)^{\wedge}(1/n) - 1$$

where *fv* equals the future investment value, *pv* equals the present investment value, and *n* equals the number of years interest will be earned. (Note that this formula assumes a one-time investment. For other interest rate calculations— for example, those involving a series of payments such as an IRA—the formulas are more complex and therefore aren't covered here.)

The Calculator keystrokes you type to solve this formula are

```
( fv / pv ) x^y ( 1 / n ) - 1 =
```

For example, suppose you can have a balance of $17,000 in your company's profit-sharing plan, and a financial planner has suggested that you should have $500,000 in retirement savings in 20 years. You could use this interest-rate formula to determine what sort of annual return your investment would need to produce:

```
( 500000 / 17000 )  x^y ( 1 / 20 ) - 1 =
```

The Calculator display will show .1842027196401, which means that your $17,000 needs to earn interest at a rate of 18.42 percent to grow to $500,000 in 20 years. (You could also specify the period of time in months instead of years. In that case, the interest rate calculated would be a monthly rate.)

A Calculator Limitation You Should Know About

The Windows Calculator is great for many numeric calculations, but you should know about its limitations. It doesn't reliably subtract decimal numbers that are close in value to one another, because it has problems rounding them off correctly. For example, if your checkbook had a balance of $137.27, and you wrote a check for $137.26, the Calculator would give you a balance of $0.009999999999991 instead of $.01. Of course, you probably wouldn't knowingly use the Calculator to subtract such a set of numbers, but if you were doing a series of calculations that included such subtraction, your final value might be inaccurate.

Use the Statistics Box to Keep Track of Numbers

Like many calculators, the Windows Calculator lets you keep a running tally of numbers with its memory features. When you want to add (or subtract) a number from the value in memory, you press the MS (memory store) key. But for more control over such a tally, use the scientific view's Statistics Box (accessed by clicking on the Calculator's Sta key), shown in Figure 6.4. The Statistics Box Calculator's Sta key lets you store numbers in memory separately and visibly. You can place the value for a series of equations into the Statistics Box, and then come back to it later when you need it.

FIGURE 6.4

The Statistics Box can be accessed when Calculator is in scientific view; use it to store a collection of separate values.

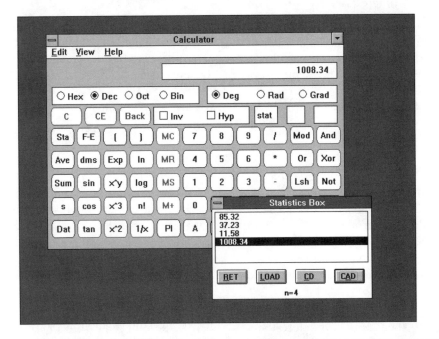

To verify that you've entered the correct values in a long series of additions and subtractions—for example, a checkbook balance—you would open the Statistics Box, click on the Ret button, enter the first value in the Calculator, and click on Dat at the bottom left of the Calculator. The first value will be visible in the Statistics Box. To subtract subsequent values, you would enter each successive value, press the Dat key, and press the minus key. All the values you entered would remain visible in the Statistics Box.

You can also place many values (such as monthly receipts) in the box and then use the Calculator's options to sum, average, or calculate the standard deviation on those values. You can use the following Calculator keys to process the numbers in the Statistics Box: S (standard deviation of the numbers), Ave (average of the numbers), and Sum (sum of numbers).

In addition, you can load numbers from the Statistics Box back into the Calculator by selecting the number in the box and clicking on the LOAD button in the Statistics Box.

Calculator Keyboard Shortcuts

Keyboard shortcuts for the Windows Calculator are shown in Table 6.2.

TABLE 6.2

Calculator Keyboard Shortcuts

Key	Action
F1	Displays help about Calculator
F9	Applies positive or negative sign
comma (,)	Inserts decimal point
R	Calculates reciprocal of number
Ctrl+C	Copies selected material to Clipboard
Ctrl+L	Clears memory contents
Ctrl+M	Stores value in memory
Ctrl+P	Adds displayed number to memory
Ctrl+R	Retrieves value from memory
Ctrl+V	Pastes selected material from Clipboard
@	Squares the number

Calendar

Personal information managers have long been a kind of application that few users felt were important enough to actually go out and buy. Windows skirts this dilemma by including with the operating system many basic PIM elements, in particular the Calendar. You can use it to manage your schedule in a number of ways and to test whether you want or need to move to a more full-featured PIM.

Print Blank Calendar Pages

When you select the Print option from the Calendar's File menu and specify a range of dates for which you'd like printed appointment sheets, you'll find out that Calendar won't print any of the days that are blank. And on the days that it does print, it won't print times for which no appointments are scheduled. To trick Calendar into printing all of these time slots or all of the blank days within the range, you'll have to type a space in each timeline entry so that Calendar thinks there is text describing an appointment there.

Personalize Calendar Output

As in many of the Windows Accessories, you can include special information in headers and footers in Calendar. By including special symbols in the Header and Footer text boxes of the File menu's Page Setup dialog box (Figure 6.5), you can enter the date, time, filename, and page number on each page, along with any other personalized text that you'd like to appear.

FIGURE 6.5

Use formatting codes to add customized headers and footers to your printed Calendar pages.

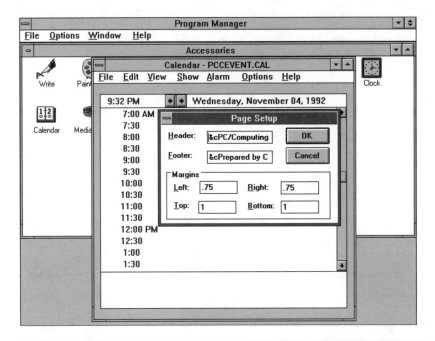

By default, Calendar prints the filename as the header and the page number as the footer. Use the codes shown here to add information and formatting to your headers and footers in Calendar or in other accessories' headers and footers:

&d Current date

&p Page numbers

&f Filename

&l Text justified at the left margin

&r Text justified at the right margin

&c Text centered between the margins

&t Current time

Start Your Day by Previewing Appointments

If you add the Calendar to your Startup Group in Windows 3.1, you won't have to remember to check your personal calendar for your daily appointments—it will automatically appear first thing. To do this, create an icon for your personal calendar in Program Manager and place it in the Startup group. For example, if your calendar is named MYCAL.CAL, specify this on the Command Line in the Program Item Properties dialog box. Then position the icon in the rightmost position in the Startup group window so that it is the last program to load at startup and remains on your screen.

Special Times

If you regularly schedule meetings on the hour or half hour, you'll want to set the Calendar's time interval to 30 or 60 minutes. (Open the Day Settings dialog box from the Options menu.) But what if you then have a very important 11:15 appointment, for which you want to set the alarm? Instead of changing your interval setting to 15 minutes and making your calendar endlessly long, or recording your appointment in a less-accurate time slot just because it's available, you can enter the exact time by using the Special Time option (press F7 or select Special Time from the Options menu). This displays the Special Time dialog box (Figure 6.6), which lets you insert a nonstandard time into your calendar. Once it appears as a time slot, you can go ahead and record your meeting and set the alarm, just as you would with any standard time slot.

FIGURE 6.6

The Special Time dialog box allows you to enter Calendar appointments that occur at odd time intervals.

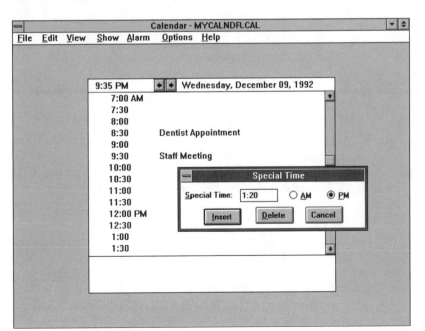

Calendar Keyboard Shortcuts

Table 6.3 lists the keyboard shortcuts for Calendar.

TABLE 6.3

Calendar Keyboard Shortcuts

Key	Action
F1	Displays Calendar Help
F4	Shows the date
F5	Sets and unsets the alarm
F6	Marks a date
F7	Inserts a special time
F8	Views a selected day
F9	Views a month
Ctrl+C	Copies material to Clipboard
Ctrl+V	Pastes material from Clipboard
Ctrl+X	Cuts material to Clipboard
Ctrl+PgUp	Shows the previous day or month
Ctrl+PgDown	Shows the next day or month
Tab	Moves between calendar area and scratch pad at bottom of Calendar screen
Ctrl+Home	In day view, moves to starting time
Ctrl+End	In day view, moves 12 hours from starting time

Cardfile

Often, when users say they need a database, what they really need is a Rolodex. Windows Cardfile provides a solid flat-file record keeper, for free. Anyone who only needs to track customers, suppliers, or the like should certainly try Cardfile before buying a separate Rolodex-type program.

Fit More Cards on a Printed Page

When you select the Print All option from Cardfile's File menu, you'll get a printout of every card in the file. With the default margin settings, only four cards fit on a printed page. To increase that number to five, select Page Setup from the File menu and reduce the top and bottom margins to no more than 0.75 inches. To conserve more page space, print the file without headers and footers by deleting the text and formatting codes in the Header and Footer sections of the Page Setup dialog box.

Dialing with Cardfile

If you use Cardfile to keep track of phone numbers and addresses, you can have it also dial the phone for you. But if you have other numeric information on the card, such as a nine-digit zip code, Cardfile may get confused and try dialing that number instead. To avoid this problem, set up your cards so that the phone number is the first set of numbers that Cardfile encounters. To do this on an existing card, place the name and phone number on the Cardfile's index line (select Index from the Edit menu; you'll see the dialog box shown in Figure 6.7). To add a new card with this format, press F7 and, in the Add dialog box, enter the name of the person or business, a space, and then the phone number all on the same line; then press OK. Now you can fill out the rest of the information in the body of the card: address, contact information, or notes.

FIGURE 6.7

Entering a phone number on a card's index line tells Cardfile that this number, not other numeric information such as a zip code, is the correct one to dial.

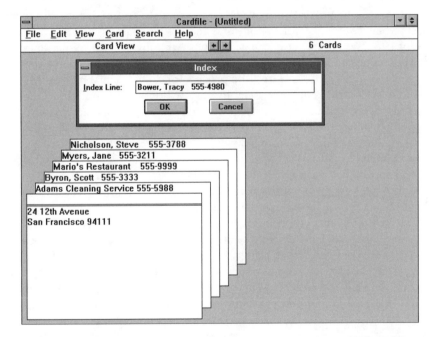

Quick Card Finds

To quickly get to a Cardfile record, there's a shortcut key combination that eliminates the need to use the Search command when your card database has more records than you can see on screen at one time. In Windows 3.0, simply press Ctrl+*letter key* to jump to the first card that begins with that letter. In Windows 3.1, this key combination is Ctrl+Shift+*letter key*.

Dial Internal Extensions

You can get Cardfile to dial numbers that contain fewer digits than a regular phone number by using hyphens in the empty spaces. Cardfile will treat the extension as a standard phone number because it's at least six digits long, but it will ignore the hyphens when it actually dials the phone. For example, if you want to be able to dial the extensions of co-workers in your office, fill out the index line of their cards as follows:

```
Fred --6088
Gayle --6029
```

If there are other numbers on the card that are six digits or more (such as a zip code), you may have to select the phone number with your mouse so that Cardfile knows that it is the correct number to dial.

Convert Cards to Text

Put your Cardfile records to use by converting them to ASCII format. For example, say you want to take your phone and address database and do a mail/merge in Word for Windows. You can accomplish this by printing your database directly to a text file. To do so, you need to set up your default printer with the Generic/Text Only option. Here's the process for doing so in Windows 3.1.

Go into Control Panel and select Printers. Choose Add and select Generic/ Text only. Select Install; you may be prompted for a Windows setup disk so that Windows can copy the appropriate driver for this printer option to your system. Choose Connect and, in the drop-down list of Ports, select File. Finally, select Set as Default.

To create a text file in Cardfile that is as clean as possible, requiring the least amount of work for your word processor. You should perform a few formatting changes before you print the cards. Select Page Setup from the File menu, delete the text in the Header and Footer boxes, and set all the margins to zero, as shown in Figure 6.8. This eliminates the default header and footer and gets rid of extra spaces in the text file. Finally, select Print All from the File menu; you will be prompted for the name of the file to which you want to output. You can now open this file in Word for Windows (or any other word processor) and set up your mail merge. Of course, there will still be extra spaces and paragraph marks that you'll have to get rid of before the file will be usable.

Autodialing Long Numbers in Windows 3.0

Cardfile's Autodial option in Windows 3.0 limits the length of the phone number that can be dialed to 14 characters. (Windows 3.1 does not have this limit.) To get around this limitation, avoid using unnecessary hyphens or commas to separate groups of numbers. For example, 9, 678-555-1234 can just as easily be specified as 96785551234. This way you'll have all 14 spaces for the actual phone number. If the number you want to dial requires even more room than that— perhaps you're dialing an international number—in the Autodial dialog box consider moving the first six digits of the phone number to the Prefix box located below the Phone Number box.

FIGURE 6.8

Change the settings in Cardfile's Page Setup dialog box to make a clean ASCII text file that you can open in a word processor.

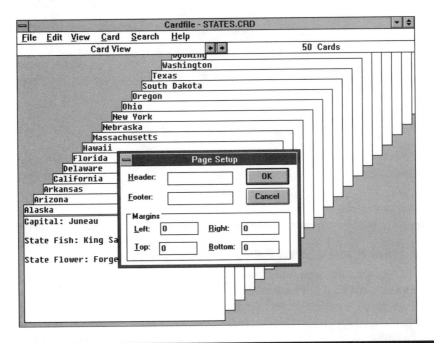

Cardfile Keyboard Shortcuts

Table 6.4 shows keyboard shortcuts for Cardfile.

Notepad Know-How

Notepad is a great place to edit ASCII text, such as the contents of a Windows "read me" file, or to jot some quick text you want to print. It doesn't have the power of a true word processor (it has terrible file import and export capabilities, for example), but then it doesn't have their dangers, either (it won't mistakenly save an ASCII file in another file format).

Turn On Word Wrap

When you're using Notepad to create lists or reminders for yourself, there's nothing more annoying than having the lines of text go on seemingly forever. Fortunately, you can just turn on the Word Wrap option on the Edit menu; this option wraps the text to fit the current Notepad window. If you shrink or enlarge the window while Word Wrap is selected, the text will move to fill the space accordingly.

TABLE 6.4

Cardfile Keyboard Shortcuts

Key	Action
Alt+Backspace	Undoes the last command
F1	Displays Cardfile help
F3	Finds the next instance of a specified search string
F4	Goes to a specified search string
F5	Autodials a number on a selected card
F6	Opens an index line on a selected card
F7	Adds a new card
PgUp	Goes to previous card
PgDn	Goes to next card
Ctrl+Home	Goes to first card in stack
Ctrl+End	Goes to last card in stack

Add Time and Date to Printed Documents

One of Notepad's niftiest features is its time/date stamp, which lets you enter the current time and date in your documents simply by pressing the F5 key. If you use Notepad for notes to yourself, this feature is especially handy for keeping track of what happened when.

Notepad also gives you another way to add the current date and time to printed Notepad documents, by using custom page formatting. From the File menu, select Page Setup to display the Page Setup dialog box. In the Header text box, you should see the default header code &f, which prints the filename at the top of each page. Type **&d, &t** into the Header box; this will make Notepad include the date and time at the top of every page each time the document is printed.

Format Headers and Footers in Notepad

As in Cardfile, Calendar, and Write, you can use formatting codes in your headers and footers to change their printed appearance. The default header is &f, which prints the filename at the top of the document. The default footer is Page &p, which prints the current page number at the bottom of each page. The code &l aligns header or footer text on the left, &r aligns text on the right, and &c centers the text. For the &l and &r codes to take effect in Notepad, they must be the very first item in the Header or Footer text box; otherwise Notepad will ignore them and center text by default.

Create a Log of Your Work Day

If you'd like to keep better track of your time, let Notepad help you by maintaining an activity log. Open a new file in Notepad and add the word **.LOG** (you must use capital letters) at the top of the page. This tells Notepad to stamp the date and time at the end of the file every time it is opened. Save the document with an easy-to-remember name such as DAYLOG.TXT. To use this log, simply open it whenever you need to make an entry and add your activities below the time/date stamp that appears. When you are ready to record your next activity, select Open again, even though the file is already loaded into Notepad. (If you haven't saved your previous additions to the file, Notepad will ask if you want to do so before displaying the Open dialog box.) Select the file; reopening it causes the new time and date to appear.

Notepad Keyboard Shortcuts

Table 6.5 shows the keyboard shortcuts for Notepad.

TABLE 6.5

Notepad Keyboard Shortcuts

Key	Action
F1	Displays Notepad Help
F3	Finds the next instance of a specified search string
F5	Inserts the time/date stamp at the insertion point
Ctrl+C	Copies material to Clipboard
Ctrl+V	Pastes material to Clipboard
Ctrl+X	Cuts material to Clipboard
Ctrl+Z	Undoes previous operation

Paintbrush Pointers

Paintbrush may be the most fully featured of Windows' small applications, and it is definitely the most integrated into the environment as a whole. Paintbrush appears when you tinker with on-screen colors or edit icons; it's a fundamental element of Windows. As a stand-alone application, Paintbrush is strong enough to compete with commercial alternatives.

Quick Duplicates

To make copies of an object that you've drawn in Paintbrush, do the following: Select the Scissors or Pick tool, both of which are at the top of the Toolbox. The one on the left, Scissors, picks irregular shapes; the one on the right, Pick, selects rectangular shapes (see Figure 6.9). Outline the object, hold down the Shift key while you click once on the object, release the Shift key, and then drag the copy wherever you want it. You can repeat this process as many times as you'd like. If you continue to hold down the Shift key while you drag the object, you'll draw multiple copies of the selected object, as shown in Figure 6.10.

FIGURE 6.9

Paintbrush's Pick tools allow you to select both rectangular and irregular shapes (for example, the leaf here). When either is used to select an object, a Pick file menu appears on Paintbrush's menu bar.

Scissors tool

Pick tool

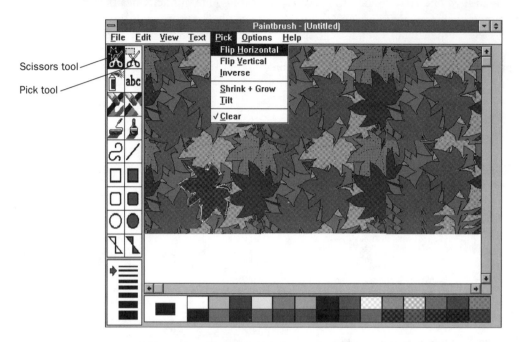

Perfect Lines and Shapes

The Shift key again comes in handy when you are drawing lines, squares, and circles. When you select one of these drawing tools, holding down the Shift key while you drag with the mouse will produce a line oriented vertically, horizontally, or at a 45-degree angle; a perfect square (as opposed to a rectangle); or a perfect circle (as opposed to an ellipse).

Easy Erasing

As you work on your Paintbrush creation you'll probably find yourself wanting to fine-tune each change you make. Pressing the Backspace key after you have completed a task such as drawing a line or adding color calls up an eraser that works just on your most recent change. The mouse pointer turns into a square with an x inside it. Holding down the left mouse button while you drag the mouse erases whatever part of the object you touch. This eraser works only for the most recent addition or change to the drawing; if you try to erase a part of the drawing that was created before the last change, nothing happens. To erase these older parts of the drawing, select the Eraser icon in the Toolbox.

FIGURE 6.10

Duplicate objects in Paintbrush by holding the Shift key while you click on the original.

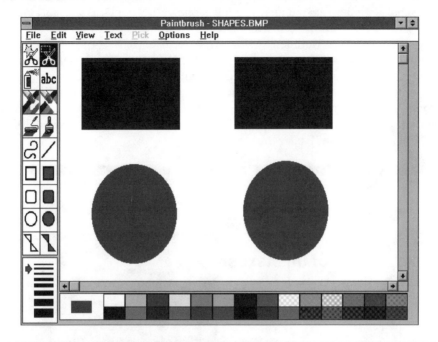

More Zoom

If you want to do some detailed work on a section of an image, you can choose the Zoom In command from the View menu. You can then select the area you'd like to see in detail. But the scope of the area you can zoom in on depends on the size of the overall image. (To check the size of the image, select Image Attributes from the Options menu.) If the image is very small, the box that appears to let you select the zoom-in area is also very small. If this doesn't cover enough ground for you, copy the image to a larger size and then zoom in on it.

Save the image you are working on just in case you make some changes that you don't like. Now select the entire image with the Pick tool, select Copy from the Edit menu, and choose New from the File menu. Before pasting the copy of the image, set the Image Attributes (found on the Options menu) to a larger width and height than the original drawing. When you paste in the image, it will appear to be the same size, but when you select Zoom In, the selection box is larger. You can now zoom in on the entire area that you want, which enables you to make the desired changes.

To return the image to its original size, copy it again and set the Image Attributes of this third drawing to match those of the original. This third drawing, which has your changes and has the same width and height dimensions as the original, is the file you'll want to save. The original and interim copy may be deleted.

Special Text Effects

When you add text to your Paintbrush creations you'll notice the choices Outline and Shadow on the Text menu. If you select one of these options and start typing text, you may not see these special effects. If you're using a white background, they won't appear as outlined or shadowed because white is the color used to create these effects. (Note that you cannot change this color.) But any other background color, with a contrasting foreground color used for the text, will give you outlined or shadowed text, as shown in Figure 6.11. To change the background color on a new drawing, click with the right mouse button on the color you want, and then select File, New. To change the background on an existing drawing, use the Paint Roller tool.

FIGURE 6.11

Use any background color except white to create outlined or shadowed text.

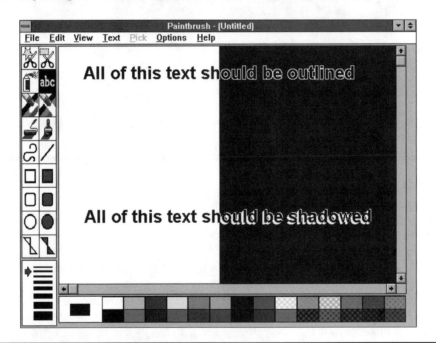

Paintbrush Keyboard Shortcuts

Table 6.6 shows keyboard shortcuts for use in Paintbrush.

Tapping into Terminal

Terminal has its limits, but if what you need is reliable dial-up and connection, this application is all you require. I actually use Terminal to dial MCI mail on the road from my notebook. Why take up valuable disk space when a perfectly adequate program is already part of Windows?

TABLE 6.6

Paintbrush Keyboard Shortcuts

Key	Action
F1	Displays Paintbrush Help
Ins	Alternative to clicking the left mouse button
Del	Alternative to clicking the right mouse button
F9+Ins	Alternative to double-clicking the left mouse button
F9+Del	Alternative to double-clicking the right mouse button
Shift+Up Arrow, Shift+Down Arrow	Moves up or down one line
Home	Scrolls to top of work area
End	Scrolls to end of work area
Shift+Home	Scrolls to left edge of work area
Shift+End	Scrolls to right edge of work area
Shift+PgUp	Scrolls left one screen
Shift+PgDn	Scrolls right one screen
Tab	Moves among Toolbox, Linesize box, Palette, and drawing area
Shift+Tab	Moves in reverse order among Toolbox, Linesize box, Palette, and drawing area
Ctrl+B	Boldfaces selected text
Ctrl+C	Copies selected item to the Clipboard
Ctrl+I	Italicizes selected text
Ctrl+N	Zooms in on the screen
Ctrl+O	Zooms out from the screen
Ctrl+P	Enlarges drawing to fill the entire screen
Ctrl+S	Saves drawing
Ctrl+U	Underlines selected text
Ctrl+V	Pastes material from Clipboard
Ctrl+X	Cuts material to Clipboard
Ctrl+Z	Undoes previous operation

Print Selected Terminal Text

Terminal offers you a few options for capturing the contents of a communications session. You can enable Printer Echo, which sends all the information from your screen to the printer; you can save incoming text to a file; and you can save the buffer contents by copying it to the Clipboard. All of these methods work well, but if you only want to print (and not save) certain text selections, you can copy the information directly from the screen (or the buffer) to the Clipboard. Use the mouse to highlight the text you want, and copy it to the Clipboard. Then paste the copied text into Notepad or Write. At this point, you can print the text.

Increase the Buffer Size

The buffer in Terminal is a holding tank for what transpires during a communications session. Everything that you see on your screen is stored in this buffer. But because buffers can hold only a limited amount of information, the most recent information from your session replaces the old. A buffer can be an extremely valuable resource because it allows you to see where you've been. If a screenful of information scrolls by too fast, you can scroll through the buffer to see what you missed.

You can also use a buffer to capture information from your session that you want to save or print. You can select the buffer contents and copy them to the Clipboard, where you can save the data as a file or send it to the printer. If you regularly copy the buffer contents to the Clipboard, paste them into a document file (for instance, in Write), and then clear them before resuming your session, you have a way of recording and saving the entire session, no matter how many lines of text it contains. Since it has all these valuable uses, you can see why you'd want the buffer to be as large as possible. The default size is only 100 lines. To change the buffer size to the maximum value of 399 lines (or less), choose Terminal Preferences from the Settings menu and change the number in the Buffer Lines text box. Any number from 25 to 399 is a valid setting.

Turn Off Call Waiting

If you share one telephone line for voice and data purposes, call waiting can cause connection problems when your computer and modem are using the phone line. Of course, you don't want to give up your call waiting, and fortunately you don't need to. You can temporarily turn off call waiting for a call by entering a code before you dial the phone number.

Have Terminal do this automatically each time you dial out by adding the code as a regular dialing prefix. To do so, select Modem Commands from the Settings menu and add the numeric code in the Dial Prefix box (see Figure 6.12). The default Prefix setting is ATDT, so, for example, you would type **70** after that to create ATDT*70. In many calling areas, *70 is the code to turn off call waiting. If this doesn't work, check with your phone service to find out which code you must use.

Work Around Noisy Phone Lines

If you consistently have a problem with noisy phone lines when you are using Terminal, it may help to lower the baud rate that you are using. Try dropping down to the next lowest setting and see if the condition of the phone lines improves. To do so, choose Communications from the Settings menu and choose a lower baud rate. For example, if you are currently communicating at 9600 baud, try 4800 and see if that helps.

FIGURE 6.12

Adding the numeric code *70 to Terminal's Modem Commands dialog box turns off the call waiting feature on most telephones.

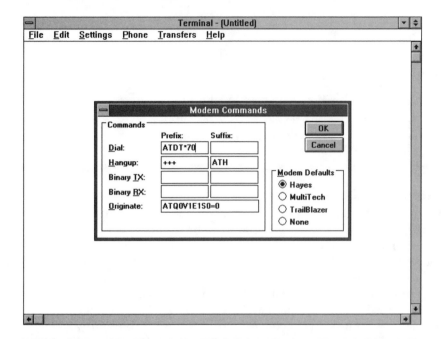

Run Terminal Maximized

When you start Terminal, you'll notice that it doesn't automatically run maximized. However, if you'd like it to start maximized so that you can see more buffer lines, you can edit your WIN.INI file and tell it to do so. Open WIN.INI in SYSEDIT or a text editor and find the [Terminal] section. Type the line **Maximized=1** at the bottom of this section, and then save your changes. For this change to take effect, you have to exit and then restart Windows.

Terminal Keyboard Shortcuts

The keyboard shortcuts for Terminal are shown in Table 6.7.

Make the Most of the Macro Recorder

Windows' Macro Recorder took a lot of heat in the early days as one of the least well-developed parts of the environment. It seemed to be the component written last and most hastily. Even in Windows 3.1 the recorder is less than spectacular, but it can be quite useful if you are aware of its quirks and limitations. These tips provide direct benefits from Recorder and will help you become familiar with how to use the program effectively.

TABLE 6.7

Terminal Keyboard Shortcuts

Key	Action
F1	Displays Terminal Help
Ctrl+C	Copies material to Clipboard
Ctrl+V	Pastes material from Clipboard
Ctrl+Ins	Copies selected text to Clipboard
Shift+Ins	Sends Clipboard contents to remote system
Ctrl+Shift+Ins	Sends selected text to remote system

Avoid the Mouse

When using Windows' Macro Recorder, you should always use keyboard commands, not mouse clicks. Mouse clicks can be recorded, but they may not play back correctly because their position is recorded relative to the upper-left corner of the window. Since your programs' windows aren't always the same size, the actions you take with the mouse in one window won't always achieve the same effect when played back in another window. To make sure that the mouse isn't recorded for the current macro, select Macro, Record and choose the Ignore Mouse setting in the Record Mouse drop-down list box. To avoid recording mouse actions for any macro, select Options, Preferences and then Ignore Mouse in the Record Mouse box (see Figure 6.13).

Use Macros to Resize Windows

Almost any task you repeat is a candidate for a Recorder macro. A good test of Recorder's power is to replicate the shortcuts, found in earlier versions of Windows, that maximize, minimize, and restore a window (Alt+F10, Alt+F9, and Alt+F5, respectively). While these handy keyboard shortcuts were not included in Windows 3.0 or 3.1, with the help of Recorder you can use the following instructions to restore them to your Windows system.

Open the Recorder and activate any program whose window can be maximized, such as Program Manager. Then press Alt+Tab as many times as necessary, until Recorder becomes the active window again. Give the macro a name that describes what it does. In the Shortcut Key area of the Record Macro dialog box, put an x in the Alt check box (remove the x from the other check boxes, if necessary) and press F10. (Or, if you prefer, click on the downward-pointing arrow and choose F10 from the drop-down list.) The shortcut key for your macro is now set to Alt+F10.

In the To drop-down list box in the Playback section of the dialog box, choose Any Application. This step is important. By default, Recorder macros operate only on the applications in which they are recorded. Because you want your maximize macro to affect whatever window is active when you run it, this step changes the default playback option to Any Application.

FIGURE 6.13

Select Ignore Mouse from Recorder's Default Preferences dialog box to record only keystroke actions when you're creating Windows macros.

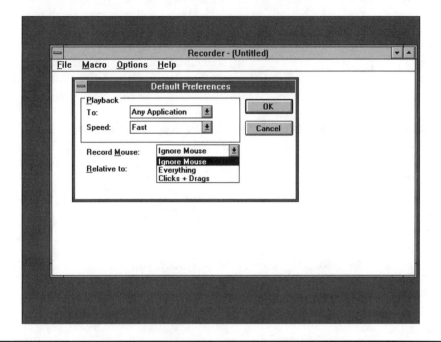

With the dialog box filled out, click on the Start button. Recorder shrinks to a blinking icon and returns you to the application you were in before you activated Recorder. The blinking icon is your signal that the tape is running. Everything you do now will be saved for posterity.

Press Alt+spacebar, x to maximize whatever application you're now in. (Remember to use keyboard techniques.) Then press Ctrl+Break to turn off the Recorder. Recorder responds with another dialog box. Choose Save Macro and click on OK; you now have a keyboard shortcut for maximizing application windows. Try activating an unmaximized window and pressing Alt+F10 just to make sure your macro is working as it should.

You can follow the same procedure to create minimize and restore macros. To make your macros available for future Windows sessions, return to Recorder, choose the File menu's Save command, and give the file a name such as SYS-MAC. (Recorder will assign it the extension .REC.) You can then make this macro file a regular resident of your Windows desktop by adding the line

```
Load=SYS-MAC.REC
```

to your WIN.INI file. With this command in WIN.INI, your macros will be available during each work session.

View Macros

In Recorder you cannot edit previously recorded macros, as you can in many applications such as Microsoft Word for Windows. However, you can review their contents. If a macro isn't working quite right, this will give you a way to study the recorded events and debug the macro. To peek at a macro's contents, start the Recorder, select Open from the File menu, and specify the macro that you want to look at. Hold down the Shift key while choosing Properties from the Macro menu. You'll now see a dialog box that shows all the actions contained in the macro.

Start Recorder Macros from Other Applications

You can call a Windows Recorder macro from within a Windows application or when you start Windows by using Recorder's command-line shortcut keys. In the following example, STARTUP.REC is the name of the Recorder macro; Ctrl+Shift+Alt+Home is the hotkey sequence that invokes STARTUP.REC.

```
WIN RECORDER-H^+%HOME STARTUP
```

This command will load Windows, load Recorder, and fire up the STARTUP macro. The -H portion tells Recorder that a macro shortcut-key sequence follows. The ^+%HOME portion tells Recorder which shortcut-key macro to execute (Recorder cares only about the shortcut-key sequence assigned to the macro).

On the command line, Recorder requires you to use special symbols when specifying the Ctrl, Shift, and Alt keys: ^ specifies Ctrl, + specifies Shift, and % specifies Alt. For example, %END specifies Alt+End. Therefore, ^+%HOME specifies Ctrl+Shift+Alt+Home.

Assign Macros to Icons

You can assign an icon to any macro that you create with Recorder; then you can run the macro simply by double-clicking on its icon. You can do this because of the command-line shortcut keys that Recorder recognizes. When you are creating a new program item for the macro, use the following syntax to specify the command line in the Program Item Properties dialog box:

```
RECORDER.EXE [-H shortcut key] [filename.rec]
```

Use the special symbols (^, +, and %) in place of the Ctrl, Shift, and Alt keys, respectively.

Create Demonstrations with Macro Recorder

Teach your employees how to take full advantage of a Windows application by creating a customized demonstration that profiles critical Windows program features. This is only one potential use for the Macro Recorder. Because you can use the Macro Recorder to automate virtually all Windows operations—including keyboard commands and mouse procedures—it's the perfect tool for setting up personalized, real-world demos. When new employees come on board, introduce them to your PC operations by replaying a Recorder macro. Voilà! an instant demonstration.

Assign Macros for Key Combinations

If there are function keys that you seldom use—for example, the F11 or F12 key—put them to work by assigning a Recorder macro to them. One convenient option is to assign a two-key combination to them. For example, if you find it awkward to press Ctrl+Esc when you want to call up Task Manager, assign that key combination to a function key for a command that's easy to execute every time.

Stop Recording Quickly

If you need to stop or pause while recording a macro, press Ctrl+Break. This keystroke combination will suspend the replaying of a Recorder macro.

Use Recorder to Assign Shortcut Keys in Windows 3.0

In Windows 3.1, you can define a shortcut key for each icon. If a shortcut key is assigned to an application, you can quickly start the application without hunting down the icon and then double-clicking it. To achieve this same result in Windows 3.0, you can use the Recorder to create a macro that launches a specific application—for example, Cardfile. If you already have a file of macros that you use every day, open that file so you can add this new macro to it.

A macro is worthless if you can't remember the keystrokes to activate it, so it's a good idea to use mnemonically significant shortcuts for each application launcher you create. For starting Cardfile, you can use Ctrl+Shift+C. Choose the Macro command in the Record menu, fill out a name for the macro, and specify the shortcut key you want to use. Click the Start button. Now hold down the Alt key and press Tab as many times as necessary to activate the Program Manager window. If Program Manager is active already, hold down Alt anyway and tab through all the programs on your desktop until you come back to Program Manager. (Don't worry if you go around more than once; Recorder cares only about where you end up.)

In Program Manager, press Alt+F, R to execute the File Run command. (Remember to use keyboard rather than mouse techniques when recording a macro.) Fill out the dialog box by typing **cardfile** in the Command Line text box and press Enter (the keyboard equivalent of clicking on OK). You can also include the name of a data file (including its full path) to load into Cardfile if you wish. In a moment, Cardfile appears. As a final (optional) step, press Alt+spacebar, x to maximize Cardfile. Now press Ctrl+Break to stop the recording. In the dialog box that appears, choose Save Macro and click OK. Now pressing the shortcut key should automatically start Cardfile.

Because you can't predict where icons will be at playback time, in the recording you must activate Program Manager and launch Cardfile with keystrokes rather than mouse actions. And because the Program Manager item in the Task List window isn't located in any predictable position, you can't activate Program Manager by pressing Ctrl+Esc and scrolling through the list. Finally, if Program Manager is already the current window when you begin recording, you must cycle around once to *actively* select it; unless you do this, your macro will fail if Program Manager is minimized at playback time.

Character Map

Being able to see what you get makes choices so much simpler. In the case of graphical characters, that has not often been possible in the past. You had to type a complex key sequence to get an ANSI or high ASCII character, and even then might see nothing but an embedded code on your screen. Windows 3.1 provides a Character Map that lets you see *all* the characters your typefaces provide. That's straightforward, but a benefit nonetheless. Character Map is also discussed in Chapter 8 under font housekeeping.

Easy Extended Characters

Character Map allows you to easily incorporate special characters into your documents, such as extended ANSI characters, trademark symbols, and foreign language characters. To locate a specific character, launch Character Map and view the characters available for each font. It's best to use a character from the same typeface as the rest of your document, but if you can't find the desired character there, try other typefaces, especially Symbol or Wingdings. If you have a hard time discerning what each character is because it's so small in the map, move the mouse pointer to it and hold down the left mouse button. A close-up of the character will pop up. Once you've located the character, click on it to select it. It should appear in the Character to Copy text box above the map. Select Copy to place it on the Clipboard. Then switch back to your document, position the cursor where you want the character to appear, and select Paste; it's as simple as that.

If the character doesn't appear after you've pasted it, make sure you have its corresponding font selected in your document: Paste may not automatically switch to the font that the special character requires if it's different from the one you're currently using. Once the character is pasted into your document, you can format it as italic, bold, and so on, if you like.

Multimedia Applets

Windows 3.1 adds two applets that indicate the impact of the multimedia future on the Windows environment: Sound Recorder and Media Player. Both are rather sketchy programs, more demonstration projects than truly useful applications. However, they do perform real work, and if you are multimedia-minded, they are a good place to begin familiarizing yourself with the new world of computer-controlled sound and video.

Play .WAV Files All the Way Through

If you are using Microsoft's PC speaker driver to play .WAV files on a PC without a sound board, the .WAV files that you play in Sound Recorder may not play all the way through. To fix this, change the speaker's Drivers settings in the Control Panel. Select your speaker driver and move the scroll bar for the Seconds to Limit Playback option all the way to the right.

Sound Recorder Keyboard Shortcuts

The keyboard shortcuts for the Sound Recorder are shown in Table 6.8.

TABLE 6.8

Sound Recorder Keyboard Shortcuts

Key	Action
Tab	Moves among buttons
Shift+Tab	Moves among buttons in the reverse direction
PgUp	Moves backward one second
PgDn	Moves forward one second
Home	Moves to beginning of sound
End	Moves to end of sound

Solitaire Secrets

Even Windows games have little, hidden aspects. So that you can be sophisticated even when you are being frivolous, here are some tips on Windows Solitaire. Be a hit at parties, amaze your friends!

Surprise Yourself with Random Card Backs

The first time that you play the Solitaire game included with Windows, the card back option that is shown is selected randomly. This means that each time you play you'll get to use a different deck of cards. But if you ever select a deck yourself you'll lose this option, and there's no setting for it in the Select Card Back box (displayed by selecting Game, Deck).

To revert to using random decks in Windows 3.1, edit the SOL.INI file that contains setting information for Solitaire. It's located in the Windows directory. Open the file in Notepad or another text editor and find the entry that says BACKS=. Delete this entry and then save the file. The next time you play, a card back will be selected at random. If you have no other special settings selected in Solitaire, it's easier just to delete the entire SOL.INI file instead of editing it, because BACK= will be the only entry in the file. Windows will recreate the SOL-.INI file the next time you play Solitaire.

Quick Stacks

It gets tedious dragging a card from its row to the correct upper stack, especially if you're having a successful game where suit stacks are quickly building up. Well, you don't have to drag any more; double-click instead. When you turn over a card that belongs in one of the four stacks, simply double-clicking on it will send it to the correct destination. This saves time too!

No Missed Opportunities

There's no way to guarantee you'll win at the Solitaire game included with Windows, but you increase your chances by using the Drag feature. Select Options from Solitaire's Game menu and choose Outline dragging. With this option turned on, moving a card over a stack that the card can legally be placed on causes that stack to change to an outline image.

To make sure you don't miss any moves that might help you, keep Outline dragging turned on. Every time you flip over a new card, pick it up and sweep across all the stacks. You'll easily spot any opportunities you might have missed. It's a good idea too, from time to time, to pick up the cards already placed on stacks and sweep them across the other stacks to make sure some opportunities haven't appeared during the game.

Cheating to Get the Card You Need

Suppose you're approaching the end of a game and you need a particular card. You click on the deck to draw three cards. The card you need is the second one down, but you can't move the top card to get to it.

You know you can't go to Options and choose Draw One because it blows your game: Solitaire will redeal the cards. Instead, click Undo to return the three cards to the deck; then hold down Ctrl+Alt+Shift and click the deck again. Only one card turns over! As long as you hold down those three keys you can go through the deck one card at a time!

Keyboard Shortcuts for Windows Accessories

The keyboard shortcuts that you can use with most of the Windows Accessories are shown in Table 6.9.

TABLE 6.9

Keyboard Shortcuts for Windows Accessories

Key	Action
F1	Displays context-sensitive help
Alt+F, N	File, New
Alt+F, O	File, Open
Alt+F, S	File, Save
Alt+F, A	File, Save As
Alt+F, P	File, Print
Alt+F, X	Close file and exit accessory
Ctrl+C	Copies material to Clipboard
Ctrl+V	Pastes material from Clipboard
Ctrl+X	Cuts material to Clipboard

With the Alt-key combinations, you can first press Alt and then press the two letters, one after another. You needn't press the keys simultaneously.

*F*ILE MANAGER

EVEN THE MOST GLORIOUS EDIFICE HAS ONE FACADE THAT ISN'T AS GRAND AS all the others. Even the best hitter in baseball has a particular pitch he's weak at. For Windows, the weak aspect is unquestionably File Manager, the program that allows you to manage files, directories, and disk drives.

In Windows 3.0, File Manager was so bad it was the single biggest reason, we feel, that Windows users reported spending a fair amount of time back in character-mode DOS. It was easier to mash that DOS button and do it the old way than to face the rigors of File Manager.

In Windows 3.1, File Manager has been hugely improved, which is to say that now it's barely adequate. It's inscrutable, rather than confounding.

When it comes to File Manager you have three choices: One, you can bag it and drop to DOS for your file operations, which is like reverting to bike pedals for getting your Ferrari uphill. Two, you can check out one of the many commercial alternatives to File Manager. It's a given in the PC business that any weakness in a popular program will draw potential replacement programs like a trash can draws flies. Your third choice is the courageous one: Dig in and work with File Manager. Use the extensibility and customizability of Windows to improve File Manager to suit your tastes. That's what we've done. To make your journey into the File Manager jungle easier (and a lot less time-consuming) than ours was, we offer here a veritable road map of shortcuts and suggestions for taming the wild subdirectory and handling other such adventures of the Windows outback.

File Manager Housekeeping

The essential reason for the File Manager's existence is the selection, movement, and manipulation of the files stored on your PC. In DOS, this was all done at the command line, a process that was remarkably swift if you knew your way around the commands, and utterly impenetrable if you didn't. By replacing commands with mouse clicks and the command line with graphics displays, the File Manager has greatly simplified these processes for the uninitiated, and hugely slowed them down for the expert. But remember, you can always drop back down to the DOS prompt for file handling if you're a DOS guru. With the techniques offered here though, you may find File Manager performance improved enough to be acceptable.

Selecting Files

In DOS, you could manage a single file reasonably, and handling a complete directory wasn't too hard. But working with groups of files smaller than a whole directory was a major headache under DOS. Whole products were created to fill this gap. Under Windows, the File Manager makes it possible to select different sets of files, but leaves the process a bit confusing. Try these ideas to make file selection smoother.

Fast File Manager Selections   Windows' File Manager offers a couple of mouse shortcuts for file selection. To select a contiguous group of files, point to the first filename and then hold down the Shift key while clicking on the filename at the end of the group. If you want to select a group of files that are not contiguous, hold down the Ctrl key as you point to each filename in the File Manager directory window, and click with the left mouse button. You can also use this trick to deselect individual files in a group if you change your mind.

Selecting Even More Files in the File Manager   Making multiple file selections in File Manager is straightforward enough: Just press Shift and click on filenames to highlight contiguous files or subdirectories, or press Ctrl and click for noncontiguous selections. However, here are some even easier ways for quick file or subdirectory processing. Press Shift+F8 to enable the *selection cursor*—a blinking, dotted line that lets you select any number of files by first pressing the spacebar on the file to select it and then using the arrow keys to advance to the next file. To select all files in a subdirectory, press Shift+slash (/). To copy all the highlighted files at once, drag the mouse from one of the highlighted files to another disk drive or subdirectory.

The Sort by Type and By File Type Options Are Different   Here's something to keep in mind: The File Manager's View menu options (Sort by Type and By File Type) are quite different. When you select Sort by Type, you get a list of files sorted by extension. Files with no extension come first and then the other files, in alphabetical order by extension. Selecting By File Type gives you much more power. Clicking this option displays the dialog box shown in Figure 7.1, which lets you choose the files you want to display. Check Programs and you'll see just program files (such as *.COM, *.EXE or *.PIF files). Check Documents and you'll see only files with extensions associated with applications. You can even request to see ordinarily hidden system files. Select as many file type options as you wish.

Caveats When Viewing by File Type   One big limitation to viewing by file type is how confusing it can get. When you select a subset of files to view, File Manager gives no indication that this isn't your complete directory listing. If you exit File Manager with this display, and you have checked Save Settings on Exit, the subset screen will return when File Manager is reloaded. Even if you press the F5 key, which forces File Manager to reread the disk, the display will not change.

FIGURE 7.1

Select Programs in the By File Type dialog box to display files with .COM, .EXE, and .PIF extensions.

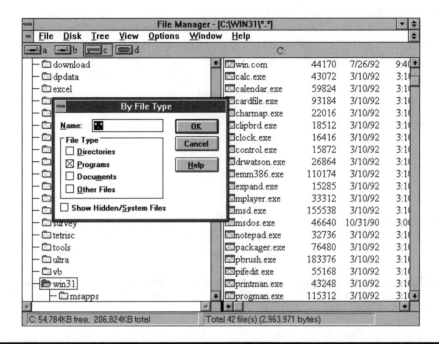

Believe it or not, Windows has no natural way around this problem. But there is one (and apparently only one) approach that works. To get back to your complete directory listing after viewing by file type, first make sure that Name and Sort by Name are checked on the View menu. Then select By File Type again. Make sure that *.* appears in the Name box and that Directories, Programs, Documents, and Other Files have all been checked under File Type. Choose OK, and you'll get your complete listing back.

Quickly Collapsing the Directory Tree   File Manager provides a keyboard shortcut for expanding all the branches of your directory tree (Shift+*), but doesn't have a keyboard shortcut to collapse them. You can, however, accomplish this with your trusty mouse. Double-click on the root directory. The entire directory tree will disappear from the directory tree window, and all you'll see is the root directory. Double-click on it again to reveal its directories, but not their subdirectories. You can use this mouse shortcut to collapse individual directories as well.

File Tweaks and Traps

Once created, files have a habit of never staying still. They need to be copied, saved, protected, archived, and otherwise altered across their natural lives. As with so many areas, the File Manager handles these chores, but somewhat less than elegantly. Avoid much mouse clicking and mouth cursing by using these tips.

File Naming for Efficiency   Here's a simple time saver: File Manager always places files that begin with numerals at the beginning of its displays. After that, it sorts alphabetically by first letter, unless you give other instructions. So, give files you access often names that begin with numerals, such as 1GETIT.COM or 1DOS.PIF. That way, these filenames will always top your directory listings. Also, name files you want grouped together with the same first letter.

Hide Files from File Manager (and Yourself)   File Manager helps prevent you from accidentally deleting or changing important files by enabling you to mark files as read-only. But these read-only files can still be deleted like any other files, even though Windows brings a dialog box asking if you in fact want to delete the file, as shown in Figure 7.2 (unless you have turned off this option by selecting Confirmation from the Options menu and checking the appropriate check box). Increase the protection of these important files by also hiding them from view. If you can't see them, chances are you won't accidentally delete or rewrite them. Hiding critical files can also keep them away from prying eyes.

FIGURE 7.2

File Manager prompts you before deleting a read-only file when you have selected the Confirmation option.

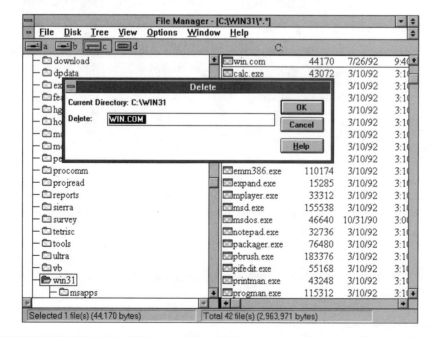

You can set a file's attributes to read-only and hidden at the same time. Select the name of the file, choose Properties from the File menu, check the Read-Only and Hidden check boxes, and then choose OK. To ensure that these files won't be visible in File Manager, choose By File Type from the View menu and make sure that the Show Hidden/System Files box is not marked.

NOTE If you use File Manager's Search feature, it will find hidden as well as nonhidden files that match the search description.

You can also apply this technique to entire subdirectories. If you share a PC with other users, you may want to mark the subdirectory where you store your files as hidden, but not read-only.

Copy Files within the Same Drive If you select a file and drag it to another directory located on the same drive, Windows asks if you want to move the file to the new location. If you want to place a copy of the file in the new directory but still retain the old one, you have to hold down the Ctrl key while you drag the file. A confirmation box still appears, but this one correctly asks if you want to copy the file to the new directory.

Refreshing Floppy Drive Listings It can be frustrating to get an accurate file listing of a floppy disk in File Manager unless you know which command to issue. For example, if you review the contents of one floppy disk and can't find the file you are looking for, you'll try another floppy disk. But when you click the drive icon for the disk drive, for example B:, all you get is the listing from the first disk. Windows is showing you the directory it has stored in memory for that drive; it is not reading the drive anew. You can try closing the window and reselecting the drive icon, but to no avail; you'll still see the contents of the previous floppy disk. Even switching temporarily to another disk drive doesn't do the trick. Short of exiting from File Manager and starting it all over again, what can you do?

Actually, the answer is quite simple and will make you wonder why you spent all that time trying to get an accurate floppy listing! Just press the F5 key or choose the Refresh command from the Window menu. Voilà! An updated listing of the current floppy disk. Repeat the command every time you insert a new floppy disk into the drive.

Copy and Move Files to Floppies If you need to copy a file from one drive to another, for example, from your hard disk to a floppy, you simply drag the filename to the drive icon and release it. But what if you want to move the file instead? Holding down the Alt key while you drag the file tells Windows that you want to put the file in a new location altogether, rather than creating another copy of it. If you have selected the Mouse Action option (Windows 3.1) or Mouse Operation option (Windows 3.0) in the Confirmation dialog box, Windows will ask if you do indeed want to move the file to the new location, as shown in Figure 7.3.

FIGURE 7.3

When you hold down the Alt key as you drag a file to another drive icon, Windows confirms that you want to move, not copy, the file.

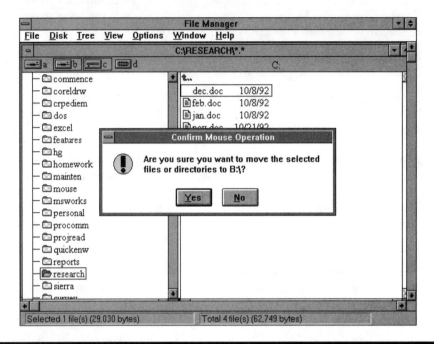

Search Out Temporary Files   If you're having trouble locating a file or group of files because your directories and subdirectories contain so many of them, use File Manager's Search feature. You can tell Search to look for specific words, file extensions, or even wildcards.

Put this capability to work by using it to rid your hard disk of old temp files that may be lurking about. Windows is supposed to delete these temp files when it's done with them, but any Windows user can tell you that that's not always the case. Before you select the Search option, make sure that the root directory is selected so that you can search the entire disk drive. Also, select Partial Details from the View menu and check Last Modification Date. Choose Search from the File menu, and mark the Search All Subdirectories box (if not already marked). In the Search For box, type ***.tmp**. File Manager then gives you a listing of all these files, as you can see in Figure 7.4. Because you asked for last modification date, the list will be sorted by the date of last usage. If the file dates are old, go ahead and delete them from within Windows, but if the files are from your current session leave them alone!

A Caution on Searches   Only move files from a Search Results window with the mouse. If you drag a file into or out of this window, it will update to include the change. However, if you do the same operation using keystrokes, the Search Results window will not automatically reflect the changes.

FIGURE 7.4

Use File Manager's Search feature to easily rid your hard disk of old temp files.

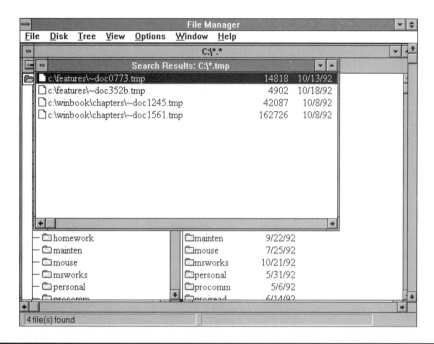

Search Multiple Layers   Remember that you can search a set of files multiple times. This means that you can search for a preliminary set of files that meet one criterion and then search that subset for a second pattern. In this way you can pinpoint your searches and keep to a minimum the wait while File Manager pores over your directories.

Use View to Find Files by Date   If you want to place the files that you have altered most recently first, select Sort by Date from the File Manager's View menu. If you want to see the dates the files were saved, check Partial Details on the View menu. Then, in the Partial Details dialog box, shown in Figure 7.5, check Last Modification Date.

File Manager's Quick Deletes   The File Manager's default settings for deleting files are wisely geared for the cautious, but the constant query "Delete file...?" can be annoying if you have entire subdirectories to clear. To remove the safety net and shave minutes off your file management chores, select File Manager's Options menu and choose Confirmation. If you delete multiple files in the same subdirectory, click on the first option, File Delete, to deselect it. If you're going to remove whole nested subdirectories, click on the second option, Directory Delete, to deselect it. To play it safe again once you've deleted your files, reselect both options, or make sure that Save Settings on Exit is not checked in the File Manager Options menu.

FIGURE 7.5

Selecting Last Modification Date in the Partial Details dialog box lists files by date, with the most recent topping the list.

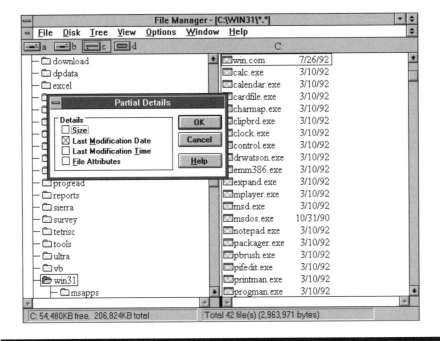

Printing Directory Listings from File Manager

Windows' File Manager doesn't provide a way to print directory listings, but you can create a batch file that will do the job. Using a text editor such as Notepad, create a one-line batch file like the following (substitute your printer port for LPT1 if it is different):

```
DIR %1 > LPT1
```

Save the file with a name like PRINTDIR.BAT, and make sure that it is located in a directory that is in your PATH statement. Now when you want to print a directory listing from File Manager, choose the Run command from the File menu and type **printdir.bat** (or whatever you named the batch file) followed by the desired directory in the Command Line text box. For example, to get a listing of your REPORTS directory, type

```
printdir.bat c:\reports
```

A DOS screen will appear and then disappear as the directory listing is sent to the printer.

Another, somewhat quicker option for the DOS savvy is to select Run from the File Manager's File menu. In the Command Line text box of the resulting dialog box, type

```
command.com /c dir> lpt1
```

This runs a copy of COMMAND.COM, the DOS command processor, and orders it to print your directory listing on printer LPT1.

The only limitation of this trick is if you have a .PIF file for DOS called COMMAND.PIF. If you do, that file, not a native COMMAND.COM, will run here. An easy fix is to instead name your DOS-session .PIF file DOS.PIF.

Finding File Facts Fast   When a file or directory is selected in File Manager, you can press Alt+Enter to call up a Properties dialog box that gives you detailed file information. The dialog box includes the filename, file size, last modification date, path, and file attributes, as shown in Figure 7.6.

FIGURE 7.6 ▬▬▬▬▬▬▬▬▬▬▬▬▬▬▬▬▬▬▬▬▬▬▬▬▬▬▬▬▬▬▬▬▬▬▬▬

File Manager's Properties dialog box supplies detailed file information.

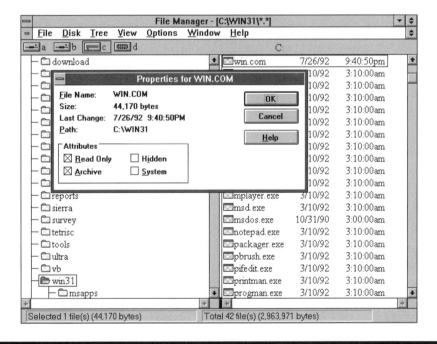

Get More Information on All Files   Usually, File Manager only lists file and directory names. However, you can instruct it to tell you far more about your files. From the View menu, select All File Details. Now your listings should include name, size in bytes, date and time last modified, and all file attributes for every file.

Too much info? Go back and check Partial Details from the View menu instead. Now you'll see a dialog box (shown earlier, in Figure 7.5) that lets you select what information you want on your files. The information you select here will remain in force for all files until you uncheck this choice on the View menu. If you have Save Settings on Exit selected, this will become your default listing.

Starting Programs from the File Manager   You can start programs from the File Manager in one of several ways:

- Double-click on a selected program's File Manager icon or on the icon of a document associated with the application (for more on association see "Take Advantage of Associations," later in this chapter).

- Drag the icon for an associated document onto the icon of its application.

- Select Run from the File menu, and enter the application's startup command into the Run dialog box.

- Select an associated document and press Enter or click on Open in the File menu.

Some Windows applications offer still other options, such as dragging an associated document icon into an open application window or onto the application's title bar. The preceding options should work for every Windows application.

Starting DOS Programs from the File Manager   You can also start DOS programs from the File Manager, as long as you have created .PIF files for them. Open a window on the WINDOWS directory on your C drive (or wherever you have Windows loaded). Double-click on the .PIF file for the DOS program you want; it will run.

Installing Windows Programs with the File Manager   Install applications in Windows through the File Manager by double-clicking on the application's startup file. To find this file, open the application's directory, select By File Type from the View menu, check Programs in the dialog box, and uncheck the other three check boxes. Study the resulting list for a file with a name like STARTUP-.EXE or INSTALL.EXE. Click on this program and the application's setup routine will run.

The Fast Way to Change the Active Drive   Even quicker than clicking on a drive icon is changing the active drive in File Manager by pressing Ctrl+*drive letter*. For example, to see a listing of the contents in your A drive, press Ctrl+A.

Quick Formats   You don't have to exit to DOS to format floppy disks, because Windows 3.1's File Manager lets you do so through its Disk menu. Speed up the process of formatting a floppy by selecting the Quick Format option in the Format Disk dialog box shown in Figure 7.7 (select Format Disk from the Disk menu). This process is faster than a regular format because it does not check the disk for bad sectors. Quick Format only works with disks that have been previously formatted. Use it when you are *sure* that the disk is problem-free (that is, it has been recently formatted and is fairly new) so that you don't end up saving a file to a bad disk sector and losing important information.

FIGURE 7.7

Speed up floppy-disk formatting by choosing the Quick Format option from the Format Disk dialog box, as explained in the Help text shown here.

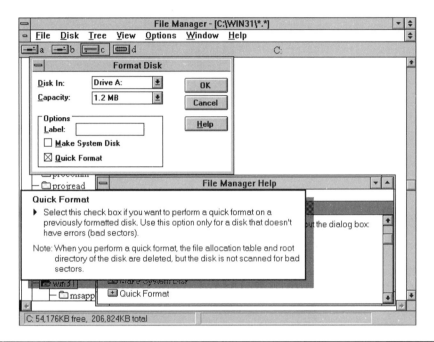

Minimizing File Manager for Quick Access Minimizing makes sense for any Windows application you think you'll use later, but it's particularly valuable with the File Manager. Every time you load File Manager, it reads your entire disk structure, wasting precious time. If you minimize it instead of closing it on first use, you can get back to the File Manager much faster by using the Task List or by clicking on the File Manager icon.

If you want to make this process automatic, pull down the File Manager Options menu and check Minimize on Use. Then put a copy of the File Manager in your StartUp program group. A minimized File Manager will appear each time you start Windows.

Using File Manager for Daily Backups Use the File Manager for a quick daily backup of each day's work to a floppy disk. In the Options menu, select Confirmation and make sure each box in the dialog box has been checked so that you won't have to okay any overwriting of old versions of today's files. Then, before you end your work, go to the File Manager and open whatever directory you've worked in. Select Sort by Date from the View menu. You'll see your new files at the beginning of the directory listing. Select these files by clicking to select the first one and then holding down the Shift key while clicking on the last file name. Click on Copy from the File menu (or press F8). In the dialog box, note the drive and directory you want the files saved to, as shown in Figure 7.8. Make sure to uncheck File Replace after your backup, so you don't inadvertently overwrite files during your other work.

FIGURE 7.8

Tell Windows where you want to copy the selected files by specifying the location in the Copy dialog box.

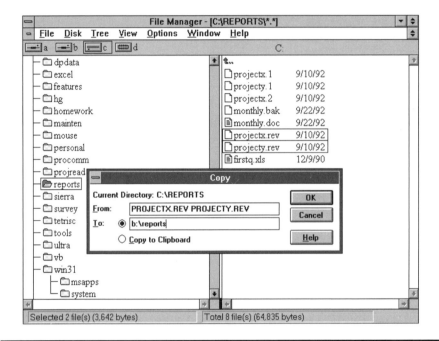

Take Advantage of Associations

One of the many conveniences Windows offers you is the ability to load a data file and the program that created it by simply double-clicking on the data file's icon.

The trick is in the data file's extension. Windows rides atop DOS and uses DOS's outdated file system, so data files don't automatically reveal which programs created them, as Macintosh files do. But Windows can be taught to associate certain file extensions with specific programs. For example, for Windows to open NOTEPAD.EXE anytime you double-click on a file with the extension .TXT, Windows must first be told that all .TXT files belong to Notepad. Fortunately, many applications provide Windows with linkage information when you install them, and those that don't can still be linked to their data files by means of a simple procedure in the File Manager. Once files are associated, they take on new powers that you can use to manage your system more efficiently.

Establishing Associations To establish an association, follow these steps:

1. Run File Manager, either by double-clicking on its icon in Program Manager or by pulling down Program Manager's File menu, choosing Run, and typing **winfile**.

2. Find a file that has the extension that you want to associate, for example *.XYZ. You'll notice that next to it (and all the other filenames) is a small icon, as shown in Figure 7.9. Document and data files, such as this one, are marked by rectangles with a bent corner.

FIGURE 7.9

File Manager denotes document and data files with bent corners on the icon; blank faces indicate unassociated files, and striped icons indicate files that are associated with applications.

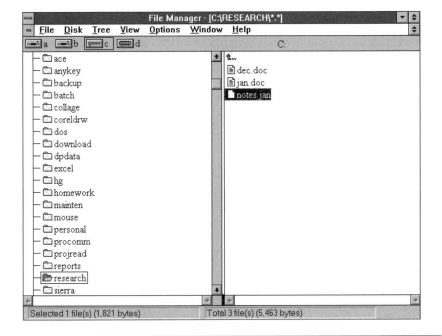

3. Pull down File Manager's File menu and choose the Associate command. A dialog box like the one shown in Figure 7.10 appears.

4. In the text box at the top, you enter the file extension you want to associate.

5. At the bottom is a list of the various applications you can associate the file with. Select one and click on OK.

All files that have the specified extension will now be associated with that application. That's all there is to it!

FIGURE 7.10

Associate a data file with an application so that you can automatically launch it from File Manager.

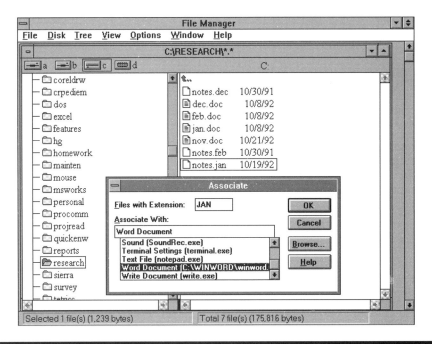

When you click on OK in the Associate dialog box, all of the icons next to the .XYZ files instantly change. They're still dog-eared, but they now bear little black stripes. A striped, dog-eared icon denotes a document file associated with a program. This means that any .XYZ file that you select (not just the specific one that you associated) can be launched from File Manager.

Change Predefined Associations File Manager can run a program and open an associated file when you click on the file's name, but it doesn't always work the way you want. If you want to look at .PCX files in Publisher Paintbrush, for example, the default association to the Windows Paintbrush accessory won't help you. Fortunately, creating and editing file associations is simple. Select a data file's name from any open subdirectory in File Manager, and then select the File menu's Associate option. Enter the path and filename of the program you want to open when you double-click on the filename and then press Enter or click on OK. (To find the file name, you can use the Browse button in the Associate dialog box. It displays the dialog box shown in Figure 7.11.) To get a list of existing file associations, open your WIN.INI file and scroll the [Extensions] section. You can also associate files and applications by directly editing the WIN.INI yourself. This is discussed in more detail in Chapter 2.

FIGURE 7.11

Use the Browse feature to locate the correct program to associate with the selected file.

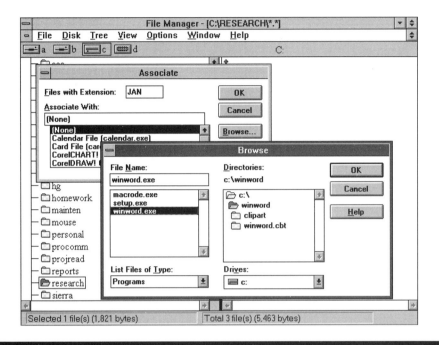

Quick Check for Associated Files If you double-click on the icon of a data file that is not associated with a program, you'll receive a message to that effect. To avoid getting this dialog box, you can do a quick check before you double-click on the file icon. The icon next to the filename will be blank if it is not associated; if it is associated you will see little lines across the icons, as shown in Figure 7.12.

Loading an Unassociated Data File If a data file is not associated with an application, you can still run it from File Manager. Select the file and then drag it and release it on top of the executable file for that application. Windows will ask if you want to start the application with that specific file, as shown in Figure 7.13. Select Yes and the application will start with the file loaded.

For example, to start the Word for Windows document file MYNOTES-.DEC, drag it and release it onto the file WINWORD.EXE. To carry out this dragging and dropping operation, it's probably easiest to display two tiled directory windows if the document file and application file are not located in the same directory (as in Figure 7.13).

NOTE Make sure both the file you want to drag and the executable file you want to drop it on are visible on screen before you begin the process. You can't scroll through a directory window while dragging a file.

FIGURE 7.12

Data files that are associated with applications have striped icons next to their names; files that aren't associated have blank icons.

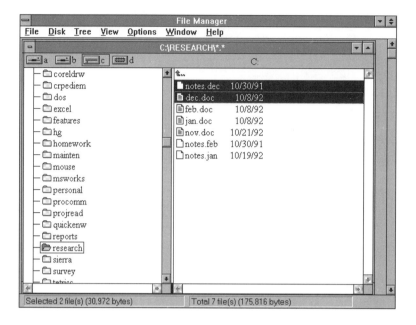

FIGURE 7.13

Drag an unassociated data file onto its application's executable file to start it from File Manager.

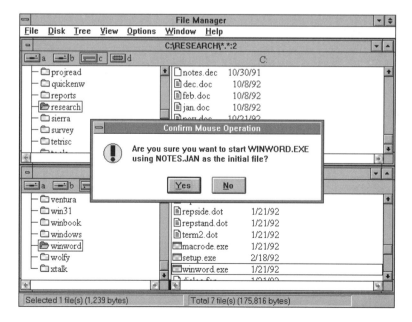

Quicker File Manager Access in Windows 3.0   Getting to the File Manager takes considerably more time in Windows 3.0 than in Windows 3.1 because the old version of File Manager reads the directory contents of the entire active drive when it loads. In Windows 3.1, this time-consuming behavior is eliminated. If you haven't upgraded to Windows 3.1 and don't like waiting for File Manager to cycle through the drive, you can gain control of File Manager more quickly by using a variation on the procedure described in the previous section.

Select the File Manager icon from the Program Manager's Main program group. Pull down the File menu and select Properties. In the Program Item Properties dialog box for your File Manager icon, change the path from C:\WIN-FILE.EXE to point to a drive on your system that contains fewer directories and files. An excellent candidate is a RAM drive, if you have one, because it contains few files. For example, for a RAM drive D, the new command line would read D:\WINFILE.EXE. Windows will tell you that the path is invalid, but just select OK to make it accept the changes.

Getting the Most from Windows 3.1 File Manager

If this were a book about Windows 3.0 exclusively, this section wouldn't exist. That's because the Windows 3.0 File Manager was so weak the problem was getting it to work, not getting the greatest benefit from it. Under Windows 3.1, however, the File Manager is solid enough to offer some worthwhile tricks for the savvy user, such as those that follow.

File Manager Drag and Drop Techniques

One of the great boons of the File Manager, once you get the knack of it, is the ability to replace typed or menu-driven file operations with simple drag and drop on-screen procedures. The notion of literally taking a file from *here* and putting it *there* makes eminent sense.

Drag and Drop Basics   In File Manager, you can move or copy files by simply dragging their icons from one spot and dropping those icons on another with the mouse. You control what happens when you drag an icon by the key you hold down while moving the mouse. Here are the basic combinations:

Action	Result
Drag (no key pressed)	Moves a file among directories of a single drive or copies a file between drives or into any Program Manager group (since this doesn't actually move the file, just the icon)
Drag+Shift or Drag+Alt	Moves a file between drives
Drag+Ctrl	Copies a file on a single drive or between drives

You Don't Need Open Windows to Drag and Drop   You can move and copy between open directory windows, but you don't have to. You can drag and drop to a minimized directory window, to a folder icon in a directory tree window, or to a disk drive icon. If you use a minimized directory of a disk drive icon, the dragged files will go into the logged directory.

Combine Associations with Drag and Drop   If a file extension is associated with a file type defined in Windows 3.1's Registration Database, not only can you start the application (as in Windows 3.0), but you can also print the file, add its icon to a Program Manager group, and even embed the file in another document all by dragging and dropping. We talk about these particular tricks in Chapters 8 and 9 and elsewhere in this chapter. Here, we'll deal with the basics of the Registration Database itself.

The Registration Database, new to Windows 3.1, contains a listing of the file types that Windows recognizes. To register a file type, you need to run the utility Registration Info Editor by typing **regedit** in the File Manager's Run dialog box (select Run from the File menu). To add a new file type, select Add a File Type from the Edit menu. A dialog box like the one shown in Figure 7.14 will appear, which you then fill out for the application. Before you attempt to add an application's file type to the Registration Database, you should make sure that the application supports drag and drop capabilities. You also need to find out the macro commands and command-line options supported by the application so that you can properly fill out the information in the Registration Info Editor. Check your application's documentation or contact the manufacturer for this information.

FIGURE 7.14

Add an application to the Registration Database by filling out the information in the Modify File Type dialog box.

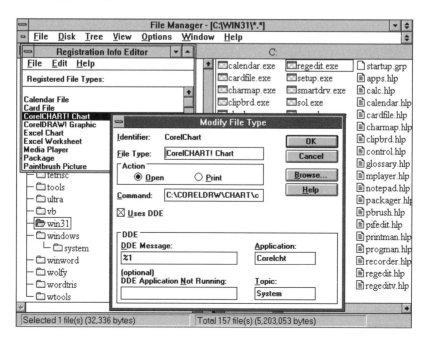

Immediate Drag and Drop   Add copies of the File Manager and Print Manager icons to your StartUp group so that they'll be readily available. With many applications now supporting drag and drop printing, you'll want to keep these two managers around all of the time to take advantage of this feature. We'll cover printing tricks in detail in Chapter 8.

Drag and Drop to Nowhere   If you change your mind about a drag and drop operation after you have selected files and started moving them, simply drag them anyplace on the screen that *isn't* a directory window. This will cancel the procedure and return the files to their original spot.

Taming the File Manager Screen

At first, the notion of being able to view all files and directories on the screen sounds great. Think about it for a minute, though. Add to an already crowded Windows screen the wealth of information contained in a complex scheme of directories and subdirectories and you wind up with a visual nightmare. To be most effective, the File Manager's screen displays must be carefully managed.

Make File Manager Easier to Read   Another new feature of the Windows 3.1 File Manager is that you can change the font that is used to display the file and directory listings. You can enlarge the font so that it's easier to make out individual files in crowded directories, or you can decrease the font size to fit more information on the screen at one time. You can even change the style of the font, such as making it uppercase or boldfaced. For instance, a large, boldfaced font in uppercase may be helpful for those who are visually impaired.

To change the File Manager font, select Font from the Options menu to call up the Font dialog box seen in Figure 7.15. You'll see the selection of your installed fonts that Windows recognizes as potential system fonts, as well as available point size and format options. Make your selections and click on OK. Your fonts will change immediately.

NOTE   Your font changes will remain in effect after you exit File Manager, even if you haven't checked Save Settings on Exit. To restore your original fonts, you'll have to reselect them from the Font dialog box.

Resize File Manager Window Panes   Using your mouse, you can easily change the proportions of the directory tree pane and the directory contents pane. Grab the line that divides the window into these two sections (it's located just to the right of the scroll bar) and drag it to the left or right, depending on which side you want to make bigger or smaller. See Figure 7.16, in which the size of the directory tree pane has been greatly reduced. If you don't have many branching subdirectories, you probably have extra space on the directory tree side. Move the border line so that the space can be used to display more files on screen at one time. Once you adjust the width of these panes, make sure that the Save Settings on Exit option is selected so that the newly sized window will remain in place the next time you use File Manager.

FIGURE 7.15

The Font option lets you change the font used to display File Manager listings.

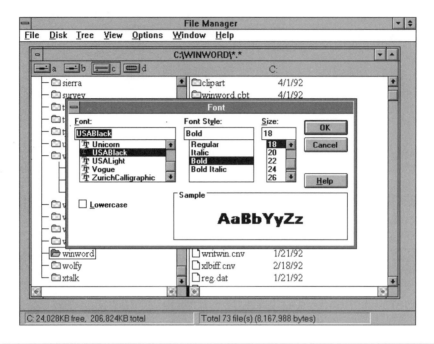

Control the Files You See in Windows Getting multiple directory windows open in the File Manager can be confusing. If you click on New Window in the Window menu, you get a replica of whatever window is already open. You can then work with that window to look at something new. But how inefficient! Here's a method that's much better.

When you want to open a new window from the same drive as the one you already have on screen, but with a different directory listing, highlight the directory folder you want. Press Shift while double-clicking on the highlighted folder. You'll get a new window that displays that directory. If you want to open a new window onto a new drive, just double-click on the drive's icon.

Get Rid of the Directory Tree File Manager defaults to a two-window arrangement: one window with the directory tree for the drive, and the other with the contents of the selected directory. Unless you are planning to hunt around on the drive a great deal, the tree listing may be superfluous. You can get rid of it, and simplify your File Manager screens, in two ways. To get rid of the tree temporarily, use your mouse to grab the slide bar that separates the windows. Drag it all the way to the left, covering the tree. If you want the tree removed permanently, go to the View menu and click on Directory Only.

To move around without the tree, click on any directory or subdirectory to open it; to move to the next highest level in the directory tree, click on the bent arrow at the top of any open listing or press Home+Enter.

FIGURE 7.16

You can adjust the width of the directory tree pane and the directory contents pane by dragging the border with the mouse.

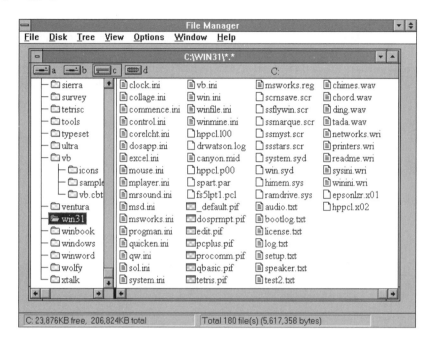

Put File Windows Side by Side   Windows 3.1 enables you to view the contents of two drives at once. To do so, select the Tile command from the Window menu. When you do this, you'll notice that the two drive windows are stacked horizontally. To make the windows line up next to one another so that you can easily compare the contents, press Shift+F4 or hold down the Shift key while you choose Tile from the Window menu.

Side-by-Side Windows for Drag and Drop   The most efficient way to arrange windows, if you plan to move many files from one directory or drive to another, is side by side. That way you can easily drag your files over to their new location. To get two File Manager windows arranged in this way, first press Shift while double-clicking on the first directory's icon. This opens a window for that directory. Repeat the process for the second window (or refer to the earlier section in this chapter, "Control the Files You See in Windows"). When both windows are open, press Shift+F4 to tile them. Now they will be side by side, and you can easily drag your files between them.

Put File Manager and Program Manager Side by Side   Positioning File Manager and Program Manager side by side is a bit trickier. The File Manager Tile key sequence won't work. What to do? Call up the Windows Task List by clicking any open space on the desktop or by pressing Ctrl+Esc. Click on the Tile button in the Task List dialog box. This will place the Program Manager and File Manager windows side by side, as shown in Figure 7.17.

FIGURE 7.17

Tiling Program Manager and File Manager side by side makes it easy to add program items to Program Manager groups with drag and drop.

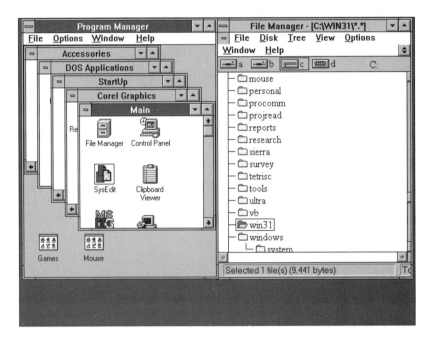

Use File Manager as Your Primary Shell   With all of these File Manager improvements, you might find yourself working very well in this improved shell. And if you liked the good old days of the MS-DOS Executive, try using the File Manager instead of Program Manager as your primary shell. The File Manager in Windows 3.1 is about twice as fast as the File Manager in Windows 3.0. And if you get rid of the directory tree window by selecting the View menu and choosing Tree Only, it even looks and feels the same as the old Windows 2 shell, MS-DOS Executive.

File Manager Keyboard Shortcuts

One way to effectively manage the File Manager screen display is to use keyboard shortcuts to move around in File Manager windows as quickly as possible. Table 7.1 lists the File Manager keyboard shortcuts.

TABLE 7.1

Keyboard Shortcuts for File Manager

Shortcut	Action
Home	Goes to the root directory in the directory tree window or first file in the directory list
End	Goes to the last directory or last file in the list
PgUp	Goes to the first visible file or directory in the current window
PgDn	Goes to the last visible file or directory in the current window
letter	Goes to the next file or directory whose name starts with the specified letter
Ctrl+/	Selects all files and directories in a directory window
Ctrl+\	Deselects all files and directories in a directory window
F5	Refreshes the listing in a directory window
F7	Moves a selected file or files to the destination you note
F8	Copies a selected file or files to the destination you note
Backspace	Selects the parent directory or current directory
Spacebar	Selects or deselects a file or directory when choosing files not listed contiguously
Del	Deletes a selected file (upon confirmation)
Ctrl+*letter*	Selects the specified disk drive
- (hyphen)	Collapses the selected directory
+ (plus sign)	Expands selected directory
* (asterisk)	Expands the entire directory branch
Tab or F6	Moves between the directory tree and directory contents panes and drive indicator
Ctrl+Tab	Moves from one directory window to another

8 Managing Fonts and Printing

DEPENDING ON YOUR POINT OF VIEW, PRINTING UNDER WINDOWS IS A GLASS either half-full or half-empty. On the one hand, printing is easier than ever with Windows because all applications print the same way, use the same printer drivers, interact with the Print Manager for printer housekeeping, and have access to a cornucopia of beautiful typefaces. On the other hand, printing remains a major Windows deficiency: The font situation is volatile and complicated; printer management still requires significant hand work and knowledge of printer basics; font management becomes a new headache, particularly for the many business users who don't know much about type; and printing performance can be adversely affected by driver and memory limitations, graphical complexity, and many other factors. In short, printing and fonts represent the kind of Windows situation where tips and tricks make an especially large difference. We wouldn't be surprised if this is one of the chapters at the top of most readers' reference lists.

Font Magic

It used to be so easy. All you could see on a DOS screen was a single font. And all you had to deal with were a few codes for boldfacing or italic. Later, as applications grew more complex, typefaces still were not an issue even for most word processors, and they had virtually no role in other applications.

Under Windows, in a way, every application is a desktop publishing program. Fonts, page design, and other graphical elements play a huge role, in both the screen display and the printed output of every Windows application. As a result, the care and feeding of fonts has become a necessary skill for the sophisticated Windows user. We've broken this skill into three parts:

- Font Housekeeping, which involves the loading, unloading, and management of the files that generate on-screen and printer fonts

- Advanced Font Secrets, tips that let you do more with fonts than you might have thought reasonably possible

- TrueType, tips on the new font standard built into Windows 3.1

Font Housekeeping

Fonts are an area where the basics still remain a bit beyond the understanding of otherwise savvy users. That makes sense, since document design is hardly part of the standard training process for either business or computing. So, we've compiled some advice and strategies to make sure your font basics are well in hand.

Keep Track of the Differences between Screen and Printer Fonts *Screen fonts* are the letters that Windows creates on your display screen; *printer fonts* are the characters a printer actually puts on paper. Some printers come with fonts permanently installed. Others allow the user to load fonts into the printer. These loadable fonts are called *soft fonts*, since they can be changed.

Screen fonts come in two types: raster fonts and scalable fonts. Raster fonts are of a fixed style and size. Scalable fonts consist of equations that can calculate the look of one style of character in many sizes. In the case of scalable fonts, such as TrueType and PostScript, what Windows draws on the screen is essentially identical to what the printer prints. The screen font matches the printer font. In the case of raster fonts, however, Windows will use the available screen font that most closely matches the selected printer font. This match is not always made in heaven, resulting in documents that may look decidedly different on paper than they did on screen. The simple way to avoid this problem is to move to scalable fonts for your Windows work. TrueType and PostScript, both scalable font formats, are discussed later in this chapter.

Install Screen Fonts You install screen fonts by double-clicking on the Fonts icon in the Control Panel, and then clicking on the Add button. By default, Windows searches your WINDOWS subdirectory for any font files. You can direct it to other drives and files by using the Drives and Directories list boxes at the bottom of the Add Fonts dialog box. Generally fonts are stored in the SYSTEMS subdirectory.

Since fonts usually come on slow floppy disks, you can speed font installation by copying the files for fonts you know you want into the SYSTEM subdirectory before starting the installation.

Load Only the Fonts You'll Use Most printers and many desktop publishing applications come with a starter set of fonts. If you're working in Windows, the list of installed fonts in the WIN.INI file expands every time you load a new font. Sometimes you're asked to specify which fonts to load when you install a new printer or Windows application, but in many cases the installation process simply loads all fonts that come with the product.

Each installed font takes up memory, which can make applications run more slowly. Some programs, such as PageMaker, are slowed even further because, when you use a command that references the list of fonts, they read the specifications of every font. The longer the list, the longer the command takes to execute.

One way to handle font overload is to add and delete fonts through the Windows Control Panel. If you regularly produce documents using different fonts, create a different WIN.INI for each document or department that uses a different font set.

First, make lists of the fonts you need for each set of documents. Say that document set A (reports) uses only Times and Helvetica, and set B (a newsletter) uses only Palatino. Add Helvetica to each list of fonts, since it is used in most Windows dialog boxes and, if you remove it, the dialog boxes will be hard to read.

Next, start Windows and use Notepad or another text editor to make a copy of WIN.INI, which includes all installed fonts, and name the copy WIN.ALL. Then use the Windows Control Panel to delete all the fonts except those you use in set A. WIN.INI is automatically updated. Make a copy of the new WIN.INI and name it WIN.A.

Repeat this step for each document set. In our example, you next use the Fonts icon in the Control Panel to delete all fonts except those used in set B, plus Helvetica, and then copy the new WIN.INI and name it WIN.B.

You now have three versions of WIN.INI—WIN.ALL, WIN.A, and WIN.B—each with a different set of fonts. To start Windows with one font set, copy the file, name it WIN.INI and restart Windows.

NOTE When you change your Windows configuration, you'll change WIN.INI, and you'll have to modify each of your alternates. This may make the solution more trouble than the problem. This tip works best when your Windows setup is stable.

Remember, Removing Fonts Isn't the Same as Deleting Them   One reason to be prudent in loading fonts is that removing a font via the Control Panel doesn't delete its file from the hard drive. The font merely disappears from WIN.INI. To remove a font from the drive, you have to use File Manager or drop down to DOS to delete its files.

Access a Host of Special Characters   You can enter characters other than the alphabet, such as the ANSI.SYS graphics primitives discussed in Chapter 4 (see "ANSI.SYS Metastrings and Graphic Characters"), by entering them from the numeric keypad. But this technique is cumbersome and doesn't let you see what other, unexpected characters may be available.

Windows 3.1 offers an easy, graphical way to see all the characters available. Go to the Accessories program group and double-click on the Character Map icon. You'll see the display that looks something like a keyboard, with the characters represented by every key, as shown in Figure 8.1. Click on the Font drop-down list box in the upper-left corner, and you'll see a list of all fonts in your system. Click on a font and its characters appear on the keyboard. When you double-click on a symbol, it appears in the Characters to Copy box in the upper-right corner. When you have selected all the characters you want, as in Figure 8.2, click on Copy and they will be copied into the Clipboard. From the Clipboard you can paste the characters into any Windows program. In some cases, such as Windows Paintbrush, you may have to manually select the font the character comes from in the receiving application before it will appear properly on the screen.

FIGURE 8.1

Windows' Character Map lets you access extended characters instantly; holding down the left mouse button gives you a close-up view of the selected character.

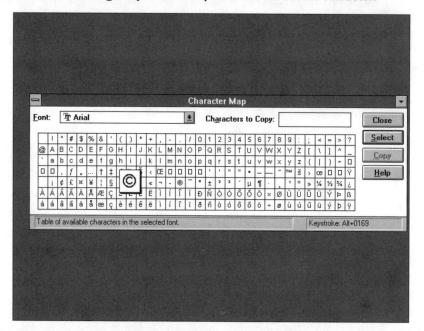

FIGURE 8.2

Select all the characters that you want to copy into your document, and then choose Copy to place them into the Clipboard.

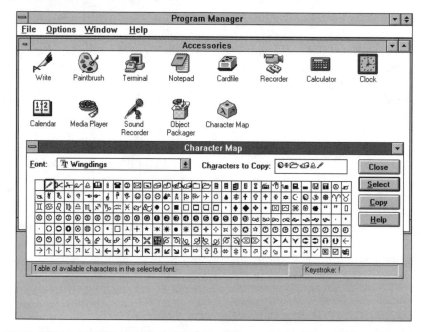

Copy Installed Soft Fonts to a New Printer   When you install soft fonts for use by Windows, a listing for each font is placed in the section of the WIN.INI file that contains settings for the specific printer and port you are using. Because these soft fonts are installed for a printer on a specific port, they will not automatically appear if you change printers. Instead of having to reinstall all of the fonts for the new printer, select Printers from the Control Panel and click on Setup. You'll see a dialog box named for the active printer. Click on the Fonts button. Then, choose the Copy Fonts To New Port button in the Font Installer dialog box that appears. The fonts will be copied to the new printer port and will be available for your use.

Troubleshoot HP LaserJet Soft Fonts   If you click Printers, Setup, Font Installer but can't get Windows to accept soft fonts for your HP LaserJet printer, make sure that you have installed the HP LaserJet II or LaserJet III. The original HP laser printer wouldn't accept soft fonts.

Retain Soft Fonts When Reinstalling Windows   When you install soft fonts to your hard disk through the Windows Control Panel, they are stored in a directory on your hard disk, and an entry for each of them is listed in the WIN.INI file, in the section for your specific installed printer. If you have to reinstall Windows for some reason, you'll lose all of these soft font settings. To avoid having to do this, take advantage of the Control Panel's ability to generate a summary file of all the soft fonts installed on your system. This file, FINSTALL.DIR, will contain all of the necessary WIN.INI settings.

To create this important file choose the Printers icon in the Control Panel, click on Setup and select the Fonts button to bring up Windows' Font Installer. Hold down the Ctrl+Shift key combination while you click on the Exit button. A dialog box like the one in Figure 8.3 will appear, asking if you want to create the FINSTALL.DIR file. You can accept the default directory proposed by Windows or choose your own. It's easiest to use the directory where your soft fonts are located. Each time you add or remove soft fonts from your system you should recreate the FINSTALL.DIR file.

After you have reinstalled Windows, here's how you use the FINSTALL-.DIR file to install your font settings: Again in the Control Panel, choose Printers, click on Setup, then select Fonts from the active printer's dialog box, and hold down Ctrl+Shift while clicking on the Add Fonts button. A special dialog box appears in which you can specify the path and filename of your FINSTALL.DIR file. Then a Font Installer dialog box appears, allowing you to select the fonts you want to install. Once you've selected the fonts, choose Move and specify the directory where the fonts are already installed. The fonts will now appear in the Windows Fonts list, showing that they are installed on your system.

Preload PostScript Fonts for Faster Printing   If you use PostScript fonts when printing from Windows, you can save time by preloading them. This means that fonts won't have to be downloaded to your printer every time you use them. Of course, you have to download the fonts before you run Windows for them to be available for your entire Windows session.

FIGURE 8.3

Create the file FINSTALL.DIR to have a record of the soft fonts that are installed on your system.

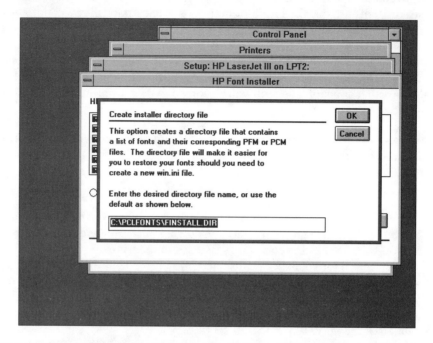

To stop Windows from downloading fonts on the fly, you have to edit your WIN.INI file. Open the WIN.INI in SysEdit or a text editor and find the section that contains settings for your printer. You'll see a listing of font files that are used by the printer. Notice that a font may be listed twice: once with a .PFM extension and once with a .PFB extension. The file with the .PFB extension is the one that instructs Windows to download the font to the printer each time it is used in a print job. Delete the lines with the .PFB extensions.

If you are using a soft font package, such as Adobe Type Manager, it will probably include a utility to batch-download the fonts you'll use while in Windows. If not, you can use a third-party utility or create your own batch file using the appropriate commands for your system. Adobe Type Manager is covered in more detail in Chapter 15.

Advanced Font Secrets

Once you have a selection of fonts available for your Windows screen and printers, there's no end to the variations you can achieve. The idea behind all the tricks that follow is that *every* part of Windows is affected by fonts, and that *all* of those fonts can be managed by you.

Change Font Names   If you add to your system a new PCL soft or scalable font (one that supports PCL, the printer control language of HP LaserJets and compatibles) that has the same name as an existing font, you can eliminate confusion for yourself by changing the font name in Windows' HP Font Installer. To access the Font Installer, select Printers in the Control Panel, select the PCL printer, and choose Fonts. From the list of installed fonts, select the one whose name you want to change. Select Edit, and in the dialog box that pops up specify the new font name, as shown in Figure 8.4. (Note that you cannot change the name of a cartridge font.) This new name will appear in the list of installed fonts, as well as in the font list of Windows applications. When you are changing the name of the font, be sure not to change any of the other Font settings unless you are familiar with editing and creating fonts.

FIGURE 8.4

The HP Font Installer allows you to change the names of soft fonts.

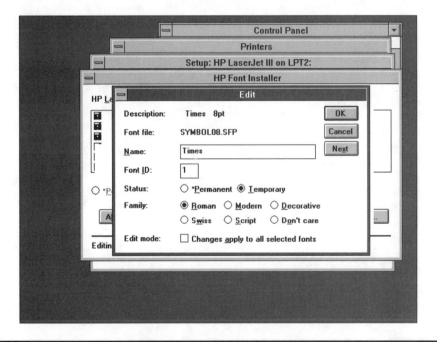

Utilize Excel's Preview Font in Any Application   Excel 3.0 and 4.0 users are certainly familiar with the program's Print Preview feature, but they probably don't know that the typeface used to preview documents can be utilized by other Windows applications. For example, open up Windows Paintbrush, select Fonts from the Text menu and scroll through the list of available fonts. You'll notice that a font named Preview is not among them. Then switch to Excel, open a spreadsheet, and select Print Preview from the File menu. Now, when you switch back to Paintbrush, the Preview font is available for your use.

You can also make sure that the Preview font is *always* available to those applications that can use it. Start the Control Panel, select Fonts, choose Add, and highlight the Excel directory in the Directories list box. When you select Excel the word Preview appears in the List of Fonts box, telling you that this font is available within that directory, as shown in Figure 8.5. If you are using Windows 3.1, you should also make sure that the Copy Fonts to Windows Directory check box is selected, so that Windows will always find the font. If you are using Windows 3.0, you should copy the font file to your WINDOWS\SYSTEM directory manually to provide for this. Finally, select OK. Now the Preview font will be available to Paintbrush and other Windows applications that will recognize it, regardless of whether or not you use Excel.

FIGURE 8.5

In the Control Panel's Add Fonts dialog box, select the Excel directory to install the Preview font for use by the rest of Windows.

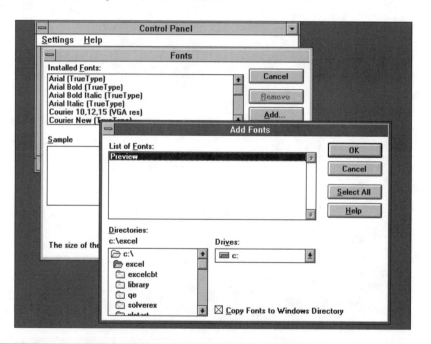

Change the System Font Size Windows assigns default system fonts based upon the kind of video display you have. These fonts appear in menus and title bars. Most of the time, the default fonts work fine. However, if you find the system font too small for comfort, you can change it.

The trick is to edit those lines in the SYSTEM.INI file that define default screen fonts. They are in the [boot] section of the file. (This section of SYSTEM.INI was discussed in Chapter 2, and you should review that material if you want to edit these lines.)

If you have a Super VGA display, the most common Windows option, you can enlarge the system font by switching to the font used by IBM's 8514/A video format. To do this, find the following lines in SYSTEM.INI and edit them so they look exactly like this:

```
[boot]
fixed.fon=8514fix.fon
oemfonts.fon=8514oem.fon
fonts.fon=8514sys.fon
```

The first line defines the fixed-width font used by some older Windows applications. Using 8514 here will enlarge the font in Notepad, Windows' built-in text editor, as shown in Figure 8.6.

FIGURE 8.6

By editing the SYSTEM.INI file, you can tell Windows to use larger fonts on your SVGA display for Windows applications such as Notepad.

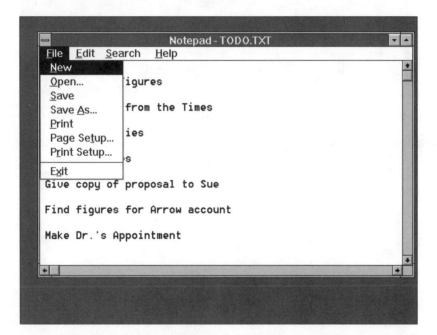

The second line describes a version of the DOS system font used by the Windows Clipboard. This is the font used if you save data from a Windows program to the Clipboard and then paste it into a DOS program. The third line changes the type in Windows menus and title bars, as shown in Figure 8.7.

If, when you start up this configuration, Windows delivers an error message that it can't find these fonts, expand and load them from Windows installation Disk 1.

FIGURE 8.7

Make Windows menus and title bars easier to see by using larger, 8514 fonts on your SVGA display.

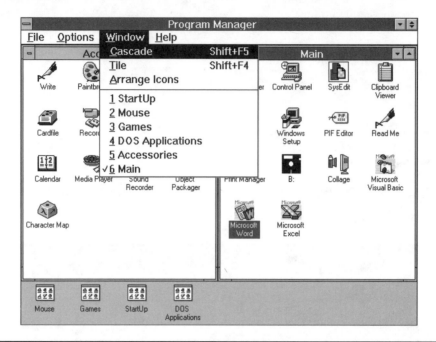

Change the System Font Typeface Not only can you control the size of your Windows system fonts, you can vary the type style as well. To do this, you need to add a line to the [Windows] section of the WIN.INI file that describes the typeface you wish to use.

The line you add should appear in the [Windows] section, just ahead of the Beep= statement and should look like this:

```
[windows]
SystemFont=xxx.fon
Beep=yes
```

Here, *xxx* denotes the name of the typeface you plan to use. You can use any installed typeface for your system font, but not all typefaces work well. Windows has on-screen fonts in both raster (dot-pattern) and vector (line-drawing) forms. Vector fonts create huge letters when used as menu and title type, so avoid them. Raster fonts work much better. Among the commonly installed Windows fonts, Modern, Script, and Roman are vector fonts. Courier (shown in Figure 8.8), Helvetica, Times Roman, and Symbol are raster fonts. Symbol shouldn't be used for system fonts, because it produces an unreadable (though amusing) array of Greek and scientific characters in your menus and title bars.

Windows Small font should also be avoided, because it yields menus with type too tiny to read.

Change the typeface that Windows uses to display screen fonts by adding a line to your WIN.INI file; the font selected here is Courier.

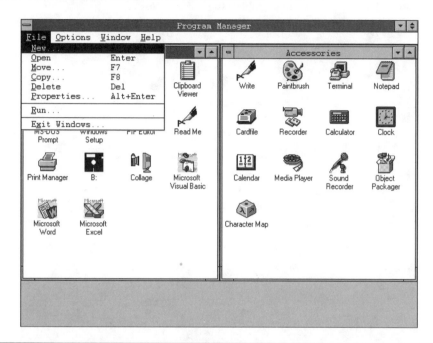

Windows raster fonts are specific to various monitors. You should make sure you have the proper version of the font installed for the screen font format you have defined in SYSTEM.INI, as described in the previous tip. The root name for each raster font file ends in a letter that denotes which video format it's for. They are as follows:

A   CGA

B   EGA

C   60 dot-per-inch printers

D   120 dot-per-inch printers

E   VGA

F   8514/A

So, HELVE.FON is the Helvetica font for VGA monitors; HELVF.FON is Helvetica for the 8514/A screen. You'll find all your available fonts listed in the WINDOWS/SYSTEM subdirectory with the file extension .FON.

By using this tip and the previous one you can mix and match system font sizes and styles to fit your individual needs; as an example, see the 8514 Serif font used in Figure 8.9.

FIGURE 8.9

The Windows screen font used here is Serif, one of the many choices that you can make available to your system by editing the WIN.INI file.

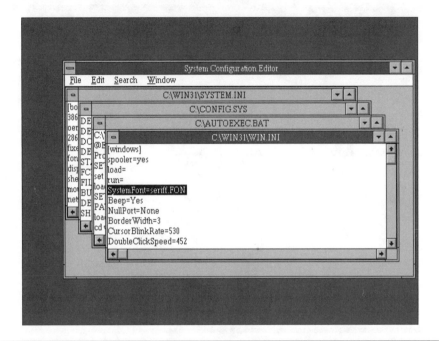

Change the System Font for DOS Programs   You can alter the font used by DOS applications running under Windows as well. To do this, the DOS program must be running in a window. Load the DOS program. If running in a window isn't the default for the application's PIF, press Alt+Enter to put the program in a window. Click on the Control menu box in the upper-left corner. You'll see Fonts as a menu option. Select it, and a dialog box offers a selection of available character settings. At the bottom, a small screen area shows how each selection looks. Make your choice, click on OK, and your DOS program will have a new font. If you want this change to be permanent, make sure to check the Save Setting box in the Font Selection dialog box before leaving it.

Change the Font in Icons   You can even change the font that appears inside icons, if you wish. Windows defaults to the MS Sans Serif 8-point typeface, which is easy to read when small. But you can make the font bigger if you have a sight problem, or more ornate if you just like to fiddle with the look of things.

Icon fonts are set in the WIN.INI file, under the [desktop] section (as discussed in Chapter 2). To change the default, enter these three lines in that section (if they don't already exist):

```
IconTitleFaceName=
IconTitleStyle=
IconTitleSize=
```

On the first line, you can specify the name of just about any raster or True-Type font—for instance, Times New Roman. (Symbol and Script will not work, however.) If you want to boldface your icon type, place a 1 after the equal sign on the second line. On the third line, specify a point size of either 8 (the default), 10, or 12. For icons, 12-point type is enormous; it would be used only for visually impaired users.

Change the Font in Other Windows Elements   Changing the font in dialog boxes, list boxes, text boxes, and other windows screen elements is trickier than altering icon fonts. Windows provides no way to change any of these elements independently. You can only change them by substituting a new font for the default MS Sans Serif 8-point default system font. To do this, go to the [fonts] section of WIN.INI. Find the line that describes MS Sans Serif for the monitor you use. For instance, the line for a VGA monitor should look like this:

```
[fonts]
MS Sans Serif 8,10,12,14,18,24 (VGA res)=SSERIFE.FON
```

To make the font bigger, you could substitute the wider 8514/A version of MS Sans Serif. Then the line would read

```
[fonts]
MS Sans Serif 8,10,12,14,18,24 (VGA res)=SSERIFF.FON
```

When you save WIN.INI with the new settings and restart Windows (or force Windows to write your changes to disk, as discussed in Chapter 1), the new font will be in place.

TrueType

Windows 3.1 marks a major step forward in simplifying the Windows font situation. In version 3.1, Microsoft has introduced a new font family, called TrueType. TrueType fonts are scalable—that is, a single file can represent characters in many sizes. Raster fonts require separate files for different point sizes. This gives TrueType many of the advantages previously available only through PostScript. However, TrueType fonts don't require special PostScript printers or PostScript interpreters; they work with any printer. Also, since they come bundled with

Windows, they provide a unified scalable font approach that any application can utilize. Previously, some applications couldn't run in Windows without the additional expense of having PostScript software and devices installed; other applications couldn't provide the benefits of scalable fonts. TrueType pushes those problems into the past.

Yet, since TrueType is new, it requires new understanding, both of how to derive the greatest benefit and how it affects what has gone before. That's the thrust of this section.

Use Font Substitutions to Avoid Confusion   Users who have upgraded to Windows 3.1 will undoubtedly be working with documents that were created under the previous version of Windows. Windows 3.0 didn't have TrueType fonts and, in fact, contained a few fonts that are no longer found in Windows 3.1, such as the Helv font. Or maybe you've been using Adobe Type Manager with Windows 3.1, but you've decided that you'd rather do all your work with True-Type. To be able to work flawlessly with these non-TrueType documents, Windows translates instructions to use these old fonts into requests for corresponding TrueType fonts. This process is controlled by a new section of the WIN.INI file called [FontSubstitutes]. As you can see in Figure 8.10, this section lists the TrueType font on the left side of the equal sign and on the right lists the Windows 3.0 font for which it will be substituted.

FIGURE 8.10

Add the names of fonts that you want to be replaced by TrueType equivalents to the [FontSubstitutes] section of the WIN.INI file.

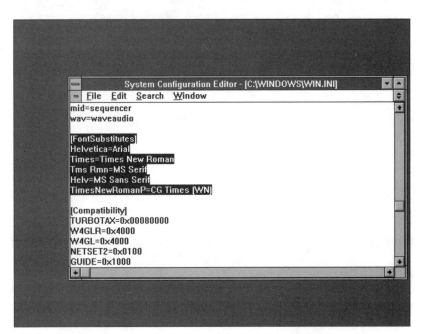

You can add new font substitutions to the list by editing your WIN.INI file and adding the names of the TrueType font and the original font. Be sure to follow the format used in the substitutions already listed in the WIN.INI.

How to Keep Font Names Straight If you are a new TrueType user and can't get used to the new Windows 3.1 typeface names, such as Arial, here's a way to keep them straight. Open your WIN.INI file in SysEdit or a text editor and look for the [FontSubstitutes] section. You'll find a listing of the old font names that you were used to using and their new TrueType equivalents. Copy this section to the Windows Clipboard and print it as a handy reference.

Delete Fonts You Don't Use If you are using TrueType along with other soft font collections, such as Adobe Type Manager, save disk space by getting rid of the duplicate typefaces you'll never use. For example, how many different Courier typefaces do you need, especially if you find little reason to use Courier fonts in your documents?

Many Windows applications also include their own soft fonts, which are installed on your hard disk. If these include fonts that you'll never use—for example, entire extended character sets—delete these as well to save precious disk space. You can also save disk and memory space by only keeping certain sizes of each typeface on your hard disk. A recommended range (it should cover your needs) are the following point sizes in each typeface: 6, 7, 8, 9, 10, 11, 12, 14, 18, 24, 30, 48, 60, 72. If keeping all of these fonts on your hard disk still takes up more space than you like, load only the point sizes that you will use regularly for your documents—for example, a 10- or 12-point size in regular, bold, and italic, 14-point bold for headlines, and 6-point regular for footnotes.

If you're using Hewlett-Packard's printer control language (PCL) fonts on a laser printer, you should install bold fonts in sizes of 14 points or greater only. At lower point sizes Windows can simulate bold text effectively. You can also do without loading bold italic fonts, because they aren't used very much, and when you do need them your PCL driver will simulate them.

How to Use TrueType Fonts Only Once you've experimented with True-Type, you may decide you don't want to fuss with raster (bitmapped) fonts anymore. No problem. Open the Fonts section of the Control Panel and click on the TrueType button. Make sure the Enable TrueType Fonts box is checked, and then check the box below it—Show Only TrueType Fonts in Applications. When you return to your application, you'll see only the TrueType fonts installed on your system.

Printer support for TrueType fonts depends upon the type of printer you have. If you have a PostScript printer, there are plenty of options, all of them buried deep inside the setup dialog boxes for your specific printer driver. Click on the Printers icon in the Control Panel and, with the PostScript driver selected, click on the Setup button. Click on the Options button and then the Advanced button. In the TrueType section of this final dialog box, you choose to download the fonts to your printer as Adobe Type 1 or Type 3 fonts; for best performance, however, use the Fonts Substitutes Table, mapping the TrueType Arial typeface to the printer's native Helvetica, Times New Roman to Times, Courier New to Courier, and so on.

With a Hewlett-Packard LaserJet Series II or III, the tactic is slightly different. You can't download TrueType fonts to the LaserJet, but you can send them as graphics directly to the printer. Choose Setup and then Options from the Printers dialog box; then check the Print TrueType as Graphics box.

Troubleshooting TrueType   If an error message tells you that a TrueType font is causing a Windows error, chances are that you have a corrupted font file. But how do you find out which one is the culprit if you are using several fonts at once? Open the Control Panel and select Fonts; then select each entry in the Installed Fonts list and note the line at the bottom of the dialog box that tells you how much disk space the font occupies. TrueType fonts generally take up about 70K of disk space. If you notice that one of the TrueType fonts that you select reports a font size of 0 or 2K, that font is corrupted. Get rid of it by selecting the Remove button and then making sure that the Delete Font File From Disk box is checked in the resulting dialog box. Once you have done this, reinstall the font from your original disks.

Printer Power

Printing under Windows is easier than it was under DOS, but that's like saying that having your fingernails pulled out is less painful than having your arm sawed off. It's still not pretty or even close to automatic. These tips for navigating the shoals of output will come in handy. The tips focus on the Print Manager; loading, changing, and configuring printers; PostScript printing; and printer troubleshooting.

Print Manager Secrets

The Print Manager, located in the Accessories program group of the Program Manager, is Windows' hub for managing the documents you send to the printer. As with so many aspects of Windows, there's a lot more to Print Manager than meets the eye—if you know where to look.

Drag and Drop with Print Manager   You can print files quickly by using Windows' drag and drop feature. The files you want to print must belong to an application that is registered in the Registration Editor and whose extensions are associated with their native Windows application. (For information on setting up drag and drop, see Chapter 7; the Registration Editor is covered in Chapter 9).

For you to print a file Print Manager must be running iconized at the bottom of your screen. From File Manager, select the desired file, drag it to the Print Manager icon, and release the mouse button. That's all there is to it. Because you need to have access to the Print Manager icon, it is a good idea to automatically start File Manager at a size that doesn't occupy the entire screen, as shown in Figure 8.11.

FIGURE 8.11

Keep the File Manager in a window that is not maximized, and keep Print Manager iconized so that you can easily accommodate drag and drop printing.

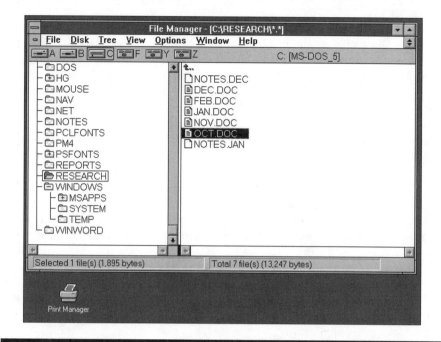

Change Your Priorities   Print Manager allows you specify how important a print job is by assigning it a priority—low, medium, or high. The priority level you used for the last document you printed will be applied to your current document unless you change the setting. The default setting is medium.

To speed up printing, choose Options from the Print Manager menu and select High Priority. In contrast, if a printing job that is spooled to Print Manager is slowing down your ability to work in other Windows applications, make sure that the setting is Medium or Low Priority, not High.

Batch Print   *Batch printing* is the process by which you send several documents to the printer at once, instead of printing them individually. It's especially convenient if you share a printer that's not located close to your desk and you don't want to keep making trips to retrieve your documents, or when the printer you use is busy and you don't feel like putting your print jobs in the printer queue along with everyone else's files. You can wait until the printer is idle—such as in the evening when you leave work—and retrieve your documents from the printer tray in the morning, when you return. Batch printing can also come in handy when you don't want to spare any of your system's resources while the Print Manager sends a document to your printer.

To accomplish batch printing with Print Manager, you simply set your default printer to pause (Ctrl+P). From within your Windows applications, you can still choose Print just as if Print Manager were ready to send these jobs to the printer. What happens instead is that Print Manager holds them in a queue until you choose resume (Ctrl+R). The documents are then sent to the printer consecutively.

Print to Disk If you want to print a file on another computer that may not have Windows installed, or you wish to carry with you a ready-to-print version of a file, use the print-to-file technique. This method substitutes a disk file for the printer at the end of the process. To use this feature, open the Print Manager and select Printer Setup from the Options menu. Pick the printer you think you'll be using later; it must be installed on your PC, but doesn't need to be currently attached. If you don't know, try HP LaserJet or Epson dot-matrix printers; they are safe options. Click on Connect and then choose FILE as the port to use. Click on OK and close the dialog box.

Another common use of this approach is in high-end desktop publishing. Here, the print-to-file method allows you to create a form of the document that can be transported to distant typesetting-service bureaus or imported into complex design programs. Parameters for the ultimate output device are then set by the application, not by Print Manager.

When you set Print to File, printing from your application will bring up a Print to File dialog box that creates the filename and other basics of your document file. Fill it out and click on OK. Your document will become a file that can be transmitted, printed at any time with the DOS PRINT command, or imported into other applications.

Quickly Cancel All Printing The fastest way to stop all printing under Windows is to exit the Print Manager. Click once on the Print Manager's icon and you'll see the Control menu for the Print Manager. Click on Close and you'll be prompted to confirm the choice. Click on Yes, and every print job beyond what's already loaded in the printer's buffers will go away.

Print Manager Keyboard Shortcuts

Here are keyboard shortcuts for the Print Manager:

Shortcut	Action
F1	Brings up context-sensitive help
F5	Refreshes the screen
Ctrl+Up Arrow	Moves file up in the print queue
Ctrl+Down Arrow	Moves file down in the print queue
Alt+P	Pauses printing
Alt+R	Resumes printing

Printer Tips

A common misconception among Windows users is that the Print Manager handles printers. It doesn't. It handles print jobs. *Printer* control is accessed by clicking the Printers icon in the Control Panel. When the task at hand is loading, changing, or configuring a printer or managing the print drivers, clicking the Printers icon is the key.

Get On-Line Help for Any Printer   To get on-line help for any printer you have or are considering getting, go to the Control Panel and double-click on the Printers icon. You'll see a list of the printers installed on your system. If you want information on a printer not on this list, click on Add and then select the printer you want from the list that appears. Click on Install, and you'll be prompted to insert Windows' Setup disks with printer drivers on them. Follow the on-screen instructions. Finally, click on Connect, even if the printer isn't really attached to your PC.

Once the printer you want to know about is installed, click on Setup or Fonts (the button that appears varies with the printer). Now when you click on Help you'll get pages of information about that printer, its fonts, and its performance.

Find Out about Your PostScript (or Other Kind of) Printer   You can find out all sorts of information about your PostScript printer by printing out a little-known file called TESTPS.TXT. You'll find it in your WINDOWS/SYSTEM subdirectory. This file is a PostScript program that, when copied to the port your printer is on, prints your printer's settings.

Another file worth looking over is PRINTERS.WRI, which contains a ton of general information about all kinds of printing with Windows. Topics include International Characters, Switch Settings, Printer Memory, and much more. It's in the WINDOWS directory.

Install the Same Printer Twice   You can save yourself the time it takes to reconfigure printer settings by installing the same printer twice, located on the same port, in Control Panel. For example, you can configure the printer with a specific type of emulation and then install it again in its regular native mode. Or you can install the printer once with legal-sized paper and once with letter-sized paper. To install the printer twice, treat each instance as if it were actually a separate printer.

For example, suppose you're using Windows 3.1 and you have an HP LaserJet III with a PostScript font cartridge, and you want to install it twice—first in its own mode with legal-sized paper and then as a PostScript printer with letter-sized paper. To do this, from the Control Panel, choose Printers. Then choose Add and select HP LaserJet III from the List of Printers. Choose Install (you may prompted to insert a Windows disk with the appropriate driver) and then Setup. In the Setup dialog box, change the paper size to Legal by scrolling through the drop-down list, and make any other changes that you desire. Select OK to return to the Printers dialog box. If the printer is not listed on the correct port, choose Connect and select the port that the printer is hooked up to.

To install the HP LaserJet III as a PostScript printer, choose Apple Laser-Writer from the List of Printers. If the driver is not already installed on your system, you will be asked to insert a Windows disk. Choose Install and then Setup. In the next dialog box, choose the options that you require, and then select OK. If this printer is not listed as being connected to the same port as the HP Laser-Jet, select Connect and assign it to the same port as the previous entry. Remember, while you can have more than one listing of a printer on a single port, only one can be active at a time. To activate a printer, highlight it in the Installed Printers list and click on the Set As Default Printer command button.

In Windows 3.0 you can also configure a printer more than once on the same port, but the buttons that you choose in the Control Panel have slightly different names.

Make Multiple Printers Active on a Single Port   You can attach more than one printer to a single Windows port using a switch box. However, to move from one printer to the other, you not only have to flip the switch, you have to access Control Panel to change your active Windows printer. Obviously, this makes having printers share a port hardly worth the trouble. Happily, you can work around this problem by creating aliases for your printer port.

An alias is a statement you add to the [ports] section of the WIN.INI file that matches a port name you create with the actual physical port. To create aliases for an HP LaserJet and a PostScript printer, both on port LPT1, add these lines to the [ports] section of your WIN.INI:

```
LPT1.HP=LPT1:
LPT1.PS=LPT1:
```

To avoid any unexpected problems, it is wise to name your aliases with a physical port name followed by an extension that indicates the printer type. Since the colon (:) has meaning in this context, don't use this character in port aliases. Finally, note that Windows limits the total number of ports described to ten, including aliases, so make sure you aren't exceeding this limit. If you have more than ten ports listed, only the first ten work. One way to avoid this problem is to remove the lines automatically included in WIN.INI for ports you may not have. (You can also comment them out by putting a semicolon before them) If, for example, you only have one printer port, remove the LPT2= and LPT3= lines from WIN.INI to keep down the number of ports. When you have entered the alias lines, save WIN.INI, and then restart Windows.

Once Windows is restarted, click on the Printers icon in the Control Panel. Select one of your printers from the Installed Printers list box. Then click on the Connect button. This brings up the Connect dialog box, which contains a list of available ports. Among these will be your alias for the selected printer. Click on the alias, and click on OK. Check to make sure the Set As Default Printer button is marked in the Printers dialog box. Then click on Close in this dialog box. Repeat this process for the second printer.

When you are done, either printer will be active and available on LPT1 when you select it from any Windows application. You know the process worked if the Printer Setup dialog box in your application says something like:

```
PCL/HP LaserJet on LPT1.HP
PostScript Printer on LPT1.PS
```

One caveat: Since both printers use the same port, only use one printer at a time. Make sure all print jobs on the first printer are complete before changing printers and sending anything to the second; otherwise you'll get trash on both.

If a particular printer won't work when assigned to an alias, simply assign that printer to the actual port name and save aliases for other devices. The actual port and aliased ports can coexist.

Install Multiple Printers on Laptops   The secret here is simple: Since your laptop will be many places and you can't know what printers you'll find there, make things easy on yourself by installing several printers. That way, you'll be able to select one that works wherever you are. A good basic set to include would be a Hewlett-Packard LaserJet II, an Epson dot-matrix printer, and a Apple LaserWriter PostScript printer.

You install each printer as described in the tip "Get On-Line Help for Any Printer."

Installing a Printer That's Not Listed in Control Panel   Ideally, there will be a Windows printer driver written for your specific printer in Windows 3.1. If such a driver isn't listed in the Control Panel's printer list, however, there are a few things you can do. If you have upgraded from version 3.0, you can check those Windows disks to see if a driver for that printer was included with the previous version of Windows. Windows 3.0 drivers will work correctly with Windows 3.1. You can also call Microsoft to see if your printer driver is available in their Windows Driver Library, or use your modem to call their Product Support Download Service and download it yourself. If a driver is not available from Microsoft, contact your printer manufacturer and see if they have one available. Many manufacturers have on-line bulletin boards, which are another good source of drivers. If all else fails, check your printer to see what emulation modes it supports, and use the driver for a printer that it emulates. This is the least desirable solution because emulating another printer means that your own printer's capabilities may not be fully utilized.

If you are using a laser printer for which you can't find a driver and it's compatible with a Hewlett-Packard LaserJet printer, use the HP LaserJet Plus driver. If your printer is PostScript-compatible and you don't have the correct driver for it, use the Apple LaserWriter Plus driver. If you're using a color PostScript printer, use the QMS-ColorScript driver. If you're using a 9-pin dot-matrix printer, see if it is IBM- or Epson-compatible. If so, use the IBM Proprinter, the

Epson FX-80 (for narrow carriage printers), or the Epson FX-100 (for wide carriage printers) driver. If you're using a 24-pin dot-matrix printer that's IBM- or Epson-compatible, use the IBM Proprinter X24 or Epson LQ-1500 driver, respectively.

Control Printing for Individual Documents   Many Windows applications, such as Word for Windows and Excel, let you control printer settings for a specific document. For example, in Word for Windows you can choose the Page Setup option from the Format menu to set the document for landscape or portrait printing, as well as for specifying the paper source. If your application supports such options, use these settings instead of making changes from the Printer Setup option in the application's File menu or from the Control Panel. This will save you the trouble of changing the printer setup every time you decide, for example, to print a document in landscape mode, and then back to portrait once you are done. This is because Page Setup ties these settings to the document only, not as the new default.

Speed Up Printing by Using Just What You Need   You can speed up printing by thinking about what your needs are before you create and print your documents. If your document doesn't require any special style, stick to normal text if you can. Using bold and italic fonts makes for more complex documents that take longer to print. Likewise, documents composed of several different typefaces will take longer to print.

When it comes to printing you'll also want to consider the purpose of the print job. If this is just a rough copy, opt for lower resolution or use a draft mode, if your application offers one.

The Fastest Way to Print Text from Any Program   It's often useful to print unformatted output from a word processor or other text-based Windows application. Here is a way to do this from any such application. You'll need to install an additional printer driver, so have your Windows disks handy. Start Control Panel, pick Printers, and then click on the Add button. On the resulting list, the first choice is Generic/Text Only. Double-click to install TTY.DRV from the Windows disk for which you are prompted.

After picking OK, choose the Configure button and scroll the list of ports until you find FILE. Clicking on this entry attaches the Generic Text printer to a disk file instead of a port, and enables you to choose the filename when you print. After choosing OK, activate the printer with the Set As Default Printer radio button in the Printer dialog box.

Most applications let you switch from the default printer to the Generic Text printer without going out to Control Panel. For example, in Word for Windows, use the Printer Setup menu item from the File menu. If you choose the text printer, you'll be prompted for a filename when you print.

NOTE   Print only unjustified text this way. The result of printing justified text—at least in some Windows applications—is bizarre.

Speed Up PostScript Printing

To speed up printing on a PostScript printer that supports downloadable fonts, use those fonts instead of TrueType fonts. You'll be able to print faster and use less printer memory. To enable the use of printer fonts, select your PostScript printer in the Printers dialog box. Click the Setup button. In the resulting dialog box, click Options. In the Options dialog box, click Advanced. Click on the check box that says Use Printer Fonts For All TrueType Fonts.

You can also speed up PostScript printing by mapping TrueType fonts to a PostScript printer font by using Font Substitution. For details on how to set up Font Substitutions, see "Use Font Substitutions to Avoid Confusion," earlier in this chapter. If your PostScript printer doesn't support downloadable soft fonts, you'll have to use printer fonts to represent TrueType fonts in documents.

Print PostScript Error Information Windows 3.1 contains an option for PostScript printers that provides a printout of error information when you encounter a PostScript printing problem. This information will be printed after your document has printed, and armed with this information you, or the technical support representative that you call, will be able to get to the root of the problem more quickly. To choose this option, select Printers in the Control Panel, select Setup, and mark the Print PostScript Error Information check box.

Print Every PostScript Document to a Unique File If you are creating PostScript documents under Windows, you have the option of printing directly to a file instead of to the printer. To set up this option, open the Control Panel and choose the PostScript printer from the Installed Printer list. Choose Connect, and choose the port named File in the Ports section of the dialog box that appears. Then choose OK. Next, select Setup, Options, Advanced, and choose Encapsulated PostScript File in the Print To dialog box. Leave the text box that asks for the filename blank so that a Print To File dialog box prompts you for a new filename each time you print to disk, as shown in Figure 8.12. If you're prompted each and every time, you're less likely to overwrite an existing print file. (The Print Setup Options dialog box retains any name entered there.) Also, the Print To File dialog box lets you enter more than twice as many characters for the filename (53 as opposed to 19), which is handy when you've got a filename and path like C:\PROJECTS\PC_COMP\GRAFIC_A.PS.

Printing in Landscape Mode with an HP DeskJet DeskJet printers can't use internal, downloadable, or cartridge fonts to print in landscape mode. To be able to do this, you have to use Window's vector screen fonts. Create your document using a font such as Modern or Roman so that you can print it in landscape mode.

Printer Troubleshooting

Printers are complicated, finicky devices. Windows, too, is complex. At the juncture of these two multifaceted worlds, many things can go wrong, and isolating the problem can be infuriating. Here are some of the common ills that Windows printing is heir to and some solutions from the trenches.

FIGURE 8.12

When a filename is not already specified in the Control Panel, you are prompted for a filename every time you print a PostScript file to disk.

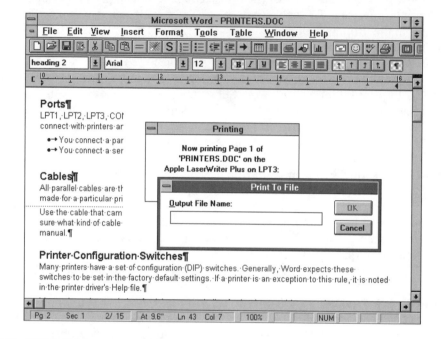

Responding to Printer Port Error Messages

When you receive an error message telling you that Print Manager cannot write to your printer port, it can be a bit frustrating because Windows' error messages are often maddeningly uninformative. This generic error message usually means the printer has gone off-line. Here's what to check for if you receive this message:

- Verify that the printer is receiving power and that it's on-line.

- Running out of paper can cause this message to appear, so check the paper tray too.

- A loose printer cable may be the problem, so check connections if necessary.

After you have verified that the printer is on-line again, press Ctrl+Esc to bring up the Task Manager; then switch to the Windows Print Manager. If you have more than one printer, make sure the active printer is selected (to select it, just click once on its listing) and then click on the Resume button.

Normally, the rest of your document will print correctly from the point at which the printer stopped.

When You Can Print from DOS but Not Windows If you can't print from within Windows but you can print directly from DOS, here are some trouble-shooting tips to help you solve the problem:

■ Check the printer settings in Control Panel to make sure that everything is set up properly.

■ Make sure that the printer you are trying to use is designated as the default printer. To check that it is, highlight it and then click on the Set as Default Printer command button.

■ Click on the Connect button and make sure the correct port is selected. Likewise, choose Setup and make sure that these settings are correct.

■ Check the TEMP statement in your AUTOEXEC.BAT file. Windows uses temporary files when printing, and if it doesn't have a place to put these files it may be unable to print. Open AUTOEXEC.BAT in SysEdit or a text editor and find the line that starts with SET TEMP=. Make sure that the line points to a directory that actually exists. Many people use C:\TEMP or C:\WINDOWS\TEMP, but any directory will do the trick. If there isn't a TEMP statement in your AUTOEXEC.BAT file, create a directory for the temporary files and then add a SET TEMP line in AU-TOEXEC.BAT to point to it. Save your new AUTOEXEC.BAT file, re-boot your computer, start Windows, and try printing again.

■ Finally, recognize that some non-Windows programs aren't "well be-haved" in the way they print. These programs may only be able to print when you exit Windows. If that is the case, you'll simply have to live with it, or upgrade to a more modern application.

A Last-Resort Troubleshooting Trick If nothing else works to get Windows operating with your printer, try installing LPT1.DOS, LPT2.DOS, or LPTI.OS2. These designations cause Windows to think that it's printing to a file, but the output will still actually flow to the LPT1 or LPT2 printer ports. Connect to these ports by clicking on the Printers icon in Control Panel, clicking on Connect, selecting one of these options from the Ports list, and then clicking on Connect.

If you don't see these alternatives in the Ports list, open your WIN.INI file, find the [ports] section, and add the lines:

```
LPT1.DOS=
LPT2.DOS=
LPT1.OS2=
```

Save the edited WIN.INI, and the names should now appear in the Ports list.

This method often solves problems when printing through an electronic switch or peer-to-peer network.

PostScript Troubleshooting Tip: Is It Connected? It's hard to test whether PostScript printers are properly connected to a PC, because they don't respond to the DOS PRINTSCREEN command, which is a long-valued way to make sure dot-matrix and laser printers alike receive print input from the machine. To get a similar response from a PostScript printer, move to the DOS prompt and type

```
COPY.CON LPT1
SHOWPAGE
CTRL+Z ENTER
```

This sends the PostScript SHOWPAGE command out the LPT1 port. On the first line, use whatever port your PostScript printer is actually connected to. If your printer is connected properly, it will process a single blank page. If it doesn't, there's a problem between the printer and the PC port.

Formatting Problems When Printing If your printed document doesn't look the way you think it should, check for these potential problems:

- Check out your fonts. If you aren't using TrueType or another scalable font, your printer may be substituting one of its own character sets for the one your application showed on screen. They may not match. Use the advice in the "Font Magic" section of this chapter to reduce the likelihood of this problem.

- Check out the information in the Setup dialog box found under the Printers icon in the Control Panel. Perhaps you have Landscape orientation checked instead of Portrait, or have selected printer options that limit margins or otherwise alter page makeup.

- Make sure that your application has the same printer installed as the Print Manager. Occasionally, applications retain printer settings from previous uses that may not match what you set up for this Windows session.

9 GETTING WINDOWS APPLICATIONS TO WORK TOGETHER

CONVENTIONAL WISDOM ABOUT WINDOWS HOLDS THAT ITS KEY CONTRIBU-tion to computing is graphics. As is usual with conventional wisdom, that's only partly correct. Windows graphics are important but only because they make possible a much more important benefit: application integration. In DOS, each application is an island, isolated, totally dominating its surroundings, unassail-able by other programs and hardly able to share with them at all. In Windows, each program and document is treated as an independent object (represented by a graphic icon). Objects are malleable, can flow into one another, can borrow elements from each other. So the graphic character of Windows naturally leads toward greater integration of applications.

It is this ability to integrate that makes Windows so special. Before Windows, every PC ran the same operating system, the same applications, in the same way, all the time, everywhere. What kind of competitive advantage is possible with those kinds of cornerstones? But, with Windows' talent for integration, one per-son can use a PC more effectively than another by mixing applications, docu-ments, and knowledge. You can make a better recipe from the basic ingredients than the other guy. Now, with Windows, your PC can really cook!

Basic Windows Integration

Windows is an integrating environment right down to its roots. From the mo-ment it loads, Windows lets programs share the screen, run side by side, and pass resources back and forth. In that sense, virtually every tip in this book is about some aspect of integration. Here, though, we'll look at some tricks completely focused on getting applications to run side by side most productively.

Load Applications as Icons

If you are working in one Windows application and would like to load another one so that you can easily switch to it, you can automatically load the second ap-plication minimized. For example, if you are working in Write in one window and want easy access to the Calculator, but aren't ready to use it yet, switch to Program Manager and hold down the Shift key while double-clicking on the icon. Calculator will be running, but it will appear minimized at the bottom of your screen, as in Figure 9.1, ready for you switch to it with Windows' shortcut keys—Alt+Tab or Alt+Esc.

Loading an application minimized means that it doesn't get in your way, but it's immediately available to you with a click of the mouse.

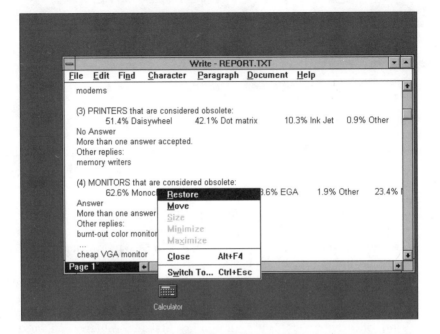

Make the Windows Clipboard Work for You

The most fundamental integration tool built into windows is the Clipboard. Here, information culled from any Windows program (and most DOS programs) can be stored and pasted into any other program. The notion of cut-and-paste as a way to move information is basic to Windows, and the Clipboard makes it happen. With a little imagination, you can use Clipboard cutting and pasting for all kinds of interesting results, as shown in the tips that follow.

Screen Captures with Clipboard   If you need to paste a screen image into a Windows application, just press the Print Screen key on your keyboard. Your cursor will vanish for a moment as the screen image is copied to the Clipboard. If you open the Clipboard Viewer (double-click on the Clipboard icon in the Main program group) you'll see a copy of it there, as shown in Figure 9.2. You can then insert the image into any application by using the Paste command from the Edit menu or pressing Shift+Ins. To copy the active window only, press Alt+PrScr.

Copy Text from DOS Apps   You can use the Clipboard's copy-and-paste capabilities with a DOS application running under Windows, provided that the DOS application is running in a window. Use the mouse to highlight the desired text, open the Control menu in the upper-left corner of the window, and choose Copy from the Edit menu. To copy the entire DOS screen of information, press the Print Screen key and the information will be copied to the Clipboard.

Use the Windows Clipboard to Convert Formats   The Windows Clipboard is a versatile utility because it can copy and paste data that's in many different formats. This feature is useful for transferring data that's in one format into an application that isn't compatible with that specific format. For example, you can paste a formatted text document from a word processor into a communications program that handles only ASCII files. Instead of having the formatting characters appear as gibberish in the communications program, the Clipboard will remove all the formatting, and paste in the document as plain ASCII text.

Keyboard Shortcuts: Clipboard   Mice are nice, but the keyboard is often quicker for Clipboard actions. Most Windows programs that support the Clipboard offer a common set of keyboard shortcuts, including Shift+Del for Cut, Ctrl+Ins for Copy, and Shift+Ins for Paste. Newer applications have switched to Ctrl+X for Cut, Ctrl+C for Copy, and Ctrl+V for Paste, but they still support the older shortcuts as well.

FIGURE 9.2	

When you press the Print Screen key, the image of your desktop is copied to the Clipboard; to verify that it's there, open the Clipboard Viewer.

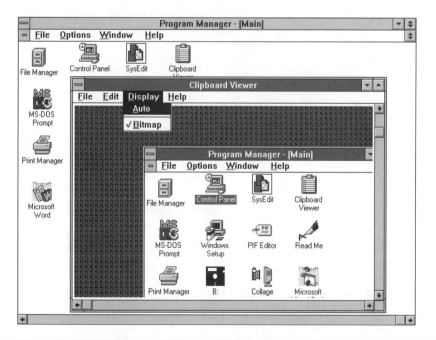

Use Macros to Integrate Windows Applications

Virtually all Windows applications offer sophisticated macro recording capabilities that allow you to create scripts for application tasks. Often, these macros can extend to other applications from the same vendor, or even to other Windows programs. The macro recording capabilities of several dozen popular Windows applications are presented in detail in Part 2 of this book.

Windows' Own Macro Recorder Integrates Applications Too   Windows provides its own macro recorder, which can record and play back keystrokes or mouse actions from Windows itself and from just about any application that can run under Windows. The advantage of Windows' macro recorder is that it can integrate both application and Windows tasks into a single operation. Windows' macro recorder is covered fully in Chapter 6.

Make Sure You Remove Windows Applications Safely

One of the dangers of running applications together is that one can bring down many. One unexpected place this can happen is when an application is deleted. Few, if any, Windows applications include a routine for removing the application from your system. Before you start hastily deleting files, make sure that removing the app doesn't interfere with any of your other Windows applications, or Windows itself. Here's a systematic approach to removing a Windows application:

1. Use SysEdit or a text editor to open your WIN.INI file and locate any sections or lines that refer to the application, then delete them. If you are in doubt about a line's or section's function, do not delete it.

2. Save the edited WIN.INI file.

3. Open your CONFIG.SYS and AUTOEXEC.BAT files and also look for lines or references to the specific application. Remove or change these as well.

4. If you have any data files saved within the application's directory, make sure to move them or copy them to a floppy if you will need them later.

5. Then use the File Manager to delete the application's directory and all of its subdirectories and files.

6. Finally, in Program Manager, remove the application's icon by selecting it and choosing Delete from the File menu or pressing the Delete key. Windows will ask you to confirm that you want to delete this item, as shown in Figure 9.3.

FIGURE 9.3

When you attempt to delete an icon from Program Manager, you will be asked to confirm your action.

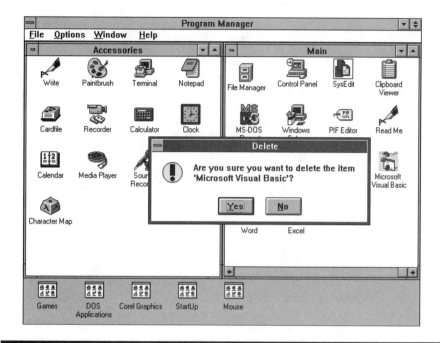

Coping with Conflicts

Applications running together in Windows 3.0 provoked endless arrays of unrecoverable application errors (UAEs)—the problem from which no program returns. Officially, UAEs are gone in Windows 3.1. In truth, while they are far less devastating, come with much better information on their source, and have a dandy new name (general protection faults), these application collisions remain a headache. We've included information here on both techniques for working with Windows 3.0 UAEs and Windows 3.1 problems. Even if you have already upgraded to 3.1, some of the 3.0 tips covered here may still be of value.

The Lingering Spectre of Windows 3.0 UAEs

If you receive a UAE that results in the termination of your current application, the error was probably caused by the application writing to a region of memory it doesn't have access to. When this happens, whatever is already stored in that area of memory can become corrupted. As a result, Windows becomes unstable. Once an application causes this UAE, other applications that you run may generate the same error, even though they are not the cause of the problem.

To avoid this situation, exit Windows and reboot your computer as soon as the application is terminated. Then check the following to find out the cause of the UAE:

- Are you running Windows applications that were designed for Windows 2.*x*? These older applications should only be run in Real mode, as you are told by Windows when you attempt to start them in Standard or Enhanced mode.

- Was an incorrect machine or network selected during Windows setup? Check the installed settings by running the Windows Setup program from the DOS prompt and entering the correct settings.

- Are incompatible TSRs running on your system? Remove all TSRs and see if the application now runs without errors. If it does, try adding the TSRs back one at a time to isolate the one causing the problem.

- Do you have a page-mapping conflict when running in Enhanced mode? To test for this conflict, run Windows in Standard mode (WIN/S). If there is no problem in Standard mode, you'll have to determine which memory address is causing the problem. Open your SYSTEM.INI file in SysEdit or a text editor, and add the following line to the [386Enh] section to exclude Windows from using the adapter segment area of memory:

```
EMMExclude=A000-EFFF
```

Now exit Windows, restart it again in Enhanced mode, and run the problematic application. If the problem is solved, try pinpointing the exact location of the hardware that is causing memory conflicts so that you don't have to exclude the entire area.

- Are you using a correct version of DOS? Systems often come with versions of DOS customized for their brand of PC, and these should be used rather than a generic version of DOS. Likewise, these DOS versions should only be used on the brand of machine with which they're supplied.

- Are free system resources low? To find out, use the About command in the Program Manager's Help menu to see if they are below 20 percent. If they are, you'll need to keep fewer windows or applications open in future Windows sessions to avoid UAEs. Get in the habit of regularly checking free system resources so that when they start getting low you can close windows and applications to prevent a UAE.

- Do you have enough file handles available for applications? UAEs are often caused when the system doesn't have any file handles available for an application. You should increase the FILES= command in your CONFIG.SYS file to meet the high demands of Windows, which generally has multiple applications open at once. The default number of file handles that DOS has available is only 8, but Windows users will need to up the ante to around 50.

■ Is your environment large enough? Applications that are denied environment space are another cause of UAEs. Increasing the environment to 1 or 2K should alleviate the problem. To make this change, edit your CONFIG.SYS file so that the line

```
SHELL=C:\DOS\COMMAND.COM
```

includes the E switch for specifying the environment variable. To set the environment to 2K, change the line to read

```
SHELL=C:\DOS\COMMAND.COM/E:2048
```

Keep the Dr. Watson Utility on Call

In Windows 3.1, UAEs are a thing of the past; they've been renamed general protection faults. While a name change doesn't make them any less daunting, at least now you've got some help in tracking down the cause of these system errors. Windows 3.1 comes with a handy diagnostic utility called Dr. Watson, which provides you with feedback when an application error occurs. Unfortunately, Dr. Watson won't do you any good unless you manually install it on your system. To add Dr. Watson so that it runs in the background every time you start Windows, make the StartUp group the active window in Program Manager, choose New from the File menu, click on OK to select Program Item in the New Program Object dialog box, fill in Dr. Watson as the description, and specify DRWATSON.EXE in the Command Line text box.

Once you've installed Dr. Watson, you'll be ready if an application error occurs, because the program creates a log with detailed system information of what happened. Armed with DRWATSON.LOG, you can troubleshoot problems yourself or provide valuable detail when you to talk to technical support people.

Dr. Watson will also work with Windows 3.0; you just need to download it, along with a file called TOOLBOX.DLL, and place it in your Windows directory. You can download Dr. Watson from the Microsoft Product Support Download Service. The number is (206) 637-9009, and the filename is WW0440.EXE.

To automatically start Dr. Watson in version 3.0, you have to edit your WIN.INI file using a text editor such as Notepad or SysEdit. In the [windows] section of the file, which should be the first section, add DRWATSON.EXE to the Load= line. If there's already a program after Load=, just leave a space between it and DRWATSON.EXE. Once you've done so, the first few lines of WIN.INI might look like this:

```
[windows]
Load=DRWATSON.EXE
Run=
Beep=Yes
Spooler=Yes
```

Advanced Windows Integration

The real meat of Windows integration doesn't lie on the desktop or in the Clipboard. It can be found in the rich tools Windows makes available to programmers, and through them to users, for tying together applications—their information, commands, and capabilities—to create customized programs. Two approaches dominate this area: dynamic data exchange (DDE) and its newer partner, object linking and embedding (OLE). We'll take a quick look at both here.

Get the Most from DDE

Do you wish you could get someone else to exchange information between Windows apps instead of relying on yourself and the trusty Windows Clipboard? Call up dynamic data exchange instead. When it works, it's slicker than a rain-soaked L.A. freeway. But when it doesn't, it's enough to make you scream at your computer. DDE links are fragile, so you'll find it useful to understand how they are built, how they operate, and how to fix them when they go awry.

A DDE link (called a *conversation*) is formed by two Windows programs, called the *server* and *client* applications. (The server application is the source of the data.) Both parties must support DDE, and these days, most general-purpose Windows programs do. Excel, Word for Windows, Ami Pro, WordPerfect for Windows, and 1-2-3 for Windows, for example, are all on the roster. The server application supplies data to the client and updates it either automatically or on demand. One common DDE scenario is a spreadsheet server application providing figures for a table in a client word processor.

Setting up the link is straightforward. Select the data in your server program and either press Ctrl+Ins or use the Copy command on the program's Edit menu. Then open the client document, put your cursor where you want the data to appear, and use the client program's Paste Link command, like the one shown in Figure 9.4 (sometimes it's a subset of the Edit menu's Paste Special option). That's all there is to it.

If the Paste Link command is unavailable (gray), you won't be able to establish a link. There are two possible causes for this. Either you've copied data from a program that isn't DDE-capable or the copied data came from a file that wasn't saved to disk. Many DDE server programs refuse to link data until it has been saved at least once.

Once you've set up the link, you need to know about three potential problems: performance drag, inability to find the server's data, and inability to launch the server app. To help you cope with these hazards, your client program should provide you with a command called Edit Links, Link Options, Change Links, just plain Links, or something similar.

Most DDE clients create automatic links that are almost instantly updated whenever the data from the server changes. An automatic link is also commonly called a *hotlink*. If you don't need continuous updating, you can improve the performance of your client application by changing the automatic link to an inactive or manual one. When you want to update your client document thereafter, just select the link and click the Update button.

FIGURE 9.4

Use the client program's Paste Link command to set up a link to the server application.

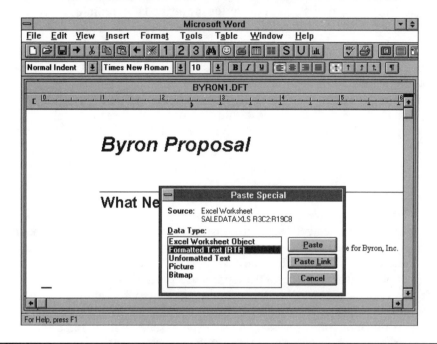

In the example of linking a spreadsheet range to a table in a word processing document, it's important to know how the link is defined. You could create a link to the cell range that you desire—for example A1:F5. But if you change the layout of your worksheet, the desired information will reside in some other range and your document will be connected to a meaningless patch of cells. The solution is to name the spreadsheet range and then tell the document to look for the named range rather than the cell addresses.

If you ever move or rename your server document, you have to edit the link that's been created. To fix the link, point to the new location of the server document.

A more difficult problem sometimes arises when you try to refresh a DDE link to a server document that is not open. Your client program in that case should offer to launch the server application and document for you. Under some circumstances, you might accept the offer, look at an hourglass pointer awhile, and then receive a maddeningly uninformative failure message from the client application. If this happens, check the following:

- Do you have enough memory and system resources to launch the server program? Switch to Program Manager and use the About Program Manager option on the Help menu to check. If you're low on either memory or system resources, close a few programs and then try again.

- Is the server program stored in a directory in your DOS path? If it isn't, quit Windows, modify your AUTOEXEC.BAT file to change the path, then reboot or simply type **autoexec** at the DOS prompt, and then try again.

If memory is plentiful and the server is in the path, something else may be spoiling your fun. Excel 3.0, for example, may refuse to launch via DDE if any add-in macros (.XLA files) are stored in your XLSTART directory. But you won't find that information in the Excel manuals.

The bottom line is that you should test any DDE link thoroughly before you depend on it. And bear in mind that although DDE will hang around forever on the macro level because of the volume of code that's already been written to use it, you can expect object linking and embedding to supersede many DDE functions.

OLE Secrets

Object linking and embedding (OLE) is new to Windows 3.1. It represents a huge potential benefit for users and is a sign of the extraordinary customizability that lies ahead for PC applications. While DDE creates a user-configurable channel between applications, OLE goes much further. OLE allows you to link programs in complex ways and to actually place one program within another program's document. Through OLE, for instance, not only a copy of a spreadsheet, or the data drawn across a link to a spreadsheet, but the full capabilities of the spreadsheet program could be plunked in the middle of a word processor's report document. It works as follows.

Windows' OLE capability allows you to create an object—such as a drawing or sound file—in one Windows application and then insert it into another file. This object can either be *linked*, in which case it actually exists in a separate file, or *embedded*, in which case it exists within the primary file. For example, suppose you are working on a Write document and you use OLE to tie a Paintbrush drawing to it. If the drawing is linked, when you double-click on it, you get the parent application (Paintbrush) with the original document window as it was saved to disk. If the drawing is embedded, when you double-click on it, you get a window from the parent application that points to the embedded data. (Furthermore, the File menu changes to read Update rather than Save, and Exit and Return rather than just Exit.)

As we discuss OLE, you'll need to be familiar with the following terms:

- *Object:* Data encapsulated in a document so that it can be displayed and manipulated by the user. This creates a so-called compound document. Any kind of data can be made into an object if it was created in a Windows application that supports OLE.

- *Package:* The icon that represents the object that is embedded in a document.

- *Client application:* A Windows application that can accept, display, and store objects. The client application stores information about embedded objects: the page position, how the object is activated, and which server application is associated with the object.

- *Server application:* A Windows application in which you can edit an object that is embedded in the client application.

- *Source document:* The file where the data or object was originally created.

- *Destination document:* The document where the data is embedded or linked.

Although Windows' applets, such as the Clipboard, and programming services, such as dynamic link libraries (DLLs), facilitate OLE, it's Windows applications that make OLE work. The server application provides data that is either linked to or embedded in a client application's document. Linked data is updated whenever you modify the original document. On the other hand, embedded data isn't modified until you click on it, which launches the server app from within the client document.

Setting Up an OLE Link   When setting up an OLE link (from a spreadsheet program, for instance), you first copy data from the server application. This sends the selection to the Clipboard in several formats—a bitmapped image of the data (.BMP or metafile), the data in its native file format (such as .XLS for Excel), and others, such as Rich Text Format (.RTF). It also sends an OLE marker file called Link.

In the client application's compound document, you choose the OLE paste command (Paste Special, Paste Link, or another variant, depending on the application). This command sends a call to OLE'S DLLs, which in turn search the Clipboard for the Link marker file. If the call finds Link, the client application then calls the OLE DLLs to ask the server application to make a link.

Making the link takes two steps: First, the data is pasted from the Clipboard to the client application's file. Then the client app's paste operation attaches reminders that the link exists to the original data file and to the document in the client application.

The server file's reminder tells it to contact the OLE libraries anytime someone modifies the data that has been pasted into the client document. The client file's reminder tells it to alert the OLE libraries whenever the file is opened. If the server file's data has changed, the client file also changes.

Embedding an Object   Setting up object embedding is similar to the linking process in that you copy data in several formats to the Clipboard, but is different in that it also stores code that acts as a pointer to the server application, rather than to a data file.

From the client application, you choose the OLE Paste command, and the client app sends the data, screen representation, and pointer to the server application. The embedding process is then complete.

When you double-click on the embedded object, the client application uses the pointer to search the OLE DLLs for the OLE Registry, which records every OLE-capable application you've installed. This finds the server app's code.

Once the client app locates the server program, the Registry calls a library function, which in turn launches the server program (or brings it to the foreground if it's already running in the background). The client application then sends the embedded graphics object to the server application that just came up. Once you've made and saved modifications, the link updates the embedded object and closes the server app (or returns it to the background).

When to Link and When to Embed   The only challenge to using OLE is deciding whether to link or embed. Linking stores only a pointer to the server data, while embedding stores a copy of the data in the client program. If you're tying together data from various corners of your hard disk or network, you can avoid unnecessary file fattening by linking instead of embedding. Linking is also preferable when the same data must be available to different client documents.

On the other hand, use embedding when the client document is likely to go off-line from the server. Getting that linked-in sound annotation to speak may be a little tough if you're on the road and the server's back home. You should also choose embedding if there's a possibility you may move or rename the server document. Linked objects have memory, but they can't find documents that have been moved.

Register Applications That Support OLE   In order to take advantage of OLE, a Windows application must be registered in the Registration Database. Many newer Windows applications come with a registration file (.REG) that contains information about how the application uses OLE. To install an existing .REG file into the database, run the Registration Editor from Program Manager by selecting Run from the File menu and typing **regedit** in the Command Line text box. Then, from the Registration Editor's File menu, choose Merge Registration File. Locate the .REG file for the application that you want to add to the database, and then select OK. The file will be added to the database, and the application will be able to take advantage of OLE functionality.

Another way to merge a registration file into the database is through File Manager. Locate the .REG file in File Manager and double-click on it to install it automatically.

Quickly Restoring the Registration Database   If you've tinkered with settings in the registration files for your Windows applications, you may end up with a Registration Database that is corrupted. But never fear, you can restore the database to its original condition. To do so, exit Windows and delete the file REG.DAT, which is located in the WINDOWS directory. Restart Windows and run the File Manager. In the WINDOWS\SYSTEM subdirectory, locate the file SETUP.REG and double-click on it.

A message appears to confirm that the information has been registered. The database now contains the original registration information that was installed with Windows. If any of your other applications have .REG files, you can add them to the restored database by choosing Merge Registration File from the File menu, as described in the previous section.

Drag and Drop OLE   You can use Windows' drag and drop capabilities to easily embed objects in documents, provided that the server application has been written for Windows 3.1. If you are using an older Windows application, you have to use the Object Packager (described in the next section) to embed the object. Of course, if you use drag and drop from File Manager you will be embedding entire files, such as a spreadsheet, instead of just part of one, for instance a range of cells.

For example, to embed an Excel spreadsheet in a Write document, follow these steps:

1. Have Write running in one window and File Manager running in another so that they are both visible on the screen at the same time.

2. In File Manager, select the name of the file that you want to embed, and drag it to the spot in the Write document where you want the package to appear.

3. When you release the file an Excel package will appear, as shown in Figure 9.5.

FIGURE 9.5

Embed an object in a document by dragging and dropping it from the File Manager to the destination document.

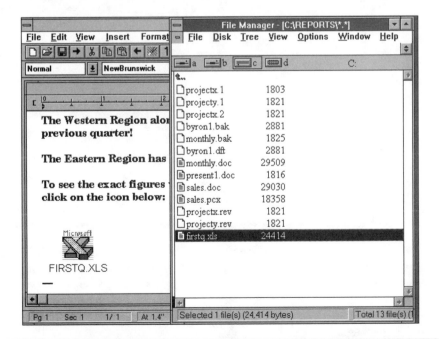

The only drawback to embedding large objects, such as a sound file, is that the object is a duplicate of the original file. This means that you are using precious hard disk space to store the same file twice.

Take Advantage of Object Packager Object linking and embedding is a great way to funnel data between two applications, but for this integration to work, both programs must support OLE. Fortunately, Windows 3.1 ships with an accessory called Object Packager (its icon is shown in Figure 9.6), which offers a way around the OLE-support requirement. Object Packager lets you embed an iconic representation of a data object into another application (which must still support OLE as a client application). But the embedded data need not originate in an OLE server. For example, you could create a Cardfile database of all of your .INI files, like that shown in Figure 9.7. Each card describes a program's initialization file and includes a Notepad icon that represents the file in question. Double-click on the icon to call up Notepad, with the appropriate .INI file loaded and ready to edit.

FIGURE 9.6

Object Packager is located in the Accessories group.

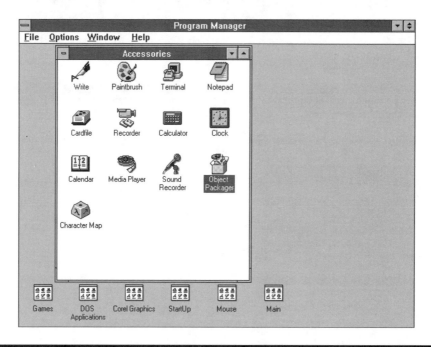

Without Object Packager, this link would be impossible to make, because although Cardfile in Windows 3.1 is an OLE client application, Notepad doesn't know a thing about OLE. The linkage is possible only because the program that did the embedding—namely Object Packager—is an OLE server. And Object Packager can encapsulate any data file, regardless of its origin, into an object package.

FIGURE 9.7

The Notepad file 123W.INI is embedded in the Cardfile document INIFILES.CRD and can be launched by double-clicking on the package (icon).

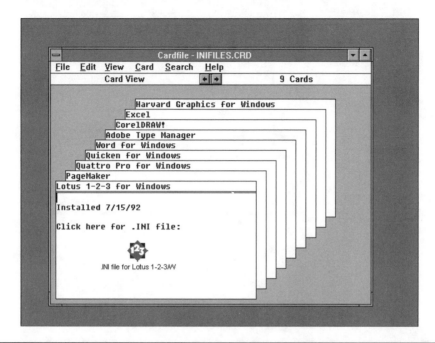

For the click-and-edit procedure to work, the .INI extension must be associated with the application NOTEPAD.EXE. If this association doesn't already exist on your system, you can create it by using the Associate command in File Manager's File menu.

There are several ways to create a packaged object, but we'll follow one of the more straightforward methods here. In a File Manager window, select the file you want to package and choose the Copy command from the File menu (or cut to the chase by pressing F8, the keyboard shortcut). In the dialog box that appears (shown in Figure 9.8), choose the Copy to Clipboard option and click on OK. Now start Object Packager, which appears in the Accessories program group by default.

Object Packager has two windows, named Appearance and Content. Select the Content window and pull down the Edit menu. Now you can use either the Paste or Paste Link command to create your package. The choice between these two commands is important. When you transfer your finished package to your client application, you will be embedding that package, not linking it. It's a given that the packages themselves cannot be linked, but what's *inside* the package can be either embedded or linked data. If you create the package with Object Packager's Paste command, you'll be embedding. If you use Paste Link, you'll be linking.

FIGURE 9.8

Create a package by copying the contents of a file to the Clipboard and then pasting it into the Object Packager.

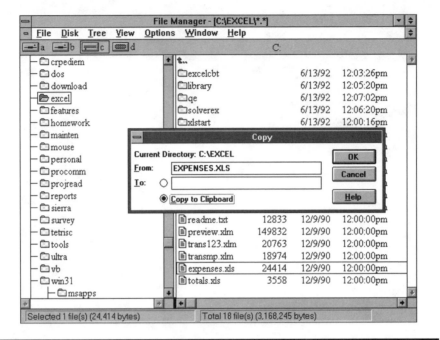

The pros and cons here are exactly the same as they are for any other linking-versus-embedding decision. The short form of the decision is this: Choose embedding if you want to encapsulate the entire source file and ensure that it will always be available, in its current form, to the client document. Choose linking if you want to encapsulate only a pointer to the source file. You should also choose linking if you plan to include the package in many different client documents and you want to ensure that each client is hooked up to exactly the same data.

In the case of the .INI file database, where all you need are pointers to the .INI files, linking makes sense and embedding does not. Embedding would not only create an overweight Cardfile document but also store frozen copies of the .INI files. As soon as an .INI's parent application made changes to the .INI file, the Cardfile document would be out of date.

Once you choose Paste or Paste Link, you can customize the package in several ways—not the least of which is changing the icon and the descriptive text, as shown in Figure 9.9.

When the package is ready, use the Edit menu's Copy Package command to put it on the loading dock—the Windows Clipboard. The rest of the procedure is standard OLE. Just activate your client program and use the appropriate Paste command.

FIGURE 9.9

Object Packager lets you customize the label used for your package.

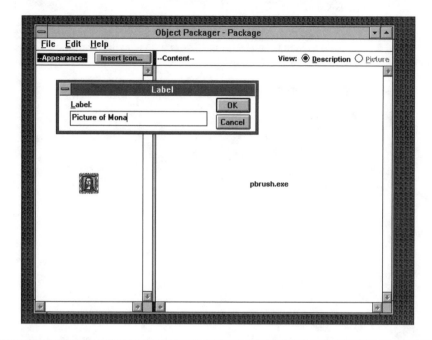

This example shows how Object Packager can connect an OLE client document to a non-OLE document. But Object Packager's talents don't end there. Using it, you can also embed an iconic representation of data from an OLE server application. This technique annotates compound documents with tidy icons instead of cluttering client documents with visible data. Interested readers can check annotations by clicking the icons; browsers can choose to skip right over them. You can even create an elaborate hypertext document by embedding additional packages within packaged files.

Object Packager has another important virtue: You can use this program to embed a Windows command line attached to an icon. For example, you can package startup commands for your DOS applications, your Excel macros, and your favorite games. If the program you use most often is an OLE server, you can use it to create a launch document full of program-starter packages. With a little imagination, you'll find that once you get started with the Object Packager, the possibilities are virtually endless.

Embed a Windows Accessory Because the Object Packager allows you to embed most any kind of data, you can use it to embed a Windows accessory, not a specific data file, into an application. For example, if you were editing a large document such as an annual report in your word processing program, you might want the ability to easily access the Notepad, where you could jot down notes about the report, things to do, whatever comes to mind. Embed a package for

Notepad and place it at the beginning of the report. If your word processor can split the screen so that the top part is always in view, you will have instant access to the Notepad, as shown in Figure 9.10.

FIGURE 9.10

This Word for Windows screen is split so that the embedded object, Notepad, is easily accessible from anywhere in the document.

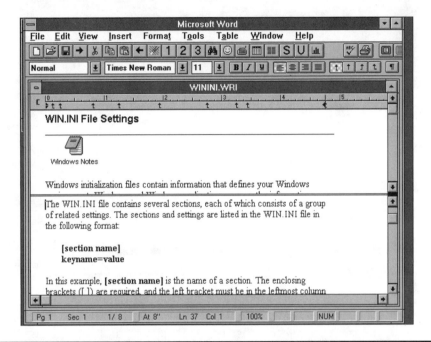

To create the Notepad package, start the Object Packager and activate the Content window by clicking on it or using the Tab key. From the Edit menu, select Command Line, and enter **notepad.exe** in the Command text box. Activate the Appearance window, and select the Insert Icon button. From the Insert Icon dialog box, choose an icon or select Browse to have access to more icon choices, as shown in Figure 9.11. Next choose Label from the Edit menu and type in a label for the icon. Finally, select Copy Package from the Edit menu. In your word processor, position the cursor where you want the icon to appear, select Paste Special, and choose the object.

Reinstall Windows 3.1 without Losing OLE Functionality If you are planning to reinstall Windows 3.1 to a new location, you don't want to have go through the trouble of reregistering all your Windows applications that support OLE. Reregistering applications usually means spending time reinstalling the applications, because for many apps that's the only way to properly register them in the database. You can avoid going through this time-consuming process by copying your existing REG.DAT file into the new location where you'll be installing Windows.

FIGURE 9.11

Use the Browse command to locate the icon you want to use to represent the object.

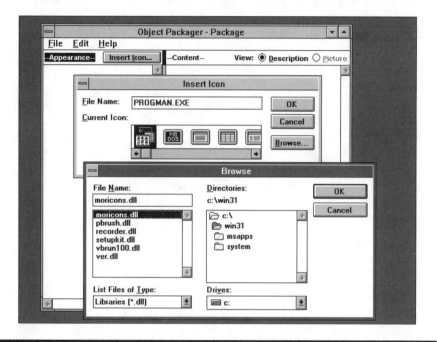

If you've already installed Windows to the new location and just realized that this means recreating your Registration Database, you can still avoid reinstalling Windows applications if you haven't yet deleted your previous copy of Windows. Exit to DOS and copy the REG.DAT file from the old Windows directory into the new one. Start Windows and then start the Registration Editor. Select the file SETUP.REG and double-click on it to execute it. Setup will read the information in the REG.DAT file and make sure that your new Windows installation uses these OLE settings.

Quicker Objects Some Windows applications that support OLE have a command that will save you time when creating objects to embed within that application. When you want to embed an object, select the Insert Object command and select the type of object that you want to embed. For example, in Microsoft Word for Windows you can choose the Insert Object command from the Insert menu and then select the appropriate object, as shown in Figure 9.12. This shortcut saves you from having to switch to the server application and copy the desired information to the Clipboard; the object is automatically placed into the document once it is created or retrieved.

FIGURE 9.12

Many applications, including Microsoft Word for Windows, have an Insert Object command, which is a shortcut for creating and pasting objects into an application.

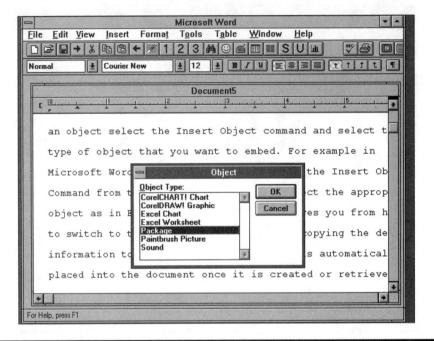

Troubleshooting OLE

If an object that is embedded in an application does not launch the server application when it is double-clicked, check your WINDOWS\SYSTEM subdirectory for the files OLECLI.DLL and OLESRV.DLL. OLE will not work if either of these files is missing. If they are there, one or both of the files may be corrupted. To restore these important files you'll have to expand them from your original Windows disks and place them in the SYSTEM subdirectory.

Application Development Tools for Windows Integration

All of the integration methods described in this chapter can be manipulated in various ways by the many application development tools available for the Windows environment. These range from sophisticated scripting tools, such as Asymetrix Toolbook, through programs designed to integrate data from other applications, like Borland's ObjectVision, to complete programming languages, such as Microsoft's Visual Basic. The three products mentioned here are covered in Part 2 of this book. An excellent source for understanding how to use all Windows development tools to create custom applications is Paul Bonner's *PC/Computing Customizing Windows 3.1* (Ziff-Davis Press, 1992).

10 SECRETS FOR RUNNING WINDOWS ON NETWORKS

WINDOWS AND NETWORKS ARE NATURAL PARTNERS. FIRST OF ALL, BOTH EX-
ploded in popularity recently, although both had been hanging around the pe-
riphery of the PC business for years. They also share the characteristic of trying
to mask extreme system complexity so that users can access great power without
having to wade through confusing layers of plumbing. Finally, and most importantly, they complement each other's requirements: Windows needs vast resources and excels at integrating disparate elements; these are what networks
provide. Networks cry out for a user environment that allows comprehensible
visual metaphors to substitute for hard-to-understand network operations; Windows provides this. So, the two have heightened each other's functionality and
increased each other's popularity.

Still, for the user and the network manager, the marriage between Windows
and networking is not entirely smooth. Windows is a complicated piece of work,
as is any network operating system. Since Windows has to be able to work with
all common networks, this complexity increases further, and results in inevitable
friction along the borders between Windows and any networking system. When
the borders between systems are long and intricate, as with Windows and networks, a weak link somewhere is inevitable.

This chapter delves into how you can make the union of Windows and networks as smooth as possible, how to shore up those weak links and avoid any unexpected obstacles along the path of network integration.

Setup Tips for Network Administrators

Why is Windows worth all the sweat and toil that it brings network administrators? Two simple reasons: cost and inevitability.

Since Windows is exploding through corporate computing, any wise systems
professional will want to deploy it in the most cost-effective way possible. Buying workstation licenses for Windows as a network environment is cheaper than
buying a retail copy for each PC. If a network is already in place, using it to distribute Windows makes inescapable economic sense.

Where a network doesn't yet exist, Windows provides the easiest, most robust
way to begin networking. In fact, Windows is so popular that implementing a network that required leaving Windows behind would probably spark a user riot. So,
the coordinated growth of Windows and networks is an inevitable by-product of
the increased use of and interest in desktop systems in corporations today.

What this comes down to, in the end, is a bit of advice to network administrators: Sure, implementing Windows on a network is a bother, but don't stand in the way of progress, get the network licenses you need and get to work. You'll achieve real benefits if you do, and you'll save yourself a wave of user complaints and problems down the line.

Optimizing Windows on a Network

Making a network Windows installation as smooth and powerful as possible requires something there is precious little of in PCdom: planning. Don't install first and try to make it work second. When it comes to networks, plan, plan, plan. From preinstallation through server tinkering, you should have a solid plan before you take a step. Here, we walk through the process of implementing Windows networks, from the very beginning.

Decisions to Make before Installation   Options for installing Windows on a network vary greatly. Before you jump into this task, there are a few things you'll need to decide based upon the network's capacity and limitations, as well as your own judgment as to what makes the most sense for your organization. Before you jump into the task, ask yourself the following questions to ensure that you install Windows in the best way possible for your situation:

- How much disk space is available on the server and network workstations? If you want to install a separate copy of Windows onto each workstation, you'll need to allow approximately 10Mb of disk space per workstation for it. Can you afford that precious real estate, or would you rather install the majority of the Windows files on the server? The latter requires around 16Mb of space and then uses only a minimal amount of workstation space for individual user files.

- Do you want to run Windows Setup from the server or from the actual Windows disks? Whether you install the Windows files on the server or each workstation, you still need to run the Setup program to configure Windows for use on each specific workstation. You can do this as you would for a stand-alone PC, using the Windows disks, or you can run the program from the file server where you've copied the necessary Windows files.

- How much say do you want each user to have in setting up Windows on his or her workstation? Do you want to allow the user to choose options, such as printers, fonts, display drivers, and where Windows files are located, or do you want to automate the entire process?

- Does Windows out of the box meet your needs? Windows' default configuration may suit your network setup just fine, but in other cases it's just a starting point. You'll install custom applications, add restrictions to groups, and maybe even introduce standard wallpaper with your company logo on it. If you know that you'll be making such changes to the Windows environment of each and every workstation, you can save yourself lots of time by creating a set of instructions for customizing Windows before you install it anywhere.

Ensure a Problem-Free Network Installation   Once you've made the preceding decisions, you're ready for installation, right? Wrong. Make sure that the Windows Setup on your network is error-free by turning off any network messaging services temporarily that allow messages to pop up on your computer screen. Other TSRs that can automatically appear should also be disabled. If one of these programs happens to pop up during Windows Setup, there's a good chance the installation will fail.

Using Setup's Command-Line Options

Setup offers a number of command-line choices that can prove helpful for network installations. Use these to tailor each installation to your particular requirements.

/A Option   The /A switch is for the Administrative Setup option. Use it to copy all the Windows files from the setup disks to the network server. Issuing the command SETUP /A does not install a working copy of Windows on the server. It simply expands the files and marks them as read-only (so that they can be used by more than one person at a time), preparing them to be used for installation on workstations. When the files are placed on the server, tiny files with disk names such as DISK1 are created and placed in the network directory. Don't delete these files. They are needed for the network installation process.

/N: Network Setup   The Network Setup option, /N, is used from the workstation itself when you want to prepare it to run a shared copy of Windows from the network. Only the few Windows files that contain information about that specific workstation and its user's preferences are copied to the workstation's hard disk. These files include WINDOWS.INI and SYSTEM.INI; they are stored in a separate Windows directory on the workstation's hard disk or in the user's private network directory.

/H: Batch Mode Setup   The /H switch for Batch Mode Setup is the option that enables you to set up Windows on many workstations, just the way you want it, with the least amount of work for you and your network users. It works in conjunction with a system settings file that you've predefined. Batch Mode Setup eliminates the need for users to make any choices about the hardware they're using with Windows, and it allows you to install hardware that's not included as a standard Windows option.

Once you've created the system settings file, it is placed in a directory where it can be accessed by users, or it can be copied directly to the workstation itself. With the custom settings file in place, either you or the workstation user can run SETUP /H from the workstation.

Even if you aren't setting up Windows on a network, the system settings file that you define can come in handy. Use it to custom-install Windows on stand-alone PCs in your organization. The predefined settings can be called up from a regular setup routine run directly from the Windows disks, rather than from a network file server.

The proper syntax for using the /H option to run Setup from a network server is

```
SETUP /H:[drive:\path]filename /N
```

The *filename* points to the system settings file that you've created. If you've placed the system settings file in the same network directory as the Windows files, there's no need to include the drive and path.

For example, you might create a system settings file named PRINT-ERS.SHH that contains the correct settings for the network printers in your organization. The correct Windows setup command would be

```
SETUP /H:PRINTERS.SHH/N
```

Creating a System Settings File to Use with Batch Mode Setup

The system settings file that you will use with Batch Mode Setup can be named anything you'd like, as long as it fits the eight-character limitation that DOS imposes. Regardless of the name, the settings file must have the extension .SHH for Windows Setup to recognize it.

A template for a system settings file is included on Windows Disk 1: SET-UP.SHH. If you have previously used the SETUP /A option to copy all the Windows files to a file server, you will find SETUP.SHH there. Since this file is a simple text file, you can modify it with any text editor that can save ASCII files.

The system settings file can contain any of the sections listed here:

- [sysinfo] tells Setup whether to include the System Configuration screen, which allows the user to confirm or change the machine type, display, mouse driver, and network installed.

- [configuration] sets hardware choices for those components appearing in the System Configuration screen, as well as keyboard type and layout, and the language used.

- [windir] tells Setup where to install the Windows files for that workstation.

- [userinfo] tells Setup what to specify as the user name and company name.

- [dontinstall] tells Windows which of the optional components (README files, accessories, games, screen savers, and wallpaper) you don't want installed on the user's system.

- [options] tells Windows whether to offer the user the options of setting up applications and starting the Windows tutorial.

- [printers] tells Windows which printers to install.

■ [endinstall] tells Windows what to do when it is successfully installed, including modifying the CONFIG.SYS and AUTOEXEC.BAT files on the user's system, returning to DOS, and restarting Windows.

Preparing to Create a System Settings File   In order to set many of the options in the .SHH file, you need to refer to other system settings located in Windows' SETUP.INF, CONTROL.INF, SYSTEM.INI, and WIN.INI files. You are already familiar with the two .INI files, especially if you've read Chapter 2's line-by-line explanations of how they work. CONTROL.INF and SETUP.INF, however, may be new to you.

These files are used by Windows Setup and contain important information that tells how to proceed given the type of system you have and the choices you specify. Think of SETUP.INF and CONTROL.INF as all of the possible lists of instructions to be used every time Windows is installed. Obviously, looking to these two files for all possible contingencies isn't realistic. While they contain settings for most types of hardware and user preferences, they can't cover everything. But that's actually good news for you because it means you can edit these files yourself to tailor them to the exact needs of your organization.

SETUP.INF and CONTROL.INF are text files, just like WIN.INI and SYSTEM.INI. If you'll be creating a system settings file and you don't know the proper terms to use, it's a good idea to print these two files for reference.

You'll find SETUP.INF on Windows Disk 1. CONTROL.INF and SETUP.INF are created when Windows is installed. If you've used the SETUP /A option to copy the contents of the Windows disks onto the network server, you'll find them there, along with the master files for WIN.INI and SYSTEM.INI, which are WIN.SRC and SYSTEM.SRC.

[sysinfo]   The [sysinfo] section of the system settings file specifies whether the System Information screen (pictured in Figure 10.1) is displayed during the DOS portion of Windows setup. The screen lists the current settings for the machine type, display type, mouse driver, and network installed. The user either confirms this information or makes the changes necessary to match his or her workstation's system configuration.

Disable this screen if you've already selected the correct settings by way of the other entries in the .SHH file, and you don't want users to think they may need to change this information.

To suppress the screen, add the line showsysinfo=no, or leave the section blank. (The default setting is no.) To display this screen, add the line showsysinfo=yes beneath the [sysinfo] heading in your system settings file.

[configuration]   The [configuration] section of the system settings file allows you to tell Windows about the hardware setup for each user's system. You can specify the machine type, display type, mouse driver, network installed, keyboard type and layout, and the language used.

FIGURE 10.1

The system settings file's [sysinfo] section is used to suppress this screen in Windows Setup.

```
Windows Setup

    If your computer or network appears on the Hardware Compatibility List
    with an asterisk next to it, press F1 before continuing.

    System Information
        Computer:          MS-DOS System
        Display:           VGA
        Mouse:             Microsoft, or IBM PS/2
        Keyboard:          Enhanced 101 or 102 key US and Non US keyboards
        Keyboard Layout:   US
        Language:          English (American)
        Codepage:          English (437)
        Network:           No Network Installed

        Complete Changes: Accept the configuration shown above.

    To change a system setting, press the UP or DOWN ARROW key to
    move the highlight to the setting you want to change. Then press
    ENTER to see alternatives for that item. When you have finished
    changing your settings, select the "Complete Changes" option
    to quit Setup.

    ENTER=Continue   F1=Help   F3=Exit
```

If you only specify some of the available [configuration] entries in the system settings file, the detected or default settings will be used for those items not listed. The following entries are valid for the configuration section:

■ machine= specifies the machine type by using one of the correct profile strings that are listed in the SETUP.INF file's [machine] section. For example, to specify a Hewlett-Packard workstation as the machine type, open the SETUP.INF file in a text editor that can handle such a large file (at over 59K it's too big for Notepad to handle); Write is a convenient choice. Locate the [machine] section in this file. You can do so quickly by using Write's Find command. Now locate the correct profile string from the list, as shown in Figure 10.2. Note that the string is the text that is listed in the left-hand column. The explanation, in this case "Hewlett-Packard: all machines" is in quotation marks. Scan the quoted text to find the proper machine type; then note the profile string to its left. Copy the string, in this case hewlett_packard, and paste it back into the system settings file, making the new entry read machine= hewlett_packard.

■ display= sets the type of display by using the correct profile string from the [display] section of the SETUP.INF file. You'll need to locate the correct item in the SETUP.INF file (as described in the preceding paragraph). Then, either copy and paste it into your .SHH file (which ensures that you get it exactly right) or note the proper syntax and type it in the .SHH file yourself. For example, to set the display for use with an XGA adapter at 640 × 480 resolution, you would enter display=xgalo.

FIGURE 10.2

In the SETUP.INF file, the profile string is the highlighted text on the left side of the screen; here the profile string is used by Windows to identify the proper system.

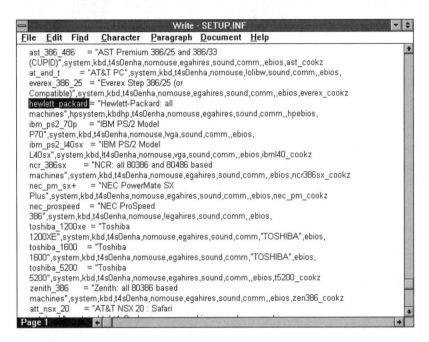

- mouse= sets the type of pointing device that will be used on the system. Once again, you'll have to refer to the SETUP.INF file and find this information in the [pointing.device] section. For example, to specify a Mouse Systems serial bus mouse in the system settings file, you would enter mouse=msmouse2.

- network= sets the kind of network you are using (type and version number) in the system settings file by using the correct string or strings from the [network] section of the SETUP.INF file. For example, to tell Windows that you are using Banyan VINES version 4.1 as your network operating system, you would first locate the string banyan. Now scan down the file to see if there is a section listing entries for the different versions of VINES. In this example, the section is clearly labeled [banyan.versions]. The correct profile string for version 4.1 is listed as *xx*041000. The version number will follow the first string, separated by a forward slash (/). The complete Banyan VINES entry for the system settings file would be network=banyan/041000.

- keyboard= sets the type of keyboard being used in the system settings file. Locate the correct entry in the [keyboard.types] section of the SETUP.INF file and enter it in the .SHH file. For example, the entry specifying that the workstation has an Enhanced 101 keyboard would be keyboard=t4s0enha.

■ language= sets the language that will be used by specifying the correct entry from the [language] section of the SETUP.INF file. For example, the entry in the system settings file to set the language to Spanish would read language=esp.

■ kblayout= sets the keyboard layout for the workstation by specifying the correct entry from the [keyboard.tables] section of the SETUP.INF file. For example, the line to specify Spanish as the language would read kblayout=spadll.

For each of the individual entries used in the preceding examples, the complete listing for the [configuration] section of the system settings file would look like this:

```
[configuration]
machine=hewlett_packard
display=xgalo
mouse=msmouse2
network=banyan/041000
keyboard=t4s0enha
language=esp
kblayout=spadll
```

These entries tell Windows Setup that this is a Hewlett-Packard workstation with an XGA display adapter, Mouse Systems bus mouse, Banyan VINES 4.1, 101 Enhanced keyboard with Spanish layout, and that the user will be using the Spanish language.

[windir] The [windir] section sets the directory where the Windows files for this user's installation will be stored. If you don't specify a directory in this section, or if your entry is invalid, the user will be prompted for the Windows directory during setup. The SETUP.INF file also contains an entry called defdir= for setting the Windows directory in the [data] section, but the setting you specify here in the system settings file will override it. For example, the line in the [windir] section to install Windows in the WIN31 directory on drive C would be C:\WIN31.

[userinfo] Set the user name and company name that Windows prompts for during setup by entering that information in the [userinfo] section. Each entry can be up to 30 characters long. If there are spaces in the name—for example, separating the first and last name—the name must be in quotation marks.

If Windows is set up as a shared copy running on a network, you won't need to specify a user name because you already did so in using the SETUP /A option to copy the files to the network server. For individual workstations that are setting up Windows, a user name is required; you'll be prompted during setup if one isn't specified. In both cases, the company name is optional. For example, to tell Windows that Jane Doe, an employee of Allied, will be using this workstation, you would use this setting:

```
"Jane Doe"
Allied
```

[dontinstall] Use the [dontinstall] section of the system settings file to tell Windows Setup which optional components you'd like to forgo. Whether you can't spare the disk space, you don't want the distraction, or you've got another utility that does the job, Setup can install only some of the items or none at all. However, within a particular optional category—for example, README files—you have to install all the items or none of them. For instance, you can't just install the NETWORKS.WRI file; if you want any one file, you're stuck with them all.

If there isn't a [dontinstall] entry in the system settings file, Windows will install all of the README files, accessories, games, screen savers, and wallpaper. The following entries are valid for the [dontinstall] section:

- readmes tells Windows not to install these README files: NET-WORKS.WRI, PRINTERS.WRI, README.WRI, SYSINI.WRI, and WININI.WRI.

- accessories tells Windows not to install these accessories and their associated help files: Calculator, Calendar, Cardfile, Character Map, Clipboard Viewer, Clock, Dr. Watson, Media Player, Notepad, Object Packager, Paintbrush, Recorder, Sound Recorder, Terminal, and the Windows Tutorial.

- games tells Windows not to install Solitaire and Minesweeper and their associated help files.

- screensavers tells Windows not to install its included screen savers: blank (default), Flying Windows, Marquee, Mystify, and Starfield Simulation.

- bitmaps tells Windows not to install the following bitmap files (which can be used as desktop wallpaper): 256 colors, Arcade, Arches, Argyle, Cars, Castle, Chintz, Egypt, Flock, Honey, Leaves, Marble, Red Brick, Rivets, Squares, Tartan, Thatch, Windows Logo, and Zigzag.

[options] The [options] section lets you tell Windows if you want users to be able to set up applications during Windows Setup, if you want to let them pick what's installed, and whether to start the Windows Tutorial after a successful installation. The following entries are valid for the [options] section of the system settings file. Note that if no entry appears in the [options] section and you are using a system settings file to automate setup, Windows will not provide users with any of these options.

- setupapps tells Windows to let users set up the applications that they choose during setup. If this entry is found in the system settings file, users have the option of telling Windows which applications, including both DOS and Windows apps, they want to set up on their system for use with Windows.

- autosetupapps tells Windows to automatically set up all of the applications that it finds on the user's hard disk, without giving the user a choice in what he or she wants installed.

- tutorial tells Windows to automatically start the Windows Tutorial upon completion of setup.

[printers]   The [printers] section in a system settings file lets you specify which printers to install during setup. As in the hardware entries discussed previously, you need to locate the string used to identify your printer. This time, however, you need to refer to the CONTROL.INF file, rather than the SETUP.INF file. Look for the [io.device] section and locate the printers that users will have access to from Windows. As with the name and company entries in the [userinfo] section, the printer name will be enclosed in quotation marks if it contains any blank spaces.

You also need to tell Windows which ports the printer will be using. You can't just specify the correct port, as in LPT1; you must use the same syntax as WIN.INI's [port] section, which adds a colon to the end of the port name. The valid WIN.INI entries include LPT1:, LPT2:, COM1:, and COM2:.

The printer name and its port will be separated by a comma in the system settings file. For example, to tell Windows that your users will be printing to a HP LaserJet II on LPT1 and an Epson LQ-1170 on COM2, the entries in [printers] section would be these:

```
"HP LaserJet Series II", LPT1:
"Epson LQ-1170 ESC/P 2", COM2:
```

If you omit this section from your system settings file, no printers will be installed.

[endinstall]   The [endinstall] section tells Windows what should happen to the system once Windows is installed. Entries in this section tell Windows whether to modify the user's CONFIG.SYS and AUTOEXEC.BAT files or save the proposed changes in a separate file and whether to exit to DOS, restart Windows, or reboot the system. The following are valid entries for the [endinstall] section:

- configfiles= tells Windows Setup to make the necessary changes to the AUTOEXEC.BAT and CONFIG.SYS files, such as including Windows in the PATH statement or adding a command to run SMARTdrive, if you set the value of the statement to read configfiles=modify. In this case, the old AUTOEXEC.BAT and CONFIG.SYS files are renamed AUTOEXEC.OLD and CONFIG.OLD, respectively. If files named AUTOEXEC.OLD and CONFIG.OLD are already present, these older files will be renamed with the file extension .000, as in AUTOEXEC.000.

To prevent Setup from changing the CONFIG.SYS and AUTOEXEC-.BAT, set this entry to configfiles=save. The original files will remain unchanged, but the proposed changes will be incorporated into new copies of the CONFIG.SYS and AUTOEXEC.BAT files named CON-FIG.WIN and AUTOEXEC.WIN, respectively. This enables you to re-view the changes later and make them yourself.

- endopt= tells Windows what action the system should take once instal-lation is complete. To return to DOS, make the line read endopt=exit. To restart Windows after Setup, make the line read endopt=restart. To reboot the system after Setup, change the line to read endopt=reboot. However, if the reboot option is specified in the system settings file, but Windows was set up to run from a shared directory on the server, the machine will be returned to DOS instead of rebooting.

Automating Setup with the SETUP.INF File

The Setup Information file (SETUP.INF), like WIN.INI and SYSTEM.INI, is composed of sections that are identified by brackets, for example [setup]. You saw that these files are useful references for creating system settings files (.SHH) to automate the setup process on a network. Now you'll see how you can use these files directly, to customize Setup on your network: for example, to add an installation choice for a printer driver that doesn't ship with Windows; to re-move unnecessary choices from Setup options, such as mouse drivers or display drivers that your organization doesn't use; or to add a custom application to the list of those that Windows recognizes and will automatically set up on the work-station during setup.

As always, here's a word of caution before tinkering with such powerful Windows files: Remember to back up the SETUP.INF file before you attempt to customize it. In case you do forget to save the previous version of SET-UP.INF, keep the Windows disks handy; SETUP.INF is located on Disk 1 in un-compressed format.

Before you attempt any additions or changes to SETUP.INF, it's a good idea to familiarize yourself with its contents. The file is commented throughout, so you'll be able to figure out what each section does and how the corresponding settings work. Here's a brief look at the file's contents:

- [setup] tells Windows where to find on-line help for the Setup program.

- [run] tells Windows which programs, if any, should be run after Setup is complete.

- [dialog] tells Windows what text should appear in the Setup dialog boxes.

- [data] provides the default settings and requirements for installing Windows, such as minimum disk space and memory required, and the default directory, keyboard, and language used.

- [winexec] tells the DOS part of Windows Setup which kernel file to use for the Windows portion of Setup.

- [disks] tells Windows which disks to prompt the user for during installation.

- [oemdisks] tells Windows what additional disks to ask for during installation.

- [user] tells Windows where the temp file containing the user's name and company is located.

- [windows] tells the DOS portion of Setup which files to copy into the WINDOWS directory.

- [windows.system] contains information about which files to copy into the SYSTEM subdirectory.

- [windows.system.386] contains both information about which files should be copied to the SYSTEM subdirectory for 386 PCs and additional instructions for use if the machine uses the Qualitas expanded memory managers Bluemax or 386Max.

- [shell] tells Windows what to use as the program shell. The default is Program Manager.

- [display] contains information for display drivers used by Windows.

- [.3gr] contains a listing of the font files used with specific 386 grabbers.

- [keyboard.drivers] contains entries that match short names for the keyboard driver filenames to the actual filenames.

- [keyboard.types] contains entries that define short names to be used in place of the keyboard descriptions that appear in Setup dialog boxes.

- [keyboard.tables] contains entries that define short names to be used in place of the DLL filenames, and tells Windows where they are located.

- [codepages] defines code pages used for international support.

- [pointing.device] lists drivers for pointing devices supported by Windows.

- [dos.mouse.driver] tells Windows which DOS mouse driver to use with which Windows mouse driver.

- [lmouse] contains settings for the Logitech DOS mouse drivers.

- [network] lists networks supported by Windows and any corresponding files, such as help files, as well as the names of sections that need to be added or modified to .INI files.

- [Network_Version] provides Windows with information for specific versions of a network operating system.

- [Network_Specific] lists entries for specific networks describing changes to be made to the .INI files.

- [sysfonts] lists system font files used by Windows.

- [fixedfonts] lists fixed-pitch font files used by Windows.

- [oemfonts] lists OEM system font files used by Windows.

- [win.copy] lists files that Windows Setup needs to copy to the WINDOWS directory or its SYSTEM subdirectory for 286 PCs.

- [win.copy.net] lists files that Windows Setup needs to copy to the WINDOWS directory or its SYSTEM subdirectory for network workstations not including 386 or higher PCs.

- [win.copy.net.386] lists files that Windows Setup needs to copy to the WINDOWS directory or its SYSTEM subdirectory for 386 or higher PCs on a network.

- [win.copy.386] lists files that Windows Setup needs to copy to the WINDOWS directory or its SYSTEM subdirectory for unnetworked 386 or higher PCs.

- [DelFiles] lists files to delete when upgrading to Windows 3.1.

- [RenFiles] lists files to rename when upgrading to Windows 3.1.

- [win_copyFiles] lists files that need to be copied when you choose to install specific components, games, screen savers, and accessories.

- [new.groups] tells Setup what Program Manager group changes to make for an upgrade from version 3.0 to 3.1.

- [progman.groups] tells Setup which Program Manager groups to create for a new installation of Windows 3.1.

- [group#] tells Windows what items should be in each Program Manager group.

- [fonts] lists vector and raster screen font files used by Windows.

- [ttfonts] lists TrueType font files used by Windows.

- [compatibility] lists the filenames of drivers whose references Windows will remove from the CONFIG.SYS because they may cause problems with Windows.

- [incompTSR1] lists the filenames of TSRs and drivers that have been known to cause problems during Windows Setup.

- [incompTSR2] lists the filenames of TSRs and drivers that have been known to cause problems when running with Windows.

- [block_devices] lists block devices known to cause problems with Windows.

- [installable.drivers] contains information for multimedia drivers, such as those for sound boards, used by Windows.

- [translate] lists the Windows 3.0 OEMSETUP.INF filenames and their equivalents in Windows 3.1.

- [update.files] lists filenames of drivers that should be updated to the version on the Windows 3.1 disks.

- [ini.upd.patches] lists the temporary filenames of .INI file sections that are updated when upgrading from Windows 3.0 to 3.1.

- [blowaway] tells Windows that this is the end of Setup information that it needs in SETUP.INF.

- [ini.upd.31] lists the lines of .INI files that will be updated in Windows 3.1.

- [system] contains entries that define short names to be used by Windows in place of actual driver names.

- [machine] contains information for installing the appropriate files for each type of system.

- [special_adapter] lists information for using special adapters with Windows.

- [ebios] lists the filenames needed for extended BIOS support on different systems.

- [language] lists the language DLLs used by Windows for systems that need language support other than English.

Add Custom Choices to System Information Screens   If the workstations on your network use a device that isn't supported by Windows, such as a trackball or off-brand mouse, you can add a menu choice for it to the Setup routine. Of course, you will need to get the driver that allows the device to work with Windows from the manufacturer.

First, copy the driver into the same shared directory as the rest of the Windows files. Next, open the SETUP.INF file in a text editor and locate the [pointing.device] section. You'll see a comment that shows the appropriate syntax for the section:

```
;profile = mouse driver, mouse description, VMD, optional work section
```

Below that you'll see the first entry:

```
hpmouse  = 2:hpmouse.drv, "HP Mouse (HP-HIL)", x:*vmd
```

The semicolon identifies that what comes after it is a remark and not file information. Now, here's what the rest of the entry means:

- *profile* is a text string that's used in place of the longer filename to identify the driver. In the example, it's hpmouse.

- *mouse driver* is the actual filename, which ends in .DRV and is preceded by the number of the disk that contains it. Because the custom driver will not be found on a disk, just use 1; Windows will ignore the number because Setup is being run from the file server. In the example, the setting is 2:hpmouse.drv.

- *mouse description* is the text that will appear as the choice in Windows Setup. In the example, it's "HP Mouse (HP-HIL)".

- *VMD* stands for virtual mouse device and specifies the driver that allows the pointing device to be used with DOS applications in 386 Enhanced mode. This file ends with the extension .386. Many pointing devices use the VMD that's part of WIN386.EXE and don't need a separate file. As with the mouse driver filename, the disk number precedes the entry if it is a separate file from WIN386.EXE. In the example, this setting is *x*:*.vmd. The *x* means that you don't need to specify the disk number where the file is located.

- *optional work section* refers to any additional information that's needed by Windows to use the driver file. In the preceding example, no additional information is required.

Add a custom choice by creating an entry for your pointing device following the syntax just described. By editing other sections of the SETUP.INF file, you can add other configuration choices to Windows Setup. For display adapters, edit the [display] section, for keyboard drivers edit the [keyboard.drivers] section, and for network drivers edit the [network] section.

Streamlining User Options in Setup with SETUP.INF and CONTROL.INF

While editing the SETUP.INF lets you add custom choices to hardware menus, you can also use it to remove menu items so that users aren't overwhelmed by the number of choices. SETUP.INF lets you remove choices for the type of system, display, keyboard, network, and pointing device. Similarly, CONTROL.INF lets you remove menu options for any printers that you don't want.

If you've created a system settings file to completely automate Windows installation on your network, the myriad menu choices aren't a problem because the user never sees them. But if each user will be going through the Windows setup process on his or her workstation, you may want to make things easier by leaving only those choices that correspond to the available printers. That way users won't have to wonder if they're selecting the correct driver. For example, is it the HP LaserJet Plus, the HP LaserJet Series II, or the HP LaserJet IID?

To remove the choices you don't want, go to the corresponding section in the .INF file—for example, [machine]—and delete the choices you don't want to appear in Setup menus.

For instance, to remove printer choices from the Setup menu and prevent them from appearing in the Control Panel printer list, follow these steps: Open CONTROL.INF in a text editor and locate the [io.device] section. You'll see a list like that in Figure 10.3. Then delete lines for any printers that you know you will never use or don't plan to add to the network. For example, you may decide to delete the lines for plotters, such as these for some of the Hewlett-Packard plotters. (Note that these lines are highlighted in the figure.)

```
6:HPPLOT.DRV,"HP 7470A [HP Plotter]","CONTINUOUSSCALING"
6:HPPLOT.DRV,"HP 7475A [HP Plotter]","CONTINUOUSSCALING"
6:HPPLOT.DRV,"HP 7550A [HP Plotter]","CONTINUOUSSCALING"
6:HPPLOT.DRV,"HP 7580A [HP Plotter]","CONTINUOUSSCALING"
6:HPPLOT.DRV,"HP 7580B [HP Plotter]","CONTINUOUSSCALING"
6:HPPLOT.DRV,"HP 7585A [HP Plotter]","CONTINUOUSSCALING"
6:HPPLOT.DRV,"HP 7585B [HP Plotter]","CONTINUOUSSCALING"
6:HPPLOT.DRV,"HP 7586B [HP Plotter]","CONTINUOUSSCALING"
6:HPPLOT.DRV,"HP ColorPro [HP Plotter]","CONTINUOUSSCALING"
```

FIGURE 10.3

The [io.device] section of the CONTROL.INF file lists all the printer choices available for installation with Windows; deleting these entries removes them from the Printers list in the Control Panel.

Although deleting extraneous entries helps make Windows setup a more straightforward process for users, avoid deleting entries for any device that you may possibly want to add to the network one day.

As in the preceding tip for adding setup choices, edit the [display] section to remove display adapter choices, the [keyboard.drivers] section for keyboard choices, and the [network] section for network choices.

Copy Additional Windows Files to Workstations with SETUP.INF You can edit the SETUP.INF file so that you can copy additional Windows files to each workstation's directory. Perhaps you'd like to make sure that the Microsoft Diagnostics Utility is installed locally on all of the workstations so that they'll have access to it even when the network drive can't be accessed. (See Chapter 3, "Find Out about the Memory You Have in Your System" for more details on this handy program.)

To add MSD.EXE to each workstation when Windows is installed, you need to add an entry to the section that controls the files copied for your specific type of PC (networked or unnetworked, 286 or 386 and above).

Open SETUP.INF in a text editor and locate the first section pertaining to copying files, [win.copy]. Notice that the remark beneath it tells you that these entries are for 286 systems only. Below [win.copy] are sections called [win.copy.net], [win.copy.net.win386], and [win.copy.win386]. These are for networked 286 systems, networked 386 and higher systems, and stand-alone 386 or higher systems, respectively.

If your network was composed of all 386 and 486 systems, you'd make changes to the [win.copy.net.win386] section. Entries to the various copy-files sections can either be references to entire lists of files that are contained in their own sections or simply to an individual file. Regardless of the kind of entry, it must point to the user's Windows directory as the destination for the copied files. 0: is the number Windows uses to refer to the location of the system's WINDOWS directory. References to 1: through 7: stand for the original Windows disks.

There are two ways to add the single file that executes MSD.EXE from the network server to the workstation's WINDOWS directory. One way is to add the file to the bottom of the list under the [net] section, which, as you can see from the existing entries in the [win.copy.net.win386] section, is automatically copied to such systems. The new [net] section might look like this:

```
[net]
6:CONTROL.SRC,     "Windows User Files"
5:WINVER
5:MSD.EXE
```

The other choice is to add the file to the [win.copy.net.win386] section itself. This entry would read

```
5:MSD.EXE, 0:
```

Note that the 5: that stands for setup Disk 5 is ignored by Setup because the file is actually located in the shared directory on the server.

If you choose to install existing groups of files to the workstation's disk, such as those in the [win.devices.win386] section (HIMEM.SYS, EMM386.EXE, SMARTDRV.EXE, and RAMDRIVE.EXE), you can do so by pointing to this group. For example, you can add the line **#win.devices.win386, 0:**. The # sign tells Windows that you are pointing to a group of files that is defined in the SETUP.INF file.

Install Custom Apps with SETUP.INF   Take the previous tip one step further by having Windows copy non-Windows files to workstations during Setup. For instance, you can tell Windows to copy custom Windows applications, such as a database management program, or commercial Windows applications, such as a screen saver or utilities program.

The files you want to copy may be either on a floppy disk or in the same directory as the Windows files on the network server. If the files are on a floppy disk, you'll need to assign a disk number to it. Remember that the Windows 3.1 disks are numbered 1 through 7.

For example, to copy a set of custom Windows utilities called RCOUTILS (and made up of the four files, RPHONE.EXE, RINFO.EXE, RUTIL.HLP, and RUTILS.DLL), which are contained on a single floppy disk, you would do the following:

1. First assign this disk the number 8, as shown in Figure 10.4. Locate the [disks] section in SETUP.INF, and add a line assigning the number, like this:

   ```
   8 =. ,"R. Company Utilities",disk8
   ```

2. The disk tag, disk8, corresponds to the disk's volume label, assigned in DOS when you format a floppy disk. If the R. Company Utilities disk doesn't have a volume label, you must assign one. Windows File Manager allows you to add a label to a disk that's already formatted by selecting the Label Disk choice from the Disk menu.

3. Next, add a reference to Disk 8 in the appropriate [win.copy] section for the workstations on your network. Since our network has all 386 and 486 workstations, we would use the [win.copy.net.win386] section. The addition for the utilities would look like these entries:

   ```
   [win.copy.net.win386]
   ; copy this section for network setup on 386 machines
   #net,        0:
   8:rphone.exe, 0:
   8:rinfo.exe,  0:
   8:rutil.hlp,  0:
   8:rutil.dll,  0:
   ```

FIGURE 10.4

The [disks] section of the SETUP.INF file tells Windows which disks it will use during Setup; adding entries lets you copy custom files to workstations during Windows Setup.

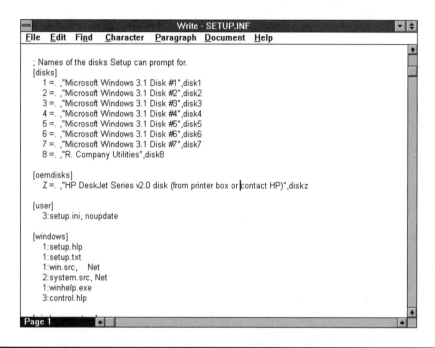

```
; Names of the disks Setup can prompt for.
[disks]
    1 =. ,"Microsoft Windows 3.1 Disk #1",disk1
    2 =. ,"Microsoft Windows 3.1 Disk #2",disk2
    3 =. ,"Microsoft Windows 3.1 Disk #3",disk3
    4 =. ,"Microsoft Windows 3.1 Disk #4",disk4
    5 =. ,"Microsoft Windows 3.1 Disk #5",disk5
    6 =. ,"Microsoft Windows 3.1 Disk #6",disk6
    7 =. ,"Microsoft Windows 3.1 Disk #7",disk7
    8 =. ,"R. Company Utilities",disk8

[oemdisks]
    Z =. ,"HP DeskJet Series v2.0 disk (from printer box or contact HP)",diskz

[user]
    3:setup.ini, noupdate

[windows]
    1:setup.hlp
    1:setup.txt
    1:win.src,    Net
    2:system.src, Net
    1:winhelp.exe
    3:control.hlp
```

If the utilities were located in the shared Windows directory on the network, in the preceding entry 8: would be replaced the with any number from 1: through 7:(since Setup ignores the number of the Windows disk if the files are located on the server).

If you want to copy many files to network workstations, or if your workstations include 286s as well as 386s and higher, you'll want to use a different method for copying files. As in the previous tip, where we placed a reference to a copy-files section ([win.devices.win386]) also defined in SETUP.INF, we can define a new copy-files section that contains our utilities and then simply reference this in the [win.copy] sections for our workstations.

For example, let's create a copy-files section named [rutils]. This new section should be placed near similar sections in the SETUP.INF file, such as [win.devices.win386], [win.other], and [win.shell]. The new section defining R. Company's utility collection would look like this:

```
[rutils]
8:rinfo.exe, "RInfo Utility", rinfo
8:rphone.exe, "RPhone Utility", rphone
8:rutil.hlp, "RHelp Utility"
```

The last file, RUTIL.DLL, would be added to the [win.dependents] copy-file section, which is used to copy DLLs to the corresponding programs (identified here by the profile strings rinfo and rphone) that use them. The new entry would look like these lines:

```
[win.dependents]
pbrush   = 4:PBRUSH.DLL
recorder = 3:RECORDER.DLL
wintutor = 4:WINTUTOR.DAT
rinfo    = 8:RUTIL.DLL
rphone   = 8:RUTIL.DLL
```

Finally, you need to add a reference to the [rutils] section to the [win.copy-.net.win386] section. It would look like this:

```
#net,        0:
#rutils,     0:rutils
```

The 0:rutils entry tells Windows to copy the files to the WINDOWS subdirectory RUTILS.

Create Custom Program Groups   You can also customize SETUP.INF to create Program Manager groups that contain only the items that you want. You can change the contents of existing groups or create entirely new ones.

For new installations of Windows 3.1, you'll use the [progman.groups] section in the SETUP.INF file. If, however, you are upgrading from 3.0, you'll refer to the [new.groups] section. Remember, if you're using Windows Write it's quickest to use the Find command, as shown in Figure 10.5.

You'll notice that the last line of the [progman.groups] section identifies the StartUp group. To add a new group called Sales, you'd add a new entry like this:

```
group6=SalesTools
```

Now that the group has been established, you must create a section called [group6] that defines its contents. Scroll down in SETUP.INF file until you locate the place where other Program Manager groups are defined, with headings like [group3] and [group4]. Add the [group6] section, following the format of the other group listings. For example, you might enter the following:

```
[group6]
"Calendar", CALENDAR.EXE,,, calendar
"Calculator", CALC.EXE,,, calc
"Excel", F:\EXCEL\EXCEL.EXE,,, excel
```

Because the Windows application Excel is not located in the WINDOWS directory, you must specify its path.

FIGURE 10.5

It's easy to edit .INF files such as SETUP.INF in Write; use Write's Find command to locate the precise section you need.

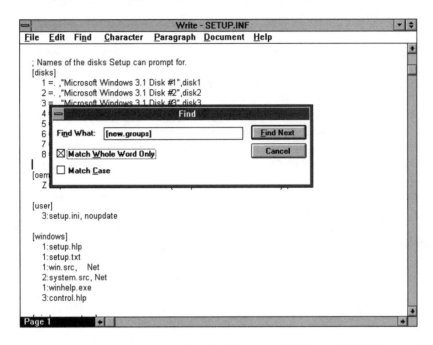

Alternatively, you can edit the existing group definitions by deleting some programs from one group while adding them to another. For example, you could move the Clipboard Viewer from Group 3 (Main) to Group 4 (Accessories) by cutting the line from [group3] and pasting it into [group4].

On the other hand, you might want to get rid of some Program Manager group items altogether. For example, if your users will not be taking advantage of any of Windows' multimedia capabilities, you can create a less cluttered desktop by removing icons for applications such as the Sound Recorder and Media Player. If you decide to use these capabilities later, you can simply add the icons. Unlike the [dontinstall] section of the system settings file discussed earlier, the files for these applications are installed on your system; they just aren't visible in the default Program Manager groups.

Create a Custom Working Environment   In the preceding section, you saw how to create Program Manager groups that contain exactly the items you need. You can customize and standardize the look of the Windows desktop by adding your own bitmaps to be used as wallpaper. For example, you might want to make your company logo the required wallpaper on your network. To do this, locate the [win.bmps] section of the SETUP.INF file; you'll see listings for the various bitmaps that are included with Windows. Then add an entry for the bitmap, in this case COLOGO.BMP, like this:

```
5:COLOGO.BMP,    "Our Logo Wallpaper",898
```

The number 898 is the size of the COLOGO.BMP file, and as mentioned before, 5: refers to the Windows disk that contains the file. Since we've copied the CO-LOGO.BMP to the shared network directory, 5: just serves as a placeholder here and is ignored by Windows Setup.

While you're in the [win.bmps] section, delete any bitmaps that you don't want users to install as wallpaper on their desktops. You can also remove entries from the other section, [win.scrs], if you plan to use an alternate screen saver, such as a commercial Windows product like Intermission or After Dark.

Replace Program Manager Before Windows Is Installed   If you plan on installing a third-party program such as Norton Desktop in place of the Windows shell Program Manager, you can make this switch while Windows is installed.

To do so, locate the [shell] section of the SETUP.INF file. It will look like this:

```
[shell]
progman.exe, "Program Manager"
```

Then replace it with the following:

```
[shell]
ndw.exe, "Norton Desktop"
```

Each network workstation will be started with Norton Desktop as the shell.

Force Network Setup   If you want to make sure that network users set up a shared copy of Windows from the files located on the server, you can edit SET-UP.INF to force this option. If a user forgets to use the /N switch (SETUP /N) for installing a shared copy of Windows on the workstation, Setup will automatically do so instead of installing a local copy of Windows.

To ensure a network setup, make sure that the line netsetup=true is in the [data] section of the SETUP.INF file. The default is netsetup=false.

Automating Setup with the APPS.INF and CONTROL.SRC Files

Another .INF file you'll want to be familiar with is APPS.INF. This file contains information for installing applications with Windows. You can edit this file to install PIF information for your own DOS applications during Windows Setup on a network. If you're unclear about the contents of .PIF files, refer to Chapter 4 for a quick refresher before proceeding.

CONTROL.SRC is the master file for the Windows Control Panel's initialization file (CONTROL.INI). In Chapter 5's "Tips for Control Panel Control," we looked briefly at how you can edit CONTROL.INI once Windows is installed, to customize the Windows desktop. Here you'll see how to make these changes before Windows is set up.

APPS.INF Contents   Like the CONTROL.INF file discussed previously, the APPS.INF file is in the WINDOWS\SYSTEM subdirectory. And like the other .INF files we've discussed, it is made up of sections defined by bracketed entries. You can use a text editor to make additions and changes to APPS.INF to provide for a custom Windows installation. You'll be able to add PIF information for DOS applications that aren't automatically recognized by Windows Setup. And if you will be using DOS applications that have common executable filenames, such as EDIT.EXE, you can make sure that APPS.INF recognizes them and configures them correctly.

APPS.INF is made up of five main sections:

- [dialog] tells Windows what text should appear in the Setup Applications dialog box.

- [base_PIFs] contains instructions for creating a batch file that creates the _DEFAULT.PIF file and settings for COMMAND.COM.

- [enha_dosprompt] contains memory requirement information for running the DOS prompt in Enhanced mode.

- [dontfind] tells Windows which applications to ignore during Setup.

- [pif] contains listings of PIF information for DOS applications that Windows will recognize and set up during installation. The information includes the executable filename, the .PIF filename, the window title, the startup directory, the close-window-on-exit flag, the icon filename, the icon number, a reference to PIF settings for Standard mode section, a reference to the section that defines applications with the same .EXE filename, and a reference to the section that contains optimized PIF settings.

Automatically Install DOS Programs with APPS.INF   To add PIF information for DOS applications that will be used on your network, you need to add entries to the [pif] section of APPS.INF. If you are uncertain whether a DOS application is already listed in the APPS.INF file, scan the existing entries in the [pif] section. The applications are listed in alphabetical order according to executable filename. The syntax for entries in this section is as follows:

```
exe file = PIF name, window title, startup directory, close-window-on-exit flag,
icon filename, icon number, reference to standard PIF settings section,
reference to enhanced PIF settings section, reference to ambiguous .EXE files
section, reference to optimized PIFs section
```

As a specific example, let's look at the first entry in the section:

```
123.COM = 123,"Lotus 1-2-3",,cwe,,3,std_gra_256,enha_123c
```

The following lists what each setting means. (Note that the first four settings refer to the first four text boxes that are defined for an application in the PIF Editor, as shown in Figure 10.6.)

FIGURE 10.6

The four text boxes in the PIF Editor—Program Filename, Window Title, Optional Parameters, and Start-up Directory—correspond to the first four settings for entries in APPS.INF's [pif] section.

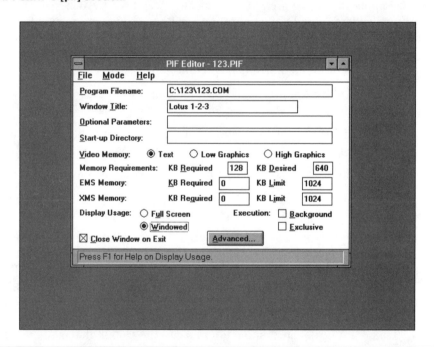

- *exe file* represents the name of the application's executable file. In the example it's 123.COM.

- *PIF name* tells Windows what name to give to the program information file that contains the settings for running the application with Windows, in this case Lotus 1-2-3. In the example the PIF will be called 123.PIF.

- *window title* is the title that will appear when the DOS application is running in a window, as pictured in Figure 10.7. In the example, the window will be entitled "Lotus 1-2-3."

FIGURE 10.7

The *window title* setting in an entry of APPS.INF's [pif] section defines the title that's displayed for a windowed DOS application.

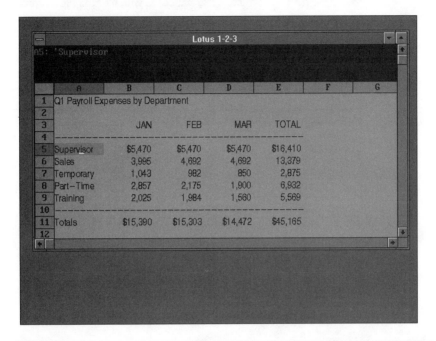

- *startup directory* is the working directory for the application. In the preceding example, no directory is specified (note the two consecutive commas). This means that Lotus 1-2-3 will start in the directory that Windows determines, usually the directory where the application's executable file is located. If you want to make sure that users save their data files in a specific directory that's different from the program directory, note it here.

- *close-window-on-exit flag* tells Windows whether to close the application's window when the user exits from the application. In the example, the setting is cwe (close window on exit). If cwe is not specified, the application won't be closed on exit.

- *icon filename* stands for the filename that contains the icon to be used for this application. In the example, the setting is blank, which means that Windows will use the default file PROGMAN.EXE as the icon source. Some of the icon choices for Lotus 1-2-3 are shown in Figure 10.8.

- *icon number* is the number of the icon to be used. In the example, the setting is 3, which means that the third icon in the PROGMAN.EXE file will be used (as shown in Figure 10.8).

FIGURE 10.8

The *icon filename* setting for an entry in APPS.INF's [pif] section corresponds to the source file that contains the icons to be used to represent the DOS application in Windows Program Manager; the icon number entry indicates which of the file's icons will be used.

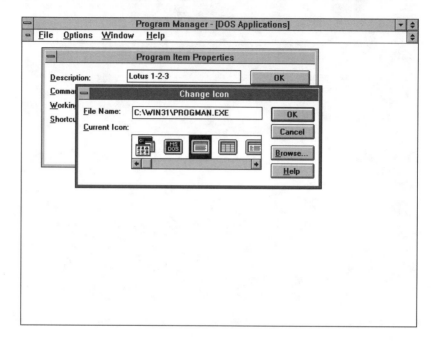

■ *reference to standard PIF settings section* tells Windows the name of the section in APPS.INF that contains PIF settings for running the application in Standard mode. In the example, the section is titled [std_gra_256]. Scroll down through the APPS.INF to find this section. You'll find a section that looks like this:

```
[std_gra_256]
minconvmem   = 256
videomode    = gra ; Graphics mode app
```

This section tells Windows that the minimum conventional memory required by Lotus 1-2-3 is 256K (which corresponds to the Memory Requirements section of the PIF Editor), and the video mode setting to be used is Graphics/Multiple Text (which corresponds to the Video Mode section of the PIF Editor). See Figure 10.9 to locate these sections in the PIF Editor.

FIGURE 10.9

All of a program's PIF settings can be set by entries in the APPS.INF's [pif] section.

```
 ┌─────────────────────────────────────────────────────┐
 │  ─              PIF Editor - [Untitled]        ▼ ▲   │
 │  File   Mode   Help                                  │
 │                                                      │
 │  Program Filename:   [                            ]  │
 │  Window Title:       [                            ]  │
 │  Optional Parameters:[                            ]  │
 │  Start-up Directory: [                            ]  │
 │  Video Mode:         ◉ Text   ○ Graphics/Multiple Text│
 │  Memory Requirements:  KB Required [128]             │
 │  XMS Memory:    KB Required [0]    KB Limit [0]      │
 │  Directly Modifies:  □ COM1   □ COM3   □ Keyboard   │
 │                      □ COM2   □ COM4                 │
 │  □ No Screen Exchange      □ Prevent Program Switch  │
 │  ⊠ Close Window on Exit    □ No Save Screen          │
 │  Reserve Shortcut Keys: □ Alt+Tab □ Alt+Esc □ Ctrl+Esc│
 │                         □ PrtSc   □ Alt+PrtSc        │
 │  ┌─────────────────────────────────────────────────┐│
 │  │ Press F1 for Help on Program Filename.           ││
 │  └─────────────────────────────────────────────────┘│
 └─────────────────────────────────────────────────────┘
```

NOTE Settings aren't specified for the rest of the PIF Editor sections, such as XMS Memory and Directly Modifies, because Windows uses a section of the APPS.INF called [std_dflt] as the default PIF settings. Locate this section and review the settings, comparing them to the PIF Editor settings. If you don't need to make any changes to the defaults for your application, leave the reference to a standard PIF settings section blank. You'll notice that other options for the settings are shown as comments in the section to help you determine if you need to make any changes.

The [std_dflt] section looks like this:

```
[std_dflt]
; default is text mode app which does not directly modify COM ports
;; Other Possible options are given for reference
; ( (or) means entry corresponds to radio button group)
minconvmem  = 128
videomode   = txt    ; (or) gra
xmsmem      = 0,0    ; ##,, ## (min, max)
checkboxes  =        ; 1,c2,c3,c4,kbd,nse,pps,ata,aes,ces,psc,aps,nss
```

■ *reference to enhanced PIF settings section.* As with the default section for running DOS applications in Standard mode, APPS.INF contains the section [enha_dflt], which contains default settings for running in Enhanced mode. In the preceding example, with Lotus 1-2-3, an addition section specifically for Lotus 1-2-3 is required: [enha_123c]. If you don't specify an enhanced PIF settings section, Windows will refer to the [enha_dflt] section, which contains the following settings:

```
[enha_dflt]
; default is as follows
;
; Other possible options are given for reference
; ( (or) means entry corresponds to radio button group )
;
convmem       = 128,640   ; ##,## (Required, Limit)
emsmem        = 0,1024     ; ##,## (Required, Limit)
xmsmem        = 0,1024     ; ##,## (Required, Limit)
dispusage     = fs         ; (or) win
execflags     =            ; bgd, exc
multaskopt    = 50,100     ; ##,## (Bgd Pri, Fgd Pri)
procmemflags  = dit,hma    ; eml,xml,lam
dispoptvideo  = txt        ; (or) lgr,hgr
dispoptports  = hgr        ; txt,lgr
dispflags     = emt        ; rvm
otheroptions  = afp        ; cwa,ata,aes,ces,psc,aps,asp,aen
```

- *reference to ambiguous .EXE files section* tells Windows the name of the section that lists other applications with the same .EXE filename. In the Lotus 1-2-3 example, there is no reference. This means that there aren't any known programs that have an executable file with the name 123.COM.

- *reference to optimized PIFs section* points to another section defined in the APPS.INF file, which contains settings for running the application with specific settings different from those defined in the [enhanced] or [standard] sections. In our example, no additional section is required. You might define an optional section when you want to create more than one PIF for a single application. For information on why you'd want to have multiple PIFs, see Chapter 4's "Make Two PIFs for the Same Application."

Now that you're familiar with the ins and outs of the APPS.INF file's [pif] section, you can add entries for custom DOS applications on your network.

Automatically Ignore the DOS Apps You Choose at Setup   Windows uses the [dontfind] section of the APPS.INF to avoid installing duplicate copies of Windows applications—for example, Write, Paintbrush, and Calculator. The section consists of a listing of executable filenames that Windows should overlook when it's searching the hard disk for applications to install.

Put this section to work for you by adding the names of existing DOS applications on the network that you don't want to be set up for use with Windows. The section is organized alphabetically, as shown here:

```
[dontfind]
apm.exe
```

```
calc.exe
calendar.exe
cardfile.exe
charmap.exe
clipbrd.exe
clock.exe
```

Simply add the executable filenames of other DOS applications in the appropriate place.

Exclude Sections of Control Panel by Editing CONTROL.SCR CONTROL.INI, the Control Panel initialization file, contains settings for the Windows Control Panel, including those governing which of its modules (Colors, Desktop, and so on) are loaded. In Chapter 5 we showed how to edit this file to keep other users from being able to make any changes to a system by denying them access to specific sections of the Control Panel.

While CONTROL.INI isn't created until after Windows is installed, you can apply these same tricks before Windows is set up on your network by going right to the source: CONTROL.SRC, the master file for CONTROL.INI. If you've copied the Windows files to the network server you'll find CONTROL.SRC there.

You can add a section to the CONTROL.SRC file called [Don't Load]. Below this heading, list the modules of the Control Panel that you don't want users to have access to. For example, if you don't want users to waste time changing the look of a standard desktop, or if you don't want them to be able to change printers, you could exclude the Desktop and Printers sections from loading into Control Panel. The new section of CONTROL.SRC would look like this:

```
[Don't Load]
Desktop=1
Printers=1
```

The setting of 1 (0 can be used in its place) tells Windows not to load these sections of the Control Panel. Their icons will not be visible in the Control Panel, as shown in Figure 10.10. To grant access to these Control Panel sections later, you'll have to remove the [Don't Load] section from CONTROL.INI.

Windows Maintenance on a Network

The preceding techniques for gaining the most control from a Windows network installation aren't just useful for Windows Setup. Use them to make system changes, such as hardware and software upgrades, a one-step process. We'll also provide new ways, such as editing the PROGMAN.INI file, to easily maintain Windows on a network.

FIGURE 10.10

The Control Panel is missing the Desktop and Printers icons because those modules were included in the CONTROL.INI's [Don't Load] section.

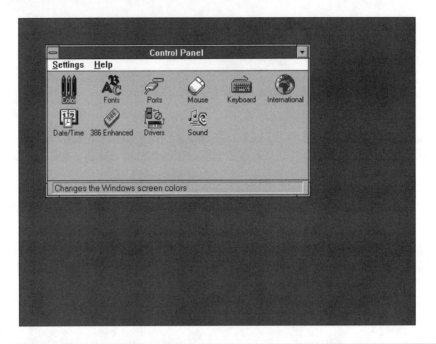

Quickly Setting Up Windows on Multiple Servers   If your business has more than one network server, you may find yourself installing the Windows files to each of these. Save yourself the trouble of shuffling through the Windows disks by copying the files from the original server to another shared server on the network. To do so, type **setup /a** from the directory that contains the Windows files on the original server. You can then specify a new directory on the network to install Windows into. The files will be copied to this location and marked as read-only. You'll also be prompted for a company name and group name, allowing you to make these entries distinct from those used in the Windows directory on the other server. Note that using the DOS COPY command will not yield the same results.

Create Shared Program Groups   You can create a Program Manager group which is accessible to all Windows users on your network. To do so, create the desired group in Program Manager, adding all of the programs that you want it to contain. For example, say you've created a group called Orders, with the group filename, ORDERS.GRP. Copy the file ORDERS.GRP to the shared network directory that contains the Windows files, marking it as read-only.

Now each workstation user will need to select the File menu from the Program Manager and specify that they want to create a New Program group. In the Program Group Properties box, shown in Figure 10.11, each user need only specify the path and .GRP filename that you've already created, in this case Y:\WINDOWS\SALESTEA.GRP. The group will automatically be created on the workstation.

FIGURE 10.11

Network users can set up shared Program Manager groups on their system by specifying the correct group file that you have previously created.

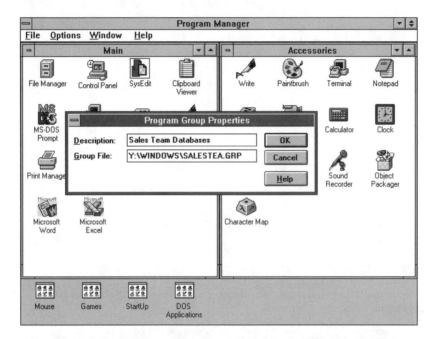

Setting User Restrictions in the PROGMAN.INI File PROGMAN.INI is the initialization file for the Windows Program Manager. Edit this file to restrict user actions—for example, to prevent users from being able to run programs that aren't represented by an icon, and to keep users from exiting Windows. You can accomplish this by adding a [restrictions] sections to the PROGMAN.INI. The [restrictions] section can contain the following:

- NoRun=1 removes the Run command from the Program Manager's File menu, as shown in Figure 10.12.

- NoFileMenu=1 removes the entire File menu from Program Manager, as shown in Figure 10.13.

- NoClose=1 prohibits users from exiting Windows by making the Exit option unavailable, as shown in Figure 10.14.

- NoSaveSettings=1 prohibits users from saving changes made to Program Manager. In Figure 10.15, note that the Save Settings on Exit choice in the Options menu is unavailable.

FIGURE 10.12

Editing the user's PROGMAN.INI file and adding a [restrictions] section allows you to remove the Run command from the Program Manager's File menu.

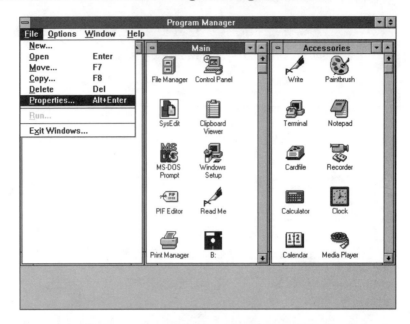

FIGURE 10.13

You can use the [restrictions] section of PROGMAN.INI to remove the entire File menu from Program Manager, thereby preventing users from making changes to existing program groups.

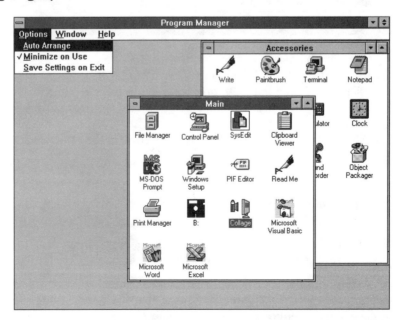

FIGURE 10.14

You can make the Close option unavailable to users by editing the PROGMAN.INI file, thus preventing users from exiting the environment.

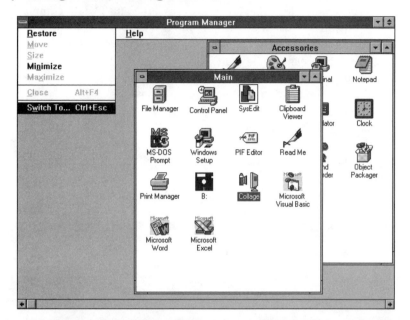

FIGURE 10.15

The Save Settings on Exit option is dimmed, meaning that users are unable to save changes made to the Windows desktop.

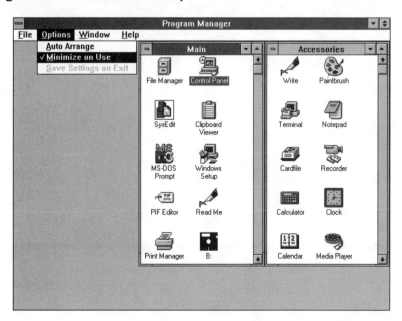

- EditLevel= sets editing privileges for the user:

    0 (the default) allows all Program Manager changes.

    1 removes access to the New, Move, Copy, and Delete commands on the File menu when a program group is selected. Users won't be able to add, change, or delete existing Program Manager groups.

    2 removes access to the New, Move, Copy, and Delete commands on the File menu at all times. Users won't be able to add, change, or delete Program Manager groups or program items.

    3 provides for restrictions in EditLevel=2 and also restricts users from changing command lines in the Program Item Properties dialog box for selected program items or groups. It also restricts users from making any changes to Program Group Properties. (See Figure 10.16.)

    4 provides all the restrictions in EditLevel=3 and restricts users from making any changes in Program Item Properties dialog boxes.

FIGURE 10.16

If the EditLevel in PROGMAN.INI is set to 3, users cannot make changes to program items in the Program Item Properties dialog box.

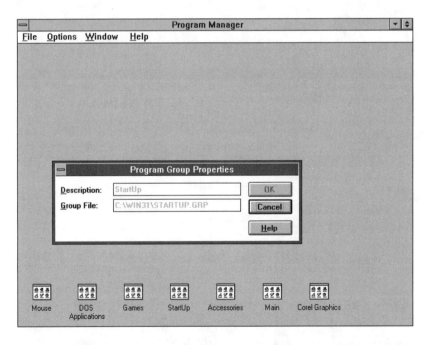

For example, to remove the File menu from the Program Manager and prevent users from making any changes to Program Manager items, you would change the [restrictions] section to look like this:

```
[restrictions]
```

```
NoFileMenu=1
EditLevel=4
```

Running Setup for an Update with a New System Settings File   Create a system settings file (.SHH) that contains updated settings for the [configuration] section when you need to update system settings across the network, such as installing new drivers. Create the file as explained in the beginning of the chapter, but to ensure that Windows reinstalls the new drivers or devices that you've specified in the file, you'll want to alter the names used for drivers just slightly. Otherwise Windows will ignore new [configuration] settings in favor of those already installed under the driver's name.

Force Windows to accept the new setting by putting an exclamation point before the name of the new device. For example, to force a new display driver to be set up, you would use an entry in the [configuration] section like this:

```
display=!svga
```

Optimizing Network Performance

Network performance is a gossamer goal. Every possible advantage should be brought to bear to attain it. If you've followed the steps so far, you should have a stable Windows network configuration. Use the tips that follow to maximize your system's performance in the three key areas: basic setup, SYS.INI management, and that old bugaboo, printing.

Fine-tuning Windows Performance on a Network

Get better performance from Windows running on a network by keeping the following in mind:

- Set the lastdrive= statement in the CONFIG.SYS to a drive that's toward the beginning of the alphabet (like J, as opposed to Z), if possible. (This isn't recommended for NetWare LANs, which use the back end of the alphabet for network drivers.) For example, if the network contains disk drives that you don't need access to, exclude them from the lastdrive= statement.

- When setting up swap files for use on a workstation, avoid using a network drive for a temporary or permanent swap file.

- Avoid loading network applications into high memory if you experience any problems running Windows.

- Likewise, if you are loading network drivers and other device drivers into upper memory and you experience problems running Windows, remove these drivers and try loading them in conventional memory.

- For a shared copy of Windows running from a network drive, make sure that the user's personal WINDOWS directory, as well as the shared WINDOWS directory, is included on the PATH statement in

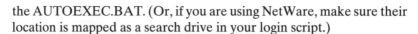

the AUTOEXEC.BAT. (Or, if you are using NetWare, make sure their location is mapped as a search drive in your login script.)

■ If you're having problems running a shared copy of Windows, make sure that the DOS command, SHARE, is not executed on the workstation.

Fine-tuning SYSTEM.INI for Network Use

You may have mastered the intricacies of your PC's SYSTEM.INI file (as described in Chapter 2), but running Windows on a network may bring unexpected performance, making it necessary to reevaluate the current settings. The following tips highlight those entries that are relevant to optimizing Windows on a network. Some of what we discuss here lies in territory we advised you to stay away from in Chapter 2. Here, however, we assume somewhat greater sophistication, commensurate with the greater need for precise control that comes with networking. But our original warning holds: Be careful when you work with these areas of SYSTEM.INI. This is the system equivalent of open heart surgery!

[Boot] Section Entries The [Boot] Section contains information about basic settings that are established when Windows starts.

■ CachedFileHandles=*number* tells Windows the number of recently used executable files and dynamic link library files (DLLs) that may remain open at one time (*number* can be from 2 to 12; the default is 12). While we warned you in Chapter 2 against changing this setting, you may need to if you have problems running a shared copy of Windows from a server. Some networks limit the number of files that can be open on a server at one time; try setting this entry to a lower number.

■ Network.drv=*filename* tells Windows the name of the network driver to use. You can change this setting by running Windows Setup and selecting a new Network setting.

[Standard] Section Entries The [Standard] section of the SYSTEM.INI defines the parameters Windows uses when running in Standard mode.

■ Int28Filter=*number*, in Standard mode, determines the percentage of Int28h interrupts that are made visible to applications that were loaded before Windows. With the default setting of 10, Windows makes every tenth interrupt visible. Increasing the setting improves Windows' performance, but may interfere with network software. Experiment to find the best setting for your system.

■ NetHeapSize=*kilobytes* determines the size of the conventional memory buffer that Windows uses for transferring data over a network in Standard mode. (The default for *kilobytes* is 8.) If an application is not running correctly, it may be because your network needs a larger buffer than the default of 8. Increasing this value decreases available conventional memory, but may be necessary for some networks. On the other hand, many networks can run perfectly with a setting of 4, increasing the amount of conventional memory available to applications.

[NonWindowsApps] Section Entries The [NonWindowsApps] section provides Windows with some basic operating information for running DOS applications.

- NetAsynchSwitching=0|1 specifies whether your system can switch away from an application running in Standard mode after it has made an asynchronous network BIOS call. (The default setting is 0.) A setting of 1 allows this task switching, but use it only if you are certain that the application will not receive network messages while you are switched away from it.

[386Enh] Section Entries The [386Enh] settings help Windows take the fullest advantage of the 386 processor and define the settings for running Windows in 386 Enhanced mode. If you experience problems running Windows on a network in 386 Enhanced mode, you'll want to examine these settings.

- EMMExclude=*paragraph-range* prevents Windows from scanning a designated range of memory. (There is no default.) Many network adapter cards require this entry to be set to the range of memory used by the card.

- FileSysChange=Off|On determines whether File Manager is notified when a non-Windows application creates, deletes, copies, moves, renames, or modifies a file. (The default is On for 386 Enhanced mode, Off for Standard mode.) If you're having problems running a non-Windows network application, try disabling this setting.

- InDOSPolling=Off|On is another entry we told you in Chapter 2 not to edit, but you may need to change this setting to On because some memory-resident software requires this setting. (The default is Off.)

- Int28Critical=Off|On, when set to On (the default), indicates some memory-resident software needs this setting switched to On. This setting is required by some networks that use virtual devices to perform internal task switching in response to Int28h.

- Network=*filename* tells Windows the type of network that will be running in 386 Enhanced mode. The filename is that of the network driver.

- NetAsynchFallback=Off|On and NetAsynchTimeout=*seconds* determine whether Windows attempts to rescue a failing asynchronous NET-Bios request. (The former defaults to Off and the latter to 5.0.) Normally, if Windows doesn't have enough space in its global network buffer to handle this request, the request fails. If NetAsynchFallback is on, however, Windows allocates a buffer in local memory and prevents any other virtual machine from running until the time specified by NetAsynchTimeout.

- NetDMASize=*kilobytes* specifies the size of the DMA buffer used for NetBIOS transport software, if a NetBIOS network is installed. (The default is 32 on MCA computers, 0 on all others.) Windows uses the larger of this setting and the DMABufferSize setting.

- NetHeapSize=*kilobytes* determines the size of the conventional-memory buffer that Windows uses in 386 Enhanced mode for transferring data over a network. (The default is 12.) Increasing this value decreases available conventional memory, but may be necessary for some networks. The NetHeapSize is always rounded up to the next 4K boundary.

- ReflectDOSInt2A=Off|On specifies whether Windows should reflect or consume Int2Ah interrupts. Some software requires this be set to On. (The default is Off.)

- TimerCriticalSection=*milliseconds* tells Windows to go into a critical section around all timer interrupt code, specifying the time-out period. (The default is 0.) During this time-out period, multitasking or switching is prohibited. A non-zero positive value means that only one virtual machine at a time receives timer interrupts. Some network software requires that this value be set. Check your documentation. Settings other than zero will slow Windows' performance.

- TokenRingSearch=Off|On determines whether Windows searches for a Token-Ring network adapter on AT-architecture machines. (The default is On.)

- UniqueDOSPSP=On|Off, if On, tells Windows to start every application at a unique address. (The default is On for networks based on Microsoft Network or LAN Manager, Off for all other networks.) The amount of memory between the addresses of two applications is the PSPIncrement described next. Some networks use these addresses to identify network processes, and an Off setting might cause one application to fail when you exit another.

- PSPIncrement=number sets the amount of additional memory that Windows should reserve in each successive virtual machine when UniqueDOSPSP=On. (The default is 2.)

Printing Tips

Printing in Windows can be a headache, printing in Windows on a network can be an office nightmare. Nothing makes users madder than printing a file, hiking down the hall to the network printer, standing there for 10 minutes, and then having nothing happen. That's not much of a productivity enhancement, either. Getting printing to work right is a critical element of any Windows network setup.

Printing on a Diskless Workstation   If you're working on a diskless workstation, Print Manager needs a TEMP directory to spool print jobs to. If a diskless workstation does not have a TEMP directory set up in its AUTOEXEC.BAT file, Windows will not be able to spool print jobs. Normally, if no TEMP directory is set, Windows defaults to the root directory of drive C, but in the case of a diskless workstation, this location does not exist.

To avoid printing problems on such a diskless workstation, make sure that the AUTOEXEC.BAT contains a TEMP= statement that points to a valid network directory.

Taking Advantage of Print Manager on a Network   One of the biggest advantages to running Windows on a network is access to more than one printer. Get the most from the printers on your network by maneuvering around Print Manager so that you can get your files printed exactly when you need them and right where you want them.

Print Manager lets you monitor network print queues, allowing you to decide whether to use your default printer or send your files to another network printer that you have access to when the print queue is full of other users' files. To check on the status of your own files on the network print queue, select Refresh from Print Manager's File menu (or press F5). If your files aren't in the process of printing yet, choose the Selected Net Queue command from the File menu. This will show you all the files, not just your own, waiting for the network printer. If the queue is too long for your liking, select the Other Net Queue command from the File menu and have a look at the other printer's queue.

If you'd rather print your files on the second printer, return to the original queue, select the files by highlighting them, and choose Delete. Now make sure you're connected to the second printer by choosing Network Connections and making the proper connection. Once this is set, return to the Windows application and choose Print again, sending the print jobs to the correct network printer.

Troubleshooting Techniques for Printing   If you're unable to print from Windows on a network, check the following:

- Are you using the correct version of the network driver? If you're not sure, contact the manufacturer to find out about the most recent version.

- Are the network printers connected? In the Control Panel, choose the Printers icon, select Connect, select Network, and note if there are any established network connections. If there aren't, select Browse, choose the correct printer, and establish a connection.

- Can you print over the network outside of Windows? If not, there is a problem with the network, not Windows.

- Try printing without the Print Manager.

- Choose LPT1.DOS rather than LPT1 as your printer port.

- From Windows, try printing a file to disk. This can help determine whether the problem is in Windows or the network. If you select an application such as Write, there is a Print to File option available in the Print dialog box, as shown in Figure 10.17.

FIGURE 10.17

Print a file to disk by marking the option in the Windows application's Print dialog box; you can then copy this file directly to the printer to test if your network printing capabilities are working outside of Windows.

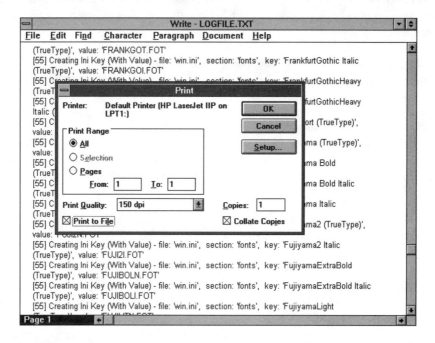

If the test application doesn't have a Print to File option, you'll first need to set up this option in Control Panel:

1. Choose Printers.

2. Select Add.

3. Choose Generic/Text Only from the list of printers.

4. Select Install.

5. Choose Connect.

6. Select File from the Ports box.

7. Select OK.

8. Select Set as Default Printer.

9. Exit Control Panel and print a file to disk.

Once the file is printed to disk, exit Windows and try copying the file to the network printer using the command COPY *filename* LPT1. If it prints, there's most likely a problem with your network configuration.

If the file does not print from DOS, try reinstalling the Windows printer driver on your system.

A Printing Workaround   If you cannot print from Windows on your network, but you can print from DOS, here's a workaround to try until you get the problem solved:

1. From the Control Panel, select Printers.

2. Locate your printer in the list of supported devices, and select Connect.

3. In the Connect dialog box, make sure the Fast Printing Direct To Port check box is off.

4. Then select OK to return to the Printers dialog box, and select Close.

Changing the Fast Printing Direct to Port option sends the print job directly to DOS to be processed. This trick may not work for large files, however.

Tips for Specific Networks

No two networks run the same way, so Windows can't interact with different networks in precisely the same way. General network tips, such as we've had so far in this chapter, are valuable. However, no one actually implements a general network. You will be choosing and living with a specific networking product. Use the following tips with the network you've chosen, or use them to get a feel for different network systems (and the problems they bring) before you buy.

Novell NetWare Tips

NetWare has been the dominant PC networking system for nearly a decade. Known for superb file-handling capabilities, huge capacity, hardware independence, and almost mind-numbing complexity, NetWare takes a lot of care and feeding, but offers great payback for the effort. Many of these tips focus on avoiding the inevitable confusion that comes with NetWare's complexity.

Make Sure Your Shell Is Current   If you're running Windows on a Novell network, make sure the NetWare shell you are using is version 3.26 or later. Windows 3.1 includes this updated version, NETX.COM.

Running in Standard Mode   If you plan to run Windows in Standard mode on a Novell network, you'll have to remember to load the TSR, TBM12.COM. So that you don't have to remember to unload it from memory once you've exited Windows, create a batch file that does this for you. The file would contain the following lines:

```
TBM12
WIN
TBM12/U
```

Logging In and Out   Novell Netware users should log in to the network before starting Windows and log out after exiting Windows. Do not attempt to log out from a DOS session within Windows.

Increase FILES Access   Netware only allows you access to 40 files at a time. Working in Windows means that those can be used up before you know it. To increase the available file handles, you need to edit the SHELL.CFG file, as well as your CONFIG.SYS file. Open SHELL.CFG in a text editor and add the following line:

```
file handles=60
```

Next, open your CONFIG.SYS file in a text editor and locate the FILES= statement. Increase the current number to 60. The line would look like this:

```
Files=60
```

SYSTEM.INI Settings   To make sure a PC running Novell NetWare with Windows doesn't time-out a network connection, you may need to make the following addition to the [386Enh] section of the SYSTEM.INI:

```
TimerCriticalSection=10000
```

Settings for Diskless Workstations   A major improvement to performance for workstations without hard disks is to reduce the size of the temporary swap file's paging size to 128 or 256K. This prevents huge packet runs over the net. Also don't forget Show Dots=On, in SHELL.CFG. Otherwise you will not see . and .. in directory listings.

Troubleshooting Techniques for Printing   If you're having problems printing from Windows on a NetWare network, check the following:

- Do you have a valid SET TEMP statement in your AUTOEXEC-.BAT? Windows won't be able to print correctly unless the DOS TEMP variable is set to a valid directory to which you have complete access.

- Is the printer configured correctly? Verify that the correct Windows printer driver is installed and that the appropriate port is selected for output.

- Do you have the correct NetWare shell version? Windows 3.1 with DOS 5.0 requires the NetWare shell version 3.26. If that is not loaded, check with your NetWare dealer or support representative for an update.

- Is the Windows NetWare driver installed? Run Windows SETUP from Program Manager and check that Novell NetWare is shown as the installed network driver.

■ Are you using the proper NetWare print configuration? Check to make sure your settings match the following using the Netware PRINTCON utility:

Suppress Form Feed should be set to Yes. Windows places a form feed command at the end of its print jobs, so Netware does not need an additional form feed.

Since Windows is often printing bitmap graphics, File Contents must be set to Byte Stream to avoid NetWare's automatic expansion of tab characters. Byte values resembling tab characters occur randomly within bitmap graphic output; if these are expanded to spaces, the output will be garbled.

The Print Banner should be disabled (set to No) to avoid garbled printing.

Setting Auto Endcap to No prevents NetWare from timing out the print job while it is in progress.

Enable Timeout should also be set to No to avoid timing out the print job while in progress.

If you experience fragmented or garbled print jobs, make sure the Print Banner, Auto Endcap, and Enable Timeout settings are correct.

If you cannot set these options globally by using the PRINTCON utility, you may specify them on your CAPTURE command line. The command would look like this:

```
CAPTURE NB NA TI=0 NFF NT
```

NB is used to specify that no banner page be printed, the NA (No Automatic endcap) option is the same as setting Auto Endcap to No in PRINTCON. TI=0 (timeout) is the same as setting Enable Timeout to No. NFF (no form feed) is the same as Suppress Form Feed set to Yes in PRINTCON. NT (no tab expansion) is similar to setting File Contents to Byte Stream.

3Com Networks

3Com's networking system comes in more flavors and has gone through more changes than NetWare. These are tips that apply to most 3Com software. 3Com's networks tend to be most popular where a variety of different kinds of hardware sit on users' desks.

SYSTEM.INI Settings   If you're using 3Com's 3+Share or 3+Open network, add the following entries to the SYSTEM.INI's [386Enh] section:

```
TimerCriticalSection=10000
UniqueDOSPSP=True
PSPIncrement=5
```

Check Your PATH Windows Setup makes changes to a workstation's AU-TOEXEC.BAT file, including making sure that the WINDOWS directory is located ahead of any conflicting directories in the PATH statement. But 3Com's 3+Share network may change the path when a user logs in. You may need to change the network log-in procedure to guarantee that the PATH statement is set correctly to run Windows on the workstation.

3Station and All ChargeCards If your 3Com network contains 3Com 3Station diskless workstations with All ChargeCards, make sure that the system is not configured to load the network drivers in the upper memory area. This configuration causes the system to run unreliably in Standard mode.

Artisoft LANtastic Tips

LANtastic is a peer-to-peer network, which means that all the linked PCs share management chores, rather than a single central server handling them. Lauded as the easiest network to install and use, LANtastic is great for small offices and PC-only networks with moderate power requirements.

SYSTEM.INI Settings When Windows is installed on an Artisoft LANtastic network, an EMMExclude= entry is added to the [386Enh] section of the SYSTEM.INI file. This setting is required for the LANtastic Enhanced 2mbps network adapter. And if you change the memory address setting of this adapter, you'll need to change this setting to reflect the new address of the adapter.

The exact entries for LANtastic versions 3.*x* are

```
EMMExclude=D800-DFFF
InDOSPolling=True
NetHeapSize=76
NetAsynchFallback=True
NetAsynchTimeout=50
```

For version 4.*x* they are

```
EMMExclude=D800-DFFF
NetHeapSize=64
NetAsynchFallback=True
NetAsynchTimeout=50
PerVMFiles=0
```

How to Create a Permanent Swap File When Windows in running on a LANtastic server, you will be unable to create a permanent swap file for a workstation. To do so, restart the workstation but don't load the server software. Create the swap file in Windows and then restart the network software.

Format Floppies   When Windows is run from a LANtastic server, users will be unable to format floppy disks from File Manager. You can, however, shell to DOS, and use the FORMAT command to format a floppy disk.

Printing in LANtastic 3.x   To successfully print on LANtastic 3.*x* network over Windows, you'll need to turn off the Fast Printing Direct to Port option in the Control Panel's Printers section. Also, set your printer port to LPT*n*.DOS, where *n* is the LPT port number. You should also disable the Print Manager.

Banyan VINES Tips

VINES is a Unix-based network that excels at wide-area connectivity. In VINES you can literally click on a printer in London from your PC in San Francisco and print halfway around the globe. Since VINES already goes to some lengths to mask the complexity of its inner workings, it has a somewhat more arm's-length interaction with Windows, at least so far. Windows and VINES will work on the same system, but they don't really work together.

Start VINES First   Remember to log onto VINES before starting Windows. If you don't, you'll receive an error message telling you that you won't be able to use VINES functions from within Windows.

SYSTEM.INI Settings   For VINES versions 4.0*x*, the following changes are made to the [386Enh] section of the SYSTEM.INI:

```
TimerCriticalSection=5000
UniqueDOSPSP=True
PSPIncrement=5
```

For VINES versions 4.1*x*, these changes are made to the [386Enh] section of the SYSTEM.INI:

```
Network=*dosnet, *vnetbios, vvinesd.386
TimerCriticalSection=5000
UniqueDOSPSP=True
PSPIncrement=5
```

Printing in VINES 4.0x   If you're using VINES 4.0*x* and have print jobs that are timing out, use the VINES SETPRINT utility to remove the time-out on your printer port. The command would be as follows:

```
SETPRINT LPTx servicename/D:INFINITE
```

x is the printer port and *servicename* is the network print queue.

NetBIOS, Standard Mode, and DOS apps   If you are running Windows in Standard mode and load NetBIOS before Windows, you may not be able to access any DOS applications. You'll have to load Windows in Standard mode first and then load NetBIOS from within Windows.

Microsoft LAN Manager Tips

Microsoft's LAN Manager hasn't been a very popular networking choice. It has, however, been a rather influential product all the same. That's because many other products, including recent versions of 3Com and Ungermann-Bass networks, have been based to varying degrees on LAN Manager. In other words, the following tips may apply to products of many names. Check your network documentation to find out if the networking software you use is based on LAN Manager and, if so, which exact version.

SYSTEM.INI Settings   For LAN Manager Basic, the following changes are made to the [386Enh] section of the SYSTEM.INI:

```
network=*dosnet, *vnetbios, lanman10.386
TimerCriticalSection=10000
UniqueDOSPSP=True
PSPIncrement=5
```

For LAN Manager 2.0 Enhanced, this change is made to the [386Enh] section of the SYSTEM.INI:

```
network=*vnetbios, *dosnet
TimerCriticalSection=10000
UniqueDOSPSP=True
PSPIncrement=5
```

For LAN Manager 2.1 Enhanced, this change is made to the [boot] section of the SYSTEM.INI:

```
network.drv=lanman21.drv
```

while the following changes are made to the [386Enh] section of the SYSTEM.INI:

```
TimerCriticalSection=10000
UniqueDOSPSP=True
PSPIncrement=5
```

LAN Manager and Expanded Memory   If you run Windows in 386 Enhanced mode on LAN Manager, it's a good idea to avoid using expanded memory. If you do use expanded memory, watch out for the system slowing down and occasionally locking up on you. To turn off the use of expanded memory, you'll need to edit the LANMAN.INI file.

Open LANMAN.INI in a text editor and locate the [workstation] section. Find the line lim= and change it to read lim=no. Save the file and restart the workstation.

Removing WinPopup LAN Manager Enhanced has a pop-up feature that allows you to receive incoming messages broadcast on the network. To run compatibly through Windows, these must be accessed through LAN Manager's WinPopup utility. To disable this utility and support for the pop-up services (since messages popping up in the middle of critical work may infuriate users), do the following:

1. Open LANMAN.INI in a text editor such as Notepad.

2. Locate the [workstation] section and find the line WRKSERVICES=.

3. Remove NETPOPUP or MINIPOP from the WRKSERVICES= line, but retain the MESSENGER entry.

4. Save the file, exit from the network, and start it again.

WinPopup will no longer appear, and any messages received will not be displayed in Windows but will be written to the MESSAGES.LOG file that is in the LOGS subdirectory under the LANMAN.DOS directory. You can view MESSAGES.LOG using a text editor such as Notepad if you want to review the messages received during a Windows session.

DEC Pathworks

DEC Pathworks stands a notch above other networks in terms of what it aims to do. Pathworks wants to provide an entire network environment, much as Windows provides a desktop environment. Pathworks, coming as it does from DEC, presumes a much more varied, multiplatform system than most PC-centric local area networks do. Since both systems involved are complex in their own right, the interface between Pathworks and Windows requires careful tending.

SYSTEM.INI Settings For DEC Pathworks 4.0 and above, the following changes are made to the [386Enh] section of the SYSTEM.INI:

```
Network=*dosnet, denet.386, decnb.386
TimerCriticalSection=10000
```

If you have problems running NetBIOS applications, try replacing the preceding decnb.386 entry with *vnetbios. The entry would look like this instead:

```
Network=*dosnet, denet.386, *vnetbios
```

A CONFIG.SYS Change You May Need to Make   If you're having difficulty starting Windows on a DEC Pathworks network, or if you're having problems opening and copying files, you may need to increase the FILES= setting in your CONFIG.SYS file to FILES=30.

PART 2

Power Secrets for Windows Applications

359
GETTING THE MOST FROM WINDOWS WORD PROCESSORS

415
SPREADSHEET TIPS

457
DRAWING AND PRESENTATION PACKAGE TIPS

475
COMMUNICATIONS PROGRAMS

487
WINDOWS ENHANCEMENTS, UTILITIES, AND PROGRAMMING TOOLS

513
PAGE LAYOUT PACKAGES

525
PERSONAL PRODUCTIVITY TOOLS

GETTING THE MOST FROM WINDOWS WORD PROCESSORS

WINDOWS HAS TRANSFORMED WORD PROCESSING. SUDDENLY, THE LONG-desired goal of "what you see is what you get" (WYSIWYG) document creation has become possible. In truth, Windows moved word processing from text to documents. The new capabilities of Windows spurred the creation of new products. Three have come to dominate the market: Ami Pro from Lotus, Microsoft Word, and WordPerfect for Windows. Recently, WordStar, one of the leading word processors of the early PC years, joined the Windows fray.

In this chapter, we offer numerous secrets, workarounds, and little-known features you can use to get the most from each of these products.

Ami Professional

Ami Pro has the advantage of always having been graphical. It never had to worry about problems inherent in converting from a DOS text version to a graphical user interface. Many consider Ami Pro, with its smart icons and rich formatting capabilities, the most Windows-like word processor. However, understanding all the new ideas Ami Pro brings, and getting at all those features, can be daunting. Here are ways to extract the most from Ami Pro.

Formatting Tips

Ami Pro offers virtually limitless formatting options. The tips that follow give you a sense of what you can accomplish.

Change Attributes Quickly Ami Pro's Replace function goes one better than changing ASCII characters—it can also edit formatting. To replace underlining with italics, for example, select Find & Replace from the Edit menu, and enter the asterisk (*) wildcard in both the Find and the Replace With text boxes. Now click on Attributes, check off the appropriate Find Attributes and Replace Attributes boxes, and click on OK. To change combinations of attributes (such as bold and italics), check off the appropriate selections, choose Options, and select Exact Attributes under Find Options. Now choose either Find or Replace All and Ami Pro will do the rest.

Create Drop Caps   Oversize, "dropped" initial characters at the beginning of selected paragraphs add class to a document. Here's how to set up drop caps in Ami Pro:

1. Create a frame and double-click in it.

2. Type the letter you want to be the drop cap.

3. Select Modify Frame Layout from the Frame menu.

4. Click on Type and make sure that the active choice under Text Wrap Around is No Wrap Around and that the choice under Placement is Where Placed.

5. Choose Transparent under Display.

6. Select the Size & Position option, and then select Clear Margins.

7. Click on Lines & Shadows, and select white as your line color, making sure that there's no shadow selected.

8. Double-click in your frame, highlight the letter, and select Text, Alignment, and Center.

9. Finally, select the desired font and point size from the Text menu.

SmartIcons Tips

Ami Pro moves beyond menus as a metaphor for program operations. Its Smart-Icons allow almost any activity the user requires to be described by a button. This feature has been adopted by other word processors, as well as by other Lotus applications.

Identify SmartIcons   Press any SmartIcon with the right mouse button (click and hold down the mouse button) to find out what it does. A description of its function will appear in the title bar at the top of your screen, as shown in Figure 11.1. To identify other SmartIcons, select SmartIcons from the Tools menu and choose Customize. Click on icons in the Standard Icons or Current Palette boxes to see their descriptions. The exceptions are icons that link to other software; they must be placed in the SmartIcon bar before you can get a description.

Larger SmartIcons on SVGA Displays   If you work in 1024×768 video mode, consider creating more-legible SmartIcons by substituting the ones from the 800×600 resolution set. From the DOS prompt, enter the Ami Pro directory and rename the high-resolution SmartIcon bar with the command

```
REN AMIICN8.DLL  AMIICN8.OLD
```

Then copy the lower-resolution toolbar with the command

```
COPY AMIICNV.DLL AMIICN8.DLL
```

Now restart Ami Pro.

FIGURE 11.1

Press a SmartIcon with the right mouse button to see a description of what it does.

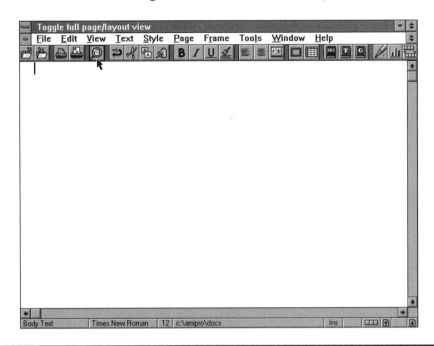

Linking Icons   Ami Pro can create links with several open Windows applications, but it won't do this automatically. First, you must place the applications' custom icons in the SmartIcons bar. Choose SmartIcons from the Tools menu and select Customize. Drag the icon that represents your application to the Current Palette box. Click on OK. When you return to the main screen, the icon you've selected will appear in the SmartIcons bar. Click on the application icon and your software application will run from within Ami Pro.

Using Handy Ami Pro Macros

The macro capabilities of Ami Pro approach the level of true programming, yet you can create macros without typing any code!

Macros 101   Making macros doesn't always involve typing lists of code. Record keystrokes into a macro by selecting Macros from the Tools menu and then selecting Record. Or you can select Quick Record for a macro dedicated to the current document only. Either way, the basic steps are these:

1. Name your macro in the Macro File text box.

2. Assign the macro to any combination of Shift or Ctrl and another key, except Shift+F1 and any combination using the F10 key.

3. Click on OK, and start to record your macro by pressing the required keystrokes.

4. When you have finished recording, select Macros from the Tools menu and select End Record.

5. Save the keystrokes to a macro file. Save a large macro file as an Ami Pro file (.SAM) instead of as a macro file (.SMM), to alleviate worries about losing the file in the development process.

6. Select Macros from the Tools menu, and then select Edit to fix any keystroke errors, double-check parameters, and include steps you missed.

7. To run the macro, choose Macro from the Tools menu, select the macro's name, and choose Run.

Repeating Macros   To create a repeating macro—or to run another macro after one has finished—select Macros from the Tools menu, select Edit, and open the macro file. Go to the end of the file, and on the line above

```
end function
```

enter **type** and the macro's shortcut key combination. Repeating macros continue executing until they reach the end of a document, and then prompt you to start again or quit.

Fix INDEXALL.SMM   Among the sample macros included with Ami Pro is one called INDEXALL.SMM, which automatically marks every instance of a selected word in your document for inclusion in the document's index. Unfortunately, every time you run IndexAll it leaves the cursor at the end of your document. If you want to continue moving through your document selecting other words for inclusion in the index, you've got to scroll back to the point where you left off.

You can automate this process by changing the code in the idx() function in the INDEXALL.SMM file, as follows (add the lines shown in bold):

```
function idx()
defstr word;
if assign(&word, curshade$()) = ""
message("Select word to mark for index.")
return 0
endif
MarkBookMark("indextemp", AddBookMark)
type("[esc][esc][esc][ctrlhome]")
while (1)
go = replace("", "", "", word, "")
if go <> 1
```

```
break
endif
FieldAdd("Index ""{word} "" #")
wend
MarkBookMark("indextemp",  FindBookMark)
MarkBookMark("indextemp",  DeleteBookMark)
end function
```

You have added three new lines that each use the MarkBookMark command to manipulate a temporary bookmark called "indextemp." The first uses the parameter AddBookMark to instruct Ami Pro to create "indextemp" at the current cursor position. This takes place immediately before the macro initiates the search for additional instances of the selected word, and thus "indextemp" serves as a marker for the point at which the search began. The second MarkBookMark command is issued after all instances of the selected word have been added to the index. It uses the parameter FindBookMark to move the cursor back to the "indextemp" bookmark. Finally, the third MarkBookMark command uses the parameter DeleteBookMark to instruct Ami Pro to delete the bookmark called "indextemp."

Getting a Word Count on the Status Bar   The following short macro will make an up-to-the-minute character and word count appear on the Ami Pro status line. Name the macro WC.SMM and assign it the shortcut key Ctrl+C. Then, whenever you press Ctrl+C, a message giving you the character and word counts will appear on the status line.

```
function wc()
Messages (ON)
Type("[enter][enter][up]")
FieldAdd("NumChars"    )
A=CurWord$()
F=FieldPrev( )
Type(" [backspace]")
FieldAdd("NumWords"    )
B=CurWord$()
F=FieldPrev( )
Type(" [backspace]")
Type("[left][del][del]")
StatusBarMsg("{A} characters in {B} words.")
Pause (020)
StatusBarMsg("")
Messages (OFF)
end function
```

The Ami Pro macro language doesn't contain keywords for obtaining word or character counts, but Ami Pro's Power Fields feature does support those functions. So, after opening a couple of blank lines in your document, the macro inserts the NumChars power field, obtains its current value, and deletes it. Then it inserts a NumWords power field, gets its current value, and deletes that before closing the blank lines and posting the character and word count on Ami Pro's status line. It may look complex, but it takes only a second before a message such as the following appears on Ami Pro's status line:

```
4597 characters in 726 words.
```

The Pause (020) followed by StatusBarMsg("") clears the status line after the word count has displayed for 2 seconds, restoring normal status line functions (among them font and style selection).

A Macro for Generating Automatic Paragraph Indents   Here's a simple macro that automatically indents a paragraph 1 inch from the left and right margins. To create it, choose Macros from the Tools menu, type a macro name and an optional description, and choose Edit. In the macro-editing screen, type the following line between the Sub MAIN and End Sub commands:

```
FormatParagraph .LeftIndent="1"+Chr$(34),.RightIndent="1"+Chr$(34)
```

Then choose Save All from the File menu and Close from the File menu.

To give the macro a shortcut key, choose Options from the Tool menu, and then select Keyboard. Make sure the Macros option button under Show is selected, and point to the macro's name in the Macros list. In the Shortcut Key box, choose a shortcut key, and then choose Add, Close. Pressing the shortcut key with the insertion point anywhere in a paragraph will now indent the paragraph 1 inch on both sides.

Speed Tips

Like all Windows applications, Ami Pro pays a price in speed for its graphics and complexity. Here are a couple of ways to speed things up.

Speed Up Data Entry   To speed up data entry, protect the label cells in Ami Pro forms—making the cursor jump only into cells where information needs to be entered. To activate cell protection, highlight any cells with form information, and then go the Table menu and choose Protect. Next, select Modify Table Layout from the Table menu, and under Options choose Honor Protection. Now permanent form-label cells are protected.

Faster Screen Repainting   When resizing or moving graphics, or just scrolling on a page, speed things up by hiding the graphics elements of the page. First add the Show/Hide pictures icon to your SmartIcons bar. Select SmartIcons from the Tools menu and choose Customize. In the Standard Icons box, find the

Show/Hide Pictures icon (a man with a cap, shown in Figure 11.2). Drag this icon to the Current Palette box, and click on OK. Click on the icon; an X appears over the man in the cap, replacing any graphics in your document with appropriately sized Xs and filenames. Click on the icon a second time to bring the graphics back.

FIGURE 11.2

Use the Show/Hide Pictures icon to turn off the screen display of graphics (and speed up the screen refresh) in your document.

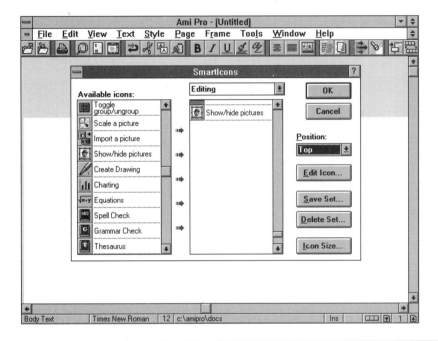

Helpful How-Tos

These tips, which don't fit neatly into any category, show just how high-end Ami Pro can get.

Drawing Bezier Curves To draw Bezier curves—curved lines with inflection points—create a frame and select Drawing from the Tools menu. Click on the Arc icon (just to the left of the abc icon) and draw a curved line within the frame. Next, select the Pointer icon and double-click on the line. This will produce four black handles for manipulating the line and four handles for rotating the line. You can use these to create an S-shape, for example, by dragging the two center handles in opposite directions.

Spell-Check Technical Documents Nothing is more frustrating than trying to spell-check a document that contains program code, mathematical formulae, or other technical material that your spell checker flags as misspelled when it isn't. You can eliminate most of these occurrences by deselecting either the Check Words with Numbers or Check Words with Initial Caps check boxes (or both) in the Spell Check Options dialog box. (To get to this dialog box, choose Spell Check from the Tools menu. Then click on Options in the Spell Check dialog box.) Doing so will eliminate most of the false errors that occur when you spell-check technical material.

Word for Windows

In pre-Windows days, Word was something of a conundrum—incredibly powerful and almost impossible to use. Early Windows versions carried some of this baggage. However, Word has improved vastly with each Windows release. Today, it is a market leader and a surprisingly easy-to-fathom application. Still, tips for finding all of Word's neat features should be welcomed by most users.

Text-Manipulation Tips

The text capabilities of Word approach those of desktop publishing packages. They are numerous and not entirely user-friendly. Here are some strategies.

Use Spike Instead of Clipboard   If you compile documents by cutting and pasting from a variety of files, get to know Word for Windows' Spike. This unheralded feature, which takes its name from the spindle on which you skewer odd scraps of paper, works much like its namesake. Unlike the Clipboard, the Spike accumulates *all* the text you send to it in a buffer, without clearing the buffer each time. Use the Unspike command to insert the contents of the Spike in your document.

Here's the method: Highlight the text to spike, and press Ctrl+F3. Repeat the process for all the text you need. To unspike the accumulated text—and empty the Spike—press Ctrl+Shift+F3. Alternatively, select Glossary from the Edit menu, highlight Spike, and click on Insert. Unlike using Ctrl+Shift+F3, selecting the Glossary entry doesn't empty the Spike, which means you can paste spiked text many times. If you want to wipe out formats and fonts used in a spiked text's previous location, click on Insert as Plain Text in the Glossary dialog box.

Speed Up Copies and Moves   Copy text swiftly from one location to another without using the Clipboard by selecting the text you want to copy, pressing Shift+F2, moving the cursor to the new location, and pressing Enter. Follow the same procedure for moves, substituting F2 for Shift+F2.

Manipulating Text with the Right Mouse Button   While Spike is a handy feature for moving text, it's less helpful when you want to copy text from various locations and paste the resulting compilation into a new location. Often the quickest way to accomplish this is by opening a second document window.

Open the document you'll be copying from, and then open a new window: Choose File, New, and then click on OK. Then choose Window, Arrange All to place the two open document windows one on top of the other. Select the first block of text from your original document. Move the mouse cursor into the second window (Document 2), and without clicking a mouse button to move the insertion point to the second window, press Ctrl+Shift and click on the right mouse button. Word copies the selected text to the second window. If you need space between text blocks, press Enter to insert a blank line after the text, and repeat the process with the next block of text that you want to copy.

If you wish to reinsert the text in the original document after you've collected all the blocks you want to copy, select the text in the second window and place the mouse pointer on the insertion point in the first window. Then hold down Ctrl+Shift (pressing the Ctrl key first), and click on the right mouse button. To move text instead of copying it, hold down the Ctrl key, point to the new location, and click the right mouse button.

Speedy Mouse and Keyboard Text Selection   Anyone coming from the world of DOS word processing must at least occasionally want to select words, sentences, or paragraphs by using key combinations rather than the mouse. Word for Windows enables you to select characters, words, and paragraphs by using various key combinations and mouse movements.

If you've ever tried to select a single character, say, to format with a different attribute, you know how tricky this can be with the mouse. The easiest way is to move the insertion point to one side of the character you want to select and then hold down the Shift key while pressing the Right Arrow or Left Arrow key to select one character at a time. To select individual words, hold down Ctrl+ Shift and press either Right Arrow or Left Arrow. Pressing the arrow again while holding down Ctrl+Shift extends the selection to the next word.

Sentences are equally easy to select, using a combination of keyboard and mouse. Place the insertion point anywhere in the sentence, hold down Ctrl, and click the sentence with the mouse. There's also a strictly keyboard method. Use the arrow keys to move the insertion point to the sentence you want to highlight. Press F8 once to toggle Word for Window's Extend mode (In Extend mode, the letters "EXT" appear in the status bar at the bottom of the screen and F8 takes on powerful highlighting functions.) When EXT appears, pressing F8 a second time selects the word the insertion point is on. Pressing F8 a third time selects the entire sentence. To select the entire paragraph, press F8 a fourth time. Pressing F8 a fifth time selects the entire document. Unfortunately, this method does not allow you to highlight two or more words, sentences, or paragraphs in a row. To exit Extend mode, press the Escape key.

There are other ways to select paragraphs, too. Place the mouse in the left margin (known as the selection bar) so that the arrow points inward at the paragraph you want to select; then double-click to select the paragraph, as shown in Figure 11.3. (You can select a single line of text at a time by using this method but single-clicking.) Or, place the cursor at the beginning (or end) of the paragraph, and press Ctrl+Shift+Down Arrow (or Up Arrow). If you place the cursor in the middle of the paragraph, this method selects from the point of the cursor to the end (or beginning) of the paragraph. Subsequent pressings of the Down Arrow (while keeping Ctrl+Shift held down) extend the selection paragraph by paragraph, assuming the paragraphs are not separated by blank lines.

FIGURE 11.3

Quickly select a paragraph by double-clicking in the left-margin selection bar.

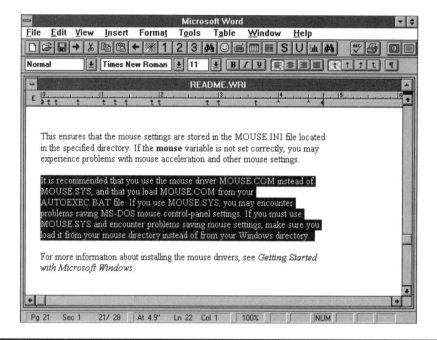

You can also select pages or all the text to the top or bottom of the document from the insertion point by combining Ctrl+Shift with Home, End, PgUp, or PgDn. To quickly select the entire document, press Ctrl+5 (on the numeric keypad) or place the mouse cursor at the far left edge of the screen, press Ctrl, and click once.

Word for Windows also offers a nifty way to extend selections with the mouse. You may be aware that Word for Windows 2.0 lets you move text in your document by selecting it, reclicking it, and dragging it to a new location. You can also adjust your selection area by pressing Shift, reclicking on the selected text, and dragging above or below the selection. As you move the mouse, the highlighted selection changes length. Or you can press Shift, move the mouse cursor to the point where you want the selection to end, and click; the selection will extend to your insertion point.

Text Selection Macros   For keyboard purists, Word for Windows' keyboard sentence and paragraph selection options leave something to be desired, since none of the methods it provides will both select the entire first sentence or paragraph and let you extend your selections to subsequent sentences or paragraphs with an additional keystroke. The following macros do both of those things, as long as your insertion point is contained anywhere before the period in a sentence or before the last period in a paragraph. Enter them by selecting Macro from the Tools menu.

In the Macro Name field of the Macro dialog box, type the name you want to give the sentence macro; **SelectSentence** is a good choice. Click on the Edit button. Type the Word BASIC listing that appears here, making sure that you enter all characters and spacings correctly:

```
Sub MAIN
If Len(Selection$()) = 1 Then
SentRight
SentLeft
ExtendSelection
SentRight
Cancel
ElseIf Len(Selection$()) > 1 Then
ExtendSelection
SentRight
Cancel
End If
End Sub
```

Choose Save All from the File menu, and exit the macro generator by double-clicking on the Control menu box to the left of the File menu. Next, assign the macro a key combination. Choose Options from the Tools menu, and select Keyboard icon. Scroll down in the Macro box until you find the macro name. Click on SelectSentence, click the check boxes for Ctrl and Shift, and then type **s** in the Key box. Make sure it says "unassigned" next to the Currently heading, then click on the Add command button.

To try out your new macro now, press Ctrl+Shift+S to select a single sentence. Press this key combination again to select the next sentence.

Repeat this process for the SelectParagraph macro. Begin by entering the following macro:

```
Sub MAIN
If Len(Selection$()) = 1 Then
ParaDown
ParaUp
ExtendSelection
ParaDown
Cancel
ElseIf Len(Selection$()) > 1 Then
ExtendSelection
ParaDown
Cancel
```

```
End If
End Sub
```

Then save the macro and assign it to the Ctrl+Shift+P key combination, following the steps just described.

Turn on Text Boundaries for More Accurate Page Layout   When performing desktop publishing tasks in Page Layout view, be sure to turn on text boundaries. With boundaries turned on, Word displays the margins of text columns, headers and footers, footnotes, and so on. This helps you place page elements precisely. Choose Options from the Tools menu and choose the View icon. Then select Text Boundaries in the Show Text With box. While you're in the View Options screen, you might also want to select the Line Breaks And Fonts As Printed and Table Gridlines check boxes to further enhance the accuracy of text placement.

Use the Clipboard in Search-and-Replace Operations   Without using the Clipboard, you can specify a maximum of 255 characters of text in the Replace dialog box (choose Replace from the Edit menu). To specify more replacement text, copy the text to the Clipboard, then type **^c** in the Replace With box and press Enter. This might be useful for replacing boilerplate sections of a contract or replacing a graphic image with another that you copy to the Clipboard.

Redefine the Insert Key to Paste from the Clipboard   Many Word for Windows users never use overtype mode (which replaces existing characters with whatever you type) and thus have little use for the normal toggle function of the Insert key. Since insert is an intuitive function, it makes sense to redefine the Insert key to paste text from the Clipboard. To do so, choose Options from the Tools menu, and choose the General icon. Then select Use the INS Key for Paste, as shown in Figure 11.4.

Use Copy and Paste for Easy Searches   If you're trying to locate obscure text strings or you're searching for phrases that appear in separate documents, using Word's copy-and-paste feature can make this a breeze. Select the text you want to search for, copy it to the Clipboard by pressing Ctrl+C or selecting Copy from the Edit menu, and then select Find or Replace from the Edit menu. Place the cursor in the box that asks for the search string, and press Ctrl+V. Your text string appears without any typing on your part.

   Note that this shortcut works only for text; you can't use it to search for special formatting characters, such as paragraph marks.

Formatting Tips

Basic formatting in Word for Windows is straightforward. But there are clever tricks even proficient Word users may not know.

FIGURE 11.4

Redefine the Insert key to paste text from the Clipboard by selecting the option in Tools' General Options dialog box.

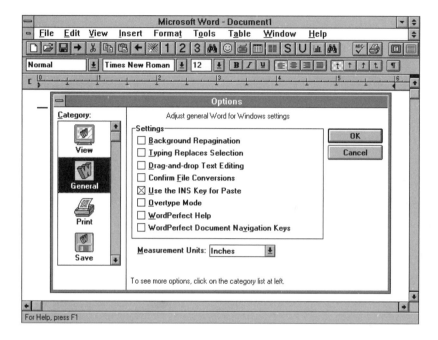

Pasting Paragraph Formatting Copying text from one location to another in a Word for Windows document becomes second nature quickly, but it's also surprisingly easy to copy paragraph formatting. This trick can be a real lifesaver when it's time to copy those indents and tab settings you struggled to get just right. First, select the paragraph you want to reformat. Then hold down the Ctrl and Shift keys simultaneously, point to the paragraph whose formatting you want to copy, and click the left mouse button once.

Clean Up Text Files That Have Been Downloaded If you regularly download files containing extra hard returns at the ends of lines, you'll appreciate these tricks for handling the most common reformatting chores:

■ Use global search and replace to remove extra hard returns. Word for Windows uses [^p] to stand for a hard return. To catch extra hard returns, first replace two sequential hard returns (and hard return-space-hard return combinations) with a character string that doesn't occur elsewhere in the document; &$@ is usually a safe choice. Next, replace the space-hard return sequence with a space, and then replace a single hard return with a space. To restore a line between paragraphs, replace the unique character string (&$@) with two carriage returns.

- Tables and formatted lists require special handling. Replacing hard returns in those sections will usually make a mess of formatting. Before performing global search-and-replace operations, replace hard returns in a table with a unique string. After reformatting the main text, you can restore hard returns in place of each instance of the unique string.

- Replace [Space][Space] with [Space] throughout the document. You may need to do this several times to delete occurrences of more than two spaces, or odd numbers of spaces. Before replacing extra spaces, check the file to see if tab characters at the beginning of paragraphs were replaced with spaces. If so, replace each occurrence of a hard return followed by multiple spaces with a hard return and a tab character.

Draw Lines   Most users draw lines or fill-in blanks by pressing the underscore key repeatedly. But that solution can force you to do a lot of trial-and-error reformatting, especially if you change text or fonts. A surer route to elegant and precise lines uses tabs and leaders; it's not at all intuitive, but it's easy once you learn how. Suppose you want to draw a line 2 inches long, beginning exactly 4 inches from the left margin. Using the ruler or the Format Tabs dialog box, insert two left-aligned tabs, one at 4" and another at 6". Next, open the Tabs dialog box (select Tabs from the Format menu), select the Tab Position at 6", click on the button next to Leader 4, and click on OK to save the new tab settings. Now, when you press the Tab key twice, you'll see an unbroken line on the screen, and on your printed page.

View Style Names On the Screen   To display the style names for each paragraph in your document, choose Options from the Tools menu and choose the View icon. Then type or select a number in the Style Area Width box, and choose OK. The style names will appear in the left margin. You can resize the style area on the fly (to display long style names or show more of the typing area) by dragging the vertical line that separates it from the text area. To close the style area, just drag the vertical divider all the way to the left, off the screen.

Insert Multiple Bullets and Symbols Quickly   To insert multiple copies of a Word for Windows symbol in a document (for example, a copyright symbol or a special type of bullet), you don't have to choose Insert, Symbol for each one. Instead, choose Insert, Symbol, select a symbol set from the Symbols From list, and double-click on the desired symbol. Before pressing another key, press F4 (Repeat Command) to insert multiple copies of the symbol.

Avoid Breaking Hyphenated Words   The fastest way to insert hyphens after you finish typing a document is to choose Hyphenation from the Tools menu and make sure the Confirm box is unchecked before clicking on OK. But Word for Windows' hyphenation routine won't catch places where word wrap has broken hyphenated words between lines. When you don't want word wrap to split a hyphenated word or combination, such as 1-25-93, press Ctrl+Shift+hyphen to insert an "unbreakable" hyphen.

Change Font Sizes in a Flash   To quickly increase or decrease the size of the current font, press Ctrl+F2 or Ctrl+Shift+F2. The new size will appear in the font size box in the ruler. (You can also select existing text and use these key combinations to change its size.) With scalable fonts, Word for Windows changes the size in 1-point increments. For example, if the current font size is 20.5 points, the next biggest size is 21.5 points. If the font isn't scalable, Word chooses the next available size.

Change Cases Quickly   After you've applied character formatting to text, you can apply it to other text—or type similarly formatted text elsewhere in the document—by selecting the characters you want to format or positioning the insertion point and pressing F4, which repeats your last command. Alternatively, choose Edit, Repeat Formatting.

     Using the mouse is even quicker: Select the text you want to format; then move the mouse pointer to the text that has the format you want to copy, hold down Ctrl+Shift, and click. To copy paragraph formatting (tabs, alignment, hanging indents, and so on) position the cursor in the paragraph you want to format; then move the mouse pointer into the selection bar of the paragraph that contains the formatting you want to copy (the selection bar is the area in the left margin where the cursor turns into an arrow), and hold down Ctrl+Shift while you click. If you accidentally move the insertion point twice instead of immediately reapplying the format, you can still copy the formatting by choosing Edit, Repeat Formatting.

Change Margins in the Middle of a Page   If you use the Page Setup option in the Format menu to adjust margins in the middle of a page, Word for Windows may not start the new margins at the insertion point. To change the margins from the insertion point forward, choose Insert, Break; then choose Continuous in the Section Break box, and click on OK. Finally, choose Format, Page Setup, make sure the Margins button is selected, set the new margins, choose This Point Forward in the Apply To box, and choose OK. To indent just a few paragraphs, it's much simpler to select the paragraphs and choose the Paragraph command in the Format menu or adjust the margin arrows on the ruler.

Make Short Work of Long Listings   Word makes light work of formatting repetitive material such as catalog listings, price lists, and spec sheets. To simplify formatting, use the Next Style feature to automatically format body text after a heading. Choose Style from the Format menu and select Define, type or select the heading style name in the Style Name text box, and choose or type a style name in the Next Style box. Choose Change, and then choose Yes when Word asks if you want to change the standard style. Choose Close to return to the document. When you apply the heading style and press Enter at the end of a heading, Word automatically switches to the next style.

Choose Your Own Bullet Styles Word can automatically format lists with bullets from any font that's available with your printer—from happy faces to twisted arrows. Simply select the list to which you want to add bullets and select a new bullet character by choosing Bullets and Numbering from the Tools menu and clicking on the New Bullet command button. In the Symbol dialog box, shown in Figure 11.5, choose a symbol set (from one of your installed fonts); then click on a symbol and choose OK twice. Placing the mouse pointer on a symbol and clicking the left mouse button produces a larger rendition of that symbol (see Figure 11.5). The Wingdings font is a particularly good source of ornamental bullets.

FIGURE 11.5

Create custom bullets by selecting any symbol you choose and adding it to Word for Windows' standard offerings.

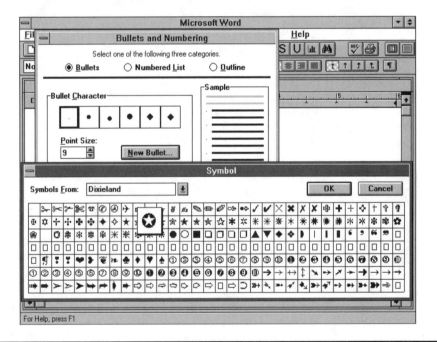

Use Dialog Boxes for Precise Formatting Word for Windows' ruler is designed to let you set page, column, and paragraph margins quickly with the mouse. When you're working with precise alignments, however, you may find it easier to set margins with dialog boxes.

For example, to set text margins in a frame, click on Select Border in the Format menu, choose the border you want, and click on OK. (To add a Frame to a document, select Frame from the Insert menu.) Choose Paragraph from the Format menu, and set left, right, and first-line margins for the frame text. To insert space between the top and bottom of the text and the frame borders, specify measurements for Before and After in the Spacing area of the Paragraph dialog box.

Suppress Blank Lines at the Top of the Page   If a document's paragraph spacing is set to greater than one line and any portion of the paragraph appears at the top of a page, extra space appears at the top of the page. To suppress the extra space and force the first line on the page to be placed at the top margin, add the entry SuppressTopSpacing=Y to your WIN.INI file.

This adjustment is often necessary for double-spaced legal documents. Choose Options from the Tools menu, and select the WIN.INI icon from the category list. In the Options box, type **SuppressTopSpacing**. In the Setting box, type **y**. Click on the Set button to record the change, and then click on the Close button to exit the dialog box.

Keyboard Shortcuts for Formatting   Use Ctrl+key combinations to format a paragraph or document and bypass Word for Windows' cumbersome series of menu selections. First, select the relevant text, and then use one of the following key combinations:

Ctrl+1   Single-spaced lines

Ctrl+2   Double-spaced lines

Ctrl+5   1 1/2-spaced lines

Ctrl+E   Centered lines

Ctrl+J   Justified lines

Ctrl+L   Left-aligned lines

Ctrl+O   Open space before

Ctrl+R   Right-aligned lines

Speed Tips

Word has a reputation, left over from early versions, of being noticeably sluggish. The program is quicker than it gets credit for. Every possible speed advantage can help, however. Here are several.

Select Entire Document   To select the entire document for a global change, move the cursor into the left margin until it changes from an I-beam to an arrow; then press Ctrl and the left mouse button. Alternatively, press Ctrl+5 (use the numeric keypad). To select a whole table, press Alt+5 (use the keypad).

Use Quick-Click Shortcuts   Word for Windows offers lots of double-click mouse shortcuts to reach various options panels and dialog boxes:

- Double-click on any blank area of the toolbar for toolbar-customizing options.

- Double-click on any blank area of the ribbon for character-formatting options.

- Double-click on the top half of the ruler for paragraph-formatting options.

- Double-click on the bottom half of the ruler for tab-formatting options.

- Double-click on the status bar at the bottom of the screen for the Go To dialog box.

- Double-click on an inserted symbol for the Symbol palette.

Download Once, Print Many   When you print multiple copies of a document using Bitstream FaceLift or other downloadable fonts, you may be wasting time. Word for Windows' File Print option allows you to set multiple copies, but the program downloads fonts for each copy you choose. When you're making five or more copies, this amounts to a lot of dead time. Instead, select Printer Setup from the File menu and click on the Setup button. Change the number of copies in the Setup dialog box to the appropriate number, and then issue the Print command. Remember to change the number of copies back to normal afterwards.

Save Time by Using Outline Mode   If you think you'll need to reorder text as you edit a long document, you can save lots of time by formatting the sections with standard heading styles from the NORMAL.DOT template. (Choose NORMAL from the New dialog box that Word displays when you choose New from the File menu.) When you use standard headings, you can reorganize the text by simply moving the headings in Outline view.

Speed Indexing with Glossaries   When you create an index that contains repetitions of a subject heading, you can generate the index more quickly by assigning that heading to a glossary item. Create the first index entry, select it and choose Glossary from the Edit menu, select a name from the Glossary Name list box (or type one in), and then choose Define. To insert the index item at other locations in the document, type the glossary name and press F3.

Turbocharge Word for Windows   Word for Windows 2.0 is already fast, but take some or all of these steps to make it even faster:

- Make sure you select Normal and Draft view (on the View menu).

- Turn off background repagination (select Options from the Tools menu and choose the General icon) and automatic save (select Options from the Tools menu and choose the Save icon).

- Turn off table borders (choose Border from the Format menu) and gridlines (select Gridlines from the Table menu) if they are on.

- Add the line

  `CacheSize=2024`

to the Microsoft Word 2.0 Application setting of the WIN.INI section (select Options from the Tools menu and then choose the WIN.INI icon).

■ If you use lots of graphics, increase the

```
BitmapMemory=
```

size of the Microsoft Word 2.0 Application setting in Word for Windows' WIN.INI section (or add this line). The default value is 256. For most uses involving graphics, a setting of 1024 should suffice.

■ Another option for increasing scroll rate with graphics is to turn on the Picture Placeholders option (select Options from the Tools menu and then select the View icon). This replaces on-screen graphics with a box outline that is the same size as the graphic. The graphic will still appear in Print Preview, and will print normally.

■ Create a 2Mb RAM drive (using a RAM drive utility) and direct Word for Windows' temp files to it (in your AUTOEXEC.BAT file).

Table Tips

Word innovated the inclusion of tables and columns in Windows documents. Again, the basics are fairly easy to handle. What may not be as clear is just how much you can do with these features.

Splitting a Table   If you want to insert text between parts of a Word for Windows table, or break a table into two sections, try this trick: Position the cursor where you want the break, and press Ctrl+Shift+Enter. Word does the rest.

Save Time with Table Shortcuts   Here are some savvy shortcuts to use with Word for Windows tables:

■ To easily insert a blank line above a table that you've put at the top of your document, place the cursor in the top row of the table and choose Split Table from the Table menu.

■ To quickly highlight a table column, position the mouse cursor on the top line of the top cell of the column until it changes to a downward-pointing arrow, and click the right mouse button.

■ To quickly insert a new cell, row, or column in an existing table, highlight the cell or group of cells to the left of or above the place where you want the new cell(s) to appear and click on the Table button on the toolbar, which is located on the right-hand side of the toolbar (see Figure 11.6). The Insert Cell dialog box will pop up when there's more than one possible location for the insert.

FIGURE 11.6

Word's table icon can be used to insert rows and columns into an existing table, as well as for adding an entire table to your document.

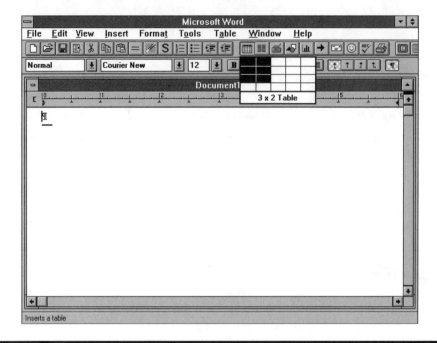

- To adjust the width of an individual cell without adjusting the overall width of the table, highlight the cell (place the mouse cursor on the left border of the cell so that the cursor points to the right, and click), hold down the Ctrl key, and drag the right border to the left or right. The cell to the right expands or contracts to compensate for the adjustment.

- To adjust the width of an individual column of cells, highlight the column using second tip in this list, and follow the procedure in the previous tip.

Editing Columns Quickly   When editing in Word for Windows, most people use only the left mouse button for blocking portions of their document. This works fine unless you're dealing with columns of information, where line-by-line editing fast becomes tedious and time-consuming. The solution is the right mouse button. Click the right button at one corner and drag to the opposite corner of the column you want to highlight. This enables you to select any rectangle of text or graphics anywhere on the screen.

Keep Headings in View   Working in a table or data-entry merge screen can be frustrating when the top row (with the headings) scrolls off the screen. To keep the headings in view, split the window and open a second view of the document.

Do this by clicking the mouse on the black bar atop the vertical scroll bar on the right side of the screen. Hold down the mouse button and drag downward. The screen will split into two windows, each with its own version of the open document. Your changes are reflected in both copies of the document, but only the document in the active window scrolls while you work.

Create Easy Fill-in-the-Blank Forms   One quick way to create blank lines for return coupons and other response forms is to create a table with a row for each line in the form and just one column, as follows:

1. Choose Table, Insert Table, and specify one column and the desired number of rows. (Don't use the table tool in the toolbar because it requires you to specify a fixed column width.)

2. Choose Column Width from the Table menu, set Column Width to the desired width of the fill-in form, and choose OK.

3. Make sure that the table's grid lines are on. If they aren't, choose Options from the Tool menu, making sure View is selected under Category and that Table Gridlines is selected under Show Text Width.

4. Type the data-entry prompts (Name, Address, and so on) within the table cells, adjusting their positions with the spacebar and checking your results with Print Preview.

5. Select the table by moving the mouse cursor above the table until it turns into a downward-pointing arrow, and then clicking.

6. Format the cells with the Border command on the Format menu.

7. In the Border Cells dialog box, click on a line type in the Line box.

8. In the sample table in the Border box, click on the vertical lines and the top horizontal line to remove them, and click on OK. (This step generally requires a bit of trial and error.) Word for Windows formats the table with lines in each row.

Create Complex Forms with Word Tables   With some planning, you can use the Tables feature to create extremely complex forms. The basic procedure is to draw the form on paper, and then create a table with a sufficient number of columns to accommodate all the data-entry cells. Keep in mind that it's much easier to merge cells than to split them, because Word won't let you split cells that haven't first been merged. Thus, it's better to start with too many columns than too few.

After creating the basic table, you can merge cells and move and format cell borders to create the form. To shade a cell, select it by clicking on its left border. Then choose Border from the Format menu, click on Shading, and specify the type of shading you want in the Shading dialog box that appears.

Bottom-Align Multiple Text Columns   When laying out desktop-published documents, you frequently need to align the bottom edges of columns to fit them around a boxed advertisement, a pull-quote, or the like. To make these adjustments efficiently, you need to see most of the page. To zoom in, switch to Page Layout view so that columns are displayed side by side; then choose Zoom from the View menu, choose 50%, and click on OK. To insert a column break, position the insertion point and press Ctrl+Shift+Enter, or choose Break from the Insert menu, select Column Break, and click on OK. To align column bottoms, move the insertion point to the end of the text and choose Break from the Insert menu. In the Break dialog box, choose Continuous, and then click on OK.

Format Columns and Rows from the Ruler   To cycle through Word for Windows' two rulers (three if you're working with tables), click on the symbol at the left end of the ruler. You can use the rulers to work with tables, but it's usually frustrating to try to precisely align row, column, and cell widths using the ruler and the mouse.

You'll find it quicker and easier to set exact measurements in dialog boxes. To display table-related dialog boxes quickly, place the insertion point in a table and click on the symbol at the left end of the ruler until it becomes a left bracket ([). Double-clicking just above the ruler line displays the Paragraph dialog box, where you can specify alignment of text in table cells. Double-clicking just below the ruler line displays the Column Width dialog box, where you can define column widths and the space between columns. You can set widths for all columns in a table without exiting the dialog box, by clicking on the Previous Column and Next Column buttons.

Perform Precise Adjustments on Column Widths   Here's an undocumented table feature: To quickly perform precise adjustments on the table column widths, click on the left end of the ruler until the left bracket ([) symbol is displayed; then double-click on the T-shaped column marker that you want to adjust (just below the ruler). Word displays the Column Width dialog box, where you can specify column width and spacing between columns in increments of 100ths of an inch. To set the width of other columns without leaving the dialog box, click on the Previous Column or Next Column button.

Save Table Formats as Glossaries   If you frequently use a specific table or table format, you can store it as a glossary entry and retrieve it with a couple of mouse clicks. To store a table format, select it and save it as a glossary entry by choosing Glossary from the Edit menu, typing a glossary name in the Glossary Name list box, and choosing Define.

To retrieve the table, type its glossary name where you want it to appear in the document and press F3; or choose Glossary from the Edit menu, enter the table name, and click on Insert. When you insert the table in a document, you can quickly add new rows by pressing Tab at the end of the table's last row. This is very useful for creating phone-message and memo forms.

Toolbar Tips

Word's Toolbar is pretty straightforward. But, even here, a couple of nifty tricks are possible.

Add Scalable Zooms to the Toolbar If you've ever wanted to quickly step back from a document for a bird's-eye view, or zoom in for a closer look, Word for Windows has a tool with which to do it. The Zoom Arrow mounts on the toolbar and pops down when you press it, as shown in Figure 11.7, allowing you to select any zoom size from 25 to 200 percent (by dragging and releasing it).

FIGURE 11.7

Adding the Zoom Arrow to the Toolbar allows you to instantly view your document in whatever View you choose.

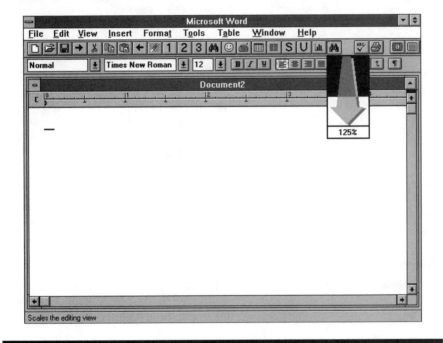

To load the button for the Zoom Arrow, choose Options from the Tool menu, and select the Toolbar. Under Tool to Change, select the button you want to replace. Click the Commands radio button on the right to open the Commands list box. Scroll through the list box to the command ViewZoom, and select it. Next, choose an icon from the Button list; the binoculars are a good choice. Click on the Change button and then on the Close button. The new toolbar button will appear immediately. To save the change permanently, choose Save All on the File menu.

Save Space with the Toolbar For most Windows users, screen space is at a premium. Sure, you can open lots of Windows, but where do you put them all on a 14-inch monitor? With Word for Windows 2.0's toolbar, ruler, ribbon, status bar, and scroll bars all displayed on your screen, there's precious little space left to show the text of long documents. The more text you can see at once, the faster you'll be able to refine and format your work.

You'll probably want to leave the toolbar and ribbon on the screen most of the time. But suppose you use the ruler and status bar only occasionally. By default, Word for Windows requires that you choose or deselect the ruler from the View menu to display or hide it. And to display or hide the status bar, you must select Options from the Tools menu, choose the View icon, and click the Status Bar box.

A good solution for getting the ruler and status bar on and off the screen fast is to mount them on the toolbar as buttons. That way you can toggle the ruler and status bar on and off as needed. This also works for the toolbar and ribbon, if you find you use these infrequently. At 800×600 resolution, Word for Windows provides a maximum of 30 spaces for buttons on the toolbar, including the spaces that separate clusters of buttons. (At 640×480 resolution, you're limited to fewer buttons, the number of which depends on the number of blank spaces you use, because of the reduced width of the screen display.)

To mount the ruler as a button on the toolbar in Word for Windows 2.0, select Options from the Tools menu and choose the Toolbar icon. Choose a location for the button under Tools to Change, and under Button pick the icon to represent the function of toggling the ruler. Next, click on the Commands option button under Show, on the right. Scroll down in the Commands list box until you can see the ViewRuler entry. Click on it, and then click on the Change button. Your new button will appear immediately. Click on the Close button to exit. Follow the same procedure to mount a status bar button, choosing the command ViewStatusBar in the Commands list box. ViewToolbar, ViewRibbon, and other view commands are also available.

Macro Tips

Word offers solid macro recording that will be no problem for anyone familiar with programming, but it may seem a bit complex for the nonprogrammer. Here are some ways to get the most from it, while writing the least code.

Create Macros that Run Automatically   You can create macros that Word will run automatically whenever you start the program, create a new document, open or close a document, or quit Word. Create these macros as usual, but name them AUTOEXEC, AUTONEW, AUTOOPEN, AUTOCLOSE, and AUTOEXIT, respectively.

You'll find these macros especially helpful for temporary use with special projects. For example, you can save lots of time opening long documents and finding your place if you create an AUTOOPEN macro that finds your previous place. Just name the macro AUTOOPEN, press Shift-F5 (Go Back), and turn off the macro recorder. You could also create an AUTOEXEC macro that switches to the document directory you're using for a special project when you start Word.

A Macro to Highlight Notes If you're making comments on someone's document, format your entries in color so that they'll stand out from the other text. To create a macro that formats selected text in red, select Tools, Macro, type a name for the macro, and click on Edit. Between the Sub MAIN and End Sub commands, type the following line:

```
FormatCharacter .Color = 6
```

Close the file. When Word asks you if you want to keep the changes, answer Yes. To assign a shortcut key, choose Options from the Tools menu, and then Keyboard. Click on the Macro button, point to the macro's name, choose a shortcut key, and click on Add and Close. To locate your comments, choose Find from the Edit menu, choose Character, and select Red under Color.

A Macro for Repeated Searches If you repeatedly open the Find dialog box (select Find from the Edit menu) to locate a specific text string while editing a long document, write a macro to do the job. Start by selecting Macro from the Tools menu, typing a name for the macro, and clicking on Edit. Between the Sub MAIN and End Sub lines, type

```
EditFind .Find= "string"
```

where *string* is the text you're looking for. Close the macro and answer Yes when Word asks if you want to save the changes. Assign a shortcut key as discussed in the preceding tip.

   When you need to search for another long text string, simply edit the macro to find the new string; the shortcut key will still work.

Spruce Up Documents with Don't-Miss Macros Word for Windows 2.0 ships with a set of about 20 macros that you can peruse and experiment with by using Word to open the file NEWMACRO.DOC in your \WINWORD subdirectory. One of these is the Watermarks macro, which lets you print "Confidential" or "Draft" as a diagonal, light-gray background to a document. The macro works with PostScript printers only. Another macro creates dropped capital letters. A third lets you copy macros from one template to another.

   To add a macro to your repertoire, select Open from the File menu and locate the file named NEWMACRO.DOC in the WINWORD directory. When you open it, a document explaining how to use it appears and a dialog box listing the available macros should pop up automatically. Select the name of the desired macro and choose Install. You can then specify which template you want it added to (Normal is the default) and assign it a shortcut key. If you're unsure about adding a macro, select the Demo button to get a quick demonstration of what the macro does. Once you install a macro, you will be returned to the list of macros, where you can either add another macro or select Cancel and then choose Close from the File menu to close the NEWMACRO template.

SmartQuotes Macro One of the touches that distinguishes a typeset document from a typewritten one is the presence of special publishing symbols, such as true quotation marks. With Word for Windows (or just about any Windows program), you can insert double open quotes and close quotes by holding down the Alt key and typing 0147 or 0148 on the numeric keypad. But why force yourself to remember nonintuitive codes? Here's a short macro that inserts the appropriate punctuation.

Select Macro from the Tools menu and choose Edit, name the macro Smart-Quotes (no spaces allowed in the Macro Name list box), and press Enter or click on OK. Now type the following text directly into the macro editor. Where you see [Alt+0147] or [Alt+0148], hold down the Alt key and type the specified numbers on the numeric keypad (remember to turn on Num Lock first). If you've entered the symbols correctly, you should see a double quote between two standard quote marks.

```
Sub MAIN
SelSize = CharLeft(1, 1)
If SelSize = 0 Then
Insert "[Alt+0147]"
Goto ENDIT
End If
A$ = Selection$()
If A$ = Chr$(32) Then
CharRight 1
Insert "[Alt+0147]"
Goto ENDIT
Else
CharRight 1
Insert "[Alt+0148]"
Goto ENDIT
End If
ENDIT:
End Sub
```

To save the macro, press Ctrl+F4 and answer Yes to the dialog box. To assign the macro to an easy-to-remember mnemonic, select Record Macro from the Tools menu, highlight SmartQuotes in the Macro Names list box, press Ctrl+Shift+Q, and then press Enter. Now, whenever you press Ctrl+Shift+Q, Word for Windows checks whether the cursor is at the first character in the document; if so, it returns an open quote. Otherwise, it looks at the character to the left of the cursor; if it finds a space or a carriage return, it returns an open quote. If none of the above conditions are true, Word inserts a close quote.

A Macro for Automatic Paragraph Indents   Here's a simple macro that automatically indents a paragraph 1 inch from the left and right margins. To create this macro, choose Macro from the Tools menu, type a macro name and an optional description, and choose Edit. In the macro-editing screen, type the following line between the Sub MAIN and End Sub commands:

```
FormatParagraph .LeftIndent="1"
```

Setting Your Own Defaults

Word for Windows' extensive use of defaults, many of which aren't made entirely clear to the user, is probably the biggest gripe about the program. Don't gripe, change them.

Change the .DOC Default   When you click on Open in the File menu in Word for Windows, the dialog box comes up with the wildcard filename *.DOC already in place. Word for Windows assumes that you give all documents a .DOC extension—not a good assumption considering all the more informative three-character extensions possible. If you aren't always looking for .DOC files, you have to change the default manually each time.

Change the default so that the dialog box, for example, appears with *.* each time, or displays another extension that works better for you. First, open any file; then click on the Macros option in the Tools menu and select the Commands radio button. Look for a macro called FileOpen; this is the code that controls the action of the File Open dialog box. If FileOpen doesn't appear in the list of available macros, click on the box next to Show Global Macros, or just type in the name FileOpen and click on the Edit button. The code that makes up that macro will appear in the macro editor. It should look like this:

```
Sub MAIN
Dim dlg As FileOpen
GetCurValues dlg
Dialog dlg
Super FileOpen dlg
End Sub
```

If you want to be presented with a *.* option in the Open dialog box, insert three lines so that the macro listing reads as follows:

```
Sub MAIN
On Error Goto ENDER
Dim dlg As FileOpen
GetCurValues dlg
dlg.NAME ="*.*"
```

```
Dialog dlg
Super FileOpen dlg
ENDER:
End Sub
```

If you want to use a wildcard filename other than *.*, include the pattern you want within the quotes in the line beginning with dlg. The lines beginning with On Error and ENDER eliminate an error box that appears if you cancel the dialog box without choosing a file. Note the colon at the end of ENDER on the next-to-last line.

Now close the file. You'll be asked if you want to save it; click on Yes. Then exit Word for Windows. You'll be asked if you want to save global changes to the glossary and commands; click on Yes again. When you reenter Word for Windows and open a file, the dialog box gives you the filename pattern you want.

Change the Default Font   If you don't like the default font you're using in Word for Windows, change it by working with NORMAL.DOT, the default template that the program uses as the initial document format. (If your document is based on another template, apply these suggestions to it.)

Open a document based on the NORMAL.DOT template and choose Style from the Format menu, then click the Define button. Select Normal from the list of styles (if it isn't already selected), and under Options, place an X in the Add to Template box. Click on the Character button or press Alt+C. Select the font you want as the default. Choose OK to close the Character dialog box, click on Apply to close the Style dialog box, and click on Yes in the box that pops up.

When you quit Word or when Word completes an autosave, the program asks if you want to save the global changes. To make the font you selected the default font, choose Yes.

Change the Default Document Directory   Word for Windows 2.0 lets you set the default document directory to any path you'd like. Select Options from the Tools menu and select the WIN.INI icon. Click on Microsoft Word 2.0 in the Application drop-down list box. In the Startup Options box, locate and select the line that begins INI-path=. Then, in the Setting box, type the path of the subdirectory to which you'd like Word for Windows to default, and click on the Set button. Click on the Close button, and restart Word for Windows to make the changes take effect.

Change the Date Default   When you insert a date field into a Word for Windows document, the program uses the short date format defined in the Windows Control Panel. To customize this setting for Word, open WIN.INI and add the line dateformat= under the [Microsoft Word] heading. Use any of the formats available under Word's Insert Field Date option. For example, for a normal long date format, insert the line dateformat=MMM dd, yyyy.

Make Boilerplate Text with the Glossary   Most people who word process use the same or very similar blocks of text repeatedly. Saving boilerplate text and reusing it not only saves time, it prevents errors. In Word for Windows, you do this via the glossary (select Glossary from the Edit menu). If you haven't used this feature, you might not realize that glossary entries store formatting as well as text, letting you skip repeated trips to the ribbon or Format menu.

Let's say the words "1993 Earnings Forecast" should appear in 12-point Palatino bold italic throughout your annual report. Choose Character from the Format menu, select those font attributes, and type the text anywhere on your page. With the cursor just after the "t" in "Forecast," return to the Character dialog box and restore your normal font attribute settings. Before saving "1993 Earnings Forecast" as a glossary entry, add an extra character space after "Forecast." Highlight the phrase, including the trailing space (but not the end-of-paragraph marker if you've entered one), and select Glossary from the Edit menu. Enter a brief, memorable name for the new glossary entry—something like "ef"—in the Glossary Name text box, and click on the Define button. To make the entry permanent, select Save All from the File menu.

To place the formatted phrase anywhere in your documents, locate the insertion point where you want the text, type the glossary name, and press F3. Word for Windows automatically inserts the formatted text, replacing the glossary name you typed. The normally-formatted trailing space lets you continue typing without requiring you to revert to your normal font settings each time you insert a glossary entry.

Automatically Load the Last Document You Worked On   Do you want to pick up where you left off last time? It's easy to get Word for Windows to automatically load the last document you edited whenever you start the program. In the Windows' Program Manager, click once on the Word for Windows icon, and then select Properties from the File menu. In the Program Item Properties dialog box that pops up, there's an icon description and a Command Line text box containing the command that opens the program. Edit this line so that the command reads WINWORD.EXE /MFILE1. Now whenever you click on the Word for Windows icon, the program will open and load the last file you saved. Consider making two Word for Windows icons, one to reopen a file and another to start the program only.

Word for Windows opens files at the top of the first page. To return to the place you were working when you saved the document, press Shift+F5. Repeating this key combination will take you to the last three places that you edited in the document.

Navigation Tips

Word offers some handy ways to scoot around large documents, if you know the tricks.

Go Back to Where You Left Off   When you open a document, press Shift+F5 (Go Back) to return to where you were working when you lasted saved the file.

Word stores the last three working locations, even if they're in different windows. This is tremendously useful when you have to copy text and want to return quickly to your point of origin.

Jump Back and Forth in Long Documents   To view a distant area of a long document and return immediately to your previous location, use the vertical scroll bar to move to the new area, and then press the spacebar. Word redisplays the area where you were working. (It also inserts a space at the cursor, so be sure to delete the space when you get back to the original location.)

Scroll to the Left Edge of the Page   You can't scroll horizontally into the left margin in Normal view unless you hold down the Shift while you click on the left scroll arrow.

Navigate through Your Document Quickly   Navigate quickly from page to page in your Word for Windows documents. To make a speedy jump to another page or a bookmark, double-click anywhere on the status bar at the bottom of the document window. The Go To dialog box pops up, allowing you to enter a page number or click on a named bookmark.

File Management Tips

File handling in Word for Windows can be more flexible than it might at first appear. Try these ideas.

Open Several Files at Once   When you need to work with several open documents at the same time, it's quickest to open all the files at once, but you can't do this from the Open dialog box (File, Open). To open several files, choose Find File from the File menu. Hold down the Ctrl key, click on the names of the files you want to open, and then choose Open.

You can also accomplish this with the keyboard: In the Find File dialog box, press Shift+F8 in a file list, use the arrow keys to move to a filename, and press the spacebar to select a file. To deselect a file, press the spacebar again. To select two or more contiguous files in the list, hold down the Shift key as you move through the filenames with the arrow keys or the cursor.

Keep Versions Current for Group Documents   Does your work group share printed draft revisions of reports and other documents? In the rush to meet deadlines, versions can often get switched. To ensure that you're working on the latest version, format a header as hidden text and print drafts with hidden text displayed. Insert author, time, and date fields; comment and edit time fields; and any other fields you wish in the header.

To create hidden text, open the header as you normally would (choose Header/Footer from the View menu), choose Character from the Format menu, and select the Hidden check box. Now you can type in text that will be hidden. Word displays hidden text with a dotted underline. To display hidden text, click on the paragraph mark at the right end of the ruler. To do this by default, choose

Options from the Tools menu, choose the View icon, and select Hidden Text to place an X in the check box. To insert fields, choose Field from the Insert menu, select a field in the Insert Field Type box, and click on OK.

Word for Windows doesn't display hidden text in the Print Preview screen. To print the document with the hidden text visible, choose Print from the File menu, set any options in the dialog box, choose Options, select the Hidden Text check box, and click on OK twice.

Selective File Searches   When searching with the Find File command on the File menu, narrow your searches. Searching for "for" locates files with "foreign," "fork," "forde," and so on. To locate the word "for," type the search text in double quotes and followed by a space, as in **"for "**. Always enclose search text in double quotes if it contains spaces or punctuation. Also be aware that Word interprets the ampersand (&) as a logical and. If you search for "Mutt & Jeff," Word locates files that contain both words, but not necessarily the phrase "Mutt & Jeff."

Mail Merge Tips

Word provides unique features for automated letter creation. If you have to produce large document mailings, these tips will help you get from PC to post office faster.

Create Envelopes on the Fly   If you know you'll be printing an envelope while you're typing a letter, mark the addressee and return address with special bookmarks that tell Word for Windows to insert the address text into the Create Envelope dialog box. Select the return address, choose Bookmark from the Insert menu, type **EnvelopeReturn** in the Bookmark Name text box, and click on OK. Select the addressee, choose Bookmark from the Insert menu, type **EnvelopeAddress** in the Bookmark name text box, and click on OK. When you select Create Envelope from the Tools menu, Word automatically displays the addressee and return address in the Create Envelope dialog box.

Make an Envelope File for Frequent Addresses   If you often address envelopes to the same individual, create an envelope file. Open a new document, choose Create Envelope from the Tools menu, type the person's address (and a return address, if needed), and choose Add to Document. Save the file under an appropriate name, for example, SMITH.ENV. To print an envelope, choose Print from the File menu, type **0** in the From and To boxes, and click on OK. (Specifying a range from page 0 to page 0 tells Word to print only an envelope.)

Unlink Time and Date Fields   It's annoying to press the Update Field key (F9) to update field codes and have Word for Windows update date or time fields that you don't want to change. (You wouldn't want a past due invoice to go out with the current date, would you?) To prevent this, you can unlink date and time fields by pressing Ctrl+Shift+F9 (Unlink Field) while the cursor is on the field.

Help Tips

Help is generally considered a rather static part of any application. However, you can even squeeze a bit of extra value from Word for Windows' internal help system with these tricks.

Get Help for Unavailable Menu Items   Sometimes it's convenient to display help for a menu item that's grayed (not currently available). In such cases, you can't select the menu item and press F1 (Help). Instead, select the grayed command using the keyboard, and press F1, or hold down the left mouse button, drag to select the grayed menu item, keep the mouse button depressed, and press F1.

Annotate Help Screens with Your Own Notes   If you call Microsoft's help line and obtain information about Word for Windows that isn't included in the *User's Guide,* you can place it in an on-line help screen for easy reference. Display the help screen you want to annotate, choose Annotate from the Edit menu, type the note, and choose Save. Word for Windows places a paper clip symbol to the left of the help screen's title, as shown in Figure 11.8, to remind you that you've created an annotation. To display the note, choose Annotate from the Edit menu, or click on the paper clip symbol.

FIGURE 11.8

Notes to Word for Windows' Help files will be marked with a paper clip symbol, which you can click on to access the notes.

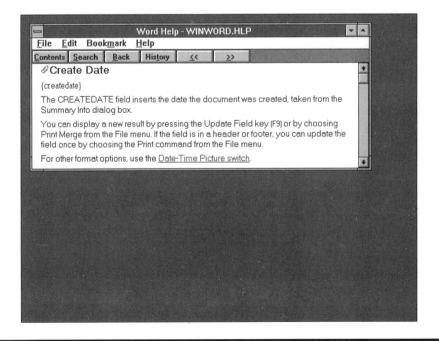

Access Help Screens Quickly   If you often refer to the same help screen, you can mark it with a bookmark and jump to it immediately. Open the help screen, choose Define from the Bookmark menu, enter a bookmark name, and then click on OK. To return to the menu, choose Help (from the standard menu bar, *not* the help system's menu bar), Help Index, Bookmark, and select the help screen by the name you assigned to it. To speed the process even more, record a macro that displays the Help Bookmark menu.

Get Fast Help for Fields   Word fields aren't listed in Word's *User's Guide*, oddly enough. The fastest way to find out about available fields is to choose Field from the Insert menu, point to a field title in the Insert Field Type list, and press F1. Word displays the help screen for that field.

Spell-Checking Tips

Spell-checking is not as tightly integrated into Word as it is in some programs. So these ideas can help make this function more responsive to your needs.

Check Spelling with a Single Keystroke   Are you uncertain how to spell a word? Move the insertion point onto the word and press F7. If the word is spelled correctly, Word displays a message to that effect; if not, it displays the Spelling dialog box and offers alternative spellings. You can choose one of these, or click on the name of a custom dictionary, and then click on Add. This is a great way to build a custom dictionary as you're working on a document.

Be Selective with Spell-Checking   Spell-checking documents that contain parts lists, technical data, and other alphanumeric codes can be extremely annoying. To skip entries that combine numbers and letters, choose Spelling from the Tools menu, and then click on Options. Then check Words with Numbers under Ignore. You can also tell Word to skip technical material by selecting lists and tables as you type them and give them No Proofing status. To do this, select the text and choose Language from the Format menu. Then choose (no proofing) and click on OK. Word will ignore the text during a spell-checking session.

Edit Your Document while Spell-Checking   Activate the document window in the middle of a spell-checking session by pressing Ctrl+Tab. Edit text as needed, then click on Start in the Spelling dialog box to restart the spell-checker. This is much quicker than canceling the session and rechecking spelling from the insertion point forward.

WordPerfect for Windows

WordPerfect dominated the DOS word processor market, but came late to the party for Windows. This means WordPerfect for Windows hasn't gone through as many versions as its competitors, and is still somewhat rough around the edges. It also bears the burden of maintaining approaches WordPerfect popularized under DOS, which may not be entirely natural for the Windows environment. Tips can be a big help here.

Text Manipulation Tips

These three tips make some basic text operations easier than they might otherwise be.

Select Text Easily   With the insertion point on a word, quickly double-click the left mouse button to select it. Click the mouse quickly three times to select a sentence. Hold down the Shift key while clicking the left mouse button three times to select from the current word to the end of the sentence. Click the mouse button four times quickly to select a paragraph; hold down the Shift key while clicking to select from the current word to the end of a paragraph. Click once at a starting point, press Shift, and click at another point to select the text between the two points. Or click and drag the cursor between two points to select text.

Move Text Quickly   If you accidentally delete text, both of WordPerfect's modes let you quickly restore it. In Windows mode, choose Undelete from the Edit menu or press Alt+Shift+Backspace, and then click on Restore.

You can use this capability to move text, if you are careful. Block the text you wish to move, and then delete it. Move the cursor to where you want to place the text. Then follow the steps for restoring it given previously, and the text will reappear in the new spot. You can restore only the last three deletions, so be careful not to make too many deletions before you reposition the cursor.

Enhance On-Screen Text Readability   If the font and display you're using in WordPerfect for Windows produce on-screen text that's too small to read easily, here's a workaround. This works best if your main body text is mostly 12-point Times Roman or a similar font and if you normally use 1-inch left and right margins.

Go to the top of the document and change the margins to 0.5 inches on both the left and right. Now select 14-point Helvetica type. The font displayed on the screen is readable, and the lines break approximately where they will when you remove these temporary codes and restore 1-inch margins with 12-point type for final printing.

To make the process easier, create a couple of macros—one to insert the temporary codes and one to remove them—and assign both to your Button Bar or to the Macro menu.

Formatting Tips

There are lots of opportunities for clever workarounds and unexpected benefits in the area of formatting in WordPerfect for Windows.

Speed the Font Attribute Switch   You can switch font attributes quickly by using the Right Arrow key to end the attribute. When you apply an attribute (Ctrl+F8), WordPerfect actually enters a pair of attribute codes (one for on and one for off) but leaves your cursor between them. After typing whatever text you want in that attribute, press the Right Arrow key to jump over the off attribute code, and you're back in normal type.

Use Dot Leaders   When creating a two-column table of contents, an invoice, or a similar listing in WordPerfect, use dot leaders to link the left column to the right. The quickest way to do this is to type the left column and press Flush Right (Alt+ F6) twice. WordPerfect for Windows fills the line with dots, and as you enter the right column of data, it remains aligned to the right margin without wrapping.

Create Check Boxes   Create small check boxes for forms in WordPerfect for Windows. Create an empty figure box anchored to a character, and then size it with the mouse or the menus. A box size of 0.25 inches by 0.25 inches is handy for most forms. You can put the box into a style or macro to insert it easily into new documents.

Box Your Page   To create a box around an entire page, put a full-page figure box in a header. Turn off Wrap Text Around Box so that your text will be contained inside the box. You may need to adjust the margins so that the text will align correctly within the box.

Underline for Emphasis   Underline a heading for emphasis. Position the insertion point at the beginning of the heading. Choose Line from the Graphics menu, and select Horizontal. Then click on OK when the Create Horizontal Line dialog box appears. Click on the line and use its handles to change its thickness, length, or position.

Set Custom Line Spacing   WordPerfect for Windows includes a Fixed Line Height command that lets you set vertical spacing for sections of your document with much greater control than traditional word processors do. For example, you can use the following sequences to set vertical spacing to .25 inch: Choose Layout, Line, Height; click the Fixed radio button; and fill in the measurement. Then click on OK to save the setting. The measurement you enter represents the baseline-to-baseline distance between lines. (The *baseline* is an imaginary line that marks the bottom of letters, excluding descenders.)

Move Tabs en Masse   Move or copy several tabs at once in WordPerfect for Windows by using the mouse and the ruler. First, use the mouse to select a group of tab markers in the ruler. Be sure to start by positioning the mouse pointer between two tab markers; if you start with it on a tab marker, you will simply move that one marker.

Now click and drag the pointer across all the tabs you want to work with. A shaded area will cover all those markers. Release the left mouse button and position the arrow anywhere in the gray area. Now click and drag the shaded area to the location on the ruler where you want to position the tabs.

Ordinarily, this simply moves the tab markers without affecting any other markers. But if you hold down the Shift key while moving the shaded area, the shaded tabs will replace any tabs in the area you move them to. If you hold down the Ctrl key while moving the shaded tabs, they are copied to a new area without affecting any existing tabs. And if you hold down both Ctrl and Shift, the copies of the shaded tabs replace any existing tabs in the area they've been moved to, and they also remain in the original location.

You can delete an entire series of tabs by shading them and dragging them below the ruler.

Undo Margins Quickly Using the ruler in WordPerfect for Windows is the easiest way to change your margins. Simply click and drag either of the margin markers. But if you change your mind in midstream, drag the mouse pointer off the ruler toward the top of the screen and release the mouse button. The margin marker will return to its original position.

Globally Change Footnotes You can include separate margins and font codes in any footnote or endnote you create. However, if you want the style for any of these to be different from your main body text, it's a hassle to set margins and fonts for individual footnotes or endnotes. And the Option menus in Word-Perfect for Windows doesn't allow you to set margins and fonts that apply to all footnotes and endnotes.

The solution is to use the Document Initial Codes and Initial Font settings. These are different from the Initial Codes setting found when you select Preferences from the File menu and from the Initial Font setting established with the Printer Setup dialog box. Document Initial Codes and Initial Font settings apply only to the individual document you're working with as you establish the settings.

To set a document's initial codes in WordPerfect for Windows, choose Document from the Layout menu, and choose Initial Codes. In DOS mode, press Setup (Shift+F1), Initial Settings (4), and Initial Codes (5). Enter any codes you want to apply to the entire document and your footnotes and endnotes. To set a document's initial font, choose Document from the Layout menu, choose Initial Codes, and select a font from the list box that appears. In DOS mode, press Format (Shift+F8), Document (3), Initial Base Font (3), and select a font from the list that appears.

If you want your main body text to be different from your footnote/endnote text after you've saved those settings, include any formatting and font instructions at the beginning of the document. But any time you create footnotes or endnotes, the formatting in the Initial Codes and Initial Font settings will apply to the notes. You can apply the same technique to headers and footers.

Button Bar Tips

The Button Bar is WordPerfect for Windows' way of displaying functions graphically. You can customize it precisely by using the following tricks.

Create Buttons to Switch Button Bars If you have more than one Word-Perfect for Windows Button Bar and switch among them for different tasks, create macros that load the different bars. Then assign those macros to the Button

Bars so that each bar has buttons to call up other Button Bars. To create the first macro, open a new file, and type the following lines:

```
Application (WP;WPWP;Default;"wpwpUS.WCP")
ButtonBarOpen
(
FileName:"c:\wpwin\macros\mybar.wwb"
)
```

If necessary, modify the FileName line to match the name of your Button Bar. Save the file in your macros directory as CALLBAR1.WCM. Now choose Button Bar Setup from the View menu, and then choose Edit. In the Edit Button Bar dialog box, choose Assign Macro to Button, select CALLBAR1.WWB from the list that appears, and click on Assign. A new button named Callbar1 will appear on the current Button Bar. Click on it to display the buttons saved as MYBAR.WWB.

Create similar macros for as many Button Bar configurations as you've set up, and assign them to all the other Button Bars.

Trick Your Font Button   You can assign fonts to the Font button on WordPerfect for Windows' ruler, but if you're using a scalable font, the ruler doesn't let you assign a specific point size. However, you can get around the problem by fooling the Ruler Fonts menu. Before opening the menu, choose Select Printer from the File menu, and click on your printer's name. Next choose Setup from the Select Printer dialog box, and then choose Cartridges/Fonts and Select. Now select a cartridge from the list that contains a font similar to a scalable typeface you use. For example, if your typeface is CG Times (Scalable) on an HP Laser-Jet III, tell WordPerfect that you have the HP ProCollection cartridge installed in your printer.

Close the printer setup menu and choose Font from the Font menu, and then click on Assign to Ruler. Among the new selections in the Font List list box is Times Roman in 8-, 10-, and 12-point fonts. Select any sizes you use and assign them to the ruler. Click on OK twice to return to your document. Now when you click on the Font button, click on TmsRmn 10pt(Pro) whenever you want to print in 10-point CG Times. You may have to experiment to find a cartridge with fonts that WordPerfect will treat as your printer's scalable fonts, but the experimentation pays off in convenient font access.

Display More Buttons   If you find yourself running out of space for buttons on WordPerfect for Windows' Button Bar, choose Button Bar Setup from the View menu, choose Options, and select Text Only and Left or Right. This displays the Button Bar on the left or right side of the screen without the icons, which allows you to display twice as many buttons, as shown in Figure 11.9.

FIGURE 11.9

Fit more buttons on the screen by selecting Text Only and lining up the buttons vertically on one side of the screen.

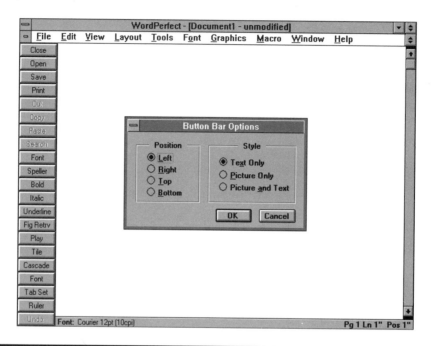

Switch Button Bars   If you still cannot display all the WordPerfect for Windows buttons you'd like, create separate button collections for separate tasks. For example, create one set for ordinary editing and another set for mail merge. Now include a button that switches to the other button set on each of the bars.

First, create two macros, each of which sets up one of the Button Bars. Choose Record from the Macro menu and give the macro a name that will identify the appropriate Button Bar, because the macro's name will be used on the button when you later add the macro to the bar.

With the Macro Facility running, select Button Bar Setup from the View menu, choose Select, and choose the appropriate Button Bar set. Then stop the macro recording.

Because you can't assign a macro to a Button Bar until it's been compiled, replay the macro you just recorded by selecting Run from the Macro menu and entering the name of the macro. The Button Bar associated with that macro will appear on the screen.

Now use View, Button Bar Setup, Select to choose your other Button Bar—the one to which you want to assign this macro. Then choose View, Button Bar Setup, Edit, Assign Macro to Button. Finally, choose the macro that you just recorded from the list box and choose Assign.

Repeat the process for your other Button Bar. If you have more than two Button Bars, you can create as many buttons as you need on each of them to display any of the other Button Bars.

Keyboard Tips

The keyboard retains more importance in WordPerfect for Windows than other Windows word processors, an expression of the program's DOS roots. You can edit and manipulate keystrokes to great advantage in this application.

Reassign the Select Toggle   The handiest key you can reassign using WordPerfect for Windows' Keyboard Editor is also one of the most overlooked. It's the 5 key on the numeric keypad. Assigning the Select toggle function to this key is particularly useful. Use it to turn on Select, and your hand is already positioned to move the cursor to extend the selection.

To assign the Select toggle—or some other function of your choice—to the 5 key on the numeric keypad, choose Preferences from the File menu, and then choose Keyboard. If the keyboard you want to edit is not already selected, click on Select and then choose the desired keyboard from the list box that appears. Choose Edit to bring up the Keyboard Editor dialog box.

In the Keyboard Editor, scroll through the Assignable Items list until you reach SelectToggle. Now press 5 on the numeric keypad (first making sure that Num Lock is on). In the Change Assignment area of the dialog box, next to the Keystroke label, you'll see the word "Clear." This is WordPerfect's name for the 5 key on the numeric keypad. Click on the Assign button—don't try to tab to it. The word "Clear" should appear in the Current Keystrokes list in the upper-right corner of the dialog box. Click on OK to save the change.

Additional Character Sets   WordPerfect 5.1 enabled you to select special characters—from the copyright symbol to Hebrew letters—through a series of Byzantine keystrokes. Inserting an entire word or sentence using a foreign alphabet was extremely tedious. WordPerfect for Windows makes the process a snap. Press Ctrl+W, click and hold down the left mouse button in the Set box, and the program pops up a list of available character sets, as shown in Figure 11.10. Move to the one you want and release the mouse button. Point and click to choose a character. To insert a single character, click the Insert and Close buttons. To continue, click the Insert button and repeat the process until you're done.

Mutate Keyboard Macros   When you assign a macro to a WordPerfect for Windows keyboard layout, the macro code becomes a permanent part of the layout. If you revise the macro, the changes will not be reflected in the macro the next time you run it from the keyboard assignment.

One solution is to enter the Keyboard Editor (choose Preferences from the File menu, choose Keyboard, and then choose Edit), unassign the macro, and then reassign it—a tiresome procedure. Another solution is to create macros that run other macros, if you expect to revise them frequently. The following code runs a macro called LETTHEAD.WCM—in this example a macro to enter letterhead information, which you might need to change from time to time. Copy this code into a new document and save it with the name RUN-LETT.WCM in the directory in which you normally store your macros.

```
Application (WP;WPWP;Default;"WPWPUS.WCD")
CHAIN ("C:\WPWIN\MACROS\LETTHEAD.WCM")
```

You'll need to substitute the name of your own macro and macro directory if they differ from the ones in this example.

FIGURE 11.10

Add special characters to your documents by calling up WordPerfect's available character sets and selecting the desired character.

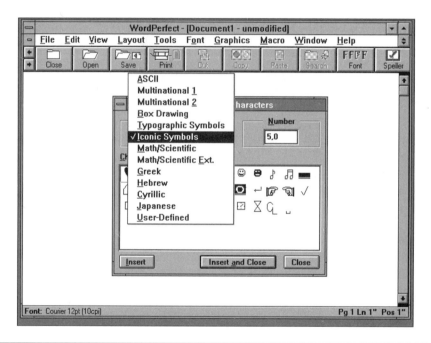

Assign RUNLETT.WCM to any of the eligible keystrokes on your favorite keyboard layout. One drawback is that the CHAIN command cannot run a macro that isn't compiled, so be sure to run any revised macro manually before trying to run it via the keyboard assignment. (You should test-run a revised macro, anyway, to make sure it works.)

Edit the CUA Keyboard WordPerfect for Windows supplies five keyboard layouts. One imitates many of the WordPerfect for DOS keystrokes. The default keyboard conforms to the CUA (common user access) interface that most Windows applications use. If you use other Windows programs, it makes sense to go with the CUA keyboard even if you're used to the WordPerfect for DOS layout.

The problem with the CUA keyboard is that you can't customize it, unlike the DOS keyboard. But you can make a copy of the CUA keyboard, which you can then edit.

Load the CUA keyboard by choosing Preferences from the File menu and then choosing Keyboard, Default (CUA), Create. When the Keyboard Editor dialog box appears, choose Save As and save the CUA keyboard with a name such as MYCUA.WWK. Now you can select Preferences from the File menu to select MYCUA.WWK as your active keyboard. Use the Keyboard Editor to customize it.

Assign Macro Keys on the Fly   WordPerfect for Windows allows you to assign macros to Ctrl+key and Ctrl+Shift+key combinations by using the Keyboard Editor, which you access by choosing Preferences from the File menu, and then choosing Keyboard. But there's an easier way to assign macros to those keystroke combinations.

When you begin to record a macro and WordPerfect wants you to name the macro in the Record Macro dialog box, press the Ctrl+key or Ctrl+Shift+key combination for that macro. WordPerfect will automatically insert a name for the macro based on the key combination. For example, pressing Ctrl+E inserts the macro name CTRLE.WCM. Pressing Ctrl+Shift+E inserts the name CTRLSFTE.WCM.

Macros named this way can be used without first being assigned to a specific keyboard layout. If, however, you're using a keyboard layout that already has macro or WordPerfect commands assigned to the same Ctrl+key or Ctrl+Shift+key combination, the previous assignment overrides the new macro.

Navigation Tips

Find your way around documents with these tips.

Recover Cursor Position   If you've ever lost your position in a file by pressing PgDn instead of the Down Arrow, it's easy to return to where you were. Choose Go To from the Edit menu, and choose Last Position to get back to where you came from.

Create Invisible Place Markers   It's convenient to leave place markers, such as **, in a long document so that you can easily find passages that you want to revise. But if you forget to remove the markers, they'll show up when you print the document.

Since WordPerfect can search for formatting codes as well as text, you can use the codes as place markers. Avoid codes that may be used for normal purposes, such as boldfacing and underlining codes. Instead, choose a format code that's not likely to be used in your document and that won't affect the printout. For example, you could use the code that controls the mixture of colors in hard copy (unless you have a color printer, that is). In WordPerfect for Windows, choose Color from the Font menu, and then click on OK. To search for the color code, choose Search from the Edit menu, and then choose Codes, Color, and click on OK.

Orient Yourself in 200% View   It's easy to get lost on a page preview in WordPerfect for Windows when it's magnified at 200 percent. To figure out which part of the page you're looking at in 200% print preview, click anywhere on the page; WordPerfect superimposes a small image of the entire page, with a red box around the portion that's currently enlarged (see Figure 11.11). The small image uses "greeked" lines instead of actual characters to indicate text, but you can move the red box anywhere in the full-page view to change your position in the close-up view.

FIGURE 11.11

Find out where you are when viewing a magnified document by clicking anywhere on the page to call up a small image of the page showing your location.

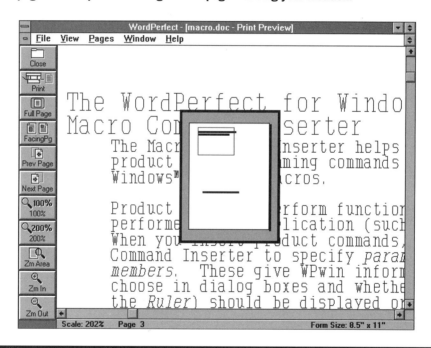

Code Tips

Codes for formatting and other operations aren't common among Windows programs, but they do have an important role in WordPerfect for Windows. Here are ways to make the codes do what you need.

Resizing Reveal Codes   Resize Reveal Codes to see more of the codes embedded in your document and fix errors or delete formatting more quickly. On the vertical scroll bar, above the up arrow or below the down arrow, are small areas that are shaded black. When you position your pointer on either of these black bands, the pointer turns into a double-headed arrow. Click and then drag to display and size Reveal Codes. To resize or eliminate Reveal Codes, position your pointer on the bar separating the document from the Reveal Codes portion. The pointer will turn into a double-headed arrow. Click and drag to resize, or double-click to eliminate Reveal Codes.

Auto Code Placement   Some formatting codes belong in a particular place in a document. Margin and justification codes belong at the beginning of a paragraph, while Center Page belongs at the beginning of a page. With Auto Code Placement on (the default setting), WordPerfect automatically moves margins, justification, line spacing, and other codes to the beginning of the paragraph where they are inserted, and moves codes such as Center Page and Page Size to the beginning of the page in which they are entered. To toggle Auto Code placement on or off, choose Preferences from the File menu, choose Environment, and click on the Auto Code Placement check box.

When to Suppress Auto Code Placement   WordPerfect for Windows' Auto Code Placement feature can cause confusion for users who've developed their own shortcuts. For example, DOS WordPerfect users may employ the trick of entering a header code somewhere below the top of a document's first page, knowing that the header won't print until the second page. This way you can avoid having to enter the commands to suppress the header on the first page.

Auto Code Placement spoils the trick, however, by automatically placing the header code at the top of the page. If you find that your headers are printing on the first page when you don't expect them to, either suppress them manually or turn off Auto Code Placement. To do this, choose Preferences from the File menu, choose Environment, and uncheck the Auto Code Placement check box.

Delete Formatting Codes   If you find that deletion keystrokes skip over formatting codes you want to delete in WordPerfect for Windows, there are two solutions: The first is to choose Preferences from the File menu, choose Environment, and check the Confirm on Code Deletion box. When this box is checked, a confirmation box appears any time a deletion keystroke would remove a code. When Confirm on Code Deletion is unchecked, deletion keystrokes skip over codes entirely. Another solution is to open the Reveal Codes window. Then deletion keys will zap codes as well as regular text.

Prevent Disappearing Codes   In WordPerfect for DOS, you can backspace or use the Delete key without deleting formatting codes such as those for boldfacing or italics. WordPerfect for Windows, however, will delete these formatting codes without any warning unless you make a change in the Preferences dialog box.

Choose Preferences from the File menu, choose Environment, and check the Confirm on Code Deletion box. You must exit WordPerfect and run it again for the change to take effect, but the next time you start to erase a formatting code, WordPerfect will present a dialog box asking you to confirm the deletion.

Display Carriage Returns When downloading files by modem, it's hard to know which lines end with a hard return unless the hard returns are displayed on the screen. Use any one of the 1,700 extended characters as a substitute for the hard-return character—just type a number into the proper entry in the preference screens. Among those that can be displayed on EGA and VGA screens are the paragraph mark, which looks like a backward P (20); a right-pointing double angle-bracket character (175); and a small dot that displays in the middle of the line (249).

In WordPerfect for Windows, choose Preferences from the File menu, choose Display, and position the cursor in the Hard Return Character box. Either type the numbers while holding down the Alt key (remember to use the numeric keypad) or press Ctrl+W to bring up the Characters dialog box, which will display hundreds of possibilities.

Update Document Settings If you change your initial codes—which Word-Perfect uses to contain your default settings—you can easily update the settings for an old document by retrieving it into a blank screen into which you have typed only a space or return. The new initial codes are part of the new, nearly blank document, and retrieving the old document into the new one strips out the old document's initial codes and uses only its text and in-line formatting. If necessary, you can delete the initial space or hard return and then save the old document under its original name. Note that this also removes any document summary the original file may have had.

File Management Tips

WordPerfect for Windows provides excellent file-handling power. Use all of it with tips like these.

Access Files Quickly WordPerfect for Windows' Quick List is handy not only for changing directories but also for getting fast access to specific files.

Select Open from the File menu. Select Quick List if it is not already displayed, and then click on Edit Quick List and Add. In the Directory/Filename text box, enter the complete path and filename of the file you want to add to the list. In the Descriptive Name text box, enter the description of the file that you want to add, and click on OK.

The next time you want to retrieve the file, all you have to do is double-click on its descriptive name from the Quick List in the Open File dialog box.

Save File Manager Settings WordPerfect for Windows' File Manager allows you to customize the layout of the various windows that display files and their contents. You can also save your custom layout. To change File Manager so that it always opens with a layout you've designed, load the File Manager. Choose Preferences from the File menu (or select its icon in the WordPerfect

Program Manager group), and then choose Environment. Then select Save Current Layout on Exit. Once you have the layout you want to use regularly, exit File Manager.

The next time you run WordPerfect's File Manager, it will automatically display your custom layout. But you have to take one more step to make sure you don't lose it. After you've opened the File Manager a second time, again choose Preferences from the File menu, and then choose Environment. This time uncheck the Save Current Layout on Exit box. This ensures that any temporary changes you make aren't saved the next time you exit File Manager.

Simplify Routine File Management Chores   In WordPerfect for Windows, use the Options button in the Open File dialog box to perform many routine file management chores. Open the dialog box by selecting Open from the File menu. Select any file you want to delete, move, rename, or copy, and then place the mouse pointer on the Options button and click and hold down the mouse button. Then choose Delete, Copy, or Move/Rename. In WordPerfect DOS mode, press List Files (F5) and select the Delete, Copy, or Move/Rename option.

Search Across Directories   WordPerfect for Windows lets you search for files in several subdirectories (or throughout all directories on a drive) based on their filenames or on words included within the files. Choose Open from the File menu. Then choose Options, Find, Find Files (or Find Words), and type in the names or words.

An asterisk (*) in a word can stand for any number of letters. A search for cat* would find files that contain cat, catalog, and catapult, for example. As with the DOS * wildcard, characters in the filename that appear after the * will be ignored.

A question mark (?) in a word stands for any one character. A search for ?at finds files with cat, hat, or rat.

Enter words separated by spaces or semicolons to find files that contain all those words. Arizona California or Arizona;California will find files that contain both the words "Arizona" and "California."

Enter words separated by commas or vertical lines to find files that contain either one or both of the words. Arizona,California or Arizona | California finds files that contain the word "Arizona" and files that contain the word "California."

Enter two words separated by a hyphen or an exclamation point to find files that contain the first word unless they also contain the second word. Arizona-California or Arizona!California will find files that contain the word "Arizona" as long as those files do not contain the word "California" as well.

To find files containing phrases that include a space, put quotation marks around the search phrase(s). For example, "bird house";"dog house" finds files that contain both the phrases "bird house" and "dog house."

To narrow a search under Windows, select Search Results List. Under DOS, select Find Again and do another search on the files presented from the first search. Under Windows, select the appropriate radio button to apply the search to the current directory, subtree, or drive.

View File Summary Information   While the File Open dialog box is open in WordPerfect for Windows, click on any filename to find out the size of the file and the time and date of its creation or last update. The information will appear near the top of the dialog box, next to the File Info: label.

Create Multiple Quick Lists   WordPerfect for Windows' Quick List is helpful—unless it becomes overcrowded with descriptive names. The solution is to create two versions of the file that keeps track of your Quick List. Use one to display a Quick List that, for example, displays directories with files that relate to your daytime job, and use the other file to display directories that relate to your side business.

The file that keeps a record of your Quick List entries is WPC.INI, which is stored in your main WINDOWS directory. Before doing anything with WPC-.INI, make a backup copy that you can restore if something goes wrong. Then edit your Quick List so that it contains only the directories for your daytime job files. Save the list and copy WPC.INI to WPCDAY.INI. Then reedit your Quick List so that it contains only entries for your part-time business, and save the list again. Now copy WPC.INI to WPCNITE.INI.

To use the different Quick Lists, create two batch files for launching Windows. DAY.BAT consists of these two lines:

```
COPY C:\WINDOWS\WPCDAY.INI C:\WINDOWS\WPC.INI
WIN
```

NITE.BAT consists of these lines:

```
COPY C:\WINDOWS\WPCNITE.INI C:\WINDOWS\WPC.INI
WIN
```

Run DAY to load Windows when you want to work with your daytime files and NITE when you want to work with your part-time business files. To change from one Quick List to another, exit WordPerfect and Windows and reload both using the other batch file.

Easy ASCII File Saves   When you write a message to upload on an electronic bulletin board or to share with someone who doesn't use WordPerfect for Windows, use this macro to save the document. If the file's already named, the macro changes the file extension to .TXT and leaves the original intact. If you haven't already saved the file, the macro prompts you for a filename and adds the .TXT extension. To create the macro, open a new file and type the following lines:

```
Application (WP;WPWP;Default;"wpwpUS.WCP")
GetWPData(MacroVariable:FullFilename;SystemVariable:Name!)
If (FullFilename = "")
```

```
Call (NoName@)
EndIf
StrPos(Dot;".";FullFilename)
If (Dot=0)
SubStr(PartName;1;8;FullFileName)
FirstPartName:=Partname + "."
Go (ChangeName@)
EndIf
SubStr(FirstPartName;1;Dot;FullFilename)
Label (ChangeName@)
NewName:=FirstPartName + "txt"
FileSave
(
    FileName:NewName;
    ExportType:160
)
Go (End@)
Label (NoName@)
Beep
GetString (FullFilename;LENGTH=12;"Enter a name for this
  file:";"Name File")
Return
Label (End@)
```

Save the file in your MACROS directory as SAVETEXT.WCM. To replay the macro, choose Play from the Macro menu and enter **savetext** in the dialog box. Or assign the macro to your Button Bar, to the Macro menu, or to the keyboard, and replay it from there.

Put Paths and Filenames in Headers   Use the following macro in WordPerfect for Windows to automatically insert the path and name of a document into a header. Type the macro code into a new document and save it as NAME-HEAD.WCM in the directory where you usually store WordPerfect for Windows macros.

```
APPLICATION(WP;WPWP;Default;"WPWPUS.WCD")
LABEL(START@)
GetWPData (MacroVariable: DocName; SystemVariable: Name!)
IF (DocName="")
FileSaveAsDlg ()
GO (Start@)
ENDIF
```

```
GetWPData (MacroVariable: PathName; SystemVariable: Path!)
ASSIGN  FullName; PathName + DocName)
PosDocVeryTop ()
HeaderFooter (Operation: Create!; Item: HeaderA!)
Type (FullName)
```

The macro uses a command to determine the current document's name and path name. (If you haven't named the file yet, the macro opens the Save As dialog box so that you can do so.) Then it inserts the path and filename into the header editing screen. The screen remains open, allowing you to add text or formatting changes.

To edit the macro so that it works with a footer, change HeaderA! to FooterA!.

Add Long Filenames to File Manager   The Open File dialog box in Word-Perfect for Windows doesn't display the long document names available in the DOS version's List Files display. But WordPerfect for Windows' File Manager displays long filenames, summary screen information, and other data that isn't displayed in the Open File dialog box.

Run the WordPerfect File Manager by selecting File Manager from the File menu. Select File List from the View menu for a list of files in the current directory. In the Column Manager—the bar at the top of the File List window that displays filenames—click and hold down the mouse button on any empty space. A menu will appear with the items that you can choose to display in the file directory. Select Desc. Name to add descriptive filenames to the directory information.

If you choose to save this view of the File List, note that because WordPerfect must read descriptive filenames from each file in a directory, opening File Manager and changing directories may become slower.

Customize File Manager Listings   In WordPerfect for Windows, it's easy to change the order of items displayed in File Manager's File List, Quick List, and Search Results windows and the amount of space devoted to each item. If you want to change the order of items—say, move descriptive filenames to the far left—click on the item you want to move in the Column Manager, at the top of the window, and drag it to where you want it to appear. The columns of information will realign to match your changes.

To delete a column from the directory listing, drag its heading off the Column Manager. To change the amount of space devoted to a column of information, move the mouse pointer to either side of the column's heading box until a two-way arrow appears. Drag to the right or left to increase or decrease the size of the box.

Customize Document Summaries   When you use the Extract feature in the Document Summary dialog box (accessed by selecting Document from the Layout menu and then selecting Summary), WordPerfect automatically adds the first 400 characters from the current document to the Abstract text box. If the characters RE: appear in those 400 words, WordPerfect inserts the first 160 characters that follow RE: into the Subject text box. (If it encounters a carriage return before it reaches the 160th character, the insertion ends there.)

RE: is the default because it appears in many memos, but if you create documents that contain a different heading and you'd like to search files for that information, change the Subject Search text setting. Choose Preferences from the File menu and choose Document Summary. The Document Summary Preference dialog box will appear, with RE: already entered in the Subject Search text box. Simply replace RE: with any text that you prefer, such as Subject: or TO:, and click on OK to save the setting.

To change RE: to something else in DOS mode, press Setup (Shift+F1), Document Management/Summary (4), and Subject Search Text (2).

Table Tips

Tables are a particular strength of WordPerfect for Windows. The following tips will give you a head start when working with tables in this Windows word processor.

Convert Columns to Tables   If you have columns of information in tabbed or parallel-column format, consider converting the material into a table. Tables provide more formatting options and can include mathematical operations. Converting tabular information to tables is a snap.

In WordPerfect for Windows, select tabbed or columnar text using the mouse or cursor keys. Then click on the Table button on the ruler and choose Tabular Columns. Or choose Tables from the Layout menu and choose Create.

Enter the Reveal Codes screen in WordPerfect for Windows by selecting Reveal Codes from the View menu. Find the table code [Tbl Def:...], highlight it, and press Del. WordPerfect for Windows will present a dialog box asking if you want to delete the entire table, its contents (text only), or its table structure (leave text). Choose Table Structure and click on OK.

Change Table Column Widths   Changing the widths of columns in tables is simple if you display the ruler in WordPerfect for Windows (the toggle for displaying the ruler is on the View menu). Place the insertion point anywhere in a table and inverted triangles appear across the top of the ruler, aligned with the edges of the columns. To change the width of a column, click and drag the corresponding triangle.

Dragging the column marker widens or narrows the column and adjusts all other columns to the right of the changed column; the table width remains unchanged. Holding down the Shift key when you're moving the column marker causes the next column to the right to expand or shrink to make up the difference; the table width remains the same. Holding down the Ctrl key while dragging a table marker doesn't affect the other columns; instead, it widens or narrows the table accordingly.

Control Column Gutters   The ruler in WordPerfect for Windows gives you easy control of the size and number of columns. To change the size of the gutter (the white space between columns), click and drag either of the two triangles that indicate the edges of the gutter. To move the position of the gutter, which effectively changes the width of the column, click and drag anywhere in the shaded area between the two markers. To delete a gutter entirely, which reduces the number of columns, click and drag the shaded area below the ruler.

Correct Table Displays   If the widths of cells in a WordPerfect for Windows table seem to grow inexplicably, causing the table to expand beyond the right side of the screen, correct the problem by using the Display Pitch setting.

Display Pitch doesn't affect printing, nor does it have an appreciable effect on how the text outside of tables is displayed. But if Display Pitch is set to Auto, tables tend to insert more white space than is needed.

To correct the problem, choose Document from the Layout menu and then choose Display Pitch. In the Display Pitch dialog box, you'll probably see that the Auto radio button is chosen and that the number next to the Manual button is more than 100 percent. Click on the Manual button, change the setting to 100, and click on OK.

Speed Tips

WordPerfect is no speed demon. These tips can help.

Go Straight to the Open File Dialog Box   Create a macro that displays the Open File dialog box each time you launch WordPerfect for Windows, and you can get to work immediately. To create the macro, open a new document and type the following:

```
Application (WP;WPWP;Default)
FileOpenDlg()
```

Save the file as OPENFILE.WCM in the directory that holds your macros—normally \WPWIN\MACROS.

Now close WordPerfect and open the group in the Windows Program Manager that contains WordPerfect for Windows. Highlight WordPerfect's icon by clicking on it once. Then use the mouse to select Properties from the File menu. Move to the Command Line text box, press the End key followed by the spacebar to move the cursor clear of the filename WPWIN.EXE, and type **/m-openfile**. Click on OK. Now launch WordPerfect for Windows by double-clicking on its icon. As soon as WordPerfect is loaded, it will automatically display the Open File dialog box.

Double-Click to Display Dialog Boxes   A shortcut for displaying dialog boxes in WordPerfect for Windows is to double-click on any of the ruler buttons. This brings up the associated dialog box and eliminates the need to keep similar buttons on your button bar.

Printer Tips

Standard printing is no problem in WordPerfect for Windows. These ideas can help with special printing situations.

Print Rotated Type   If your printer can handle graphics, you can print both portrait and landscape text on the same page. Choose Text Box from the Graphics menu, and choose Create. After entering your text, choose Rotate before you close the box.

WordPerfect will print these rotated text boxes as graphics, so this technique is not limited to laser printers or printers with landscape fonts. Under the text box's Options menu, change Borders to None to eliminate the box that surrounds the landscape text.

Print Files to Disk   A print-to-disk file includes all the formatting a document would have if it were printed on paper. There are two reasons to create print-to-disk files. One is that you can later copy the file directly to a printer, which is handy if you'll be using a printer connected to a PC without WordPerfect on it. The other reason is to create an ASCII file that includes your indents, spacing, heading, and other formatting touches.

In WordPerfect for Windows, print to disk by choosing Select Printer from the File menu, selecting the DOS Text Printer, and clicking on Setup. In the Printer Setup dialog box, click and hold down the mouse button on the Port option under Destination. From the resulting drop-down menu, select File as the destination and enter the filename you want to print to in the box underneath.

When you want to print to disk, select the Print to Disk Printer to send the output automatically to a file named PRNTDISK.TMP. If you already have a file with that name from an earlier print-to-disk operation, it will be overwritten without warning.

Print Page *x* of *y* Headers   Use the following macro in WordPerfect for Windows to insert a line in a document header that reads Page *x* of *y*, where *x* is the current page number and *y* is the total number of pages in the document. Type the following macro code into a new document and save it as PAGE-HEAD.WCM in the directory where you normally store WordPerfect for Windows macros.

```
APPLICATION(WP;WPWP;Default;"WPWPUS.WCD")
PosDocBottom ()
GetWPData (MacroVariable: LastPage;
SystemVariable: Page!)
NUMSTR (LastPageText; ; LastPage)
PosDocVeryTop ()
HeaderFooter (Operation: Create!; Item:
HeaderA!)
Type ("Page ")
```

```
PageNumberInsert ()
Type (" of " + LastPageText)
```

The macro moves to the last page of your document, determines its page number, and stores the information as a variable. Then it moves to the top of the document, where it opens the header editing screen and inserts the text that includes the total number of pages along with WordPerfect's code for the current page number. The macro leaves the header editing screen open so that you can include any other text or formatting you want.

Run this macro just before you print. If you've added or deleted text in the document since you last ran the macro, the total number of pages may have changed. To edit the macro so that it works with a footer, change the parameter HeaderA! to FooterA!.

Prevent Words from Wrapping   Here's a trick to make sure words that belong together, such as names and titles, print on the same line. Press and release the Home key before you press the spacebar that separates the words. This method works only if you're using the VATP51 keyboard, but you can also press Ctrl+spacebar. Unless you replace the nonbreaking space, the words will always appear on the same line. It's so simple you might not think you've done it right. To check, choose Reveal Codes from the View menu. You'll see the space enclosed within brackets.

Macro Tips

There's lots of macro potential here. Use these macro ideas as the basis for your own automation projects.

Change Macro Menu Selections   WordPerfect for Windows lets you assign macros to the Macro menu so that you can run them by clicking on their titles. But the menu can accommodate only nine macros. Here's a way to use more macros with the menu feature, which is handy if you create different sets of macros for different tasks.

For each group of macros that you want to use, create a macro that deletes the macros currently assigned to the menu and assigns the new set. For example, suppose you have a set of macros for saving files in different word processing formats. To assign this set to the Macro menu, you'd create a macro called CONVERT.WCM, for example, that looks like this:

```
Application (WP;WPWP;DEFAULT;"wpwpUS.WCP")
MacroMenuDelete()
MacroMenuAppend (
"Save as  ASCII"; "SAVETEXT.WCM";
"Save as  WordStar file";  SAVEWS.WCM";
"Save as  Ami Pro file"; "SAVEAMI.WCM";
"Save as  WinWord file"; "SAVEWORD.WCM";
```

```
"Save as  XyWrite file"; "SAVEXY.WCM";
"Save as  MultiMate file"; "SAVEMULT.WCM";
"Save as  DisplayWrite file"; "SAVEDISP.WCM";
"Save as  Rich Text Format"; "SAVERTF.WCM";
"Restore  normal menu"; "NORMENU.WCM"
)
```

The MacroMenuDelete command erases the current selections from the Macro menu. The MacroMenuAppend command adds new entries to the menu. The first phrase in quotation marks in each line is the description that appears in the menu. The second phrase in each line is the name of the macro that will run when you click on that menu entry. Of course, the phrases and macro file-names you'll use will differ. Note the semicolons that separate the items.

The last line runs a macro named NORMMENU.WCM—a variation of this macro to restore your normal Macro menu selections. By including a similar line in each of your menu-assignment macros, you'll always have a menu selection that lets you switch back to your usual menu with a click of the mouse.

Include Dialog Boxes in Macros If you want to record a WordPerfect for Windows macro to open a dialog box so that a user can make selections on the fly, you have to use a poorly documented feature. Without this trick, if you try to record a macro that opens a dialog box but makes no changes in it, the dialog box won't come up at all when you run the macros. And if you do make a change in the dialog box without this trick, your macro will record those changes automatically, without asking for user input.

As you're recording the macro, open any dialog box and change any one of the items. Click on the small square in the upper-right corner of the dialog box (the square appears only when you're recording a macro). Now close the dialog box as if you wanted to save your change. Complete your macro and stop recording.

The changes you make in the dialog box will apply to whatever document you have open when you record the macro, so be sure to record your actions in a dummy document. When you play the macro later, however, the changes you included as you recorded it will not appear. The dialog box will simply open so that you can change any of the selections.

WordStar for Windows

WordStar for Windows, like WordPerfect for Windows, brings a successful DOS history to the Windows environment. WordStar has not hewed as close to the DOS tree as WordPerfect, which means more natural operation in some ways, but more confusion for traditional customers in another.

Speed Tips

Speed was the watchword of WordStar in DOS. It's not quite that way in Windows, but these tips will help.

Quick Searches Old-time WordStar users will find that the Windows version's global find and replace takes too long. Since Windows' screen updates account for much of the environment's sluggishness, you can accelerate the process by cutting out WordStar for Windows' default scrolling. After selecting Find and Replace from the Edit menu and entering the parameters to find and replace, click on Don't Ask, and then deselect View Context. The last step ensures a quicker search.

Speedy Scrolling Scrolling through a document containing graphics is noticeably slower than scrolling through a text-only file. Unless you are working on graphics, invoke WordStar for Windows' text-only view to speed things up. Select Preferences from the Edit menu, select View, find the Text Only choice, and turn it on for quick scrolling; turn it off when you need to work on graphics.

Disable an Annoying Printer Message WordStar for Windows' persistent startup reminder to activate printer connections soon gets annoying. To avoid the message and to save yourself the trouble of having to activate the printer every time you want to print with a new template, select Open from the File menu and, under File Type, choose Templates. Select the default template (usually DEFAULT.WST) and press Enter. From the File menu's Printer Setup option, select the appropriate printer, click on OK, and then save the document. To keep the pesky reminder at bay, repeat this procedure for every template in the template directory.

Formatting Tips

Formatting in WordStar for DOS took a lot of knowledge of arcane key sequences. That's not necessary in Windows, but sometimes is still faster for the knowledgeable user.

Style Bar Shortcuts With the default WordStar for Windows keystroke configuration, avoid using the mouse to click on the style bar's text formatting boxes. It's quicker to use the following keyboard shortcuts.

Style	Ctrl+Y
Font	Ctrl+F
Size	Ctrl+Z

Note that you can't use these keystrokes in the WordStar and WordStar 2000 keyboard configurations.

New Border Style WordStar for Windows enables you to create new line styles for frame borders. First, create the line style by selecting Layout, Modify Frame Style, Borders, Create Line Styles. While you're still in Modify Frame Styles' Borders option, select the appropriate Style (All, Left, Right-Top, or

Bottom). Go to the last choice within the style; it will be the line style you just created. Select it and click on OK. When you go back to your document, you will see your new line style as the border of the frame.

Add Blank Lines to Forms   There's a trick to creating a table with blank rows to use as a form. First, create a table frame and use the Table-Format Table dialog box to specify the number of rows you want. You can also set the number and width of every column in the same dialog box by manipulating markers on the ruler line. Don't use Table-Insert Row unless you are also entering text in the new row; if you leave the cells empty, you'll see only the default number of rows when you reopen the document.

Drawing and Graphics Tips

The mere notion of drawing and graphics associated with WordStar shows how far this program has come from its DOS progenitors.

Making the Most of the Arc Tool   The Arc tool does more than just drawing curves; you can use it to draw straight lines or construct various shapes. Hold down the Shift key while dragging with the mouse to draw straight lines. To construct shapes, drag the cursor to draw additional lines. If you make a mistake, press Backspace to delete the last line. To close a series of lines into a single shape to which you can apply fill patterns and fill colors, click near the starting point. Or leave the shape open by double-clicking after drawing the last curve.

Correct Inverse Video Mode   If a graphic imported into WordStar for Windows appears like a photographic negative, click inside the frame and choose the Select tool—the solid arrow in the tool bar. Click on the image and, when the square handles indicate that it's selected, press the spacebar. This process toggles between inverse and regular video modes.

Refresh the Screen   Periodically, WordStar for Windows screens distort or hide images or display other eccentricities. Press Ctrl and the backslash key (\) to refresh the screen. This usually solves the problem.

SPREADSHEET TIPS

SPREADSHEETS HAVE LED THE WAY IN WINDOWS APPLICATIONS. MUCH AS Lotus 1-2-3 carried the early days of DOS by providing a unique, new set of benefits, Excel pushed the spreadsheet envelope under Windows. Excel's success spurred Lotus and Borland to respond with Windows spreadsheets of their own.

With their combination of computational demands, formatting requirements, and graphical display, spreadsheets naturally lend themselves to Windows. Excel, Lotus 1-2-3 for Windows, and Borland's Quattro Pro for Windows are all among the most powerful and innovative Windows programs. They are so rich that it's hard for even a sophisticated user to mine their every aspect. That's prime territory for tips. So this is a big chapter, as big as the benefit users can glean from using Windows spreadsheets to the max.

Excel

Excel set a high bar for Windows spreadsheets, initiating a whole wave of new ideas about formatting, output, and basic operation of financial applications. It has stayed at the head of the pack with a series of new versions. The tips here refer to both of the most recent versions, 3.0 and 4.0. Where we simply say "Excel," we mean tips that work for either Excel version 3.0 or 4.0. Those exclusive to Excel 4.0 are specified by version number.

Start-up and Shutdown Tips

You don't have to start Excel as a blank sheet, and you don't have to shut it down one sheet at a time, if you use these tricks.

Add Current Files to a Start-up Directory   Any macro sheet, chart, or worksheet present in a directory called XLSTART will be opened automatically each time you start Excel. Make sure the XLSTART directory is directly beneath the directory that holds the main Excel program file, EXCEL.EXE.

Bypass the Blank Worksheet   Normally, when you start Excel 4.0 you get a blank worksheet. Use the /N command-line switch to start Excel without any worksheet loaded. In the Program Manager, add the /N switch to the Command Line text box of the File Properties dialog box. Your command line should look something like this, depending on your subdirectory structure:

```
C:\EXCEL\EXCEL.EXE /N
```

Another way to start Excel 4.0 without a blank worksheet is to add the line open=/e to your EXCEL4.INI file. This is a plain text file, similar in structure to WIN.INI, SYSTEM.INI, and other initialization files used by Windows. You'll find it in your WINDOWS subdirectory.

Before modifying EXCEL4.INI, back it up. Then open the file with a plain text editor, such as Notepad. (Do not use a word processor or any other program that adds formatting information to the files it saves.) Look for the heading [Microsoft Excel]. Then, anywhere between that heading and the next bracketed heading (if any), add the line

```
open=/e
```

Save the modified .INI file and start Excel. No blank worksheet!

Use the Save Workspace Option   A lot of work in Excel can be repetitive—reiterations of monthly and annual budgets, forecasts, time lines, and the like. Templates and specialized macro worksheets automate the drudgery, but they make for a complex workspace. Excel's Save Workspace option helps tie things together neatly. Choose Save Workspace from the File menu and give a name to the whole shebang: template, macro worksheet, and all. Workspace files have the extension .XLW, and they appear on the File menu's list of recently opened files, ready to recreate at the click of a mouse button.

Take Advantage of Global Macros   If you don't want to have to remember to open a macro sheet each time you want to use a macro, consider Excel 4.0's global macro sheet. Excel manages the global macro sheet automatically, and any macro recorded on it is available each time you start Excel. When you record a new macro with the Record command on the Macro menu, Excel prompts you for the location of the macro sheet. Choose Global Macro Sheet, and the macro will be available at all times. To add an existing macro to the global macro sheet, you need to first display the global macro sheet by selecting Unhide from the Window menu and choosing GLOBAL.XLM. (This won't be an option if you don't have any macros on the global macro sheet, by the way.) Then, open the macro sheet that you want to make global, and cut-and-paste it into the global macro sheet.

Save Worksheets Automatically   Do you like the AutoSave feature in Word for Windows, which automatically saves your document every so often? Duplicate this feature in Excel with the Excel AutoSave macro. Put the AUTOSAVE.XLA file into the XLSTART directory to have it loaded automatically each time you start Excel. AUTOSAVE.XLA is in the LIBRARY subdirectory if you used Excel's default installation routine.

Close All Your Windows at Once   If you routinely work with a lot of worksheets on the screen at one time, it's pretty tedious to close each worksheet individually. Instead of either selecting Close from the File menu or double-clicking in the upper-left corner of each worksheet, you can just hold down the Shift key while you click on the File menu. The Close item will now say Close All and will give you the opportunity to save each or all of the open worksheets before closing.

Keyboard Shortcuts

Keystrokes remain an efficient way to move around in big spreadsheets, even under Windows. Here are tricks for moving quickly in Excel worksheets.

Keyboard Shortcuts for Selecting Columns and Rows   If you have a single cell selected, to select its entire row in Excel, press Shift+spacebar. To select its entire column, press Ctrl+spacebar. If you have more than one adjacent cell selected in a row, pressing Ctrl+spacebar will select multiple columns. Similarly, if you have more than one adjacent cell selected in a column, pressing Shift+spacebar will select multiple rows. For instance, if you have three cells selected in a single column, pressing Shift+spacebar will select all three corresponding rows.

Time- and Date-Stamp Documents   Excel offers convenient keyboard shortcuts for date- and time-stamping your worksheet. To enter the current date, press the semicolon key while holding down the Ctrl key. For the current time, press the semicolon key while holding down both Ctrl and Shift (in other words, press Ctrl+:).

   After you press either key combination, Excel leaves you on the formula bar—in case you want to use the date or time string as part of a larger formula. So if you just want to know what time it is, you can press Ctrl+Shift+;, read the information that appears on the formula line, and then press Esc.

Copy Value from Cell Above   Ctrl+" is Excel's "ditto" key. It copies the value from the cell above the current cell. If you're in A2, for example, Ctrl+" enters the value of A1. If the cell above contains a formula, this ditto-key shortcut gives you the value of that formula, not the formula itself.

Copy Formula from Cell Above   Like Ctrl+", Ctrl+' copies into the current cell the entry stored in the cell above. But there's a crucial difference: Where Ctrl+" copies the *value* of the cell above, Ctrl+' copies the *formula* in the cell above. Moreover, it copies this formula *exactly*, without updating relative references. For example, if cell C1 contains the formula =2*A1, and you press Ctrl+' at C2, Excel enters the formula =2*A1 in C2. However, if you performed this copy operation by dragging C1's fill handle or by using the Copy and Paste options on the Edit menu, the result at C2 would be =2*A2.

Use Excel's Undo and Repeat Commands   When building and editing worksheet models, you can save yourself a lot of time by memorizing the keyboard shortcuts for Excel's Repeat and Undo commands. The shortcut for Repeat is

Alt+Enter, and the shortcut for Undo is Alt+Backspace. Unfortunately, because of horizontal space limitations, Excel doesn't display these shortcuts next to the associated commands on the Edit menu. It does display a different shortcut, Ctrl+Z, next to the Undo command. Ctrl+Z works fine as an Undo shortcut, but you may find Alt+Enter and Alt+Backspace easier to remember. Think of Enter as a go-ahead command and Backspace as a signal to retreat.

Make Entries in Many Cells at Once   To enter the same formula or value in several cells at once, select the entire range, type the formula or value, then press Ctrl+Enter. Ctrl+Enter saves you the trouble of replicating cell entries. When you terminate an entry with this keyboard combination, Excel behaves as though you had used the Copy and Paste commands on the Edit menu to copy the active cell into all selected cells, updating relative references in the process.

Instant Argument Reference   While entering a function, press Ctrl+A to see a list of the function's arguments. Do you find it hard to remember the order in which you're supposed to enter arguments for the PMT function? No problem. Type **=pmt**, and then press Ctrl+A. Excel 4.0 supplies the opening parenthesis and fills out the remainder of the formula with the names of the required and optional arguments. Just replace those argument names with the values or references you want to use. The Ctrl+A shortcut works with all of Excel 4.0's built-in and add-in functions, and you can type it immediately after the function name or right after the opening parenthesis.

Mouse Tips

Keystrokes still have power in Excel, but mice can do some things keyboards can't, especially dragging and dropping, and marking worksheet areas. Here are some tricks.

Double-Click Tricks   Depending on where you do it, double-clicking in an Excel worksheet can perform many shortcuts. The following are a few examples; spend a little time double-clicking around, and you'll probably find more.

- To change the column width to fit the longest text in any cell, double-click on the line between two column letters.

- To bring up the Format Pattern dialog box for a graphical element, double-click on the element.

- To clear more space on the screen for your worksheet, double-click on the worksheet's title bar or the lower-right corner box (directly below the down scroll arrow). The worksheet's title bar disappears, leaving only the application's title bar.

- When you want to return the worksheet's title bar to the screen, double-click on the lower-right corner box again.

Use Drag and Drop for Copies and Moves   The simplest way to move a cell or range is often to drag it with the mouse. (This capability is provided with Excel 4.0 only.) Just position your mouse pointer on any border of the cell or range you want to move. When the pointer changes from a cross to an arrow, press and hold down the mouse button, drag the selection to its destination, and release the mouse button. To copy a cell or range, follow the same procedure, but hold down the Ctrl key as you drag, making sure to release the mouse button *before* you release the Ctrl key.

NOTE   If the mouse pointer doesn't change from a cross to an arrow when you put it on a cell boundary, you may have Excel 4.0's drag-and-drop feature turned off. To turn it on, choose Workspace from the Options menu and select the Cell Drag and Drop check box.

Save Time with Excel's Context-Sensitive Help Menus   If you have the mouse pointer positioned over a cell in Excel 4.0, just click the right mouse button once to bring up a list of actions that make sense in the current context. For example, if you click the right mouse button while the mouse pointer is positioned over a cell, you'll get a brief menu of the actions you can perform on that cell, as shown in Figure 12.1. Since you don't have to move up to the menu bar and back to carry out commands, these "menus on demand" are great time-savers.

FIGURE 12.1

Access Excel 4.0's context-sensitive menus by clicking the right mouse button.

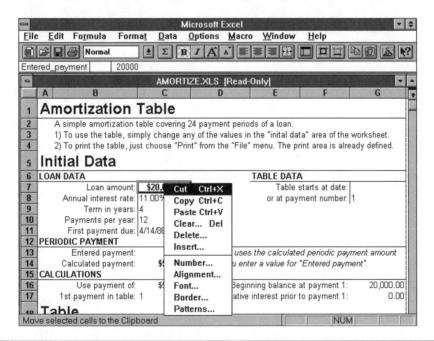

Quick Formula Reviews Double-click on a formula cell to select its *precedent* cells (the cells that make up the formula). For example, if cell Z100 reads

```
=AVERAGE(A1,B14,D13,C6:C12,X99)
```

and you can't quite recall what's in each of those cells, just double-click on Z100. Excel 4.0 will select each cell referenced in the formula. If you can't see them all at once because they're scattered all over your screen, just press Enter repeatedly. Excel 4.0 will move from one selected cell to the next, showing you the current value of each cell (on the worksheet) and the formula from which that value is derived (on the formula bar). If the cell you double-click on contains an external reference, Excel 4.0 will activate the external worksheet—loading it from disk, if necessary.

After you've inspected a cell's precedents in this manner, you can return quickly to the formula cell by using the GoTo command on the Formula menu. Goto presents a list of all your recent "went from" addresses. At the top of this list, you'll find the cell you double-clicked on. Select it in the list, click on OK, and you're right back where you started from.

When you double-click a formula cell in Excel 3.0, it will not select the entire range, but it will position the cursor in the first cell that is referenced. It will also open other worksheets from a reference.

Quick Note Review If a cell has a note attached, double-click on the cell to read the note. If you double-click on a cell that has a note associated with it, Excel displays the Cell Note dialog box, letting you read and edit the note. If a cell contains both references to other cells and a note, double-clicking brings up the note, not the formula precedents.

Create Series Automatically with AutoFill Perhaps the most brilliant innovation in Excel 4.0 is AutoFill. This feature lets you create column and row headings, date and time series, and numeric series just by dragging with the mouse. To create a row of month headings, for example, type **January** (or **Jan**) in the first cell where you want the headings to appear. Then drag the little black square at the lower-right corner of the cell (the *fill handle*). Make sure the mouse pointer changes to a plus sign (+). Excel 4.0 fills the area you drag over with the succeeding month names. To create headings for alternate months, type **Jan** in one cell and **Mar** in the next. Then select both cells and drag the handle; you get May, Jul, Sep, and so on.

NOTE If you don't see a fill handle on the active cell, choose Workspace from the Options menu and select the Cell Drag and Drop check box.

You can fill in any linear series of numbers or dates with AutoFill. You can even use it to create a series of month-ending dates. To do this, type two month-ending dates in adjacent cells; then select both cells and drag the handle. (If you extend a single month-ending date, Excel 4.0 increments by days instead of by months.) You can also use this feature to create other common label series, such as Division 1, Division 2, and so on. If you extend a text item that ends with a number, Excel 4.0 replicates the text and increments the number.

Use AutoFill to Replicate Formulas   You can also use AutoFill to copy a formula into an adjacent range, updating relative references in the process. For example, suppose cell D10 contains the formula =D9+C10. If you drag the fill handle to the right, you get =E9+D10 at E10, =F9+E10 at F10, and so on.

Formula and Function Tips

Excel has some unique formula features that these tips take advantage of.

Flawless Functions   Excel doesn't care whether you use upper- or lowercase letters in your functions, but if the function is spelled correctly, the program automatically capitalizes the function name. If you see a lowercase function name in the formula bar, you'll know it contains an error. Eliminate typos by using the Paste option on the Formula menu to plant all your formula names in the appropriate cells.

Use Intersections   The space character is Excel 4.0's *intersection operator*, which means that a reference of the form

```
Address1 Address2
```

denotes the cell at the intersection of *Address1* and *Address2*. You can use this feature to improve the readability of your formulas. If you're working with a rectangular block of cells bounded by column and row labels, start by assigning names to each column and row in the block: Select the entire block, choose Create Names from the Formula menu, and click on OK to accept the defaults in the dialog box. Once you've done this, you can reference any cell in the block by its row and column names. For example, you could reference a cell at the intersection of a row labeled South and a column labeled April as either April South or South April. To build a formula that adds the South figures for April and May, type

```
=April South + May South
```

To sum a range of South figures—say April through June—type

```
=SUM((April South):(June South))
```

Easier Random Integers   Use RANDBETWEEN to create bounded random integers. Want a random integer between 1 and 100? You can use

```
=INT(RAND()*100)+1
```

but it's much simpler to type

```
=RANDBETWEEN(1,100)
```

The RANDBETWEEN function is a handy item included in ADDINFNS-.XLA, a set of add-in functions shipped with Excel 4.0. It doesn't do anything you couldn't do yourself, but it's a real convenience if you have trouble remembering how to manipulate RAND(). To install the add-in, choose Add-ins from the Options menu, click on Add, and then select ADDINFNS.XLA from the list.

More-Readable Formulas   Use spaces to make formulas more readable. Unlike most spreadsheet programs, Excel 4.0 does not object to space characters in formulas—nor does it "helpfully" remove them for you. If inserting space between formula operands helps you decode your work later on, by all means do so.

Template Tips

Excel templates provide rich turf for tipsters.

Take Advantage of Templates   Excel's Save As command includes an option (on the Save File as Type drop-down list box) that lets you save a file as a template. Template files can store labels, formats, formulas, and anything else that normal Excel files can store, and you can create templates from charts and macro sheets as well as worksheets. Templates serve as models into which you can enter data, so they are ideal for any kind of recurrent work.

To use a template, just load it from disk as you would any other file. Excel will require that you give the file a new name when you save it, ensuring that your template stays intact and available for reuse.

Immediate Access to Templates   If you find yourself using particular template files repeatedly, store them in the XLSTART subdirectory of your Excel 4.0 program directory. (If you don't already have a directory named XLSTART immediately subordinate to the directory containing your Excel program files, you can use the Windows File Manager to create one.) When you use the New command in Excel's File menu, any templates stored in XLSTART appear in Excel's list of file types. For example, if you store a template named EX-PENSE.XLT in XLSTART, the list that appears when you choose New from the File menu will include the standard choices (Worksheet, Chart, and so on) plus a new item called Expense.

A Template with Your Own Defaults   To override Excel's worksheet defaults, create a template named SHEET and store it in the XLSTART directory. Do you tire of seeing grid lines on your worksheets? Open a blank worksheet, turn off the grid lines (with the Display command on the Options menu), and then use the Save As command to save the blank worksheet as a template. Name it SHEET.XLT and store it in the XLSTART directory. Once you've done this, all new worksheets will arrive without grid lines. You can use this technique to express yourself on virtually any of Excel's settings.

Formatting Tips

As with Windows word processors, the principal problem with formatting in Windows spreadsheets is how much of it there is. These tips note a few of the best ideas in this sprawling area.

Create More Readable Rows   Make long, information-dense printouts easier to read by simulating the effect of green-bar computer paper. First, select alternating rows of the worksheet by holding down the Ctrl key while selecting every other row. Then use the Patterns command on the Format menu to create a light gray background. When you click on OK, your printout will have a gray background that helps your eye follow the lines of the report, as shown in Figure 12.2.

FIGURE 12.2

Make rows easier to follow by creating the effect of green-bar computer paper on your worksheets.

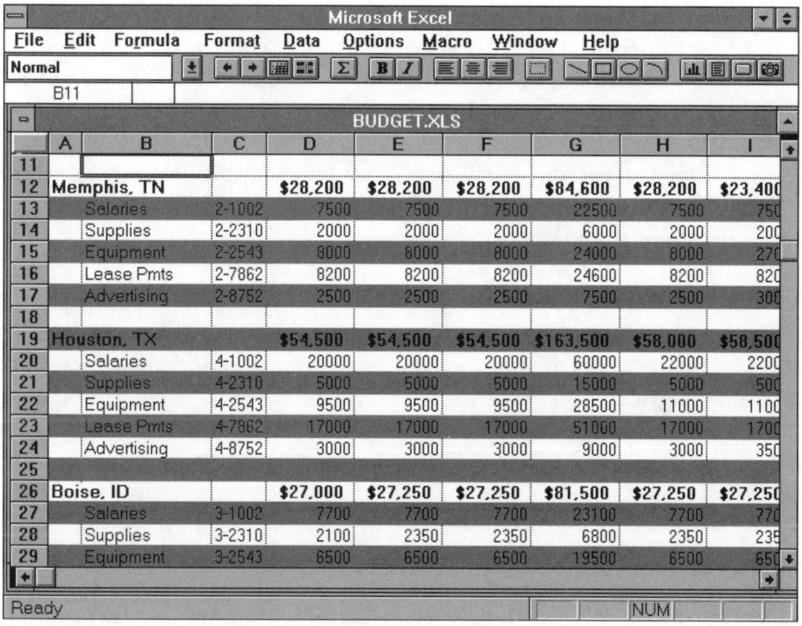

Insert Special Characters in Graphs and Worksheets   Take advantage of the Windows environment to gain access to special characters. If you often create worksheets that use international currencies, for example, you can insert the symbol for the Japanese yen (¥) or the British pound sterling (£). To access these symbols, make sure that your Num Lock is turned on. Then, while holding down the Alt key, use the numeric keypad (*not* the numbers across the top of your keyboard) to enter the number **0165** for the Japanese yen or **0163** for the British pound. Other interesting symbols include the cents sign (¢, 0162) and the copyright symbol (©, 0169).

If you use these symbols often, you might create them on a separate worksheet. When you're ready to use one, just copy it to the Windows Clipboard and then paste it to your Excel worksheet. Another option is to use Windows' Character Map to insert special characters.

NOTE   Once you've put a special character in a cell with a number, that number will no longer be included in calculations unless you develop a custom number format that includes the symbol.

Create Styles by Example   Named styles help you achieve a consistent look in your worksheets. Unfortunately, the complexity of the Format menu's Style command (and its associated dialog boxes) discourages many users from taking advantage of this feature. However, you can use styles effectively without ever visiting the Style dialog boxes. Just format your cells in the normal manner, using Number, Font, and other commands on the Format menu. Whenever you think you might want to reuse some combination of formatting attributes—say, centered 12-point Arial bold italic type—just click on the style box near the left edge of Excel's standard toolbar. This drops down a list box, as shown in Figure 12.3. Then type a name such as **Main Heading** for your combination of formatting attributes, and press Enter. That's all you need to do to define a style. From then on, within the current worksheet, you can reapply those formatting attributes just by selecting the cells you want to format, clicking the down arrow next to the style box, and choosing the name of the style you want.

Fit Text to Columns   You're about to print a worksheet with a long column of labels, and you don't want any words to come out truncated. Instead of scrolling down and checking each cell before printing, use Excel's Best Fit option to make the column just wide enough for the longest element in it. Highlight the column that you want to adjust (or the whole worksheet), select Column Width from the Format menu, click on Best Fit, and Excel will calculate the optimum width and make the necessary adjustments.

Discover Mac Date Formats   Macs and PCs save dates in different formats, a fact that drives Excel users crazy when they try to share files between the two hardware platforms. Fortunately, there's an easy fix—albeit one buried deep within the menus of Excel for Windows: Select Calculation from the Options menu. Under Sheet Options, click on the 1904 Date System check box; the dates within your spreadsheet will display using the Mac's date system.

FIGURE 12.3

Create styles to easily apply formatting attributes to your Excel documents.

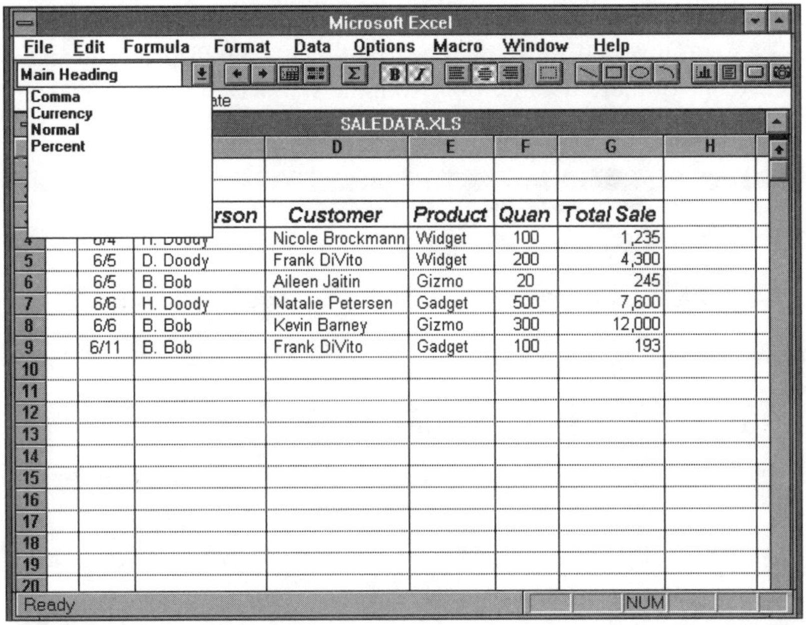

Toolbar Tips

The toolbar in Excel is similar to the Toolbar in Word for Windows. It's customizable and far more powerful than many users realize.

Use Toolbar Icons That Give You Two Tools in One   Excel 4.0's customizable toolbars are a great way to organize the tools you'll use most often. To save even more space, use tools that work one way unshifted but perform a different function in combination with the Shift key. For example, if you just click on the Enlarge Font tool, your text will grow one size larger for each click. But if you click on the Enlarge Font tool while holding down the Shift key, your text will shrink with each mouse click. Because one tool can perform two jobs, there's no need to display the tools for both tasks, so you have another slot to play with. There are dozens of tools that behave this way; see Excel 4.0's documentation for a complete list.

Use Toolbar Icons to Increase and Decrease Decimal Precision   Two of Excel 4.0's handiest toolbar icons allow you to add and remove precision from the current numeric format, one decimal place at a time. For example, if a cell is formatted to show two decimal places, you can double-click on the first of these icons to make it show four decimal places. These icons are on the Formatting toolbar, not on the default standard toolbar. (See Figure 12.4.) To access the Formatting toolbar, select Toolbars from the Options menu and select Formatting in the Show Toolbars list. You can move these icons to the standard toolbar by selecting Toolbars from the Options menu and clicking on the Customize button. (Depending on the resolution of your display, you may need to remove one or more default tools from the standard toolbar to make room for the newcomers.)

FIGURE 12.4

You can use these two icons on the Formatting toolbar to increase and decrease decimal precision.

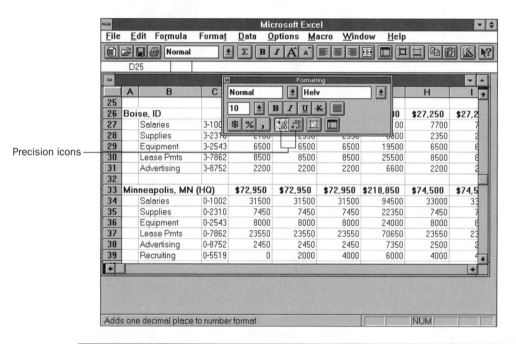

Precision icons

Use Toolbar Icons for Pasting Formats Only or Values Only   At times it's convenient to copy only selected attributes of a cell, such as the cell's value or display format. You can do that with the Paste Special command on the Edit menu, but it's a time-consuming task, particularly since the Paste Special dialog box offers no fewer than ten radio buttons and two check boxes. To make this job simple, use the Paste-Formats and Paste-Value toolbar icons. The Paste-Format tool is the third tool from the right on the default standard toolbar. To add the Paste-Value tool to the standard toolbar, select Toolbars from the Options menu, click on the Customize button, and select Edit from the Categories list. Then drag the Paste-Value tool onto the standard toolbar. (You may have to remove a default tool to make room for it.)

Worksheet Tips

Here are a couple notions for getting the most out of Excel worksheets.

Check Worksheets for Logical Errors Use the Auditor feature in Excel 4.0 to get a "bird's-eye" view of the worksheet. First, open the AUDIT.XLA macro. (It's located in the LIBRARY subdirectory if you used the default installation procedure.) Then select Worksheet Auditor from the Formula menu. When the Worksheet Auditor dialog box appears, choose Map Worksheet. Excel will display another worksheet, like the one shown in Figure 12.5, with each cell in your worksheet represented by a single character: T for text, F for formula, 9 for number, L for logical, and # for error. By looking for patterns of letters, you can more easily spot logical errors in your worksheet.

FIGURE 12.5

Check for errors in your worksheets by looking at a schematic view.

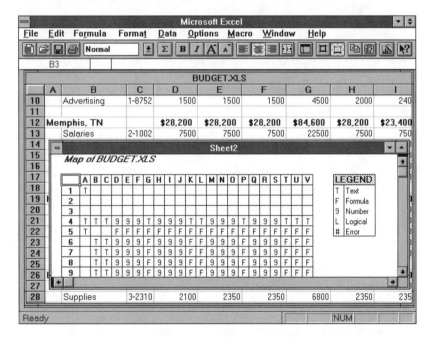

View the Same Worksheet in Two Windows When you want to see two widely separated parts of a worksheet at the same time, open a new window. You can split an Excel worksheet window into horizontal or vertical panes and then "freeze" the panes. But a simpler way to keep disjunct sections of a worksheet in view is to open a new window using the New Window command on the Window menu. The second window becomes a display unit in its own right, which you can size and move independently of the first. Place a copy of the worksheet in this window, and view any part you want while maintaining your original position in the first window.

Jazz Up Your Worksheets and Graphs with OLE   Use Excel 4.0's support for object linking and embedding (OLE) to include information from other applications that support OLE. Use the Insert Object command on the Edit menu to display a list of objects that have been "registered" in your system. For example, if you have a sound card installed in your system, use the Sound object to add voice annotation to a worksheet or graph—Excel will display a small icon of a microphone. Anyone looking at the file can double-click on the microphone icon to play back the voice message (provided they have a sound card). Other OLE-compliant applications included with Windows 3.1 include Write and Paintbrush, letting you embed .WRI files and .BMP images, respectively. Finally, if you have Microsoft's Word for Windows, you will have access to several other OLE-compliant applications, including an equation editor, a basic drawing package, and a utility to add special effects to text.

Data Entry Tips

You can build your worksheets more quickly with ideas like these.

Fill a Range with Dates in Excel 3.0   Excel's 4.0 Autofill feature makes short work of filling in series of numbers, dates, and so on. To insert a range off dates in Excel 3.0, you can use the Series command on the Data menu:

1. Enter a starting date into the first cell of the range.

2. From the Format menu, change the cell format to Number General to get the five-digit date serial number. (Excel automatically formats the entry as a date.)

3. Beginning at the starting date's cell, select the entire range of cells you want to fill.

4. Make sure that you're using the long menus, and then choose Series from the Data menu.

5. Indicate whether you want to enter the series in rows or columns.

6. Choose Date for the Type, and then choose a Date Unit interval (Day, Weekday, Month, or Year).

7. Leave the step value at 1, and click on OK or press Enter.

8. Finally, format the range with your preferred date style.

Select Multiple Groups   For those times when you'd like to apply formatting to several cells or groups of cells that are not adjacent, Excel lets you make multiple cell selections and act on all of them as a group. With the keyboard, select the first cell, press F8, and use the direction keys to extend the selection. Press

Shift+F8 to keep that selection. Then move to the first cell of the next range you want to select. Repeat this procedure to add selections. If you're using a mouse, drag through the first selection, then hold down the Ctrl key and drag through each additional selection.

Accelerating Data Entry   Save time by eliminating excess keystrokes during data entry. When you're entering data into several adjacent cells, highlight all the cells as a range. As you begin typing, Excel places the first value into the upper-left cell of the range. Simply press Enter to move to the next cell down (or across, if you've highlighted a single row). Press Shift+Enter to move up a cell, Tab to move right, and Shift+Tab to move left. Avoid using the arrow keys, which will undo the selection.

Quick Dollars-and-Cents Values   For quick entry of dollars-and-cents values, use the Fixed Decimal option (choose Workspace from the Options menu). The Fixed Decimal option in the Workspace Options dialog box lets you scale all inputs by a common factor. Setting this option to two decimal places, for example, allows you to enter $101.25 by typing **10125**, $0.25 by typing **25**, and so on, as long as the Currency style is selected. You can turn the option on and off at any time. If you're entering a long column of numbers, you can save additional keystrokes by choosing Workspace from the Options menu and selecting the Move Selection after Enter check box.

Add New Records Quickly   The simplest way to append new data to an existing database is to use the Form command on Excel's Data menu. Click on the New button to tell Excel you want to create a new record. Fill out the dialog box, and click on Close; your database automatically expands to include the new entry.

Enter Data into Several Worksheets at Once   Use the Group Edit command on the Options menu to set up parallel worksheets. Any time you need to enter the same data or formats into several worksheets at once, you can save yourself time by calling on the Group Edit command. Open all the sheets that you're going to use; then choose Group Edit from the Options menu and select the name of each worksheet in the list box that appears. From that point on, any changes you make to the current worksheet will be reproduced in all other worksheets in the group. To get out of group-edit mode, choose Group Edit again and deselect the worksheets. Alternatively, you can simply navigate to one of the other group worksheets by pressing Ctrl+F6, pointing with the mouse, or selecting the correct filename Window from the listing on the Window menu.

Button Tips

In addition to its toolbar, Excel lets you create buttons associated with specific actions and place them in your worksheets. You can save time and streamline your work with these buttons.

Lining Up Buttons Excel enables you to insert graphical objects such as lines, arrows, boxes, and macro buttons into your worksheet. These can enhance the look of a finished report, but if they're misaligned, the result is an unprofessional-looking mess. Fortunately, Excel has a snap-to feature (like those in page layout programs) that aligns objects to the grid lines in your worksheet. Once you've drawn the object, press Ctrl and use the left mouse button to drag the object. Instead of moving freely, the graphic will automatically align with the cells in its path.

Create a Fast-Save Button Make a quick-save button by using Excel's ability to activate macros from buttons that you draw in a worksheet. First, record a macro that saves the current worksheet: Select Record from the Macro menu, name the macro SAVE, and click on OK. Then select Stop Recorder from the Macro menu. Now create the macro button:

1. Click the button icon on the toolbar. In Excel 3.0, it's on the far right of the standard toolbar next to the camera icon, and looks like a rounded rectangle.

2. When the cursor becomes a cross, move it to the desired position for your button.

3. Now click the mouse button and drag down and across to draw the button—a box one cell across and two or three cells deep works best.

4. When you release the mouse button, a Button I label appears in the on-screen button, and a dialog box labeled Assign To Object pops up. Double-click on SAVE in the macro list to assign it to the button.

5. Now click on any part of your worksheet outside the button to activate the worksheet again.

6. Label the button by positioning the cursor on it and typing the desired text.

7. Test your work by clicking on the button. This should save all the changes you've made to your file.

Although this button saves only a few keystrokes, it reminds you to save your work frequently.

Printing Tips

Printing stands between your spreadsheet and the world. Make your worksheet look good on paper with these tactics.

Print Only What You Need Excel makes it easy to print a small section of a large worksheet and then goes one better by enabling you to select and print several sections in widely different areas. Use the mouse to highlight the first area to be printed. Then hold down Ctrl and use the scroll bars to find the next section and highlight it with the mouse. Repeat these steps until you've selected all the areas to be printed. Now select Set Print Area in the Options menu. Behind the scenes, Excel assigns the name Print_Area to your selection. When you choose Print from the File menu, the program prints the selections in the order in which you highlighted them.

To change the print area, simply define a new range and select Set Print Area from the Options menu again. To print the entire worksheet, select Define Name from the Formula menu and delete the name Print_Area.

Print or Format Multiple Ranges   Excel enables you to select discontinuous ranges of cells and print or format them with a single command—and you can use either the keyboard or the mouse to do this. With the keyboard, select the first cell, press F8, and use the direction keys to extend the selection. Press Shift+F8 to retain the selection, and then move to the first cell of the next range. Repeat the procedure to add selections. If you're using a mouse, drag through the first selection, hold down the Ctrl key, and drag through each additional selection.

Print Separate Worksheet Ranges on One Page   Use the Camera tool to print widely separated worksheet ranges on the same page. Unlike many other spreadsheet programs, Excel automatically issues a form feed at the end of every print job. Usually that's convenient. But when you want to print two or more ranges on the same piece of paper, it's inconvenient. In some cases, you can put two separated ranges onto the same printout simply by hiding the intervening rows and columns. If your worksheet's layout precludes that option, use the Camera tool to take a picture of a discontinuous area of your worksheet and place it near the other section you want to print.

To see how this works, assume you want to print two areas, Area 1 and Area 2. Choose Toolbars from the Options menu and double-click on Utility—the default home of the Camera tool in Excel 4.0—in the Show Toolbars list. (In Excel 3.0, this tool is located on the standard toolbar.) Select Area 2 and click on the Camera tool. Now put your mouse pointer at the upper-left corner of the area where you want Area 2's picture to appear and click. Excel will create an image of Area 2 in the designated spot. It may cover other worksheet data in the process, but that's not a problem; you can delete this picture as soon as you're through with it. Finally, select a range encompassing Area 1 and the picture of Area 2, choose Options, Set Print Area, and print.

Guarantee Up-to-Date Worksheets   After you've printed several versions of a worksheet and circulated them for comments, how can you tell which is the most current version? The Page Setup option on Excel's File menu lets you add a date and time stamp to your page footer, but it lacks emphasis. For more effective version control, insert the following formula in a prominent position on your worksheet:

```
="Printed "&TEXT(NOW(),"Mmmm d, yyyy hh:mm")
```

Every time you send the worksheet to the printer, this formula will translate the current system date and time to a text label that looks something like "Printed January 28, 1993 08:37." To make the time stamp really stand out, use Font from the Format menu to set the cell contents to bold italics.

Display Tips

Here are a couple of tips related to the look of Excel on the screen.

Extend Your Screen Display   If you have a lot of data to display, you can see more of the worksheet if you turn off the formula bar, the status bar, and the standard toolbar. To enable or disable these Excel features, select Workspace from the Options menu and make the appropriate selections in the Display section of the dialog box. Although you can reach features from the toolbar through menus and you won't always need the status bar, you might want to leave the formula bar enabled. It's difficult to edit the contents of a cell with the formula bar disabled.

Change the Default Font   To change the default Excel 4.0 font, add a line reading

```
"font=[fontname],[size]"
```

to Excel's .INI file in the WINDOWS subdirectory. For example, to change the default font to 11-point Arial, you would enter the line

```
"font=Arial,11"
```

Save your changes and restart to Excel to see the new font.

Find Your Place with the Show Active Cell Command   Here's a typical situation in Excel: You've just selected a large block of cells covering a space of some 30 or 40 rows. You're about to apply a command to this selection, but you need to take another look at the active cell. Unfortunately, it has scrolled off the screen. If you use the cursor keys to redisplay the active cell, you break the selection. You can scroll it into view with Scroll Lock or by moving your mouse up the scroll bar, but both are tedious, time-consuming procedures. Solution: Pull down the Formula menu and choose Show Active Cell. Simpler yet, press Ctrl+Backspace, the keyboard shortcut for Show Active Cell.

Lotus 1-2-3 for Windows

Lotus 1-2-3 for Windows aims to meld the traditional 1-2-3 approaches with the new potentials in a graphical environment. Sometimes it works; sometimes it doesn't. This makes for a unique blend of state-of-the-art ideas and rough interactions between the old and the new. Both those situations, though, can be helped greatly by savvy tips.

SmartIcon Tips

Lotus 1-2-3 for Windows' SmartIcons are compatible with those in Ami Pro. An icon from one program performs the same operation in the other.

Identify SmartIcons   SmartIcons can make access to some features faster and more efficient. Sometimes, though, it's not always easy to remember what one of the SmartIcons does. If you need a quick memory jog, just position the mouse pointer over the icon in question and press the right mouse button. 1-2-3 for Windows will display a one-line reminder in the title bar.

Move SmartIcons   You don't have to retain the default location of 1-2-3 for Windows SmartIcons. If you need more space on the top or bottom of your worksheet, select SmartIcons from the Tools menu to move the SmartIcons around. Move the icon palette to the bottom of the window (as shown in Figure 12.6), to either side, or make a "floating" icon palette in the worksheet area that you can move around at will.

FIGURE 12.6

Move your SmartIcons palette to another location on the screen by selecting SmartIcons from the Tools menu.

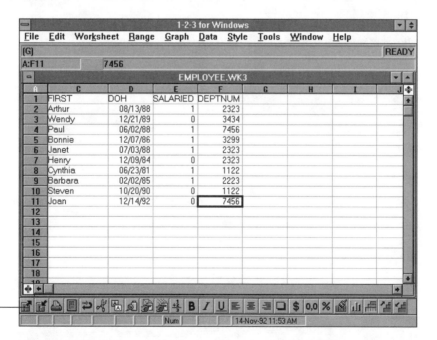

Relocated SmartIcons palette

Worksheet Tips

The worksheet is the heart of the operation in Lotus, as it is in other spreadsheets. Here are some ideas for building and manipulating worksheets quickly.

Switch Worksheets Quickly The standard ways of changing windows when you have several worksheets open—namely mouse clicks on the title bar or selecting options from the Window menu—aren't always the quickest. Here are some speedy keyboard shortcuts. You initiate the shortcuts by pressing Ctrl+End, which brings up the word "File" in the status bar next to the current date and time.

Ctrl+End, Ctrl+PgUp	Move to the next file
Ctrl+End, Ctrl+PgDn	Move to the previous file
Ctrl+End, End	Move to the last file opened
Ctrl+End, Home	Move to the first file opened

Edit Cells in Title Rows and Columns Select Titles from the Worksheet menu and pick the Both option to "freeze" the rows above and the columns to the left of the cursor so that they remain visible. (See Figure 12.7.) As you move through the worksheet, you'll always see the row and column labels that identify your data.

FIGURE 12.7

Select the Both option in the Worksheet Titles box to keep row and column labels visible as you move through the worksheet.

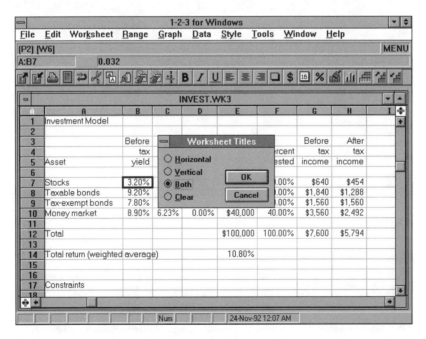

Once you've invoked the command, however, you can't use your arrow keys to move into the title region, so it's inconvenient to edit a misspelled or incorrect title or to add a title to a new row or column. Here's a handy trick for editing a label in the title area without clearing your titles: Press the GoTo key (F5), and then use the arrow keys to move into the title area. To get out of the title area and return to Ready mode, just press Enter.

Use Separate Sheets to Keep Elements Straight Let 1-2-3's three-dimensionality help you maintain worksheet order by segregating functionally distinct modeling areas. With the help of the Worksheet, Insert, Sheet command (select Insert from the Worksheet menu and select the radio button marked Sheet), you can pack up to 256 row-and-column grids into a single 1-2-3 file. Use one for titles and a description of your model, a second for input values, a third for calculations, another for reports, and so on. If you write macros, it's especially desirable to put them on their own page. That way, you won't inadvertently destroy macro code by deleting worksheet rows or insert space into code by adding new rows to your model.

Tips for Moving, Entering, and Copying Data

These tips will speed the building and rearrangement of Lotus 1-2-3 worksheets.

The Safest Way to Move Cells There are three ways to move cells on a 1-2-3 for Windows worksheet: with the classic-menu /Move command, with the Edit menu's Move Cells command, and with the Cut and Paste commands. Avoid the third method; it can damage the logic of your worksheet. When you move a cell with the Cut and Paste commands on the Edit menu, any relative references it may contain are updated. If cell A3 has the formula +A1, for example, cutting and pasting it to B3 makes it read +B1. (Of course, this could not happen if you used the absolute reference A1.) When you use /Move or Move Cells on the Edit menu, references are not updated. Moreover, if the cell you move is itself referenced elsewhere on the worksheet, the cut-and-paste procedure does not change the referencing formulas to point to the cell's new location, but the other two methods do.

Copy Values, Not Formulas To freeze the current values from a range of formulas, select the range, choose Quick Copy from the Edit menu, select the Convert to Values check box, and click on OK.

Copying External-Reference Formulas If you copy an external-reference formula with the Copy and Paste commands on the Edit menu, 1-2-3 treats the reference as absolute, even if you've written it to be relative. Worse, if you use Copy and Paste to replicate an external-reference formula in several adjacent cells at once, the reference will be treated as absolute in the first target cell and relative in each remaining target cell. To avoid these hazards, use either Quick Copy on the Edit menu or the SmartFill function included with the SmartPak. (See the section "SmartPak Tips" on page 441 for more information about SmartPak.)

Quick Date Entries When you're creating a schedule in 1-2-3 for Windows, use Data Fill to create all your date entries. To fill cells A4 through A34 with consecutive dates starting January 1, 1993, for example, select the Fill command in the Data menu, and enter **@DATE(93,1,1)** in the Start box. To generate a daily list, select 1 as the Step value, and insert any large number in the Stop box—press any number four or five times and press Enter or click on OK. For a list of weekly dates, use 7 as the step value.

Formatting Tips

Formatting is perhaps not as strong an area in Lotus 1-2-3 for Windows as in other Windows spreadsheets. But you can make it stronger with these ideas.

Remove Style Attributes   You can remove numeric formats from a 1-2-3 range quickly and easily by choosing the Format command in the Range menu and clicking on the Reset button. But there's no comparable button for resetting style attributes: color, shading, borders, alignment, and fonts. To restore default style settings to a range without deleting the contents of the range, choose the Edit menu's Clear Special command. Then deselect the Cell Contents check box, shown in Figure 12.8.

FIGURE 12.8

Use Lotus 1-2-3 for Window's Clear Special command to remove style attributes from cell contents.

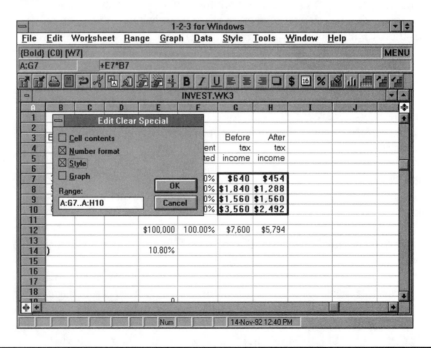

If you just want to remove some aspect of a cell, such as the numeric formatting or a style assignment, use the Clear Special command on the Edit menu to delete only the element that you don't want.

CAUTION 1-2-3 does not leave check-box options the way you last set them. Thus, even if you use Clear Special only for deleting style attributes, you'll need to make the same check-box selections each time.

Delete Formatting and Cell Contents Pressing the Delete key erases a cell's contents but leaves the formatting and style information in place. You can clean a cell out entirely by using the Clear Special command (on the Edit menu) with its default check-box settings, but a simpler technique is to press Shift+Del. This action cuts the cell and all its attributes to the Clipboard, leaving you with a blank, unformatted, unstyled cell. A mouse alternative for Shift+Del is the Scissors SmartIcon.

Copy Style Attributes The Edit menu's Quick Copy command includes a check box labeled Styles Only that allows you to copy styling attributes—colors, fonts, alignment, borders, and shading—from one range to another. Use this command, in preference to the Format-Painting SmartIcon, when you want to copy styles but not numeric formats.

Easy Dates and Times If you assign the Automatic format to a range of cells by selecting Format from the Range menu and scrolling down to Automatic, you can then enter dates and times without using formulas. For example, if you type **7/9/93** into an Automatic format cell, 1-2-3 recognizes your entry as a date and gives you 07/09/93. The same formatting technique allows you to enter currency values with dollar signs and commas. In general, if a cell has been given the Automatic format, you can type an entry the way you expect to see it displayed.

Format Multiple Worksheets When 1-2-3's Group mode is on, style and formatting changes that you make to any worksheet page are copied instantly into all other pages in your worksheet. Changes to cell contents are not copied. To turn Group mode on, choose the Worksheet Global Settings command in the Worksheet menu and select the Group Mode check box. The word "Group" will appear in the status panel at the bottom of your screen, as shown in Figure 12.9.

Name Frequently Used Styles If you expect to use a particular combination of attributes in many different places on a worksheet, you can save yourself a little trouble by using the Name command on the Style menu. For example, suppose you plan to begin each page of a multisheet worksheet with a heading in 24-point Arial bold, centered across five columns, with red letters on a green-stippled background. Start by assigning the appropriate style attributes to the first of these headings. Then choose Name from the Style menu. You'll see a dialog box with eight numbered slots. In the first slot, type a six-character name for the style (for example, **Head01**) and a description of up to 36 characters (for example, **24-Arial bold, red on shaded green**). When you want to reuse this style combination, pull down the Style menu and choose the appropriate slot number.

NOTE You cannot assign numeric formatting to a named style.

FIGURE 12.9

The word "Group" in the status bar at the bottom of the screen means Group mode is
on and any style or formatting changes made to one worksheet page are reflected on
all the other pages.

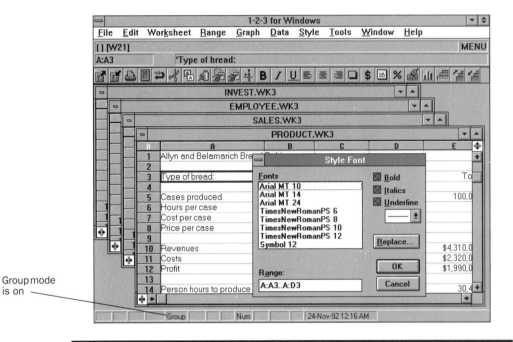

Group mode
is on

Copy Styles and Formats   The default SmartIcon palette includes a handy
Paintbrush icon that lets you copy both style attributes and numeric formats, but
not cell contents, from one range to another. Simply select the source range containing the styles and formats you want to copy, click on the Paintbrush icon, and
then drag the mouse across the target range. The mouse pointer will change
from an arrow to a paintbrush as you do this. One caveat: The target range must
be on the same worksheet page as the source range; 1-2-3 will let you navigate
(by keyboard) to other pages and will appear to copy your source range, but no
copy will occur.

Create Centered Headings   The Align Over Columns check box, in the
Style Alignment dialog box, makes it a snap to center headings over a range of
columns. Just type the label you want to center in the leftmost cell of the range.
Then choose Alignment from the Style menu, select Align Over Columns and
Center, and click on OK (see Figure 12.10). Alternatively, you may use the
Alignment option to set up the heading range first, and then type the label
later. If you do this, though, you need to type the centered-label prefix character (^) at the beginning of your label. Otherwise, 1-2-3 will align your label
flush left within the heading field, even though you have previously selected
the Center option.

FIGURE 12.10

Center column titles with 1-2-3's Style Alignment option.

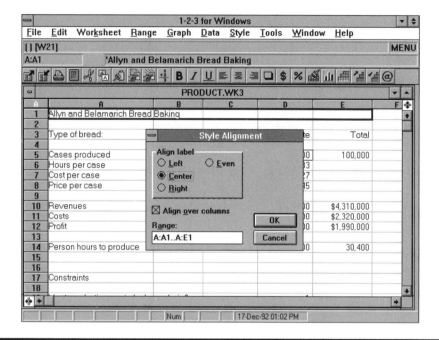

Formula and Function Tips

Increase the calculation clout of Lotus 1-2-3 spreadsheets with these tactics.

Easy Functions   1-2-3 includes an "at-sign" (@) SmartIcon that can simplify the job of entering functions. When you click on this icon, the program presents an alphabetical list of all available functions. You can then use the scroll bar or the cursor keys to locate the function you need. The @ icon is not part of the default SmartIcon palette, but you can add it by choosing SmartIcons from the Tools menu and clicking on the Customize button. Scroll through the box labeled Standard icons until you locate the function icon (it's in the top row, just about halfway through the available icons). Click on it to select it, select Add, and it will appear in the current palette. Select OK to exit the Tools SmartIcons dialog box. If you're working on a standard VGA screen, you may need to remove one icon from the palette to make room for the addition.

Shorten Calculation Time   Chances are some of your spreadsheets contain formulas that calculate the same values over and over again. For instance, if a worksheet still contains an @SUM formula that you used to calculate final sales figures for the previous quarter, 1-2-3 will continue to calculate the same figure whenever you recalculate the spreadsheet. Shorten recalc time by turning these formulas into values. To turn a single cell into its current value, press Edit (F2),

Calc (F9), Enter. Your worksheets will recalculate faster if you eliminate formulas that have already served their purpose.

Take Advantage of the @PMT Function   If you're thinking of buying or refinancing a home, you'll want to know about Lotus 1-2-3's financial functions. The @PMT function uses the syntax

```
@PMT(principal,int,term)
```

where *principal* is the amount loaned, *int* is the interest rate, and *term* is the term of the loan. The interest rate should reflect the period each payment covers (as opposed to an annual rate), and the term is the total number of payments (not years) over the course of the loan.

   If you want to find out what the monthly payments will be if you borrow $95,000 for 15 years at an 8.05% annual interest rate, enter the formula

```
@pmt(95000,.0805/12,15*12)
```

Dividing .0805 by 12 converts the yearly interest rate into a monthly rate, and multiplying the number of years by 12 supplies the function with the total number of payments.

Quicker What-If Scenarios   What-if experimenting is easier when you place formula arguments in separate cells and reference those cells. For example, if you're using the @PMT function described above, you can put the formula

```
@PMT(B2,C2/12,D2*12)
```

in cell A2. Enter the amount borrowed in cell B2, the yearly interest rate in C2, and the number of years in the term in D2. Add identifying labels for principal, interest, and term in row 1.

   If you want to see the effect on your monthly payments of a change in the amount borrowed, interest rate, or term, you won't have to retype the whole formula. Just enter different numbers in the appropriate cells.

Retain Formulas in Templates   You can transform a spreadsheet designed to handle a specific situation into a general template for analyzing similar situations. To retain formulas and labels while zeroing out numerical data for an entire spreadsheet, first press Home to return the cursor to cell A1. Then select Combine from the File menu, choose Subtract Entire-File, and enter the name of the file currently in memory. Next choose Save from the File menu and enter a new filename; this will be the name of your template for the file.

   Be aware, however, that any cell that contains a calculation that you regard as data but 1-2-3 regards as a formula (such as 12/5) will not go to zero. Also, there may be certain numbers, for example tax percentages, that aren't restricted to a particular case. If that's so, remember to reenter such numbers in the appropriate cells of your template.

Display Days of the Week   You can display the day of the week a particular date falls on by combining three handy 1-2-3 @functions:

- @DATEVALUE takes a label that looks like a date and turns it into a number that 1-2-3 uses to perform date arithmetic. Each date is assigned the number of days that have elapsed since the turn of the century.

- @MOD finds the remainder left when its first argument is divided by its second argument.

- The first argument of @CHOOSE chooses between the remaining arguments. The remaining arguments are assigned numbers starting with 0. @CHOOSE returns the argument whose designated number matches the first argument.

To use these three functions to display days of the week, follow this example: In cell B2, enter an apostrophe and the date of your choice in mm/dd/yy format. The apostrophe ensures that your entry will be interpreted as a label and not as a calculated number.

In cell B3, type

```
@choose(@mod(@datevalue(B2),7),"Saturday","Sunday","Monday",
 "Tuesday","Wednesday","Thursday","Friday")
```

@DATEVALUE turns the contents of B2 into a date number. @MOD returns the remainder of this date number when divided by 7.

The difference between any two date numbers that fall on the same day of the week is always an exact multiple of seven (the number of days in a week). Consequently, the date numbers of any two dates that fall on the same day of the week have the same remainder when divided by seven. The @CHOOSE function turns this remainder into a day of the week.

If you want to find the day of the week another date falls on, just type that date as a label in cell B2.

SmartPak Tips

Lotus has provided three free upgrades to 1-2-3 for Windows since its initial release in the fall of 1991. Unless the company has begun shipping version 2.0 by the time you read this, you should be working with version 1.1, and you should also have received an add-in macro called SmartPak. If you don't have these items, request them from Lotus by calling (800) 872-3387, extension 6866, or download them from the LOTUSA forum on CompuServe (GO LOTUSA). To check the version number, select About 1-2-3 from the Help menu.

Use SmartPak to Create Crosstabs   Included in SmartPak is a CrossTab macro that lets you summarize information stored in a 1-2-3 database. Select the range you want to cross-tabulate, choose SmartPak from the Tools menu, and then pick CrossTab. The macro will prompt you for a field to use for row headings, a field to use for column headings, and the field whose values you want to summarize. You may apply any of five statistical functions to the value field: @SUM, @AVG, @COUNT, @MIN, or @MAX.

One caveat: Because the CrossTab macro doesn't include an option to gather numeric or date values into groups, you may need to preprocess your database before running it through the tabulator. For example, suppose you have a database that records financial transactions and has fields named Date, Amount, Account, Payee, and Category. If you want SmartPak to create a crosstab that shows how much you spent per month in each category, you'll first need to create a new field that extracts the month from each transaction date. Then you can tell the CrossTab macro to use Category as its row field, Month as its column field, and Amount as the field to summarize.

Use SmartPak's Preset Formatting   The SmartFormat section of Lotus's SmartPak add-in lets you choose from nine preset formatting combinations—five in color and four in black and white. If you find Lotus's designs suitable, you can use SmartFormat to enliven whole worksheet blocks with a single stroke. If you like to work with color on the screen but you print in black and white, you may also want to use SmartFormat as a quick palette-switcher. Before printing, select the range you're going to print, pull down the Tools menu, choose Smart-Pak, and choose SmartFormat from the cascading menu. Then select one of the four black-and-white options in the dialog box that appears.

Create Series with SmartFill   The SmartFill component of Lotus's Smart-Pak add-in makes it easy to create headings for month names. Just type **January** in one cell, select that cell plus the rest of your month-heading range, choose SmartPak from the Tools menu, and then select SmartFill from the cascading submenu. 1-2-3 will supply the rest of your month names automatically. If you want your headings to display only every other month, start by creating the first two—January and March, for example. Then select *both* headings, extend the selection, and call up SmartFill.

NOTE   You can also select the SmartIcons option from the Tools menu and then use the Customize command to put a SmartFill icon on the palette. (To learn how to do this, choose Index from the Help menu, search for SmartIcons, and then choose the topic named Tools SmartIcons Customize.) You then use this SmartIcon just as you do the SmartFill menu item.

You can use SmartFill to create numeric series and series of labels that include a mixture of text and numbers (for example, Division 1, Division 2, and so on). The principle is the same as for date series: Create either a one-cell or a two-cell pattern, and then extend that pattern and invoke SmartFill. If your pattern includes only one cell, SmartFill increments by 1. If it includes two, SmartFill bases its action on the interval between the two.

CAUTION Be sure the range into which you extend a SmartFill pattern is blank. The macro overwrites anything in its path—without issuing a warning.

Use SmartFill to Create an End-of-Month Date Series If you ask SmartFill to extend a series that begins with two month-ending dates, the program is clever enough to recognize that you want a whole series of month-ending dates, not a series based on the number of days between the pattern cells. Begin with July 31 and August 31, and you'll get September 30 next (not the mythical 31st). The caution from the previous tip holds here, too.

Create Custom SmartFill Sequences One of SmartFill's better features is its willingness to let you design your own sequences. Suppose you frequently need to create the following set of labels: Pitcher, Catcher, 1st Base, 2nd Base, 3rd Base, Shortstop, Left Field, Center Field, Right Field, and DH. Use Notepad or another plain text editor to open the file SMARTFLL.INI (it's in your 1-2-3 for Windows program directory), and add a new [SET #] section. As soon as you save the modified .INI file, you can use the new SmartFill set in your worksheets. (You don't have to restart 1-2-3 for Windows to make the additions available.)

Lotus has supplied two custom sequences as examples—one that enters the names of all of Lotus Windows products and another that enters the names of the planets. Therefore, if you leave those examples in place, your first custom sequence will go under the heading [SET 3], the second under [SET 4], and so on. Each set can specify up to 99 items. If any of the items is a label beginning with a number (for example, 1st base), you must include a label-prefix character—an apostrophe, carat, or double-quote mark, depending on your alignment preference. And if any of your entries begin with numbers or include internal uppercase letters, you should add the optional line case=exact. Otherwise, if your first pattern entry begins with a capital letter, 1-2-3 will capitalize the first alphabetical character of every other entry, so you'll see 1St base, 2Nd base, and so on.

Display and Printing Tips

Here are some ways to make Lotus 1-2-3 look better on screen and on paper.

Easier-to-Read LCDs The gray background used by 1-2-3 for Windows dialog boxes creates a stylish appearance on a color VGA screen. If you find it a hindrance on your LCD, you can turn it off by modifying the 123W.INI file. Open the file with a plain text editor, such as Notepad, search for the line that begins

```
;Great_looking_dialogs=
```

and replace whatever is to the right of the equal sign with a 0. Then save the file and restart 1-2-3.

Two Views, One Window   Since 1-2-3 for Windows won't let you open two windows on the same file, use the split-screen feature to divide one window into "panes." Grab a button with double-headed arrows from the left of the horizontal scroll bar or above the vertical scroll bar—the mouse pointer changes to a cross with a horizontal two-headed arrow when you find the right spot. Then drag the button out or down—the vertical line that appears in the worksheet shows where the file will be split when you release the mouse button. This doesn't affect the file contents on disk; it's just a way to look at two different parts of the worksheet.

Draft-Mode Printouts   As in releases 2.*x* and 3.*x*, /Print in 1-2-3 for Windows gets you a fast plain-text printout, no matter how your worksheet appears on screen. However, even if you have previously specified a print range when you select the Print command from the File menu, you still need to tell /Print what range you want to print. The File menu's Print command and its classic-menu counterpart (:Print) maintain one print range, and /Print maintains another. To specify the range, press the / key, select Print from the menu that appears, select Printer, Range, and enter a range.

Print Multiple Ranges on the Same Page   The Windows-menu File Print command automatically issues form feeds at the end of each print job. To combine separated worksheet areas on a single page, you can use the classic-menu counterpart, /Print, just as you would in one of the DOS versions of 1-2-3. The program will print your selection without ejecting the final page. Then you can use the /Print, Printer, Line command to advance the page a line or two, define your next print range with /Print Printer, Range, and so on.

Print Multiple Copies   In porting 1-2-3 to Windows, Lotus disabled the classic-menu :Print, Settings, Copies command. (This command was part of the WYSI-WYG menu tree in 1-2-3 release 2.*x* and release 3.*x*.) To get more than one copy of a printout, choose Printer Setup from the File menu, click the Setup button, and change the number in the Copies box. You can print as many copies as you want this way, but you'll have to collate them yourself. Be aware that 1-2-3 will not record your Copies setting when you save your file; the program resets this parameter to 1 when you quit.

Set Printing Defaults   You can easily set up 1-2-3 so that it always prints the name of your company at the top of each page, the current date at the bottom, and so on. You can make any combination of the program's Page Setup options the default, just by selecting Page Setup from the File menu, setting the options as you want them, and clicking on the Update button.

Save Different Printing Defaults   1-2-3's Page Setup dialog box includes a Save button that lets you record the current settings in a file. Thus, if you use particular headers and footers, margin settings, or other printing options again and again, you can save yourself time and trouble (and ensure consistency) by encapsulating those settings in files. Just click on Save and supply a filename (1-2-3 will add the extension .AL3). To reuse a group of settings, go back to the Page Setup box dialog and click on Retrieve.

Performance Tips

If you want to speed up Lotus 1-2-3 for Windows, try these approaches.

Use Draft Mode   1-2-3's draft-mode display option provides faster screen performance. In this mode, the program does not display any style attributes (such as bold and italic) on the screen, but it still uses them in printouts. It also suppresses the display of grid lines, recreating the unlined look of 1-2-3 releases 2.*x* and 3.*x*. You can toggle in and out of draft mode by choosing Display Options from the Window menu and selecting the Draft check box. To make draft mode the permanent default, click on the Update button before you leave the Display Options dialog box. Note that in draft mode, you can select ranges by dragging with the mouse, but 1-2-3 won't highlight the selection. In addition, you cannot change column widths by dragging with the mouse.

Conserve Memory by Turning Off Undo   1-2-3's Undo command consumes quite a bit of memory. If you're working with very large files, you may need to turn off Undo. To do so, choose User Setup from the Tools menu and deselect the Enable Edit Undo check box. Note that if the MEM indicator appears at the bottom of your screen, you may first need to quit the program. Then restart, turn off Undo, reload your file, and try again.

Conserve Memory by Knowing the Limits of Your Worksheet   Formatted cells take up memory, even if the cell contains no data. If you have formatted cells that contain no data, shrink your spreadsheet with the Extract command on the File menu. To do this, highlight the range containing data, choose Extract from the File menu, choose Formulas, enter a name for your modified spreadsheet, and press Enter.

Speaking of cells with no data, to quickly find out the area of a worksheet that does contain data, press End and then Home. Suppose that pressing End, Home lands you in cell R217. This means that any cell outside the range A1..R217 is blank—that is, it contains no data and is not specially formatted. You may not have made any changes to cell R217 itself; however, at least one cell in row 217 and one cell in column R are not blank.

Turn Off Screen Refresh for Speedy Macro Execution   To accelerate the execution of a macro, turn off the Windows screen refresh feature whenever you can. Use 1-2-3 for Windows' {WINDOWSOFF} command at the start of a macro to turn off screen refresh, and insert {WINDOWSOFF} again at the end to turn refresh back on. This not only speeds execution, it also improves the look of your screen during macro execution by suppressing high-speed scrolling and cell updates.

Tips for Users of Classic 1-2-3

DOS Lotus 1-2-3 users have built up a lot of muscle memory over a decade of using spreadsheets. If you fall into that category, here are some ideas that will help you cope more effectively with the new graphical world.

Movable Menus   Longtime 1-2-3 users instinctively press the slash key (/) to access the Lotus menu structure as shown in Figure 12.11. In 1-2-3 for Windows, that same key brings up the "1-2-3 Classic" menu bar. If the menu's default location gets in your way, click somewhere within the title bar and drag it elsewhere, perhaps toward the bottom of the screen. Once it's there, it will reappear there every time you press the slash key. Alternatively, press the colon key (:) for Release 3.1's Classic menu, which lets you access that version's graphical features.

FIGURE 12.11

Longtime 1-2-3 users can access the Classic menu by instinctively pressing the / key.

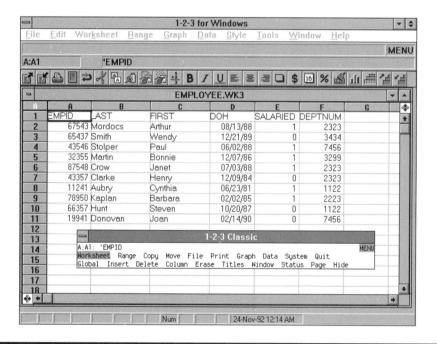

Classic 1-2-3 Users Can Learn Windows Commands   1-2-3 for Windows' Help system can do a lot to ease the transition from classic menus to native Windows menus. If you press F1 while highlighting any classic-menu command, a Windows Help message tells you where to find the equivalent command on the pull-down menus.

Switch to Another Windows Application   When you're working in a 1-2-3 dialog box, or in the classic-menu window, you may not be able to switch to another Windows program by pressing Alt+Tab. In most cases, however, you can switch away by pressing Ctrl+Esc to summon the Windows Task List. If you've used Program Manager to assign a keyboard shortcut to the program you want to switch to, that shortcut will still be available as well.

File-Linking Tips

Linking across spreadsheets is critical for Windows spreadsheets. These tips maximize this function in Lotus 1-2-3 for Windows.

Easy Links   Suppose you want to write a formula in SHEET2.WK3 that grabs the value at A1 of SHEET1.WK3. Both worksheets are open in memory and you've maximized the current document window. You type a plus sign in SHEET2.WK3 and click the Window menu to activate SHEET1. 1-2-3 for Windows beeps; the Window menu, the scroll bars, and the SmartIcon palette are all unavailable while you're in the middle of creating a formula. Fortunately, you don't have to write that external-reference formula out by hand. Start by tiling SHEET2 and SHEET1. Make sure both the cell you're working in and the cell to which you want to link are visible. Type your plus sign, and click in the desired cell in the other worksheet. 1-2-3 will create the linking formula for you.

Update Specific Links Only   To update only specific file links, copy the range that contains the link to itself.

Quattro Pro for Windows

Generally considered the most innovative of DOS spreadsheets, Quattro Pro is a latecomer to the Windows wars. However, in an interesting reprise on DOS history (where Quattro was the last major player to appear), Quattro Pro for Windows bears a slew of innovations that set it apart from other programs. We start here with tips about some of those new ideas.

Page Tips

Quattro Pro for Windows contains a new metaphor for building spreadsheets. It structures sheets like pages in a notebook. In this way, many spreadsheets can be viewed as part of a whole divisional budget for part of a corporation, for instance. Working with these fresh ideas offers some unique new options in Quattro Pro for Windows.

Name Pages   When building multipage spreadsheet notebooks in Quattro Pro for Windows, assign names to each page. The names will help you remember the structure of your notebook. Because page names can be used in formulas, just like cell and range names, they can also help you document the logic of your model. For example, suppose the first four pages of your notebook are named 1990, 1991, 1992, and 1993. If you write a formula to average the values at cell F10 on each of the first four pages, Quattro Pro will automatically spell that formula as:

```
@AVG(1990..1993:F10)
```

which is easier to read and understand than the equivalent

```
@AVG(A..D:F10)
```

To name a notebook page, position the cursor on its tab at the bottom of the worksheet grid and click the right mouse button. Quattro Pro will activate the page you selected and at the same time display its property inspector, as shown in Figure 12.12. The first option in the Active Page property inspector lets you assign or edit the page's name.

FIGURE 12.12

To name a notebook page, right-click on its tab and call up this dialog box.

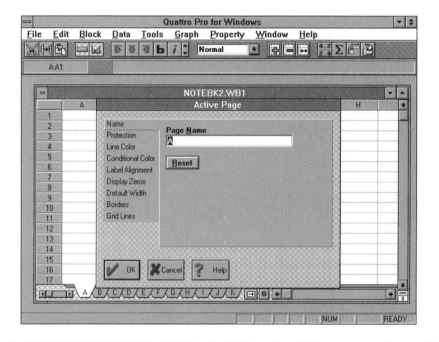

Name Groups of Pages   You may also sometimes find it useful to assign names to groups of consecutive pages—to create named sections within your notebooks. For example, you could assign the name LastFourYears to a block of pages named 1990, 1991, 1992, and 1993. You could then create formulas that reference the entire block by its name. For example, if pages 1990 through 1993 were named LastFourYears, you could find the average value of cell F10 on these four pages by writing the formula

```
@AVG(LastFourYears:F10)
```

To assign a name to a group of consecutive pages, choose Define Group from the Tools menu. In the dialog box, supply the name for the group, the first page of the group (either the page's letter coordinate or its name, if you've named the page), and the last page of the group.

Print Groups of Pages at Once　If you use consecutive pages to store parallel worksheets—divisional expense figures, for example—you'll appreciate Quattro Pro's ability to print them all with a single command. Just select a block that begins on the first page of the group, hold down the Shift key, and click on the page tab for the last page of the group. Then choose the Print command on the File menu. In the dialog box that appears, click on the Options button. The Print between 3D Pages section of the ensuing dialog box lets you choose between having each page printed on a separate piece of paper or combining the whole works. If you do the latter, you can tell the program how many lines of separation you want. Once you've expressed your preferences, return to the Print dialog box and click on the Preview button to see how it's all going to look.

Protect Pages　Put critical data on its own page and turn on protection for that page. Like many other spreadsheet programs, including the DOS versions of Quattro Pro, Quattro Pro for Windows assigns the "protected" attribute to all cells by default but leaves protection globally disabled. To make the protection effective, you have to use an enabling command. Unlike other programs, however, Quattro Pro lets you apply the enabling command on a per-page basis. Thus, you can have protection on for certain pages of your notebook and off for others. If there are particular portions of a model that you do not want anyone—yourself included—to modify, put those elements on their own pages and turn protection on for just those pages. To enable protection for a page, right-click on its page tab. Then click on the word "Protection" and click on the Enable option button.

Data Entry Tips

Data entry is key in Quattro Pro, as in other Windows spreadsheets. Use these notions to get the best performance possible.

Create Rows and Columns Quickly　You can use Quattro Pro's SpeedFill feature to create both column headings and row headings in a single stroke. For example, you can quickly fill in column headings for the months of the year and row headings for Group 1, Group 2, and so on. Type **January** at B1 and **Group 1** at A2. Select the range A1 through M10 (or whatever range you want to fill) and click the SpeedFill icon—the second icon from the right on the default worksheet SpeedBar. Quattro Pro for Windows fills out the row and column labels for you.

SpeedFill can also work with discontinuous selections. So another way to use SpeedFill for row and column headings at the same time is to select the column headings, hold down the Ctrl key while selecting the row headings, and then click on the SpeedFill icon.

Enter Formatted Dates　If you start a cell entry with Ctrl+Shift+D, and then type a date in a recognized date format, Quattro Pro will convert your entry to the appropriate serial date value and display it as a formatted date. For example, to enter the date July 4, 1993, you can press Ctrl+Shift+D and then enter **7/4/93** or 4-Jul-93. Quattro Pro will record the value 34154 and display it in the format you typed. You can also enter times in much the same manner. To enter 3 p.m. in a cell, for example, you can press Ctrl+Shift+D and then enter **3:00 PM**.

Dates Only   If you have earmarked an entire range for dates, you may want to take advantage of another Quattro Pro data entry feature. Select the range and right-click anywhere within it to get the object inspector for the range. Choose Data Entry Input, and then select the Dates Only option button. Now begin entering dates in your range, in the format you want Quattro Pro to use for display. For example, type **11/16/93** if you want Quattro Pro to display that date in the "long international" date format.

CAUTION   If you apply the dates-only data entry property to a cell, you must remove that property before you can enter any other kind of data in the cell. Even if you just want to increment a date by appending a +1 to its value in the formula bar, you must remove the dates-only property.

Formatting Tips

One reason Quattro Pro for Windows was late to market is that the DOS version of Quattro Pro was nearly as good at formatting and graphics as most Windows programs. Now, the Windows version of Quattro Pro offers some clever new formatting options.

Speed Formatting   Quattro Pro for Windows' SpeedFormat icon, which is at the right end of the default worksheet SpeedBar, offers a handy set of pleasing formatting combinations (see Figure 12.13). You can use it to instantly transform a drab block of numbers and labels into something stylish and arresting. In some cases, however, you may want to use only selected elements of a formatting combination. If you like the colors and type styles, but don't want the dollar signs, deselect the Numeric Format check box in the SpeedFormat dialog box. Similarly, if you want to skip the gray shading in the rightmost column and bottom row, deselect Column Total and Row Total.

Copy Formatting   When you select Copy from the Block menu, all properties and contents of the source range, apart from column widths, are replicated. If you want to transfer the properties only, leaving cell contents behind, select the Copy command from the Edit menu instead of Block. Then paste with the Paste Special command. In the Paste Special dialog box, deselect the Contents check box.

Delete Cell Formatting   As in the DOS versions of Quattro Pro, pressing the Delete key in Quattro Pro for Windows deletes the contents of a cell while leaving all the formatting information in place. To clean out a cell completely, returning it to its default condition, press Shift+Delete instead of Delete. This cuts the cell to the Clipboard, taking with it all properties except for column width.

FIGURE 12.13

Click on the SpeedFormat icon to easily change style attributes in your spreadsheets.

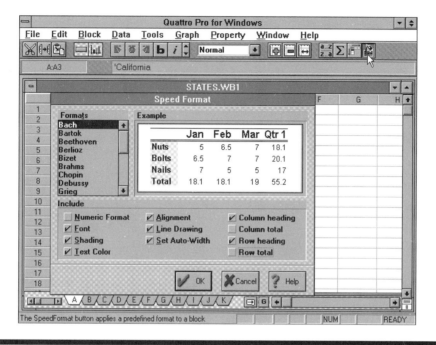

Perfect Column Widths   The double-headed blue arrow near the right side of Quattro Pro for Windows' default SpeedBar (shown in Figure 12.14) automatically adjusts a column's width to accommodate the contents of the current cell and any cells below in the same column. Here's one nifty thing about this feature: If you have spillover labels near the top of a column and you select any cell below the labels, the Automatic Width icon will adjust the column's width for everything below the labels but continue to let the labels above spill into adjacent columns.

Create Custom Formats   Need a display format that's not included in Quattro Pro's default set? Use the Active Block property inspector to create your own. Select the block you want to format, right-click anywhere on the block, and select User Defined at the bottom of the format list. In the right side of the dialog box, click on the arrow to reveal the drop-down list box, and then define your custom format. You can use custom formats to replace a numeric display with text (for example, to hide cell contents with the word "Confidential"), add units to a numeric display, spell out dates more fully, include weekday names in date displays, and so on.

Quattro Pro also allows you to specify value-dependent display colors. This formatting feature, however, must be applied to entire notebook pages; you can't incorporate conditional colors into a custom numeric format and apply it only to a particular cell or range. To specify value-dependent colors, right-click on a page tab and choose Conditional Color.

FIGURE 12.14

The double-headed arrow icon automatically adjusts the width of columns.

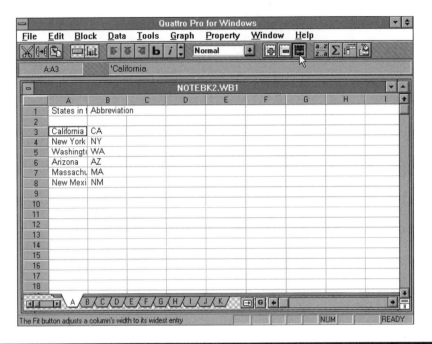

Tips for Moving Data

The new concepts in Quattro Pro for Windows bring new ways to move data.

Drag and Drop Single Cells   Quattro Pro lets you move and copy work-sheet blocks by dragging with the mouse. When you click on a block selection, the mouse pointer changes from an arrow to a hand. To move the block, just drag it and drop it at its new destination. (The program will warn you if you accidentally drop the block onto an area of the worksheet that already contains data.) If you want to copy the block instead of moving it, hold down the Ctrl key while you drag.

Unfortunately these conveniences are not available for single-cell copies and moves. When you click on a single cell, the pointer does not change to a hand. In some cases, however, you can overcome this limitation just by grabbing the cell you want to drag *and* one of its neighbors. For example, suppose you want to move the data in A1 to cell D10. If A2 happens to be blank, try dragging both A1 and A2.

The Best Way to Move Cells and Ranges   You can use two different menu commands to move Quattro Pro cells and ranges. You can transfer cells via the Clipboard, using the Cut and Paste commands on the Edit menu. Or you can use the Move command on the Block menu. Use the latter; the former is dangerous.

If you cut and paste a formula cell via the Clipboard, any relative references it may contain are left unchanged—as they should be. If cell A3 contains the formula +A1, and you cut-and-paste it to B3, it still says +A1 when it arrives at B3. But the Clipboard maintains a copy of that cut cell, and should you paste it a second time, Quattro Pro will (incorrectly) update its relative references. For example, if you paste the same cell a second time at C3, the formula changes to +C1—probably not what you had in mind.

And that's not all. Suppose the cell you cut to the Clipboard is referenced by a formula somewhere else. Suppose, for example, that cell A4 contains the formula 2*A3. As soon as you cut A3 to the Clipboard, the formula at A4 returns 0, because it now references a blank cell. When you paste, all is well again. Paste at B3, for example, and A4's formula changes from +A3 to +B3. But what if you get interrupted in the middle of your work and forget to paste that formula? Now you have a damaged worksheet.

Play it safe and stick with the Move command on the Block menu for relocating worksheet cells. Reserve the Cut command on the Edit menu for two purposes: moving graphic objects and erasing all attributes (contents and formatting information) from a cell.

Move Data across Pages   The Copy command on the Block menu presents a simple dialog box with a From line and a To line. Your current selection always appears as a default on the From and To lines. To specify the target for your copy operation, select the To line and then point. If the target is on a different notebook page, point to the target's page tab. You can even use this technique to copy a cell or range from one page into several pages at once. For example, to copy A1..F1 from page A to pages B through F, you could select A1..F1, choose the Copy command from the Block menu, tab to the To line, click on the page tab for page B, hold down the Shift key, click on the page tab for page F, and then click on OK.

Move Data across Notebooks   The To and From ranges in a block move or block copy operation may be in different notebooks, but you can't point to a target range in another notebook unless that range is already visible on the screen. Therefore, if you plan to move data between notebooks with Move or Copy on the Block menu, it's a good idea to arrange your screen with the Window menu's Tile command before going to the Block menu.

How to Extend Selections   When you click the mouse on any selected block of cells, the pointer changes to a hand, indicating that Quattro Pro expects you to initiate a drag and drop maneuver. This behavior has both virtues and drawbacks. It makes it easy to drag and drop, but it makes it awkward to extend a selection. If you've already selected A1..A2, for example, and you want to add A3 to the selection, you can't simply drag the mouse from A1 to A3, because Quattro Pro will interpret that action as a command to relocate A1 and A2. The simplest way to extend the selection in this case is to hold down the Shift key while clicking on A3 (or whatever cell you want to extend the selection to). Alternatively, you can click anywhere on the worksheet to break the original selection, and then drag the mouse from A1 to A3.

Display and Printing Tips

There are tricks you can use to improve the look and feel of Quattro Pro both on-screen and in printouts.

View Different Parts of a Notebook at Once   When you need to see two or more parts of a notebook at the same time, use the New View command on the Window menu. This command lets you open multiple windows on a common notebook file. Each new window can be sized and positioned independently of every other. The New View command is handy when you need to see two or more notebook pages at the same time. You may also find it a convenient way to keep widely separated sections of a single notebook page in view.

Turn Off Grid Lines and Frames   If you're using particular notebook pages as repositories of display text (a title page for a notebook, for example), consider turning off the worksheet frame for those pages. You'll free up some window room by doing so. Similarly, on pages devoted to database tables, you might want to turn off horizontal grid lines, leaving just the vertical lines to separate your database fields. Quattro Pro provides unusual flexibility in these matters, allowing you to turn off and on both the grid lines and the worksheet frame— horizontally, vertically, or both—on a page-by-page basis. To change page settings, select Active Page from the Properties menu or right-click on the page tab.

Set Display Zero Preferences   Unlike the DOS versions of Quattro Pro, Quattro Pro for Windows records your preferences about the display of zero values when you save your file. If you always want your zeros suppressed, you no longer need to write an autoexec macro to take care of this detail. What's more, in Quattro Pro for Windows you can control the display of zeros on a per-page basis. To turn the zeros on or off for any page, right-click on its page tab and choose the property labeled Display Zeros.

Set Properties for Maximized Documents   Normally, you set document-wide properties in Quattro Pro by right-clicking on the document window's title bar. To turn off automatic recalculation, for example, you right-click on the title bar of your notebook and select Recalc Setting options. But if you maximize your document window, you no longer have a document title bar. In that case, you can set document-wide properties by choosing the Property menu's Active Notebook command or by pressing its keyboard shortcut, Shift+F12.

Printing Multiple Copies   Don't use your printer driver's Setup dialog box to specify copies or orientation. Quattro Pro for Windows' Print dialog box includes a Copies setting. To specify multiple copies of a printout, use this File menu option, not the Copies setting in your printer driver's own setup dialog box. Quattro Pro ignores the latter setting! Similarly, to switch between portrait and landscape orientation, use Quattro Pro's Page Setup dialog box, not the Orientation setting in your printer driver's setup dialog box. The latter has no effect on Quattro Pro's behavior.

Print Files to Disk   Use the Printer Setup command on the File menu to redirect a printout to a disk file. Quattro Pro's Printer Setup command makes it easy to send a printout to a disk file. Just select the Redirect To File check box and specify a filename. A handy Browse button is available to help you find names of files you've used before.

Preview Color as Black and White   Use the File menu's Print Preview option to see how color formatting will appear on a black-and-white printout. Your colorful worksheet may look dazzling on the VGA screen, but will it play on paper? Quattro Pro's Print Preview screen includes a Color button that removes some of the guesswork. You can use this button to toggle your preview between color and monochrome. If the monochrome rendition looks intolerably muddy, try applying one of Quattro Pro's SpeedFormats to your print range. Several of these "canned" formats are designed specifically for monochrome screens and printers.

Tips for Quick Access

Here are a couple of final shortcuts to get to specific areas of Quattro Pro for Windows quickly.

Quickly Move to Graphs   The last page of any Quattro Pro's notebook is called the *graphs page*. All graphs associated with a file are stored here, along with any slide shows, custom dialog boxes, or custom SpeedBars you create. Contrary to your expectation, perhaps, the direct route to the graphs page is not the G symbol at the bottom of the notebook window (which puts you in Group mode) but the arrow to the left of the "G." Click here to go forthwith to the graphs page. Click here again to return to whatever page you left.

To return directly to the first page in your notebook, press Ctrl+Home. Unfortunately, this keystroke combination is inactive if you're on the graphs page. To get from there to page 1, you must return first to a worksheet page and then press Ctrl+Home. One quick way to do this is to hold down the Ctrl key and press PgUp, Home.

Get to the Most Recently Used Files   To reuse a file that you've had open during a working session, open the drop-down File Name list. To do so, select Open from the File menu. Quattro Pro's Open File dialog box includes a handy drop-down arrow to the right of the File Name line. Click here to see the names of all files you've opened during the current session. To reopen a file, just select its name.

13 DRAWING AND PRESENTATION PACKAGE TIPS

THE GRAPHIC PRESENTATION OF INFORMATION REPRESENTS A KEY TO BUSINESS creativity and efficiency. Under DOS, PCs were mediocre at all aspects of graphics. With its character-mode origins, DOS was never a hospitable home for artistic and design pursuits.

Windows offers a much more natural environment for graphics. For the first time, PCs have some of the graphical gifts that have made Macintoshes so popular. As an entirely graphical environment, it's no surprise that Windows should attract a new crop of graphics-oriented software. But what may be surprising is the characteristic that most definitively separates Windows' graphics applications from all other software. It's not merely how they produce pictures and fancy type, but how they interact with other programs. The biggest role for graphics packages in Windows is to provide drawing and display tools that spreadsheets, databases, word processors, and other programs can share.

As we've mentioned before, in Windows no program stands alone, and that's eminently true for graphics packages.

So here we look at both the basic operations of Windows graphics programs—image creation, slide production and the like—and the ability of these programs to spread design and drawing power to other applications.

Aldus Persuasion

It's not surprising, considering Aldus' background in desktop publishing, that Persuasion builds presentations from a text core. In this program, you first create an outline, then you fill in the outline with the text you want displayed, and then Persuasion automatically builds a presentation for you.

This makes Persuasion one of the swiftest and easiest to use of graphics programs—as long as you stick with what it gives you automatically. When you want it your way, Persuasion can become much more challenging. So that is the focus of many of our tips here.

Slide and Presentation Tips

If you want something in your presentation that *isn't* part of Persuasion's automatic repertoire, try these tricks from expert users.

Incorporate Graduated Fills into Your Slides Graduated fills aren't restricted to backgrounds; you can use them in portions of a slide. For example, to fill a rectangular area in a single slide, select Slide Master from the View menu.

Then, from the Master pull-down menu, select Set Background. In the Set Background dialog box, click on the Fills drop-down list box and choose the graduated fill. (Make sure that the Use Background Master box is *not* checked.) Next use the Square Corner tool (it looks like a box) to block out areas not covered by the rectangle. Assign these blocks a solid fill by choosing Fills from the Show menu and then choosing Solid. Assign the same blocks a solid color using Colors from the Show menu. When you've masked every area but the rectangle, the graduated fill shows up only there.

Number Your Slides Automatically　Unlike the Macintosh version of the program, PC Persuasion does not have a page number placeholder feature. In order to number your slides, use a universal Background master. Select the Text tool and press Ctrl+Shift+3 (make sure to use the 3 on the numeric keypad). A # will appear on the Background master, as shown in Figure 13.1. The slides will automatically be numbered from one upwards.

FIGURE 13.1

Persuasion automatically numbers slides if the slide numbering option (the # box in this figure) is added to the universal Background master that you are using for your presentation.

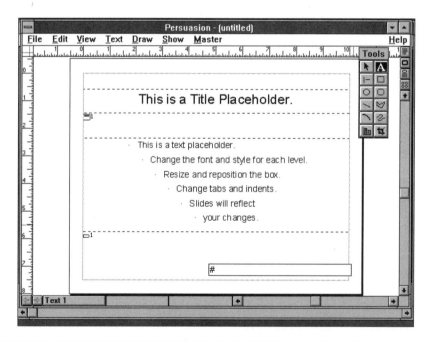

Make Thumbnails of Your Presentation　To create a thumbnail view of your presentation for use as a handout or outline, select Handout Master from the View menu. Four slide copy placeholders and four title placeholders appear on the handout master sheet. To add more slides, choose the Master menu's Add

Slide Copy option. To add more Title placeholders, select Add Title from the Master menu. With a little sizing, 12 slide copy placeholders (thumbnails) fit nicely on a page. You may need to delete the lines provided for note taking for all of the slide copy placeholders to fit.

Create a Defaults Stylesheet To retain standard defaults for each new presentation you make, open the file NEW.AT2 as an Original file. Select Open from the File menu. In the Open dialog box, select the directory containing NEW.AT2 (usually PR2US). Choose NEW.AT2 from the Files list box. Under Open at the bottom of the dialog box, click on the original option button. Set your default Background master colors, fills, target printers, and other elements, and then save the file. Now every time you create new presentations by selecting New from the Open menu, your defaults will be in effect.

System and Operation Tips

Here's a potpourri of tips for squeezing the most power from Persuasion through wise use of the program itself and the system beneath it.

Breeze through Data Sheets The best way to enter data quickly in a data sheet is to highlight the entire range where you plan to enter the data. Input data in the first cell, press Enter, and you'll immediately move to the next cell in the highlighted range.

Create Perfectly Spaced Duplicates Persuasion has a little known multiple duplication feature that automatically offsets duplicates. First, select and copy the original object, and then paste it. This creates a duplicate in the center of the slide. Move the duplicate where you want it, and then press Ctrl+K. This pastes a second copy in the same relative position as the first copy is to the original (two lines down, two slides apart, whatever). Repeat this process as often as necessary to create more copies.

Change Organization Charts Effortlessly It's easy to change the bottom level of a Persuasion organization chart. First, select the chart, and select Org Chart Info from the Draw menu. In the Org Chart Info dialog box, set the lowest organization chart level by double-clicking on one of the options: Boxed List, Horizontal Boxes, List, or Vertical List Right.

Slimming Down the ALDUS.INI File for Faster Loading Persuasion loads every import and export filter whenever you start the program. If startup is too sluggish, check which filters you have installed, and remove the unnecessary ones. Here's how. Select the Help menu, hold down Ctrl and click on About Persuasion. You'll get a complete list of filters and dictionaries installed. Note the ones you don't want, and then open the ALDUS.INI file in Notepad. Find the lines that contain the filter names and prefix each one with a semicolon. This prevents the line from loading, but lets you run it when you need to by simply removing the semicolon.

Viewing TrueType Fonts If you're using one of the MAGICorp printer drivers that comes with Persuasion, Windows TrueType fonts won't be visible to you. In order to have access to these fonts, you must use a Windows printer driver. To change the current driver, get into Program Manager's Main group, select Printers from the Control Panel and choose the appropriate driver for your printer.

CorelDRAW!

The Canadian program CorelDRAW! offers a vast array of drawing tools, clip art, display options, and other nifty features. Hailed since its introduction as the first drawing package that nonprofessionals could use, CorelDRAW! is now in its third version, and probably offers the widest single-product smorgasbord of graphics possibilities in the market today.

CorelDRAW!'s 150 fonts are so numerous that scrolling down the list to Zürich Calligraphic can rival a Friday afternoon commute in trying your patience. These tips will assist you in getting more from this huge array of typefaces.

Rename Fonts to Typeface Standards Like many type products, CorelDRAW! uses nonstandard names to identify many fonts to avoid copyright infringement. If you know fonts, keeping track of the substitute names can be downright confusing. Fortunately, Corel's Typeface Reference Chart provides translations of the fake font names, and with a little work you can rename them in the menus. Use Notepad to open WIN.INI and go to the section headed [CorelDrawFonts]. Change the font name at the beginning of each line to the common name, ensuring that you leave no gaps between words—use the underscore to separate them. Don't alter the rest of the line, as it contains data that refers to Corel's font files. When you're done, save the file and restart Windows.

Even solidly performing graphics software can do with a bit of extra oomph and improved printing speed. That's where these tricks come in.

Disable Thumbnails CorelDRAW! displays a handy thumbnail preview of a file's contents so that you don't waste time opening the wrong drawing, but the thumbnail itself slows down operations such as saves. If your complex drawing takes too long to save, try disabling the thumbnail. In versions prior to 3.0, open Notepad and, from your CORELDRW directory, open CORELDRW.INI. Use the Search function to get to the line

```
CDRHeaderResolution=1
```

Change the 1 value to 0, and then save the file. This sacrifices the preview, but can save long minutes of drawing time. To bring back the thumbnails, change the 0 value back to 1. In version 3.0, select Options in the Open Drawing dialog box and deselect the Preview check box. You'll see a diagonal line in the Preview window instead of the thumbnail.

Speed Up Screen Redraws   When the preview window is showing, you can speed up Corel's notoriously sluggish redrawing by previewing only a particular part of the design at one time. Choose Preview Selected Only from the Display menu to limit the preview to the section you're working on.

Eliminate Banding in Fountain Fills   Fountain fills look attractive on screen, but can print with distinctly unimpressive banding. To improve the look of laser-printed fills, choose Print from the File menu to bring up the Print Options dialog box and increase the number of Fountain Stripes. Start out at around 80, or slightly higher if the filled area is large. However, since increasing the number of stripes slows screen redraw, use only five stripes until you need to print.

Add Nonprinting Notes   Complex CorelDRAW! graphics often require annotations (you might want to remind yourself or someone else of special output instructions, for example), but you'll seldom want such notes to print. Fortunately CorelDRAW! enables you to write nonprinting notes. Choose the Text tool, click on the page as usual, and write your note. Then set the line and fill for the text to None. The words will appear in wireframe views of the page, as shown in Figure 13.2, but will neither preview (as shown in Figure 13.3) nor print.

FIGURE 13.2

Add nonprinting notes to your CorelDRAW! graphics, and the notes will only appear in the wireframe view. This lets you annotate your work.

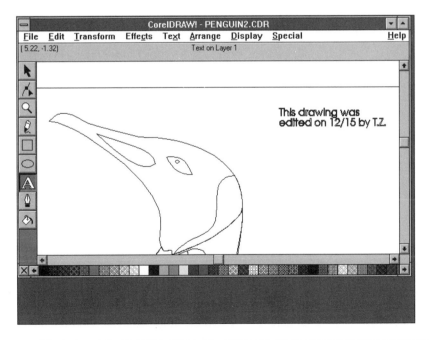

FIGURE 13.3

The note does not appear in the preview screen or when the drawing is printed.

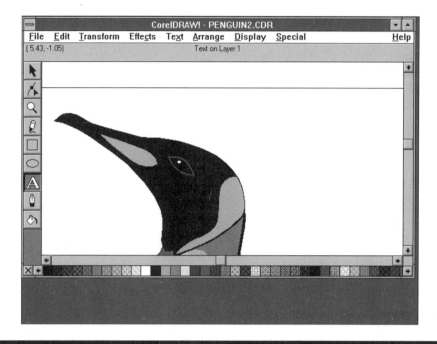

Lotus Freelance for Windows

One of the easiest presentation packages to use, Freelance enables you to create straightforward slide shows almost effortlessly. The tips here show a few ways to push the operation of this solid performer.

Skip the Opening Screen   To skip the "Welcome to Freelance Graphics" screen, you can add the /Q parameter to Freelance's command line in Program Manager: Select the Freelance icon in Program Manager, choose Properties from the File menu, and add the /Q parameter to the command line—for example, C:\FLW\FLW.EXE/Q. The next time you start Freelance, the welcome screen will be omitted.

You can also skip Freelance's opening screen by editing the FLW.INI file found in the WINDOWS directory. Open FLW.INI in Notepad or another text editor, locate the line that reads Skip Welcome=0, change the 0 to a 1 so the new line reads Skip Welcome=1, and save the changes to FLW.INI. The next time you start Freelance, the welcome screen will be bypassed and Freelance will be opened with the last SmartMaster that was in use.

Import a Drawing onto a Blank Page   When you are importing a drawing into Freelance for Windows, the Import function is not accessible unless a SmartMaster is selected. To get around this limitation and import the drawing onto a blank white page instead of onto a SmartMaster, select New from the File menu and choose NOMASTER.MAS as the SmartMaster file for the presentation. NOMASTER.MAS is a blank SmartMaster.

View All Your SmartIcons   The number of SmartIcons visible depends upon the position of the SmartIcon Palette. If it is in the Top or Bottom position, only 27 SmartIcons are visible; if it is in the Left or Right position, only 17 are visible. To view all of your SmartIcons, change the position of the palette to floating and increase its size: Choose SmartIcons from the Tools menu, select the Floating position, and click on OK. Click and drag on one of the corners of the palette until all the icons are visible.

Printing Hatch Patterns with a Hewlett-Packard LaserJet III   When you print a presentation that contains hatch patterns on a Hewlett-Packard LaserJet III, the patterns often appear as shades of gray, even though they look fine on the screen. This happens because the printer resolution is set at 300 dpi, making the hatch patterns print very closely together. To see the hatch patterns, change the printer resolution to 150 dpi. Unfortunately, if you are using ATM fonts in the same presentation, they will appear jagged at the lower resolution. In this case you should change to an internal HP font, such as CGTimes, which will print correctly at a resolution of 150 dpi.

Minimize Freelance's Disk Space   Freelance takes up about 12 megabytes of disk space, including the tutorial, and there are no options to install only certain components upon setup. To regain some of the space once Freelance is installed, consider deleting the tutorial once you are finished with it. SmartMasters that you aren't ever likely to use are also likely candidates for deletion. In the Freelance manuals, you can preview the SmartMasters and decide which ones you don't need. You can always reinstall these .MAS files later or save them to a floppy disk so that you can easily copy them to your system if you decide that you need them.

If you are on a network with other Freelance users, create a MASTERS directory on the network that can be shared. Store the contents of the MASTERS subdirectory, which includes symbols, palettes, and SmartMasters, which take up about 6 megabytes of disk space. Once the files are copied to the network drive, edit the MASTERS directory path so that Freelance will be able to find the files. Select User Setup from the Tools menu, select Directories, and specify the new network path.

Harvard Graphics for Windows

Harvard Graphics utterly dominated DOS presentation graphics. Now, the product has migrated to Windows. This is a good news/bad news situation. The good news is that Harvard Graphics for Windows brings compatibility and a natural migration path for the horde of customers for the DOS versions. The bad news is that the burden of maintaining that DOS past limits the freedom with which Harvard Graphics can exercise new Windows possibilities.

These tips run the gamut from basic charting à la DOS to high-end features new to Windows.

Drawing and Charting Tips

Harvard Graphics established the basics of charting that all products now use. These tips show how to get more from a most solid set of charting tools.

Highlighting Sections of an Organization Chart   To draw attention to a specific section of an organization chart in Harvard Graphics for Windows, such as a division or workgroup, change the color or attributes of this section. To accomplish this easily, select one of the boxes and change the attributes as you desire. Then simply use the eyedropper tool to transfer these attributes to those of the other boxes in the section.

Quick Chart Resizing   When you select the Add Chart to Slide option from the Chart menu, Harvard Graphics for Windows automatically places the chart full-screen, on top of your current chart or drawing. Quickly resize the new chart by clicking on it to select it, and then dragging on one of its corners or sides until it is the desired size.

Create Pictographs   Bar charts are great ways of showing off data, but a more effective way is to use a shape or graphic to represent the barred data. This type of representation is called a pictograph. To create a pictograph in Harvard Graphics for Windows, create a chart and select the chart element that you want to fill. Choose the Bitmap option from the Color icon, and set the bitmap to vertical tiling (see Figure 13.4).

A Slice of Pie   To reposition a slice of a pie chart, select the slice by double-clicking on it. When the selection handles appear inside the slice, drag it to the desired location.

Create Transparent Chart Backgrounds   If a slide contains a chart, the slide background is not visible through the chart frame by default. To make the slide background visible through the chart, select the chart frame by clicking on it, click on the color icon, and choose None as the fill color.

Easy Duplicate Objects   To duplicate an object you've already drawn, select the object and hold down the Ctrl key while dragging the object to the desired location for the copy. When you release the Ctrl key, a duplicate object is inserted in the new location, while the original object does not move. To align a duplicate object with the original, hold down the Shift and Ctrl keys as you drag the object to the desired location. It will snap to the proper vertical or horizontal line.

FIGURE 13.4

Jazz up bar charts in Harvard Graphics by creating pictographs of the data.

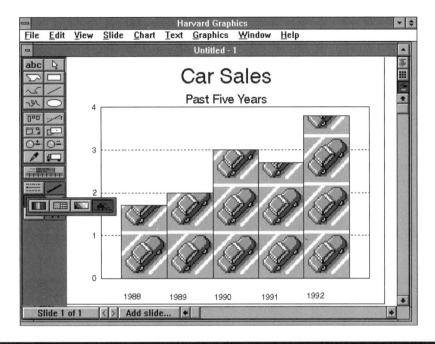

Presentation and Printing Tips

You can improve your custom presentations and printer performance with the tips below.

Copying Slides between Presentations   When copying a slide from one presentation to another, make sure that both presentations have the same printer setup. For example, if one presentation is set up for PostScript, a pasted chart could look very different even though the other options remain the same. This difference results from different margin settings for each different device. Locate each presentation; then select Printer Setup from the File menu to see what output is in place.

Share Backgrounds among Presentations   To transfer a background from one presentation to another, open the presentation that contains the desired background, as well as the presentation that you want to transfer it to. Select Arrange Tiled from the Window menu. Select a slide that contains the desired background from the first presentation and choose Copy to copy the slide and its background to the Clipboard. Click on the second presentation and select Paste from the Edit menu to bring the slide into the presentation from the Clipboard. In the Paste Background dialog box, select a new name for the slide and select Rename. From the Slide menu, choose Background, Apply, and the newly named background will appear in the list of choices. Select the background and it will be applied to all of the slides in the new presentation. Remember to delete the slide that you pasted in from the original presentation.

Custom Handouts   Harvard Graphics for Windows lets you create and print handouts for your presentation. To do so, choose Setup from the File menu, click on the Handouts option button, and select the desired layout. To customize these handouts, go into the Slide Editor and choose Edit Handouts Master from the Slide menu. Add text, drawings, borders, or other elements to give your presentation a personal touch.

Import ASCII Files into the Outliner   When importing ASCII text files into the Outliner, Harvard Graphics for Windows creates a separate slide each time it encounters a hard carriage return. You can remedy the situation and consolidate these slides after Harvard Graphics is finished importing the text. By placing the cursor at the top line of a slide and pressing the Tab key, you can bring the slide's text into the previous slide. It will appear as a bulleted item. Likewise, if the ASCII document you are importing into Harvard Graphics contains Tabs, each Tab will appear as a bullet in the Harvard Graphics slides.

Speed Up PostScript Printing   If printing to a PostScript printer seems to take forever, make sure that you are using PostScript, not Bitstream, fonts (such as Dutch or Swiss). To change an existing presentation to a PostScript font, choose Change Presentation Font from the Presentation menu, and choose a PostScript font, such as Times or Helvetica. PostScript font names are preceded by an asterisk. To avoid using a Bitstream font in the future, select a PostScript presentation style (any style that begins with a P) and save it as your default style.

Best Printing for Slides   For best results when printing a presentation, set up the printer that you intend to use before you begin creating the slides. Because text appearance and line spacing values vary from one output device to another, selecting the output device before you even create the presentation ensures that you get the results you expect.

Micrografx Designer, Draw, and Charisma

Micrografx was the first Windows software developer. Over the decade since Windows 1.0, this Texas company has amassed an unmatched knowledge of Windows' intricacies, along with the most complete line of Windows graphics products.

Micrografx's greatest success has been with design professionals who have come to rely upon powerful products, such as Designer and Charisma. With the release of Windows 3.0 and 3.1, the company is reaching out to a wider audience with Windows Draw, a fun and easy-to-use set of basic drawing tools.

This section covers all three Micrografx products.

Tips for Charisma, Draw, and Designer

Because they share some operating modules, Micrografx's programs handle some tasks identically. These tips will work with more than one Micrografx program.

Change the Default Path for Saving Files   There are two options for changing the default path that Designer or Charisma uses to save files. From the File menu, choose Open, type the path that you want the files saved to (such as C:\PRESENTS), select Save, and then choose OK. Or you can add a line to the WIN.INI file's [Charisma] or [Designer] section. For Charisma, add the line path=*path*, for example

```
path=C:\PRESENTS
```

For Designer add a line that says drawings=*path*, for example

```
drawings=C:\DRAWINGS
```

Center Text within an Object   In Micrografx Draw, Charisma, or Designer, it's easy to center text within an object that you've drawn. To do so, draw the object and select it by clicking on it. Then hold down the Shift key while you select the Text tool. When you begin typing, the text will be centered within the object.

Customize Your Toolbox   Charisma and Designer allow you to customize your toolbox, sparing you wasted time and confusion by having just the tools you use readily available to you. Because the tools you need will depend upon the drawings you do, it makes sense to take note of which tools or commands you frequently access before making any changes to the toolbox. (Every command has a tool icon that corresponds to it.) Even if you don't want to make any additions or deletions to the current toolbox, you can always change the order of icons so that they are grouped together in clusters that make sense to the way you work. For example, you can position all of the drawing tools near one another.

To add or delete tools, select the Tools command from the View menu. You'll see a menu bar that's a duplicate of the regular one. Selecting or deselecting a command on the menu bar determines whether its tool appears in the toolbox.

Three tools you'll want to add to your collection are the Pattern Color, Line Color, and Background Color tools (these show up in the toolbox as PC, LC, and BC, respectively). These tools make it easy for you to get to color palettes for each item, and they also show you the color for each element of the selected object. In a layered object, being able to see these colors is helpful if you want to change colors, but you're not sure which item is which color.

If you've got so many items in your toolbox that you don't have enough room to add any more, here's what you can do to free up some space without losing any functionality: Delete the Square and Circle tools because you can draw squares and circles with the Rectangle and Ellipse tool. To draw a perfect square with the Rectangle tool, hold down the Ctrl key while you draw. Likewise, you can draw a circle with the Ellipse tool by holding down the Ctrl key as you drag.

Finally, you can change the order of items in the toolbox. If you've added new items (nondefault tools) to the toolbox, they'll be positioned at the bottom. You won't be able to insert them elsewhere—for instance, near other tools that perform similar actions. To change the order of tools, you need to edit WIN.INI. Before opening WIN.INI, determine the desired tool position by counting down how many tools from the Pointer tool (which is the first tool and cannot be moved or deleted) it is. For example, if you want the Rounded Rectangle tool to occupy the position of the seventh tool on the toolbar, you'd be counting six down from the pointer.

Now open up WIN.INI in SysEdit or a text editor and locate the [Charisma] or [Designer] section. Find the line that begins with Tools=. After the equal sign, you'll notice a series of numbers separated by spaces, with 1 being the first. These numbers represent each of the tools in the toolbox. Go to end of the line and locate the number that corresponds with the Rounded Rectangle (424). Select the number and cut it; then go back to the beginning of the line. Count over seven groups of numbers and insert 424 there, followed by a space. The next time you start Charisma or Designer, the Rounded Rectangle will occupy the position you selected.

Tips for Micrografx Designer

Here are a few secrets specific to Designer, Micrografx's toolkit for sophisticated graphic artists.

Easy Global Changes   Once your drawing begins to get complicated, you'll often want to change something common to many different objects—say the shade of a red pattern color. Don't waste time highlighting different objects; go straight to the File menu's Select option. This enables you to choose all objects with specific properties, such as background color, lines, patterns, and font. Select can also seek out objects with a combination of properties, such as a red pattern color with a blue line.

Import File Fix   Occasionally, Designer imports a bitmap or vector file with the colors reversed. This happens most often with AutoCAD.DXF files, so there's a fix built into the DXF input dialog box: Simply select the Reverse Black/White box. If you get negative images from a TIFF file import, it's probably in compressed format. You can fix reversed TIFF images by opening the file in another program and saving it as an uncompressed TIFF file.

Output to a Plotter   Designer's CAD-like capabilities make its drawing files a natural for output on a plotter, but if you're using outline fonts, plotters won't print the text. Select Text Font to check that this is the case, and if so, convert fonts to vectors by selecting Text Convert to curves and pressing OK. Once converted to curves, text can be manipulated like any drawing, but you can't edit it, so use this technique just before sending your illustration to the plotter.

Use Replace for Fine-Tuning   Designer's Replace function makes it easy for you to do precision drawing and detailing on an object without having to work on a small scale and deal with zoom, even if your image size is very small. Replace takes an object that is copied or pasted to the Clipboard and then lets you paste it on top of a different shape whose dimensions you want it to take on. For example, if you've drawn a small circle that you want to do a great deal of work on, copy it to the Clipboard. Next draw a large square, the size of which is comfortable for doing the kind of editing that you plan for the circle. Select Replace, and the copy of the circle replaces the square, but retains its large dimension. Once you've done your editing, choose Cut from the Edit menu to place the large circle on the Clipboard, select the original small circle, and choose Replace. The edited circle will appear back in its original size.

Troubleshooting Font Cache Problems   If you notice that you are using up a great deal of system resources when working in Designer, chances are it's a font cache problem. To stop this resource drain, edit your WIN.INI file to match the following:

```
[Micrografx Fonts 4.0]
Font Cache=0
Character Cache=0
Bitmap Cache=0
```

Setting these values to zero means that Designer uses the minimum values for each cache (3, 1,024, and 100, respectively).

Charisma Tips

Charisma is a sports car among graphics programs. It's a subtle and sophisticated package that offers ultimate control over the creation of business graphics. It is aimed at departments that produce business shows and presentations fulltime. Charisma is all about customization, which is what these tips home in on.

Create Custom Bullets   You can draw an image in Charisma and save it as a bullet that is always available to you. To do so, draw the image, select it, and assign it a symbol ID. Open the File menu, choose Save As, give the bullet a name (keep the .DRW extension), and save it to the Templates directory. Next, select Bullet from the Options menu and choose Open. You'll be presented with a list of files; open the one that you just saved.

Windows Draw Tips

Windows Draw is by far the simplest of Micrografx's offerings. Draw's straight-forward nature makes it easy to use, but masks surprising power. These tips aim to unlock some of that hidden clout.

Delete Portions of Shapes and Lines Precisely   In creating your drawings, you'll find it handy to use the following technique for deleting unwanted parts of shapes or lines. First select the shape—for instance, a square—and then select the Pointer tool from the toolbox and choose Reshape Points from the button area. Handles will appear at various points on the symbol. Next select the segment of the shape that you want to delete. You do this by defining the area bordered by endpoints. The default endpoints lie at each corner of the selected shape (in this case, the square). If you want to delete an area less than an entire square, you'll need to define new endpoints.

To create a new endpoint, choose the Duplicate command from the Edit menu and choose Button 1 where you want to add the point. Now select one of the desired endpoints, choose the Arrange command from the Change menu, and select Disconnect. Repeat these steps to select the other endpoint of the segment. Press Esc to exit this mode and from the Change menu select Arrange, Disconnect again. Finally, just select the segment and press Delete to get rid of it (or move it away from the rest of the drawing by dragging it).

Alternatively, you can delete a shape's endpoint by selecting it and pressing the Delete key.

Microsoft PowerPoint

PowerPoint is one of the oldest Windows presentation packages, and its operation shows it. Many tasks that are automatic, or nearly so, in most packages in this chapter take ingenuity and effort in PowerPoint. Feature-rich, but tough to handle, PowerPoint is a natural breeding ground for potent tips, such as those that follow.

Drawing Tips

Get better use from PowerPoint's drawing tools with these tricks.

Precision Drawing   Hold down the Shift key along with the left mouse button to control drawing tools. Shift used with the Oval, Rectangle, or Rounded Rectangle tools will help create perfect circles, squares, or rounded corner squares. Use Shift with the Line tool to guarantee that the lines meet at a 90-degree angle. And for resizing graphics to their original size, select the graphic, hold down Shift, and double-click on one of the corner sizing-boxes.

Add Embossing   To create an embossing effect in PowerPoint, draw the object you want to emboss and fill it in with the main background color. Select Copy from the Edit menu and then choose Paste from the Edit menu. Choose Paste again, so that you have three copies of the object on your slide. Select each copy in turn, filling one with a lighter shade than the background object, and the other with a darker shade. Overlap the three objects so that the lightest is slightly visible above the upper-left corner of the main object, and the darkest is slightly visible below the lower-right corner. Select the main object and use the Bring to Front command to ensure that it stays in front.

Create Shaded Objects   There's no specific command for creating shaded objects in PowerPoint. But to do so, first create a slide that has the color and shading desired for the object. Draw the object you want—for example, an oval—and make sure that it is unfilled. Choose Opaque from the Draw menu. Copy this object and then Paste it as a Picture into your presentation in the Slide view. The object becomes a shaded object that can be cropped, resized, and placed anywhere on the slide.

Display Object Measurements   The guides in PowerPoint allow you to center objects effortlessly, but they're also handy as a measuring tool. When you move the guides, the measurement displayed is the offset from the center, shown in inches. To view the offset from your starting position, click on the guide and drag it to the desired position.

Presentation Tips

Progressing from idea to finished presentation is not automatic in PowerPoint. These ideas should make the process easier.

Two Ways to Reorganize   If you're doing a major reorganization of a presentation, select the Slide Sorter from the View menu to see the changes as you delete or reorder slides. However, if you know exactly what changes you want to make—and your slides are clearly labeled—it saves time to use the Title Sorter view because the program doesn't have to redraw each slide to reflect every change.

Sharing Slide Masters   In PowerPoint, you can select Slide Master from the View menu to create templates that ensure slide consistency throughout your presentation. If you're in a time crunch, use Slide Master to create a new presentation. Open the presentation where you created the Slide Master, and select New from the File menu. When prompted for a presentation format, select the option Use Format of Active Presentation. If you've already started on the new presentation, switch to the original presentation, select Slide Master from the View menu, and then, from the Edit menu, choose Select All followed by Copy. Then switch back to the new presentation. From the View menu, select Slide Master, and then choose Edit, Paste.

Custom Defaults   If you don't like PowerPoint's presentation defaults, customize a new presentation and make it the new default presentation. Don't forget to include all of these items: color scheme, format of the Slide Master, Notes Master, and Handout Page, object attributes (such as opaque, framed, and filled), slide size, slide orientation, text styles, and word processing format (such as indents, tabs, and line spacing). When you're done designing your ideal presentation, select Save As from the File menu and name the file DEFAULT.PPT. Now when you choose New from the File menu, the presentations created will be based upon these attributes.

Create Speaker Notes PowerPoint creates presentation handouts by using thumbnail views of your slides. But for handouts with more substance, include your speaker notes. By making your notes into slides, you can quickly create a separate presentation to generate complete handouts for the original presentation.

Open the original presentation and select Title Sorter from the View menu, insert blank slides between each existing slide by using New Slide from the Edit menu. Save the file under a different name before proceeding. Choose Notes from the View menu, click next to your notes to select the text, and then select Copy from the Edit menu. Next, choose Slide from the View menu, advance to the first blank slide, and choose Paste from the Edit menu to paste your notes into it. Repeat this process for all the slides. Finally, select Print from the File menu, choose Handout, pick the number of images you want per page (2, 4, or 6), and press Enter.

Best-Looking Black-and-White Handouts For the best-looking handouts, you'll want to use a black-and-white color palette that reflects what the slides will look like on your monochrome printer. To create a monochrome color scheme for the slide images on your notes and handout pages, you must temporarily change the color scheme of your presentation slides. To do so follow these steps:

1. Save any changes that you have made to your presentation and close the file.

2. Open an untitled copy of the file. (This is so you don't affect the original presentation.)

3. Switch to Slides view.

4. From the Color menu, choose Color Scheme.

5. In the Color Scheme dialog box, select the Choose A Scheme button.

6. In the Choose A Scheme dialog box, choose White for the background color, choose Black for the foreground color, and choose the set of accents that consists of six black color swatches. Then choose the OK button to return to the Color Scheme dialog box.

7. In the Color Scheme dialog box, choose the Shade Background button.

8. In the Shade Background dialog box, clear the None check box to turn off any background shading. Then choose the OK button to return to the Color Scheme dialog box.

9. In the Color Scheme dialog box, select the All Slides option and then choose the Apply button to have the monochrome color scheme applied to the entire presentation.

10. Print your notes and/or handout pages with this new color scheme in place.

Type Size Rules of Thumb Here are some good rules of thumb for using type in PowerPoint presentations. The following numbers reflect point size.

Output	Largest	Average	Smallest
On-screen	36	24	18
Overhead	24	18	12
35-mm slide	36	24	18
Printed flip charts	24	18	12

Integrating PowerPoint with Other Microsoft Applications

A positive feature of PowerPoint is how well it interacts with other Microsoft Windows applications. That's the focus of these tips.

Define Quick Access Keys Insert charts, graphs, and worksheets into your presentations more quickly by assigning quick menu access keys to your Insert options. This involves editing WIN.INI, but it's a simple process. Open WIN.INI in Notepad and go to the [Embedding] section. For each entry, go to the second argument after the equal sign and place an ampersand (&) in front of the letter you want to use as a quick key. Here's how the section should read after you're done:

```
ExcelWorksheet=Worksheet created by Microsoft Excel, Excel &Worksheet, Excel.exe,
picture
ExcelChart=Chart created by Microsoft Excel, Excel&Chart, Excel.exe, picture
Graph=Business Graphs from Powerpoint Graph, &Graph, PPtGraph.exe, picture
```

Save the edited WIN.INI file. Now when you choose Insert from the File menu, the quick key letter will be underlined: <u>G</u>raph, Excel <u>C</u>hart, Excel <u>W</u>orksheet.

Share Dictionaries with Word for Windows If you use Word for Windows as well as PowerPoint, save over 233K of disk space by letting these two applications share a common dictionary and spell checker. In the File Manager, go to the Word for Windows directory, and copy the files LEX-AM.DLL and LEX-AM.DAT to a floppy disk as a safety measure. Next, go to the PowerPoint directory, rename the file SPELL-AM.DLL as LEX-AM.DLL. Move this file and LEX-AM.DAT to the Word for Windows directory, replacing the existing files with the same names. Word for Windows spelling will work as if nothing's changed, but the next time you select PowerPoint's Spelling option on the Text menu, a message will appear asking where SPELL-AM.DLL is. Type in the path of the renamed file:

```
C:\WINWORD\LEX-AM.DLL
```

and press OK. Caution: While Word for Windows can use PowerPoint's dictionary and spell checker, the reverse is not true.

Publisher's Paintbrush

Publisher's Paintbrush is a full-featured Windows package which offers image creation, editing, and enhancement, as well as scanner control. Here are a few tips for getting the most from this program.

Save Everything in Its Place   To save a new configuration of tool boxes, file dimensions, and so on whenever you leave the program, open WIN.INI in a text editor, find the [pupb] section, and change the line Config On Exit=0 to Config On Exit=1.

Resize, Don't Distort   To maintain the aspect ratio of an image when resizing, hold down the Shift key before dragging the image's frame with the mouse.

14. COMMUNICATIONS PROGRAMS

IN COMMUNICATIONS, MORE THAN IN PERHAPS ANY OTHER AREA, WINDOWS has opened the door to new products and approaches. Communications software in DOS was essentially metaphor free; it had no standard look and feel. Windows offers the opportunity to put the basics of communication behind easier-to-comprehend facades and to use more advanced communications facilities for entirely new purposes.

With its recurring patterns of access and use, communications-related software lends itself superbly to shortcuts, once you know how to get the connection you want.

This chapter looks at four key products. The old: Procomm and Crosstalk, venerable leaders of DOS comm software. The new: Dynacomm, one of the most progressive of all Windows applications. And the future: Lotus Notes, an application that turns communications into an engine for mobile group creation and the manipulation of information.

Procomm Plus for Windows

Procomm is a well-known name in communications software (its DOS version is the standby for many PC users). Many have used this venerable program since its shareware days and its new Windows version has been long-awaited. These tips will help you get started with this Windows newcomer.

More Readable Terminal Text If you have difficulty reading the text that scrolls by in Procomm Plus for Windows' terminal window, change the default font used. First, you'll need to change the user settings to tell Procomm Plus not to automatically adjust the incoming text: Select the Setup icon, double-click on User Settings, select the No autosize option, and then OK. Next, double-click on Terminal, Font Select, and then choose the typeface and size you would like to use. Select OK twice to exit the Terminal Settings dialog box. Finally, select Save from the File menu and exit the Procomm Plus for Windows' setup.

View More Icons You can change Procomm Plus for Windows' display options to fit more Action Bar icons on-screen at one time. To do so you'll have to rerun the setup program for Procomm Plus for Windows. Exit Windows and from the \WINDOWS directory start the setup program. Use the arrow keys to get to the Display option and press Enter to scroll the options. Select a display driver that supports an 800 × 600 resolution (provided your display can acco-modate this setting). Exit setup and restart Windows. Now Procomm Plus for Windows will have access to more on-screen real estate and you'll be able to see all of the program's available icons.

Quickly Use Procomm's Options   Here's a quick way to access Procomm Plus for Windows' GIF Viewer, Dialog Editor, and Windows User Builder with-out having to switch to Program Manager to select their icons: Simply click on the control box in the upper-left corner of the window; the three choices will be listed there.

Change the GIF Viewer Directory   You can customize Procomm Plus for Windows to automatically run the GIF Viewer from whatever directory you specify. By making this change, you'll be able to start this utility in the directory that contains all of your .GIF files. Run the GIF Viewer by selecting the option from the choices displayed from the control box (as in the preceding tip). Find the directory that you want the GIF Viewer to run in and click on the Set De-fault button. The next time you open the GIF Viewer it will be in the directory you specified.

Use Your Mouse While On-Line   While you're connected to an on-line ser-vice or BBS in Windows, you don't have to give up using the mouse in favor of the keyboard. Select Procomm Plus for Windows' Setup icon, select User Set-tings, and, in the Mouse Double Click section, select the Send Character option. If you are hooking up to a service or BBS that requires a carriage return to be sent after each menu choice is selected, you'll need to select the Add CR box as well. Select OK, and then choose Save from the File menu to keep the new mouse settings.

Crosstalk for Windows

Crosstalk was one of the earliest PC communications programs. Over the years it has grown steadily more complex, with scripting functions, multiple versions, terminal emulation, and protocol support bolted onto a simple dial-up package. In Windows, Crosstalk aims both to innovate and maintain the past. It's a tough job, but one that creates many opportunities for tips.

Tips for Dialing and On-Line Sessions

You can automate just about any aspect of Crosstalk's basic operation, if you know the right tricks.

Easy Redialing   Use Crosstalk's dialing queues to dial several phone entries repeatedly, until a connection is made. Here's how to set up a dialing queue: First, choose the Actions menu's Dial option. Drag the mouse cursor over con-secutive phone entries you want included in the queue, or hold down the Ctrl key while clicking with the left mouse button to select noncontiguous files.

When you've marked all the relevant entries, click on the Dial button. Crosstalk cycles through the appropriate numbers for however many times you specified in the Dial dialog box. Once an entry is successfully contacted, Crosstalk removes that entry from the queue. After you sign off, Crosstalk automatically resumes dialing the remaining entries.

Instant Replay of On-Line Sessions   Each time you connect to a remote system, a timer appears on the far right side of the status line to display the length of the session. Double-click on this timer to enter Crosstalk's scroll buffer—a block of memory that stores the most recent events of the session. The scroll bars that appear let you navigate through the contents of this buffer. Double-click on the timer a second time to toggle off the scroll buffer and return to normal Crosstalk operations.

No-Key Keyboard Entry   The next time you're using Crosstalk for Windows with a remote system, such as CompuServe, that uses numbered menus, try the following time-saving tip: Point to the number that identifies the option you want and double-click the left mouse button. Crosstalk reads the number under the mouse pointer and transmits it back to the remote system, just as if you had entered the number at the keyboard.

Copy Tables Painlessly   If you download figures such as the day's stock quotes from an on-line service to put into an Excel worksheet, don't waste time with Windows' cut-and-paste routine. Crosstalk's Copy Table command can move formatted rows and columns of data and won't involve finicky cell-by-cell editing. After downloading the data, double-click on Crosstalk's on-screen timer to activate the scroll buffer. Hold down the left mouse button and drag with your mouse to highlight the data to be transferred. Select Copy Table from the Edit menu. As the marked section is transferred to the Windows Clipboard, Crosstalk inserts special characters that identify it as tabular data. When you paste the data into an Excel worksheet, each item goes into a separate cell.

Tips for Handling Setup and COM Ports

You can fine-tune the operation of the hardware beneath Crosstalk with these tips.

Status Bar Shortcuts   If the status bar lists an option you want to modify, don't bother pulling down the Settings menu, just double-click on the status bar entry. For example, double-click on the current terminal setting and Crosstalk cycles through the various available terminal emulations, as shown in Figure 14.1. Note that Crosstalk builds in a few safety checks here. You can't, for example, change the COM port setting when you're on-line.

FIGURE 14.1

Quickly change Crosstalk settings by double-clicking on the appropriate item in the status bar at the top of the screen.

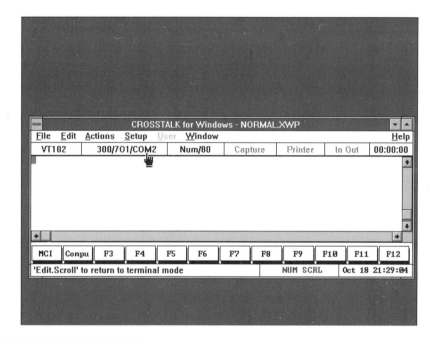

Customizing Program Groups You can use New Call to create icons in your Crosstalk program group, so you can call selected on-line services such as CompuServe and MCI Mail with the click of a mouse. The following procedure enables you to do the same for other information services and bulletin boards that New Call doesn't support. First, select Setup and identify the connect number, user ID, and other file transfer options for the bulletin board in question. Then choose Save As from the File menu, give the session a name, and click on the Save As Program Manager Icon option. In the Icon Description field, enter a short description to appear under the icon. Click on the Next Icon or Previous Icon buttons until you see an icon you want to associate with this session, and then click on OK. The new icon will now appear in Crosstalk's Program Manager group, ready to run like any other Windows application.

Eliminating LEARN Script Conflicts Unlike the other versions of the program, Crosstalk for Windows tucks away its learn capability into a script called LEARN, which can run either as the startup script or as an Actions Script while on-line or off-line. This mode has a problem with graphics. If you select Yes when a BBS asks, "Do you want graphics?" you risk being disconnected. To be safe, select No when you're running LEARN; then afterward change the script to Yes.

Minimizing Data Loss and Retransmission Some high-speed modems run too quickly for the PC to which they are attached, resulting in data loss, retransmission, and a noticeable drop in throughput rate. If you notice too many retransmitted blocks, increase the size of Crosstalk's COM port buffer. If necessary, terminate the current on-line session. Then select Setup, System, and click on the More button. Click on the 16K button to increase Crosstalk's COM buffer to the largest available size, and then choose OK.

Recognizing Ports with Windows 3.0 If you receive an error message telling you the COM port you're addressing is assigned to a DOS program, it isn't necessarily so. The problem may be Windows 3.0's difficulties in addressing modems connected to COM3 or COM4 (version 3.1 directly supports COM3 and COM4). Crosstalk for Windows' SETCOM.EXE utility eliminates these COM conflicts by writing serial port addresses to your system's BIOS. From the DOS prompt, enter **setcom**, and the utility writes the default addresses for COM ports 1 through 4 (03F8, 02F8, 03E8, and 02E8 respectively) to your BIOS. To specify nonstandard addresses for one or more COM ports, enter **setcom** followed by the hex addresses of all four ports in order. If this solves the problem, insert the command either in AUTOEXEC.BAT or as the first command in a batch file that runs Windows.

Dynacomm

Dynacomm is a communications program crafted with Windows in mind. Not only does this application take advantage of Windows graphics to make basic communications tasks easier to follow, it attains new levels of programming and integration. Essentially, Dynacomm assumes it is providing communications services to aid some other application. This makes it far easier to use Dynacomm as a communications adjunct to other Windows programs than it was with older communications packages.

The tips in this section begin with scripting, one of Dynacomm's most notable features.

Scripting Tips

All major communications packages provide some level of scripting for controlling dial-up sessions and the uploading and downloading of data. Dynacomm, however, goes scripting one better, offering a near-programming-language level of complexity.

Here are tips for getting the most from this singular communications control environment.

Scripts without Scripting If you want to write an automatic login script for some particular host and don't really want to have to learn about Dynacomm's script language, you can use the RECORDER script. When the RECORDER script is executed, you are prompted for the name and description of the script you will be creating. After you've provided the name and description, Dynacomm will record the successive send and receive commands, writing them to a script. When the RECORDER is stopped, you can edit the login script or compile it and use it as is.

Help for Script Debugging   If you're having problems determining why a particular script is not working, take advantage of Dynacomm's DEBUG command. Add the DEBUG command, followed by the script name, to the beginning of the script. The next time the script is run, it will create a file that contains a listing of how each command was executed. You can use this text listing to locate trouble spots.

Table Variables in Scripts   Dynacomm's script language allows you to refer to specific fields of a structured table using the form @R5.2—where 5 refers to the table and 2 refers to the field—and to use a variable rather than an integer to refer to the field number, as in @R5.Field%. However, don't use a variable expression for the table number; this causes an error during script compilation. If you want to use a variable instead of a table name, enclose the variable within parentheses as follows:

```
@R(%Table).2
```

Graphic Boxes Made Simple   Dynacomm doesn't include a graphic dialog box editor, so designing dialog boxes for use in scripts can take hours of tedious statement editing. You can dramatically cut the amount of time you spend re-editing these script statements by downloading a public-domain graphic dialog box editor called DLGED.EXE from the Future Soft Engineering section (Library 4) of CompuServe's WINAPA forum. DLGED.EXE makes it easy to design dialog boxes—complete with list boxes, buttons, and other controls—and generates the Dynacomm code needed to include them in scripts.

Customize Your Keyboard   Within a Dynacomm script you can remap selected keys, or even the entire keyboard if you choose. For example, you might find it convenient to run a script with a single keypress. You can remap characters, strings, escape sequences and control sequences. For example, the script command

```
KEY F2 "Ziffnet"
```

would map the F2 key to display the string "ZiffNet."

Once you've remapped all of the desired keys, save and compile the script. After you run it, the keys that you've remapped will be available to you.

On-Line Session Tips

While integration is Dynacomm's big attraction, the program does provide all the communications basics. These tips will help you get the most from Dynacomm dial-up sessions.

Define New Function Keys   It's easy to change the settings of the function key buttons at the bottom of a Dynacomm terminal session. For instance, to create a function key that instructs a remote system to scan new messages, open the Settings Function Keys dialog box by selecting Function Keys from the Settings menu, name the button Scan New, and type **Scan New Messages** into the Command field. To send an Enter command after the command string, add the characters ^M at the end as follows:

```
Scan New Messages^M
```

Instant CompuServe File Transfer   Dynacomm can bypass some of the finicky work involved in CompuServe file transfers. From the Settings menu, select Terminal Emulation's CompuServe option. This automatically activates Dynacomm's support for the CompuServe Quick B binary file transfer protocol. When you're ready to upload or download a file, instruct CompuServe to use that protocol and Dynacomm will automatically start the transfer.

Terminal Text Print   To print text from the terminal windows, first select it with your mouse. Then select Copy Special from the Edit menu and use the Printer option to send the selected data to the printer.

Capturing On-Line Sessions to Disk   Save time on-line by capturing your on-line session to a file on disk for later reference. Select Receive Text File from the Transfers menu and supply the dialog box that pops up with a filename. Then proceed with your on-line session. You can pause or stop the disk capture at any time by clicking on the appropriate button on the file transfer progress bar at the bottom of the screen. Until you do so, everything that happens in the terminal window will be saved to disk.

Quick Text Scanning   Unlike structured tables, text tables are standard ASCII text files with records on separate lines. So you can use Dynacomm's commands for reading and evaluating records in text tables with any ASCII text file. This trick can come in handy in several instances. For example, spool a series of messages to disk in an ASCII file, and you can use the text table commands to read through the file for the message's sender, subject matter, and other details.

Troubleshooting Tips

Because it brings many new ideas to communications, Dynacomm can be confusing when problems occur. Try these tricks when trouble arises.

Keep Dynacomm 3.0's Path Short   Dynacomm version 3.0 issues a general protection (GP) fault when you try to access the Windows Help system. Some machines might display the message "Help topic does not exist" instead of the GP fault message. This happens because Dynacomm 3.0 only allows a buffer size of 34 bytes to hold the path name of the help file. So if your Dynacomm directory is nested too deeply within other directories, this problem will occur.

For example, a path such as

```
C:\WIN\WINAPPS\NEWAPPS\DYNACOMM\DYNACOMM.HLP
```

would cause such a GP fault. If you won't be running Windows Help for Dynacomm, you may not care if the path name is too long, but chances are that sooner or later you'll want to use Help.

Troubleshooting Carrier Detection under Windows 3.1   If you're having trouble dialing out after first starting Dynacomm in Windows 3.1, try turning Carrier Detection off. You'll find this option when you choose Communications from the Settings menu. Turning off this option makes Dynacomm use a slower but more reliable method for determining connection.

Restoring the Correct Font in Dynacomm under Windows 3.1   If you're running Dynacomm under Windows 3.1 and notice that you're seeing extra spaces between characters, you'll have to select another screen font for Dynacomm to use. To do so, select Terminal Preferences from the Settings menu; try using Terminal or Fixedsys. The extra spacing results because Dynacomm uses the SYSTEM font by default in Windows 3.1, a different font than that used under 3.0.

Smooth High-Speed Transfers   If you're attempting to do a high-speed transfer (9600 baud or higher), but keep getting corrupted files or unfinished transfers, the trouble may result from Windows interrupting the session if you have other applications running. To fix this problem, choose Communications from the Settings menu and increase the Read Yield Count from the default value of 80 to 300 or more. When you increase this setting, Dynacomm can process more information before giving up control to Windows.

Lotus Notes

What is Lotus Notes? It is an electronic mail system—but much more. It is a remote accessing package—but goes far beyond that. It is a document management package—but that's not all. Notes is that rarity in the PC universe: an absolutely unique program. Perhaps the best way to describe Notes is as a program that combines communications and document management functions to form an environment where groups can create, manipulate, and manage information regardless of physical location. Notes is so flexible that it can be used in situations ranging from keeping track of letters to building a Supreme Court brief.

If you are already a Notes user, these tips will help you navigate one of the most complex products in computing. If you aren't a Notes user yet, these tips provide a glimpse of your future.

Address Tips

Underlying much of what Notes can do is the ability to get documents to individuals or groups, wherever they may be. This requires sophisticated address management, which is what these tips focus on.

Quick Addresses   A quick way to address a Notes message and get it on its way is simply to type the recipient's last name in the To field. If the last name is not unique, Notes presents you with a list of choices and lets you choose the correct one. You can also use this shortcut to address notes to more than one person; just separate each last name with a comma.

Create Custom Groups in Your Personal Address Book   If you find yourself continually sending Notes to the same several people, save yourself lots of time by creating a group in your personal address book. To create a group, select Group from the Compose menu and enter the names of the individual Notes users you want to include. Name the group and then save it; you'll be able to send mail to group members by typing the group name in the To field. Notes even lets you specify existing group names when defining a new group, giving you still more flexibility.

Share Groups   After you've carefully constructed the private groups that you'll want to use regularly, you might want to share them with others in your office. To do so, you'll need to copy their member listing by highlighting this information in your address book and selecting Copy from the Edit menu. Next compose a message to the person or persons with whom you want to share the group. Within the message, paste the text containing the names of the group members by placing the cursor in the correct spot and selecting Paste from the Edit menu. When the message is received, that person will have to create the group in his or her own address book, but at least he or she won't have to retype the long list of names. Instead he or she can paste them in the correct field.

Mail Tips

Although it can do much more, Notes does perform all the functions of an E-mail system. Here we offer some ideas for making Notes E-mail sing.

Tips for Running Notes Remotely   One of the biggest complaints of users running Notes remotely is that it takes too much time to send and receive all of your messages. If you're the recipient of a great deal of mail every day or if the databases that you use are constantly being updated, you know the wait can be unnerving. To speed up the process of sending and receiving mail, follow these suggestions, which break down the process into separate components, minimizing the amount of time and effort required on your part.

When you want to receive mail only—such as first thing in the morning or at the end of the day—select Database from the File menu, choose Exchange, and then select the following options: Selected Databases, Receive Documents from Server, Hangup When Done. Make sure that none of the other available options are marked. Before calling in, make sure that your mailbox icon is opened.

When you want to send mail only—such as when you've composed replies to all of your previously collected messages—select Database from the File menu, choose Exchange, and then select the following options: Transfer Outgoing Mail, Hangup When Done.

Finally, when you want to send and receive mail in the same session, choose Database from the File menu, choose Exchange, and then select the following options: Selected Databases, Receive Documents from Server, Transfer Outgoing Mail, Hangup When Done.

Keep Tabs on Incoming Mail   Instead of periodically checking your mailbox and all of your databases to see if you have any new messages or if there are new additions to a critical database, let Notes give you the answer in response to a single keystroke. From the View menu, select the Show Unread option; below the title of each database is a small box containing a number, as shown in Figure 14.2. This number reflects the total unread message count for that database. Unfortunately, Notes can't update this count on its own; you'll have to press the F9 key to tell it to scan for new documents.

FIGURE 14.2

The number of unread messages appears in the box below the database title.

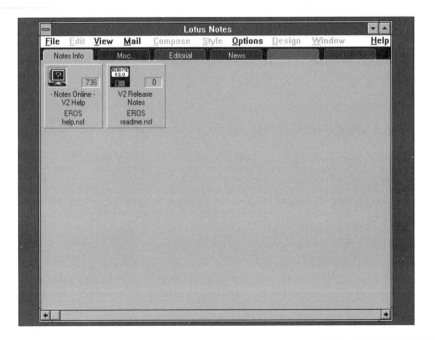

You can also tell Notes to update this count automatically each time you start it. From the Options menu, choose Scan Unread, choose Setup, and then select the databases that you want to be updated regularly. Mark the option that says Start Scanner at Notes Startup.

Now when you open the database you find yourself at the first unread item or topic. If you click on the Unread down arrow on the tool bar, you go to the next unread item in that view. If there are no more unread items in that view, but the Scan Unread dialog box shows a number of unread items still remaining in that database, select a new view from the View menu and then reopen the database. If there are items in the database that are not visible in any view that you select, Notes tells you that it can open the item but that you cannot navigate from it. If you selected more than one database in Setup, the scanner proceeds to the next database automatically, or you can choose Next Unread and go to the next database whenever you want.

Hear Your Incoming Mail   Activating the unread count in Notes, as just described, is handy for getting a visual reminder that you have mail waiting for you in your mailbox, but it doesn't help if you spend the majority of your time outside of Notes in other Windows applications. In this situation, you should activate Notes' Mail Notify option, which beeps every time you receive an incoming message. To turn on this feature, select Preferences from the Options menu and choose Mail Notify. Notes can alert you that you have a message only if the program is currently open and running, either full-screened or minimized.

Pasting from Word for Windows 2.0 to Notes   Word for Windows 2.0 users may have experienced difficulty in trying to paste text into a Notes message or database item that was placed on the Clipboard from Word for Windows. When you select Paste from Notes' Edit menu, you end up with a Word for Windows icon, not the text you expected. The solution to trouble-free pasting is selecting the Paste Special command from the Edit menu instead. You'll then need to select the desired format; Rich Text format will work just fine.

Keyboard Shortcuts

Finally, here are a few suggestions for using your keyboard in Notes.

Keep Notes Secure   You don't have to exit Notes to have your password lock Notes for you. If you're leaving your desk for lunch or to go to a meeting, press the F5 key to lock your Notes databases. If someone tries to open one of your databases or read an already open database, Notes prompts for your password, as shown in Figure 14.3. If the password is entered incorrectly, Notes produces the message, "Wrong Password."

FIGURE 14.3

Keep Notes secure by activating the password feature (press F5) when you're away from your desk.

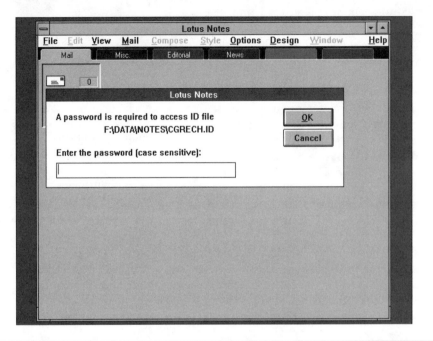

Shortcuts Here are keys to use for screening important Notes functions quickly.

F5   Activates security feature

F9   Updates message unread count

Ctrl+E   Gives you access to edit mode

Alt+F9   Minimizes Notes

Esc   Sends and/or saves messages

Letter   Jumps to the first item in the database that begins
               with the specified letter

WINDOWS ENHANCEMENTS, UTILITIES, AND PROGRAMMING TOOLS

AS A NEW, GRAPHICAL ENVIRONMENT, WINDOWS HAS SPURRED THE CREATION of never-before-seen types of programs. These applications improve, alter, or deepen Windows operations in specific areas. Some provide fresh font alternatives, both for screen and printout. Others offer alternatives to the Program Manager or other utility enhancements to the basic Windows environment. And still others deliver customizing and integration tools for graphical applications.

All of the programs covered in this chapter demonstrate the power of one of Windows' most admirable features: extensibility. If you don't like the way a particular part of Windows runs or a specific feature of a Windows application, you can change it. This is an environment you can truly make your own.

The tips that follow represent a quick recipe kit for customizing your Windows environment.

Adobe Type Manager

Adobe Type Manager (ATM) was a huge hit under Windows 3.0, where it provided all the font management tools Microsoft left out. Built-in fonts are much improved in Windows 3.1, with Microsoft's introduction of TrueType. However, ATM remains a valuable program because it provides access to the widely used fonts of PostScript, the type-programming language that dominates professional desktop publishing.

If you work with type for a living, ATM is essential to the Windows setup. For others, it can be a powerful partner to your TrueType fonts.

These tips deal with the two fundamental areas of ATM: fonts and printing.

Font Tips

Much of what ATM accomplishes with fonts is automatic and invisible: Install the program, and fonts just appear! But you can achieve special effects with a bit of savvy.

Smaller ATM Fonts   Adobe Type Manager starts rendering fonts at 9 points. If you want to overwrite the default (in order to render fonts as small as 4 points), open the ATM.INI file and, in the [Settings] section, change the 9 to a 4 in the line that reads

```
SynonymPSBegin=9
```

Then save the file and restart Windows.

Quick Bullets If you're using a non-PostScript printer, just press Shift+Esc when using an ATM font, and you'll get a bullet. (For a bullet that prints to a PostScript printer, select Windows' Symbol font, turn on Num Lock, hold down the Alt key, type **0153** on the numeric keypad, and release the Alt key (alternatively, you can use the Character Map, as described in Chapter 6.)

Setting the Font Cache for Maximum Performance If you routinely work with documents containing several fonts, consider increasing your font cache to improve performance. Double-click on the ATM Control Panel icon (found in Program Manager's Main program group) or select Run from File Manager's File menu to run ATMCNTRL.EXE. Then use the scroll bar buttons under Font Cache to increase the cache size, as shown in Figure 15.1. Depending on your usage and the amount of memory in your PC, you can set the font cache from 64K to 8,192K—192K is a good starting figure. A good rule of thumb is to increase the font cache by 96K for every 1 megabyte of extended memory you have above 1 megabyte. For example, if you had a 4 megabyte computer, you would set the font cache to 288K. Keep in mind that the more memory you allocate to the ATM font cache, the less memory Windows has available for other Windows applications. If you increase or decrease the ATM font cache, your changes will not take effect until after you exit and restart Windows.

FIGURE 15.1

Improve ATM's performance by increasing the font cache size if you have the memory to spare.

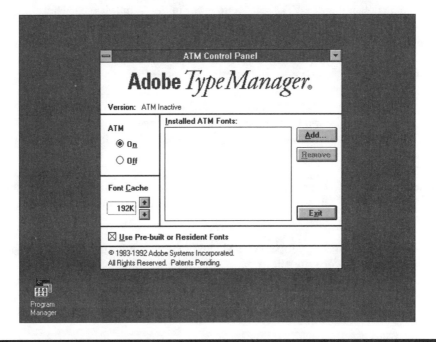

Substitute Fonts   ATM can substitute fonts to simplify the exchange of documents containing fonts that aren't on your system. For example, if you use Tms Rmn and receive files containing a look-alike font called Times, open the ATM-.INI file (usually found in the same directory as Windows) and look for the section called [Aliases]. Then enter the line **Tms Rmn=Times**. ATM does the rest behind the scenes.

Remove Multiple Fonts at One Time   Clicking on the ATM Control Panel's Remove button allows you to remove PostScript Type 1 fonts from the ATM program. To remove fonts, you first need to select the fonts to be removed from the list of installed ATM fonts. You can highlight a range of fonts by holding down the mouse button and scrolling through the list of fonts, or you can pick and choose fonts by holding down the Ctrl key and clicking on the font names. Once you have selected the fonts that you wish to remove, click on the Remove button. You are prompted for confirmation before each font is removed from the ATM program. You can, however, click on the No Confirmation to Remove Fonts option if you don't want to be prompted as the fonts are removed from the ATM program. You must exit and restart Windows in order for your changes to take effect. Incidentally, removing fonts from the ATM program does not delete them from your hard disk.

Printing and Problem-Solving Tips

PostScript was the first language to describe both on-screen fonts and printer output. ATM is an expression of PostScript, so it too offers significant control over PostScript printers and presents problems with printers that don't have PostScript installed. These tips deal with both issues.

Speed Up Printing   Speed up printing with ATM by using the fonts that are already available in the printer. For example, if you are using ATM with a LaserJet or other PCL printer, ensure that the Use Pre-built or Resident Fonts check box is turned on. If it isn't, ATM builds a bitmap of the text in the relevant font, resulting in slower printing times. But keep in mind that if your application supports auto-kerning, ATM fonts will be kerned, but prebuilt or resident bitmap fonts will not be. Also note that some typefaces have a different look than the ATM PostScript fonts. For example, the ATM Courier is quite different from the Courier found in the Hewlett-Packard LaserJets. If you change the printing resolution on your printer, the ATM fonts will change accordingly, whereas the prebuilt or resident fonts will not.

Using ATM with a PostScript Printer   If you receive an error message telling you that the ATM fonts and PostScript fonts don't match, ATM is detecting a difference between the available printer fonts and those installed in ATM. Check the following:

■ Make sure that any additional PostScript fonts that you have installed for ATM are also listed in your WIN.INI as well as in the ATM.INI file. Both of these files are in the WINDOWS directory. If you do not have any soft font entries in the WIN.INI file under the PostScript Printer Definition [PostScript, *port*] where *port* is your PostScript printer port name, you will need to add the fonts again using the ATM Control Panel.

■ To add fonts, first verify that your PostScript printer is the default printer. You can do this by opening the Windows Control Panel and double-clicking on Printers. The default printer will be listed at the top of the Printers dialog box. If it is not the current, default printer, double-click on the printer you wish to be the default printer. Click on OK to exit. Run the ATM Control Panel and then click on the Add button. Select the directory containing your .PFM files—this is usually the PSFONTS\PFM directory. Highlight all the fonts listed in the directory and click on Add. You need to restart Windows for the changes to take effect.

■ If you have a PostScript printer but do not have a PostScript Printer Entry [PostScript, *port*] in your WIN.INI file, you need to add one. Open the Windows Control Panel and double-click on Printers. Click on Add and select the correct printer provided in the printer listing. Click on Install and insert the correct Windows disk if and when you are prompted to do so. Once you have installed the new printer, click on Configure to set the printer port, and then click on Setup. Verify that these options are correct and then click on OK three times to return to the Windows Control Panel.

Troubleshooting an Inactive Version Number   The version number section in the ATM Control Panel tells users what version of the program they have on their system. If the version number ever reports "inactive," ATM has been disabled and is not currently running. This might occur if the SYSTEM.INI file gets modified by another software program's installation process. If the ATM Control Panel is reporting that the version is inactive, verify that your SYSTEM.INI file contains the following statements:

```
system.drv=atmsys.drv
atm.system.drv=system.drv
```

Disabling ATM for Troubleshooting   If you're getting garbled output from Windows, you'll want to disable ATM to see if it's the cause of your problems. First open the SYSTEM.INI with SysEdit or Notepad and locate the [boot] section. Find the lines that read

```
SYSTEM.DRV=ATMSYS.DRV
ATM.SYSTEM.DRV=SYSTEM.DRV
```

Comment these lines out by placing semicolons in front of them.

Now you'll need to add a new line to the [boot] section that sets the SYSTEM.DRV to itself. The new line would read

```
SYSTEM.DRV=SYSTEM.DRV
```

Save your changes to the SYSTEM.INI. Next open WIN.INI and look for any lines that begin with *Softfontx=*, and remark them out as well. Save the WIN.INI and then restart Windows. Try printing a document using one of Windows' native fonts. If your output is fine, ATM was the problem; try reinstalling it and test printing again.

Bitstream Facelift

Bitstream offers Facelift, an alternative to ATM that supports Bitstream's own font formats.

Font Tips

As with other font products, Bitstream Facelift offers special capabilities to the sophisticated user.

Fine-Tuning Your Font Cache Fine-tuning your font cache under the Parameters option can make Facelift perform at warp speed—so long as you remember that a bigger cache isn't always better. Windows itself needs memory, and if Facelift is hogging too much, the overall performance will suffer. If your PC has 2Mb of memory, set the cache no higher than 256K. For PCs with 4Mb or more, 512K is the maximum. Another factor is maximum cache height, which determines the character size that can be stored there. Set it at the maximum (128 pixels) only if you use a 300 dpi printer, print large headlines, and have at least 2Mb of PC memory. And finally, increase Windows' performance with Facelift by checking the Save Cache to Disk box.

Cure Character Substitution If you type one character and another shows up on the screen, don't immediately blame your typing skills. Your disk-based font cache may be corrupted. Select Parameters and check the filename (usually CACHEDMP.CCH) and its location. Then go into File Manager and delete the file. Facelift will rebuild the cache the next time you run Windows. If this problem recurs, go into Parameters and turn off the Save Cache to Disk box. Optimize your hard disk with a disk management utility before trying out a disk-based cache again.

Banning Font Substitutions A native Windows vector font is usually faster than a Facelift one, so it pays to prevent Facelift from substituting its fonts for Windows' own. To do so, open WIN.INI in SysEdit or Notepad. Locate the section labeled [Typefaces], find the line that begins Active=, and in the next line down, enter

```
NoSubstVectFonts=1
```

Then save the changes and restart Windows.

Setup and Operation Tips

You can fine-tune the way Facelift works for you by using the tips that follow.

Setting Thresholds   If you're not bothered by how faithfully a font is rendered at small point sizes—where you'd need a magnifying glass to tell the difference—set higher thresholds in Parameters. The threshold sets the point size at which Windows fonts replace Facelift fonts. Since printed documents need faithful fonts more than monitors do, set printer thresholds around 6 points and monitors around 8 points. Check out higher values to see how they look. Some Facelift typefaces fare better than others, so Facelift lets you override the global threshold settings: Under Typeface, select the font name and check Threshold Inactive to override the default settings.

Setting Printer Resolution   Because Facelift sends characters as graphics to most printers, the graphic resolution of the printer is important in determining the quality of output. When Facelift is active, the resolution of the printer should be set to the highest choice. (Set the resolution by selecting Printers in the Windows Control Panel). Hewlett-Packard LaserJets and DeskJets work best at 300 dpi. For other printers, choose the highest setting possible for graphics resolution.

Know When to Turn Off Facelift   In general day-to-day use, there is no reason to toggle Facelift on and off. But if you are changing any hardware in your system, such as a printer or monitor, it is a good idea to turn Facelift off. Turn it back on after you have installed the new components and restart Windows. When you do, Facelift will rewrite the necessary lines to the WIN.INI and SYSTEM.INI files. This refreshes Facelift and ensures that any changes made during the hardware setup will not conflict with Facelift.

Know When Not to Use a Font Cache   While there are performance benefits to be gained by using a sizable print cache (see "Fine-Tuning Your Font Cache," earlier), this strategy doesn't pay for everyone. If you are always changing the fonts that you use, you won't be utilizing the cache as much as someone who sticks with just one or two fonts all the time. A good-sized font cache also slows down Windows because every time that you start and quit Windows the cache must be opened and dumped, respectively.

Troubleshooting Tips

Because Facelift represents neither the standard printer language (PostScript) nor the built-in Windows font format (TrueType), solving problems in Facelift may require a bit of work on your part. These troubleshooting strategies should help.

Hewlett-Packard Printers If you're having problems printing scalable fonts from Bitstream Facelift to a Hewlett-Packard PCL printer, it may be because the graphics resolution is not being correctly detected by the printer. Try resetting the graphics resolution to fix this problem. In the Control Panel, choose Printers, select Setup, and, in the Resolution box, select 75 dots per inch. Then choose OK and exit to the Control Panel. Reopen the Printers section and repeat the process, this time setting the resolution to 300 dpi. Now try printing and see if the problem has been resolved.

Editing WIN.INI to Change Facelift Settings Edit your WIN.INI to apply the following Bitstream Facelift settings.

- Facelift can dither (alter the fill pattern) of characters on color screens and printers, but Windows does not support this feature. To disable dithering, insert the line NoDitheredColors=1 into the [Typefaces] section of the WIN.INI file.

- If incorrect colors print on the HP PaintJet, insert the line NoCacheColorChars=1 into the [Typefaces] section of the WIN.INI file.

- If you use Facelift's HP Softfonts option to generate soft fonts for the HP LaserJet III, you will receive the following message: "Can only generate softfonts for a HP/PCL LaserJet and compatibles. The HPPCL driver is not currently selected as the default driver in Windows. Generate fonts anyway?" If the LaserJet III is set up as the default printer and you still receive this message after verifying printer setup and restarting Windows, open WIN.INI in SysEdit or Notepad and locate the [HPPCL] section. Copy each *SoftFontx=* line, and insert it into the [HPPCL5A,LPTx] section. For example, go to the [HPPCL] section and copy the line:

```
SoftFont1=C:\PCLFONTS\BI100NU0.PFM,C:\PCLFONTS\BI100NU0.ANP
```

  Place it under the [HPPCL5A, LPT1] section of the WIN.INI file. Save the changes to the WIN.INI, restart Windows, and you should be able to print without receiving the error message.

- If you cannot print small characters on your color dot-matrix printer, add the line NoCacheColorChars=1 to the WIN.INI [Typefaces] section.

Character Map Problems If you're using Character Map and select a Facelift font, the characters may not look right, but when you click on them to get a closer view the correct character should appear. This problem usually occurs when the typeface is at sizes of 9 points or lower. If this inconsistency bothers you, you need to change Facelift's Screen Threshold from the default of 9 to a lower number. Select the Parameters icon, change the Threshold for Screen setting in the resulting dialog box to something like 4, and change the Threshold for Printer setting to a number lower than the one you specified for the screen threshold.

Disable Facelift for Troubleshooting If you're getting garbled output from Windows, you'll want to disable Facelift to see if it's the cause of your problems. First open the SYSTEM.INI with SysEdit or Notepad and locate the following line:

```
display.drv=shellscr.drv
```

Edit this line to read DISPLAY.DRV=*system display driver*. For example, if your display driver were VGA.DRV the line would now read as follows:

```
display.drv=vga.drv
```

Next you need to change the entry beginning with DISPLAY.ORG=, specifying your original display driver before Facelift was installed. The line would read DISPLAY.ORG=VGA.DRV, but you should comment it out with a semicolon.

Next you need to make changes to the WIN.INI. Open it in SysEdit or Notepad and locate the [Typefaces] section. In this case you'll comment out the entire section, including the section name. For example, the first few lines would look like this:

```
;[Typefaces]
;Active=1
;CacheFonts=8
```

Save changes to the WIN.INI and restart Windows. Try printing now to see if Facelift was causing the problem.

Norton Desktop for Windows

A brilliant innovation, Norton Desktop for Windows combines the values of the Norton Utilities for DOS (disk doctoring, system analysis, and the like) with a cleverly reworked Windows desktop. It operates as a virtual replacement for the Windows Program Manager, greatly enhancing disk access and the organization of the screen.

These tips examine Norton Desktop's use as a pseudo-File Manager, ways to make it run swiftly, and handling any rough spots in its interaction with native Windows.

File Tips

You can use Norton Desktop for much of what File Manager should do. When you have the right know-how, Desktop does a much better job!

Select Multiple Files   Unless you make a habit of using the right mouse button, you might overlook one of the most useful selection features of Norton Desktop for Windows: the ability to select multiple files or directories with a single keystroke. Open the Drive Window, and from either the Tree Pane or the File Pane, position the cursor over a file or directory name, press the right mouse button, and drag to select multiple files or directories, as shown in Figure 15.2. Let go of the right button to finish selecting.

FIGURE 15.2

Select multiple files in Norton Desktop by using the right mouse button.

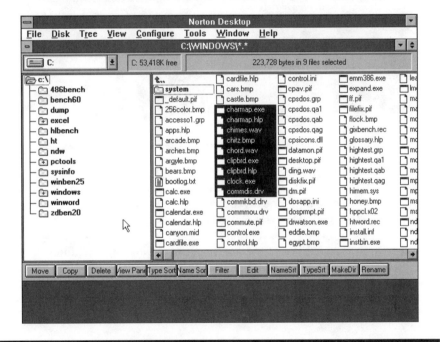

View More Files   Use Viewer to browse through a stack of files quickly and easily. Double-click on the disk drive icon or press Ctrl+W and scroll to the correct drive to bring up the Drive window. Then find the subdirectory containing the relevant files. Press Ctrl and click on each of the files (or use the right mouse button without Ctrl as explained in the preceding tip) to select them; then click on one with the left button, and drag them all to the Viewer icon. Norton automatically loads the Viewer utility and cascades the files you selected. Select Tile from the Window menu to view the files side by side, as shown in Figure 15.3.

FIGURE 15.3

Quickly and easily view several files at once by dragging them to the Viewer icon.

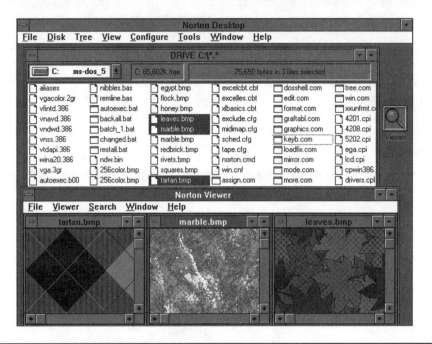

Hidden Batch Builder File   Norton Desktop ships with several sample batch builder files, but the installation routine often misses a handy routine that inserts a reminder of the date and time on the Desktop's title bar. Check your Norton Desktop directory for NDWTIME.WBT, and if it's not there, crack out your program disks. First, copy the program NPACK.EXE from the Emergency disk to your Norton Desktop directory, and then insert the disk containing all your WB$ files. Copy NDWTIME.WB$ to your Norton Desktop directory, and then issue the following command from the DOS prompt:

```
NPACK NDWTIME.WB$ NDWTIME.WBT
```

Now return to Windows and select Run from the File menu, Browse for NDWTIME.WBT, select it, and click on OK. The title bar now contains a date and time reminder. To make this a permanent feature whenever you start Windows, select Run from the File menu again, highlight the line C:\NDW\ NDWTIME.WBT, and press Shift+Del to cut it to the Clipboard. Next, open WIN.INI in Notepad and paste the contents of the Clipboard in the line beginning RUN=. Separate the batch loader command from any others in the line with a semicolon.

Quick File Copies and Moves   To copy files quickly, select them in the File Pane and use the mouse to drag and drop them onto a target subdirectory icon in the Tree Pane. Move files in the same way by pressing and holding down the Alt key after you've selected the files but before you grab and drag them. This technique works for moving whole trees, too.

Type Your Way to a File   Norton Desktop for Windows lets you type your way to a file or subdirectory in the Drive Window. To get to a directory—especially when you've got another one selected in the Tree Pane—just type its name. A search box drops down showing what you've typed, and the Tree Pane shows a framed subdirectory beginning with the letters you've typed so far. When more than one directory contains the letters you've typed, Norton Desktop lets you choose from these possibilities using the arrow keys. As you type in more letters, the search narrows until you find the directory you want. Then press Enter to select it and to list the files it contains in the adjacent File Pane. To cross over to the File Pane, click in it first. The process works the same there, except that when you press Enter, you launch the selected file or its associated application.

Performance Tips

With proper care and feeding, Desktop runs no slower than native Windows, and in some cases it runs even faster.

Improve Loading Time   Norton Desktop loads onto your system faster if all of its .DLL files are located contiguously on your hard disk. Also, placing these .DLL files along with .EXE files at the beginning of the disk improves performance. To configure your disk to optimize performance, start by running Speed-Disk (disk defragger) from the Emergency disk that comes with Desktop. When the Recommendation dialog box appears, choose Configure. Choose Directory Order and make sure that the Windows and Desktop directories are located first. If they aren't, move them to this position. Next choose Files to Place First from the Configure menu and type *.exe on the first line and *.dll on the second to put these files first on your disk. From the Optimization menu, choose Optimization Method, select Full with File Reorder, and choose Begin Optimization.

You'll also want to delete any Quick Access groups that you do not use, to save Norton Desktop from having to load them into memory.

Improve Shutdown Time   For the quickest exit from Windows with Norton Desktop, make sure that the Save Configuration on Exit option is not selected, so that Norton does not have to spend time saving your configuration to disk. To make sure this setting is off, choose Preferences from the Configure menu and deselect it.

Tell Erase Protect to Ignore Windows Temp Files   Erase Protect is a Norton Desktop TSR that works with SmartErase, protecting files that are deleted by placing them in a temporary trash can for a certain amount of time before they are purged from your disk. But with the many temporary files that Windows and its applications can produce, this feature can waste resources and slow your system by protecting useless files. To get around this, tell SmartErase which files you don't want it to protect. From the Configure menu select SmartErase, and select the All Files Except Those Listed option. In the File Extensions text box, type

```
*.tmp *.swp *.bin *.dat *.qag *.grp
```

and any other extensions that you know are temporary files or that you don't want protected, such as backup copies of files (with a .BAK extension).

Disable SmartErase to Improve Performance SmartErase safely stores deleted files in a subdirectory so that you can retrieve accidental deletions days after you make the mistake, but it soaks up both RAM and hard-disk space. Norton Desktop can retrieve deleted files immediately even when SmartErase is disabled. If that's all you need, select Configure, SmartErase, and then deselect the Enable SmartErase Protection box. Erased files will no longer be stored in a special subdirectory, but you can still see and unerase them by double-clicking on the SmartErase icon.

This method still loads Erase Protect software in memory. To free up that extra memory, open AUTOEXEC.BAT in a text editor and find the line that reads EP /ON. Change the line to REM EP /ON and then reboot. To avoid having the message "Erase Protect is not loaded and cannot be enabled" interrupt Windows startup, open NDW.INI in Notepad or another text editor. Look for the SmartErase heading followed by the line EPWarning=1. Change it to read EPWarning=0, and kiss the error message goodbye.

Quick Access to Privacy and Safety Desktop's screen blanker, Sleeper, sports two features that are easy to miss, but which can be invaluable. One enables you to blank the screen quickly; the other keeps it safe from prying eyes until you enter a password to restore it. Click on the Sleeper icon, and, under Preferences, click on one corner in the Sleep Now box. Select the Use Sleep Corners box, and, once you've clicked on OK, you can blank the screen any time by moving your mouse into the appropriate corner. Alternatively, select a sleep hotkey, and use that to blank your screen. Enabling a password is just as easy. In the main Sleeper dialog box, click on password, and follow the instructions.

AutoStart Your Applications Norton Desktop can start applications automatically when it loads. Just place their group box icons directly into the AutoStart group box (which is generated during Desktop's install routine), and the next time you launch Desktop those programs will load as well.

Update Quick Access Groups Norton Desktop automatically converts Windows group boxes into Quick Access groups upon installation. But if you've used Program Manager as your shell for a while and you've created a new group, or if Desktop misses one, here's how to update in Norton Desktop: Ensure that the

Quick Access dialog box is open; then choose New from the File menu, and select Group in the Type box. Click on the Group File Name field, and either type the path and filename or click on Browse and locate the correct .GRP file in your WINDOWS subdirectory. Don't bother filling in the Title, since Desktop requires you to use the name of the Windows group. If you want to change the name, wait until the group is converted. Then select it, choose Properties from the File menu, and change the name under Title. Be forewarned: Too many Quick Access groups will slow down loading, so be selective when creating groups.

Troubleshooting Tips

You may run into rough spots where Desktop meets native Windows. These tips can help with some of the more common problems.

Reverting to Program Manager   You get the most from Norton Desktop if you install it as your Windows shell—but if you do, it's easy to switch back to Windows' Program Manager. Or you may need to revert to Program Manager for Windows troubleshooting. To do so, open SYSTEM.INI, edit the Shell line to read SHELL=PROGMAN.EXE, and restart Windows. Or to switch to Program Manager occasionally, set up a Program Manager icon in Desktop. Open the directory listing for your Windows subdirectory, click on the filename PROGMAN.EXE, and then drag and drop it onto your desktop for double-click program launching.

Applications Run Minimized   If all of your Windows applications are running minimized and you haven't set them up to do so, the problem may be an old version of the file SHELL.DLL. Delete the existing copy of SHELL.DLL on your system and copy the version from your Desktop disks into the Windows SYSTEM subdirectory. Restart Windows and try running your applications now.

Applications Not Displaying Free System Resources and Memory Information   If you're having problems getting Free System Resources and Memory Readings for your Windows application, or if Desktop's System Information refuses to run or generates a general protection fault, the problem may be an old copy of TOOLHELP.DLL. As before, delete the file from your Windows SYSTEM directory and retrieve the version on the Desktop disks. You'll need to expand the file using the NPACK.EXE file found on your Fixit disk. To do so, copy both NPACK.EXE and TOOLHELP.DL$ from the Norton disks into your Windows SYSTEM subdirectory. The syntax for unpacking the file is

```
NPACK TOOLHELP.DL$ TOOLHELP.DLL
```

Remember to delete the file TOOLHELP.DL$ before you restart Windows.

Wrong Version Error Message   If you're receiving error messages telling you "Wrong Version," the problem is probably caused by another .DLL file that's not current. Locate the file VER.DLL and delete it. Copy the VER.DLL file from the Desktop disks into your Windows SYSTEM subdirectory and see if this solves the problem.

Viewer Won't Display All Files   If Viewer will not display all kinds of files, the problem may also result from an incorrect version of VER.DLL. As before, delete the existing version and copy the file from your Desktop's disks to your Windows SYSTEM subdirectory.

General Protection Faults   If you are consistently receiving General Protection Faults, the cause is most likely older versions of .DLLs. Locate and rename all of the .DLL files in your Windows SYSTEM subdirectory. For example, replace their extensions with .OLD. Exit Windows and restart it. If the problems seem to be eliminated, try adding the .DLL files back to your system one by one by renaming the extension back to .DLL. Once you locate the problematic file, you'll need to get a replacement.

PC Tools

The utilities that enhanced DOS 5.0 were derived from PC Tools, so this suite of utilities has a good handle on working within the framework that supports Windows. PC Tools has been described as the Swiss Army knife of software, an eclectic set of useful gadgets. Most of the programs in this application are simple and straightforward. Our tips offer advice on a few ways to improve the overall operation of PC Tools.

Tell PC Tools That You're Left-Handed   Use PC Tools' SET statements to change the mouse parameters at the command line or in your AUTOEXEC-.BAT file. The /LE switch exchanges the left and right mouse buttons. To execute the switch from the AUTOEXEC.BAT file, add a line that says

```
SET PCTOOLS = /LE
```

Or from the command line before starting Windows, type

```
PCCONFIG/VIDEO/LE
```

Quick Exit   Use PC Tools' CP Launcher to make a hasty exit from a Windows session in any active application. Click on the Control menu icon (the bar in the upper-left corner of your active window), select the CP Launcher option from the bottom of the list, and click on Exit Windows. Choosing OK in the subsequent dialog box tells CP Launcher to shut down any active Windows applications and return you to the DOS system prompt. Don't worry, CP Launcher prompts you to save changes to any open files that you've modified.

Enable Virus Scan Using PC Tools' Scheduler to automate virus scans not only protects your PC, it does so without intruding into your normal work. To automate a PC Tools virus scan, double-click on the CP Backup icon in your PC Tools program group. Click on the Backup button. Select any disks you want scanned from the Backup From window, and, in the Method window, select Virus Scan Only. Click on the Reporting icon and specify Report to File. Click on Save Setup, activate Safe File Selections, and call this new configuration VSCAN. Click on the Scheduler icon and choose Backup. From the Setup File list, select VSCAN, select Add, and enter a day and time for the scans to take place. Then choose OK and close the Add Backup Scheduler Item dialog box. Choose OK to store the information and exit the Backup Schedule dialog box.

Assuming your PC and Scheduler are both active at the specified time for the scan, Backup does the rest, producing a report for you to review in Notepad at your convenience.

Disable PC Tools If you need to disable PC Tools for some reason, you'll need to do the following: Open the SYSTEM.INI file in SysEdit or Notepad and, in the [boot] section, locate the lines:

```
MOUSE.DRV=C:\PCTOOLS\SYSTEM\COMMMOU.DRV
KEYBOARD.DRV=C:\PCTOOLS\SYSTEM\COMMKBD.DRV
```

Comment out these lines by placing a semicolon in front of them. In their place add the following lines:

```
MOUSE.DRV=MOUSE.DRV
KEYBOARD.DRV=KEYBOARD.DRV
```

In the [386Enh] section, locate the lines:

```
DEVICE=VDMAD.386
DEVICE=VFD.386
```

As before, comment out these lines by placing a semicolon in front of them. Then add the following lines to the [386Enh] section:

```
DEVICE=*VDMAD
DEVICE=*VFD
```

Save the SYSTEM.INI and then open the WIN.INI file in SYSEDIT or Notepad. Comment out the LOAD= and RUN= lines in the [Windows] section by placing a semicolon in front of them. Save these changes and restart Windows.

Asymetrix Toolbook

The graphical programming system called Toolbook was created by Paul Allen, longtime partner and former roommate of Bill Gates, Microsoft's chairman. It is designed to allow quick creation of graphical applications. Toolbook is far too complex to cover thoroughly in a book like this; whole books have been dedicated to its use. Here we offer some standout tips from folks who have worked with the product a lot. These are shortcuts you can use once you have the Toolbook basics in hand.

Box and OpenScript Tips

Toolbook bases its programs on two tools: Boxes, which you build on screen, and scripts, which you create with the product's OpenScript language. These tips improve operation of these essential Toolbook elements.

Make a List Box Use Tab Stops   It is not easy to display list box data in columns because tabs aren't normally recognized in list boxes. To enable a list box to use tab stops when displaying data, identify the dlgBox item that determines the style of the list box, and add the value LBS_USETABSTOPS from WINDOWS.H. This value is 80 hex or 128 decimal.

To specify the location of the tab stops, you need to send the list box a message before it is displayed. This requires a modified version of TBKDLG.DLL, which is available from Asymetrix's bulletin board. This version allows you to modify the dialog box after dialog() has been called, allowing you to add functionality to your boxes.

Dialog Box Tips   Modifying the dlgBox property allows you customize your dialog box. The first item of the dlgBox property is the dialog frame style. The System menu is present in a box because the WS_SYSMENU value is present here (80000 hex or 524288 decimal). By subtracting 524288 from item 1 of the dlgBox property, you can remove the System menu.

If you want to prevent the user from moving the dialog box or activating other applications, you can make the dialog box system-modal by adding the value of DS_SYSMODAL to the dialog frame style. This value is 2.

The box's location is stored in the second and third items of the dlgBox property, and its caption is stored in the ninth item. Adjusting these values allows you to change the box location and caption without having to recreate the dialog box.

Keep Book Size Trim   To keep the size of your books to a minimum during development, place the following handler in your book script or system book script and send the compact command whenever you want to compact your books. This technique is easier and faster than accomplishing the same process via menus.

```
to handle compact
    push name of this book onto bookNames
```

```
    push name of this book onto bookNames
    set chars charCount(item 2 of bookNames) - 2 to\
        charcount(item 2 of bookNames) of item 2 of \
        bookNames to "bak"
    save as item 2 of bookNames, false
    save as item 1 of bookNames, true
    linkDLL "tbkfile.dll"
        .INT removeFile(STRING)
    and
    get removeFile(item 2 of bookNames) of this book
    unlinkDLL "tbkfile.dll"
end
```

Advance to Next Field or Focus with Enter To make the Enter key advance the focus to the next field or record field on a data-entry screen, place the following handler in the page or background script of your book:

```
to handle keychar key
    if key is keyEnter and object of focus is "field"
    - replace "field" with "recordfield" if desired
    send keydown keyTab to focus
    else
        forward
    end
end
```

Get at Scripts through the Back Door If you find that you can't get at a script because you've somehow locked yourself out, take heart: You can still get at it, although you may have to go through the back door.

You can edit the script of any object in a book, regardless of whether the book is running in the current instance or even running at all. To edit the script of a book that you can't open for some reason, open another instance of Toolbook, show the command window, type

```
edit script of book "c:\toolbook\sample.tbk"
```

and then press Enter. Of course, your book name will be different, but this allows you to edit the script of the other book without having to open it. You can edit the script of any object in a book in the same fashion. For example, you can enter

```
edit button "OK" of page 3 of book "c:\toolbook\sample.tbk"
```

Smart Techniques for Using Toolbook

The voices of experience say that these approaches will make your Toolbook development easier and your Toolbook programs better.

Easy Mutually Exclusive Buttons   You can make a group of radio buttons mutually exclusive with fewer lines of OpenScript than you might think. First group the radio buttons together, and then set the group script to the following:

```
to handle buttonDown
set checked of self to false
end
to handle buttonUp
set checked of target to true
end
```

In this context, self refers to the group, but target refers to the object in the group that received the message. You would probably want to do more in the buttonUp handler, of course, but this is all it takes to make the group mutually exclusive.

Limit Style of User Input   You can limit user input to all uppercase, lowercase, or non-echoing by adding a line to an edit control's style value. For example, to specify that only uppercase input be accepted, the correct command is

```
ES_UPPERCASE is 8
```

For lowercase input only, use this line:

```
ES_LOWERCASE is 16
```

And for non-echoing input, the line is

```
ES_PASSWORD is 32
```

Use Filters from Other Windows Applications   Although Toolbook comes with filters for importing .EPS, .CGM, .DRW, and .TIF format graphics files, you can also use compatible filters from other software such as Microsoft Word for Windows.

In the [Toolbook Filters] section of the WIN.INI file, make an entry in the format:

```
file description(ext)=filter filename,EXT
```

For example, you could enter

```
PCX Graphics(.pcx)=c:\win\msapps\grphflt\pcximp.flt,PCX
```

The prompt text to the left of the equal sign will then appear in the Import Graphics dialog box as a filter option.

Conserve Local Memory   If you are doing a lot of moving around from page to page and particularly from book to book, turning off the recording of all that navigation can save a lot of memory space. There are two steps involved, as shown in the following OpenScript statements:

```
set sysHistoryRecord to false
clear sysHistory
```

The first statement turns off the navigation recording, while the second clears out memory. When you consider that sysHistory is a list of up to 100 pages to which the user has navigated, the references to which could be 40 or more characters each, you can see that this could save you up to 4K of local memory.

Search List Boxes   You can't normally use the search command in list boxes, but if you set the fieldType to wordWrap, you'll be able to do so. Once you're finished with the search, change the fieldType back again.

Take Advantage of the Forward Command   Use of the forward command in handlers for system generated messages such as enterBook, enterPage, leave-Page, leaveField, keyUp, keyChar, and so on is critical. This is particularly true if you are using system books, which you are if you are using Multimedia Tool-book, Daybook, or Instant Database, or if you have specified a startupSysBook in your WIN.INI file or set any sysBooks explicitly in your script. If you do not forward some messages, such as a keyUp or keyChar message, Toolbook does not get a chance to process the message normally. For instance, if you handle keyChar messages to check for certain keys, the character does not appear in the field unless you forward the message. For example, you could enter

```
to handle keyChar key
if key = keyEnter
send keyDown keyTab
else
forward
end
end
```

In this example, pressing the Enter key would set the focus to the next field in the tabbing order. If the forward statement were not included, no characters would appear in the field.

If you are using a system book, as Multimedia Toolbook does, failing to include the forward statement in an enterBook handler would prevent the system book from executing any script in an enterBook handler. In Multimedia Toolbook, it would prevent your application from initializing the devices it needs and linking the .DLLs used in multimedia applications.

ObjectVision

ObjectVision from Borland is another of the Windows programs that defy typical description. In one sense, this is a forms package, putting data into user-designed on-screen reports. But it is also an application generator, because the forms are imbued with all the functionality of Borland's database and spreadsheet applications and are backed by an unusual visual design language. Perhaps the best way to describe ObjectVision is as an integration tool that puts a common business filter, the form, over Windows application processes.

These tips will help you with the basic ObjectVision task of getting data into the forms. They also describe methods for getting applications built quickly.

Data Entry Tips

The value of ObjectVision is in the union of on-screen forms and the data generated by business applications. These tips help get the data where you need it.

Change the Default Field Font   To change the default font used to print a FIELD value, enter the editing tool and click the right mouse button on the field button. Select the Value Font. Your choice will be retained as the default font.

Flexible Insertions   When you're designing an application, make it easy for the user to enter data—use Auto Insert instead of @Insert. Auto Insert works the same way, but after entering values in an Insert Record, instead of finding an Enter button, you can move off that record by pressing Enter, F3 (@Previous), F4 (@Next), F5 (@PageUp), F6 (@PageDn), or F7 (@Top).

Prevent Mixed Cases   To prevent data entry in mixed cases, make a field convert all data entered into uppercase. Use the following value tree on the field:

```
@UPPER(fieldname)
```

To create an initial cap field for proper names and so on, enter the following expression on a single line:

```
@PROPER(fieldname)
```

Timesaving Tips

As in any development environment, ObjectVision can be greatly aided by time-saving tips gathered through experience. Try these ideas for streamlining your ObjectVision chores.

Keep Track of Timing   Keep track of the sequence and timing of events with ObjectVision's debugging tracer. Designed to work with an AUX (mono) monitor, this facility can also write to a text file. The catch? You have to create the file before running the program. In this example, save an empty text file called OUTPUT.TXT in the C:\DATA directory. Activate the tracer to write a sequence into the file by inserting the following lines in WIN.INI's [ObjectVision] section. Edit the last line to reflect any different directory names or filenames you may have.

```
EnableAuxPrintf=Yes
TraceEvents=1
TraceObjects=1
AuxName=C:\data\output.txt
```

Autoload Applications   To speed up loading an ObjectVision application you're working on, start Windows, ObjectVision, and the application from the DOS prompt. First, open WIN.INI and ensure that the [Extensions] section contains a line linking the file extension .OVD with the startup command for ObjectVision. If this checks out—and it will if ObjectVision is correctly installed—loading the app from DOS is as simple as typing

```
Win filename.ovd
```

where *filename.ovd* is the name and path to your ObjectVision application. This is an ideal candidate for a short batch file or line in AUTOEXEC.BAT.

View Object Properties   To set or just view the properties for a particular object in Designer mode, click once on the right mouse button.

Add a Deletion Warning   When you're assigning the delete function to a button,

```
@delete("linkname")
```

will do the job, but won't warn you that you're about to delete a record. Insert a comma followed by 1 before the closing parenthesis; that is, use

```
@delete("linkname",1)
```

to bring up such a warning.

Cutting Tables   There's a trick to deleting rows and columns in an ObjectVision table. To remove a row, select the entire table object, grab the lower handle, and drag it upwards. You will see a small box with the number of rows. Continue dragging upwards until this number decrements. To delete columns, click once within a cell in a column to select the individual column object, and drag a corner handle to the left or right until the outline is a single line. The program prompts you to choose whether to delete the column, as shown in Figure 15.4. Delete a row of values by moving the table currency indicator to the row in question and issuing an @delete function, which you can attach to a button or any field's event tree.

FIGURE 15.4

Delete rows and columns in ObjectVision by dragging upon its boundaries to bring up this dialog box.

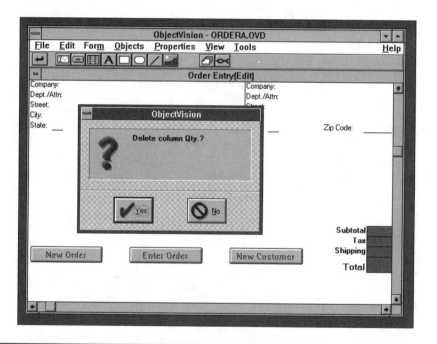

Cut and Paste Forms   Don't duplicate development work. Open ready-made ObjectVision applications and use Windows' standard Cut or Copy commands to move entire forms, trees, or parts of forms to the Clipboard. Then paste them into another ObjectVision application.

Visual Basic

Visual Basic is Microsoft's language that melds the easy programming style of BASIC with on-screen interface building. In Visual Basic, you "draw" the way your application should look, and then code the actions associated with the on-screen parts.

Visual Basic provides a complete development universe for the user with a modest understanding of BASIC programming concepts.

These tips focus on building solid program routines and achieving the best program performance.

Function and Routine Tips

Building screens in Visual Basic is so straightforward that it requires little explanation and presents few opportunities for tips. However, the code that makes the screen functional is a tougher proposition. These tips should help you build better Visual Basic routines.

Use DOEVENTS   Use the DOEVENTS() function regularly, particularly when your Visual Basic application interacts with other Windows applications. Otherwise, Visual Basic may hog the processor, not giving other applications a chance to respond to the keystrokes or DDE messages your Visual Basic application is sending. DOEVENTS() tells Visual Basic to yield processor control to any other applications that may be clamoring for it. Invoke the function as follows:

```
JUNK%=DOEVENTS()
```

Minimize and Restore Routine   Do you want to minimize and restore several forms in a Visual Basic application at once? It's easy. Simply set the MinButton property to false for all but the main form, and then include the following routine under the main form's Repaint subroutine:

```
SUB MainForm.Repaint ()
IF MainForm.WindowState=1 THEN
SecondForm.Hide
ThirdForm.Hide
Etc.Hide
Else
SecondForm.Show
ThirdForm.Show
Etc.Show
END IF
END SUB
```

Whenever you minimize the main form (thus setting its WindowState to 1) the other forms will be hidden. Whenever you restore it, the others will be shown.

Key Sequences Routine   The key sequences routine allows you to funnel Ctrl, Shift, or Alt key sequences to command buttons or menus located on the main form, even if a secondary form has the input focus at the time that the user issues the command. To pass the keystrokes from the active form to another form in a multiform application, create a function like the following for the form that's going to do the passing:

```
Function PassKeys (Keycode As Integer, Shift As Integer)
OtherForm.SetFocus
ShiftDown% = (Shift And SHIFT_MASK) > 0
AltDown% = (Shift And ALT_MASK) > 0
CtrlDown% = (Shift And CTRL_MASK) > 0
SendString$ = " "
If ShiftDown% Then SendString$ = " +" + SendString$
If AltDown% Then SendString$ = " %" + SendString$
If CtrlDown% Then SendString$ = " ^" + SendString$
SendString$ = SendString$ + Chr$(Keycode)
SendKeys SendString$
End Function
```

To use the function, include the following command under the KeyUp procedure for *every* control on the form that will do the passing:

```
Junk=Passkeys(Keycode As Integer, Shift As Integer)
```

You must also include the following definitions from the standard CONSTANT.TXT file in your Global module:

```
Global Const SHIFT_MASK = 1
Global Const CTRL_MASK = 2
Global Const ALT_MASK = 4
```

The Shift variable is a bit field, which contains individual bits that signify the status of the Shift, Alt, and Ctrl keys. You can't examine these bits directly from Visual Basic. Instead, to test whether one of those keys was pressed, you have to evaluate it against the mask for that key found in CONSTANT.TXT, using a Boolean AND expression.

Make DEFINT Global   The DEFINT declaration is not global, even if you include it in the Global module. If you want to designate all untyped variables as integers, you must issue the DEFINT A-Z command in the declarations section of each module in your program.

Turn the Pointer into an Hourglass during Program Delays   Let your users know that your application is performing an operation that takes some time. Use the following routine so users are not left guessing as to why nothing seems to be happening:

```
Sub Form_Click ()
    SavedPointer = Screen.MousePointer    ' Save mouse pointer.
    Screen.MousePointer = 11              ' 11# = hourglass.
    For i = 1 To 10000: Next i            ' Some lengthy operation.
    Screen.MousePointer = SavedPointer    ' set to previous mouse pointer.
End Sub
```

Set Properties for Multiple Controls   When you're setting a series of properties for multiple controls, don't set all the properties for the first control before moving on to the next. Save yourself a good deal of time by selecting a property, setting it for the first control, and then clicking on the other controls one by one to set the same property for them. Once you've finished with that property, select the next property you want to change and repeat the process.

Performance Tips

Visual Basic programs, while simple, are real applications and can be aided by typical development tricks. Try these for compact, quick-running code.

Keep .EXE Files Trim   The size of the compiled .EXE program that Visual Basic will create from your application tends to grow each time you modify and save your application. To compress it, making the .EXE file as compact and efficient as possible, open each module in your application and, in turn, select Code, Save Text, and then Load Text, replacing the existing code with the text file of its code that you just saved. Once you've done that for each module, select Make EXE from the File menu right away.

Speed and Memory Considerations   To speed up the process of showing and hiding forms, load all forms into memory as your application loads, and then simply show or hide them when needed. If, on the other hand, you want to reduce your application's memory usage, simply load its first form into memory as the application loads, and then load and unload subsequent forms as you need them.

Get a Complete API Function Library   Are you trying to figure out the proper way to call a particular Windows API function from your Visual Basic program? Download WINAPI.TXT from the MSBASIC forum on CompuServe. It contains the correct form for every API function that you can call from within Visual Basic.

Access .INI Files from Visual Basic

There are several Windows API Functions that enable Visual Basic to retrieve and write information from or to a Windows .INI file. You can use the following Declare statements in a Visual Basic global module or in the General Declarations of a Visual Basic form to manipulate the contents of .INI files:

- Declare Function GetProfileInt% Lib "Kernel"(ByVal lpAppName$, ByVal lpKeyName$, ByVal nDefault%)

- Declare Function GetProfileString% Lib "Kernel" (ByVal lpApp-Name$, ByVal lpKeyName$, ByVal lpDefault$, ByVal lpReturned-String$, ByVal nSize%)

- Declare Function WriteProfileString% Lib "Kernel"(ByVal lpApp-Name$, ByVal lpKeyName$, ByVal lpString$)

- Declare Function GetPrivateProfileInt% Lib "Kernel" (ByVal lpApp-Name$, ByVal lpKeyName$, ByVal nDefault%, ByVal lpFileName$)

- Declare Function GetPrivateProfileString% Lib "Kernel" (ByVal lp-AppName$, ByVal lpKeyName$, ByVal lpDefault$, ByVal lpRe-turnedString$, ByVal nSize%, ByVal lpFileName$)

- Declare Function WritePrivateProfileString% Lib "Kernel" (ByVal lpAppName$, ByVal lpKeyName$, ByVal lpString$, ByVal lpFile-Name$)

These arguments are used in the preceding functions:

lpAppName$	Specifies the name of a Windows application that appears in the initialization file
lpKeyName$	Specifies the key name that appears in the initialization file
*n*Default$	Specifies the default value for the given key if the key cannot be found in the initialization file
lpFileName$	Points to a string that names the initialization file. If lpFileName does not contain a path to the file, Windows searches for the file in the WINDOWS directory
lpDefault$	Specifies the default value for the given key if the key cannot be found in the initialization file
lpReturnedString$	Specifies the buffer that receives the character string
*n*Size%	Specifies the maximum number of characters (including the last null character) to be copied to the buffer
lpString$	Specifies the string that contains the new key value

PAGE LAYOUT PACKAGES

WHEN WINDOWS 3.0 FIRST CAME OUT, SKEPTICS LEAPT UP AND PROCLAIMED, "Sure, it's *pretty,* but what kind of application needs all those cutes?" "Well," replied defensive Windows supporters, "how about desktop publishing!"

In fact, desktop publishing—the union of text handling, page makeup, and graphics editing—is a uniquely graphical application. This was the "Trojan application" that led the charge of Apple Macintoshes into corporate offices. On PCs, desktop publishing was virtually nonexistent (apart from the brave, but fundamentally inadequate, attempts of Ventura Publisher) until Windows appeared. Since then, PCs have begun slowly to make their mark in this area. Macs still rule where desktop publishing is concerned, but PCs are no longer a joke.

Desktop publishing software, by its very nature, tends to be complex, tough for nongraphicists to fathom, and tough on the underlying system. These tips touch on all those aspects of three representative products: PageMaker, the market leader; Ventura Publisher, the Windows flavor of a DOS diehard; and Microsoft Publisher, an attempt to bring desktop publishing to a broader audience.

PageMaker

PageMaker established desktop publishing on PCs. In the early days of Windows it was one of the few applications that could effectively demonstrate the graphics potential of this new system. PageMaker blends text manipulation, graphics control, and design features in a package that rivals professional typesetting for publication creation.

Our tips move, as the program does, from straightforward text to questions of design and page production.

Text Tips

You can manipulate text in wondrous ways in PageMaker, but the power isn't always obvious. These ideas produce special text effects.

Move Text in a Straight Line   To move a text block quickly and accurately in a straight line, hold down the Shift key before you drag. The four-headed arrow that appears when you drag text will turn into a two-headed one (as shown in Figure 16.1), and the text block's movement will be restricted to either the vertical or horizontal axis—whichever you move it along first.

FIGURE 16.1

Move text blocks in a straight line by holding down the Shift key as you drag them.

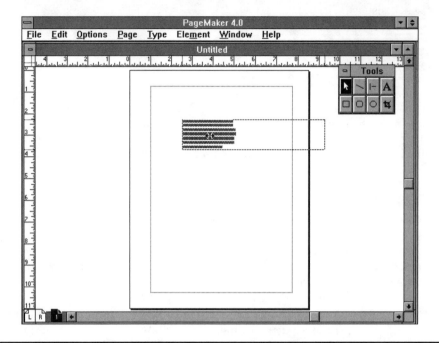

Edit Rotated Text   You can't edit rotated text in the layout view, but you don't have to unrotate it to make changes. Edit it in the Story Editor instead. Just point to the text, and then triple-click with the mouse to load it in the Story Editor. Here you can change the text or typestyle at will. When you're done, double-click on the Story Editor's Control menu box to close the Story Editor and enact your changes.

Using the New Line Character   To start a new line without invoking the formatting for a new paragraph (in a two-line headline, for example), use the new line character (Shift+Enter). This is especially useful when the current style calls for indents or a blank line before or after a paragraph—the new line character will break the line without adding the spacing.

Create Drop Caps   There's no easy way to create drop caps in PageMaker, but it is possible. First, cut the initial letter and paste it outside the text block. Then enlarge it to the approximate size desired. Shorten the window shade handles to fit the character's width. Next, drag the letter back into the text, aligning the bottom of the character with the baseline of your first paragraph.

Now comes the tricky part. Pull a temporary guide down from the horizontal ruler and align it with the baseline of the line following the drop cap. (That is, if the drop cap extends to line four, place the ruler at line five.) Using the pointer tool, select the main text block, and then roll the shade up to the bottom of the drop cap, so that only the lines under the character are showing. Resize the block displayed to fit next to the drop cap. Now, click on the bottom handle (it should be red) to pick up the remaining text. Paste this text below the drop cap; it should return to its original margins. Finally, align the first line of the major text block with the temporary guide you inserted before.

Graphics and Document Tips

Publications aren't made of text alone. The ability to integrate graphics to create compound documents is one of PageMaker's strongest features. These tips make it stronger still.

Anchor Graphics to Text   For a logo that marks the end of a story, or a chart that's permanently tied to a section of a report, use an inline graphic. Inline graphics are anchored to their position in the text, not to the page. To create an inline graphic, highlight a regular graphic, cut it to the Clipboard, select the text tool, place the cursor at the insertion point, and paste.

Position Duplicate Graphics   To position duplicate graphics, first copy the original, and then paste it. This creates a duplicate that overlaps the original. Move the duplicate where you want it, and then press Ctrl+Shift+P. This pastes a second copy in the same relative position to the first copy as the first copy is to the original, as shown in Figure 16.2. You can repeat the Ctrl+Shift+P keystroke as often as you need to create more copies. You can use this trick to place duplicates in exactly the same position on different pages; just copy the first duplicate to a new page, and repeatedly press Ctrl+Shift+P.

Preview Documents   Before printing a long PageMaker document, quickly preview each page on the screen to check for obvious errors. First, press Alt+Shift or Alt+Ctrl, select the Page menu, and click on Fit in Window. Then press Shift and select Go to Page. Keep holding down Shift until the first page is drawn, and then watch for errors as PageMaker cycles through each page. When you're done, you can press Escape to exit from the continuous loop.

Open a Single View   To open a single view (say 200% magnification) on all the pages in your document, open the Page menu, hold down the Alt and Ctrl keys, and select the view. Now you can move from page to page without changing your magnification.

Faster Startup   PageMaker loads every import and export filter and dictionary installed whenever you start the program. If startup is too sluggish for you, check which filters you have installed and remove the unnecessary ones. Here's how: Select the Help menu, hold down Ctrl, and click on About PageMaker. You'll get a complete list of filters and dictionaries. Note the ones you don't want, and then open the ALDUS.INI file in Notepad. Find the lines that contain the condemned filter names and prefix each one with a semicolon. This prevents the line from loading, but gives you the option of using the filter or dictionary when you need to.

FIGURE 16.2

Easily position duplicate graphics in PageMaker by pressing Ctrl+Shift+P.

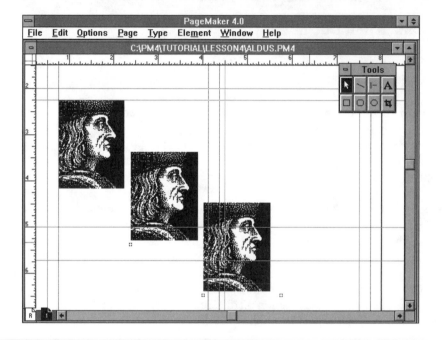

Saved by PageMaker's Temporary File PageMaker has an autostore feature that can really save your skin after a system crash. Every time you invoke a major function—including a move to another page—the program saves your changes in a temporary file. If your system crashes while you're working on a file, PageMaker loads the temporary file the next time you call up the main one. If you're working on an unnamed new file during a crash, look for a filename like ~PM4280E.TMP in your Windows temporary directory (usually \TEMP).

Quick Story Imports The quickest way to bring a story from another Page-Maker document into your current publication is to import it directly from an un-opened file. The Place command on the File menu can read PageMaker files into a new document just as easily as a graphics or a text file—but with .PM4 files, you have more options. The command brings up a dialog box listing each of the different stories in a document, supplying the first few words of each one to make the stories easy to recognize. Select the one(s) you want, or select all of them, and click on OK to bring them into the current document. This trick also comes in handy for salvaging stories from a damaged file that you can't open in the usual way.

Ventura Publisher

The loyal opposition to PageMaker's majority position, Xerox's Ventura Publisher, is considered by some simpler and by others more inscrutable than the market leader. Ventura's niche seems to be small businesses and individuals with moderate document-creation needs. Ventura has DOS origins, having gone to the huge trouble of creating its own graphic environment in DOS so that some publishing power was possible on a PC. As is often the case with DOS-derived programs, Ventura has some areas that can be hard to follow and occasional compatibility issues.

The tips in this section look at ways to push the power of the product, use some of its better hidden features, and troubleshoot problems.

Formatting Tips

Here is a bit of advice on accessing some formatting features of Ventura that may not be obvious.

Format a Single Page   A standard format is the best way to lay out a whole report or book, but sometimes you might want the opening page to be more dramatic than the rest of the document. Select the Remove Page command from the Chapter menu to change the design of one page without affecting the underlying page-frame format in the rest of the document.

Create Multicolumn Headlines   There's an easy way to place a headline over several columns in a multicolumn document. Select tagging mode (the paragraph icon). Click on the headline that you want to span multiple columns. Choose Alignment from the Paragraph menu. In the Overall Width box (shown in Figure 16.3), select Frame-Wide. Click on OK. The Frame-Wide setting applied to this headline tag overrides the multicolumn format of the underlying page.

Split Captions   Some book designs put illustration caption labels, such as "Figure 3-5," in the margin to the left or right of the illustration, while keeping the caption text itself directly below the illustration. Ventura won't automatically split the caption in this way, but try this: Use the Anchors & Caption option on the Frame menu to add a caption frame and label to the right or left of the illustration frame. Select the illustration frame, create a box using the Box Text tool, and then size and position it below the illustration. Enter your caption text in the Box Text box. Give the illustration frame enough additional vertical padding by selecting the Sizing & Scaling option from the Frame menu and changing the settings in the Sizing & Scaling dialog box to prevent your body text from overlapping the box.

Use Descriptive Style Sheet Names   When using Ventura Publisher for short documents such as fliers, create a style sheet using tag names that describe text and font attributes instead of using generic titles like Headline or Subtitle. For example, for centered 12-point Palatino text, use the tag PTO CTR 12p, and for justified and indented 16-point Avante Garde, use the tag AVGD JF IN 16p. You'll be able to tell at a glance each tag's font and basic attributes. To make style sheets easier to reuse, use descriptive titles prefaced by double ampersands to ensure that they appear at the top of the list in the style sheet dialog box— &&PALAVG.STY, for instance.

FIGURE 16.3

Create headlines that span more than one column by selecting Frame-Wide in the Alignment dialog box.

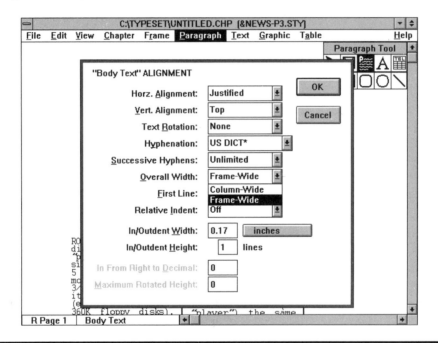

Fast Framing When drawing several text boxes or frames in succession, use the Box Text or Add Frame tool. Hold down the Shift key as you draw with the tool. When you release the mouse button, the cursor remains in its Box Tool or Add Frame shape, so you can draw another box or frame without selecting the tool again.

Cut and Paste Tables to New Documents With the Table Edit tool you can cut or copy an entire table and paste it into another part of your document. However, you can't paste it into a new document, because it will vanish from the Clipboard when you close the original document. Instead, cut or copy the table as before, and then use the Add Frame tool to create a new frame in your document (you'll only need it temporarily). Select the new frame with the pointer tool, and then paste the table into it. Finally, cut the entire frame to the Clipboard, open the new document, and paste in the table-laden frame. Cut and paste the table into your document and delete the temporary frame.

Make Fractions with the Equation Generator   Unlike other Windows programs, Ventura Publisher doesn't use the handy symbols for the fractions $1/2$ and $1/4$, which are built into most PostScript and TrueType fonts (generated by pressing Alt+0189 and Alt+0188, respectively). Use Ventura's equation generator for fractions instead. Before importing your document into Ventura, use your word processor to enter the simple equation code in your document. For the $1/2$ symbol, type **<$E 1/2>**; for $1/4$, type **<$E 1/4>**; and so on. You can even build macros so that you can enter the codes with a single keystroke. Ventura automatically converts the codes into fractions when you load the text.

Quick Hanging Quotes   You've seen magazine article pull-quotes where the opening quotation mark lies outside the left text margin. Ventura doesn't automatically create such hanging punctuation, but you can manage it using Ventura's Special Effects command. First create a new tag for hung quotes. Then, select Special Effects from the Paragraph menu and choose Bullet. At Bullet Char enter **169** (the open quote ASCII code), and at Indent After Bullet, enter a value half the point size of the call-out type; adjust this value later to get attractive spacing between the quote and the text block. To align the text in a column, select Spacing from the Paragraph menu and decrease the In From Left value by the same amount.

Speed Tips

Desktop publishing programs are notoriously slow, and Ventura is no exception. These tips will get the program running as quickly as possible.

Replay Recent Dialog Boxes   Avoid reselecting nested menu options to repeat the last operation you performed. Press Ctrl+X to redisplay the most recently used dialog box. This technique is especially helpful when you are trying to determine the best cropping and sizing for an imported graphic.

Speed Up Program Loading   If it takes too long to load Ventura Publisher on your system, tell the program to stop rebuilding the soft fonts on your system each time it is loaded. These fonts don't need to be rebuilt until new ones are added to your system. To do this, rename ENVIRONMENT.WID to a new width table name. Then use that width table in your style sheets. The ENVIRONMENT.WID table is rebuilt from the fonts listed in the Windows printer driver and your WIN.INI file each time it is loaded. To rebuild the table, rename it back to ENVIRONMENT.WID and restart Ventura.

Print Multiple Copies Faster   When printing multiple copies, the Print window's Copies option works only if you select Collated Copies. If you don't collate, you can't enter a number in the Copies box. However, collating (printing the pages in successive order multiple times, instead of printing multiple copies of each page in successive order) takes dramatically longer than printing in the normal manner. To get around this, click on the Setup box to bring up the Windows printer setup screen, and enter the number of copies you want under the Copies option. Then print as usual.

Troubleshooting Tips

If problems crop up in your use of Ventura, check out these workarounds.

File Not Found Messages   Improperly copied Ventura chapters usually open with a string of "file not found" messages because the locations of text and graphics files on the copy don't match the pointers in the chapter file. When you get caught like this, organize the text and graphics files into sub-directories and jot down the path names you've used. Then make a backup copy of the chapter file and open it in a word processor. Look for entries like this at the head of the file:

```
#G 07 e:\1_book\command.eps 0040 0100 00FA
#I 03 e:\1_book\1_type\graphics\pc.tif * 0021 0021
```

Edit the drive specs and path names at the head of the chapter file so they reflect the correct location of the files. Then save the file as text-only (ASCII).

An Error Message while Loading a Large Document   If you receive an error message when trying to load a large document, try increasing the memory allocated to Ventura Publisher. Choose About from the Help menu, and, in the dialog box that appears, increase the memory settings, as shown in Figure 16.4. If you need help with these settings, press F1. Save your changes and restart the program; then try loading the document again.

System Faults when Using Text Menu   If you receive UAEs or GP faults when selecting items in the Text menu or when choosing Alignment of Text from the Paragraph menu, the cause may be a third-party display driver. If you are using a driver that didn't come with Windows, check with the manufacturer to see if there is an update that works with Ventura Publisher.

Printer Troubleshooting   If your PostScript printer stalls frequently and doesn't print your Ventura document, try resetting the Transmission Retry and the Job Timeout settings in the printer driver configuration dialog box. To increase the settings, choose the Printers icon from the Windows Control Panel.

If graphics don't print on Hewlett-Packard printers or compatibles, make sure that the printer resolution is set to 300 dpi. To increase this setting, choose the Printers icon from the Windows Control Panel.

Microsoft Publisher

Microsoft came to desktop publishing late and on a small scale. This package has a decidedly low-end feel. You wouldn't use Publisher to produce a book, but it would work fine for an employee newsletter or marketing pamphlet.

The tips here focus on getting a bit of high-end oomph from this low-end application.

FIGURE 16.4

If you're having trouble loading a large document, try increasing the memory allocated to Ventura.

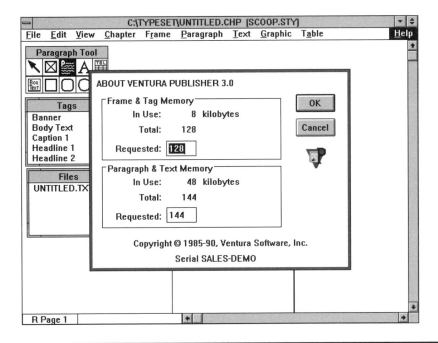

Drawing and Text Tips

Most operations in Publisher are straightforward. Try these ideas for a few drawing and text capabilities that you might otherwise miss.

Create Identical Objects   To quickly create a number of identical objects in succession, lock the Drawing tool by clicking it with the right mouse button, and then execute the drawing as many times as desired. When you're finished, unlock the Drawing tool by choosing the Selection tool (the arrow on the far left of the Toolbar).

Perfect Shapes   As in many drawing and page-layout packages, you can create perfect squares, circles, and straight lines in Publisher by holding down the Shift key and dragging while the Drawing tool is selected.

Perfect Kerning   Use kerning when you want to position characters more precisely by setting the exact amount of space between each character. To access this Publisher feature, choose Spacing Between Characters from the Format menu and increase or decrease the setting as desired, selecting Squeeze Letters Together or Move Letters Apart. Of course, before you set the spacing you'll need to select the characters to be kerned.

Keep in mind that Publisher adjusts the space following *each* character, even the last one. For example, if you choose an entire word to be kerned, the spacing will be adjusted for each letter, including the last one, where more space will be added. If you're centering kerned text, you may notice that it doesn't quite appear to be even. This may be because space was added after the last letter. To avoid this problem, don't select the last letter in a word, phrase, or sentence that you are kerning.

Custom Bullets   You can create custom bullets to be used for emphasis by manipulating the BorderArt that's included with Publisher. Draw a rectangle where you want to place the bullet and then choose BorderArt from the Layout menu. From the BorderArt dialog box (shown in Figure 16.5) select the pattern that you want to use as a single bullet. Set the point size of the bullet to match the size of the text that you plan to use in the bulleted item and then select OK. The rectangle that you drew will contain the patterned border. Grab the selection handles on the rectangle and pull it from the top to the bottom to create a single line; then pull from the left to the right until the rectangle's border becomes a single point. If the bullet is not located exactly where you want it, move it to the correct location. If you'll be creating several bulleted items, select the bullet and copy it to the Clipboard so that you can paste it to a new location.

FIGURE 16.5

You can use Microsoft Publisher's BorderArt to create custom bullets.

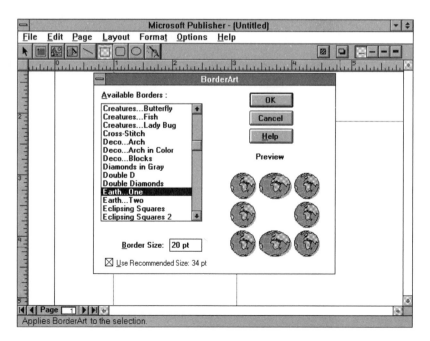

Search for Special Characters As in other Windows applications, you can use Publisher's Find or Replace command to locate special formatting characters within text. You can specify the following characters in the Find and Replace dialog boxes:

?	Wildcard character
^-	Optional hyphen
^~	Nonbreaking hyphen
^n	Line break
^p	End of a paragraph
^s	Nonbreaking space
^t	Tab stop
^w	White space

Superimpose Text You can create the effect of superimposed text by manipulating text contained in two separate text frames. Place one frame on the background page (select Go to Background from the Page menu to get to the background page) and the other on the foreground page. Format the foreground frame as transparent by selecting Shading from the Layout menu and selecting the first style. The word clear will appear in the Preview box. Then position the foreground text frame over the text frame in the background until you have the desired effect (see Figure 16.6). Remember, though, that an object on the background page will appear on each page in your document unless you select Ignore Background from the Page menu when working on the other pages. Make sure to select this option so that the text frame appears only on the page with the superimposed effect.

Page-Numbering and Exiting Tips

If you use these techniques, you can get more control over page-numbering procedures than you might think. Plus, we'll tell you the fastest way to get out of Publisher.

Custom Page Numbers Publisher can automatically number the pages of your publication. From the Page menu, choose Go to Background. On the background page, create a text frame where you want to place the page numbers. Then choose Insert Page Numbers from the Page menu. A pound sign (#) will appear in the frame as a placeholder for the actual number of each page. You can now customize the style of your page numbers by selecting the pound sign and changing the typeface, font size, style, and alignment.

FIGURE 16.6

Create superimposed text in your documents by using two separate text frames—one on the foreground and one on the background.

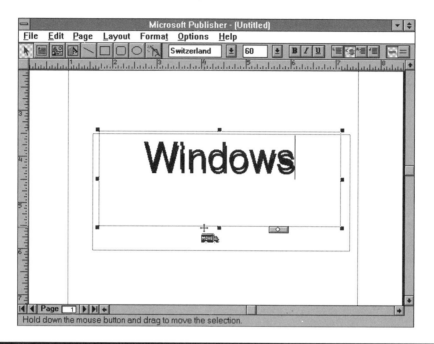

Suppress Page Numbering   Automatic page numbering is convenient, but there will sometimes be pages in your document that you don't want numbered. You have two options for suppressing page numbers on a specific page. Try this method first: Select the Box Drawing tool from the Toolbar and draw a box over the area on the page that contains the page number. Use the color white as the fill and border color. Try printing the page to see if the "white-out" worked. If not, you can choose Ignore Background from the Page menu. If you select this option, however, no background objects will show for that particular page.

Number Facing Pages   Publisher can also automatically number pages that will be facing one another. Start with a right-hand page and, as when inserting regular page numbers, select Go to Background from the Page menu. Create a text frame where you want the page number to appear on the right-hand page. Choose Insert Page Numbers from the Page menu and then select Layout Guides from the Layout menu. Select the Create Two Backgrounds with Mirrored Guides check box and then choose OK. Publisher will create a second background for the left-hand page that mirrors the background for the right-hand page.

Quick Getaway   Pressing the F3 key lets you quickly exit Publisher. If you have not saved your latest changes, Publisher asks you if you want to save them.

PERSONAL PRODUCTIVITY TOOLS

THIS CHAPTER COVERS A POTPOURRI OF PROGRAMS THAT HAVE ONE THING IN common: They aim to improve some common business task for individuals. In some cases it's managing projects—keeping track of resources, producing reports, measuring how long it will take to get work done. In other cases, it's money—balancing accounts, writing checks, paying bills. A few programs deliver a little of everything.

As the programs in this chapter run the gamut, so do the tips. Look over this chapter even if you don't currently use any of these products. Many of the ideas will translate to other similar applications.

Microsoft Project

Project management is a natural for the Windows environment. It combines aspects of databases, graphics programs, spreadsheets, and document managers to deliver information on the status of work in progress. Microsoft Project, a long-time DOS standard for this kind of work, is exemplary of how Windows makes project management easier and more powerful.

We have a healthy crop of tips here, not because the product has problems, but because it can do so much.

Viewing Tips

Producing coherent reports about the status of projects is the key to project management. These tips improve the performance of Views, the slices of data Microsoft Project provides.

Customize Your Views   On the left side of the Gantt Chart, Project normally displays the Task Table with plan data. To show critical information, change the default display to show project costs or variances. Choose Define Views from the Views menu, and then select Gantt Chart from the list of charts and tables. In the Table box, scroll through the list to select Costs or Variances. In the Filter box, choose Critical or In-Progress Tasks. Click on OK, and then click on Set to make those choices the default view.

Show Separate Files in a Single Window   If your department's projects are managed in separate files, merge the files into a single window to present them in a single Gantt chart. First open all the relevant files (up to a maximum of eight); then choose New Window from the Window menu. Select all the files in the list, and click on OK. Project opens a window that includes all the files. Although the files remain separate, you can filter, sort, and report on a merged project as if it were a single file. You can even save it by choosing Save Workspace from the File menu. To differentiate between files in a merged window, choose Define Tables from the Tables menu and edit the Plan table to add the Project field to the table definition.

Create a Filter to Show Summary Tasks   Project doesn't come with a filter to display only summary tasks, but you can create one. For starters you'll have to identify the summary tasks by marking their fields: Select Form from the Edit menu and select the Marked box. You can then create a filter to display only these marked tasks by selecting the Field Name as Op, the Test as Marked, and Equals as Yes.

View All of a Resource's Tasks   To view all of the tasks to which a single resource is assigned, you might try to filter a project on the Resource Names column. But using this view doesn't always display all of the tasks to which a resource is assigned because the maximum column width is only 256 characters (ellipses at the end of the list inform you if there are more tasks). An easy way to see all of the tasks is to place the Resource Sheet in the top part of the Project screen and then move the Task Sheet or Gantt Chart to the bottom of the screen. When you select a resource name in the Resource Sheet, all of its associated tasks will appear in the Task Sheet or Gantt Chart.

Create Base Calendars   If several resources have similar work schedules, create a base calendar to represent them collectively. Choose Base Calendars from the Options menu, and choose New to create a new calendar or Copy to start with an existing calendar. Give the new calendar a name, set the dates and times, and then save and use it.

Task and Task-Sheet Tips

Accurate reports demand accurate underlying information. These tips should help you structure the underpinnings for a project.

Assign Resources to Many Tasks at Once   You can save time by assigning multiple resources to a single task at the same time. First select the group of tasks to which you want to assign the same resources. Then select Form from the Edit menu. In the Resources field, type in each resource separated by a comma (or the default List Separator that you've selected). For example, you might enter

```
Steve,Wendy,Mark,David
```

If each resource will be allocated at a different level—for example, with Steve and David working 100 percent, and Wendy and Mark only 50 percent—you'll have to insert the value in brackets after each name. For this example, the text in the Resources field would read

```
Steve,Wendy[.5],Mark[.5],David
```

These percentages will be applied to all of the selected tasks.

Add New Tasks to a Project Already in Progress   When you add a new task to a project that is already in progress, it will automatically be scheduled according to the project's start date. To view the project's start date, select Project Info from the Options menu. Assigning this start date to the task doesn't make sense if your project is already underway and the task will have a very different time frame. To schedule the task according to the day that you've added it to the project, select the constraint Start No Earlier Than and set that equal to the date you want the task to begin. This solution works fine unless the same task also needs to be assigned another constraint, such as Finish No Later Than, because a task can only have one constraint.

To change the start date of a task that has an existing constraint, you can add the Delay field to the task. To calculate the exact amount of delay time that you'll need to specify, first create a new task. From the Gantt Chart view, select this new task and then choose Form from the Edit menu. In the Dates section, enter the project's start date in the Scheduled Start box and enter the date the task is expected to begin in the Scheduled Finish box. Then select OK. Project will calculate the value you'll want to use in the Delay field of the original task. Delete the new task you just created—its only purpose is to calculate the delay value.

Now add the delay value to the original task: From the Entry table in the Gantt Chart view, select Define Tables from the Table menu, select the Entry table, choose Edit, select the Scheduled Start line under Field Name, and choose Insert. Click on the blank line in the Field Name column and type **delay**. Choose OK and then choose Set to make the change take effect. The delay should now appear in the table between the Duration and Scheduled Start.

Delete a Single Field in the Task Sheet   If you attempt to delete a field in a Task or Resource Sheet by selecting Cut or Delete from the Edit menu or by simply pressing the Delete key, you'll end up deleting the entire task or resource. To easily remove a single field, select it, place your pointer in the formula bar, backspace over the information, and then press Enter.

Printing a Gantt Chart without the Task Sheet   By default, the Task Sheet is printed on the left side of the page when you print a Gantt chart. To remove the Task Sheet from the printout (and prevent the left side of the page from being blank) use the following method instead of just repositioning the chart over the Task Sheet: Create a dummy Task Sheet by selecting Define Table from the Table menu and including only one field that has a width of 1. In the table's Title box, enter a space so that this area will appear blank. Save this table and it will appear on the left side of the screen (and the printout), but will not be visible because it is blank and narrow.

Keyboard Shortcuts   Don't slavishly use the mouse to navigate through your charts or select timescale units. Use these shortcuts to zoom to the top of your charts or cycle through time in a progression of hours, days, weeks, months, quarters, and years:

Alt+Home	Scrolls to the start of a project in a Gantt chart
Ctrl+Home	Scrolls to the top of a table in a Tables chart
Ctrl+* (numeric keypad)	Increases timescale units
Ctrl+/ (numeric keypad)	Decreases timescale units

Formatting Tips

Project management applications have some characteristics of desktop publishers and some features of presentation graphics software. The following tips put a shine on Project's look and feel.

Add Text to a Gantt Bar   To annotate a Gantt bar with a task's duration (or any other comments), create an invisible Gantt bar and attach text to it. Choose Palette from the Format menu and insert a row in the list beneath the definitions of Critical and Noncritical bars. Click on the down arrow in the Bar box and select the blank bar from the list. Enter the following information in the blank row:

Bar Name:	**Fake**
Show For:	**Normal**
From:	**Scheduled Start**
To:	**Scheduled Start**
Right Text:	**Duration**

Finally, click on OK. The task duration now appears on the bars of critical and noncritical tasks, but not milestones or summary tasks.

Change Colors   In Project, you can choose from various color schemes by selecting Preferences from the Options menu. But these predefined schemes may not be to your liking. You can customize them by editing Project's .INI file, WINPROJ.INI.

To change the default colors, you need to know the red-green-blue values for the colors that you want to use in their place. You can determine these numeric values by selecting Color in the Windows Control Panel, choosing Color Palette, and then choosing Define Custom Colors. Then move the custom color selector around the color palette until you've located the color you want (as you move across the spectrum it will appear in the Color|Solid box). Note the color's red-green-blue value in the boxes at the bottom of the dialog box.

Once you've identified all of the colors you want to use in your Project scheme, open the WINPROJ.INI file in Notepad or another text editor. Locate the entries labeled Form Color and Dialog Color. Delete the existing values and insert the values associated with the new color (separating the values by commas). Save your changes to WINPROJ.INI and restart Project. Your color changes will now be in effect.

Create Custom Headers, Footers, and Legends   As in many Windows applications, you can create custom headers and footers in Project's printouts by using a series of codes. You can also use these codes to format Project's legends. To use the following codes, you need to choose Page Setup from the File menu and enter the appropriate codes in the Header, Footer, and Legend boxes. Note that the codes are case sensitive.

&L	Left-align the characters that follow
&C	Center the characters that follow
&R	Right-align the characters that follow
&D	Print the current date
&T	Print the current time
&P	Print the page number
&F	Print the filename
&s	Print the project start date
&f	Print the project finish date
&v	Print the name of the view
&r	Print the name of the report
&p	Print the project name as shown in the Options Project Info dialog box
&c	Print the company name as shown in the Options Project Info dialog box
&m	Print the manager's name as shown in the Options Project Info dialog box
&d	Print the current date as shown in the Options Project Info dialog box
&&	Print a single ampersand

Use Colors and Shapes to Denote Project Milestones   To easily get an idea of a project's progress, you can use special colors or shapes to display milestones in your Gantt Charts. Select the chart and choose Palette from the Format menu. In the Show For field, select Milestone, Critical. Select the color and/or shape that you want to use to represent milestones. If you'd like to show other, less critical, milestones in a different color and shape, create a new definition for the Milestone, Noncritical. Select Milestone, Noncritical in the Show For field and select the desired color and shape. When you're done setting the milestone properties, select OK to save the changes and return to the chart.

Microsoft Works

In DOS, the notion of integrated software made a lot of sense. Since each application virtually had to build its entire operating environment—look, feel, commands, formats—maintaining that environment across a suite of products provided an obvious benefit. Even in DOS, however, integrated packages lost out to more powerful individual programs. In Windows, the ability of the operating environment to integrate applications has diminished the need for preintegrated applications. Still, some integrated applications have made the migration to Windows.

Microsoft Works is a case in point. Recast as a small set of business tools, it has made the jump from DOS to Windows. Offering a spreadsheet, word processor, and database, Works falls somewhere between Windows' applets and more complex programs.

These tips push the potential of all Works' modules.

Text Tips

Here are some ideas for getting the most from the text processor built into Works.

Keep Text in View   Use Works' Wrap for Window command to keep your work in sight at all times. When you turn on this feature, text will wrap to keep all lines visible on screen, regardless of the size of the window (see Figure 17.1). The document's margins won't be changed, and when you print the document it will still take up the full page. Select Wrap for Window from the Options menu to toggle on this handy feature.

Editing Your Custom Dictionary   You can easily add words and names to (and delete them from) your custom dictionary in Works. To add many words at a time, create a text file in the word processor that contains all the words. Then run the spell checker and let Works add each word as it flags it. These words are added to the text file CUSTOM.DIC, which is located in the WINDOWS\MSAPPS\PROOF directory. It's quicker to add words directly to the text file yourself, but caution is advised because Works sorts this file in ASCII alphabetical order and you don't want to introduce any errors. Similarly, you can delete words from the dictionary by opening CUSTOM.DIC in the word processor, locating the words, and deleting them. When you are finished editing the file, make sure to save it as Text (DOS), not Text.

FIGURE 17.1

Works' Wrap for Window option keeps all text in view, no matter what the size of the window.

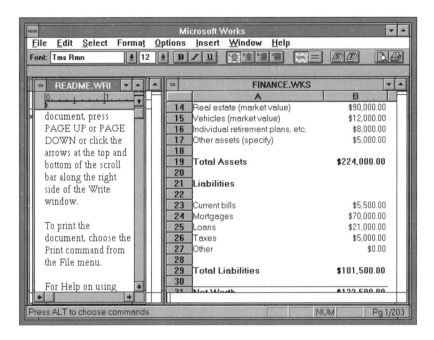

Changing the Font and Style of Headers and Footers   You can easily format headers and footers in Works by formatting the last paragraph in your documents instead of having to go through dialog boxes to format the headers and footers themselves. The headers and footers will take on the formatting of the last paragraph marker in the document. If you want the headers and footers to be formatted the same as the rest of your document, you won't need to make any changes. But if you want them in a different font you can add a paragraph marker to the document by pressing the Enter key after the last bit of text. Add a space to this new line and highlight it. Then format it in the font that you want to be used for the headers and footers.

Spreadsheet Tips

These tips bring surprising power to the Works spreadsheet module.

Protecting Some or All of the Data in a Spreadsheet   Use the Protect Data command in Works to help you save all or just some of your data from accidental changes. To protect the entire spreadsheet, simply choose Protect Data from the Options menu. To verify that this option is on, look at the Options menu and see if a check mark appears next to Protect Data. To turn off total protection and protect only selected data, press Ctrl+Home followed by Ctrl+Shift+End to select the entire worksheet. From the Format menu, select Style and then deselect the Locked check box. Now select the cells that you want protected and choose Protect Data from the Options menu. To unprotect some selected cells, choose Style from the Format menu and deselect the Locked box; then choose Protect Data from the Options menu to remove the check mark.

Rounding Numbers in the Spreadsheet and Database Take advantage of Works' rounding feature in the spreadsheet and database to make your data automatically take on the format that you choose. The Round function uses the syntax

```
=ROUND(value,number of places)
```

and can be used with cell references in place of an actual value. You can round numbers up to 14 places on either side of the decimal point. For example, to round the value in cell B4 to the nearest integer you would specify

```
=ROUND(B4,0)
```

To round the cell's value to a specific number of places to the left of the decimal point, use a negative number. For example, if the value in B4 is 102 and the cell's formula says

```
=ROUND(B4,-1)
```

the value displayed by B4 would be 100. To round the cell's value to a specific number of places to the right of a decimal point (for a decimal number), use a positive number. For example, if the value in B4 is 27.8897 and the cell's formula is

```
=ROUND(B4,2)
```

the value displayed by B4 would be 27.89.

Use Leading Zeros in Zip Codes If you enter numbers with leading zeros into Works' database or spreadsheet, such as zip codes for the Eastern United States, the zeros won't be displayed. To force Works to show these zeros, select Leading Zeros from the Format menu and enter the number of digits you want to display.

Database Tips

Pump up Works' database program with the following techniques.

Sorting on More than Three Fields Works is limited to performing a database sort on three fields at one time. To sort more than three fields, you have to conduct multiple sorts in reverse order of importance. For example, suppose you want to sort the following fields: Name, Title, Department, Salary, and Years Service. First rank the fields' order of importance to you: Salary, Years Service, Title, Name, Department. Then conduct a sort using Title, Name, and Department as the first, second, and third sort fields, respectively. Once this sort is completed, you conduct another sort where Salary is the first sort field and Years is the second sort field.

Create Multiple-Line Fields in a Form   Customize your database forms and make data entry easier by creating multiple-line fields instead of lengthy fields that span the entire screen. You can create these fields in the database's Form view by choosing Field Size from the Format menu and entering the number of lines you want the field to include. As you enter text in the field, it will automatically wrap to the next line. To jump to the next line in the field without adding any more text, press Shift+Enter. These multiple lines will only appear in Form view; the field's contents will actually be contained in a single line in list views and reports.

Tips for All Works Modules

The Works modules share a number of common facilities. These tips improve operation of the Works application environment overall.

Creating More than One Template File for Each Tool   Each of Works' modules can use only one template file, but you can get around this limit by creating additional templates that are just regular files you've marked as read-only. In the selected module—for example, the word processor—create a new document by selecting New from the File menu. Enter the template text and format it as desired. Save the file with an easy-to-remember file name, such as MYTEMP. In the Windows File Manager, locate this newly created file, select it, and choose Properties from the File menu. Select the Read Only check box in the Attributes section of the Properties dialog box.

Now when you want to use the template, open the file in Works' word processor. A message will tell you that the file is read-only; select OK. Enter the information for the document you are creating that is based on the template. When you are done, choose Save As from the File menu and give the document a unique name.

Start with a Tidy Workspace   Start each Works session in an orderly way by creating and saving a workspace that fits the way you work. Each time you start Works, all elements will be in exactly the same place each time—that means size and position of windows, as well as documents and iconized files. For example, if you're consistently working on a big project, you can have all the files at your fingertips. Set up Works just the way you want it and then select Save Workspace from the File menu. If you find that you don't want to use this same workspace each Works session, change the Options settings to reflect this preference. Choose Work Settings from the Options menu and deselect the Use Saved Workspace check box. When you *do* want to use the saved workspace—for example, when you're preparing a monthly report—change this setting in the Work Settings dialog box and restart Works. To save a new workspace, select Save Workspace from the File menu to overwrite the previous workspace.

Mouse Shortcut to Open Works' Startup Dialog Box   Quickly access Works' Startup dialog box by double-clicking anywhere on the blank background that appears once you've started Works and before you've opened any files. Calling up this dialog box allows you to create a new document, open an existing file, or use a WorksWizard.

Delrina PerForm Pro

Forms software began as an application that could create on-screen representations for common printed business forms. Over time, the software has grown far more powerful. Today, forms applications function as formatted filters through which data from the far reaches of a corporate network can be drawn. These electronic forms are "intelligent": They can manipulate and evaluate the data they display. Forms software could become one of the breakout hit categories of Windows computing.

Delrina's PerForm Pro stands among the most powerful and innovative of forms packages. Our tips examine merging data into forms, formatting and display, and pushing performance to the max.

Tool Tips

PerForm provides a wide selection of tools for creating its forms. Use these tips to sharpen those tools.

Customize Your Tools   Often when you're using the Comb tool in your forms, except when you're creating tables, you only need two areas instead of the default of four. You can change this setting to reflect your preference by double-clicking on the Comb tool and changing the number in the Number of Areas box in the Comb Spacing section from 4 to 2, or any other number that you choose, as shown in Figure 17.2.

You can also customize the Text and Fill tools to reflect your preferences. For the Text and Fill tools you can set options for the Regular or Fillable text type. To adjust these settings, select the tool, select the desired setting, and then exit the tool to save your changes.

Easy Defaults to Try   It's easy to set new defaults for PerForm Pro's tools, but it may take a bit of fine-tuning to get your forms looking exactly right. If you don't have time to experiment but want to adjust the tool defaults, try these settings: For regular text select an easy-to-read, sans serif typeface like Helvetica or Arial at 8 points; for fill text select a contrasting typeface, such as the serif font Times Roman at a size of 10 points; for regular text justification select top, left; for fill text justification select top, left as well because left, bottom justification may cause fill data to overwrite regular text; finally, for margins change the default to .02 inches to gain some valuable space that gives you more flexibility when designing your forms.

FIGURE 17.2

To change settings for the Comb tool in PerForm Pro's Designer, double-click on it to bring up the Comb Attributes dialog box.

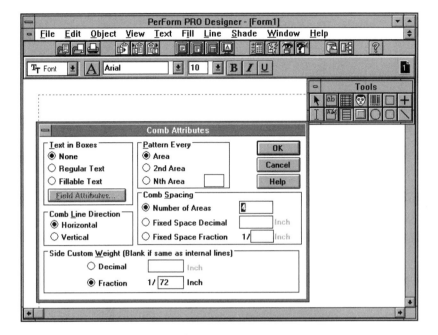

Form-Design Tips

The heart of forms software, naturally, is building efficient forms. That's the crux of the tips that follow.

Use Boxes Instead of Lines   When you're designing a form, think in terms of boxes instead of individual lines. Using individual lines to create form elements uses more memory and slows down screen redraw and printing time because PerForm Pro has more elements to keep track of. Consolidate elements by using boxes, and let elements that are located next to one another share common box borders.

Quick Table Creation   The fastest and easiest way to create tables is to use the Comb tool for the first column. With the Comb tool selected, press F7 (or choose Attributes from the Object menu) to specify the number of rows in your table. With the Comb tool still selected, press Ctrl+D (or choose Duplicate from the Object menu) to duplicate the number of columns you need.

Inserting Fillable Text in a String   When you're designing a form that will include a fillable field in the middle of a text statement—such as a name field— you may be tempted to use blank spaces to achieve the proper alignment. For example, you would type in the sentence up to the point where you want to insert the field and then add a few spaces before inserting the field. This method will work, but if you make any changes to the printer's setup or if you change printers altogether, the alignment will change and the text may overwrite part of the field. If you know that you won't be making any printer adjustments, go ahead and use the method just described, but if you do anticipate using the form on multiple printers, use a separate text box for the statement text following the field.

Easy Alignment   Keep the Designer module's Snap to Grid feature turned on to help you align form objects with ease. Even with this feature turned on, you can place objects off of the grid settings by using the Position option and specifying the desired location. To activate this feature, select Snap to Grid from the View menu. A check mark will appear to the left of the option if it is turned on.

Signing Forms Electronically and Safely   To use a scanned signature in a form, include a two-field security system. The first field should be a standard signature field with password protection. The second field should be a fillable graphic that looks up the signer's name from the signature field and brings in the scanned signature.

Data Tips

Try these tips for managing the data in your forms.

Efficient Data Sharing   To share data between several forms, such as a series of personnel documents, create a folder and set a single .DBF file as the default data file for each form in the folder. Select Form Folders from the System menu to set up the folder in PerForm Pro Filler *before* you create the data file, to allow data to flow into fields with common names in all the forms.

Lean Data Files   To minimize the size of data files, use fixed instead of variable field lengths when you set the Fill Attributes of fillable fields.

Performance Tips

Forms are iceberg software: There's a lot going on beneath their surface. As a result, forms packages can tax your PC. Try these tricks for potent performance.

Improve Printer Performance   If you're using a PostScript printer, you can speed up printing by making sure that the Enhanced Fonts on Printer option is turned off in the Designer module's Font dialog box and in Filler's Printer Setup dialog box.

On a Hewlett-Packard LaserJet printer, you can speed up printing by optimizing your use of bit-mapped images (which are memory hogs). Make sure that all of the excess blank space around a bitmap is eliminated, and, before you bring the image into the Designer, crop it in a graphics program to remove any excess.

Also minimize the use of opaque objects, angled lines, rounded-corner boxes, and white text on a shaded background when print speed is an issue.

Faster Screen Redraw   To increase the screen redraw speed in PerForm Pro Filler or Designer, select View and turn off the Show Graphics feature. In Filler, you'll also speed things up if you disable the Auto Recalc option in the View menu.

Polaris Packrat

The purpose of Packrat is to manage personal information—dates, times, appointments, phone numbers—all that critical stuff we scribble on small notes and stuff in our briefcases. So-called personal information managers have traditionally been a solution in search of a problem. However, Packrat's ability to offer organizing options to the entire Windows environment indicates how this software category may evolve in the future.

Here, we look at searching for the information you need, using Packrat's phone book, and, most importantly, at integrating this application with other Windows programs.

Searching Tips

The idea behind these tips is to make sure your electronic information files are easier to sort through than a stack of heavily scribbled-on note cards.

Quick Search on the Today Box   Use the Today Box—the one that contains the current date and time—for quick searches. Click once with the left mouse button to show all the current day's items, or click once with the right mouse button to show all items In Progress or Overdue To Do.

Partial Word Searches   Packrat searches will only match if the search string you ask for is at the beginning of a text string. To find search strings that appear somewhere other than at the beginning of a word, use the Search screen's Text Within Keys option. The keyboard shortcut for this is Alt+X while in the Search dialog box. For example, if you listed someone as Becky or Rebecca and are not sure which name to search for, the Text Within Keys option lets you successfully search for "Bec."

Phone Book Tips

Packrat has a truly innovative and fun phone book. If you know its intricacies, you can get great use from this feature.

Scroll Quickly   In the Phone Book, remember to record your entries in the format *last name, first name* so that you can quickly jump to the person you're looking for. Sort the list on the Name field, and then type the first letter of the person's last name. You'll move to the section of the Phone Book that begins with that letter. In general, when in Normal List view, typing the first letter of the desired record's key field is the quickest way to get to that section.

Dial Internal Extensions   One of Packrat's most useful features is automatic phone dialing—but the full seven-digit number in your records won't help you dial an internal extension of three, four, or five digits. Packrat's Prefix Translation provides the solution. Choose Preferences from the File menu, select Dial Info, and enter the full seven-digit number that's in your records. Then enter the number that you want Packrat to dial in its place. Click on OK to complete the command.

Tips for Using Packrat with Other Windows Applications

Packrat doesn't horde its virtues. Other Windows applications can utilize Packrat services. Here, we show you how to make it happen.

Install Excel and Word Macros   Packrat ships with macros that enable you to get more from Excel and Word for Windows. These macros add menu items to both Excel and Word for Windows that let you store and log documents into Packrat for quicker searching and launching in the future. You can also insert a name and address directly from a Packrat menu into a Word for Windows document. To install the macros in Word for Windows, open the template named PACKRAT.DOT and follow the instructions. For Excel, run START-RAT.XLM.

Use Packrat as Your WinFax Pro Phonebook   Instead of having to keep separate records of names and phone numbers for Packrat and WinFax Pro, you can have the two applications share the same phone book. First you need to open your WIN.INI file in SysEdit or a text editor and go to the end of the file. Add a new section for Packrat that looks like the following:

```
[Polaris Packrat]
File=Junkfile
```

Save your additions to WIN.INI and then open WinFax Pro. From the Phone Book menu, select Phone Book Record. In the drop-down list of phone books, select Packrat, and then choose OK.

The next time you send a fax and type the name of the intended recipient in the To box, WinFax searches your Packrat phone book for the correct fax number.

Launch Windows Applications from Packrat   Use Packrat's Disk File facility as an application launcher. To do so, create a Disk File item with the name of an existing Windows application, such as Write. For easier launching, create a Smart Button that launches Write whenever you click on it.

Quicken for Windows

Quicken is the quintessential big software hit. The idea is simple: Combine simple spreadsheet functions, basic accounting, and budgeting with the ability to actually pay bills electronically. The result has been one of the most popular and sworn-by applications in existence. Thousands of people have turned their entire personal financial lives over to Quicken, with happy results. Now migrated to Windows, Quicken shows no sign of slowing down.

Financial-Tracking Tips

These tips will help you use Quicken to keep track of your receivables and payables without excess pain.

List Charitable Donations To list all charitable donations made from all your accounts, choose Home from the Reports menu and select Itemized Categories. Click on Settings, and then Filters. Choose Select Categories to Include and select OK or press the Enter key, then Mark All to exclude them all, and then double-click on Charity to include it alone, as shown in Figure 17.3.

FIGURE 17.3

Create a report of all your charitable deductions by using filters to look at the Charity category of transactions only.

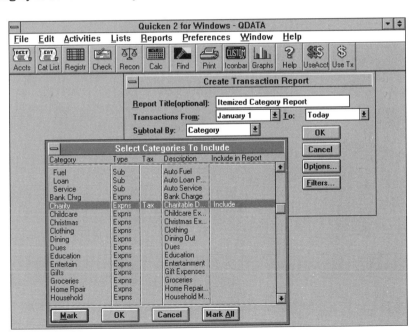

Select Home from the Reports menu, and then Itemized Categories. From the Itemized Category Report Box, name the report, select the time period the report should cover, and click on Settings. From the resulting Create Transaction Report box, set Accounts to Report On to All Accounts (or select the ones you want to draw from through the Selected Accounts option). Choose Filters and then Select Categories to Include (Alt+S) and click on OK. From the Select Categories to Include box, click on Mark All, and double-click on Charities. Also double-click on its subcategories to include them, and then click on OK. Back at the Create Transaction Report box, click on OK to compile the report.

Track 401(k)s   Most people don't trace share number and price fluctuations, so tracking a 401(k) plan as a Quicken Investment Account won't work—but using an Asset Account will. When you enter your paycheck, use a split transaction by clicking on the Splits button to show your gross salary and all deductions.

Divide your salary into two parts: taxable and nontaxable (which includes 401(k) contributions and other before-tax accounts). Using separate lines of the split, assign these two parts to two separate subcategories. Assign Salary:Taxable to a tax form (in this case W-2:Salary), but don't do the same for Salary:Nontaxable. In one line of the split, show your 401(k) deduction from your paycheck as a transfer to your 401(k) account. In other lines of the split, assign deductions for taxes to the appropriate tax categories. (You can also assign each tax category to the appropriate line of Form W-2.)

Enter CheckFree Payments   You can enter CheckFree payments directly into the Quicken for Windows register, just as with DOS-based versions of the program. To store an electronic transaction, go to the Activities menu, select CheckFree, and bring up the Electronic Payee List. Click on New and enter the Payee information. With AutoMemorize on, once you use the Electronic Payment in a transaction, the transaction is memorized and you can use Auto-Recall to recall the transaction. To view the confirmation number for a transmitted electronic payment, highlight the transaction and select Edit/Electronic Payment Info. Quicken displays the confirmation number and transmission date.

Data Entry Tips

Like all applications, Quicken has secrets that aid its operation. Try these tips for smooth sailing when working with data.

Enter the Date Quickly   Don't waste time typing the date directly in the date field. Press T to immediately enter today's date, if it doesn't appear automatically. Then, if necessary, press the plus key (+) or minus key (–) to go forward or backward a day at a time—or hold down either key to scroll through dates.

Enable AutoMemorize and AutoRecall   Avoid creating duplicates and speed the entry of data into the register by enabling the Automatic Memorization and Automatic Recall features. Automatic Memorization saves each entry as you enter it, to prevent duplication, and Automatic Recall calls up memorized items when you type in the first few letters of the payee and press Tab. Select QuickFill from the Preferences menu and select both check boxes. This is the default setting, but if you've converted data from Quicken 3 or 4, the check boxes won't be selected.

Microsoft Money

Is there a software category in which Microsoft *hasn't* dipped a giant toe? It certainly doesn't seem so. Lured by the success of Quicken, Microsoft has crafted its own Windows personal money manager. Perhaps a tad more business-oriented than Quicken, Money is a solid piece of work that's surprisingly easy to use. Our tips focus on the high-end: customizing and accounting.

Customization Tips

Try these ideas to train Money to handle affairs your way.

Customize Reports   Create custom reports that show only selected transactions or selected accounts. Create an Income and Expense report by selecting Income and Expense from the Report menu and then choose the Customize button. In the Include Transactions box, choose only the specific account—for example, your major credit card account. The result will be an expense report detailing what categories of expenses you've used your credit card for and providing totals for those expenses.

Track Other Classifications   Further classify your expenses to track income or expenses associated with special projects, rental properties, clients, and so on. Under the List menu, choose Other Classification. Choose New to create a new category and then choose the category type. Then you can enter individual items for your classification, such as names of individual properties you own. This allows you to track expenses for each classification.

Accounting Tips

Here are a few ideas for getting the most out of Money's accounting capabilities.

Automatic Deposits and Transfers   Keep track of automatic deposits and transfers automatically. For example, to set up a monthly transfer of $500 from your checking account to your savings account, enter the transaction for the first time in the checking account. In the Account Books drop-down category list, choose Transfer and then choose the savings account. Enter the transaction in the savings account and then click on the Calendar icon. You will be prompted to schedule this transaction for a certain frequency; in this case, choose Monthly, as shown in Figure 17.4. Select OK, and the transaction will occur automatically every month until you change it.

FIGURE 17.4

Schedule an automatic deposit or transfer quickly and easily by using Money's calendar icon to call up the Schedule Future Transaction dialog box.

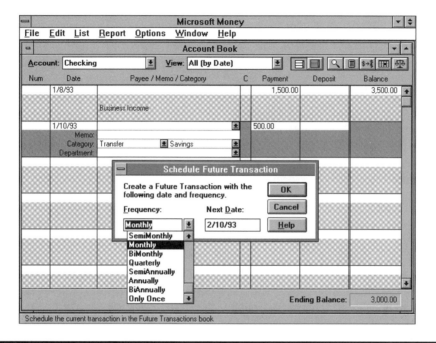

Don't Just Rely on SmartReconcile If your account doesn't balance, use Money's SmartReconcile feature to help you find the error. To use SmartReconcile, select the Use SmartReconcile radio button to help find the error in the Account Didn't Balance dialog box. But while SmartReconcile can find many types of errors in the way a transaction was entered—such as a backwards entry or one with the numbers transposed—it can't find multiple instances of errors. If the account contains a single transaction error, SmartReconcile will find it, but if you've got more than one incorrect transaction SmartReconcile will be foiled and you will have to recheck the entries yourself.

Have Multiple Payees with the Same Name Money allows you to have several payees with the same name. For example, to add a payee named Acme Inc. when you already have a payee listed as Acme Inc., do the following: From the List menu, select Payee List, select New, and, in the Name box, type **Acme Inc.**. Money will ask you to confirm that you want to add a second payee with the same name as an existing one. Now whenever you enter Acme Inc. you will be provided with the two payees with that name and will be asked to choose the correct one.

An easy way to differentiate between the payees of the same name is to add nonprinting identifying information. Place the text in curly braces and it won't be printed but will appear on the screen. For example, you could have Acme Inc. {cleaning} and Acme Inc. {locks}.

Navigation Tips

Here are some tricks for getting around Money with the least amount of effort.

Move Easily from Field to Field   If you have trouble remembering to press the Tab key to move between fields in Money, taking advantage of the Alternate Register Navigation setting will make working in Money easier. To turn on this option, select Settings from the Options menu and select the Alternate Register Navigation box. Now you can move from field to field by simply (and intuitively) pressing the Enter key. To enter a transaction, which you could normally do by pressing the Enter key, you'll have to press Ctrl+Enter or press the Enter key while in the Subcategory field.

Keyboard Shortcuts   Use these shortcuts to navigate through Money's screens without a mouse.

Register Navigation

Down Arrow	Move to the next transaction
Up Arrow	Move to the previous transaction
PgUp	Move up one screen
PgDn	Move down one screen
Ctrl+Home	Move to beginning of register
Ctrl+End	Move to end of register

Transaction Navigation

Tab	Move ahead one field
Shift+Tab	Move back one field
Up Arrow	Move up one field
Down Arrow	Move down one field
Enter	Enter a transaction

Entering Transactions

Ctrl+S	Split transaction
Ctrl+D	Insert current date
+	Increase the number or date by one
−	Decrease the number or date by one

Shift+"	Copy information from the same field in the previous transaction
Ctrl+M	Mark transaction cleared
Shift+Ctrl+M	Mark transaction as reconciled

Editing Shortcuts

Ctrl+Z	Undo previous edit
Alt+Backspace	Undo previous edit
Del	Delete selected text
Ctrl+C	Copy selected text
Ctrl+Ins	Copy selected text
Ctrl+V	Paste from the Clipboard
Shift+Ins	Paste from the Clipboard
Ctrl+X	Cut selected text
Shift+Del	Cut selected text

Command Shortcuts

Ctrl+E	Schedule a future transaction
Ctrl+P	Pay bills
F9	Balance an account
Ctrl+K	Access calculator
Ctrl+T	Switch between register views
Ctrl+O	Create a custom view
Ctrl+F	Find

■ Index

[] (square brackets), 35–36

A
About Program Manager option, 175, 176
accessories, 27, 204
    Calculator, 208–215
    Calendar, 215–218
    Cardfile, 218–221
    Character Map, 234, 265–266
    Clock, 204–205
    embedding, 305–306
    headers and footers for, 215–216, 222
    keyboard shortcuts for, 237
    Macro Recorder, 229–234, 292
    Notepad, 38, 221–223
    Object Packager, 302–305
    Paintbrush, 223–226
    Sound Recorder, 235
    Terminal, 226–229
    Write, 206–208
Acer computers, 97
activity log, creating, 222–223
Add/Remove Windows Components option,
    14, 15
Administrative Setup, 311
Adobe Type Manager, 487
    font cache, 488
    font substitution, 489
    and PostScript, 489–490
    preloading fonts, 268
    removing fonts from, 489
    small fonts, 487
    troubleshooting, 490–491
    286 machines and, 94
AfterDark, 201
ALDUS.INI file, 459
Aldus PageMaker, 513
    documents, 515–516
    graphics, 515
    text, 513–515
Aldus Persuasion, 457–460
    copying objects, 459
    editing ALDUS.INI file, 459
    handouts, 458–459
    presentations, 458–459
    slides, 457–458

aliases, 282
AllEMSLocked= setting, 73
All File Details option, 247–248
AllVMsExclusive= setting, 73
ALR computers, 96
AltKeyDelay= setting, 73
AltPasteDelay= setting, 73
Ami Pro, 359
    automatic paragraph indents, 364
    counting words, 363–364
    drawing Bezier curves, 365
    formatting, 359–360
    INDEXALL.SMM macro, 362–363
    macros for, 361–364
    SmartIcons, 360–361
    speeding up, 364–365
    spell-checking, 365–366
    WC.SMM macro, 363–364
ANSI.SYS file
    and Apricot computers, 98
    color settings, 165–166
    creating DOS prompts with, 161
    cursor positioning, 166
    display attributes, 166
    graphic characters, 165, 167
    metastrings, 165–167
APPEND command (DOS)
    avoiding, 156
    removing from AUTOEXEC.BAT, 5
applets. *See* accessories
applications. *See also* accessories; *names of*
    applications; non-Windows applications
    deleting, 292–293
    installing with File Manager, 248
    integrating, 289–293
    loading minimized, 289–290
    registering, 300
applications development tools, 308
    Asymetrix Toolbook, 502–506
    Object Vision, 506–508
    Visual Basic, 508–512
APPS.INF file, 30, 136, 330
    [base_PIFs] section, 331
    contents of, 331
    defined, 330
    [dialog] section, 331

[dontfind] section, 331, 336–337
[enha_dosprompt] section, 331
[pif] section, 331–336
Apricot computers, 98
Artisoft LANtastic, 352–353
ASCII files
    cleaning up in Word for Windows, 371–372
    saving in WordPerfect for Windows, 404–405
    sending via Clipboard, 153
    using Notepad for, 221–223
ASP Integrity Toolkit, 5
ASSIGN command (DOS), avoiding, 156
Associate option, 16, 172, 191–192, 251–252
associations, 15–16, 191–192
    creating, 251–252
    editing, 252–253
    listing, 252–253
    predefined, 252–253
    using drag and drop with, 256
    WIN.INI file settings, 52–53
AST computers, 96
Asymetrix Toolbook, 308, 502–506
    boxes, 502
    OpenScript, 502–503
ATM. *See* Adobe Type Manager
A20 handlers, 20–21
audio, troubleshooting, 124
Auto Arrange option, 173
AutoCAD, running from Windows, 19
AUTOEXEC.BAT file
    changing path references in, 11
    mouse driver in, 5–6, 116, 117
    optimizing for non-Windows applications, 142–146
    potential conflicts with Windows, 5
    SET TEMP= command, 287
    skipping logo in, 32
    TSRs in, 4–5, 20, 105–106
AutoRestoreScreen= setting, 73
A_WindowPosition= setting, 57

B

background execution, non-Windows applications, 141, 159
backing up
    .INI files, 14, 37, 38
    using File Manager, 249–250
Banyan VINES, 353–354
Basic Input/Output System (BIOS). *See* BIOS
batch files
    creating Windows icons for, 154–156
    for printing directory listings, 246–247
    running, 153–154
    for starting Windows, 31–32
    switching between VGA and SVGA with, 120
Batch Mode Setup
    defined, 311–312
    system settings file for, 312–319
batch printing, 279–280
Beep= setting, 42

BIOS, 95–97
    problems with, 96–97
    when to replace, 95
Bitstream Facelift, 491
    and Character Map, 493–494
    font cache, 491, 492
    font substitution, 491–492
    setup, 492
    troubleshooting, 493–494
    286 machines and, 94
blink rate, cursor, 124
.BMP files, 27, 182, 183
Boolean values, .INI file settings, 36, 43
boot disks
    creating, 8
    troubleshooting system from, 8, 21–22
BOOTLOG.TXT file, 16
BOOT.SYS file, 106–107
Border Width option, 177
BorderWidth= setting, 42
Borland Object Vision, 308, 506–508
Browse button, 174, 175
buffering, double, 109–110
buffers, specifying, 20, 143
bullets, ATM fonts, 488
By File Type option (File Manager)
    problems with, 240–241
    restoring complete listing, 241
    vs. Sort by Type option, 240

C

Calculator, 27, 208
    financial calculations, 208–213
    future value calculations, 210–211
    interest rate calculations, 212–213
    keyboard shortcuts, 214–215
    limitation of, 213
    loan balance calculations, 210
    loan payment calculations, 209–210
    lump-sum investment calculations, 210–212
    running tally, 213–214
    Statistics Box, 213–214
    term calculations, 211–212
Calendar, 27, 215
    keyboard shortcuts, 218
    personalizing output, 215–216
    previewing appointments, 216–217
    printing blank calendars, 215
    setting nonstandard times, 217
call waiting, turning off in Terminal, 228
Cardfile, 27, 218
    dialing long numbers, 220–221
    keyboard shortcuts, 219, 222
    phone numbers in, 219, 220–221
    printing more cards per page, 218
CD-ROM drives, 124–125
CGA80WOA.FON file, 30, 74
CGA40WOA.FON file, 30, 73
CGANoSnow= setting, 73
Character Map, 27, 234, 265–266
    accessing special characters, 265–266
    and Bitstream Facelift, 493–494

characters, special, 265–266
CHKDSK command (DOS)
    for hard disk maintenance, 113
    when not to use, 156
.CHK files, 113
client applications, defined, 298–299
Clipboard
    CLIPBRD files, 27
    converting formats with, 291
    copying special characters to, 265
    keyboard shortcuts, 291
    screen capture with, 183, 202, 290–291
    using with DOS graphics, 141, 152
    using with non-Windows applications,
        150–153, 290–291
clock, displaying as icon, 190–191, 205
Clock accessory, 27, 204–205
code segments, padding, 21
Color dialog box, 184–185
Color icon, 125–126, 184–188
color schemes, 184
    built-in, 185
    with custom colors, 185–186
    modifying, 185
    WIN.INI file settings, 63–64
COMBoostTime= setting, 76
COMdrv30= setting, 76
COMIrqSharing= setting, 76, 112
COMMAND.COM file, 8
CommandEnvSize= setting, 87
COMM.DRV file, 69–70
communication ports. *See* COM ports
communications programs, 141–142, 153
    Crosstalk for Windows, 476–479
    Dynacomm, 479–482
    Lotus Notes, 482–486
    Procomm Plus for Windows, 475–476
Compaq computers, 98
COM ports
    support for more than four, 112
    using COM3 or COM4, 111–112
    Windows 3.0 vs. 3.1, 111–112
CompuServe
    Microsoft Knowledge Base, 33
    Windows Advanced Users forum, 33
    Windows New Users forum, 33
COMxAutoAssign= setting, 74
COMxBase= setting, 75
COMxBuffer= setting, 75
COMxFIFO= setting, 75
COMxIRQ= setting, 75
COMxProtocol= setting, 75–76
CONFIG.SYS file
    file handles and buffers in, 20
    mouse driver in, 116
    optimizing for non-Windows applications,
        142–146
    order of drivers in, 5
    stacks in, 26
    TSRs in, 4–5
CONTROL.EXE file, 174

CONTROL.INF file
    as basis for .SHH file, 313
    customizing user options, 323–325
CONTROL.INI file, 181–182, 337
Control Panel
    accessing with Run option, 181
    Color icon, 125–126, 184–188
    Desktop icon, 177, 182–184, 190
    excluding sections of, 337, 338
    Fonts icon, 264
    hiding icons, 181–182
    International icon, 118
    keyboard access to, 180
    LaserTools, 107
    Mouse icon, 117–118
    Ports icon, 111
    Printers icon, 267, 269
    Settings menu, 180
    Sound icon, 182
    386 Enhanced icon, 115, 182
CONTROL.SRC file
    defined, 331
    excluding sections of Control Panel with, 337
conventional memory, defined, 100
CoolSwitch= setting, 42
copying
    formatting in Word for Windows, 371
    vs. moving, 243
    Paintbrush objects, 223–224, 225
    program items, 171
CorelDRAW!, 460
    fonts, 460
    previewing, 460–462
    printing, 460–462
COURx.FON file, 28
CPWIN386.CPL file, 30
Crosstalk for Windows, 476
    COM ports, 479
    dialing, 476–477
    on-line sessions, 477
    setup, 477–478
cursor
    blink rate, 124
    color of, 188
    keyboard shortcuts, 198
CursorBlinkRate= setting, 43
custom colors, 185–186
Custom Setup, 6–7
C_WindowPosition= setting, 57

D

data files
    associating, 172, 191–192, 251, 252, 253, 254
    loading from icons, 191–192, 253, 254
    unassociated, loading from File Manager,
        253–254
DATA Physician Plus, 5
DDE (dynamic data exchange), 296–298
    editing links, 297
    vs. OLE (object linking and embedding), 298
    refreshing links, 297
    setting up links, 296

DDEML.DLL file, 28
DEC Pathworks, 355–356
_DEFAULT.PIF file, 85
DefaultQueueSize= setting, 43
Define Custom Colors option, 185–186
deleting
    device drivers, 28, 122
    files, 112–113, 245
    fonts, 28, 29, 265, 277
    non-Windows applications, 147
    program items, 171
    vs. removing fonts, 28, 265
    Windows applications, 292–293
Delrina PerForm Pro, 534
    data, 536–537
    forms design, 535–536
    tools, 534–535
desktop
    adding patterns to colors, 186
    colors for, 184–188
    customizing patterns, 183–184
    wallpaper choices, 182–183
    wallpaper vs. patterns, 183
    window adjustments, 177
    WIN.INI file settings, 50
Desktop icon, 177, 190
desktop publishing software
    Microsoft Publisher, 520–524
    PageMaker, 513–516
    Ventura Publisher, 517–520
destination documents, defined, 299
development tools, 308, 502–512
Device Contention option, 182
device drivers
    available on-line, 33
    deleting, 28, 122
    for displays, 120, 121–122
    loading into high memory, 143–144
    mouse, 5–6, 116, 117, 135
    for printers, 28, 127, 283–284
    for SCSI hardware, 113
    troubleshooting, 144
    updating, 24, 33
    video, 120, 121–122
DEVICEHIGH= command, 143, 144
DeviceNotSelectedTimeout= setting, 44
Device= setting, 44
dialog boxes, keyboard shortcuts, 198–199
directories
    collapsing tree display, 241
    deleting tree display, 258
    expanding tree display, 241
    moving Windows 3.1 after installation, 9–11
    printing, 246–247
    Properties dialog box, 247
    resizing tree pane, 257, 259
DisablePositionSave= setting, 87–88
disk cache, 22, 108–109. *See also* SMARTDrive
    for 286 machines, 92–93
    and expanded vs. extended memory, 108
disk-compression utilities, 114
    SMARTDrive and, 114

swap files and, 114
diskless workstations
    and Novell NetWare, 350
    printing from, 346–347
disks, floppy
    booting from, 8, 21–22
    formatting in File Manager, 248–249
    refreshing File Manager listing, 243
    for Windows 3.1, 7–8, 10
display drivers
    files for, 120
    installing, 121–122
displays
    notebook, 125–126
    troubleshooting, 120–121
DMABufferIn= setting, 76
DMABufferSize= setting, 76
Documents= setting, 44–45
DOS (disk operating system). *See* MS-DOS
DOSAPP.FON file, 30
DOS applications. *See* non-Windows
    applications
DOS-extended applications
    running, 19
DOSKEY command (DOS), 145
DOSPrint= setting, 45
DOSPromptExitInstruc= setting, 76–77, 150
DOSPROMPT.PIF file, 149
DOS prompts, fun, 161–167. *See also* MS-DOS
    icon
DOS protected-mode interface (DPMI), 19
DOS sessions. *See also* non-Windows
    applications
    changing default directory, 150
    creating Windows reminder message for,
        160
    exiting before turn off system, 160
    special DOS prompts for, 161–167
    starting windowed, 149
    windowed vs. full-screen, 149
DOSX.EXE file, 29
double buffering, 109–110
DoubleClickHeight= setting, 45
DoubleClickSpeed= setting, 45–46
DoubleClickWidth= setting, 45
Doubledisk program, 107
DPMI. *See* DOS protected-mode interface
Dr. Watson utility, 31, 295
Draft mode, advantage of, 95
drag and drop, 193–194
    and associations, 256
    canceling, 257
    creating program icons using, 193
    in File Manager, 255–257
    with Print Manager, 278
    side-by-side window arrangement for, 259
    unzipping files with, 154
    using with OLE, 301–302
drawing programs. *See* graphics software
driver files
    for display drivers, 120, 121–122
    installing, 121–122

old, deleting, 28, 122
drivers. *See* device drivers
drives
    active, changing in File Manager, 248
    moving Windows 3.1 after installation, 9–11
Drive= setting, 63
.DRV files, 120
DRWATSON.EXE file, 27, 31, 295
DRWATSON.LOG file, 295
DSWAP.EXE file, 29, 30
DualDisplay= setting, 77
Dynacomm, 479–482
    on-line sessions, 481
    scripting, 479–480
    troubleshooting, 481–482
dynamic data exchange (DDE). *See* DDE

E

EditLevel= setting, 179
EGA80WOA.FON file, 30, 77
EGA40WOA.FON file, 30, 77
80286 PCs, 91–95
    adding RAM to, 92
    disk caches for, 92–93
    fonts and, 94
    hard disks for, 93
    running Windows on, 17
    video cards for, 94
EISA systems, BIOS problems, 97
embedding, 299–300
    vs. linking, 298, 300, 303–304
    with Object Packager, 303–304
    using drag and drop, 301–302
    WIN.INI file settings for, 63
EMM386 program, 19, 21, 25, 102
    defined, 100
    error message, 144–145
    and Everex computers, 99
    with switches, 103, 144
    troubleshooting, 102–103, 144–145
    when to use, 27, 101, 144
EMM386.SYS file, 142, 144
EMMExclude= setting, 17, 24–25, 77–78, 121
EMMInclude= setting, 78
EMMPageFrame= setting, 78
EMMSize= setting, 78
EMS cards, 18
Epson computers, 98–99
error messages
    EMM386 program, 144–145
    "Unexpected MS-DOS Error #11," 147
Everex computers, 99
Excel, 415
    buttons, 429–430
    data entry, 428–429
    formatting, 423–425
    formulas, 421–422
    functions, 421–422
    keyboard shortcuts, 417–418
    mouse, 418–421
    printing, 430–432
    screen display, 432

    shutting down, 415, 416–417
    startup, 415–416
    templates, 422–423
    Toolbar, 425–426
    using Preview font, 269–270
    worksheets, 427–428
exiting Windows, 33–34
expanded memory
    converting to extended, 102
    defined, 100
    need for, 101–102
    and non-Windows applications, 140–141
    and Standard mode, 18–19
EXPAND.EXE file, 10, 135
Express Setup, 7
extended characters. *See* special characters
extended memory
    for 386 Enhanced mode, 23
    converting expanded memory to, 102
    defined, 100
    in Standard mode, 21

F

Facelift. *See* Bitstream Facelift
FasterModeSwitch= setting, 86
FASTOPEN command (DOS), 107
FDISK command (DOS), avoiding, 156
file handles, specifying, 19, 20, 143
File Manager, 239–261
    adding to Startup group, 249, 257
    All File Details option, 247–248
    for backups, 249–250
    changing active drive in, 248
    changing screen font, 257
    and drag and drop feature, 255–257
    Format Disk option, 248–249
    installing Windows applications with, 248
    keyboard shortcuts, 260–261
    launching non-Windows applications from,
        132, 248
    loading data files from, 253–254
    minimizing, 249
    opening new windows in, 258
    Partial Details option, 248
    printing directory listings from, 246–247
    Properties dialog box, 247
    Refresh option, 243
    resizing window panes, 257, 259
    Search option, 244
    selecting files in, 240–241
    side-by-side with Program Manager,
        259–260
    Sort by Type vs. By File Type options, 240
    starting Windows applications from, 248
    using as shell, 260
    viewing file windows side-by-side, 259
    viewing options, 257–260
    Windows 3.0 vs. 3.1, 255, 260
files. *See also* data files
    associating, 16, 172, 191–192, 250–255
    backing up, 14
    copying to floppy disk, 243–244

copying vs. moving, 243
copying without installing, 10
copying on same drive, 243
decompressing, 10
deleting quickly, 245
grouping names, 242
hiding, 242–243
moving to floppy disk, 243–244
moving on same drive, 243
multiple, selecting, 240
naming, 242
for non-Windows application support,
     removing, 30
not needed, 26–31, 112–113
opening with drag and drop feature, 193–194
optional, 26–31
printing lists of, 246–247
read-only, 242
selecting, 240–241
sorting, 240–241
sorting by date, 245, 246
for Standard mode, removing, 29
temporary, searching for, 244, 245
for 386 Enhanced mode, removing, 30
unnecessary, deleting, 112–113
unzipping with drag and drop, 154
viewing details, 247–248
on Windows 3.1 disks, 10
FileSysChange= setting, 22, 78, 159–160
FINSTALL.DIR file, 267, 268
Fixed.fon= setting, 271
Fixedfon.fon= setting, 70, 123
.FON files, 273
font cache
     Adobe Type Manager, 488
     Bitstream Facelift, 491, 492
     when not to use, 492
FontChangeEnable= setting, 88
Font dialog box, 257, 258
Font Installer, 269
fonts, 263–278
     adding, 264–265
     in Aldus Persuasion, 460
     and ATM, 487–489
     and Bitstream Facelift, 491–492
     in CorelDRAW!, 460
     default, 270–273
     deleting from disk, 28, 29, 265
     for File Manager, 257
     in icons, changing, 274–275
     and memory, 105
     for non-Windows applications, 148, 153,
          154, 274
     for notebooks, 126
     PostScript, 264, 267–268, 489–490
     raster, 122, 264, 273, 275
     removing vs. deleting, 28, 265
     renaming, 269
     scalable, 264
     screen, 122–123, 264
     screen vs. printer, defined, 264
     smaller, 123, 487

soft, 264, 267, 268
storing, 264
system, default, 270–273
troubleshooting, 267, 278
TrueType, 94, 264, 275–278
unused, deleting, 28, 29, 277
unused, removing, 28, 264
vector, 122
for windowed DOS applications, 148, 153,
     154, 274
WIN.INI file settings, 58–60, 62, 276–277
Fonts.fon= setting, 70, 122, 271
Fonts icon, 264
font substitution, 285
     using Adobe Type Manager, 489
     using Bitstream Facelift, 491–492
     WIN.INI file settings, 58–59, 276–277
FORMAT command (DOS), avoiding, 156
Format Disk option, 248–249
formatting floppy disks, 248–249
forms software. *See* Delrina PerForm Pro
Freelance for Windows. *See* Lotus Freelance
     for Windows
Free System Resources (FSRs), 104–105
     checking status of, 175
     and Program Manager, 174–176
FSRs. *See* Free System Resources

G
general protection faults, 31, 295
Generic Text printers, 284
Global= setting, 78–79
grabber files, 120
Granularity option, 177
graphical display, 119–124
graphics software
     Aldus Persuasion, 457–460
     CorelDRAW!, 460–462
     Harvard Graphics for Windows, 463–466
     Lotus Freelance for Windows, 462–463
     Micrografx, 466–470
     Microsoft PowerPoint, 470–474
.GRB files, 112
GridGranularity= setting, 50
.GRP files, 170
     backing up, 14
     changing path references in, 11
     and reinstalling Windows, 13
     Windows 3.0 vs. 3.1, 12
.GR2 files, 120

H
hard disks, 112–116
     defragmenting, 22, 94–95
     and disk caches, 22
     files to delete, 112–113
     SCSI, 26
     troubleshooting, 26
     for 286 machines, 93
hardware. *See also* system requirements
     A20 handlers, 20–21
     moving Windows 3.1 to new system, 11

problems with specific PCs, 97–100
Harvard Graphics for Windows, 463–464
    charting, 464–465
    drawing, 464–465
    presentations, 465–466
    printing, 465–466
    slides, 465–466
hDC Power Launcher, 132
help
    for DOS users of Lotus 1-2-3, 446
    MS-DOS, 356
    with printers, 281
    WIN.INI file settings for, 56–57
    Word for Windows, 390–391
hiding files, 242–243
high memory area, 100, 142, 143
HIMEM.SYS file, 102, 103, 142, 143
    and A20 handlers, 20–21, 24
    decompressing, 10
    EISA systems and, 97
    and /M switch, 20–21, 24
    versions of, 20, 24
hotlinks, 296
HP DeskJet, landscape mode, 285
HP Font Installer, 269
HP LaserJet printers
    and Bitstream Facelift, 493
    installing as PostScript printers, 282
    troubleshooting fonts, 267
H_WindowPosition= setting, 56

I

IBM 7552 computers, 99
.ICN files, 190
.ICO files, 190
Icondraw, 189
Icon Magic, 189
IconMaster, 189
icons
    adding for SYSEDIT, 38, 39
    assigning macros to, 232
    changing, 131, 171
    changing fonts in, 274–275
    creating, 189, 190, 193
    for data files, 251, 252, 253, 254
    defined, 189
    hiding, 181–182
    loading applications as, 191
    loading data files from, 191–192
    for non-Windows applications, 131–132,
        189–190
    sources of, 174, 190
    spacing of, 190
    wrapping titles of, 190
IconSpacing= setting, 50
IconTitleFaceName= setting, 50, 275
IconTitleSize= setting, 51, 275
IconTitleStyle= setting, 275
IconTitleWrap= setting, 51
IconVerticalSpacing= setting, 51
iCountry= setting, 53
iCurrDigits= setting, 53

iCurrency= setting, 53
iDate= setting, 53
iDigits= setting, 53
IFJumpColor= setting, 57
IFPopupColor= setting, 57
iLZero= setting, 53
iMeasure= setting, 54
iNegCurr= setting, 54
.INI files. *See also* SYSTEM.INI file;
    WIN.INI file
    accessing from Visual Basic, 512
    backing up, 14, 37, 38
    changes to, 36–37
    changing path references in, 10
    editing, 37
    and reinstalling Windows, 13
    structure of, 35–37
    syntax, 36, 39
input devices. *See* keyboards; mouse
InRestoreNetConnect= setting, 63
Insert Object option, 307–308
installing Windows 3.1, 4–11
Intermission program, 201
internal stack overflow, 26
International icon, 118
interrupts, conflicts among, 25
Int28Critical= setting, 79
Int28Filter= setting, 86
IRQ lines, sharing, 76, 112
IRQ9Global= setting, 79
iTime= setting, 54
iTLZero= setting, 54

J

JOIN command (DOS)
    avoiding, 156
    removing from AUTOEXEC.BAT, 5
JumpColor= setting, 57

K

KBFLOW program, 107
KeyboardDelay= setting, 46
keyboards, 118–119
    adjusting responsiveness, 119
    non-U.S., 118
keyboard shortcuts, 195–197
    for Accessories, 237
    assigning in Windows 3.0, 233–234
    assigning in Windows 3.1, 233
    assigning macros to, 233
    Calculator, 214–215
    Calendar, 218
    Cardfile, 219, 222
    for character formatting, 198
    Clipboard, 291
    for Control Panel, 180
    for cursor movement, 198
    for dialog boxes, 198–199
    Excel, 417–418
    for expanding directory tree, 241
    File Manager, 260–261
    first-letter, 196–197

Lotus Notes, 485–486
for menus, 199–200
Microsoft Money, 544–545
Microsoft Project, 528
Notepad, 223
for on-screen windows, 200
Paintbrush, 227
PIF settings for, 138, 140
Print Manager, 280
for Program Manager, 200–201
for selecting text in Word for Windows, 367–370
Sound Recorder, 235
for task switching, 158–159, 197
for text, 197–198
using with notebooks, 126–127
Word for Windows, 375
Write, 207, 208
KeyboardSpeed= setting, 46
KeyBoostTime= setting, 26, 79, 119
KeyBufferDelay= setting, 79
KeyIdleDelay= setting, 79
KeyPasteCRSkipCount= setting, 79
KeyPasteDelay= setting, 79
KeyPasteSkipCount= setting, 79
KeyPasteTimeout= setting, 79
KRNL286.EXE file, 29
KybdReboot= setting, 80

L

landscape mode, HP DeskJet, 285
LAN Manager, 354–355
LANtastic, 352–353
laptops. *See* notebooks
LaserJet printers
and Bitstream Facelift, 493
installing as PostScript printers, 282
troubleshooting fonts, 267
LaserTools Control Panel, 107
LCD displays, 125–126
Le Menu program, 107
lines, drawing
in Word for Windows, 372
in Write, 206
linking. *See also* DDE (dynamic data exchange); OLE (object linking and embedding)
vs. embedding, 298, 300, 303–304
with Object Packager, 303–304
LOADHIGH command (DOS), 143
Load= setting, 46, 176
LocalLoadHigh= setting, 80
LocalReboot= setting, 80
LocalTSRs= setting, 88, 157
Logitech mouse, 107, 117
logo, Windows
bypassing, 15, 31–32
removing, 32
replacing, 32
logo files, 28
Lotus Freelance for Windows, 462
importing drawings, 462–463
minimizing disk space, 463

opening screen, 462
SmartIcons, 463
Lotus Notes, 482–483
address management, 483
e-mail, 483–485
keyboard shortcuts, 485–486
Lotus 1-2-3 for Windows, 432
data entry, 435–436
DOS user help, 446
file-linking, 447
formatting, 436–439
formulas, 439–441
functions, 439–441
performance, 445
printing, 444–445
screen display, 443–444
SmartIcons, 433
SmartPak, 441–443
worksheets, 433–435

M

MacroColor= setting, 57
Macro Recorder, 27, 229–234, 292
avoiding use of mouse, 230
creating demonstrations with, 232–233
viewing macros in, 232
macros, 292
in Ami Pro, 361–364
assigning key combinations to, 233
assigning to icons, 232
to resize windows, 230–231
starting from other applications, 232
stopping recording quickly, 233
for text selection in Word for Windows, 368–370
viewing, 232
in Word for Windows, 382–385
Marquee screen saver, 202
MaxCOMPort= setting, 80
MaxPagingFileSize= setting, 80
MaxPhysPage= setting, 80
MCADMA= setting, 80
MCI drivers, 28
MEM command (DOS), 143
memory, 100–111. *See also* RAM disks
added, motherboard vs. add-in boards, 92
adding to 286 machines, 92
configuring, 102
conventional, defined, 100
and disk caches, 108
and fonts, 105
how much to have, 100
needed for setup, 9
and PIFs, 139, 145
third-party memory managers, 16, 19, 103–104
memory, expanded
converting to extended, 102
defined, 100
need for, 101–102
and non-Windows applications, 140–141
and Standard mode, 18-19

memory, extended
  converting to expanded, 102
  defined, 100
  for non-Windows applications, 104
  in Standard mode, 21
  for using 386 Enhanced mode, 23
memory managers, third party, 16, 19, 103–104
memory-resident programs. *See* TSRs
MenuDropAlignment= setting, 47
menus, keyboard shortcuts, 199–200
MenuShowDelay= setting, 47
MessageBackColor= setting, 80–81
Micrografx, 466
  centering text, 467
  Charisma, 469
  customizing toolbox, 467–468
  default path, 467
  Designer, 468–469
  Draw, 470
Microsoft CD-ROM Extensions, 124–125
Microsoft Diagnostics Utility, 31, 100, 101
Microsoft Excel. *See* Excel
Microsoft LAN Manager, 354–355
Microsoft Money, 541
  accounting, 542–543
  customization, 541
  keyboard shortcuts, 544–545
  navigation, 543–545
Microsoft mouse, 116–117
Microsoft PowerPoint, 470
  drawing, 470–471
  handouts, 472–473
  integrating, 473–474
  presentations, 471–473
Microsoft Project, 525
  formatting, 528–530
  keyboard shortcuts, 528
  tasks, 526–528
  viewing, 525–526
Microsoft Publisher, 520
  drawing, 521–522
  exiting, 524
  page numbering, 523–524
  text, 521–523, 524
Microsoft Visual Basic, 308, 508–512
Microsoft Windows. *See* Windows
Microsoft Word for Windows. *See* Word for Windows
Microsoft Works, 530
  database, 532–533
  spreadsheet, 531–532
  templates, 533
  text, 530–531
  workspaces, 533–534
.MID files, 27
MIDI drivers, 28
Minimize on Use option
  for File Manager, 249
  streamlining desktop with, 173
MinTimeSlice= setting, 81
MinUserDiskSpace= setting, 81, 116
MMSYSTEM.DLL file, 28

MODERN.FON file, 28
Money. *See* Microsoft Money
MORICONS.DLL file, 27, 131, 171, 174
mouse, 116–118
  adjusting tracking speed, 117–118
  in Excel, 418–421
  Logitech, 117
  Microsoft, 116–117
  selecting files with, 240
  shortcuts, 194–195, 207–208, 375–376
  troubleshooting, 116–117
  using with non-Windows applications, 135
  using with notebooks, 126
MOUSE.COM file, 5, 116, 117
  in AUTOEXEC.BAT, 5–6, 116, 117
  latest version, 135
  loading from batch file, 135
  retrieving from Windows 3.1 disk, 135
mouse driver
  in AUTOEXEC.BAT, 5–6, 116, 117
  in CONFIG.SYS, 116
  loading from batch file, 135
  for non-Windows applications, 5–6, 116, 117, 135
Mouse icon, 117–118
MouseInDosBox= setting, 88
MOUSE.INI file, 117
MouseSoftInit= setting, 81
MouseSpeed= setting, 47
MouseSyncTime= setting, 86
MOUSE.SYS file, 116
MouseThreshold1= setting, 47
MouseThreshold2= setting, 47–48
MouseTrails= setting, 48
moving
  files, 243–244
  program items, 171
  Windows after installation, 9–11
MPLAYER files, 27
MSCDEX file, 124, 125
MSD files, 27, 31
MS-DOS
  commands to avoid, 5, 156
  exiting to, 132
  help system, 156
  LOADHIGH command, 143
  MEM command, 143
  upgrading to version 5.0, 20, 24, 142
  versions of, 20, 24, 142
MS-DOS icon, 132, 149, 150
MS-DOS Task Swapper, 156
multimedia, 124
  troubleshooting, 124–125
  WIN.INI file settings, 62
M_WindowPosition= setting, 56

N

naming files, 242
NCR computers, 99
NetAsynchFallback= setting, 81
NetAsynchSwitch= setting, 86
NetAsynchTimeout= setting, 81

NetDMASize= setting, 81
NetHeapSize= setting, 81, 86
NetWare, 349–351
NetWarn= setting, 48
networks, 309–356. *See also* SETUP.INF file
   automating Setup, 319–330
   customizing Setup choices, 322–323
   installing non-Windows applications, 331–336
   maintaining Windows, 337–343
   with multiple servers, 338
   optimizing performance, 343–349
   optimizing Windows, 310–311
   printing, 346–349
   Setup for, 310–312
   shared program groups, 338–339
   WIN.INI file settings, 62–63
NoEMMDriver= setting, 82
non-Windows applications
   assigning hotkeys to, 158–159
   and background execution, 141, 159
   changing fonts, 148, 153, 154, 274
   choosing not to install, 336–337
   and Clipboard, 150–153
   communications programs, 141–142, 153
   copying and pasting with Clipboard, 290–291
   copying DOS graphics to Windows, 152
   creating icons for, 189–190
   data file location, 140
   deleting, 147
   exiting, Windows Standard mode, 34
   exiting, Windows 386 Enhanced mode, 33–34
   expanding environment under Windows, 150
   extended, running under Windows, 19
   icons for, 131–132, 189–190
   installing after Setup, 131
   installing automatically on networks, 331–336
   installing with Windows Setup, 130–131
   launching, 131–133
   and memory, 101–102, 103, 104
   multiple, running, 141
   optimizing AUTOEXEC.BAT file for, 142–146
   optimizing CONFIG.SYS file for, 142–146
   optimizing in 386 Enhanced mode, 22
   PIF settings for, 136
   printing, 158
   and Real mode, 133–134
   running in a window, 19
   screen capture with Clipboard, 183, 290–291
   and Standard mode, 134
   switching among, 157–158
   switching to Windows with Task List, 160
   SYSTEM.INI file settings for, 87–89
   task switching from, 141
   and 386 Enhanced mode, 134–134
   troubleshooting, 146–148
   and TSRs, 157

   using Clipboard with, 141, 150–153, 290–291
   using mouse with, 135
   windowed, 135, 148, 153, 154, 157, 274
Norton Anti-Virus, 5
Norton Desktop for Windows, 132, 494–500
   file management, 495–497
   performance, 497
   reverting to Program Manager, 499
   troubleshooting, 499–500
Norton Utilities, 107
NoSaveSettings= setting, 179
notebooks, 125–128
   increasing font size, 126
   installing multiple printers for, 127, 283
   optimizing display, 125–126
   printer drivers for, 127, 281
   using keyboard shortcuts with, 126–127
   using mouse with, 126
   using style sheets with, 127
Notepad, 38, 221
   activity log, 222–223
   headers/footers, 222
   keyboard shortcuts, 223
   time/date stamp, 222
   word wrap, 221–222
   vs. Write, 206
Notes. *See* Lotus Notes
Novell NetWare, 349–351
NullPort= setting, 48

O

object linking and embedding (OLE). *See* OLE
Object Packager, 302–305
objects
   defined, 298
   embedding, 299–300
   embedding using drag and drop, 301–302
   linking vs. embedding, 300
   packaged, 302–305
   shortcut for creating, 307–308
Object Vision, 308, 506–508
   data entry, 506
   saving time, 507–508
Oemfonts.fon= setting, 70–71, 123, 271
OLE (object linking and embedding), 298–308
   creating packaged objects for, 302–305
   embedding objects, 300
   linking vs. embedding, 298, 300
   registering applications for, 300–301
   setting up links, 299
   terminology, 298–299
   troubleshooting, 308
   using drag and drop, 301–302
   using Insert Object command, 307–308
   WIN.INI file settings, 63
OLE Registry, 300
1-2-3 for Windows. *See* Lotus 1-2-3 for Windows
on-line resources, 33
organization charts
   in Aldus Persuasion, 459
   in Harvard Graphics for Windows, 464

OutlineThreshold= setting, 59
Out of Memory errors, 103, 104–105

P

packaged objects, creating, 303–304
PACKAGER files, 27
packages, defined, 298
PadCodeSegments= setting, 21
padding code segments, 21
PageBuffers= setting, 82
page layout programs
    Microsoft Publisher, 520–524
    PageMaker, 513–516
    Ventura Publisher, 517–520
PageMaker, 513–516
Page Setup dialog box (File menu)
    changing margins, 218
    header/footer options, 215–216, 222
PagingDrive= setting, 82
PagingFile= setting, 82
Paging= setting, 82
Paintbrush, 223. *See also* Publisher's Paintbrush
    duplicating objects, 223–224, 225
    erasing, 224
    keyboard shortcuts, 227
    lines and shapes in, 224
    text effects, 226
    zooming in, 225
panes. *See* windows
Paradox 3.5, running from Windows, 19
Partial Details option, 248
passwords, 201–202
Paste Link option, 296
Paste Special option, 296
PATH statement
    streamlining, 145–146
    WIN.INI file settings, 65
patterns
    adding, 186
    creating, 183–184
    vs. wallpaper, 183
Pattern= setting, 51
PBRUSH files, 27
pcAnywhere, 127
PC-Kwik, 5
PCL fonts, 269, 277
PC Tools, 107, 500
    CP Launcher, 500
    disabling, 501
    virus scan, 501
.PCX files, 183
PerForm Pro, 534–537
PermSwapDOSDrive= setting, 82
PermSwapSizeK= setting, 82
personal finance software
    Microsoft Money, 541–545
    Quicken for Windows, 539–541
personal productivity software
    Delrina PerForm Pro, 534
    Microsoft Project, 525–530
    Microsoft Works, 530–534
    Polaris Packrat, 527–538

Persuasion. *See* Aldus Persuasion
PerVMFiles= setting, 82–83
.PFB files, 268
.PFM files, 268
PIFEDIT.EXE file, 30
PIF Editor, 136
    Mode menu, 137
    writing PIFs with, 136–137
PIFs, 11, 30, 34, 135–142
    checking for, 136
    defined, 130
    and memory, 104, 139, 145
    multiple, 138
    predefined, 136
    restoring, 138
    for Standard mode, 137
    386 Enhanced mode, 137
    troubleshooting, 138–142
    writing, 136–137
Polaris Packrat, 537
    integrating, 538
    phone book, 537–538
    searching, 537
PopupColor= setting, 7
ports
    aliases for, 282–283
    COM, 111–112, 139–140
    and PIF settings, 139–140
    for printers, 64, 282–283
    WIN.INI file settings, 57–58, 64, 287
Port= setting, 63
Ports icon, 111
PostScript
    and ATM fonts, 489–490
    fonts, 264
    fonts, preloading, 267–268
    speeding up printing, 285
    troubleshooting printers, 288
Power Launcher, 132
PowerPoint, 470–474
Preview font, 269–270
printer drivers
    deleting from disk, 28
    deleting references to, 28
    for notebooks, 127
    obtaining, 283–284
printer fonts, defined, 264
printers
    Generic Text, 284
    installing on laptops, 127, 283
    installing twice, 281–282
    multiple, on one port, 282–283
    multiple configurations for, 281–282
    new, copying soft fonts to, 267
    on-line help for, 281
    PostScript, information about, 281
    troubleshooting, 285–288
Printers icon, 267, 269
PRINTERS.WRI file, 281
printing
    with ATM fonts, 489
    batch, 279–280

canceling, 280
control, document vs. Windows, 284
directory listings, 246–247
to disk, 280
on networks, 346–349
PostScript, speeding up, 285
to screen, 183, 202
speeding up, 284, 285
using temporary files, 287
Print Manager, 278
batch printing with, 279–280
changing priority level, 279
and diskless workstations, 346–347
dragging and dropping with, 278
keyboard shortcuts, 280
on networks, 347
and non-Windows applications, 158
replacing, 95
PRINTMAN files, 27
Print Screen key, 183, 202, 290
Procomm Plus for Windows, 475–476
PROGMAN.EXE file, 174
PROGMAN.INI file, 10, 177
backing up, 14
changing path references in, 10
customizing startup in, 188–189
multiple versions of, 177–179
[Restrictions] section, 179
setting network restrictions, 339–343
[Settings] section, 188–189
Windows 3.0 vs. 3.1, 12, 13
program groups, 169–179
adding program items to, 170–171
creating, 170
defined, 169
shared, creating, 338–339
for specific tasks, 171–173
streamlining, 173
Program Information Files. *See* PIFs
Program Item Properties Dialog box, 147–148,
174, 175
program items
adding to program groups, 170–171
copying, 171
defined, 169–170
deleting, 171
for loading data files, 171–172
moving, 171
properties of, 174
Program Manager
and Free System Resources (FSRs),
174–176
.GRP files, 11
keyboard shortcuts, 200–201
PROGMAN.INI file, 10, 177–179
replacing before installing, 330
restricting changes to, 179
saving settings, 173, 176–177
side-by-side with File Manager, 259–260
starting minimized, 191
programming tools
Asymetrix Toolbook, 502–506

Object Vision, 506–508
Visual Basic, 508–512
Programs= setting, 48
Project. *See* Microsoft Project
project management. *See* Microsoft Project
PROMPT command (DOS), 161
Properties dialog box (File Manager), 247
PrtSc key, 183, 202, 290
Publisher. *See* Microsoft Publisher
Publisher's Paintbrush, 470
Pyro! program, 107

Q

QEMM-386 memory manager, 16, 19
Quattro Pro for Windows, 447
data entry, 449–450
formatting, 450–452
moving data, 452–454
pages, 447–449
printing, 454–455
quick access, 455
screen display, 454
Quicken for Windows, 539
data entry, 540–541
display screen, 541
financial tracking, 539–540
quitting Windows, 33–34
quotation marks, 384

R

RAM. *See* memory
RAM disks
setting up, 104
for Standard mode, 19
storing temporary files on, 108–109
RAMDRIVE.SYS file, 28
Rampage boards, 98
RAM shadowing, 21, 26
RAMTYPE.SYS driver, 98
raster fonts, 122, 264, 273, 275
README files, 31
read-only files, 242
Real mode
defined, 17
and non-Windows applications, 133–134
system requirements, 17
when to use, 18
.REC files, 231
Recorder. *See* Macro Recorder
RECOVER command (DOS), avoiding, 156
ReflectDOSInt2A= setting, 83
Refresh option, 243
REG.DAT file, 306–307
.REG files, 300
Registration Database
defined, 256
and OLE, 300
recreating, 307
registering applications in, 300
restoring, 300–301
Registration Editor, 278, 300

reinstalling Windows, 13, 22, 26, 306–307
remote-control software, 127–128
removing Windows components, 14, 15
ReservedHighArea= setting, 83
ReservePageFrame= setting, 83
resources. *See also* Free System Resources
     (FSRs)
     leakage of, 176
     on-line, 33
.RLE files, 32
ROMAN.FON file, 28
Run option, 132
Run= setting, 49, 176

S

Save Settings on Exit option, 173
Save Settings option, 33, 173
scalable fonts, 264. *See also* TrueType fonts
scanners, 183
sCountry= setting, 54
screen captures, 183, 202, 290–291
screen fonts, 122–123
     defined, 264
     installing, 264
     raster vs. scalable, defined, 264
Screenlines= setting, 88
ScreenSaveActive= setting, 49
screen savers, 201–202
ScreenSaveTimeOut= setting, 49
.SCR files, 27
SCRIPT.FON file, 28
scroll bars, 195
SCSI drives, 125
SCSI hard disks, 26, 113
sCurrency= setting, 55
sDecimal= setting, 55
Search option (File Manager), 244–245
SELECT command (DOS), avoiding, 156
serial ports. *See* COM ports
server applications, defined, 299
SET TEMP= command, 287
SETUP.EXE file, 4, 6
SETUP.INF file, 5, 136, 313
     copying additional Windows files with,
          325–326
     creating custom working environment,
          329–330
     customizing, 319–330
     customizing program groups, 328–329
     customizing user options, 323–325
     installing custom applications with, 326–328
     list of sections, 319–322
     specifying, 6
     third-party, 121–122
Setup program
     Administrative Setup, 311
     Batch Mode Setup, 311–312
     conflicts with existing programs, 4–5
     Custom vs. Express, 6–7
     for networks, 310–312
     before running, 4–6

search for non-Windows applications,
     130–131
     troubleshooting, 7–9
SETUP.REG file, 307
SETUP.SHH file, 312–313
     [configuration] section, 312, 313–316
     creating, 313
     [dontinstall] section, 312, 317
     [endinstall] section, 313, 318–319
     [options] section, 312, 317–318
     [printers] section, 312, 318
     [sysinfo] section, 312, 313–314
     [userinfo] section, 312, 316–317
     [windir] section, 312, 316
SHARE command (DOS), 5
Shell= setting, 71
.SHH files
     creating, 312, 313
     with updated settings, 343
SideKick, 107
Sizing Grid option, 177
sLanguage= setting, 55
sLis= setting, 55
sLongDate= setting, 55
SMALLx.FON file, 28
SMARTDrive, 22, 109–111
     in AUTOEXEC.BAT file, 109
     command-line parameters for, 110–111
     and Compaq computers, 98
     in CONFIG.SYS file, 109–110
     and disk-compression utilities, 114
     element size for, 111
     forcing to write to disk, 111
     read-ahead buffer for, 110
     and SCSI hardware, 113
     for 286 machines, 92–93
     when to use, 26
SMARTDRV.EXE file, 27
SmartIcons
     in Ami Pro, 360–361
     in Lotus Freelance for Windows, 463
     in Lotus 1-2-3 for Windows, 433
SmartQuotes macro, 384
soft fonts
     copying to new printer, 267
     defined, 264
     troubleshooting, 267
     and Windows reinstallation, 267, 268
SoftIce Debugger, 5
Solitaire, 27, 235–236
     cheating at, 236
     randomizing card back selection, 235
s1159= setting, 54
sorting files
     by date, 245, 246
     by file type, 240
sound
     troubleshooting, 124
     WIN.INI file settings, 60–61
sound cards, 124
Sound.drv= setting, 71
Sound icon, 182

Sound Recorder, 27, 235
source documents, 299
SPART.PAR file, 115
special characters, adding with Character Map, 234
SPEEDFXR program, 107
Spooler= setting, 49
spreadsheets
    Excel, 415–432
    Lotus 1-2-3 for Windows, 432–447
    Microsoft Works, 531–532
    Quattro Pro for Windows, 447–455
square brackets ([]), 35–36
sShortDate= setting, 55
Stacker, 114
stack overflow, 26
Stacks= setting, 86
Standard mode
    defined, 17
    exiting non-Windows applications in, 34
    and non-Windows applications, 134
    removing support files for, 29
    SYSTEM.INI file settings for, 86
    system requirements, 17, 19
    troubleshooting, 19–22
    when to use, 18–19
starting Windows 3.1, 14–17
    avoiding startup screen, 31–32
    SYSTEM.INI file settings for, 69–72
Startup group, 188–189
    adding Calendar to, 216–217
    bypassing, 189
    File Manager in, 249, 257
    loading order in, 189
    Print Manager in, 257
    restoring, 189
sThousand= setting, 56
sTime= setting, 56
s2359= setting, 54
style sheets, customizing for notebooks, 127
SUBST command (DOS)
    avoiding, 156
    removing from AUTOEXEC.BAT, 5
    when to use, 108
SuperStor, 114
Super VGA, 119–120
    creating larger SmartIcons for, 360
    enlarging system font, 271–272
    vs. VGA, 22–23, 119–120
SVGA. *See* Super VGA
Swapdisk= setting, 19, 88–89
swap files, 112, 114–116
    permanent, 22, 114–115
    setting up, 114–116
    temporary, 114, 115–116
SwapMouseButtons= setting, 49
.SYD files, 37
SYMBOLx.FON file, 28
SYSEDIT.EXE program, 28, 31, 37
    adding icon for, 38, 39
    editing WIN.INI file with, 41
    using without mouse, 39

SYSINI.WRI file, 31
SYSINIx.TXT files, 31
System Editor. *See* SYSEDIT.EXE program
system files, backing up, 14
system fonts, changing default, 270–273
SystemFont= setting, 272
SYSTEM.INI file
    and Adobe Type Manager, 490–491
    backing up, 14
    and Bitstream Facelift, 494
    [Boot description] section, 66, 67
    [Boot] section, 66, 67, 69–72, 344
    changing path references in, 10
    and DEC Pathworks, 355
    [Drivers] section, 66, 69
    editing, 31, 37, 38
    [Keyboard] section, 66, 67
    and LANtastic, 352
    [MCI] section, 66, 69
    and Microsoft LAN Manager, 354
    more than one, 120
    [NonWindowsApp] section, 66, 69, 87–89, 345
    and Novell NetWare, 350
    optimizing for networks, 344–346
    sections not to edit, 67–69
    [Standard] section, 66, 69, 86, 344–345
    syntax, 66
    and 3Com, 351
    [386Enh] section, 66, 67, 72–85, 345–346
    and VINES, 353
    vs. WIN.INI, 35
system requirements. *See also* hardware
    for Real mode, 17
    for Standard mode, 17
    for 386 Enhanced mode, 18
SystemROMBreakPoint= setting, 16
system settings file, 312–319
SYSTEM.SRC file, 313

T
Task List
    invoking, 71
    switching from DOS to Windows
        applications with, 160
    Tiling windows from, 260
TASKMAN.EXE file, 27
TaskMan.Exe= setting, 71–72
Task Swapper, 156
task switching
    keyboard shortcuts, 197
    from non-Windows applications, 141, 160
templates
    in Excel, 422–423
    in Microsoft Works, 533
    in Write, 207
temporary files, 108
    deleting, 112
    and printing, 287
    searching File Manager for, 244, 245
    storing, 108–109

Terminal, 27, 226
    increasing buffer size, 228
    keyboard shortcuts, 230
    and noisy phone lines, 228–229
    printing selected text, 227–228
    running maximized, 229
    turning off call waiting, 228
terminate-and-stay-resident programs. *See*
        TSRs
TESTPS.TXT file, 281
text editors. *See also* word processors
    Notepad, 38, 221–223
    SYSEDIT, 31, 37, 38–39
text files
    cleaning up in Word for Windows, 371–372
    saving in WordPerfect for Windows,
        404–405
    sending via Clipboard, 153
    using Notepad for, 221–223
32BitDiskAccess= setting, 16, 72–73
3Com, 351–352
386 Enhanced dialog box, 182
386 Enhanced icon, 115, 182
386 Enhanced mode
    enhancing, 22–23
    and non-Windows applications, 134–134
    SYSTEM.INI file settings for, 72–85
    system requirements, 18, 23
    troubleshooting, 16–17, 23–26
.386 files, 30, 122
386SPART.PAR file, 115
.3GR files, 30, 120
TileWallpaper= setting, 51
TIMER.DRV driver, 28
title bar, 194
TokenRingSearch= setting, 83
Toolbook, 308, 502–506
TOOLBOX.DLL file, 295
TOOLHELP.DLL file, 28, 31
TransmissionRetryTimeout= setting, 50
troubleshooting
    Adobe Type Manager, 490–491
    audio, 124
    Bitstream Facelift, 493–494
    CD-ROM drives, 125
    device drivers, 144
    displays, 120–121
    EMM386, 102–103, 144–145
    formatting problems, 288
    HP LaserJet fonts, 267
    Microsoft mouse, 116–117
    network printing, 347–349
    non-Windows applications, 146–148
    Norton Desktop for Windows, 499–500
    Novell NetWare printing, 350–351
    OLE, 308
    PIFs, 138–142
    PostScript printers, 288
    printers, 285–288
    Setup, 7–9
    Standard mode, 19–22
    startup, 16–17

386 Enhanced mode, 16–17, 23–26
TrueType fonts, 278
TSRs, 8, 105–106
UAEs, 294–295
using boot disk for, 8, 21–22
Windows 3.1 upgrades, 12–13
TrueType fonts, 264, 275
    vs. PostScript, 275–276
    troubleshooting, 278
    for 286 machines, 94
    using only, 277–278
    WIN.INI file settings, 59–60
TSCSI.SYS driver, 108
TSRs, 105–108
    in AUTOEXEC.BAT file, 105
    avoiding, 105
    disabling before installing Windows, 4–5
    in DOS sessions, 157
    list of, 106
    and non-Windows applications, 157
    in Standard mode, 20
    troubleshooting, 8, 105–106
    in WINSTART.BAT file, 105
TTEnable= setting, 59–60
TTIfCollisions= setting, 60
TTOnly= setting, 60
TTY.DRV file, 284
.286 files, 122
286 PCs, 91–95
    adding RAM to, 92
    disk caches for, 92–93
    fonts and, 94
    hard disks for, 93
    running Windows on, 17
    video cards for, 94
.2GR files, 29, 30, 120
.TXT files, 27, 250
Txt= setting, 133

U
UAEs, 293–295
UNDELETE command (DOS), avoiding, 156
"Unexpected MS-DOS Error #11" message,
        147
unrecoverable application errors (UAEs),
        293–295
upgrading to Windows 3.1
    using Express Setup, 7
    from 3.0, 12–13
    from 2.0, 13
UsableHighArea= setting, 83
USER.EXE file, 174
UseROMFont= setting, 83–84
utilities
    Norton Desktop for Windows, 494–500
    PC Tools, 500–501

V
Vaccine program, 5
VDDx.386 file, 120
VDefend, 5

vector fonts, 122
Ventura Publisher, 517
    formatting, 517–519
    speeding up, 519
    troubleshooting, 520
VGA displays
    vs. EGA for 286 machines, 94
    problems with, 121
    vs. SVGA, 22–23, 119–120
VGALOGO.LGO file, 32
VGALOGO.RLE file, 32
VGAMonoText= setting, 84
video boards
    driver files, 120
    installing drivers, 121–122
    problems with, 121
    for 286 machines, 94
VINES, 353–354
Virex, 1.11
virtual display driver, 120
VirtualHDIRQ= setting, 17, 25, 26, 84
virtual memory. *See* RAM disk; swap files
ViruSafe, 5
Visual Basic, 308, 508–509
    accessing .INI files from, 512
    functions, 509
    performance, 511
    routines, 509–510

W
wallpaper, 182–183
    creating, 183
    vs. patterns, 183
    sources of, 183
    286 machines and, 94
WallpaperOriginX= setting, 51–52
WallpaperOriginY= setting, 51–52
Wallpaper= setting, 51
.WAV files, 27, 235
WINA20.386 file, 25–26, 146–147
WIN.CNF file, 32
WIN.COM file, 32
WIN command
    bypassing startup screen, 15, 31–32
    command-line parameters, 15–17
    using, 14–17
WindowKBRequired= setting, 84
WindowMemSize= setting, 84
Windows
    on 286 machines, 91–95
    assigning shortcut keys (3.0), 233–234
    changing default font, 270–273
    color control (3.0), 186–188
    compatibility between 3.0 and 3.1, 62
    copying files from disks (3.1), 10
    development tools, 308
    exiting, 33–34
    File Manager access (3.0), 255
    installing (3.1), 4–11
    before installing (3.1), 4–6
    modes (3.1), 17–26

moving after installation (3.1), 9–11
    optimizing on networks, 310–311
    optional files (3.1), 26–31
    and Real mode (3.0), 17, 18
    reinstalling (3.1), 13, 22, 26, 267, 268,
        306–307
    removing parts of (3.1), 14, 15
    starting, 14–17
    starting with batch file, 31–32
    startup screen, avoiding, 31–32
    UAEs (3.0), 293–295
    upgrading 3.0 to 3.1, 7, 12–13
    upgrading 2.0 to 3.1, 13
    using COM3 or COM4 (3.0), 111–112
    using Dr. Watson with (3.0), 295
    WINA20.386 file (3.0), 25–26
windows
    adjusting, 177
    border width, 177
    closing, 194
    in File Manager, 257–260
    keyboard shortcuts, 200
    macros for resizing, 230–231
    maximizing, 194
    resizing, 195
    resizing panes in File Manager, 257, 259
    scrolling through, 195
    switching among, 194
    tiling, 259
    viewing side-by-side, 259–260
\WINDOWS directory, moving, 9–10
Windows Drivers Library, 33
Windows logo
    bypassing, 15, 31–32
    removing, 32
    replacing, 32
WinExclusive= setting, 84
WINHELP.EXE file, 27
WINHELP.HLP file, 27
WIN.INI file
    and Adobe Type Manager, 491
    backing up, 14
    and Bitstream Facelift, 493, 494
    changing path references in, 10
    [Colors] section, 63–64, 186–188
    [Compatibility] section, 62
    controlling fonts in, 264–265
    creating different versions of, 264–265
    [Desktop] section, 50–52
    [Devices] section, 64–65
    editing, 31, 37, 38, 41
    [Embedding] section, 63
    [Extensions] section, 52–53, 252
    [Fonts] section, 62
    [FontSubstitutes] section, 58–59, 276–277
    [Intl] section, 53–56
    line-by-line, 40–65
    [MCI extensions] section, 62
    [Network] section, 62–63
    [Ports] section, 57–58, 287
    [PrinterPorts] section, 64

[Programs] section, 65
rewriting disk file without restarting
    Windows, 41
sections of, 39–40
[Sounds] section, 60–61
syntax, 39
vs. SYSTEM.INI, 35
[TrueType] section, 59–60
[Windows Help] section, 56–57
[Windows] section, 42–50
WININI2.TXT file, 31
WININI.TXT file, 31, 41
WININI.WRI file, 31, 41
WINMINE files, 27
WINOA386.MOD file, 30
WINOLDAP.MOD file, 29, 30
WIN.SRC file, 313
WINSTART.BAT file
    listing TSRs in, 105
    loading TSRs from, 157
WIN386.EXE file, 30
WIN386.PS2 file, 30
WIN386.SWP file, 108, 112
WinTimeSlice= setting, 84–85
WINTUTOR files, 27
.WOA files, 108, 112
Word for Windows, 366
    adding Zoom Arrow to Toolbar, 381
    annotating help, 390
    automatic paragraph indents, 385
    boilerplate text, 387
    creating forms, 379
    defaults, changing, 385–387
    drawing lines in, 372
    envelopes, 389
    file handling, 388–389
    formatting, 370–375
    help, 390–391
    macros, 382–385
    mail merge, 389
    mouse shortcuts, 375–376
    navigating, 387–388
    pasting with Insert key, 370
    redefining Insert key, 370
    speeding up, 375–377
    spell checking, 391
    tables, 377–380
    text manipulation, 366–370
    toolbars, 381–382
    using Clipboard in search and replace, 370
    using Spike, 366
WordPerfect for Windows, 391
    ASCII file saves, 404–405
    Button Bar, 394–397
    codes, 400–402
    file management, 402–407
    formatting, 392–394
    keyboard, 397–399
    macros, 397–398, 410–411
    navigation, 399–400
    printers, 409–410

    reveal codes, 400–402
    speeding up, 408
    tables, 407–408
    text capabilities, 392
word processors. *See also* text editors
    Ami Pro, 359–366
    Microsoft Works, 530–531
    Word for Windows, 366–391
    WordPerfect for Windows, 391–411
    WordStar for Windows, 411–413
    Write, 206–208
WordStar for Windows, 411
    drawing in, 413
    formatting, 412–413
    graphics in, 413
    speeding up, 411–412
working directory
    vs. PIF startup directory, 191
    setting, 147–148, 191
Works. *See* Microsoft Works
.WRI files, 27, 31
Write, 27, 206
    changing margins, 206
    creating lines, 206
    creating template, 206–207
    keyboard shortcuts, 207, 208
    mouse shortcuts, 207–208
    vs. Notepad, 206
    searching for formatting characters, 207
    using optional hyphens, 206
WSWAP.EXE file, 29
Wyse computers, 100

X
XCOPY command (DOS), 10